GUI

SOCCER WHO'S WHO

Jack Rollin

GUINNESS PUBLISHING

This edition first published 1996
Reprint 10 9 8 7 6 5 4 3 2 1 0

First edition 1984
Second edition 1986
Third edition 1989
Fourth edition 1990
Fifth edition 1991
Sixth edition 1992
Seventh edition 1993
Eighth edition 1994
Ninth edition 1995

Published in Great Britain by Guinness Publishing Ltd,
33 London Road, Enfield, Middlesex

Cover design: Ad Vantage Studios

Database Typeset in Times Roman by Wearset
Printed and bound in Great Britain by
BPC Paperbacks Ltd

A catalogue record for this book is
available from the British Library

ISBN 0-85112-013-x

FOREWORD

I am delighted to welcome the tenth edition of the *Guinness Soccer Who's Who* by Jack Rollin. It is certainly on a par with all the quality reference books in the Guinness library and will prove an invaluable help to all administrators, managers, soccer writers and supporters of football throughout the United Kingdom.

It is a difficult task to keep abreast of the changing face of personnel at clubs and Jack Rollin is to be congratulated on achieving this task successfully. There are precise details of professional players in England, Wales and Scotland which can be found by quick and easy alphabetical reference and it provides all the information necessary for a football fact-finder.

The book will occupy a prominent place on my desk and I do not hesitate to recommend it.

Gordon Taylor

Gordon Taylor,
Chief Executive, The Professional Footballers' Association

Front cover, from left:
Peter Schmeichel (Manchester United), Tony Adams (Arsenal), Jamie Redknapp (Liverpool), Mark Draper (Aston Villa), Tosh McKinlay (Celtic).
Photos: Allsport UK Ltd (Shaun Botterill/Phil Cole/David Cannon/David Rogers/Clive Mason)

INTRODUCTION

This book features the statistical League careers of all players who made FA Carling Premiership and Endsleigh Insurance League appearances during the 1995–96 season as well as those in the Scottish Premier Division and Dunfermline Athletic and Dundee United, the promoted teams from the First Division.

Other players in England who did not appear last season are also included. Club names in italics indicate temporary transfers where they have not become permanent moves in the same season. All appearances include those as substitute.

The Editor would like to thank Glenda Rollin for her invaluable assistance, Alan Elliott for providing details of Scottish League players and also acknowledge the co-operation and assistance of the FA Premier League and Football League in the compilation of this book. In particular Mike Foster of the FA Premier League and Sheila Andrew and Debbie Birch of the Football League.

Bibliography: *Rothmans Football Yearbook*

Also published by Guinness:
The Guinness Football Encyclopedia, 3rd edition
The Guinness Book of World Soccer, 2nd edition
The Guinness Record of the World Cup
The Football Fact Book
More Soccer Shorts
Leeds United Player by Player
Everton Player by Player

THE AUTHOR

Jack Rollin was born in London in 1932 and educated at King's, Harrow. There he played soccer, while later at Westcliff-on-Sea High School it was rugby. Within ten days of joining the Royal Air Force he was playing in a Welsh Cup tie for RAF Bridgnorth and in the services he learned shorthand and typing, resuming his career in journalism and covering the 1954 World Cup in Switzerland in a freelance capacity.

In 1958 an ankle injury ended his own career during which, at the age of 14, he had been offered a trial with the United States club Chicago Maroons. Played representative football for Southend Youth in the 1951 Festival of Britain and for RAF Fighter Command. He wisely declined a one-off re-appearance in 1971 against the European cup finalists Panathinaikos of Greece.

For ten years Jack Rollin was Editor of the weekly magazine *Soccer Star* and its companion monthly *World Soccer* before becoming a freelance again in 1970. Since then he has researched football for BBC Television, acted as an assistant to commentators on 'Match of the Day', spoken on radio and appeared on television programmes. He has contributed to *What's on in London* and *Radio Times* and in 1975 he won the Designers and Art Directors Association Silver Award for *Radio Times World Cup Special* for the most outstanding specialist feature of the year.

In 1972 he became one of the compilers of the *Rothmans Football Yearbook* and later became its Editor. He has provided advice on the football sections of the *Encyclopaedia Britannica* and *Guinness Book of Records.* He is a football columnist for the *Sunday Telegraph.*

Jack Rollin contributed to three part-works: *The Game* (8 vols. 1970); *Book of Football* (6 vols. 1972) and *Football Handbook* (1979–80). His articles have appeared in programmes for matches at Wembley Stadium since 1963. He has produced handbooks which include *World Soccer Digest* 1961, 1962 and 1963 and *World Cup Digest* 1966.

In 1978 he carried out the international research for the BBC Television Series 'The Game of the Century' and produced the first edition of *The Guinness Book of Soccer Facts and Feats.*

Other books he has written: *England's World Cup Triumph* (1966), *A Source Book of Football* (1971), *The History of Aldershot Football Club* (1975), *World Cup Guide* (1982), *Soccer at War 1939–45* (1985), *Soccer: The Records* (1985), *Soccer: Records, Facts and Champions* (1988), *Soccer Shorts* (1988) and *More Soccer Shorts* (1991), *The Guinness Record of the World Cup 1930–1994* (1994), *The Football Fact Book* (1990 and 1993). In 1974 he contributed the South American section for John Moynihan's *Football Fever.*

The author is married to June and has a daughter Glenda.

THE AUTHOR

Jack Rollin was born in London in 1932 and educated at King's, Harrow. There he played soccer, while later at Westcliff-on-Sea High School it was rugby. Within ten days of joining the Royal Air Force he was playing in a Welsh Cup tie for RAF Pembroke, and in the Services he learned shorthand and typing, resuming his career in journalism and covering the 1954 World Cup in Switzerland in a freelance capacity.

In 1956 an ankle injury ended his own career during which, at the age of 14, he had been offered a trial with the United States club Chicago Maroon. Played representative football for Southend Youth in the 1951 Festival of Britain and for RAF Fighter Command. He [illegible] a [illegible] performance in 1971 against the European cup finalists Panathinaikos of Greece.

For ten years Jack Rollin was Editor of the weekly magazine Soccer Star and its companion monthly World Soccer, before becoming a freelance agent in 1970. Since then he has researched football for BBC Television, acted as an assistant to commentators on Match of the Day, spoken on radio and appeared on television programmes. He has contributed to [illegible] London and Radio Times, and in 1975 he won the Designers and Art Directors Association Silver Award for Radio Times World Cup Special for the most outstanding specialist feature of the year.

In 1972 he became one of the compilers of the Rothmans Football Yearbook and later became its Editor. He has provided advice on the football sections of the Encyclopaedia Britannica and Guinness Book of Records. He is a football columnist for the Sunday Telegraph.

Jack Rollin contributed to three part-works: Book of Football (6 vols 1970–72), Football (6 vols 1977) and Football Handbook (1979–80). His articles have appeared in programmes for matches at Wembley Stadium since 1965. He has produced handbooks which include World Soccer Digest 1961, 1962 and 1963 and World Cup Digest 1966.

In 1978 he carried out the information research for the BBC Television series The Game of the Century and produced the first edition of The Guinness Book of Soccer Facts and Feats.

Other books he has written: England's World Cup Triumph (1966), A Source Book of Football (1971), The History of Aldershot Football Club (1975), World Cup Guide (1982), Soccer at War 1939–45 (1985), Soccer: The Records (1985), Soccer Records, Facts and Champions (1988), Soccer Shorts (1988) and More Soccer Shorts (1991), The Guinness Record of the World Cup 1930–1994 (1993), The Football Fact Book (1990 and 1993). In 1994 he contributed the South American section for John Motson's Football [illegible].

Jack Rollin is married to June and has a daughter, Glenda.

Season Club League Appearances/Goals

Season Club League Appearances/Goals

ABBEY, Nathanael

Born Islington 11.7.78
Goalkeeper. From Trainee.

Season	Club	Apps	Goals
1995–96	Luton T	—	—

ABBOTT, Gordon

Born Edinburgh 24.2.79
Midfield. From Falkirk Under-16.

Season	Club	Apps	Goals
1995–96	Falkirk	1	—

ABBOTT, Greg

Born Coventry 14.12.63 Ht 5 9 Wt 10 07
Midfield. From Apprentice.

Season	Club	Apps	Goals
1981–82	Coventry C	—	—
1982–83	Bradford C	11	—
1983–84		35	3
1984–85		42	6
1985–86		39	10
1986–87		33	7
1987–88		32	5
1988–89		28	4
1989–90		35	3
1990–91		26	—
1991–92	Halifax T	28	1
From Guiseley			
1992–93	Hull C	27	1
1993–94		40	6
1994–95		26	3
1995–96		31	6

ABLETT, Gary

Born Liverpool 19.11.65 Ht 6 2
Wt 12 02
Defender. From Apprentice. England Under-21, B.

Season	Club	Apps	Goals
1983–84	Liverpool	—	—
1984–85		—	—
1984–85	*Derby Co*	6	—
1985–86	Liverpool	—	—
1986–87	*Hull C*	5	—
1986–87	Liverpool	5	1
1987–88		17	—
1988–89		35	—
1989–90		15	—
1990–91		23	—
1991–92		14	—
1991–92	Everton	17	1
1992–93		40	—
1993–94		32	1
1994–95		26	3
1995–96		13	—
1995–96	*Sheffield U*	12	—

ABRAHAMS, Paul

Born Colchester 31.10.73 Ht 5 8
Wt 11 03
Forward. From Trainee.

Season	Club	Apps	Goals
1991–92	Colchester U	—	—
1992–93		23	6
1993–94		4	—
1994–95		28	2
1994–95	Brentford	10	3
1995–96		17	3
1995–96	*Colchester U*	8	2

ADAMS, Charles

Born Irvine 21.3.76 Ht 5 10 Wt 11 05
Midfield. From Kilwinning Rangers.

Season	Club	Apps	Goals
1995–96	Partick T	5	—

ADAMS, Darren

Born Newham 12.1.74 Ht 5 7 Wt 10 07
Forward. From Danson Furnace.

Season	Club	Apps	Goals
1993–94	Cardiff C	14	1
1994–95		6	—
1995–96		14	3

ADAMS, Derek

Born Aberdeen 25.6.75 Ht 5 10
Wt 11 12
Midfield. From Aberdeen.

Season	Club	Apps	Goals
1994–95	Burnley	—	—
1995–96		2	—

ADAMS, Kieran

Born St Ives 20.10.77 Ht 5 10 Wt 11 06
Midfield. From Trainee.

Season	Club	Apps	Goals
1994–95	Barnet	4	—
1995–96		1	—

ADAMS, Micky

Born Sheffield 8.11.61 Ht 5 8 Wt 11 04
Midfield. From Apprentice. England Youth.

Season	Club	Apps	Goals
1979–80	Gillingham	4	—
1980–81		13	—
1981–82		31	2
1982–83		44	3
1983–84	Coventry C	17	1

Season	Club	League Appearances/Goals	
1984–85		31	3
1985–86		31	3
1986–87		11	2
1986–87	Leeds U	17	1
1987–88		40	—
1988–89		16	1
1988–89	Southampton	8	—
1989–90		15	—
1990–91		30	—
1991–92		34	3
1992–93		38	4
1993–94		19	—
1993–94	Stoke C	10	3
1994–95	Fulham	21	7
1995–96		5	2

ADAMS, Neil

Born Stoke 23.11.65 Ht 5 8 Wt 10 12
Midfield. From Local. England Under-21.

Season	Club	Apps	Goals
1985–86	Stoke C	32	4
1986–87	Everton	12	—
1987–88		8	—
1988–89		—	—
1988–89	*Oldham Ath*	9	—
1989–90	Oldham Ath	27	4
1990–91		31	6
1991–92		26	4
1992–93		32	9
1993–94		13	—
1993–94	Norwich C	14	—
1994–95		33	3
1995–96		42	2

ADAMS, Tony

Born London 10.10.66 Ht 6 3 Wt 13 11
Defender. From Apprentice. England Schools, Youth, Under-21, B, 45 full caps.

Season	Club	Apps	Goals
1983–84	Arsenal	3	—
1984–85		16	—
1985–86		10	—
1986–87		42	6
1987–88		39	2
1988–89		36	4
1989–90		38	5
1990–91		30	1
1991–92		35	2
1992–93		35	—
1993–94		35	—
1994–95		27	3
1995–96		21	1

ADCOCK, Tony

Born Bethnal Green 27.2.63 Ht 5 10
Wt 11 09
Forward. From Apprentice.

Season	Club	Apps	Goals
1980–81	Colchester U	1	—
1981–82		40	5
1982–83		30	17
1983–84		43	26
1984–85		28	24
1985–86		33	15
1986–87		35	11
1987–88	Manchester C	15	5
1987–88	Northampton T	18	10
1988–89		46	17
1989–90		8	3
1989–90	Bradford C	28	5
1990–91		10	1
1990–91	Northampton T	21	3
1991–92		14	7
1991–92	Peterborough U	24	7
1992–93		45	16
1993–94		42	12
1994–95	Luton T	2	—
1995–96	Colchester U	41	12

ADEBOLA, Dele

Born Lagos 23.6.75 Ht 6 3 Wt 12 06
Forward. From Trainee.

Season	Club	Apps	Goals
1992–93	Crewe Alex	6	—
1993–94		—	—
1994–95		30	8
1995–96		29	8

ADEKOLA, David

Born Lagos 19.5.68 Ht 6 0 Wt 12 10
Forward.

Season	Club	Apps	Goals
1992–93	Bury	16	8
1993–94		19	4
1993–94	*Exeter C*	3	1
1994–95	Bournemouth	—	—
1994–95	Wigan Ath	4	—
1994–95	Hereford U	—	—
1995–96	Cambridge U	5	1

AGANA, Tony

Born London 2.10.63 Ht 6 0 Wt 12 02
Forward. From Weymouth.

Season	Club	Apps	Goals
1987–88	Watford	15	1
1987–88	Sheffield U	12	2
1988–89		46	24

Season Club League Appearances/Goals

Season	Club	Apps	Goals
1989–90	....	31	10
1990–91	....	16	2
1991–92	....	13	4
1991–92	Notts Co..................	13	1
1991–92	*Leeds U*..................	2	—
1992–93	Notts Co..................	29	2
1993–94	....	20	4
1994–95	....	31	3
1995–96	....	29	2

AGNEW, Paul

Born Lisburn 15.8.65 Ht 5 9 Wt 10 07
Defender. From Cliftonville. Northern Ireland Schools, Youth, Under-23.

Season	Club	Apps	Goals
1983–84	Grimsby T	1	—
1984–85	....	12	—
1985–86	....	16	—
1986–87	....	29	—
1987–88	....	38	1
1988–89	....	34	—
1989–90	....	24	2
1990–91	....	7	—
1991–92	....	24	—
1992–93	....	23	—
1993–94	....	23	—
1994–95	....	10	—
1994–95	WBA......................	14	1
1995–96	....	3	—

AGNEW, Steve

Born Shipley 9.11.65 Ht 5 10 Wt 11 01
Midfield. From Apprentice.

Season	Club	Apps	Goals
1983–84	Barnsley..................	1	—
1984–85	....	10	1
1985–86	....	2	—
1986–87	....	33	—
1987–88	....	25	6
1988–89	....	39	6
1989–90	....	46	8
1990–91	....	38	8
1991–92	Blackburn R..............	2	—
1992–93	....	—	—
1992–93	*Portsmouth*..............	5	—
1992–93	Leicester C	9	1
1993–94	....	36	3
1994–95	....	11	—
1994–95	Sunderland	16	2
1995–96	....	29	5

AGOSTINO, Paul

Born Woodville 9.6.75 Ht 5 11 Wt 12 12
Forward.

Season	Club	Apps	Goals
1992–93	Young Boys..............	12	2
1993–94	....	14	1
1994–95	....	3	—
1995–96	Bristol C..................	40	10

AINSWORTH, Gareth

Born Blackburn 10.5.73 Ht 5 9 Wt 11 09
Midfield. From Blackburn R Trainee.

Season	Club	Apps	Goals
1991–92	Preston NE..............	5	—
1992–93	Cambridge U............	4	1
1992–93	Preston NE..............	26	—
1993–94	....	38	11
1994–95	....	16	1
1995–96	....	2	—
1995–96	Lincoln C................	31	12

AISTON, Sam

Born Newcastle 21.11.76 Ht 6 0
Wt 12 10
Midfield. From Newcastle U Trainee.

Season	Club	Apps	Goals
1995–96	Sunderland	14	—

AKINBIYI, Ade

Born Hackney 10.10.74 Ht 6 1 Wt 12 09
Forward. From Trainee.

Season	Club	Apps	Goals
1992–93	Norwich C	—	—
1993–94	....	2	—
1993–94	*Hereford U*	4	2
1994–95	Norwich C	13	—
1994–95	*Brighton & HA*	7	4
1995–96	Norwich C	22	3

ALBERT, Philippe

Born Bouillon 10.8.67 Ht 6 3 Wt 13 00
Defender. Belgium 36 full caps.

Season	Club	Apps	Goals
1987–88	Charleroi..................	32	5
1988–89	....	33	2
1989–90	Mechelen	22	—
1990–91	....	32	3
1991–92	....	33	2
1992–93	Anderlecht	25	5
1993–94	....	25	4
1994–95	Newcastle U	17	2
1995–96	....	23	4

Season Club League Appearances/Goals

ALCIDE, Colin

Born Huddersfield 14.4.72 Ht 6 2
Wt 12 09
Forward. From Emley.

Season	Club	Apps	Goals
1995–96	Lincoln C	27	6

ALDOUS, Richard

Born Sheffield 2.9.76 Ht 6 2 Wt 13 00
Goalkeeper. From Trainee.

Season	Club	Apps	Goals
1994–95	Sheffield W	—	—
1995–96		—	—

ALDRIDGE, John

Born Liverpool 18.9.58 Ht 5 11
Wt 12 03
Forward. From South Liverpool. Eire 68 full caps.

Season	Club	Apps	Goals
1978–79	Newport Co	—	—
1979–80		38	14
1980–81		27	7
1981–82		36	11
1982–83		41	17
1983–84		28	20
1983–84	Oxford U	8	4
1984–85		42	30
1985–86		39	23
1986–87		25	15
1986–87	Liverpool	10	2
1987–88		36	26
1988–89		35	21
1989–90		2	1
1989–90	Real Sociedad	28	16
1990–91		35	17
1991–92	Tranmere R	43	22
1992–93		30	21
1993–94		34	21
1994–95		33	24
1995–96		45	27

ALDRIDGE, Martin

Born Northampton 6.12.74 Ht 5 11
Wt 12 02
Forward. From Trainee.

Season	Club	Apps	Goals
1991–92	Northampton T	5	—
1992–93		9	2
1993–94		29	8
1994–95		27	7
1995–96		—	—
1995–96	Oxford U	18	9

ALEXANDER, Graham

Born Coventry 10.10.71 Ht 5 10 Wt 12 02
Midfield. From Trainee.

Season	Club	Apps	Goals
1989–90	Scunthorpe U	—	—
1990–91		1	—
1991–92		36	5
1992–93		41	5
1993–94		41	4
1994–95		40	4
1995–96	Luton T	37	1

ALEXANDER, Keith

Born Nottingham 14.11.58 Ht 6 4
Wt 14 08
Forward. From Barnet.

Season	Club	Apps	Goals
1988–89	Grimsby T	44	14
1989–90		38	12
1990–91		1	—
1990–91	Stockport Co	11	—
1990–91	Lincoln C	23	3
1991–92		15	1
1992–93		7	—
1993–94		—	—
1994–95	Mansfield T	2	—
1995–96		1	—

ALLAN, Derek

Born Irving 24.12.74 Ht 6 0 Wt 12 01
Defender. From Ayr U BC.

Season	Club	Apps	Goals
1992–93	Ayr U	5	—
1992–93	Southampton	1	—
1993–94		—	—
1994–95		—	—
1995–96		—	—
1995–96	*Brighton & HA*	8	—

ALLARDYCE, Craig

Born Bolton 9.6.75 Ht 6 3 Wt 13 07
Defender. From Trainee.

Season	Club	Apps	Goals
1992–93	Preston NE	1	—
1993–94		—	—
1994–95	Blackpool	—	—
1995–96		1	—

ALLEN, Bradley

Born Harold Wood 13.9.71 Ht 5 7
Wt 10 07
Forward. From School. England Youth, Under-21.

Season	Club	Apps	Goals
1988–89	QPR	1	—

Season Club League Appearances/Goals

Season	Club	Apps	Goals
1989–90		—	—
1990–91		10	2
1991–92		11	5
1992–93		25	10
1993–94		21	7
1994–95		5	2
1995–96		8	1
1995–96	Charlton Ath	10	3

ALLEN, Chris

Born Oxford 18.11.72 Ht 6 0 Wt 12 02
Forward. From Trainee. England Under-21.

Season	Club	Apps	Goals
1990–91	Oxford U	—	—
1991–92		14	1
1992–93		31	3
1993–94		45	3
1994–95		36	2
1995–96		24	3
1995–96	*Nottingham F*	3	1

ALLEN, Clive

Born London 20.5.61 Ht 5 11 Wt 12 07
Forward. From Apprentice. England Schools, Youth, Under-21, 3 full caps. Football League.

Season	Club	Apps	Goals
1978–79	QPR	10	4
1979–80		39	28
1980–81	Arsenal	—	—
1980–81	Crystal Palace	25	9
1981–82	QPR	37	13
1982–83		25	13
1983–84		25	14
1984–85	Tottenham H	13	7
1985–86		19	9
1986–87		39	33
1987–88		34	11
1988–89	Bordeaux	19	13
1989–90	Manchester C	30	10
1990–91		20	4
1991–92		3	2
1991–92	Chelsea	16	7
1991–92	West Ham U	4	1
1992–93		27	14
1993–94		7	2
1993–94	Millwall	12	—
1994–95		—	—
1995–96	Carlisle U	3	—

ALLEN, Gavin

Born Bangor 17.6.76 Ht 6 0 Wt 10 05
Forward. From Trainee.

Season	Club	Apps	Goals
1994–95	Tranmere R	—	—
1995–96	Stockport Co	—	—

ALLEN, Graham

Born Bolton 8.4.77 Ht 6 1 Wt 11 12
Defender. From Trainee. England Youth.

Season	Club	Apps	Goals
1994–95	Everton	—	—
1995–96		—	—

ALLEN, Malcolm

Born Dioniolen 21.3.67 Ht 5 8 Wt 11 08
Forward. From Apprentice. Wales Youth, B, 14 full caps.

Season	Club	Apps	Goals
1984–85	Watford	—	—
1985–86		13	2
1986–87		4	—
1987–88		22	3
1987–88	*Aston Villa*	4	—
1988–89	Norwich C	23	5
1989–90		12	3
1989–90	Millwall	8	2
1990–91		21	7
1991–92		11	5
1992–93		41	10
1993–94	Newcastle U	9	5
1994–95		1	—
1995–96		—	—

ALLEN, Martin

Born Reading 14.8.65 Ht 5 10 Wt 11 00
Midfield. From School. England Youth, Under-21, B, Football League.

Season	Club	Apps	Goals
1983–84	QPR	—	—
1984–85		5	—
1985–86		31	3
1986–87		32	5
1987–88		38	4
1988–89		28	4
1989–90		2	—
1989–90	West Ham U	39	9
1990–91		40	3
1991–92		19	—
1992–93		34	4
1993–94		26	6
1994–95		29	2
1995–96		3	1
1995–96	Portsmouth	27	4

ALLEN, Paul

Born Aveley 28.8.62 Ht 5 7 Wt 10 04
Midfield. From Apprentice. England Youth, Under-21.

Season	Club	Apps	Goals
1979–80	West Ham U	31	2
1980–81		3	1
1981–82		28	—
1982–83		33	—
1983–84		19	—
1984–85		38	3
1985–86	Tottenham H	33	1
1986–87		37	3
1987–88		39	3
1988–89		37	1
1989–90		32	6
1990–91		36	3
1991–92		39	3
1992–93		38	3
1993–94		1	—
1993–94	Southampton	32	1
1994–95		11	—
1994–95	*Luton T*	4	—
1994–95	*Stoke C*	17	1
1995–96	Southampton	—	—
1995–96	Swindon T	27	—

ALLEN, Rory

Born Beckenham 17.10.77
Forward. From Trainee.

Season	Club	Apps	Goals
1995–96	Tottenham H	—	—

ALLINSON, Jamie

Born Stockton 15.6.78 Ht 6 1 Wt 12 00
Defender. From Trainee.

Season	Club	Apps	Goals
1995–96	Hartlepool U	4	—

ALLISON, Neil

Born Hull 20.10.73 Ht 6 2 Wt 11 10
Defender. From Trainee.

Season	Club	Apps	Goals
1990–91	Hull C	1	—
1991–92		7	—
1992–93		11	—
1993–94		28	1
1994–95		13	—
1995–96		35	2

ALLISON, Wayne

Born Huddersfield 16.10.68 Ht 6 1
Wt 12 06
Forward.

Season	Club	Apps	Goals
1986–87	Halifax T	8	4
1987–88		35	4
1988–89		41	15
1989–90	Watford	7	—
1990–91	Bristol C	37	6
1991–92		43	10
1992–93		39	4
1993–94		39	15
1994–95		37	13
1995–96	Swindon T	44	17

ALLON, Joe

Born Gateshead 12.11.66 Ht 5 11
Wt 13 06
Forward. From Trainee. England Youth.

Season	Club	Apps	Goals
1984–85	Newcastle U	1	—
1985–86		3	1
1986–87		5	1
1987–88	Swansea C	32	11
1988–89		2	—
1988–89	Hartlepool U	21	4
1989–90		45	18
1990–91		46	28
1991–92	Chelsea	11	2
1991–92	*Port Vale*	6	—
1992–93	Chelsea	3	—
1992–93	Brentford	24	6
1993–94		21	13
1993–94	*Southend U*	3	—
1993–94	Port Vale	4	2
1994–95		19	7
1995–96	Lincoln C	4	—
1995–96	Hartlepool U	22	8

ALLOTT, Mark

Born Manchester 3.10.77
Forward. From Trainee.

Season	Club	Apps	Goals
1995–96	Oldham Ath	—	—

ALSFORD, Julian

Born Poole 24.12.72 Ht 6 2 Wt 13 07
Defender. From Trainee.

Season	Club	Apps	Goals
1991–92	Watford	—	—
1992–93		5	—

Season	Club	Apps	Goals
1993–94		8	1
1994–95	Chester C	35	—
1995–96		24	—

AMMANN, Mike

Born California 8.2.71 Ht 6 2 Wt 14 04
Goalkeeper. From California State University.

Season	Club	Apps	Goals
1994–95	Charlton Ath	19	—
1995–96		11	—

AMOKACHI, Daniel

Born Nigeria 30.12.72 Ht 5 10 Wt 13 00
Forward. Nigeria full caps.

Season	Club	Apps	Goals
1990–91	FC Brugge	3	—
1991–92		26	12
1992–93		23	9
1993–94		28	14
1994–95		1	—
1994–95	Everton	18	4
1995–96		25	6

AMPADU, Kwame

Born Bradford 20.12.70 Ht 5 10
Wt 11 10
Forward. From Belvedere, Trainee. Eire Youth, Under-21.

Season	Club	Apps	Goals
1988–89	Arsenal	—	—
1989–90		2	—
1990–91		—	—
1990–91	*Plymouth Arg*	6	1
1990–91	*WBA*	7	1
1991–92	WBA	21	3
1992–93		10	—
1993–94		11	—
1993–94	Swansea C	13	—
1994–95		44	6
1995–96		43	2

ANDERSEN, Erik Bo

Born Randers 14.11.70
Forward. Denmark 8 full caps.

Season	Club	Apps	Goals
1995–96	Rangers	6	6

ANDERSEN, Leif

Born Fredrikstad 19.4.71 Ht 6 5
Wt 14 10
Defender. From Moss.

Season	Club	Apps	Goals
1995–96	Crystal Palace	16	—

ANDERSON, Colin

Born Newcastle 26.4.62 Ht 5 10
Wt 11 11
Midfield. From Apprentice.

Season	Club	Apps	Goals
1979–80	Burnley	—	—
1980–81		2	—
1981–82		4	—
1982–83	Torquay U	42	5
1983–84		39	4
1984–85		28	2
1984–85	*QPR*	—	—
1984–85	WBA	—	—
1985–86		11	—
1986–87		28	1
1987–88		23	1
1988–89		42	6
1989–90		13	—
1990–91		23	2
1991–92	Walsall	26	2
1992–93	Hereford U	35	—
1993–94		35	1
1994–95	Exeter C	21	1
1995–96		13	—

ANDERSON, Derek

Born Paisley 15.5.72 Ht 6 0 Wt 11 00
Defender. From Kilwinning Rangers.

Season	Club	Apps	Goals
1993–94	Kilmarnock	—	—
1994–95		20	—
1995–96		28	—

ANDERSON, Ijah

Born Hackney 30.12.75 Ht 5 7 Wt 10 02
Defender. From Tottenham H Trainee.

Season	Club	Apps	Goals
1994–95	Southend U	—	—
1995–96	Brentford	25	2

ANDERSON, Viv

Born Nottingham 29.8.56 Ht 6 1
Wt 13 00
Defender. From Apprentice. England Under-21, B, 30 full caps. Football League

Season	Club	Apps	Goals
1974–75	Nottingham F	16	—
1975–76		21	—
1976–77		38	1
1977–78		37	3
1978–79		40	1
1979–80		41	3
1980–81		31	—
1981–82		39	—

Season	Club	Apps	Goals
1982–83	....	25	1
1983–84	....	40	6
1984–85	Arsenal	41	3
1985–86	....	39	2
1986–87	....	40	4
1987–88	Manchester U	31	2
1988–89	....	6	—
1989–90	....	16	—
1990–91	....	1	—
1990–91	Sheffield W...............	22	2
1991–92	....	22	3
1992–93	....	26	3
1993–94	Barnsley.....................	20	3
1994–95	Middlesbrough..........	2	—
1995–96	....	—	—

ANDERTON, Darren

Born Southampton 3.3.72 Ht 6 1
Wt 12 00
Forward. From Trainee. England Youth, Under-21, 16 full caps.

Season	Club	Apps	Goals
1989–90	Portsmouth...............	—	—
1990–91	....	20	—
1991–92	....	42	7
1992–93	Tottenham H............	34	6
1993–94	....	37	6
1994–95	....	37	5
1995–96	....	8	2

ANDISON, Gary

Born Gateshead 12.12.76 Ht 5 11
Wt 12 00
Defender. From Trainee.

Season	Club	Apps	Goals
1995–96	Sheffield U................	—	—

ANDREWS, Ian

Born Nottingham 1.12.64 Ht 6 2
Wt 14 01
Goalkeeper. From Apprentice. England Youth, Under-21.

Season	Club	Apps	Goals
1982–83	Leicester C	—	—
1983–84	....	2	—
1983–84	*Swindon T*	1	—
1984–85	Leicester C	31	—
1985–86	....	39	—
1986–87	....	42	—
1987–88	....	12	—
1988–89	Celtic.........................	5	—
1988–89	*Leeds U*......................	1	—
1989–90	Celtic.........................	—	—
1989–90	Southampton.............	3	—
1990–91	....	1	—
1991–92	....	1	—
1992–93	....	—	—
1993–94	....	5	—
1994–95	....	—	—
1994–95	Bournemouth............	38	—
1995–96	....	26	—

ANDREWS, Nicky

Born London 10.10.75 Ht 5 10 Wt 11 05
Defender. From Trainee.

Season	Club	Apps	Goals
1994–95	Fulham.......................	—	—
1995–96	....	—	—

ANDREWS, Philip

Born Andover 14.9.76 Ht 5 11 Wt 10 06
Forward. From Trainee.

Season	Club	Apps	Goals
1993–94	Brighton & HA.........	5	—
1994–95	....	5	—
1995–96	....	8	—

ANDREWS, Wayne

Born Paddington 25.11.77
Midfield. From Trainee.

Season	Club	Apps	Goals
1995–96	Watford.....................	1	—

ANGEL, Mark

Born Newcastle 23.8.75 Ht 5 10
Wt 11 01
Forward. From Trainee.

Season	Club	Apps	Goals
1993–94	Sunderland	—	—
1994–95	....	—	—
1995–96	Oxford U	27	1

ANGELL, Brett

Born Marlborough 20.8.68 Ht 6 2
Wt 13 10
Forward. From Portsmouth, Cheltenham T.

Season	Club	Apps	Goals
1987–88	Derby Co..................	—	—
1988–89	Stockport Co............	26	5
1989–90	....	44	23
1990–91	Southend U	42	15
1991–92	....	43	21
1992–93	....	13	5
1993–94	....	5	4
1993–94	*Everton*	1	—
1993–94	Southend U	12	2
1993–94	Everton......................	15	1

Season	Club	League Appearances/Goals	
1994–95		4	—
1994–95	Sunderland	8	—
1995–96		2	—
1995–96	*Sheffield U*	6	2
1995–96	*WBA*	3	—

ANGUS, Terry

Born Coventry 14.1.66 Ht 6 0 Wt 13 10
Defender. From VS Rugby.

Season	Club	League Appearances/Goals	
1990–91	Northampton T	42	2
1991–92		37	2
1992–93		37	2
1993–94	Fulham	36	2
1994–95		23	—
1995–96		31	2

ANNON, Darren

Born London 17.2.72 Ht 5 5 Wt 10 11
Midfield. From Carshalton Ath.

Season	Club	League Appearances/Goals	
1993–94	Brentford	9	1
1994–95		10	1
1995–96		1	—

ANSAH, Andy

Born Lewisham 19.3.69 Ht 5 9 Wt 11 03
Forward. From Crystal Palace.

Season	Club	League Appearances/Goals	
1988–89	Brentford	7	2
1989–90		1	—
1989–90	Southend U	7	1
1990–91		40	9
1991–92		40	9
1992–93		30	7
1993–94		27	7
1994–95		9	—
1994–95	*Brentford*	3	1
1995–96	Southend U	4	—
1995–96	*Brentford*	6	1
1995–96	Peterborough U	2	1
1995–96	Gillingham	2	—

ANTHONY, Graham

Born Jarrow 9.8.75 Ht 5 8 Wt 10 08
Midfield. From Trainee.

Season	Club	League Appearances/Goals	
1993–94	Sheffield U	—	—
1994–95		1	—
1995–96		—	—
1995–96	*Scarborough*	2	—

ANTHROBUS, Steve

Born Lewisham 10.11.68 Ht 6 3
Wt 14 11
Forward.

Season	Club	League Appearances/Goals	
1986–87	Millwall	—	—
1987–88		3	—
1988–89		3	—
1989–90		15	4
1989–90	*Southend U*	—	—
1989–90	Wimbledon	10	—
1990–91		3	—
1991–92		10	—
1992–93		5	—
1993–94		—	—
1993–94	*Peterborough U*	2	—
1994–95	Wimbledon	—	—
1994–95	*Chester C*	7	—
1995–96	Shrewsbury T	39	10

APPLEBY, Matty

Born Middlesbrough 16.4.72 Ht 5 10
Wt 11 10
Defender. From Trainee.

Season	Club	League Appearances/Goals	
1989–90	Newcastle U	—	—
1990–91		1	—
1991–92		18	—
1992–93		—	—
1993–94		1	—
1993–94	*Darlington*	10	1
1994–95	Darlington	36	1
1995–96		43	6

APPLEBY, Ritchie

Born Middlesbrough 18.9.75 Ht 5 8
Wt 10 06
Midfield. From Trainee. England Youth.

Season	Club	League Appearances/Goals	
1993–94	Newcastle U	—	—
1994–95		—	—
1994–95	*Darlington*	—	—
1995–96	Ipswich T	3	—

APPLETON, Michael

Born Salford 4.12.75 Ht 5 9 Wt 11 13
Midfield. From Trainee.

Season	Club	League Appearances/Goals	
1994–95	Manchester U	—	—
1995–96		—	—
1995–96	*Lincoln C*	4	—

Season Club League Appearances/Goals

ARBER, Mark

Born South Africa 9.10.77
Defender. From Trainee.

Season	Club	Apps	Goals
1995–96	Tottenham H	—	—

ARCHDEACON, Owen

Born Glasgow 4.3.66 Ht 5 7 Wt 10 09
Midfield. From Gourock U. Scotland Youth, Under-21.

Season	Club	Apps	Goals
1982–83	Celtic	—	—
1983–84		1	—
1984–85		3	1
1985–86		23	3
1986–87		29	2
1987–88		10	1
1988–89		10	—
1989–90	Barnsley	21	3
1990–91		45	2
1991–92		40	6
1992–93		38	6
1993–94		42	2
1994–95		9	1
1995–96		38	3

ARCHER, Lee

Born Bristol 6.11.72 Ht 5 6 Wt 9 06
Midfield. From Trainee.

Season	Club	Apps	Goals
1991–92	Bristol R	5	—
1992–93		2	1
1993–94		37	5
1994–95		42	6
1995–96		19	1

ARCHER, Paul

Born Leicester 25.4.78 Ht 5 7 Wt 9 04
Midfield. From Trainee.

Season	Club	Apps	Goals
1994–95	Nottingham F	—	—
1995–96		—	—

ARDLEY, Neal

Born Epsom 1.9.72 Ht 5 11 Wt 11 09
Midfield. From Trainee. England Under-21.

Season	Club	Apps	Goals
1990–91	Wimbledon	1	—
1991–92		8	—
1992–93		26	4
1993–94		16	1
1994–95		14	1
1995–96		6	—

ARIS, Steven

Born London 27.4.78
Defender.

Season	Club	Apps	Goals
1995–96	Millwall	—	—

ARKINS, Vinny

Born Dublin 18.9.70 Ht 6 2 Wt 11 10
Forward. From Home Farm. Eire Youth, Under-21.

Season	Club	Apps	Goals
1987–88	Dundee U	—	—
1988–89		—	—
From Shamrock R			
1991–92	St Johnstone	21	5
1992–93		26	6
1993–94		1	—
From Shelbourne			
1995–96	Notts Co	23	7

ARMSTRONG, Alun

Born Gateshead 22.2.75 Ht 6 0 Wt 12 00
Forward. From School.

Season	Club	Apps	Goals
1993–94	Newcastle U	—	—
1994–95	Stockport Co	45	14
1995–96		46	13

ARMSTRONG, Chris

Born Newcastle 19.6.71 Ht 6 0 Wt 13 03
Forward. From Llay Welfare. England B.

Season	Club	Apps	Goals
1988–89	Wrexham	—	—
1989–90		22	3
1990–91		38	10
1991–92	Millwall	25	4
1992–93		3	1
1992–93	Crystal Palace	35	15
1993–94		43	22
1994–95		40	8
1995–96	Tottenham H	36	15

ARMSTRONG, Craig

Born South Shields 23.5.75 Ht 5 11 Wt 12 10
Defender. From Trainee.

Season	Club	Apps	Goals
1992–93	Nottingham F	—	—
1993–94		—	—
1994–95		—	—
1994–95	*Burnley*	4	—
1995–96	Nottingham F	—	—
1995–96	*Bristol R*	14	—

ARMSTRONG, Gordon

Born Newcastle 15.7.67 Ht 6 0 Wt 12 10
Midfield. From Apprentice.

Season	Club	Apps	Goals
1984–85	Sunderland	4	—
1985–86		14	2
1986–87		41	5
1987–88		37	5
1988–89		45	8
1989–90		46	8
1990–91		35	6
1991–92		40	10
1992–93		45	3
1993–94		26	2
1994–95		15	1
1995–96		1	—
1995–96	*Bristol C*	6	—
1995–96	*Northampton T*	4	1

ARNISON, Paul

Born Hartlepool 18.9.77 Ht 5 9
Wt 10 12
Midfield. From Trainee.

Season	Club	Apps	Goals
1995–96	Newcastle U	—	—

ARNOTT, Andy

Born Chatham 18.10.73 Ht 6 1 Wt 12 02
Forward. From Trainee.

Season	Club	Apps	Goals
1990–91	Gillingham	—	—
1991–92		19	2
1992–93		15	6
1992–93	*Manchester U*	—	—
1993–94	Gillingham	10	2
1994–95		28	2
1995–96		1	—
1995–96	Leyton Orient	19	3

ARNOTT, Doug

Born Lanark 5.8.64 Ht 5 7 Wt 10 07
Forward. From Pollok Juniors.

Season	Club	Apps	Goals
1986–87	Motherwell	1	—
1987–88		2	—
1988–89		14	1
1989–90		30	5
1990–91		29	14
1991–92		26	8
1992–93		33	6
1993–94		29	8
1994–95		27	10
1995–96		27	3

ASABA, Carl

Born London 28.1.73 Ht 6 1 Wt 12 12
Forward. From Dulwich Hamlet.

Season	Club	Apps	Goals
1994–95	Brentford	—	—
1994–95	*Colchester U*	12	2
1995–96	Brentford	10	2

ASHBEE, Ian

Born Birmingham 6.9.76 Ht 6 0
Wt 13 07
Defender. From Trainee. England Youth.

Season	Club	Apps	Goals
1994–95	Derby Co	1	—
1995–96		—	—

ASHBY, Barry

Born London 21.11.70 Ht 6 2 Wt 12 02
Defender. From Trainee.

Season	Club	Apps	Goals
1988–89	Watford	—	—
1989–90		18	1
1990–91		23	—
1991–92		21	—
1992–93		35	—
1993–94		17	2
1993–94	Brentford	8	1
1994–95		40	1
1995–96		33	1

ASHCROFT, Lee

Born Preston 7.9.72 Ht 5 10 Wt 11 02
Forward. From Trainee. England Under-21.

Season	Club	Apps	Goals
1990–91	Preston NE	14	1
1991–92		38	5
1992–93		39	7
1993–94	WBA	21	3
1994–95		38	10
1995–96		26	4
1995–96	*Notts Co*	6	—

ASHLEY, Kevin

Born Birmingham 31.12.68 Ht 5 7
Wt 11 10
Defender. From Apprentice.

Season	Club	Apps	Goals
1986–87	Birmingham C	7	—
1987–88		1	—
1988–89		15	—
1989–90		31	1
1990–91		3	—
1990–91	Wolverhampton W	16	—
1991–92		44	1

Season	Club	League Appearances/Goals	
1992–93	....	28	—
1993–94	....	—	—
1994–95	Peterborough U.........	27	—
1995–96	....	9	—
1995–96	Doncaster R...............	3	—

ASPIN, Neil

Born Gateshead 12.4.65 Ht 6 0
Wt 12 06
Defender. From Apprentice.

Season	Club	League Appearances/Goals	
1981–82	Leeds U	1	—
1982–83	....	15	—
1983–84	....	21	1
1984–85	....	32	1
1985–86	....	38	2
1986–87	....	41	1
1987–88	....	26	—
1988–89	....	33	—
1989–90	Port Vale	42	—
1990–91	....	41	1
1991–92	....	42	—
1992–93	....	35	—
1993–94	....	40	1
1994–95	....	37	—
1995–96	....	22	1

ASPINALL, Warren

Born Wigan 13.9.67 Ht 5 9 Wt 12 10
Forward. From Apprentice. England Youth.

Season	Club	League Appearances/Goals	
1984–85	Wigan Ath.................	10	1
1985–86	....	—	—
1985–86	Everton......................	1	—
1985–86	*Wigan Ath*..................	41	21
1986–87	Everton......................	6	—
1986–87	Aston Villa................	12	3
1987–88	....	32	11
1988–89	Portsmouth................	40	11
1989–90	....	3	—
1990–91	....	33	4
1991–92	....	24	4
1992–93	....	27	2
1993–94	....	5	—
1993–94	*Swansea C*.................	5	—
1993–94	Bournemouth............	24	5
1994–95	....	9	4
1994–95	*Carlisle U*..................	7	1
1995–96	Carlisle U..................	42	6

ASPRILLA, Faustino

Born Tulua 10.11.69 Ht 5 9 Wt 11 03
Forward. From Nacional. Colombia full caps.

Season	Club	League Appearances/Goals	
1992–93	Parma........................	26	7
1993–94	....	27	10
1994–95	....	25	6
1995–96	....	6	2
1995–96	Newcastle U..............	14	3

ATHERTON, Peter

Born Wigan 6.4.70 Ht 5 7 Wt 13 07
Defender. From Trainee. England Under-21.

Season	Club	League Appearances/Goals	
1987–88	Wigan Ath.................	16	—
1988–89	....	40	1
1989–90	....	46	—
1990–91	....	46	—
1991–92	....	1	—
1991–92	Coventry C...............	35	—
1992–93	....	39	—
1993–94	....	40	—
1994–95	Sheffield W...............	41	1
1995–96	....	36	—

ATKIN, Paul

Born Nottingham 3.9.69 Ht 6 0
Wt 13 00
Defender. From Trainee. England Youth.

Season	Club	League Appearances/Goals	
1987–88	Notts Co....................	—	—
1988–89	....	—	—
1988–89	Bury...........................	1	—
1989–90	....	9	1
1990–91	....	11	—
1991–92	York C......................	33	1
1992–93	....	31	2
1993–94	....	14	—
1994–95	....	34	—
1995–96	....	29	—

ATKINS, Ian

Born Birmingham 16.1.57 Ht 5 11
Wt 12 06
Midfield. From Apprentice.

Season	Club	League Appearances/Goals	
1974–75	Shrewsbury T............	—	—
1975–76	....	32	4
1976–77	....	43	7
1977–78	....	41	10
1978–79	....	44	11
1979–80	....	39	3

Season	Club	League Appearances/Goals	
1980–81		39	6
1981–82		40	17
1982–83	Sunderland	37	4
1983–84		40	2
1984–85		—	—
1984–85	Everton	6	1
1985–86		1	—
1985–86	Ipswich T	21	2
1986–87		40	1
1987–88		16	1
1987–88	Birmingham C	8	1
1988–89		40	3
1989–90		45	2
1990–91	Colchester U	—	—
1991–92	Birmingham C	8	—
1992–93		—	—
1992–93	Cambridge U	2	—
1993–94	Sunderland	—	—
1993–94	Doncaster R	7	—
1994–95		—	—
1994–95	Northampton T	—	—
1995–96		—	—

ATKINS, Mark

Born Doncaster 14.8.68 Ht 6 1 Wt 12 00
Defender. England Schools.

Season	Club	Apps	Goals
1986–87	Scunthorpe U	26	—
1987–88		22	2
1988–89	Blackburn R	46	6
1989–90		41	7
1990–91		42	4
1991–92		44	6
1992–93		31	5
1993–94		15	1
1994–95		34	6
1995–96		4	—
1995–96	Wolverhampton W	32	3

ATKINSON, Brian

Born Darlington 19.1.71 Ht 5 9
Wt 12 02
Midfield. From Trainee. England Under-21.

Season	Club	Apps	Goals
1988–89	Sunderland	3	—
1989–90		13	—
1990–91		6	—
1991–92		30	2
1992–93		36	2
1993–94		29	—
1994–95		17	—
1995–96		7	—
1995–96	*Carlisle U*	2	—

ATKINSON, Craig

Born Rotherham 29.9.77 Ht 6 0 Wt 11 02
Midfield. From Trainee. England Youth.

Season	Club	Apps	Goals
1994–95	Nottingham F	—	—
1995–96		—	—

ATKINSON, Dalian

Born Shrewsbury 21.3.68 Ht 6 0
Wt 13 10
Forward. England B.

Season	Club	Apps	Goals
1985–86	Ipswich	1	—
1986–87		8	—
1987–88		17	8
1988–89		34	10
1989–90	Sheffield W	38	10
1990–91	Real Sociedad	26	12
1991–92	Aston Villa	14	1
1992–93		28	11
1993–94		29	8
1994–95		16	3
1995–96		—	—

ATKINSON, Graeme

Born Hull 11.11.71 Ht 5 8 Wt 11 02
Midfield. From Trainee.

Season	Club	Apps	Goals
1989–90	Hull C	13	1
1990–91		16	—
1991–92		25	8
1992–93		46	6
1993–94		40	7
1994–95		9	1
1994–95	Preston NE	15	1
1995–96		44	5

ATKINSON, Paddy

Born Singapore 22.5.70 Ht 5 9 Wt 11 06
Defender. From Workington.

Season	Club	Apps	Goals
1995–96	York C	22	—

AUSTIN, Dean

Born Hemel Hempstead 26.4.70 Ht 6 0
Wt 11 06
Defender. From St. Albans C.

Season	Club	Apps	Goals
1989–90	Southend U	7	—
1990–91		44	—
1991–92		45	2
1992–93	Tottenham H	34	—
1993–94		23	—
1994–95		24	—
1995–96		28	—

AUSTIN, Kevin
Born Hackney 12.2.73 Ht 6 1 Wt 14 00
Defender. From Saffron Walden.

1993–94	Leyton Orient	30	—
1994–95		39	2
1995–96		40	1

AWFORD, Andy
Born Worcester 14.7.72 Ht 5 9 Wt 11 09
Defender. From Worcester C. England Youth, Under-21, Football League.

1988–89	Portsmouth	4	—
1989–90		—	—
1990–91		14	—
1991–92		45	—
1992–93		44	—
1993–94		35	—
1994–95		4	—
1995–96		18	1

AYORINDE, Sam
Born Lagos 20.10.74 Ht 6 0 Wt 12 07
Forward.

1995–96	Leyton Orient	1	—

AYRTON, Matthew
Born Rotherham 16.12.76 Ht 5 9
Wt 10 11
Midfield. From Trainee.

1995–96	Rotherham U	—	—

AYTON, Stuart
Born Glasgow 19.10.75 Ht 5 8 Wt 10 12
Midfield. From Rangers BC.

1992–93	Rangers	—	—
1993–94		—	—
1994–95	Partick T	1	—
1995–96		5	—

Season	Club	League Appearances/Goals	

BABB, Phil
Born Lambeth 30.11.70 Ht 6 0 Wt 12 03
Defender. From Trainee. Eire B, 20 full caps.

1988–89	Millwall	—	—
1989–90		—	—
1990–91	Bradford C	34	10
1991–92		46	4
1992–93	Coventry C	34	—
1993–94		40	3
1994–95		3	—
1994–95	Liverpool	34	—
1995–96		28	—

BADDELEY, Lee
Born Cardiff 12.7.74 Ht 6 1 Wt 12 07
Defender. From Trainee. Wales Under-21.

1990–91	Cardiff C	2	—
1991–92		18	—
1992–93		8	—
1993–94		30	—
1994–95		36	1
1995–96		30	—

BAGAYOKO, Salif
Born Manosque 9.5.77 Ht 6 0 Wt 12 00
Forward. From Trainee.

1995–96	Middlesbrough	—	—

BAGNALL, John
Born Southport 23.11.73 Ht 6 0
Wt 12 00
Goalkeeper. From Preston NE.

1993–94	Chester C	—	—
1994–95		—	—
1994–95	Wigan Ath	—	—
1995–96	Bury	—	—
1995–96	Chester C	—	—

BAILEY, Danny
Born Leyton 21.5.64 Ht 5 8 Wt 12 11
Midfield. From Apprentice.

1980–81	Bournemouth	2	—
From Local			
1983–84	Torquay U	1	—
From Wealdstone			
1989–90	Exeter C	46	1
1990–91		18	1
1990–91	Reading	26	2
1991–92		24	—

Season	Club	League Appearances/Goals	
1992–93	....	—	—
1992–93	*Fulham*.....................	3	—
1992–93	Exeter C.....................	27	—
1993–94	....	34	—
1994–95	....	14	1
1995–96	....	42	1

BAILEY, Dennis

Born Lambeth 13.11.65 Ht 5 10
Wt 11 04
Forward. From Fulham, Farnborough T.

Season	Club	Apps	Goals
1987–88	Crystal Palace	5	1
1988–89	....	—	—
1988–89	*Bristol R*.....................	17	9
1989–90	Birmingham C...........	43	18
1990–91	....	32	5
1990–91	*Bristol R*.....................	6	1
1991–92	QPR	24	9
1992–93	....	15	1
1993–94	....	—	—
1993–94	*Charlton Ath*	4	—
1993–94	*Watford*......................	8	4
1994–95	QPR	—	—
1994–95	*Brentford*	6	3
1995–96	Gillingham.................	45	8

BAILEY, Gavin

Born Chesterfield 10.10.76 Ht 5 8
Wt 11 07
Forward. From Trainee.

Season	Club	Apps	Goals
1994–95	Sheffield W..............	—	—
1995–96	....	—	—

BAILEY, John

Born London 6.5.69 Ht 5 8 Wt 10 02
Midfield. From Enfield.

Season	Club	Apps	Goals
1995–96	Bournemouth............	44	4

BAILEY, Mark

Born Stoke 12.8.76 Ht 5 9 Wt 10 12
Midfield. From Trainee.

Season	Club	Apps	Goals
1994–95	Stoke C	—	—
1995–96	....		

BAIRD, Ian

Born Rotherham 1.4.64 Ht 6 0 Wt 12 12
Forward. From Apprentice. England Schools.

Season	Club	Apps	Goals
1981–82	Southampton.............	—	—
1982–83	....	11	2
1983–84	....	6	1
1983–84	*Cardiff C*.....................	12	6
1984–85	Southampton.............	5	2
1984–85	*Newcastle U*...............	5	1
1984–85	Leeds U	10	6
1985–86	....	35	12
1986–87	....	40	15
1987–88	Portsmouth................	20	1
1987–88	Leeds U	10	3
1988–89	....	43	10
1989–90	....	24	4
1989–90	Middlesbrough..........	19	5
1990–91	....	44	14
1991–92	Hearts	30	6
1992–93	....	34	9
1993–94	Bristol C.....................	19	5
1994–95	....	37	6
1995–96	....	1	—
1995–96	Plymouth Arg	27	5

BAKER, Clive

Born North Walsham 14.3.59 Ht 5 9
Wt 11 00
Goalkeeper. From Amateur.

Season	Club	Apps	Goals
1977–78	Norwich C	2	—
1978–79	....	2	—
1979–80	....	—	—
1980–81	....	—	—
1981–82	....	—	—
1982–83	....	—	—
1983–84	....	—	—
1984–85	Barnsley....................	37	—
1985–86	....	42	—
1986–87	....	39	—
1987–88	....	44	—
1988–89	....	46	—
1989–90	....	37	—
1990–91	....	46	—
1991–92	Coventry C.................	—	—
1992–93	Ipswich T	31	—
1993–94	....	15	—
1994–95	....	2	—
1995–96	....	—	—

BAKER, Desmond

Born Dublin 25.8.77 Ht 5 7 Wt 11 00
Forward. From Trainee.

Season	Club	Apps	Goals
1994–95	Manchester U	—	—
1995–96	....	—	—

BAKER, Joe

Born London 19.4.77 Ht 5 7 Wt 10 03
Midfield. From Charlton Ath Trainee.

Season	Club	App	Goals
1994–95	Leyton Orient	—	—
1995–96		20	—

BAKER, Paul

Born Newcastle 5.1.63 Ht 6 0 Wt 13 00
Forward. From Bishop Auckland.

Season	Club	App	Goals
1984–85	Southampton	—	—
1985–86	Carlisle U	35	2
1986–87		36	9
1987–88	Hartlepool U	39	19
1988–89		40	7
1989–90		43	16
1990–91		46	12
1991–92		29	13
1992–93	Motherwell	9	1
1992–93	Gillingham	21	6
1993–94		33	8
1994–95		8	2
1994–95	York C	30	13
1995–96		18	5
1995–96	Torquay U	20	4

BALDRY, Simon

Born Huddersfield 12.2.76 Ht 5 10
Wt 11 06
Forward. From Trainee.

Season	Club	App	Goals
1993–94	Huddersfield T	10	2
1994–95		11	—
1995–96		14	—

BALL, Kevin

Born Hastings 12.11.64 Ht 5 10
Wt 12 05
Defender. From Apprentice.

Season	Club	App	Goals
1983–84	Portsmouth	1	—
1984–85		—	—
1985–86		9	—
1986–87		16	—
1987–88		29	1
1988–89		14	1
1989–90		36	2
1990–91	Sunderland	33	3
1991–92		33	1
1992–93		43	3
1993–94		36	—
1994–95		42	2
1995–96		36	4

BALL, Steve

Born Colchester 2.9.69 Ht 5 11
Wt 13 00
Midfield. From Trainee.

Season	Club	App	Goals
1987–88	Arsenal	—	—
1988–89		—	—
1989–90	Colchester U	4	—
1990–91	Norwich C	—	—
1991–92		2	—
1992–93	Colchester U	24	4
1993–94		32	2
1994–95		—	—
1995–96		8	1

BALMER, Stuart

Born Falkirk 20.9.69 Ht 6 1 Wt 12 04
Defender. From Celtic BC.

Season	Club	App	Goals
1987–88	Celtic	—	—
1988–89		—	—
1989–90		—	—
1990–91	Charlton Ath	24	—
1991–92		18	—
1992–93		45	2
1993–94		31	1
1994–95		29	2
1995–96		32	1

BANGER, Nicky

Born Southampton 25.2.71 Ht 5 8
Wt 10 06
Forward. From Trainee.

Season	Club	App	Goals
1988–89	Southampton	—	—
1989–90		—	—
1990–91		6	—
1991–92		4	—
1992–93		27	6
1993–94		14	—
1994–95		4	2
1994–95	Oldham Ath	28	3
1995–96		13	2

BANKS, Steven

Born Hillingdon 9.2.72 Ht 6 0 Wt 13 02
Goalkeeper. From Trainee.

Season	Club	App	Goals
1991–92	West Ham U	—	—
1992–93		—	—
1993–94	Gillingham	29	—
1994–95		38	—
1995–96	Blackpool	24	—

BANNISTER, Gary

Born Warrington 22.7.60 Ht 5 8
Wt 11 06
Forward. From Apprentice. England Under-21.

Season	Club	Apps	Goals
1978–79	Coventry C	4	1
1979–80		7	—
1980–81		11	2
1981–82	Sheffield W	42	21
1982–83		39	20
1983–84		37	14
1984–85	QPR	42	17
1985–86		36	16
1986–87		34	15
1987–88		24	8
1987–88	Coventry C	8	1
1988–89		24	8
1989–90		11	2
1989–90	WBA	13	2
1990–91		44	13
1991–92		15	3
1991–92	*Oxford U*	10	2
1992–93	Nottingham F	31	8
1993–94	Stoke C	15	2
From Hong Kong			
1994–95	Lincoln C	29	7
1995–96	Darlington	41	10

BARACLOUGH, Ian

Born Leicester 4.12.70 Ht 6 1 Wt 12 02
Defender. From Trainee.

Season	Club	Apps	Goals
1988–89	Leicester C	—	—
1989–90		—	—
1989–90	*Wigan Ath*	9	2
1990–91	Leicester C	—	—
1990–91	*Grimsby T*	4	—
1991–92	Grimsby T	—	—
1992–93		1	—
1992–93	Lincoln C	36	5
1993–94		37	5
1994–95	Mansfield T	36	3
1995–96		11	2
1995–96	Notts Co	35	2

BARBER, Andrew

Born Darlington 4.2.79 Ht 5 9 Wt 9 08
Defender. From Trainee.

Season	Club	Apps	Goals
1995–96	Nottingham F	—	—

BARBER, Fred

Born Ferryhill 26.8.63 Ht 5 10
Wt 12 00
Goalkeeper. From Apprentice.

Season	Club	Apps	Goals
1981–82	Darlington	—	—
1982–83		12	—
1983–84		46	—
1984–85		45	—
1985–86		32	—
1985–86	Everton	—	—
1986–87		—	—
1986–87	Walsall	36	—
1987–88		46	—
1988–89		44	—
1989–90		25	—
1989–90	*Peterborough U*	6	—
1990–91	Walsall	2	—
1990–91	*Chester*	8	—
1990–91	*Blackpool*	2	—
1991–92	Peterborough U	39	—
1992–93		—	—
1992–93	*Colchester U*	10	—
1992–93	*Chesterfield*	—	—
1993–94	Peterborough U	24	—
1994–95		5	—
1994–95	Luton T	—	—
1995–96	*Ipswich T*	1	—
1995–96	*Blackpool*	1	—
1995–96	Birmingham C	1	—

BARBER, Phil

Born Tring 10.6.65 Ht 5 11
Wt 12 06
Midfield. From Aylesbury.

Season	Club	Apps	Goals
1983–84	Crystal Palace	9	2
1984–85		23	4
1985–86		39	9
1986–87		31	5
1987–88		37	7
1988–89		46	6
1989–90		30	1
1990–91		19	1
1991–92	Millwall	29	4
1992–93		46	8
1993–94		35	—
1994–95		—	—
1994–95	*Plymouth Arg*	4	—
1995–96	Bristol C	3	—
1995–96	*Mansfield T*	4	1
1995–96	*Fulham*	13	1

BARCLAY, Dominic

Born Bristol 5.9.76 Ht 5 10 Wt 11 07
Forward. From Trainee.

Season	Club	League Appearances	Goals
1993–94	Bristol C	2	—
1994–95		—	—
1995–96		2	—

BARDSLEY, David

Born Manchester 11.9.64 Ht 5 10
Wt 11 07
Defender. From Apprentice. England Youth, 2 full caps.

Season	Club	League Appearances	Goals
1981–82	Blackpool	1	—
1982–83		28	—
1983–84		16	—
1983–84	Watford	25	—
1984–85		17	—
1985–86		13	2
1986–87		41	5
1987–88		4	—
1987–88	Oxford U	34	1
1988–89		37	6
1989–90		3	—
1989–90	QPR	31	1
1990–91		38	—
1991–92		41	—
1992–93		40	3
1993–94		32	—
1994–95		30	—
1995–96		29	—

BARKER, Richard

Born Sheffield 30.5.75 Ht 6 1 Wt 13 05
Forward. From Trainee.

Season	Club	League Appearances	Goals
1993–94	Sheffield W	—	—
1994–95		—	—
1995–96		—	—
1995–96	*Doncaster R*	6	—

BARKER, Simon

Born Farnworth 4.11.64 Ht 5 9 Wt 11 07
Midfield. From Apprentice. England Under-21.

Season	Club	League Appearances	Goals
1982–83	Blackburn R	—	—
1983–84		28	3
1984–85		38	2
1985–86		41	10
1986–87		42	11
1987–88		33	9
1988–89	QPR	25	1
1989–90		28	3
1990–91		35	1
1991–92		34	6
1992–93		25	1
1993–94		37	5
1994–95		37	4
1995–96		33	5

BARKUS, Lea

Born Reading 7.12.74 Ht 5 6 Wt 10 10
Forward. From Trainee.

Season	Club	League Appearances	Goals
1991–92	Reading	6	1
1992–93		9	—
1993–94		—	—
1994–95		—	—
1995–96		—	—
1995–96	Fulham	9	1

BARLOW, Andy

Born Oldham 24.11.65 Ht 5 9 Wt 11 01
Defender.

Season	Club	League Appearances	Goals
1984–85	Oldham Ath	33	—
1985–86		26	—
1986–87		29	2
1987–88		26	—
1988–89		15	—
1989–90		44	1
1990–91		46	—
1991–92		28	2
1992–93		6	—
1993–94		6	—
1993–94	*Bradford C*	2	—
1994–95	Oldham Ath	2	—
1995–96	Blackpool	34	1

BARLOW, Martin

Born Barnstable 25.6.71 Ht 5 7
Wt 10 01
Midfield. From Trainee.

Season	Club	League Appearances	Goals
1988–89	Plymouth Arg	1	—
1989–90		1	—
1990–91		30	1
1991–92		28	3
1992–93		24	1
1993–94		26	2
1994–95		42	2
1995–96		28	5

Season Club League Appearances/Goals

BARLOW, Neil

Born Bury 24.3.78
Defender. From Trainee.

Season	Club	Apps	Goals
1995–96	Rochdale	2	—

BARLOW, Stuart

Born Liverpool 16.7.68 Ht 5 10
Wt 11 02
Forward.

Season	Club	Apps	Goals
1990–91	Everton	2	—
1991–92		7	—
1991–92	*Rotherham U*	—	—
1992–93	Everton	26	5
1993–94		22	3
1994–95		11	2
1995–96		3	—
1995–96	Oldham Ath	26	7

BARMBY, Nick

Born Hull 11.2.74 Ht 5 7 Wt 11 04
Forward. From Trainee. England Youth, B, Under-21, 9 full caps.

Season	Club	Apps	Goals
1991–92	Tottenham H	—	—
1992–93		22	6
1993–94		27	5
1994–95		38	9
1995–96	Middlesbrough	32	7

BARNARD, Darren

Born Rinteln 30.11.71 Ht 5 10 Wt 11 00
Defender. From Wokingham.

Season	Club	Apps	Goals
1990–91	Chelsea	—	—
1991–92		4	—
1992–93		13	1
1993–94		12	1
1994–95		—	—
1994–95	*Reading*	4	—
1995–96	Chelsea	—	—
1995–96	Bristol C	34	4

BARNARD, Mark

Born Sheffield 27.11.75 Ht 5 10
Wt 11 07
Defender. From Trainee.

Season	Club	Apps	Goals
1994–95	Rotherham U	—	—
1995–96	Darlington	37	3

BARNES, Bobby

Born Kingston 17.12.62 Ht 5 7 Wt 10 09
Forward. From Apprentice.

Season	Club	Apps	Goals
1980–81	West Ham U	6	1
1981–82		3	—
1982–83		—	—
1983–84		13	2
1984–85		20	2
1985–86		1	—
1985–86	*Scunthorpe U*	6	—
1985–86	Aldershot	14	8
1986–87		25	11
1987–88		10	7
1987–88	Swindon T	28	10
1988–89		17	3
1988–89	Bournemouth	10	—
1989–90		4	—
1989–90	Northampton T	37	18
1990–91		43	13
1991–92		18	6
1991–92	Peterborough U	15	5
1992–93		26	3
1993–94		8	1
1993–94	Partick T	7	—
From Hong Kong			
1995–96	Torquay U	1	—

BARNES, David

Born London 16.11.61 Ht 5 10 Wt 11 01
Defender. From Apprentice. England Youth.

Season	Club	Apps	Goals
1979–80	Coventry C	3	—
1980–81		—	—
1981–82		6	—
1981–82	Ipswich T	—	—
1982–83		6	—
1983–84		11	—
1984–85		—	—
1984–85	Wolverhampton W	23	1
1985–86		38	1
1986–87		26	2
1987–88		1	—
1987–88	Aldershot	30	—
1988–89		39	1
1989–90	Sheffield U	24	—
1990–91		28	1
1991–92		15	—
1992–93		13	—
1993–94		2	—
1993–94	Watford	5	—
1994–95		1	—
1995–96		10	—

BARNES, John

Born Jamaica 7.11.63 Ht 5 11 Wt 12 07
Midfield. From Sudbury Court. England Under-21, 79 full caps.

Season	Club	App	Goals
1981–82	Watford	36	13
1982–83		42	10
1983–84		39	11
1984–85		40	12
1985–86		39	9
1986–87		37	10
1987–88	Liverpool	38	15
1988–89		33	8
1989–90		34	22
1990–91		35	16
1991–92		12	1
1992–93		27	5
1993–94		26	3
1994–95		38	7
1995–96		36	3

BARNES, Paul

Born Leicester 16.11.67 Ht 5 10
Wt 12 00
Forward. From Apprentice.

Season	Club	App	Goals
1985–86	Notts Co	14	4
1986–87		—	—
1987–88		11	2
1988–89		15	7
1989–90		13	1
1989–90	Stoke C	5	—
1990–91		6	—
1990–91	*Chesterfield*	1	—
1991–92	Stoke C	13	3
1992–93	York C	40	21
1993–94		42	24
1994–95		36	16
1995–96		30	15
1995–96	Birmingham C	15	7

BARNES, Richard

Born Wrexham 6.9.75 Ht 5 10 Wt 11 06
Forward. From Trainee.

Season	Club	App	Goals
1994–95	Wrexham	1	—
1995–96		—	—

BARNES, Steve

Born Harrow 5.1.76 Ht 5 4 Wt 10 05
Midfield. From Welling U.

Season	Club	App	Goals
1995–96	Birmingham C	3	—

BARNESS, Anthony

Born Lewisham 25.2.72 Ht 5 10
Wt 12 01
Defender. From Trainee.

Season	Club	App	Goals
1990–91	Charlton Ath	—	—
1991–92		22	1
1992–93		5	—
1992–93	Chelsea	2	—
1993–94		—	—
1993–94	*Middlesbrough*	—	—
1994–95	Chelsea	12	—
1995–96		—	—
1995–96	*Southend U*	5	—

BARNETT, Dave

Born London 16.4.67 Ht 6 0 Wt 12 00
Defender. From Windsor & Eton.

Season	Club	App	Goals
1988–89	Colchester U	20	—
1989–90	WBA	—	—
1990–91	Walsall	5	—
From Kidderminster H			
1991–92	Barnet	4	—
1992–93		36	2
1993–94		19	1
1993–94	Birmingham C	9	—
1994–95		31	—
1995–96		—	—

BARNETT, Jason

Born Shrewsbury 21.4.76 Ht 5 9
Wt 12 04
Forward. From Trainee.

Season	Club	App	Goals
1994–95	Wolverhampton W	—	—
1995–96		—	—
1995–96	Lincoln C	32	2

BARNHOUSE, David

Born Swansea 19.3.75 Ht 5 8 Wt 10 09
Defender. From Trainee. Wales Under-21.

Season	Club	App	Goals
1991–92	Swansea C	1	—
1992–93		—	—
1993–94		3	—
1994–95		4	—
1995–96		15	—

Season Club League Appearances/Goals

BARNWELL-EDINBORO, Jamie

Born Hull 26.12.75 Ht 5 10 Wt 11 09
Forward. From Trainee.

Season	Club	Apps	Goals
1994–95	Coventry C	—	—
1995–96		1	—
1995–96	*Swansea C*	4	—
1995–96	*Wigan Ath*	10	1
1995–96	Cambridge U	7	2

BARR, Billy

Born Halifax 21.1.69 Ht 5 11 Wt 10 08
Midfield. From Trainee.

Season	Club	Apps	Goals
1987–88	Halifax T	30	—
1988–89		43	4
1989–90		23	2
1990–91		37	1
1991–92		35	3
1992–93		28	3
From Halifax T			
1994–95	Crewe Alex	34	2
1995–96		17	—

BARRAS, Tony

Born Stockton 29.3.71 Ht 6 0 Wt 13 00
Defender. From Trainee.

Season	Club	Apps	Goals
1988–89	Hartlepool U	3	—
1989–90		9	—
1990–91	Stockport Co	40	—
1991–92		42	5
1992–93		14	—
1993–94		3	—
1993–94	*Rotherham U*	5	1
1994–95	York C	31	1
1995–96		32	3

BARRETT, Earl

Born Rochdale 28.4.67 Ht 5 9 Wt 11 07
Defender. From Apprentice. England Under-21, B, 3 full caps.

Season	Club	Apps	Goals
1984–85	Manchester C	—	—
1985–86		1	—
1985–86	*Chester C*	12	—
1986–87	Manchester C	2	—
1987–88		—	—
1987–88	Oldham Ath	18	—
1988–89		44	—
1989–90		46	2
1990–91		46	3
1991–92		29	2
1991–92	Aston Villa	13	—
1992–93		42	1
1993–94		39	—
1994–95		25	—
1994–95	Everton	17	—
1995–96		8	—

BARRETT, Richard

Born Sutton Coldfield 1.11.77 Ht 5 6 Wt 9 08
Defender. From Trainee.

Season	Club	Apps	Goals
1994–95	Nottingham F	—	—
1995–96		—	—

BARRETT, Scott

Born Derby 2.4.63 Ht 6 0 Wt 13 13
Goalkeeper. From Ilkeston T.

Season	Club	Apps	Goals
1984–85	Wolverhampton W	4	—
1985–86		21	—
1986–87		5	—
1987–88	Stoke C	27	—
1988–89		17	—
1989–90		7	—
1989–90	*Colchester U*	13	—
1989–90	*Stockport Co*	10	—
1990–91	Colchester U	—	—
1991–92		—	—
1992–93	Gillingham	34	—
1993–94		13	—
1994–95		4	—
1995–96	Cambridge U	31	—

BARRICK, Dean

Born Hemsworth 30.9.69 Ht 5 9 Wt 12 05
Defender. From Trainee.

Season	Club	Apps	Goals
1987–88	Sheffield W	—	—
1988–89		8	2
1989–90		3	—
1990–91		—	—
1990–91	Rotherham U	19	2
1991–92		34	1
1992–93		46	4
1993–94	Cambridge U	44	1
1994–95		44	1
1995–96		3	1
1995–96	Preston NE	40	—

BARRON, Michael

Born Chester le Street 22.12.74 Ht 5 11
Wt 11 09
Defender. From Trainee.

Season	Club	App	Goals
1992–93	Middlesbrough	—	—
1993–94		2	—
1994–95		—	—
1995–96		1	—

BARROW, Lee

Born Worksworth 1.5.73 Ht 5 11
Wt 13 00
Defender. From Trainee.

Season	Club	App	Goals
1991–92	Notts Co	—	—
1992–93	Scarborough	11	—
1992–93	Torquay U	15	2
1993–94		20	—
1994–95		40	3
1995–96		41	—

BART-WILLIAMS, Chris

Born Freetown 16.6.74 Ht 5 11
Wt 11 00
Midfield. From Trainee. England Youth, Under-21.

Season	Club	App	Goals
1990–91	Leyton Orient	21	2
1991–92		15	—
1991–92	Sheffield W	15	—
1992–93		34	6
1993–94		37	8
1994–95		38	2
1995–96	Nottingham F	33	—

BARTLEY, Carl

Born Lambeth 6.10.76 Ht 6 2 Wt 12 13
Forward. From Trainee.

Season	Club	App	Goals
1994–95	Fulham	1	—
1995–96		—	—

BARTON, Warren

Born Stoke Newington 19.3.69 Ht 5 11
Wt 12 00
Defender. From Leytonstone/Ilford. England B, 3 full caps.

Season	Club	App	Goals
1989–90	Maidstone U	42	—
1990–91	Wimbledon	37	3
1991–92		42	1
1992–93		23	2
1993–94		39	2
1994–95		39	2
1995–96	Newcastle U	31	—

BARTRAM, Vince

Born Birmingham 7.8.68 Ht 6 2
Wt 13 07
Goalkeeper. From Local.

Season	Club	App	Goals
1985–86	Wolverhampton W	—	—
1986–87		1	—
1987–88		—	—
1988–89		—	—
1989–90		—	—
1989–90	*Blackpool*	9	—
1990–91	Wolverhampton W	4	—
1990–91	*WBA*	—	—
1991–92	Bournemouth	46	—
1992–93		45	—
1993–94		41	—
1994–95	Arsenal	11	—
1995–96			

BASHAM, Michael

Born Barking 27.9.73 Ht 6 2 Wt 13 02
Midfield. From Trainee.

Season	Club	App	Goals
1992–93	West Ham U	—	—
1993–94		—	—
1993–94	*Colchester U*	1	—
1993–94	Swansea C	5	—
1994–95		13	—
1995–96		11	1
1995–96	Peterborough U	14	1

BASS, David

Born Frimley 29.11.74 Ht 5 11 Wt 12 07
Midfield. From Trainee.

Season	Club	App	Goals
1991–92	Reading	3	—
1992–93		5	—
1993–94		1	—
1994–95		—	—
1995–96		—	—

BASS, Jonathan

Born Weston Super Mare 1.7.76 Ht 6 0
Wt 12 02
Defender. From Trainee.

Season	Club	App	Goals
1994–95	Birmingham C	—	—
1995–96		5	—

Season	Club	League Appearances/Goals	

BATES, Jamie

Born London 24.2.68 Ht 6 1 Wt 12 12
Defender. From Trainee.

1986–87	Brentford	24	1
1987–88		23	1
1988–89		36	1
1989–90		15	—
1990–91		32	2
1991–92		42	1
1992–93		24	—
1993–94		45	2
1994–95		38	2
1995–96		36	4

BATTERSBY, Tony

Born Doncaster 30.8.75 Ht 6 0 Wt 12 07
Forward. From Trainee.

1993–94	Sheffield U	—	—
1994–95		—	—
1994–95	*Southend U*	8	1
1995–96	Sheffield U	10	1
1995–96	Notts Co	21	7

BATTY, David

Born Leeds 2.12.68 Ht 5 8 Wt 12 00
Midfield. From Trainee. England Under-21, B, 17 full caps.

1987–88	Leeds U	23	1
1988–89		30	—
1989–90		42	—
1990–91		37	—
1991–92		40	2
1992–93		30	1
1993–94		9	—
1993–94	Blackburn R	26	—
1994–95		5	—
1995–96		23	1
1995–96	Newcastle U	11	1

BATTY, Mark

Born Nottingham 30.1.79
Midfield. From Trainee.

1995–96	Sheffield W	—	—

BAYES, Ashley

Born Lincoln 19.4.72 Ht 6 1 Wt 13 05
Goalkeeper. From Trainee.

1989–90	Brentford	1	—
1990–91		—	—
1991–92		1	—
1992–93		2	—
1993–94	Torquay U	32	—
1994–95		37	—
1995–96		28	—

BAYLISS, David

Born Liverpool 8.6.76 Ht 5 11 Wt 12 04
Defender. From Trainee.

1994–95	Rochdale	1	—
1995–96		28	—

BAZELEY, Darren

Born Northampton 5.10.72 Ht 5 10 Wt 11 02
Forward. From Trainee. England Under-21.

1989–90	Watford	1	—
1990–91		7	—
1991–92		34	6
1992–93		22	1
1993–94		10	1
1994–95		28	4
1995–96		41	1

BEADLE, Peter

Born London 13.5.72 Ht 6 2 Wt 13 07
Forward. From Trainee.

1988–89	Gillingham	2	—
1989–90		10	2
1990–91		22	7
1991–92		33	5
1992–93	Tottenham H	—	—
1992–93	*Bournemouth*	9	2
1993–94	Tottenham H	—	—
1993–94	*Southend U*	8	1
1994–95	Tottenham H	—	—
1994–95	Watford	20	1
1995–96		3	—
1995–96	Bristol R	27	12

BEAGRIE, Peter

Born Middlesbrough 28.11.65 Ht 5 8 Wt 12 00
Midfield. From Local. England Under-21, B.

1983–84	Middlesbrough	—	—
1984–85		7	1
1985–86		26	1
1986–87	Sheffield U	41	9
1987–88		43	2

Season	Club	League Appearances/Goals	
1988–89	Stoke C	41	7
1989–90		13	—
1989–90	Everton	19	—
1990–91		17	2
1991–92		27	3
1991–92	*Sunderland*	5	1
1992–93	Everton	22	3
1993–94		29	3
1993–94	Manchester C	9	1
1994–95		37	2
1995–96		5	—

BEALL, Matthew

Born Enfield 4.12.77 Ht 5 7 Wt 10 06
Forward. From Trainee.

Season	Club	League Appearances/Goals	
1995–96	Cambridge U	15	4

BEARD, Mark

Born Roehampton 8.10.74 Ht 5 11
Wt 11 03
Defender. From Trainee.

Season	Club	League Appearances/Goals	
1992–93	Millwall	—	—
1993–94		14	1
1994–95		31	1
1995–96	Sheffield U	20	—

BEARDSLEY, Peter

Born Newcastle 18.1.61 Ht 5 8 Wt 11 07
Forward. From Wallsend BC. England B, 59 full caps. Football League.

Season	Club	League Appearances/Goals	
1979–80	Carlisle U	39	8
1980–81		43	10
1981–82		22	4
From Vancouver Whitecaps			
1982–83	Manchester U	—	—
From Vancouver Whitecaps			
1983–84	Newcastle U	35	20
1984–85		38	17
1985–86		42	19
1986–87		32	5
1987–88	Liverpool	38	15
1988–89		37	10
1989–90		29	10
1990–91		27	11
1991–92	Everton	42	15
1992–93		39	10
1993–94	Newcastle U	35	21
1994–95		34	12
1995–96		35	8

BEARDSMORE, Russell

Born Wigan 28.9.68 Ht 5 8 Wt 10 04
Midfield. From Apprentice. England Under-21.

Season	Club	League Appearances/Goals	
1986–87	Manchester U	—	—
1987–88		—	—
1988–89		23	2
1989–90		21	2
1990–91		12	—
1991–92		—	—
1991–92	*Blackburn R*	2	—
1992–93	Manchester U	—	—
1993–94	Bournemouth	24	—
1994–95		43	3
1995–96		44	—

BEASANT, Dave

Born Ealing 20.3.59 Ht 6 4 Wt 14 03
Goalkeeper. From Edgware T. England B, 2 full caps.

Season	Club	League Appearances/Goals	
1979–80	Wimbledon	2	—
1980–81		34	—
1981–82		46	—
1982–83		46	—
1983–84		46	—
1984–85		42	—
1985–86		42	—
1986–87		42	—
1987–88		40	—
1988–89	Newcastle U	20	—
1988–89	Chelsea	22	—
1989–90		38	—
1990–91		35	—
1991–92		21	—
1992–93		17	—
1992–93	*Grimsby T*	6	—
1992–93	*Wolverhampton W*	4	—
1993–94	Chelsea	—	—
1993–94	Southampton	25	—
1994–95		13	—
1995–96		36	—

BEASLEY, Andrew

Born Sedgley 5.2.64 Ht 6 1 Wt 12 10
Goalkeeper. From Apprentice.

Season	Club	League Appearances/Goals	
1981–82	Luton T	—	—
1982–83		—	—
1983–84		—	—
1983–84	*Mansfield T*	—	—
1983–84	*Gillingham*	—	—
1984–85	Mansfield T	3	—

Season	Club	Apps	Goals
1985–86	....	—	—
1986–87	....	—	—
1986–87	*Peterborough U*.........	7	—
1987–88	Mansfield T	8	—
1987–88	*Scarborough*..............	4	—
1988–89	Mansfield T	6	—
1989–90	....	26	—
1990–91	....	42	—
1991–92	....	9	—
1992–93	....	—	—
1992–93	*Bristol R*....................	1	—
1993–94	Doncaster R	37	—
1994–95	Chesterfield	21	—
1995–96	....	11	—

BEATTIE, James

Born Lancaster 27.2.78 Ht 6 1 Wt 12 00
Forward. From Trainee.

Season	Club	Apps	Goals
1994–95	Blackburn R..............	—	—
1995–96	....	—	—

BEAUCHAMP, Joey

Born Oxford 13.3.71 Ht 5 10 Wt 12 05
Midfield. From Trainee.

Season	Club	Apps	Goals
1988–89	Oxford U	1	—
1989–90	....	3	—
1990–91	....	4	—
1991–92	....	27	7
1991–92	*Swansea C*.................	5	2
1992–93	Oxford U	44	7
1993–94	....	45	6
1994–95	West Ham U	—	—
1994–95	Swindon T	42	3
1995–96	....	3	—
1995–96	Oxford U	32	7

BEAUMONT, Chris

Born Sheffield 5.12.65 Ht 5 11 Wt 11 07
Forward. From Denaby.

Season	Club	Apps	Goals
1988–89	Rochdale.....................	34	7
1989–90	Stockport Co	22	5
1990–91	....	45	15
1991–92	....	34	2
1992–93	....	44	14
1993–94	....	32	1
1994–95	....	38	2
1995–96	....	43	—

BECKETT, Luke

Born Sheffield 25.11.76 Ht 5 11 Wt 11 02
Forward. From Trainee.

Season	Club	Apps	Goals
1995–96	Barnsley.....................	—	—

BECKFORD, Darren

Born Manchester 12.5.67 Ht 6 1
Wt 11 01
Forward. From Apprentice. England Schools, Youth.

Season	Club	Apps	Goals
1984–85	Manchester C............	4	—
1985–86	....	3	—
1985–86	*Bury*...........................	12	5
1986–87	Manchester C............	4	—
1986–87	*Port Vale*...................	11	4
1987–88	Port Vale	40	9
1988–89	....	42	20
1989–90	....	42	17
1990–91	....	43	22
1991–92	Norwich C	30	7
1992–93	....	8	1
1992–93	Oldham Ath	7	3
1993–94	....	22	6
1994–95	....	3	—
1995–96	....	20	2

BECKFORD, Jason

Born Manchester 14.2.70 Ht 5 9 Wt 14 03
Forward. From Trainee. England Youth.

Season	Club	Apps	Goals
1987–88	Manchester C............	5	—
1988–89	....	8	1
1989–90	....	5	—
1990–91	....	2	—
1990–91	*Blackburn R*..............	4	—
1991–92	Manchester C............	—	—
1991–92	*Port Vale*...................	5	1
1991–92	Birmingham C............	4	1
1992–93	....	3	1
1993–94	....	—	—
1993–94	*Bury*...........................	3	—
1994–95	Stoke C	4	—
1994–95	Millwall......................	9	—
1994–95	Northampton T..........	—	—
1995–96	....	1	—

BECKHAM, David

Born Leytonstone 2.5.75 Ht 6 0
Wt 11 02
Midfield. From Trainee. England Youth, Under-21.

Season	Club	Apps	Goals
1992–93	Manchester U	—	—

Season Club League Appearances/Goals

Season	Club	Apps	Goals
1993–94		—	—
1994–95		4	—
1994–95	*Preston NE*	5	2
1995–96	Manchester U	33	7

BEDDER, Paul

Born Leicester 8.3.77 Ht 5 8 Wt 11 03
Midfield. From Trainee.

Season	Club	Apps	Goals
1995–96	Leicester C	—	—

BEDEAU, Anthony

Born Hammersmith 24.3.79 Ht 5 9
Wt 11 01
Midfield. From Trainee.

Season	Club	Apps	Goals
1995–96	Torquay U	4	—

BEECH, Chris

Born Blackpool 16.9.74 Ht 5 10
Wt 11 00
Midfield. From Trainee.

Season	Club	Apps	Goals
1992–93	Blackpool	1	—
1993–94		35	2
1994–95		28	2
1995–96		18	—

BEECH, Chris

Born Congleton 5.11.75 Ht 5 9 Wt 11 00
Forward. From Trainee. England Schools, Youth.

Season	Club	Apps	Goals
1992–93	Manchester C	—	—
1993–94		—	—
1994–95		—	—
1995–96		—	—

BEENEY, Mark

Born Pembury 30.12.67 Ht 6 4 Wt 14 07
Goalkeeper.

Season	Club	Apps	Goals
1986–87	Gillingham	2	—
1987–88	Maidstone U	—	—
1988–89		—	—
1989–90		33	—
1989–90	*Aldershot*	7	—
1990–91	Maidstone U	17	—
1990–91	Brighton & HA	2	—
1991–92		25	—
1992–93		42	—
1992–93	Leeds U	1	—
1993–94		22	—
1994–95		—	—
1995–96		10	—

BEESLEY, Paul

Born Liverpool 21.9.65 Ht 6 1 Wt 12 06
Defender. From Marine.

Season	Club	Apps	Goals
1984–85	Wigan Ath	2	—
1985–86		17	—
1986–87		39	—
1987–88		42	1
1988–89		44	2
1989–90		11	—
1989–90	Leyton Orient	32	1
1990–91	Sheffield U	37	1
1991–92		40	2
1992–93		39	2
1993–94		25	—
1994–95		27	2
1995–96	Leeds U	10	—

BEESTON, Carl

Born Stoke 30.6.67 Ht 5 10 Wt 12 03
Midfield. From Apprentice. England Under-21.

Season	Club	Apps	Goals
1984–85	Stoke C	1	—
1985–86		5	—
1986–87		—	—
1987–88		12	—
1988–89		23	2
1989–90		38	2
1990–91		37	2
1991–92		43	3
1992–93		27	3
1993–94		—	—
1994–95		16	1
1995–96		16	—

BELL, Leon

Born Ipswich 23.9.77
Midfield. From Trainee.

Season	Club	Apps	Goals
1995–96	Ipswich T	—	—

BELL, Mick

Born Newcastle 15.11.71 Ht 5 10
Wt 11 08
Defender. From Trainee.

Season	Club	Apps	Goals
1989–90	Northampton T	6	—
1990–91		28	—

Season	Club	League Appearances	Goals
1991–92		30	4
1992–93		39	5
1993–94		38	—
1994–95		12	1
1994–95	Wycombe W	31	3
1995–96		41	1

BELLAMY, Gary

Born Worksop 4.7.62 Ht 6 2 Wt 11 05
Defender. From Apprentice.

Season	Club	League Appearances	Goals
1980–81	Chesterfield	3	—
1981–82		25	—
1982–83		42	—
1983–84		38	1
1984–85		22	2
1985–86		12	2
1986–87		42	2
1987–88	Wolverhampton W	24	2
1988–89		43	1
1989–90		39	3
1990–91		26	3
1991–92		4	—
1991–92	*Cardiff C*	9	—
1992–93	Wolverhampton W	—	—
1992–93	Leyton Orient	39	4
1993–94		29	1
1994–95		32	—
1995–96		32	1

BELLOTTI, Ross

Born Pembury 15.5.78
Goalkeeper. From Trainee.

Season	Club	League Appearances	Goals
1994–95	Exeter C	2	—
1995–96		—	—

BELSVIK, Peter

Born Lillehammer 2.10.67
Forward. From IK Start.

Season	Club	League Appearances	Goals
1995–96	Southend U	3	1

BENALI, Francis

Born Southampton 30.12.68 Ht 5 10
Wt 10 13
Defender. From Apprentice.

Season	Club	League Appearances	Goals
1986–87	Southampton	—	—
1987–88		—	—
1988–89		7	—
1989–90		27	—
1990–91		12	—
1991–92		22	—
1992–93		33	—
1993–94		37	—
1994–95		35	—
1995–96		29	—

BENJAMIN, Ian

Born Nottingham 11.12.61 Ht 5 11
Wt 13 04
Forward. From Apprentice. England Youth.

Season	Club	League Appearances	Goals
1978–79	Sheffield U	2	2
1979–80		3	1
1979–80	WBA	—	—
1980–81		2	—
1981–82	Notts Co	—	—
1982–83	Peterborough U	46	6
1983–84		34	8
1984–85	Northampton T	44	18
1985–86		46	22
1986–87		46	18
1987–88		14	1
1987–88	Cambridge U	25	2
1988–89	Chester C	22	2
1988–89	Exeter C	20	3
1989–90		12	1
1989–90	Southend U	15	4
1990–91		46	13
1991–92		45	9
1992–93		16	7
1992–93	Luton T	10	1
1993–94		3	1
1993–94	Brentford	14	2
1994–95		1	—
1994–95	Wigan Ath	17	6
1995–96		3	—

BENJAMIN, Trevor

Born Cambridge 8.2.79
Midfield. From Trainee.

Season	Club	League Appearances	Goals
1995–96	Cambridge U	5	—

BENN, Wayne

Born Pontefract 7.8.76 Ht 5 10 Wt 11 12
Defender. From Trainee.

Season	Club	League Appearances	Goals
1993–94	Bradford C	—	—
1994–95		10	—
1995–96		—	—

BENNETT, Frankie

Born Birmingham 3.1.69 Ht 5 7
Wt 12 01
Forward. From Halesowen T.

Season	Club	Apps	Goals
1992–93	Southampton	—	—
1993–94		8	1
1994–95		—	—
1995–96		11	—

BENNETT, Gary

Born Manchester 4.12.61 Ht 6 1
Wt 12 01
Defender. From Amateur.

Season	Club	Apps	Goals
1979–80	Manchester C	—	—
1980–81		—	—
1981–82	Cardiff C	19	1
1982–83		36	8
1983–84		32	2
1984–85	Sunderland	37	3
1985–86		28	3
1986–87		41	4
1987–88		38	2
1988–89		40	3
1989–90		36	3
1990–91		37	2
1991–92		39	3
1992–93		15	—
1993–94		38	—
1994–95		20	—
1995–96		—	—
1995–96	Carlisle U	26	5

BENNETT, Gary

Born Kirby 20.9.63 Ht 5 11 Wt 12 00
Forward. From Kirby T.

Season	Club	Apps	Goals
1984–85	Wigan Ath	20	3
1985–86	Chester C	43	13
1986–87		33	13
1987–88		43	10
1988–89		7	—
1988–89	Southend U	17	2
1989–90		25	4
1989–90	Chester C	8	1
1990–91		30	3
1991–92		42	11
1992–93	Wrexham	35	16
1993–94		41	32
1994–95		45	29
1995–96	Tranmere R	29	9
1995–96	Preston NE	8	1

BENNETT, Ian

Born Worksop 10.10.71 Ht 6 0 Wt 12 00
Goalkeeper. From Newcastle U Trainee.

Season	Club	Apps	Goals
1991–92	Peterborough U	7	—
1992–93		46	—
1993–94		19	—
1993–94	Birmingham C	22	—
1994–95		46	—
1995–96		24	—

BENNETT, Mickey

Born Camberwell 22.7.69 Ht 5 10
Wt 11 11
Midfield. From Apprentice. England Youth.

Season	Club	Apps	Goals
1986–87	Charlton Ath	2	—
1987–88		16	1
1988–89		11	—
1989–90		6	1
1989–90	Wimbledon	7	1
1990–91		6	—
1991–92		5	1
1992–93	Brentford	38	4
1993–94		8	—
1993–94	Charlton Ath	10	1
1994–95		14	—
1994–95	Millwall	—	—
1995–96		2	—

BENNETT, Tom

Born Falkirk 12.12.69 Ht 5 11 Wt 11 08
Defender. From Trainee.

Season	Club	Apps	Goals
1987–88	Aston Villa	—	—
1988–89	Wolverhampton W	2	—
1989–90		30	—
1990–91		26	—
1991–92		38	2
1992–93		1	—
1993–94		10	—
1994–95		8	—
1995–96	Stockport Co	24	1

BENNETT, Troy

Born Barnsley 25.12.75 Ht 5 9 Wt 11 13
Midfield. From Trainee. England Youth.

Season	Club	Apps	Goals
1992–93	Barnsley	2	—
1993–94		—	—
1994–95		—	—
1995–96		—	—

Season Club League Appearances/Goals Season Club League Appearances/Goals

BENSON, Mark

Born Dublin 7.8.78 Ht 5 5 Wt 10 05
Defender. From Trainee.

Season	Club	Apps	Goals
1995–96	Blackburn R	—	—

BENT, Junior

Born Huddersfield 1.3.70 Ht 5 6
Wt 10 09
Forward. From Trainee.

Season	Club	Apps	Goals
1987–88	Huddersfield T	7	—
1988–89		22	5
1989–90		7	1
1989–90	*Burnley*	9	3
1989–90	Bristol C	1	—
1990–91		20	2
1991–92		17	2
1991–92	*Stoke C*	1	—
1992–93	Bristol C	20	3
1993–94		20	2
1994–95		41	6
1995–96		40	2

BENT, Marcus

Born Hammersmith 19.5.78 Ht 6 3
Wt 11 13
Forward. From Trainee.

Season	Club	Apps	Goals
1995–96	Brentford	12	1

BENTLEY, Jim

Born Liverpool 11.6.76 Ht 6 1 Wt 13 00
Defender. From Trainee.

Season	Club	Apps	Goals
1993–94	Manchester C	—	—
1994–95		—	—
1995–96		—	—

BERESFORD, David

Born Middlesbrough 11.11.76 Ht 5 8
Wt 10 09
Forward. From Trainee. England Youth.

Season	Club	Apps	Goals
1993–94	Oldham Ath	1	—
1994–95		2	—
1995–96		28	2
1995–96	*Swansea C*	6	—

BERESFORD, John

Born Sheffield 4.9.66 Ht 5 5 Wt 10 12
Midfield. From Apprentice. England
Schools, Youth, B.

Season	Club	Apps	Goals
1983–84	Manchester C	—	—
1984–85		—	—
1985–86		—	—
1986–87	Barnsley	27	1
1987–88		34	3
1988–89		27	1
1988–89	Portsmouth	2	—
1989–90		28	—
1990–91		42	2
1991–92		35	6
1992–93	Newcastle U	42	1
1993–94		34	—
1994–95		33	—
1995–96		33	—

BERESFORD, Marlon

Born Lincoln 2.9.69 Ht 6 1 Wt 13 05
Goalkeeper. From Trainee.

Season	Club	Apps	Goals
1987–88	Sheffield W	—	—
1988–89		—	—
1989–90		—	—
1989–90	*Bury*	1	—
1989–90	*Ipswich T*	—	—
1990–91	Sheffield W	—	—
1990–91	*Northampton T*	13	—
1990–91	*Crewe Alex*	3	—
1991–92	Sheffield W	—	—
1991–92	*Northampton T*	15	—
1992–93	Burnley	44	—
1993–94		46	—
1994–95		40	—
1995–96		36	—

BERG, Henning

Born Eidsvoll 1.9.68 Ht 6 0 Wt 12 04
Defender. From Lillestrom. Norway
Under-21, 33 full caps.

Season	Club	Apps	Goals
1992–93	Blackburn R	4	—
1993–94		41	1
1994–95		40	1
1995–96		38	—

BERGKAMP, Dennis

Born Amsterdam 18.5.69 Ht 6 0
Wt 12 05
Forward. Holland 49 full caps.

Season	Club	Apps	Goals
1986–87	Ajax	14	2
1987–88		25	5
1988–89		30	13
1989–90		25	8
1990–91		33	25

Season	Club	League Appearances/Goals	
1991–92		30	24
1992–93		28	26
1993–94	Internazionale	31	8
1994–95		21	3
1995–96	Arsenal	33	11

BERGSSON, Gudni

Born Reykjavik 21.7.65 Ht 6 1 Wt 12 03
Defender. From Valur. Iceland Youth, Under-21, 62 full caps.

1988–89	Tottenham H	8	—
1989–90		18	—
1990–91		12	1
1991–92		28	1
1992–93		5	—
1993–94		—	—
1994–95	Bolton W	8	—
1995–96		34	4

BERKLEY, Austin

Born Gravesend 28.1.73 Ht 5 8
Wt 11 06
Midfield. From Trainee.

1990–91	Gillingham	—	—
1991–92		3	—
1992–93	Swindon T	—	—
1993–94		—	—
1994–95		1	—
1995–96	Shrewsbury T	38	1

BERNAL, Andy

Born Canberra 16.7.66 Ht 5 10 Wt 12 05
Defender. From Sporting Gijon. Australia full caps.

1992–93	Ipswich T	9	—
1993–94		—	—

From Sydney Olympic

1994–95	Reading	33	—
1995–96		34	2

BERNARD, Paul

Born Edinburgh 30.12.72 Ht 5 11
Wt 11 08
Midfield. From Trainee. Scotland Under-21, 2 full caps.

1990–91	Oldham Ath	2	1
1991–92		21	5
1992–93		33	4
1993–94		32	5
1994–95		17	2
1995–96		7	1
1995–96	Aberdeen	31	1

BERRY, Damien

Born Bury 30.3.77
Defender. From Trainee.

1995–96	Bury	—	—

BERRY, Greg

Born Essex 5.3.71 Ht 6 1 Wt 12 00
Forward. From East Thurrock.

1989–90	Leyton Orient	9	1
1990–91		35	5
1991–92		36	8
1992–93	Wimbledon	3	—
1993–94		4	1
1993–94	Millwall	10	1
1994–95		9	—
1995–96		1	—
1995–96	*Brighton & HA*	6	2
1995–96	*Leyton Orient*	7	—

BERRY, Neil

Born Edinburgh 6.4.63 Ht 6 0 Wt 12 00
Defender. From Apprentice. Scotland Youth.

1980–81	Bolton W	—	—
1981–82		3	—
1982–83		9	—
1983–84		14	—
1984–85		6	—
1984–85	Hearts	3	—
1985–86		32	2
1986–87		30	3
1987–88		35	—
1988–89		32	1
1989–90		10	1
1990–91		19	1
1991–92		—	—
1992–93		17	1
1993–94		30	—
1994–95		29	—
1995–96		19	—

Season	Club	League Appearances/Goals	

BERRY, Trevor

Born Haslemere 1.8.74 Ht 5 7
Wt 10 08
Forward. From Bournemouth.

1991–92	Aston Villa	—	—
1992–93		—	—
1993–94		—	—
1994–95		—	—
1995–96		—	—
1995–96	Rotherham U	36	7

BETT, Jim

Born Hamilton 25.11.59 Ht 5 11
Wt 12 03
Midfield. From school. Scotland Schools, Under-21, 25 full caps.

1976–77	Airdrieonians	1	—
1977–78		7	—
From Iceland and Lokeren			
1980–81	Rangers	34	4
1981–82		35	11
1982–83		35	6
From Lokeren			
1985–86	Aberdeen	24	3
1986–87		38	4
1987–88		38	10
1988–89		31	5
1989–90		30	3
1990–91		36	7
1991–92		38	1
1992–93		17	—
1993–94		6	—
1994–95	Hearts	26	2
1995–96	Dundee U	23	2

BETTNEY, Chris

Born Chesterfield 27.10.77
Midfield. From Trainee.

1995–96	Sheffield U	—	—

BETTS, Simon

Born Middlesbrough 3.3.73 Ht 5 7
Wt 11 00
Defender. From Trainee.

1991–92	Ipswich T	—	—
1992–93	Scarborough	—	—
1992–93	Colchester U	23	—
1993–94		33	1
1994–95		35	2
1995–96		45	5

BIBBO, Sal

Born Basingstoke 24.8.74 Ht 6 2
Wt 13 05
Goalkeeper. From Bournemouth.

1993–94	Sheffield U	—	—
1994–95		—	—
1994–95	*Chesterfield*	1	—
1995–96	Sheffield U	—	—

BIGGINS, Wayne

Born Sheffield 20.11.61 Ht 5 11
Wt 11 00
Forward. From Apprentice.

1979–80	Lincoln C	—	—
1980–81		8	1
From Matlock Town and King's Lynn			
1983–84	Burnley	20	8
1984–85		46	18
1985–86		12	3
1985–86	Norwich C	28	7
1986–87		31	4
1987–88		20	5
1988–89	Manchester C	32	9
1989–90	Stoke C	35	10
1990–91		38	12
1991–92		41	22
1992–93		8	2
1992–93	Barnsley	34	14
1993–94		13	2
1993–94	Celtic	9	—
1993–94	Stoke C	10	4
1994–95		17	2
1994–95	*Luton T*	7	1
1995–96	Oxford U	10	1
1995–96	Wigan Ath	18	2

BILIC, Slaven

Born Croatia 11.9.68 Ht 6 2
Wt 13 06
Defender. Croatia 23 full caps.

1988–89	Hajduk Split	3	2
1989–90		27	3
1990–91		32	2

Season	Club	League Appearances/Goals	
1991–92		20	1
1992–93		27	5
1993–94	Karlsruhe	26	2
1994–95		28	3
1995–96	West Ham U	13	—

BILLING, Peter

Born Liverpool 24.10.64 Ht 6 0
Wt 13 12
Defender. From South Liverpool.

Season	Club	Apps	Goals
1985–86	Everton	1	—
1986–87		—	—
1986–87	Crewe Alex	19	—
1987–88		32	—
1988–89		37	1
1989–90	Coventry C	18	—
1990–91		15	—
1991–92		22	1
1992–93		3	—
1992–93	*Port Vale*	12	—
1993–94	Port Vale	8	—
1994–95		6	—
1995–96	Hartlepool U	36	—

BILLY, Chris

Born Huddersfield 2.1.73 Ht 5 11
Wt 10 09
Defender. From Trainee.

Season	Club	Apps	Goals
1991–92	Huddersfield T	10	2
1992–93		13	—
1993–94		34	—
1994–95		37	2
1995–96	Plymouth Arg	32	4

BIMSON, Stuart

Born Liverpool 29.9.69 Ht 5 11
Wt 12 00
Defender. From Macclesfield.

Season	Club	Apps	Goals
1994–95	Bury	19	—
1995–96		16	—

BINGHAM, David

Born Dunfermline 3.9.70 Ht 5 10
Wt 10 07
Forward. From Oakley Utd.

Season	Club	Apps	Goals
1989–90	St Johnstone	1	—
1990–91		7	2
1991–92		9	1
1992–93		—	—
1992–93	Forfar Ath	20	6
1993–94		38	13
1994–95		36	22
1995–96		5	3
1995–96	Dunfermline Ath	15	3

BIRCH, Mark

Born Stoke 5.1.77 Ht 5 10
Wt 12 05
Defender. From Trainee.

Season	Club	Apps	Goals
1995–96	Stoke C	—	—

BIRCH, Paul

Born West Bromwich 20.11.62 Ht 5 6
Wt 10 04
Midfield. From Apprentice.

Season	Club	Apps	Goals
1980–81	Aston Villa	—	—
1981–82		—	—
1982–83		—	—
1983–84		22	2
1984–85		25	3
1985–86		27	2
1986–87		29	3
1987–88		38	6
1988–89		12	—
1989–90		12	—
1990–91		8	—
1990–91	Wolverhampton W	20	2
1991–92		45	8
1992–93		28	3
1993–94		32	1
1994–95		10	1
1995–96		7	—
1995–96	*Preston NE*	11	2

BIRD, Anthony

Born Cardiff 1.9.74 Ht 5 10
Wt 10 07
Forward. From Trainee. Wales Under-21.

Season	Club	Apps	Goals
1991–92	Cardiff C	—	—
1992–93		9	1
1993–94		35	5
1994–95		19	4
1995–96		12	3

Season	Club	League Appearances/Goals	

BISHOP, Charlie

Born Nottingham 16.2.68 Ht 5 9
Wt 13 07
Defender. From Stoke C Apprentice.

1986–87	Watford	—	—
1987–88	Bury	17	—
1988–89		38	3
1989–90		30	1
1990–91		29	2
1991–92	Barnsley	28	—
1992–93		43	—
1993–94		38	1
1994–95		8	—
1995–96		13	—
1995–96	*Preston NE*	4	—
1995–96	*Burnley*	9	—

BISHOP, Eddie

Born Liverpool 28.11.62 Ht 5 10
Wt 12 06
Midfield. From Winsford U, Northwich Vic, Altrincham, Runcorn.

1987–88	Tranmere R	5	1
1988–89		35	8
1989–90		28	7
1990–91		8	3
1990–91	Chester C	19	7
1991–92		21	4
1991–92	*Crewe Alex*	3	—
1992–93	Chester C	29	6
1993–94		18	2
1994–95		19	4
1995–96		9	5

BISHOP, Ian

Born Liverpool 29.5.65 Ht 5 9
Wt 10 12
Midfield. From Apprentice. England B.

1983–84	Everton	1	—
1983–84	*Crewe Alex*	4	—
1984–85	Everton	—	—
1984–85	Carlisle U	30	2
1985–86		36	6
1986–87		42	3
1987–88		24	3
1988–89	Bournemouth	44	2
1989–90	Manchester C	19	2
1989–90	West Ham U	17	2
1990–91		40	4
1991–92		41	1
1992–93		22	1
1993–94		36	1
1994–95		31	1
1995–96		35	1

BJORNEBYE, Stig Inge

Born Norway 11.12.69 Ht 5 10 Wt 11 09
Defender. From Rosenborg. Norway 43 full caps.

1992–93	Liverpool	11	—
1993–94		9	—
1994–95		31	—
1995–96		2	—

BLACK, Kingsley

Born Luton 22.6.68 Ht 5 9 Wt 11 12
Midfield. From School. Northern Ireland 30 full caps.

1986–87	Luton T	—	—
1987–88		13	—
1988–89		37	8
1989–90		36	11
1990–91		37	7
1991–92		4	—
1991–92	Nottingham F	25	4
1992–93		24	5
1993–94		37	3
1994–95		10	2
1994–95	*Sheffield U*	11	2
1995–96	Nottingham F	2	—
1995–96	*Millwall*	3	1

BLACK, Michael

Born Chigwell 6.10.76 Ht 5 8 Wt 11 08
Midfield. From Trainee.

1995–96	Arsenal	—	—

BLACK, Simon

Born Marston Green 9.11.75 Ht 6 1
Wt 12 00
Forward. From Trainee.

1993–94	Birmingham C	2	—
1994–95		—	—
1995–96		—	—

BLACK, Tom

Born Lanark 11.10.62 Ht 5 8 Wt 10 12
Defender. From Bellshill YM.

Season	Club	Apps	Goals
1980–81	Airdrieonians	—	—
1981–82		—	—
1982–83		5	—
1983–84		32	4
1984–85		37	1
1985–86		12	—
1986–87		24	1
1987–88		29	1
1988–89		37	4
1989–90	St Mirren	31	1
1990–91		34	2
1991–92		9	1
1992–93	Kilmarnock	10	1
1993–94		44	4
1994–95		32	5
1995–96		30	4

BLACK, Tony

Born Barrow 15.7.69 Ht 5 8 Wt 11 01
Forward. From Bamber Bridge.

Season	Club	Apps	Goals
1994–95	Wigan Ath	9	—
1995–96		21	2

BLACKMORE, Clayton

Born Neath 23.9.64 Ht 5 8 Wt 11 12
Midfield. From Apprentice. Wales Schools, Youth, Under-21, 38 full caps.

Season	Club	Apps	Goals
1982–83	Manchester U	—	—
1983–84		1	—
1984–85		1	—
1985–86		12	3
1986–87		12	1
1987–88		22	3
1988–89		28	3
1989–90		28	2
1990–91		35	4
1991–92		33	3
1992–93		14	—
1993–94		—	—
1994–95	Middlesbrough	30	2
1995–96		5	—

BLACKWELL, Dean

Born Camden 5.12.69 Ht 6 1 Wt 12 10
Defender. From Trainee. England Under-21.

Season Club League Appearances/Goals

Season	Club	Apps	Goals
1988–89	Wimbledon	—	—
1989–90		3	—
1989–90	*Plymouth Arg*	7	—
1990–91	Wimbledon	35	—
1991–92		4	1
1992–93		24	—
1993–94		18	—
1994–95		—	—
1995–96		8	—

BLACKWELL, Kevin

Born Luton 21.12.58 Ht 5 10 Wt 12 10
Goalkeeper. From Boston U, Barnet.

Season	Club	Apps	Goals
1987–88	Scarborough	21	—
1988–89		15	—
1989–90		8	—
1989–90	Notts Co	—	—
1990–91		—	—
1991–92		—	—
1992–93		—	—
1992–93	Torquay U	18	—
1993–94	Huddersfield T	1	—
1994–95		4	—
1995–96	Plymouth Arg	20	—

BLADES, Paul

Born Peterborough 5.1.65 Ht 6 0 Wt 12 00
Defender. From Apprentice. England Youth.

Season	Club	Apps	Goals
1982–83	Derby Co	6	—
1983–84		4	—
1984–85		22	—
1985–86		30	—
1986–87		16	—
1987–88		31	—
1988–89		38	1
1989–90		19	—
1990–91	Norwich C	21	—
1991–92		26	—
1992–93	Wolverhampton W	40	1
1993–94		35	1
1994–95		32	—
1995–96	Rotherham U	34	1

BLAKE, Mark

Born Portsmouth 17.12.67 Ht 6 0 Wt 12 06
Defender. From Apprentice. England Youth.

Season	Club	Apps	Goals
1985–86	Southampton	1	—
1986–87		8	1

Season	Club	League Appearances	Goals
1987–88		6	1
1988–89		3	—
1989–90		—	—
1989–90	*Colchester U*	4	1
1989–90	*Shrewsbury T*	10	—
1990–91	Shrewsbury T	46	2
1991–92		39	—
1992–93		32	1
1993–94		15	—
1994–95	Fulham	35	3
1995–96		38	5

BLAKE, Mark

Born Nottingham 16.12.70 Ht 5 11
Wt 12 09
Midfield. From Trainee. England Schools, Youth, Under-21.

Season	Club	League Appearances	Goals
1989–90	Aston Villa	9	—
1990–91		7	—
1990–91	*Wolverhampton W*	2	—
1991–92	Aston Villa	14	2
1992–93		1	—
1993–94	Portsmouth	15	—
1993–94	Leicester C	11	1
1994–95		30	3
1995–96		8	—

BLAKE, Nathan

Born Cardiff 27.1.72 Ht 5 11 Wt 13 12
Forward. From Chelsea Trainee. Wales B, Under-21, 6 full caps.

Season	Club	League Appearances	Goals
1989–90	Cardiff C	6	—
1990–91		40	4
1991–92		31	6
1992–93		34	11
1993–94		20	14
1993–94	Sheffield U	12	5
1994–95		35	17
1995–96		22	12
1995–96	Bolton W	18	1

BLAKE, Noel

Born Jamaica 12.1.62 Ht 6 2 Wt 14 02
Defender. From Walsall Amateur, Sutton Coldfield T.

Season	Club	League Appearances	Goals
1979–80	Aston Villa	3	—
1980–81		—	—
1981–82		1	—
1981–82	*Shrewsbury T*	6	—
1982–83	Aston Villa	—	—
1982–83	Birmingham C	37	3
1983–84		39	2
1984–85	Portsmouth	42	3
1985–86		42	4
1986–87		41	3
1987–88		19	—
1988–89	Leeds U	44	4
1989–90		7	—
1989–90	Stoke C	18	—
1990–91		44	3
1991–92		13	—
1991–92	*Bradford C*	6	—
1992–93	Bradford C	32	3
1993–94		7	—
1993–94	Dundee	23	2
1994–95		31	—
1995–96	Exeter C	44	2

BLAKE, Robbie

Born Middlesbrough 4.3.76 Ht 5 9
Wt 11 07
Forward. From Trainee.

Season	Club	League Appearances	Goals
1994–95	Darlington	9	—
1995–96		29	11

BLAKE, Tim

Born Merthyr 25.9.75 Ht 6 2 Wt 13 00
Defender. From Trainee.

Season	Club	League Appearances	Goals
1994–95	Coventry C	—	—
1995–96		—	—

BLAMEY, Nathan

Born Plymouth 10.6.77 Ht 5 10
Wt 11 05
Defender. From Trainee.

Season	Club	League Appearances	Goals
1995–96	Southampton	—	—

BLANEY, Steven

Born Orsett 24.3.77 Ht 6 0 Wt 13 00
Defender. From Trainee.

Season	Club	League Appearances	Goals
1995–96	West Ham U	—	—

Season Club League Appearances/Goals

BLATHERWICK, Steve

Born Nottingham 20.9.73 Ht 6 1
Wt 14 14
Defender. From Notts Co.

Season	Club	Apps	Goals
1992–93	Nottingham F	—	—
1993–94		3	—
1993–94	*Wycombe W*	2	—
1994–95	Nottingham F	—	—
1995–96		—	—
1995–96	*Hereford U*	10	1

BLINKER, Regi

Born Surinam 4.6.69 Ht 5 8 Wt 11 07
Forward. Holland 3 full caps.

Season	Club	Apps	Goals
1986–87	Feyenoord	26	1
1987–88		24	2
1988–89		1	—
1988–89	Den Bosch	25	6
1989–90	Feyenoord	31	2
1990–91		26	1
1991–92		28	5
1992–93		30	13
1993–94		29	9
1994–95		30	8
1995–96		13	4
1995–96	Sheffield W	9	2

BLISSETT, Gary

Born Manchester 29.6.64 Ht 6 0
Wt 12 07
Forward. From Manchester C, Manchester U, Altrincham.

Season	Club	Apps	Goals
1983–84	Crewe Alex	22	3
1984–85		29	9
1985–86		38	11
1986–87		33	16
1986–87	Brentford	10	5
1987–88		41	9
1988–89		36	6
1989–90		37	11
1990–91		26	10
1991–92		37	17
1992–93		46	21
1993–94	Wimbledon	18	3
1994–95		9	—
1995–96		4	—
1995–96	*Wycombe W*	4	2
1995–96	*Crewe Alex*	10	1

BLOUNT, Mark

Born Derby 5.1.74 Ht 5 10 Wt 12 04
Midfield. From Gresley R.

Season	Club	Apps	Goals
1993–94	Sheffield U	—	—
1994–95		5	—
1995–96		8	—
1995–96	Peterborough U	5	—

BLOXHAM, Robert

Born Solihull 9.10.76 Ht 5 7 Wt 10 12
Forward.

Season	Club	Apps	Goals
1995–96	Birmingham C	—	—

BLUNT, Jason

Born Penzance 16.8.77 Ht 5 8 Wt 10 10
Midfield. From Trainee. England Youth.

Season	Club	Apps	Goals
1994–95	Leeds U	—	—
1995–96		3	—

BOARDMAN, Craig

Born Barnsley 30.11.70 Ht 6 1 Wt 12 02
Defender. From Trainee.

Season	Club	Apps	Goals
1991–92	Nottingham F	—	—
1992–93		—	—
1993–94	Peterborough U	—	—
From Halifax T			
1995–96	Scarborough	9	—

BOCHENSKI, Simon

Born Worksop 6.12.75 Ht 5 8 Wt 11 13
Forward. From Trainee.

Season	Club	Apps	Goals
1994–95	Barnsley	—	—
1995–96		1	—

BODEN, Chris

Born Wolverhampton 13.10.73 Ht 5 9
Wt 11 00
Defender. From Trainee.

Season	Club	Apps	Goals
1991–92	Aston Villa	—	—
1992–93		—	—
1993–94		—	—
1993–94	*Barnsley*	4	—
1994–95	Aston Villa	1	—
1994–95	Derby Co	6	—

Season	Club	Apps	Goals
1995–96		4	—
1995–96	*Shrewsbury T*	5	—

BODIN, Paul

Born Cardiff 13.9.64 Ht 6 0 Wt 13 01
Defender. From Chelsea Amateur. Wales Youth, Under-21, 23 full caps

Season	Club	Apps	Goals
1981–82	Newport Co	—	—
1982–83	Cardiff C	31	—
1983–84		26	3
From Bath C			
1987–88	Newport Co	6	1
1987–88	Swindon T	5	1
1988–89		16	1
1989–90		41	5
1990–91		31	2
1990–91	Crystal Palace	5	—
1991–92		4	—
1991–92	*Newcastle U*	6	—
1991–92	Swindon T	21	2
1992–93		35	11
1993–94		32	7
1994–95		25	6
1995–96		33	2

BODLEY, Mick

Born Hayes 14.9.67 Ht 6 1 Wt 13 01
Defender. From Apprentice.

Season	Club	Apps	Goals
1985–86	Chelsea	—	—
1986–87		—	—
1987–88		6	1
1988–89		—	—
1988–89	Northampton T	20	—
1989–90		—	—
1990–91	Barnet	—	—
1991–92		36	1
1992–93		33	2
1993–94	Southend U	16	1
1994–95		12	—
1994–95	*Gillingham*	7	—
1994–95	*Birmingham C*	3	—
1995–96	Southend U	39	1

BOERE, Jeroen

Born Arnheim 18.11.67 Ht 6 3 Wt 13 02
Forward. From Go Ahead.

Season	Club	Apps	Goals
1993–94	West Ham U	4	—
1993–94	*Portsmouth*	5	—
1994–95	West Ham U	20	6
1994–95	*WBA*	5	—
1995–96	West Ham U	1	—
1995–96	Crystal Palace	8	1
1995–96	Southend U	6	2

BOGIE, Ian

Born Newcastle 6.12.67 Ht 5 7 Wt 10 02
Midfield. From Apprentice. England Schools.

Season	Club	Apps	Goals
1985–86	Newcastle U	—	—
1986–87		1	—
1987–88		7	—
1988–89		6	—
1988–89	Preston NE	13	1
1989–90		35	3
1990–91		31	8
1991–92	Millwall	25	—
1992–93		22	—
1993–94		4	1
1993–94	Leyton Orient	34	3
1994–95		31	2
1994–95	Port Vale	9	2
1995–96		32	3

BOHINEN, Lars

Born Vadso 8.9.69 Ht 6 1 Wt 12 01
Midfield. From Young Boys. Norway 45 full caps.

Season	Club	Apps	Goals
1988	Valerengen	15	2
1989		18	3
1990	Viking	10	—
1990–91	Young Boys	22	4
1991–92		34	2
1992–93		2	—
1993–94	Nottingham F	23	1
1994–95		34	6
1995–96		7	—
1995–96	Blackburn R	19	4

BOLAND, Willie

Born Ennis 6.8.75 Ht 5 9 Wt 11 02
Midfield. From Trainee. Eire Youth, Under-21.

Season	Club	Apps	Goals
1992–93	Coventry C	1	—
1993–94		27	—
1994–95		12	—
1995–96		3	—

BOLESAN, Mirko

Born Genoa 6.5.75
Forward. From Sestrese.

1995–96	Cardiff C	1	—

BOLLAN, Gary

Born Dundee 24.3.73 Ht 5 11 Wt 12 04
Midfield. From Celtic BC. Scotland Under-21.

1987–88	Celtic	—	—
1988–89		—	—
1989–90		—	—
1990–91	Dundee U	2	—
1991–92		10	1
1992–93		15	3
1993–94		12	—
1994–95		7	—
1994–95	Rangers	6	—
1995–96		4	—

BOLT, Danny

Born Wandsworth 5.2.76 Ht 5 7
Wt 11 06
Midfield. From Trainee.

1994–95	Fulham	2	—
1995–96		11	2

BONAR, Paul

Born Glasgow 28.12.76 Ht 5 11
Wt 10 07
Midfield. From Milngavie Wanderers.

1995–96	Airdrieonians	12	—
1995–96	Raith R	5	—

BONETTI, Ivano

Born Brescia 1.8.64
Midfield. From Torino.

1995–96	Grimsby T	19	3

BONNER, Mark

Born Ormskirk 7.6.74 Ht 5 10 Wt 11 00
Midfield. From Trainee.

1991–92	Blackpool	3	—
1992–93		15	—
1993–94		40	7
1994–95		17	—
1995–96		42	3

BOOGERS, Marco

Born Dordrecht 12.1.67 Ht 6 1 Wt 12 00
Midfield.

1986–87	DS 79	31	13
1987–88		29	5
1988–89	Utrecht	33	11
1989–90		27	4
1990–91	RKC	33	14
1991–92	Fortuna Sittard	29	13
1992–93	RKC	32	17
1993–94		32	11
1994–95		7	4
1994–95	Sparta	25	11
1995–96	West Ham U	4	—

BOOTH, Andrew

Born Huddersfield 17.3.73 Ht 6 1
Wt 12 06
Forward. From Trainee. England Under-21.

1991–92	Huddersfield T	3	—
1992–93		5	2
1993–94		26	10
1994–95		46	26
1995–96		43	16

BOOTH, Scott

Born Aberdeen 16.12.71 Ht 5 7
Wt 10 03
Forward. From Schools. Scotland Under-21, 13 full caps.

1988–89	Aberdeen	—	—
1989–90		2	—
1990–91		19	6
1991–92		33	5
1992–93		29	13
1993–94		25	4
1994–95		12	6
1995–96		24	9

BOOTHROYD, Aidy

Born Bradford 8.2.71 Ht 5 9 Wt 11 07
Defender. From Trainee.

1989–90	Huddersfield T	10	—
1990–91	Bristol R	3	—
1991–92		13	—

Season	Club	League Appearances/Goals	
1992–93	Hearts	4	—
1993–94		—	—
1993–94	Mansfield T	23	1
1994–95		36	—
1995–96		43	2

BOOTY, Martyn

Born Kirby Muxloe 30.5.71 Ht 5 8
Wt 11 02
Defender. From Trainee.

Season	Club	League Appearances/Goals	
1991–92	Coventry C	3	—
1992–93		—	—
1993–94		2	—
1993–94	Crewe Alex	31	1
1994–95		44	2
1995–96		21	2
1995–96	Reading	17	1

BORLAND, John

Born Lancaster 28.1.77 Ht 5 8 Wt 11 06
Midfield. From Trainee.

Season	Club	League Appearances/Goals	
1995–96	Burnley	1	—

BORROWS, Brian

Born Liverpool 20.12.60 Ht 5 10
Wt 11 12
Defender. From Amateur. England B.

Season	Club	League Appearances/Goals	
1979–80	Everton	—	—
1980–81		—	—
1981–82		15	—
1982–83		12	—
1982–83	Bolton W	9	—
1983–84		44	—
1984–85		42	—
1985–86	Coventry C	41	—
1986–87		41	1
1987–88		33	—
1988–89		38	1
1989–90		37	1
1990–91		38	6
1991–92		35	—
1992–93		38	2
1993–94		29	—
1993–94	*Bristol C*	6	—
1994–95	Coventry C	35	—
1995–96		21	—

BORWICK, Chris

Born Preston 30.10.76 Ht 5 10 Wt 12 07
Midfield. From Trainee.

Season	Club	League Appearances/Goals	
1995–96	Preston NE	—	—

BOS, Gijsbert

Born Spakenburg 22.3.73 Ht 6 4
Wt 12 07
Forward. From Ijsselmeervogels.

Season	Club	League Appearances/Goals	
1995–96	Lincoln C	11	5

BOSNICH, Mark

Born Fairfield 13.1.72 Ht 6 1 Wt 13 07
Goalkeeper. From Croatia Sydney.
Australia full caps.

Season	Club	League Appearances/Goals	
1989–90	Manchester U	1	—
1990–91		2	—
1991–92	Aston Villa	1	—
1992–93		17	—
1993–94		28	—
1994–95		30	—
1995–96		38	1

BOUCKEN, Kriss

Born Raratonga 7.2.77 Ht 5 9 Wt 12 00
Forward. From Trainee.

Season	Club	League Appearances/Goals	
1995–96	Rotherham U	—	—

BOUGH, Gareth

Born Nottingham 17.10.78 Ht 5 10
Wt 12 01
Goalkeeper. From Trainee.

Season	Club	League Appearances/Goals	
1995–96	Nottingham F	—	—

BOULD, Steve

Born Stoke 16.11.62 Ht 6 4 Wt 14 02
Defender. From Apprentice. England 2
full caps.

Season	Club	League Appearances/Goals	
1980–81	Stoke C	—	—
1981–82		2	—
1982–83		14	—
1982–83	*Torquay U*	9	—
1983–84	Stoke C	38	2
1984–85		38	3

Season	Club	League Appearances	Goals
1985–86		33	—
1986–87		28	1
1987–88		30	—
1988–89	Arsenal	30	2
1989–90		19	—
1990–91		38	—
1991–92		25	1
1992–93		24	1
1993–94		25	1
1994–95		31	—
1995–96		19	—

BOUND, Matthew

Born Trowbridge 9.11.72 Ht 6 2
Wt 13 09
Defender. From Trainee.

Season	Club	League Appearances	Goals
1990–91	Southampton	1	—
1991–92		—	—
1992–93		3	—
1993–94		1	—
1993–94	*Hull C*	7	1
1994–95	Southampton	—	—
1994–95	Stockport Co	14	—
1995–96		26	5
1995–96	*Lincoln C*	4	—

BOWEN, Jason

Born Merthyr 24.8.72 Ht 5 6 Wt 8 10
Midfield. From Trainee. Wales Youth, Under-21, 1 full cap.

Season	Club	League Appearances	Goals
1990–91	Swansea C	3	—
1991–92		11	—
1992–93		38	10
1993–94		41	11
1994–95		31	5
1995–96	Birmingham C	23	4

BOWEN, Mark

Born Neath 7.12.63 Ht 5 8 Wt 11 07
Defender. From Apprentice. Wales Schools, Youth, Under-21, 37 full caps.

Season	Club	League Appearances	Goals
1981–82	Tottenham H	—	—
1982–83		—	—
1983–84		7	—
1984–85		6	—
1985–86		2	1
1986–87		2	1
1987–88	Norwich C	24	1
1988–89		35	2
1989–90		38	7
1990–91		37	1
1991–92		36	3
1992–93		42	1
1993–94		41	5
1994–95		36	2
1995–96		31	2

BOWER, Danny

Born Woolwich 20.11.76
Defender. From Trainee.

Season	Club	League Appearances	Goals
1995–96	Fulham	4	—

BOWEY, Steven

Born Durham 10.7.74 Ht 5 8 Wt 10 09
Midfield. From Forest Green R.

Season	Club	League Appearances	Goals
1995–96	Bristol R	—	—

BOWLING, Ian

Born Sheffield 27.7.65 Ht 6 4 Wt 14 04
Goalkeeper. From Gainsborough T.

Season	Club	League Appearances	Goals
1988–89	Lincoln C	8	—
1989–90		—	—
1989–90	*Hartlepool U*	1	—
1990–91	Lincoln C	16	—
1991–92		20	—
1992–93		15	—
1992–93	*Bradford C*	7	—
1993–94	Bradford C	23	—
1994–95		6	—
1995–96	Mansfield T	44	—

BOWMAN, David

Born Tunbridge Wells 10.3.64 Ht 5 10
Wt 11 02
Midfield. From Salvesen BC. Scotland Under-21, 6 full caps.

Season	Club	League Appearances	Goals
1980–81	Hearts	17	1
1981–82		16	1
1982–83		39	5
1983–84		33	—
1984–85		11	1
1984–85	Coventry C	10	—
1985–86		30	2
1986–87	Dundee U	29	—

Season Club League Appearances/Goals

Season	Club	Apps	Goals
1987–88		39	1
1988–89		29	1
1989–90		24	1
1990–91		20	1
1991–92		41	3
1992–93		24	—
1993–94		35	2
1994–95		31	—
1995–96		17	—

BOWMAN, Robert

Born Durham 21.11.75 Ht 6 1 Wt 11 12
Defender. From Trainee. England Youth.

Season	Club	Apps	Goals
1992–93	Leeds U	4	—
1993–94		—	—
1994–95		—	—
1995–96		3	—

BOWRY, Bobby

Born Croydon 19.5.71 Ht 5 10 Wt 10 08
Midfield.

Season	Club	Apps	Goals
1991–92	Crystal Palace	—	—
1992–93		11	1
1993–94		21	—
1994–95		18	—
1995–96	Millwall	38	2

BOWYER, Gary

Born Manchester 26.6.71 Ht 6 1
Wt 13 04
Defender.

Season	Club	Apps	Goals
1989–90	Hereford U	14	2
1990–91	Nottingham F	—	—
1991–92		—	—
1992–93		—	—
1993–94		—	—
1994–95		—	—
1995–96	Rotherham U	27	—

BOWYER, Lee

Born London 3.1.77 Ht 5 9 Wt 9 09
Midfield. From Trainee. England Youth, Under-21.

Season	Club	Apps	Goals
1993–94	Charlton Ath	—	—
1994–95		5	—
1995–96		41	8

BOXALL, Danny

Born Croydon 24.8.77 Ht 5 8 Wt 10 05
Defender. From Trainee.

Season	Club	Apps	Goals
1994–95	Crystal Palace	—	—
1995–96		1	—

BOYCE, Robert

Born Islington 7.1.74
Forward. From Enfield.

Season	Club	Apps	Goals
1995–96	Colchester U	2	—

BOYD, Tom

Born Glasgow 24.11.65 Ht 5 11
Wt 11 04
Defender. From 'S' Form. Scotland Youth, Under-21 B, 27 full caps.

Season	Club	Apps	Goals
1983–84	Motherwell	13	—
1984–85		36	—
1985–86		31	—
1986–87		31	—
1987–88		42	2
1988–89		36	1
1989–90		33	1
1990–91		30	2
1991–92	Chelsea	23	—
1991–92	Celtic	13	1
1992–93		42	—
1993–94		38	—
1994–95		35	1
1995–96		34	—

BOYLE, Wesley

Born Portadown 30.3.79
Midfield. From Trainee.

Season	Club	Apps	Goals
1995–96	Leeds U	—	—

BRABIN, Gary

Born Liverpool 9.12.70 Ht 5 11
Wt 15 01
Midfield. From Trainee.

Season	Club	Apps	Goals
1989–90	Stockport Co	1	—
1990–91		1	—
From Runcorn			
1994–95	Doncaster R	28	8
1995–96		31	3
1995–96	Bury	5	—

BRACE, Deryn

Born Haverfordwest 15.3.75 Ht 5 7 Wt 10 12
Defender. From Trainee. Wales Under-21.

Season	Club	Apps	Goals
1993–94	Norwich C	—	—
1993–94	Wrexham	1	—
1994–95		14	—
1995–96		16	1

BRACEWELL, Paul

Born Stoke 19.7.62 Ht 5 10 Wt 12 05
Midfield. From Apprentice. England Under-21, 3 full caps.

Season	Club	Apps	Goals
1979–80	Stoke C	6	—
1980–81		40	2
1981–82		42	1
1982–83		41	2
1983–84	Sunderland	38	4
1984–85	Everton	37	2
1985–86		38	3
1986–87		—	—
1987–88		—	—
1988–89		20	2
1989–90		—	—
1989–90	Sunderland	37	2
1990–91		37	—
1991–92		39	—
1992–93	Newcastle U	25	2
1993–94		32	1
1994–95		16	—
1995–96	Sunderland	38	—

BRACEY, Lee

Born Ashford 11.9.68 Ht 6 0 Wt 13 07
Goalkeeper. From Trainee.

Season	Club	Apps	Goals
1987–88	West Ham U	—	—
1988–89	Swansea C	30	—
1989–90		31	—
1990–91		35	—
1991–92		3	—
1991–92	Halifax T	32	—
1992–93		41	—
1993–94	Bury	40	—
1994–95		6	—
1995–96		21	—

BRADBURY, Lee

Born Isle of Wight 3.7.75
Forward. From Cowes.

Season	Club	Apps	Goals
1995–96	Portsmouth	12	—
1995–96	*Exeter C*	14	5

BRADLEY, Darren

Born Birmingham 24.11.65 Ht 5 11
Wt 13 02
Defender. From Apprentice. England Youth.

Season	Club	Apps	Goals
1983–84	Aston Villa	—	—
1984–85		2	—
1985–86		18	—
1985–86	WBA	10	—
1986–87		14	1
1987–88		19	—
1988–89		26	—
1989–90		27	2
1990–91		39	1
1991–92		37	2
1992–93		42	1
1993–94		24	2
1994–95		16	—
1995–96	Walsall	45	1

BRADLEY, Russell

Born Birmingham 28.3.66 Ht 6 1
Wt 12 07
Defender. From Dudley T.

Season	Club	Apps	Goals
1987–88	Nottingham F	—	—
1988–89		—	—
1988–89	*Hereford U*	12	1
1989–90	Hereford U	33	1
1990–91		41	2
1991–92		3	—
1991–92	Halifax T	26	2
1992–93		30	1
1993–94	Scunthorpe U	34	1
1994–95		25	2
1995–96		38	1

BRADSHAW, Carl

Born Sheffield 2.10.68 Ht 5 10 Wt 11 11
Defender. From Apprentice. England Youth.

Season	Club	Apps	Goals
1986–87	Sheffield W	9	2
1986–87	*Barnsley*	6	1
1987–88	Sheffield W	20	2
1988–89		3	—
1988–89	Manchester C	5	—
1989–90		—	—
1989–90	Sheffield U	30	3
1990–91		27	1
1991–92		18	2

Season Club League Appearances/Goals

Season	Club	Apps	Goals
1992–93		32	1
1993–94		40	1
1994–95	Norwich C	26	1
1995–96		21	1

BRADSHAW, Darren

Born Sheffield 19.3.67 Ht 5 11 Wt 11 04
Midfield. From Matlock T.

Season	Club	Apps	Goals
1987–88	Chesterfield	18	—
1987–88	York C	25	1
1988–89		34	2
1989–90		—	—
1989–90	Newcastle U	12	—
1990–91		7	—
1991–92		19	—
1992–93	Peterborough U	34	—
1993–94		39	1
1994–95		—	—
1994–95	*Plymouth Arg*	6	1
1994–95	Blackpool	26	1
1995–96		25	—

BRADY, Garry

Born Glasgow 7.9.76 Ht 5 8 Wt 10 02
Midfield. From Trainee.

Season	Club	Apps	Goals
1993–94	Tottenham H	—	—
1994–95		—	—
1995–96		—	—

BRADY, Matthew

Born London 27.10.77 Ht 6 0 Wt 10 04
Midfield. From Trainee.

Season	Club	Apps	Goals
1994–95	Barnet	1	—
1995–96		2	—

BRAITHWAITE, Leon

Born Hackney 17.12.72
Forward. From Bishops Stortford.

Season	Club	Apps	Goals
1995–96	Exeter C	23	3

BRAMMER, David

Born Bromborough 28.2.75 Ht 5 10
Wt 12 00
Midfield. From Trainee.

Season	Club	Apps	Goals
1992–93	Wrexham	2	—
1993–94		22	2
1994–95		14	1
1995–96		11	2

BRANAGAN, Keith

Born Fulham 10.7.66 Ht 6 0 Wt 13 02
Goalkeeper. Eire B.

Season	Club	Apps	Goals
1983–84	Cambridge U	1	—
1984–85		19	—
1985–86		9	—
1986–87		46	—
1987–88		35	—
1987–88	Millwall	—	—
1988–89		—	—
1989–90		16	—
1989–90	*Brentford*	2	—
1990–91	Millwall	18	—
1991–92		12	—
1991–92	*Gillingham*	1	—
1991–92	*Fulham*	—	—
1992–93	Bolton W	46	—
1993–94		10	—
1994–95		43	—
1995–96		31	—

BRANCH, Graham

Born Liverpool 12.2.72 Ht 6 2 Wt 12 12
Forward. From Heswall Ath.

Season	Club	Apps	Goals
1991–92	Tranmere R	4	—
1992–93		3	—
1992–93	*Bury*	4	1
1993–94	Tranmere R	13	—
1994–95		1	—
1995–96		21	2

BRANCH, Michael

Born Liverpool 18.10.78 Ht 5 9
Wt 11 00
Forward. From Trainee. England Youth.

Season	Club	Apps	Goals
1995–96	Everton	3	—

BRANCO

Born Bage 4.4.64
Defender. From Internacional. Brazil full caps.

Season	Club	Apps	Goals
1995–96	Middlesbrough	7	—

BRANNAN, Ged

Born Liverpool 15.1.72 Ht 6 0 Wt 12 05
Defender. From Trainee.

Season	Club	Apps	Goals
1990–91	Tranmere R	18	1
1991–92		18	1

Season Club League Appearances/Goals

Season	Club	Apps	Goals
1992–93		38	1
1993–94		45	9
1994–95		41	2
1995–96		44	—

BRASS, Chris

Born Easington 24.7.75 Ht 5 9 Wt 12 06
Defender. From Trainee.

Season	Club	Apps	Goals
1993–94	Burnley	—	—
1994–95		5	—
1994–95	*Torquay U*	7	—
1995–96	Burnley	9	—

BRAY, Lee

Born Great Yarmouth 21.9.76 Ht 6 1
Wt 12 00
Goalkeeper. From Trainee.

Season	Club	Apps	Goals
1995–96	Norwich C	—	—

BRAYBROOK, Kevin

Born Basingstoke 11.2.77
Midfield. From Trainee.

Season	Club	Apps	Goals
1995–96	Portsmouth	—	—

BRAYSON, Paul

Born Newcastle 16.9.77 Ht 5 4 Wt 10 10
Forward. From Trainee. England Youth.

Season	Club	Apps	Goals
1995–96	Newcastle U	—	—

BRAZIER, Matthew

Born Whipps Cross 2.7.76 Ht 5 8
Wt 11 06
Defender. From Trainee.

Season	Club	Apps	Goals
1994–95	QPR	—	—
1995–96		11	—

BRAZIER, Philip

Born Liverpool 3.9.77
Defender. From Trainee.

Season	Club	Apps	Goals
1995–96	Liverpool	—	—

BRAZIL, Derek

Born Dublin 14.12.68 Ht 5 11 Wt 10 06
Defender. Rivermount BC. Eire Youth, Under-21, Under-23, B.

Season	Club	Apps	Goals
1985–86	Manchester U	—	—
1986–87		—	—
1987–88		—	—
1988–89		1	—
1989–90		1	—
1990–91		—	—
1990–91	*Oldham Ath*	1	—
1991–92	Manchester U	—	—
1991–92	*Swansea C*	12	1
1992–93	Cardiff C	34	—
1993–94		31	—
1994–95		30	1
1995–96		20	—

BRAZIL, Gary

Born Tunbridge Wells 19.9.62 Ht 5 11
Wt 11 04
Forward. From Crystal Palace Apprentice.

Season	Club	Apps	Goals
1980–81	Sheffield U	3	—
1981–82		1	—
1982–83		33	5
1983–84		19	2
1984–85		6	2
1984–85	*Port Vale*	6	3
1984–85	Preston NE	17	3
1985–86		43	14
1986–87		45	18
1987–88		36	14
1988–89		25	9
1988–89	Newcastle U	7	—
1989–90		16	2
1990–91	Fulham	41	4
1991–92		46	14
1992–93		30	7
1993–94		46	14
1994–95		32	7
1995–96		18	1

BREACKER, Tim

Born Bicester 2.7.65 Ht 5 11 Wt 13 00
Defender. England Under-21.

Season	Club	Apps	Goals
1983–84	Luton T	2	—
1984–85		35	—
1985–86		36	—
1986–87		29	1

Season Club League Appearances/Goals

Season	Club	Apps	Goals
1987–88		40	1
1988–89		22	—
1989–90		38	1
1990–91		8	—
1990–91	West Ham U	24	1
1991–92		34	2
1992–93		39	2
1993–94		40	3
1994–95		33	—
1995–96		22	—

BREBNER, Grant

Born Edinburgh 6.12.77 Ht 5 9
Wt 11 03
Midfield. From Trainee.

Season	Club	Apps	Goals
1994–95	Manchester U	—	—
1995–96		—	—

BRECKIN, Ian

Born Rotherham 24.7.75 Ht 5 11
Wt 11 07
Defender. From Trainee.

Season	Club	Apps	Goals
1993–94	Rotherham U	10	—
1994–95		41	2
1995–96		39	1

BREEN, Gary

Born London 12.12.73 Ht 6 2 Wt 11 12
Defender. From Charlton Ath. Eire Under-21, 6 full caps.

Season	Club	Apps	Goals
1991–92	Maidstone U	19	—
1992–93	Gillingham	29	—
1993–94		22	—
1994–95	Peterborough U	44	1
1995–96		25	—
1995–96	Birmingham C	18	1

BRENCHLEY, Scott

Born Hull 22.12.76
Midfield. From Liverpool Trainee.

Season	Club	Apps	Goals
1995–96	Chester C	—	—

BRENNAN, Jim

Born Toronto 8.5.77 Ht 5 9 Wt 12 05
Midfield. From Sora Lazio.

Season	Club	Apps	Goals
1994–95	Bristol C	—	—
1995–96		—	—

BRENNAN, Mark

Born Rossendale 4.10.65 Ht 5 9
Wt 11 01
Midfield. From Apprentice. England Youth, Under-21.

Season	Club	Apps	Goals
1982–83	Ipswich T	—	—
1983–84		19	1
1984–85		36	2
1985–86		40	3
1986–87		37	7
1987–88		36	6
1988–89	Middlesbrough	25	3
1989–90		40	3
1990–91	Manchester C	16	3
1991–92		13	3
1992–93		—	—
1992–93	Oldham Ath	14	3
1993–94		11	—
1994–95		40	1
1995–96		25	3

BRENNAN, Steve

Born Bury 24.9.76 Ht 5 9 Wt 11 00
Forward. From Trainee.

Season	Club	Apps	Goals
1995–96	Manchester C	—	—

BREVETT, Rufus

Born Derby 24.9.69 Ht 5 8 Wt 11 04
Defender. From Trainee.

Season	Club	Apps	Goals
1987–88	Doncaster R	17	—
1988–89		23	—
1989–90		42	—
1990–91		27	3
1990–91	QPR	10	—
1991–92		7	—
1992–93		15	—
1993–94		7	—
1994–95		19	—
1995–96		27	1

BREWSTER, Craig

Born Dundee 13.12.66 Ht 5 11 Wt 10 07
Midfield. From Stobwell J.

Season	Club	Apps	Goals
1985–86	Forfar Ath	16	2
1986–87		32	3
1987–88		39	2
1988–89		37	9

Season	Club	League Appearances/Goals	
1989–90		38	8
1990–91		29	11
1991–92	Raith R	42	12
1992–93		44	22
1993–94	Dundee U	33	16
1994–95		27	7
1995–96		30	17

BRIDGES, Michael

Born Whitley Bay 5.8.78 Ht 6 0
Wt 11 00
Forward. From Trainee.

Season	Club	Apps	Goals
1995–96	Sunderland	15	4

BRIEN, Tony

Born Dublin 10.2.69 Ht 5 11 Wt 11 09
Defender. From Apprentice.

Season	Club	Apps	Goals
1986–87	Leicester C	—	—
1987–88		15	1
1988–89		1	—
1988–89	Chesterfield	29	1
1989–90		43	3
1990–91		43	3
1991–92		41	—
1992–93		39	1
1993–94		9	—
1993–94	Rotherham U	26	2
1994–95		17	—
1995–96	WBA	2	—
1995–96	*Mansfield T*	4	—
1995–96	*Chester C*	8	—

BRIGHT, Mark

Born Stoke 6.6.62 Ht 6 1 Wt 13 00
Forward. From Leek T.

Season	Club	Apps	Goals
1981–82	Port Vale	2	—
1982–83		1	1
1983–84		26	9
1984–85	Leicester C	16	—
1985–86		24	6
1986–87		2	—
1986–87	Crystal Palace	28	8
1987–88		38	25
1988–89		46	20
1989–90		36	12
1990–91		32	9
1991–92		42	17
1992–93		5	1
1992–93	Sheffield W	30	11
1993–94		40	19
1994–95		37	11
1995–96		25	7

BRIGHTWELL, David

Born Lutterworth 7.1.71 Ht 6 1
Wt 13 04
Defender. From Trainee.

Season	Club	Apps	Goals
1987–88	Manchester C	—	—
1988–89		—	—
1989–90		—	—
1990–91		—	—
1990–91	*Chester C*	6	—
1991–92	Manchester C	4	—
1992–93		8	—
1993–94		22	1
1994–95		9	—
1995–96		—	—
1995–96	*Lincoln C*	5	—
1995–96	*Stoke C*	1	—
1995–96	Bradford C	22	—

BRIGHTWELL, Ian

Born Lutterworth 9.4.68 Ht 5 10
Wt 12 05
Midfield. From Congleton T. England Schools, Youth, Under-21.

Season	Club	Apps	Goals
1986–87	Manchester C	16	1
1987–88		33	5
1988–89		26	6
1989–90		28	2
1990–91		33	—
1991–92		40	1
1992–93		21	1
1993–94		7	—
1994–95		30	—
1995–96		29	—

BRIGHTWELL, Stuart

Born Easington 31.1.79 Ht 5 6 Wt 10 09
Forward. From Trainee.

Season	Club	Apps	Goals
1995–96	Manchester U	—	—

BRISCOE, Lee

Born Pontefract 30.9.75 Ht 5 11
Wt 11 05
Forward. From Trainee. England Under-21.

Season	Club	Apps	Goals
1993–94	Sheffield W	1	—

Season	Club	League Appearances/Goals	
1994–95	....	6	—
1995–96	....	26	—

BRISSETT, Jason

Born Redbridge 7.9.74 Ht 5 9 Wt 12 00
Midfield. From Arsenal Trainee.

1993–94	Peterborough U.........	30	—
1994–95	....	5	—
1994–95	Bournemouth.............	25	—
1995–96	....	43	3

BROCK, Stuart

Born Birmingham 26.9.76 Ht 6 1
Wt 12 07
Goalkeeper. From Trainee.

1994–95	Aston Villa................	—	—
1995–96	....	—	—

BRODDLE, Julian

Born Laughton 1.11.64 Ht 5 9 Wt 11 07
Midfield. From Apprentice.

1981–82	Sheffield U................	1	—
1982–83	....	—	—
1983–84	Scunthorpe U............	13	1
1984–85	....	45	14
1985–86	....	41	7
1986–87	....	38	10
1987–88	....	7	—
1987–88	Barnsley.....................	19	1
1988–89	....	38	3
1989–90	....	20	—
1989–90	Plymouth Arg	9	—
1990–91	....	—	—
1990–91	*Bradford C*	—	—
1990–91	St Mirren	10	—
1991–92	....	35	2
1992–93	Partick T.....................	6	—
1992–93	*Scunthorpe U*.............	5	—
1993–94	Raith R	18	—
1994–95	....	28	1
1995–96	....	27	—

BRODIE, Steve

Born Sunderland 14.1.73 Ht 5 6
Wt 10 08
Forward. From Trainee.

1991–92	Sunderland	—	—
1992–93	....	—	—

Season	Club	League Appearances/Goals	
1993–94	....	4	—
1994–95	....	8	—
1995–96	....	—	—
1995–96	*Doncaster R*...............	5	1

BROLIN, Tomas

Born Hudiksvall 29.11.69
Midfield. Sweden 46 full caps.

1987	Sundsvall....................	12	3
1988	....	21	6
1989	....	21	4
1990	Norrkoping................	11	7
1990–91	Parma.........................	33	7
1991–92	....	34	4
1992–93	....	22	4
1993–94	....	29	5
1994–95	....	11	—
1995–96	....	4	—
1995–96	Leeds U	19	4

BROOKE, David

Born Barnsley 23.11.75 Ht 5 8
Wt 11 02
Midfield. From Trainee.

1995–96	Barnsley.....................	—	—

BROOKER, Paul

Born Hammersmith 25.11.76 Ht 5 8
Wt 9 13
Midfield. From Trainee.

1995–96	Fulham........................	20	2

BROOKES, Mark

Born Nottingham 19.9.75 Ht 5 9
Wt 10 06
Midfield. From Trainee.

1994–95	Grimsby T	—	—
1995–96	....	—	—

BROOKS, Shaun

Born London 9.10.62 Ht 5 8 Wt 11 00
Midfield. From Apprentice. England Schools, Youth.

1979–80	Crystal Palace	1	—
1980–81	....	17	—

Season	Club	Apps	Goals
1981–82		25	2
1982–83		7	2
1983–84		4	—
1983–84	Orient	36	9
1984–85		29	5
1985–86		38	7
1986–87		45	5
1987–88	Bournemouth	37	6
1988–89		36	3
1989–90		35	4
1990–91		13	—
1991–92		7	—
1992–93		—	—
1992–93	*Stockport C*	—	—
1993–94	Bournemouth	—	—
1994–95		1	—
1994–95	Leyton Orient	9	—
1995–96		41	2

BROOMES, Marlon

Born Birmingham 28.11.77 Ht 6 0
Wt 12 12
Defender. From Trainee. England Youth.

Season	Club	Apps	Goals
1994–95	Blackburn R	—	—
1995–96		—	—

BROUGH, John

Born Heanor 8.1.73 Ht 6 0 Wt 12 11
Defender. From Trainee.

Season	Club	Apps	Goals
1991–92	Notts Co	—	—
1992–93	Shrewsbury T	14	1
1993–94		2	—
From Telford U			
1994–95	Hereford U	18	1
1995–96		22	1

BROWN, Andrew

Born Edinburgh 11.10.76 Ht 6 3
Wt 13 00
Forward. From Trainee.

Season	Club	Apps	Goals
1994–95	Leeds U	—	—
1995–96		—	—
1995–96	Hull C	—	—

BROWN, David

Born Bolton 2.10.78 Ht 5 9 Wt 12 06
Forward. From Trainee.

Season	Club	Apps	Goals
1995–96	Manchester U	—	—

BROWN, Grant

Born Sunderland 19.11.69 Ht 6 0
Wt 11 12
Defender. From Trainee.

Season	Club	Apps	Goals
1987–88	Leicester C	2	—
1988–89		12	—
1989–90	Lincoln C	34	2
1990–91		32	1
1991–92		37	1
1992–93		40	1
1993–94		38	3
1994–95		39	3
1995–96		34	—

BROWN, Greg

Born Manchester 31.7.78
Defender. From Trainee.

Season	Club	Apps	Goals
1995–96	Chester C	3	—

BROWN, John

Born Stirling 26.1.62 Ht 5 11 Wt 10 02
Defender. From Blantyre Welfare.

Season	Club	Apps	Goals
1979–80	Hamilton A	19	—
1980–81		38	6
1981–82		28	5
1982–83		9	—
1983–84		39	—
1984–85	Dundee	34	7
1985–86		29	11
1986–87		31	10
1987–88		20	3
1987–88	Rangers	9	2
1988–89		29	1
1989–90		27	1
1990–91		27	1
1991–92		25	4
1992–93		39	4
1993–94		24	—
1994–95		13	1
1995–96		14	—

BROWN, Kenny

Born Barking 11.7.67 Ht 5 10 Wt 11 06
Defender. From Apprentice.

Season	Club	Apps	Goals
1984–85	Norwich C	—	—
1985–86		—	—
1986–87		18	—

Season	Club	League Appearances	Goals
1987–88		7	—
1988–89	Plymouth Arg	39	1
1989–90		44	—
1990–91		43	3
1991–92	West Ham U	27	3
1992–93		15	2
1993–94		9	—
1994–95		9	—
1995–96		3	—
1995–96	*Huddersfield T*	5	—
1995–96	*Reading*	12	1
1995–96	*Southend U*	6	—
1995–96	*Crystal Palace*	6	2

BROWN, Linton

Born Driffield 12.4.68 Ht 5 9 Wt 11 00
Forward. From Guiseley.

Season	Club	League Appearances	Goals
1992–93	Halifax T	3	—
1992–93	Hull C	23	1
1993–94		42	9
1994–95		33	12
1995–96		23	1
1995–96	Swansea C	4	—

BROWN, Michael

Born Hartlepool 25.1.77 Ht 5 8
Wt 11 08
Midfield. From Trainee. England Under-21.

Season	Club	League Appearances	Goals
1994–95	Manchester C	—	—
1995–96		21	—

BROWN, Mickey

Born Birmingham 8.2.68 Ht 5 8
Wt 11 12
Forward. From Apprentice.

Season	Club	League Appearances	Goals
1985–86	Shrewsbury T	—	—
1986–87		22	2
1987–88		41	5
1988–89		41	—
1989–90		43	1
1990–91		43	1
1991–92	Bolton W	27	3
1992–93		6	—
1992–93	Shrewsbury T	17	1
1993–94		41	7
1994–95		9	3
1994–95	Preston NE	—	—
1995–96		10	1

BROWN, Phil

Born South Shields 30.5.59 Ht 5 11
Wt 11 08
Defender. From Local.

Season	Club	League Appearances	Goals
1978–79	Hartlepool U	—	—
1979–80		10	—
1980–81		46	1
1981–82		44	4
1982–83		44	2
1983–84		31	—
1984–85		42	1
1985–86	Halifax T	45	2
1986–87		46	12
1987–88		44	5
1988–89	Bolton W	46	4
1989–90		46	1
1990–91		45	—
1991–92		37	2
1992–93		40	5
1993–94		42	2
1994–95	Blackpool	31	5
1995–96		13	—

BROWN, Richard

Born Nottingham 13.1.67 Ht 5 10
Wt 11 02
Defender. From Derby Co, Ilkeston T.

Season	Club	League Appearances	Goals
1984–85	Sheffield W	—	—
1985–86		—	—
From Kettering T			
1990–91	Blackburn R	—	—
1990–91	*Maidstone U*	3	—
1991–92	Blackburn R	26	—
1992–93		2	—
1993–94		—	—
1994–95		—	—
1994–95	Stockport Co	1	—
1995–96	Blackpool	3	—

BROWN, Simon

Born Chelmsford 3.12.76 Ht 6 2
Wt 13 00
Goalkeeper. From Trainee.

Season	Club	League Appearances	Goals
1995–96	Tottenham H	—	—

Season	Club	League Appearances/Goals	

BROWN, Steve

Born Brighton 13.5.72 Ht 6 1 Wt 13 10
Defender. From Trainee.

1990–91	Charlton Ath	—	—
1991–92		1	—
1992–93		—	—
1993–94		19	—
1994–95		42	3
1995–96		19	—

BROWN, Steve

Born Southend 6.12.73 Ht 6 0 Wt 12 07
Forward. From Trainee.

1992–93	Southend U	10	2
1993–94	Scunthorpe U	—	—
1993–94	Colchester U	34	11
1994–95		28	6
1994–95	Gillingham	8	2
1995–96		1	—
1995–96	Lincoln C	26	3

BROWN, Steve

Born Northampton 6.7.66 Ht 6 0
Wt 11 08
Defender.

1985–86	Northampton T	—	—

From Irthlingborough D

1989–90		21	1
1990–91		40	2
1991–92		35	3
1992–93		38	9
1993–94		24	4
1993–94	Wycombe W	9	2
1994–95		40	1
1995–96		38	—

BROWN, Tom

Born Glasgow 1.4.68 Ht 5 7 Wt 10 00
Midfield. From Glenafton Ath.

1993–94	Kilmarnock	31	5
1994–95		27	4
1995–96		25	6

BROWN, Wayne

Born Southampton 14.1.77 Ht 6 1
Wt 11 06
Goalkeeper. From Trainee.

1993–94	Bristol C	1	—
1994–95		—	—
1995–96		—	—

BROWN, Wayne

Born Barking 20.8.77
Midfield. From Trainee.

1995–96	Ipswich T	—	—

BROWNE, Paul

Born Glasgow 17.2.75 Ht 6 1 Wt 12 00
Defender. From Trainee.

1993–94	Aston Villa	—	—
1994–95		—	—
1995–96		2	—

BROWNING, Marcus

Born Bristol 22.4.71 Ht 5 11 Wt 13 00
Forward. From Trainee. Wales 2 full caps.

1989–90	Bristol R	1	—
1990–91		—	—
1991–92		11	—
1992–93		19	1
1992–93	*Hereford U*	7	5
1993–94	Bristol R	31	4
1994–95		41	2
1995–96		45	4

BROWNRIGG, Andrew

Born Sheffield 2.8.76 Ht 6 0 Wt 11 12
Defender. From Trainee.

1994–95	Hereford U	8	—
1994–95	Norwich C	—	—
1995–96		—	—

BRUCE, Steve

Born Newcastle 31.12.60 Ht 6 0
Wt 13 00
Defender. From Apprentice. England Youth.

1978–79	Gillingham	—	—
1979–80		40	6
1980–81		41	4
1981–82		45	6
1982–83		39	7

Season	Club	League Appearances/Goals	
1983–84		40	6
1984–85	Norwich C	39	1
1985–86		42	8
1986–87		41	3
1987–88		19	2
1987–88	Manchester U	21	2
1988–89		38	2
1989–90		34	3
1990–91		31	13
1991–92		37	5
1992–93		42	5
1993–94		41	3
1994–95		35	2
1995–96		30	1

BRUMWELL, Phil

Born Darlington 8.8.75 Ht 5 8 Wt 11 00
Midfield. From Trainee.

1994–95	Sunderland	—	—
1995–96	Darlington	28	—

BRUNO, Pasquale

Born Lecce 19.6.62 Ht 6 0 Wt 11 07
Defender. From Fiorentina.

1995–96	Hearts	22	1

BRUNSKILL, Iain

Born Ormskirk 5.11.76 Ht 5 10
Wt 12 05
Defender. From Trainee.

1993–94	Liverpool	—	—
1994–95		—	—
1995–96		—	—

BRYAN, Marvin

Born Paddington 2.8.75 Ht 6 0 Wt 12 02
Forward. From Trainee.

1992–93	QPR	—	—
1993–94		—	—
1994–95		—	—
1994–95	*Doncaster R*	5	1
1995–96	Blackpool	46	1

BRYANT, Matthew

Born Bristol 21.9.70 Ht 6 0 Wt 13 02
Defender. From Trainee.

1989–90	Bristol C	—	—
1990–91		22	1
1990–91	*Walsall*	13	—
1991–92	Bristol C	43	2
1992–93		41	1
1993–94		28	—
1994–95		37	3
1995–96		32	—

BRYDON, Lee

Born Stockton 15.11.74 Ht 5 11
Wt 11 00
Defender. From Trainee.

1992–93	Liverpool	—	—
1993–94		—	—
1994–95		—	—
1995–96		—	—

BRYSON, Ian

Born Kilmarnock 26.11.62 Ht 5 10
Wt 12 10
Midfield.

1981–82	Kilmarnock	14	3
1982–83		28	1
1983–84		25	4
1984–85		36	3
1985–86		38	14
1986–87		32	10
1987–88		42	5
1988–89	Sheffield U	37	8
1989–90		39	9
1990–91		29	7
1991–92		34	9
1992–93		16	3
1993–94	Barnsley	16	3
1993–94	Preston NE	25	2
1994–95		41	5
1995–96		44	9

BUCHAN, James

Born Manchester 3.4.77 Ht 5 10
Wt 10 10
Midfield. From Stonehaven.

1995–96	Aberdeen	4	1

BUCKLE, Paul

Born Hatfield 16.12.70 Ht 5 7 Wt 10 10
Midfield. From Trainee.

1987–88	Brentford	1	—
1988–89		—	—
1989–90		10	—
1990–91		26	—

Season Club League Appearances/Goals

Season	Club	Apps	Goals
1991–92		15	1
1992–93		5	—
1993–94		—	—
1993–94	Torquay U	16	2
1994–95		32	3
1995–96		11	4
1995–96	Exeter C	22	2

BUCKLEY, Simon

Born Stafford 29.2.76 Ht 5 10 Wt 11 00
Forward. From Trainee.

Season	Club	Apps	Goals
1994–95	Grimsby T	—	—
1995–96		—	—

BUIST, Mark

Born Kirkcaldy 13.9.75 Ht 6 0 Wt 11 12
Midfield. From Glenrothes Strollers.

Season	Club	Apps	Goals
1994–95	Raith R	—	—
1995–96		2	—

BULL, Gary

Born West Bromwich 12.6.66 Ht 5 10
Wt 12 02
Forward.

Season	Club	Apps	Goals
1986–87	Southampton	—	—
1987–88		—	—
1987–88	Cambridge U	9	3
1988–89		10	1
From Barnet			
1991–92	Barnet	42	20
1992–93		41	17
1993–94	Nottingham F	11	—
1994–95		1	1
1994–95	*Birmingham C*	10	6
1995–96	Nottingham F	—	—
1995–96	*Brighton & HA*	10	2
1995–96	*Birmingham C*	6	—
1995–96	York C	15	8

BULL, Steve

Born Tipton 28.3.65 Ht 5 11 Wt 11 04
Forward. From Apprentice. England Under-21, B, 13 full caps.

Season	Club	Apps	Goals
1985–86	WBA	1	—
1986–87		3	2
1986–87	Wolverhampton W	30	15
1987–88		44	34
1988–89		45	37
1989–90		42	24
1990–91		43	26
1991–92		43	20
1992–93		36	16
1993–94		27	14
1994–95		31	16
1995–96		44	15

BULLIMORE, Wayne

Born Mansfield 12.9.70 Ht 5 9 Wt 12 01
Midfield. From Trainee. FA Schools.

Season	Club	Apps	Goals
1988–89	Manchester U	—	—
1989–90		—	—
1990–91		—	—
1990–91	Barnsley	—	—
1991–92		18	1
1992–93		17	—
1993–94		—	—
1993–94	Stockport Co	—	—
1993–94	Scunthorpe U	18	3
1994–95		35	6
1995–96		14	2
1995–96	Bradford C	2	—

BULLOCK, Darren

Born Worcester 12.2.69 Ht 5 8 Wt 12 07
Midfield. From Nuneaton.

Season	Club	Apps	Goals
1993–94	Huddersfield T	20	3
1994–95		39	6
1995–96		42	6

BULLOCK, Martin

Born Derby 5.3.75 Ht 5 4 Wt 10 09
Midfield. From Eastwood T.

Season	Club	Apps	Goals
1993–94	Barnsley	—	—
1994–95		29	—
1995–96		41	1

BUNCH, James

Born Sandwell 5.12.76 Ht 5 9 Wt 11 05
Defender. From Trainee.

Season	Club	Apps	Goals
1995–96	Birmingham C	—	—

BURCHELL, Lee

Born Birmingham 12.11.76 Ht 5 7
Wt 10 06
Midfield. From Trainee.

Season	Club	Apps	Goals
1993–94	Aston Villa	—	—
1994–95		—	—
1995–96		—	—

BURGESS, Daryl

Born Birmingham 20.4.71 Ht 5 11
Wt 12 03
Defender. From Trainee.

Season	Club	Apps	Goals
1989–90	WBA	34	—
1990–91		25	—
1991–92		36	2
1992–93		18	1
1993–94		43	2
1994–95		22	—
1995–96		45	2

BURKE, David

Born Liverpool 6.8.60 Ht 5 10 Wt 11 06
Defender. From Apprentice. England Youth.

Season	Club	Apps	Goals
1977–78	Bolton W	—	—
1978–79		20	1
1979–80		27	—
1980–81		22	—
1981–82	Huddersfield T	41	1
1982–83		44	1
1983–84		42	—
1984–85		31	1
1985–86		—	—
1986–87		21	—
1987–88		10	—
1987–88	Crystal Palace	31	—
1988–89		39	—
1989–90		11	—
1990–91	Bolton W	14	—
1991–92		37	—
1992–93		43	—
1993–94		12	—
1994–95	Blackpool	23	—
1995–96		—	—

BURLEY, Craig

Born Ayr 24.9.71 Ht 6 1 Wt 12 13
Midfield. From Trainee. Scotland Schools, Youth, Under-21, 12 full caps.

Season	Club	Apps	Goals
1989–90	Chelsea	—	—
1990–91		1	—
1991–92		8	—
1992–93		3	—
1993–94		23	3
1994–95		25	2
1995–96		22	—

BURLEY, George

Born Cumnock 3.6.56 Ht 5 10 Wt 11 00
Defender. From Apprentice. Scotland Schools, Youth, Under-21, Under-23, 11 full caps.

Season	Club	Apps	Goals
1973–74	Ipswich T	20	—
1974–75		31	—
1975–76		42	—
1976–77		40	2
1977–78		31	1
1978–79		38	1
1979–80		38	—
1980–81		23	—
1981–82		29	—
1982–83		31	1
1983–84		28	—
1984–85		37	—
1985–86		6	—
1985–86	Sunderland	27	—
1986–87		27	—
1987–88		—	—
1988–89	Gillingham	46	2
1989–90	Motherwell	34	—
1990–91		20	—
1990–91	Ayr U	12	—
1991–92		9	—
1992–93		33	—
1993–94		13	—
1993–94	Falkirk	1	—
1993–94	Motherwell	5	—
1994–95	Colchester U	7	—
1995–96		—	—

BURNETT, Wayne

Born London 4.9.71 Ht 5 11 Wt 12 01
Midfield. From Trainee.

Season	Club	Apps	Goals
1989–90	Leyton Orient	3	—
1990–91		1	—
1991–92		36	—
1992–93	Blackburn R	—	—
1993–94	Plymouth Arg	32	2
1994–95		32	1

Season	Club	League Appearances/Goals	
1995–96		6	—
1995–96	Bolton W	1	—

BURNHAM, Jason

Born Mansfield 8.5.73 Ht 5 10 Wt 13 03
Defender. From Notts Co Trainee, Northampton T Trainee.

1991–92	Northampton T	40	2
1992–93		31	—
1993–94		17	—
1994–95	Chester C	24	—
1995–96		40	1

BURNS, Alex

Born Bellshill 4.8.73 Ht 5 8 Wt 10 00
Midfield. From Shotts Bon-Accord.

1992–93	Motherwell	—	—
1993–94		4	1
1994–95		14	3
1995–96		28	3

BURNS, Chris

Born Manchester 9.11.67 Ht 6 1
Wt 14 01
Midfield. From Cheltenham T.

1990–91	Portsmouth	—	—
1991–92		46	8
1992–93		32	1
1993–94		12	—
1993–94	*Swansea C*	4	—
1993–94	*Bournemouth*	14	1
1994–95	Portsmouth	—	—
1994–95	Swansea C	5	—
1994–95	Northampton T	17	2
1995–96		43	7

BURNS, John

Born Dublin 4.12.77 Ht 5 8 Wt 10 08
Midfield. From Belvedere, Trainee.

1994–95	Nottingham F	—	—
1995–96		—	—

BURRIDGE, John

Born Workington 3.12.51 Ht 5 11
Wt 13 03
Goalkeeper. From Apprentice.

1968–69	Workington	1	—
1969–70		—	—
1970–71		26	—
1970–71	Blackpool	3	—
1971–72		34	—
1972–73		22	—
1973–74		30	—
1974–75		38	—
1975–76		7	—
1975–76	Aston Villa	30	—
1976–77		35	—
1977–78		—	—
1977–78	*Southend U*	6	—
1977–78	Crystal Palace	10	—
1978–79		42	—
1979–80		36	—
1980–81		—	—
1980–81	QPR	19	—
1981–82		20	—
1982–83	Wolverhampton W	42	—
1983–84		32	—
1984–85		—	—
1984–85	*Derby Co*	6	—
1984–85	Sheffield U	30	—
1985–86		42	—
1986–87		37	—
1987–88	Southampton	31	—
1988–89		31	—
1989–90		—	—
1989–90	Newcastle U	28	—
1990–91		39	—
1991–92	Hibernian	35	—
1992–93		30	—
1993–94	Newcastle U	—	—
1993–94	Scarborough	3	—
1993–94	Lincoln C	4	—
1993–94	Aberdeen	3	—
1994–95	Newcastle U	—	—
1994–95	Dumbarton	3	—
1994–95	Falkirk	3	—
1994–95	Manchester C	4	—
1995–96	Notts Co	—	—
1995–96	Darlington	3	—
1995–96	Grimsby T	—	—
1995–96	Northampton T	—	—
1995–96	Q of S	6	—

BURROWS, David

Born Dudley 25.10.68 Ht 5 10 Wt 11 08
Defender. From Apprentice. England Under-21, B.

1985–86	WBA	1	—
1986–87		15	1

Season	Club	League Appearances/Goals	
1987–88		21	—
1988–89		9	—
1988–89	Liverpool	21	—
1989–90		26	—
1990–91		35	—
1991–92		30	1
1992–93		30	2
1993–94		4	—
1993–94	West Ham U	25	1
1994–95		4	—
1994–95	Everton	19	—
1994–95	Coventry C	11	—
1995–96		11	—

BURROWS, Marc

Born Sheffield 20.12.75 Ht 5 9 Wt 10 00
Defender. From Trainee. England Youth.

1994–95	Sheffield W	—	—
1995–96		—	—

BURTON, Deon

Born Ashford 25.10.76 Ht 5 8 Wt 10 09
Forward. From Trainee.

1993–94	Portsmouth	2	—
1994–95		7	2
1995–96		32	7

BURTON, Mark

Born Barnsley 7.5.73 Ht 5 7 Wt 11 11
Midfield. From Trainee.

1991–92	Barnsley	—	—
1992–93		5	—
1993–94		—	—
1994–95		—	—
1995–96		—	—

BURTON, Sagi

Born Birmingham 25.11.77 Ht 6 2
Wt 13 00
Defender. From Trainee.

1995–96	Crystal Palace	—	—

BUSHELL, Steve

Born Manchester 28.12.72 Ht 5 9
Wt 11 05
Midfield. From Trainee.

1990–91	York C	15	—
1991–92		16	—
1992–93		8	—
1993–94		31	4
1994–95		10	1
1995–96		23	—

BUSST, David

Born Birmingham 30.6.67 Ht 6 1
Wt 12 10
Defender. From Moor Green.

1991–92	Coventry C	—	—
1992–93		10	—
1993–94		3	—
1994–95		20	2
1995–96		17	2

BUTLER, John

Born Liverpool 7.2.62 Ht 5 11 Wt 12 01
Defender. From Prescot Cables.

1981–82	Wigan Ath	1	—
1982–83		40	5
1983–84		41	3
1984–85		45	3
1985–86		36	—
1986–87		36	—
1987–88		26	1
1988–89		20	3
1988–89	Stoke C	25	1
1989–90		44	—
1990–91		31	2
1991–92		42	3
1992–93		44	1
1993–94		35	—
1994–95		41	—
1995–96	Wigan Ath	33	1

BUTLER, Lee

Born Sheffield 30.5.66 Ht 6 1 Wt 14 04
Goalkeeper. From Haworth Colliery.

1986–87	Lincoln C	30	—
1987–88	Aston Villa	—	—
1988–89		4	—
1989–90		—	—
1990–91		4	—
1990–91	*Hull C*	4	—
1991–92	Barnsley	43	—
1992–93		28	—
1993–94		37	—
1994–95		9	—
1995–96		3	—
1995–96	*Scunthorpe U*	2	—

Season Club League Appearances/Goals

BUTLER, Martin

Born Dudley 15.9.74 Ht 5 11
Wt 11 09
Forward. From Trainee.

Season	Club	Apps	Goals
1993–94	Walsall	15	3
1994–95		8	—
1995–96		28	4

BUTLER, Paul

Born Manchester 2.11.72 Ht 6 2
Wt 13 00
Defender. From Trainee.

Season	Club	Apps	Goals
1990–91	Rochdale	2	—
1991–92		25	—
1992–93		16	2
1993–94		38	2
1994–95		39	3
1995–96		38	3

BUTLER, Peter

Born Halifax 27.8.66 Ht 5 9
Wt 11 02
Midfield. From Apprentice.

Season	Club	Apps	Goals
1984–85	Huddersfield T	4	—
1985–86		1	—
1985–86	*Cambridge U*	14	1
1986–87	Bury	11	—
1986–87	Cambridge U	29	4
1987–88		26	5
1987–88	Southend U	15	3
1988–89		35	2
1989–90		41	2
1990–91		42	2
1991–92		9	—
1991–92	*Huddersfield T*	7	—
1992–93	West Ham U	39	2
1993–94		26	1
1994–95		5	—
1994–95	Notts Co	20	—
1995–96		—	—
1995–96	*Grimsby T*	3	—
1995–96	*WBA*	9	—

BUTLER, Steve

Born Birmingham 27.1.62 Ht 6 2
Wt 13 00
Forward. From Windsor & Eton, Wokingham.

Season	Club	Apps	Goals
1984–85	Brentford	3	1
1985–86		18	2

From Maidstone U

Season	Club	Apps	Goals
1989–90		44	21
1990–91		32	20
1990–91	Watford	10	1
1991–92		43	8
1992–93		9	—
1992–93	*Bournemouth*	1	—
1992–93	Cambridge U	23	6
1993–94		33	21
1994–95		37	14
1995–96		16	10
1995–96	Gillingham	20	5

BUTLER, Tony

Born Stockport 28.9.72 Ht 6 2 Wt 12 02
Defender. From Trainee.

Season	Club	Apps	Goals
1990–91	Gillingham	6	—
1991–92		5	—
1992–93		41	—
1993–94		27	1
1994–95		33	2
1995–96		36	2

BUTT, Nicky

Born Manchester 21.1.75 Ht 5 10
Wt 11 03
Midfield. From Trainee. England Youth, Under-21.

Season	Club	Apps	Goals
1992–93	Manchester U	1	—
1993–94		1	—
1994–95		22	1
1995–96		32	2

BUTTERS, Guy

Born Hillingdon 30.10.69 Ht 6 3
Wt 13 00
Defender. From Trainee. England Under-21.

Season	Club	Apps	Goals
1988–89	Tottenham H	28	1
1989–90		7	—
1989–90	*Southend U*	16	3
1990–91	Portsmouth	23	—
1991–92		33	2
1992–93		15	1
1993–94		15	1
1994–95		24	—
1994–95	*Oxford U*	3	1
1995–96	Portsmouth	37	2

BYFIELD, Darren

Born Birmingham 29.9.76 Ht 5 11
Wt 11 04
Forward. From Trainee.

1993–94	Aston Villa	—	—
1994–95		—	—
1995–96		—	—

BYNG, David

Born Walsgrave 9.7.77 Ht 6 2 Wt 13 12
Forward. From Trainee.

1993–94	Torquay U	3	2
1994–95		7	1
1995–96		14	—
1995–96	Doncaster R	—	—

BYRNE, John

Born Manchester 1.2.61 Ht 6 0 Wt 12 13
Forward. From Apprentice. Eire 23 full caps.

1978–79	York C	—	—
1979–80		9	2
1980–81		38	6
1981–82		29	6
1982–83		43	12
1983–84		46	27
1984–85		10	2
1984–85	QPR	23	3
1985–86		36	12
1986–87		40	11
1987–88		27	4
From Le Havre			
1990–91	Brighton & HA	38	9
1991–92		13	5
1991–92	Sunderland	27	7
1992–93		6	1
1992–93	Millwall	13	1
1992–93	*Brighton & HA*	7	2
1993–94	Millwall	4	—
1993–94	Oxford U	30	7
1994–95		25	11
1994–95	Brighton & HA	14	4
1995–96		25	2

BYRNE, Nicky

Born Dublin 9.10.78
Midfield.

1995–96	Leeds U	—	—

BYRNE, Paul

Born Dublin 30.6.72 Ht 5 11 Wt 13 00
Midfield. From Trainee. Eire Youth.

1989–90	Oxford U	3	—
1990–91		2	—
1991–92		1	—
From Bangor			
1993–94	Celtic	22	2
1994–95		6	2
1994–95	*Brighton & HA*	8	1
1995–96	Southend U	41	5

BYRNE, Wesley

Born Dublin 9.2.77 Ht 5 9 Wt 11 03
Defender. From Trainee.

1993–94	Middlesbrough	—	—
1994–95		—	—
1995–96		—	—

BYTHEWAY, Matthew

Born Wolverhampton 11.3.77 Ht 5 11
Wt 13 00
Defender. From Trainee.

1995–96	Wolverhampton W	—	—

Season Club League Appearances/Goals

CADETE, Jorge

Born Mozambique 27.8.68

Forward. From Sporting Lisbon. Portugal 26 full caps.

Season	Club	Apps	Goals
1995–96	Celtic	6	5

CADETTE, Richard

Born Hammersmith 21.3.65 Ht 5 7 Wt 12 00

Forward. From Wembley.

Season	Club	Apps	Goals
1984–85	Orient	21	4
1985–86	Southend U	44	24
1986–87		46	24
1987–88	Sheffield U	28	7
1988–89	Brentford	32	12
1989–90		16	1
1989–90	*Bournemouth*	8	1
1990–91	Brentford	28	6
1991–92		11	1
1991–92	Falkirk	14	3
1992–93		31	8
1993–94		39	18
1994–95		8	3
1994–95	Millwall	16	4
1995–96		1	—

CAESAR, Gus

Born London 5.3.66 Ht 6 0 Wt 12 09

Defender. From Apprentice. England Under-21.

Season	Club	Apps	Goals
1983–84	Arsenal	—	—
1984–85		—	—
1985–86		2	—
1986–87		15	—
1987–88		22	—
1988–89		2	—
1989–90		3	—
1990–91		—	—
1990–91	*QPR*	5	—
1991–92	Cambridge U	—	—
1991–92	Bristol C	10	—
1991–92	Airdrieonians	12	—
1992–93		29	—
1993–94		16	1
1994–95	Colchester U	39	1
1995–96		23	2

CAHILL, Ollie

Born Clonmel 29.9.75 Ht 5 10 Wt 11 01

Forward. From Clonmel.

Season	Club	Apps	Goals
1994–95	Northampton T	8	1
1995–96		3	—

CAIG, Tony

Born Whitehaven 11.4.74 Ht 6 0 Wt 13 04

Goalkeeper. From Trainee.

Season	Club	Apps	Goals
1992–93	Carlisle U	1	—
1993–94		20	—
1994–95		40	—
1995–96		33	—

CAIRNS, Mark

Born Edinburgh 25.9.69 Ht 6 0 Wt 13 02

Goalkeeper. From Gala Fairydean.

Season	Club	Apps	Goals
1994–95	Partick T	1	—
1995–96		3	—

CALDERHEAD, Robert

Born Liverpool 8.12.76 Ht 5 11 Wt 12 00

Midfield. From Trainee.

Season	Club	Apps	Goals
1995–96	Watford	—	—

CALDERWOOD, Colin

Born Glasgow 20.1.65 Ht 6 0 Wt 12 12

Defender. From Amateur. Scotland 14 full caps. Football League.

Season	Club	Apps	Goals
1981–82	Mansfield T	1	—
1982–83		28	—
1983–84		30	1
1984–85		41	—
1985–86	Swindon T	46	2
1986–87		46	1
1987–88		34	1
1988–89		43	4
1989–90		46	3
1990–91		23	2
1991–92		46	5
1992–93		46	2
1993–94	Tottenham H	26	—
1994–95		36	2
1995–96		29	—

Season	Club	League Appearances/Goals	

CALDWELL, Garrett

Born Princeton 6.11.73
Goalkeeper.

1995–96	Colchester U	—	—

CALDWELL, Neil

Born Glasgow 25.9.75 Ht 5 6 Wt 10 02
Midfield. From Rangers BC.

1993–94	Rangers	—	—
1994–95		1	—
1995–96	Dundee U	2	—

CALDWELL, Peter

Born Dorchester 5.6.72 Ht 6 1 Wt 13 00
Goalkeeper. From Trainee.

1991–92	QPR	—	—
1992–93		—	—
1993–94		—	—
1994–95		—	—
1995–96	Leyton Orient	28	—

CALLAGHAN, Anthony

Born Manchester 11.1.78
Defender. From Trainee.

1995–96	Manchester C	—	—

CALLAGHAN, Stuart

Born Calderbank 20.7.76 Ht 5 8
Wt 10 03
Midfield. From Blantyre BC.

1994–95	Hearts	—	—
1995–96		1	—

CALLAGHAN, Thomas

Born Glasgow 28.8.69 Ht 5 10 Wt 11 04
Midfield. From Aston Villa Trainee.

1987–88	St Mirren	—	—
1988–89		—	—
1988–89	Kilmarnock	11	—
1989–90	Falkirk	10	1
1989–90	Kilmarnock	21	2
1990–91		30	4
1991–92		8	—
1992–93	Stirling Albion	26	2
1993–94		32	2
1994–95		4	—
1994–95	Stranraer	16	—
1995–96		9	—
1995–96	Dunfermline Ath	3	—

CALLAN, Aiden

Born Stoke 8.10.76 Ht 5 9 Wt 10 12
Midfield. From Trainee.

1995–96	Stoke C	—	—

CALLIGAN, John

Born Preston 15.8.77 Ht 6 4 Wt 13 13
Forward. From Trainee.

1995–96	Preston NE	—	—

CALVERT, Mark

Born Consett 11.9.70 Ht 5 9 Wt 11 08
Midfield. From Trainee.

1988–89	Hull C	5	—
1989–90		—	—
1990–91		7	—
1991–92		11	1
1992–93		7	—
1993–94	Scarborough	42	3
1994–95		30	2
1995–96		—	—

CAME, Mark

Born Exeter 14.9.61 Ht 6 1 Wt 14 03
Defender. From Winsford U.

1983–84	Bolton W	—	—
1984–85		23	1
1985–86		35	1
1986–87		43	—
1987–88		43	5
1988–89		2	—
1989–90		19	—
1990–91		8	—
1991–92		18	—
1992–93		4	—
1992–93	Chester C	17	—
1993–94		30	1
1994–95	Exeter C	32	1
1995–96		38	4

Season	Club	League Appearances/Goals	

CAMERON, Colin

Born Kirkcaldy 23.10.72 Ht 5 6 Wt 9 06
Forward. From Lochore Welfare.

1990–91	Raith R	—	—
1991–92	*Sligo R*	—	—
1992–93	Raith R	16	1
1993–94		41	6
1994–95		35	7
1995–96		30	9
1995–96	Hearts	4	2

CAMERON, Ian

Born Glasgow 24.8.66 Ht 5 9 Wt 10 04
Midfield. From 'S' Form. Scotland Schools, Youth.

1983–84	St Mirren	8	—
1984–85		9	1
1985–86		12	—
1986–87		31	6
1987–88		41	8
1988–89		26	2
1989–90	Aberdeen	11	—
1990–91		10	1
1991–92		6	—
1992–93	Partick T	41	5
1993–94		41	1
1994–95		34	3
1995–96		35	1

CAMPBELL, Andrew

Born Stockton 18.4.79
Forward. From Trainee.

1995–96	Middlesbrough	2	—

CAMPBELL, Corey

Born London 6.3.76 Ht 5 10 Wt 11 06
Defender. From Trainee.

1994–95	Brentford	—	—
1995–96		—	—

CAMPBELL, Jamie

Born Birmingham 21.10.72 Ht 6 2 Wt 12 11
Forward. From Trainee.

1991–92	Luton T	11	—
1992–93		9	1
1993–94		16	—
1994–95		—	—
1994–95	*Mansfield T*	3	1
1994–95	*Cambridge U*	12	—
1995–96	Barnet	24	1

CAMPBELL, Kevin

Born Lambeth 4.2.70 Ht 6 1 Wt 13 08
Forward. From Trainee. England Under-21, B.

1987–88	Arsenal	1	—
1988–89		—	—
1988–89	*Leyton Orient*	16	9
1989–90	Arsenal	15	2
1989–90	*Leicester C*	11	5
1990–91	Arsenal	22	9
1991–92		31	13
1992–93		37	4
1993–94		37	14
1994–95		23	4
1995–96	Nottingham F	21	3

CAMPBELL, Neil

Born Middlesbrough 26.1.77 Ht 5 10 Wt 13 00
Forward. From Trainee.

1995–96	York C	—	—

CAMPBELL, Sol

Born Newham 18.9.74 Ht 6 1 Wt 14 01
Midfield. From Trainee. England Youth, Under-21, 2 full caps.

1992–93	Tottenham H	1	1
1993–94		34	—
1994–95		30	—
1995–96		31	1

CANHAM, Scott

Born London 5.11.74 Ht 5 8 Wt 10 13
Midfield. From Trainee.

1993–94	West Ham U	—	—
1994–95		—	—
1995–96		—	—
1995–96	*Torquay U*	3	—
1995–96	*Brentford*	14	—

Season	Club	League Appearances/Goals	

CANHAM, Tony

Born Leeds 8.6.60 Ht 5 8 Wt 11 04
Midfield. From Harrogate Railway.

1984–85	York C	3	1
1985–86		41	13
1986–87		38	9
1987–88		18	2
1988–89		41	9
1989–90		34	4
1990–91		41	5
1991–92		31	5
1992–93		29	4
1993–94		36	3
1994–95		35	2
1995–96	Hartlepool U	29	1

CANOVILLE, Dean

Born Perivale 30.11.78
Midfield. From Trainee.

1995–96	Millwall	—	—

CANTONA, Eric

Born Paris 24.5.66 Ht 6 2 Wt 14 03
Forward. France 45 full caps.

1983–84	Auxerre	2	—
1984–85		4	2
1985–86		7	—
1985–86	Martigues	—	—
1986–87	Auxerre	36	13
1987–88		32	8
1988–89	Marseille	22	5
1988–89	Bordeaux	11	6
1989–90	Montpellier	33	10
1990–91	Marseille	18	8
1991–92	Nimes	17	2
1991–92	Leeds U	15	3
1992–93		13	6
1992–93	Manchester U	22	9
1993–94		34	18
1994–95		21	12
1995–96		30	14

CAPLETON, Mel

Born London 24.10.73 Ht 5 11 Wt 12 00
Goalkeeper. From Trainee.

1992–93	Southend U	—	—
1993–94	Blackpool	—	—
1994–95		10	—
1995–96		1	—

CARBON, Matthew

Born Nottingham 8.6.75 Ht 6 2
Wt 12 04
Defender. From Trainee. England Under-21.

1992–93	Lincoln C	1	—
1993–94		9	—
1994–95		33	7
1995–96		26	3
1995–96	Derby Co	6	—

CARBONE, Anthony

Born Perth 13.10.74 Ht 5 10 Wt 11 13
Midfield. From Perth Italia.

1993–94	Nottingham F	—	—
1994–95		—	—
1995–96		—	—

CAREY, Alan

Born Greenwich 21.8.75 Ht 5 7
Wt 10 10
Defender. From Trainee.

1993–94	Reading	1	—
1994–95		2	—
1995–96		—	—

CAREY, Brian

Born Cork 31.5.68 Ht 6 3 Wt 13 12
Defender. From Cork C. Eire 3 full caps.

1989–90	Manchester U	—	—
1990–91		—	—
1990–91	*Wrexham*	3	—
1991–92	Manchester U	—	—
1991–92	*Wrexham*	13	1
1992–93	Manchester U	—	—
1993–94	Leicester C	27	—
1994–95		12	—
1995–96		19	1

CAREY, Louis

Born Bristol 22.1.77 Ht 5 11 Wt 11 05
Defender. From Trainee.

1995–96	Bristol C	23	—

CAREY, Shaun

Born Kettering 13.5.76 Ht 5 9 Wt 10 10
Midfield. From Trainee.

1994–95	Norwich C	—	—
1995–96		9	—

CARLITA

Born Angola 20.12.70 Ht 5 9 Wt 10 06
Midfield. From Farense.

Season	Club	Apps	Goals
1995–96	Coventry C	—	—

CARMICHAEL, Matt

Born Singapore 13.5.64 Ht 6 1 Wt 13 02
Forward. From Army.

Season	Club	Apps	Goals
1989–90	Lincoln C	26	5
1990–91		26	2
1991–92		40	7
1992–93		41	4
1993–94	Scunthorpe U	42	18
1994–95		20	2
1994–95	*Barnet*	3	—
1994–95	Preston NE	10	3
1995–96	Mansfield T	1	1
1995–96	Doncaster R	27	4
1995–96	Darlington	13	2

CARPENTER, Richard

Born Sheppey 30.9.72 Ht 5 11 Wt 13 02
Midfield. From Trainee.

Season	Club	Apps	Goals
1990–91	Gillingham	9	1
1991–92		3	—
1992–93		28	—
1993–94		40	3
1994–95		29	—
1995–96		12	—

CARR, Darren

Born Bristol 4.9.68 Ht 6 3 Wt 13 07
Defender. From Trainee.

Season	Club	Apps	Goals
1985–86	Bristol R	1	—
1986–87		20	—
1987–88		9	—
1987–88	Newport Co	9	—
1987–88	Sheffield U	3	—
1988–89		10	1
1989–90		—	—
1990–91		—	—
1990–91	Crewe Alex	36	—
1991–92		36	3
1992–93		32	2
1993–94	Chesterfield	28	1
1994–95		35	2
1995–96		1	—

CARR, Franz

Born Preston 24.9.66 Ht 5 6 Wt 11 12
Forward. From Apprentice. England Schools, Youth, Under-21.

Season	Club	Apps	Goals
1984–85	Blackburn R	—	—
1985–86	Nottingham F	23	3
1986–87		36	4
1987–88		22	4
1988–89		23	3
1989–90		14	1
1989–90	*Sheffield W*	12	—
1990–91	Nottingham F	13	2
1990–91	*West Ham U*	3	—
1991–92	Newcastle U	15	2
1992–93		10	1
1992–93	Sheffield U	8	3
1993–94		10	1
1994–95		—	—
1994–95	*Leicester C*	13	1
1994–95	Aston Villa	2	—
1995–96		1	—

CARR, Steve

Born Dublin 29.8.76 Ht 5 7 Wt 12 02
Defender. From Trainee. Eire Under-21.

Season	Club	Apps	Goals
1993–94	Tottenham H	1	—
1994–95		—	—
1995–96		—	—

CARRAGHER, James

Born Bootle 28.1.78
Midfield. From Trainee.

Season	Club	Apps	Goals
1995–96	Liverpool	—	—

CARRAGHER, Matthew

Born Liverpool 14.1.76 Ht 5 9 Wt 10 07
Defender. From Trainee.

Season	Club	Apps	Goals
1993–94	Wigan Ath	32	—
1994–95		41	—
1995–96		28	—

CARROLL, David

Born Paisley 20.9.66 Ht 6 0 Wt 11 09
Forward. From Ruislip Manor.

Season	Club	Apps	Goals
1993–94	Wycombe W	41	6
1994–95		41	6
1995–96		46	8

CARROLL, David

Born Blackpool 25.9.76
Midfield. From Trainee.

Season	Club	Apps	Goals
1995–96	Blackpool	—	—

CARROLL, Roy

Born Northern Ireland 30.9.77 Ht 6 2
Wt 11 09
Goalkeeper. From Trainee.

Season	Club	Apps	Goals
1995–96	Hull C	23	—

CARRUTHERS, Martin

Born Nottingham 7.8.72 Ht 5 11
Wt 11 07
Forward. From Trainee.

Season	Club	Apps	Goals
1990–91	Aston Villa	—	—
1991–92		3	—
1992–93		1	—
1992–93	*Hull C*	13	6
1993–94	Stoke C	34	5
1994–95		32	5
1995–96		24	3

CARSLEY, Lee

Born Birmingham 28.2.74 Ht 5 9
Wt 12 00
Defender. From Trainee.

Season	Club	Apps	Goals
1992–93	Derby Co	—	—
1993–94		—	—
1994–95		23	2
1995–96		35	1

CARSS, Anthony

Born Alnwick 31.3.76 Ht 5 9 Wt 11 05
Midfield. From Bradford C Trainee.

Season	Club	Apps	Goals
1994–95	Blackburn R	—	—
1995–96	Darlington	28	2

CARTER, Danny

Born Hackney 29.6.69 Ht 5 9 Wt 12 01
Midfield. From Billericay.

Season	Club	Apps	Goals
1988–89	Leyton Orient	1	—
1989–90		31	5
1990–91		42	5
1991–92		20	2
1992–93		29	3
1993–94		36	7
1994–95		29	—
1995–96	Peterborough U	37	1

Season Club League Appearances/Goals

CARTER, Jimmy

Born London 9.11.65 Ht 5 10 Wt 11 02
Midfield. From Apprentice.

Season	Club	Apps	Goals
1983–84	Crystal Palace	—	—
1984–85		—	—
1985–86	QPR	—	—
1986–87	Millwall	12	1
1987–88		26	—
1988–89		20	5
1989–90		28	2
1990–91		24	2
1990–91	Liverpool	5	—
1991–92		—	—
1991–92	Arsenal	6	—
1992–93		16	2
1993–94		—	—
1993–94	*Oxford U*	5	—
1994–95	Arsenal	3	—
1994–95	*Oxford U*	4	—
1995–96	Portsmouth	35	4

CARTER, Mark

Born Liverpool 17.12.60 Ht 5 10
Wt 12 07
Forward. From S Liverpool, Bangor C, Runcorn.

Season	Club	Apps	Goals
1991–92	Barnet	36	19
1992–93		41	11
1993–94		5	—
1993–94	Bury	36	20
1994–95		26	14
1995–96		32	16

CARTER, Tim

Born Bristol 5.10.67 Ht 6 2 Wt 13 11
Goalkeeper. From Apprentice. England Youth.

Season	Club	Apps	Goals
1985–86	Bristol R	2	—
1986–87		38	—
1987–88		7	—
1987–88	*Newport Co*	1	—
1987–88	*Carlisle U*	4	—

Season	Club	League Appearances/Goals	
1987–88	Sunderland	1	—
1988–89		2	—
1988–89	*Bristol C*	3	—
1989–90	Sunderland	18	—
1990–91		1	—
1991–92		2	—
1991–92	*Birmingham C*	2	—
1992–93	Sunderland	13	—
1993–94	Hartlepool U	18	—
1993–94	Millwall	2	—
1994–95		2	—
1995–96	Oxford U	12	—
1995–96	Millwall	4	—

CARTWRIGHT, Lee

Born Rossendale 19.9.72 Ht 5 9
Wt 11 00
Midfield. From Trainee.

1990–91	Preston NE	14	1
1991–92		33	4
1992–93		34	3
1993–94		39	1
1994–95		36	1
1995–96		26	3

CARTWRIGHT, Mark

Born Chester 13.1.73 Ht 6 2 Wt 13 06
Goalkeeper. From York C.

1994–95	Wrexham	—	—
1995–96		—	—

CASE, Jimmy

Born Liverpool 18.5.54 Ht 5 9 Wt 12 12
Midfield. From South Liverpool. England Under-23.

1973–74	Liverpool	—	—
1974–75		1	—
1975–76		27	6
1976–77		27	1
1977–78		33	5
1978–79		37	7
1979–80		37	3
1980–81		24	1
1981–82	Brighton & HA	33	3
1982–83		35	3
1983–84		35	4
1984–85		24	—
1984–85	Southampton	10	1

Season	Club	League Appearances/Goals	
1985–86		36	2
1986–87		39	3
1987–88		38	—
1988–89		34	—
1989–90		33	3
1990–91		25	1
1991–92	Bournemouth	40	1
1992–93	Halifax T	21	2
1992–93	Wrexham	4	—
1993–94	Darlington	1	—
From Sittingbourne			
1993–94	Brighton & HA	21	—
1994–95		9	—
1995–96		2	—

CASKEY, Darren

Born Basildon 21.8.74 Ht 5 8 Wt 11 09
Midfield. From Trainee. England Youth.

1991–92	Tottenham H	—	—
1992–93		—	—
1993–94		25	4
1994–95		4	—
1995–96		3	—
1995–96	*Watford*	6	1
1995–96	Reading	15	2

CASPER, Chris

Born Burnley 28.4.75 Ht 6 0 Wt 11 11
Defender. From Trainee. England Youth, Under-21.

1992–93	Manchester U	—	—
1993–94		—	—
1994–95		—	—
1995–96		—	—
1995–96	*Bournemouth*	16	1

CASSIDY, Jamie

Born Liverpool 21.11.77 Ht 5 9
Wt 10 08
Midfield. From Trainee. England Youth.

1994–95	Liverpool	—	—
1995–96		—	—

CASSIN, Graham

Born Dublin 24.3.78 Ht 5 10 Wt 11 07
Forward. From Belvedere, Trainee.

1994–95	Blackburn R	—	—
1995–96		—	—

Season	Club	League Appearances/Goals	

CASTLE, Steve

Born Barkingside 17.5.66 Ht 5 10
Wt 12 07
Midfield. From Apprentice.

1984–85	Orient	21	1
1985–86		23	4
1986–87		24	5
1987–88		42	10
1988–89		24	6
1989–90		27	7
1990–91		45	12
1991–92		37	10
1992–93	Plymouth Arg	31	11
1993–94		44	21
1994–95		26	3
1995–96	Birmingham C	15	1
1995–96	*Gillingham*	6	1

CASTLEDINE, Gary

Born Dumfries 27.3.70 Ht 5 8 Wt 11 12
Forward. From Shirebrook.

1990–91	Mansfield T	—	—
1991–92		7	—
1992–93		28	3
1993–94		21	—
1994–95		10	—
1995–96		—	—
1995–96	Chesterfield	—	—

CASTLEDINE, Stewart

Born Wandsworth 22.1.73 Ht 6 1
Wt 12 13
Midfield. From Trainee.

1991–92	Wimbledon	2	—
1992–93		—	—
1993–94		3	1
1994–95		6	1
1995–96		4	1
1995–96	*Wycombe W*	7	3

CAWLEY, Peter

Born London 15.9.65 Ht 6 4 Wt 15 07
Defender. From Chertsey.

1986–87	Wimbledon	—	—
1986–87	*Bristol R*	10	—
1987–88	Wimbledon	—	—
1988–89		1	—
1988–89	*Fulham*	5	—
1989–90	Bristol R	3	—
1990–91	Southend U	7	1
1990–91	Exeter C	7	—
1991–92	Barnet	3	—
1992–93		—	—
1992–93	Colchester U	24	3
1993–94		36	1
1994–95		23	2
1995–96		42	1

CECERE, Michele

Born Chester 4.1.68 Ht 6 0 Wt 12 12
Forward. From Apprentice.

1985–86	Oldham Ath	—	—
1986–87		14	4
1987–88		25	2
1988–89		13	2
1988–89	Huddersfield T	31	4
1989–90		23	4
1989–90	*Stockport Co*	1	—
1990–91	Huddersfield T	—	—
1990–91	Walsall	32	6
1991–92		35	8
1992–93		39	16
1993–94		6	2
1993–94	Exeter C	2	—
1994–95		28	10
1995–96		13	1

CHALK, Martyn

Born Swindon 30.8.69 Ht 5 6 Wt 10 00
Forward. From Louth U.

1990–91	Derby Co	—	—
1991–92		7	1
1992–93		—	—
1993–94		—	—
1994–95	Stockport Co	33	6
1995–96		10	—
1995–96	Wrexham	19	4

CHALLINOR, Dave

Born Chester 2.10.75 Ht 6 1 Wt 12 12
Defender. From Brombrough Pool.

1994–95	Tranmere R	—	—
1995–96		—	—

Season	Club	League Appearances/Goals	

CHALLINOR, Paul

Born Newcastle under 6.4.76 Ht 6 1
Wt 12 02
Defender. From Trainee.

1994–95	Birmingham C	—	—
1995–96		—	—

CHALLIS, Trevor

Born Paddington 23.10.75 Ht 5 8
Wt 11 00
Defender. From Trainee. England Youth, Under-21.

1994–95	QPR	—	—
1995–96		11	—

CHAMBERLAIN, Alec

Born Ramsey 30.6.64 Ht 6 2 Wt 13 06
Goalkeeper. From Ramsey T.

1981–82	Ipswich T	—	—
1982–83	Colchester U	—	—
1983–84		46	—
1984–85		46	—
1985–86		46	—
1986–87		46	—
1987–88	Everton	—	—
1987–88	*Tranmere R*	15	—
1988–89	Luton T	6	—
1989–90		38	—
1990–91		38	—
1991–92		24	—
1992–93		32	—
1992–93	*Chelsea*	—	—
1993–94	Sunderland	43	—
1994–95		18	—
1994–95	*Liverpool*	—	—
1995–96	Sunderland	29	—

CHAMBERLAIN, Mark

Born Stoke 19.11.61 Ht 5 9 Wt 12 00
Midfield. From Apprentice. England Schools, Under-21, 8 full caps.

1978–79	Port Vale	8	—
1979–80		11	—
1980–81		31	9
1981–82		46	8
1982–83	Stoke C	37	6
1983–84		40	7
1984–85		28	1
1985–86		7	3
1985–86	Sheffield W	21	2
1986–87		24	5
1987–88		21	1
1988–89	Portsmouth	28	6
1989–90		38	6
1990–91		25	2
1991–92		16	1
1992–93		41	4
1993–94		19	1
1994–95	Brighton & HA	19	2
1995–96	Exeter C	33	1

CHAMBERS, David

Born Chesterfield 16.9.76 Ht 5 11
Wt 10 10
Forward. From Trainee.

1995–96	Hull C	—	—

CHAMBERS, Leroy

Born Sheffield 25.10.72 Ht 5 11
Wt 12 00
Forward. From Trainee.

1991–92	Sheffield W	—	—
1992–93		—	—
1993–94		—	—
1994–95	Chester C	13	—
1995–96		8	1

CHANDLER, Dean

Born Ilford 6.5.76 Ht 6 1 Wt 11 02
Defender. From Trainee.

1993–94	Charlton Ath	—	—
1994–95		1	1
1995–96		1	—

CHANNING, Justin

Born Reading 19.11.68 Ht 5 11
Wt 11 07
Defender. From Apprentice. England Youth.

1986–87	QPR	2	—
1987–88		14	1
1988–89		9	1
1989–90		23	2

Season Club League Appearances/Goals

Season	Club	Apps	Goals
1990–91		5	—
1991–92		—	—
1992–93		2	1
1992–93	Bristol R	25	3
1993–94		29	5
1994–95		40	2
1995–96		36	—

CHAPMAN, Danny

Born Peckham 21.11.74 Ht 5 10
Wt 11 06
Midfield. From Trainee.

Season	Club	Apps	Goals
1992–93	Millwall	—	—
1993–94		—	—
1994–95		12	—
1995–96	Leyton Orient	38	2

CHAPMAN, Ian

Born Brighton 31.5.70 Ht 5 9 Wt 12 05
Midfield. From FA Schools, Trainee.

Season	Club	Apps	Goals
1986–87	Brighton & HA	5	—
1987–88		—	—
1988–89		19	—
1989–90		42	1
1990–91		23	—
1991–92		37	2
1992–93		34	1
1993–94		45	3
1994–95		40	4
1995–96		36	3

CHAPMAN, Lee

Born Lincoln 5.12.59 Ht 6 2 Wt 13 00
Forward. From Amateur. England Under-21, B.

Season	Club	Apps	Goals
1978–79	Stoke C	—	—
1978–79	*Plymouth Arg*	4	—
1979–80	Stoke C	17	3
1980–81		41	15
1981–82		41	16
1982–83	Arsenal	19	3
1983–84		4	1
1983–84	Sunderland	15	3
1984–85	Sheffield W	40	15
1985–86		31	10
1986–87		41	19
1987–88		37	19

From Niort

Season	Club	Apps	Goals
1988–89	Nottingham F	30	8
1989–90		18	7
1989–90	Leeds U	21	12
1990–91		38	21
1991–92		38	16
1992–93		40	13
1993–94	Portsmouth	5	2
1993–94	West Ham U	30	7
1994–95		10	—
1994–95	*Southend U*	1	1
1994–95	Ipswich T	16	1
1995–96		6	—
1995–96	*Leeds U*	2	—
1995–96	Swansea C	7	4

CHAPPLE, Phil

Born Norwich 26.11.66 Ht 6 2 Wt 12 07
Defender. From Apprentice.

Season	Club	Apps	Goals
1984–85	Norwich C	—	—
1985–86		—	—
1986–87		—	—
1987–88		—	—
1987–88	Cambridge U	6	1
1988–89		46	3
1989–90		45	5
1990–91		43	5
1991–92		29	3
1992–93		18	2
1993–94	Charlton Ath	44	5
1994–95		21	2
1995–96		16	2

CHAPPLE, Shaun

Born Swansea 14.2.73 Ht 5 11 Wt 12 03
Midfield. From Trainee. Wales Under-21.

Season	Club	Apps	Goals
1991–92	Swansea C	21	2
1992–93		4	—
1993–94		29	3
1994–95		9	2
1995–96		22	2

CHARLERY, Ken

Born Stepney 28.11.64 Ht 6 0 Wt 12 00
Forward. From Fisher Ath, Basildon U, Beckton U.

Season	Club	Apps	Goals
1989–90	Maidstone U	30	2
1990–91		29	9

Season	Club	League Appearances/Goals	
1990–91	Peterborough U	4	—
1991–92		37	16
1992–93		10	3
1992–93	Watford	32	11
1993–94		16	2
1993–94	Peterborough U	26	8
1994–95		44	16
1995–96	Birmingham C	17	4
1995–96	*Southend U*	3	—
1995–96	Peterborough U	19	7

CHARLES, Gary

Born London 13.4.70 Ht 5 9 Wt 11 08
Defender. From Trainee. England Under-21, 2 full caps.

1987–88	Nottingham F	—	—
1988–89		1	—
1988–89	*Leicester C*	8	—
1989–90	Nottingham F	1	—
1990–91		10	—
1991–92		30	1
1992–93		14	—
1993–94	Derby Co	43	1
1994–95		18	2
1994–95	Aston Villa	16	—
1995–96		34	1

CHARLES, Lee

Born Hillingdon 20.8.71 Ht 5 11
Wt 12 04
Forward. From Chertsey T.

1995–96	QPR	4	—
1995–96	*Barnet*	5	—

CHARLES, Steve

Born Sheffield 10.5.60 Ht 5 11 Wt 12 02
Midfield. From Sheffield Univ. England Schools.

1979–80	Sheffield U	14	1
1980–81		31	6
1981–82		30	1
1982–83		35	—
1983–84		11	1
1984–85		2	1
1984–85	Wrexham	32	7
1985–86		40	20
1986–87		41	10
1987–88	Mansfield T	46	12
1988–89		46	7
1989–90		43	7
1990–91		39	4
1991–92		40	6
1992–93		23	3
1992–93	*Scunthorpe U*	4	—
1992–93	Scarborough	16	3
1993–94		37	7
1994–95		40	5
1995–96		41	5

CHARLTON, Simon

Born Huddersfield 25.10.71 Ht 5 8
Wt 11 10
Defender. From Trainee. FA Schools.

1989–90	Huddersfield T	3	—
1990–91		30	—
1991–92		45	—
1992–93		46	1
1993–94	Southampton	33	1
1994–95		25	1
1995–96		26	—

CHARNOCK, Phil

Born Southport 14.2.75 Ht 5 11
Wt 11 02
Midfield. From Trainee.

1992–93	Liverpool	—	—
1993–94		—	—
1994–95		—	—
1995–96		—	—
1995–96	*Blackpool*	4	—

CHEESEWRIGHT, John

Born Hornchurch 12.1.73 Ht 6 0
Wt 12 03
Goalkeeper. From Tottenham H Trainee.

1990–91	Southend U	—	—
1991–92	Birmingham C	1	—
From Braintree T			
1993–94	Colchester U	17	—
1994–95		23	—
1995–96	Wimbledon	—	—
1995–96	Wycombe W	—	—

Season	Club	League Appearances/Goals	

CHEETHAM, Michael

Born Amsterdam 30.6.67 Ht 5 9
Wt 12 03
Midfield. From Army.

1988–89	Ipswich T	3	—
1989–90		1	—
1989–90	Cambridge U	36	10
1990–91		44	7
1991–92		22	3
1992–93		17	—
1993–94		13	2
1994–95	Chesterfield	5	—
1994–95	Colchester U	9	1
1995–96		28	2

CHENERY, Ben

Born Ipswich 28.1.77 Ht 6 1 Wt 12 05
Defender. From Trainee.

1994–95	Luton T	—	—
1995–96		2	—

CHERRY, Steve

Born Nottingham 5.8.60 Ht 6 1
Wt 13 00
Goalkeeper. From Apprentice. England Youth.

1977–78	Derby Co	—	—
1978–79		—	—
1979–80		4	—
1980–81	*Port Vale*	4	—
1981–82	Derby Co	4	—
1982–83		31	—
1983–84		38	—
1984–85	Walsall	41	—
1985–86		30	—
1986–87		—	—
1986–87	Plymouth Arg	21	—
1987–88		37	—
1988–89		15	—
1988–89	*Chesterfield*	10	—
1988–89	Notts Co	18	—
1989–90		46	—
1990–91		46	—
1991–92		42	—
1992–93		44	—
1993–94		45	—
1994–95		25	—
1995–96	Watford	4	—
1995–96	*Plymouth Arg*	16	—

CHETTLE, Steve

Born Nottingham 27.9.68 Ht 6 1
Wt 13 01
Defender. From Apprentice. England Under-21.

1986–87	Nottingham F	—	—
1987–88		30	—
1988–89		28	2
1989–90		22	1
1990–91		37	2
1991–92		22	1
1992–93		30	—
1993–94		46	1
1994–95		41	—
1995–96		37	—

CHILDS, Gary

Born Birmingham 19.4.64 Ht 5 7
Wt 10 08
Midfield. From Apprentice. England Youth.

1981–82	WBA	2	—
1982–83		—	—
1983–84		1	—
1983–84	Walsall	30	2
1984–85		40	2
1985–86		33	5
1986–87		28	8
1987–88	Birmingham C	32	1
1988–89		23	1
1989–90	Grimsby T	44	5
1990–91		25	4
1991–92		29	3
1992–93		17	—
1993–94		31	6
1994–95		25	4
1995–96		35	3

CHISHOLM, Craig

Born Glasgow 21.9.77 Ht 5 11 Wt 10 08
Midfield. From Trainee.

1994–95	Blackburn R	—	—
1995–96		—	—

CHRISTIE, Iyseden

Born Coventry 14.11.76 Ht 6 0 Wt 12 06
Forward. From Trainee.

1994–95	Coventry C	—	—
1995–96		1	—

Season	Club	League Appearances/Goals	

CHRISTIE, Kevin

Born Aberdeen 1.4.76 Ht 6 1 Wt 12 03
Midfield. From Lewis Utd.

1994–95	Aberdeen	—	—
1995–96		2	—

CLAPHAM, Jamie

Born Lincoln 7.12.75 Ht 5 9 Wt 10 08
Midfield. From Trainee.

1994–95	Tottenham H	—	—
1995–96		—	—

CLARE, Daryl

Born Jersey 1.8.78 Ht 5 8 Wt 10 06
Midfield. From Trainee.

1995–96	Grimsby T	1	—

CLARIDGE, Steve

Born Portsmouth 10.4.66 Ht 6 0
Wt 12 10
Forward. From Portsmouth, Fareham.

1984–85	Bournemouth	6	1
1985–86		1	—
From Weymouth			
1988–89	Crystal Palace	—	—
1988–89	Aldershot	37	9
1989–90		25	10
1989–90	Cambridge U	20	4
1990–91		30	12
1991–92		29	12
1992–93	Luton T	16	2
1992–93	Cambridge U	29	7
1993–94		24	11
1993–94	Birmingham C	18	7
1994–95		42	20
1995–96		28	8
1995–96	Leicester C	14	5

CLARK, Anthony

Born London 7.4.77 Ht 5 7 Wt 11 00
Forward.

1994–95	Wycombe W	1	—
1995–96		3	—

CLARK, Billy

Born Christchurch 19.5.67 Ht 6 0
Wt 12 03
Defender. From Trainee.

1984–85	Bournemouth	1	—
1985–86		1	—
1986–87		—	—
1987–88		2	—
1987–88	Bristol R	31	1
1988–89		11	—
1989–90		—	—
1990–91		14	1
1991–92		24	1
1992–93		24	1
1993–94		36	1
1994–95		42	6
1995–96		39	2

Season Club League Appearances/Goals

CLARK, Ian

Born Cleveland 23.10.74 Ht 5 11
Wt 11 02
Midfield.

1995–96	Doncaster R	23	1

CLARK, John

Born Edinburgh 22.9.64 Ht 6 0
Wt 13 01
Defender. From 'S' From. Scotland Youth.

1981–82	Dundee U	—	—
1982–83		1	—
1983–84		9	1
1984–85		10	3
1985–86		11	1
1986–87		30	3
1987–88		28	3
1988–89		20	2
1989–90		29	1
1990–91		18	2
1991–92		35	1
1992–93		37	2
1993–94		14	—
1993–94	Stoke C	12	—
1994–95		5	—
1994–95	Falkirk	31	8
1995–96		17	2
1995–96	Dunfermline Ath	11	1

CLARK, Lee

Born Wallsend 27.10.72 Ht 5 7 Wt 11 07
Midfield. From Trainee. England Youth, Under-21.

1989–90	Newcastle U	—	—
1990–91		19	2

Season	Club	Apps	Goals
1991–92		29	5
1992–93		46	9
1993–94		29	2
1994–95		19	1
1995–96		28	2

CLARK, Paul

Born Benfleet 14.9.58 Ht 5 9 Wt 13 13
Midfield. From Apprentice. England Schools, Youth.

Season	Club	Apps	Goals
1976–77	Southend U	25	—
1977–78		8	1
1977–78	Brighton & HA	26	3
1978–79		33	4
1979–80		11	2
1980–81		9	—
1981–82	*Reading*	2	—
1982–83	Southend U	31	1
1983–84		20	—
1984–85		29	1
1985–86		39	1
1986–87		46	—
1987–88		30	—
1988–89		16	—
1989–90		25	—
1990–91		40	—
1991–92	Gillingham	42	—
1992–93		35	1
1993–94		13	—
1994–95	Cambridge U	—	—
1995–96		2	—

CLARK, Richard

Born Nuneaton 6.4.77 Ht 5 11 Wt 13 04
Goalkeeper. From Trainee.

Season	Club	Apps	Goals
1993–94	Nottingham F	—	—
1994–95		—	—
1995–96		—	—

CLARK, Simon

Born London 12.3.67 Ht 6 0 Wt 12 12
Defender. From Boston U, Holbeach, Kings Lynn, Hendon, Stevenage Borough.

Season	Club	Apps	Goals
1993–94	Peterborough U	1	—
1994–95		32	—
1995–96		40	1

CLARKE, Adrian

Born Suffolk 28.9.74 Ht 5 10 Wt 11 00
Forward. From Trainee. England Schools.

Season	Club	Apps	Goals
1993–94	Arsenal	—	—
1994–95		1	—
1995–96		6	—

CLARKE, Andy

Born Islington 22.7.67 Ht 5 10 Wt 11 07
Forward. From Barnet.

Season	Club	Apps	Goals
1990–91	Wimbledon	12	3
1991–92		34	3
1992–93		33	5
1993–94		23	2
1994–95		25	1
1995–96		18	2

CLARKE, Chris

Born Barnsley 1.5.74 Ht 6 1 Wt 12 10
Goalkeeper. From Trainee.

Season	Club	Apps	Goals
1992–93	Bolton W	—	—
1993–94		—	—
1994–95	Rochdale	24	—
1995–96		6	—

CLARKE, Darrell

Born Mansfield 16.12.77 Ht 5 10 Wt 12 00
Defender. From Trainee.

Season	Club	Apps	Goals
1995–96	Mansfield T	3	—

CLARKE, Dean

Born Hereford 28.7.77 Ht 5 9 Wt 11 04
Forward. From Trainee.

Season	Club	Apps	Goals
1993–94	Hereford U	1	—
1994–95		5	—
1995–96		5	—

CLARKE, Matthew

Born Sheffield 3.11.73 Ht 6 3 Wt 11 05
Goalkeeper. From Trainee.

Season	Club	Apps	Goals
1992–93	Rotherham U	9	—
1993–94		30	—
1994–95		45	—
1995–96		40	—

CLARKE, Steve

Born Saltcoats 29.8.63 Ht 5 10 Wt 12 05
Defender. From Beith Juniors, Scotland Youth, Under-21, B, 6 full caps. Football League.

Season	Club	Apps	Goals
1981–82	St Mirren	—	—
1982–83		31	—
1983–84		33	2
1984–85		33	—
1985–86		31	3
1986–87		23	1
1986–87	Chelsea	16	—
1987–88		38	1
1988–89		36	—
1989–90		24	3
1990–91		18	1
1991–92		31	1
1992–93		20	—
1993–94		39	—
1994–95		29	—
1995–96		22	—

CLARKE, Stuart

Born Leamington 10.3.77
Midfield. From Trainee.

Season	Club	Apps	Goals
1995–96	WBA	—	—

CLARKE, Tim

Born Stourbridge 19.9.68 Ht 6 3
Wt 13 07
Goalkeeper. From Halesowen.

Season	Club	Apps	Goals
1990–91	Coventry C	—	—
1991–92	Huddersfield T	39	—
1992–93		31	—
1992–93	*Rochdale*	2	—
1993–94	Shrewsbury T	—	—
1994–95		16	—
1995–96		15	—

CLARKSON, Ian

Born Birmingham 4.12.70 Ht 5 10
Wt 12 02
Defender. From Trainee.

Season	Club	Apps	Goals
1988–89	Birmingham C	9	—
1989–90		20	—
1990–91		37	—
1991–92		42	—
1992–93		28	—
1993–94		—	—
1993–94	Stoke C	14	—
1994–95		18	—
1995–96		43	—

CLARKSON, Phil

Born Hambleton 13.11.68 Ht 5 8
Wt 11 02
Midfield. From Fleetwood.

Season	Club	Apps	Goals
1991–92	Crewe Alex	28	6
1992–93		35	13
1993–94		7	2
1994–95		23	6
1995–96		5	—
1995–96	Scunthorpe U	24	6

CLAYTON, Gary

Born Sheffield 2.2.63 Ht 5 10 Wt 12 03
Midfield. From Rotherham U Apprentice, Burton Alb.

Season	Club	Apps	Goals
1986–87	Doncaster R	35	5
1987–88	Cambridge U	45	5
1988–89		46	1
1989–90		10	1
1990–91		6	—
1990–91	*Peterborough U*	4	—
1991–92	Cambridge U	11	3
1992–93		36	3
1993–94		25	4
1993–94	Huddersfield T	17	1
1994–95		2	—
1995–96	Plymouth Arg	36	2

CLEARY, Kevin

Born Isleworth 7.9.76
Defender. From Trainee.

Season	Club	Apps	Goals
1995–96	Brentford	—	—

CLEELAND, Marc

Born Whitehaven 15.12.75 Ht 5 8
Wt 10 00
Midfield. From Trainee.

Season	Club	Apps	Goals
1995–96	Carlisle U	—	—

CLEGG, David

Born Liverpool 23.10.76 Ht 5 9
Wt 10 01
Midfield. From Trainee.

Season	Club	Apps	Goals
1994–95	Liverpool	—	—
1995–96		—	—

Season	Club	League Appearances/Goals	

CLEGG, Michael

Born Tameside 3.7.77 Ht 5 8 Wt 11 08
Defender. From Trainee.

1995–96	Manchester U	—	—

CLELAND, Alec

Born Glasgow 10.12.70 Ht 5 8 Wt 10 00
Defender. From 'S' Form. Scotland Under-21.

1987–88	Dundee U	1	—
1988–89		9	—
1989–90		15	—
1990–91		20	2
1991–92		31	4
1992–93		24	—
1993–94		33	1
1994–95		18	1
1994–95	Rangers	10	—
1995–96		25	1

CLEMENCE, Stephen

Born Liverpool 31.3.78 Ht 5 11
Wt 12 00
Midfield. From Trainee. England Youth.

1994–95	Tottenham H	—	—
1995–96		—	—

CLEMENT, Neil

Born Reading 3.10.78 Ht 5 10 Wt 10 00
Defender. From Trainee.

1995–96	Chelsea	—	—

CLIFFORD, Mark

Born Nottingham 11.9.77
Defender. From Trainee.

1994–95	Mansfield T	1	—
1995–96		—	—

CLODE, Mark

Born Plymouth 24.2.73 Ht 5 10
Wt 10 10
Defender. From Trainee.

1991–92	Plymouth Arg	—	—
1992–93		—	—
1993–94	Swansea C	28	1
1994–95		33	1
1995–96		30	—

CLOUGH, Nigel

Born Sunderland 19.3.66 Ht 5 10
Wt 12 03
Midfield. From AC Hunters. England Under-21, B, 14 full caps.

1984–85	Nottingham F	9	1
1985–86		39	15
1986–87		42	14
1987–88		34	19
1988–89		36	14
1989–90		38	9
1990–91		37	14
1991–92		34	5
1992–93		42	10
1993–94	Liverpool	27	7
1994–95		10	—
1995–96		2	—
1995–96	Manchester C	15	2

CLYDE, Darran

Born Northern Ireland 26.3.76 Ht 6 4
Wt 11 13
Defender. From Trainee.

1994–95	Barnsley	—	—
1995–96		—	—

COADY, Lewis

Born Liverpool 20.9.76 Ht 6 1 Wt 11 05
Forward. From Trainee.

1994–95	Wrexham	2	—
1995–96		—	—

COATES, Jonathan

Born Swansea 27.6.75 Ht 5 8 Wt 10 04
Forward. From Trainee. Wales Under-21.

1993–94	Swansea C	4	1
1994–95		5	—
1995–96		18	—

COATES, Scott

Born Consett 7.9.76
Defender. From Trainee.

1995–96	Sunderland	—	—

COCKERILL, Glenn

Born Grimsby 25.8.59 Ht 5 10 Wt 12 06
Midfield. From Louth U.

1976–77	Lincoln C	4	—
1977–78		13	1

Season	Club	League Appearances/Goals	
1978–79		35	6
1979–80		19	3
1979–80	Swindon T	10	1
1980–81		16	—
1981–82	Lincoln C	44	11
1982–83		38	8
1983–84		33	6
1983–84	Sheffield U	10	1
1984–85		40	7
1985–86		12	2
1985–86	Southampton	30	7
1986–87		42	7
1987–88		39	2
1988–89		34	6
1989–90		36	4
1990–91		32	2
1991–92		37	4
1992–93		23	—
1993–94		14	—
1993–94	Leyton Orient	19	2
1994–95		33	4
1995–96		38	1

CODNER, Robert

Born Walthamstow 23.1.65 Ht 5 11
Wt 13 01
Midfield. From Leicester C, Barnet.

Season	Club	Apps	Goals
1988–89	Brighton & HA	28	1
1989–90		45	9
1990–91		42	8
1991–92		45	6
1992–93		43	3
1993–94		40	8
1994–95		23	4
1995–96	Reading	4	—
1995–96	Peterborough U	2	—
1995–96	Barnet	8	—

COLCOMBE, Scott

Born West Bromwich 15.12.71 Ht 5 6
Wt 10 04
Forward. From Trainee.

Season	Club	Apps	Goals
1989–90	WBA	—	—
1990–91		—	—
1991–92	Torquay U	28	—
1992–93		24	1
1993–94		27	—
1994–95		10	—
1995–96	Doncaster R	30	3

COLDICOTT, Stacy

Born Worcester 29.4.74 Ht 5 8 Wt 11 04
Defender. From Trainee.

Season	Club	Apps	Goals
1991–92	WBA	—	—
1992–93		14	—
1993–94		5	—
1994–95		11	—
1995–96		33	—

COLE, Andy

Born Nottingham 15.10.71 Ht 5 11
Wt 11 02
Forward. From Trainee. England Youth, Under-21, B, 1 full cap. Football League.

Season	Club	Apps	Goals
1989–90	Arsenal	—	—
1990–91		1	—
1991–92		—	—
1991–92	*Fulham*	13	3
1991–92	*Bristol C*	12	8
1992–93	Bristol C	29	12
1992–93	Newcastle U	12	12
1993–94		40	34
1994–95		18	9
1994–95	Manchester U	18	12
1995–96		34	11

COLEMAN, Chris

Born Swansea 10.6.70 Ht 6 2 Wt 14 03
Defender. From Apprentice. Wales Under-21, 14 full caps.

Season	Club	Apps	Goals
1987–88	Swansea C	30	—
1988–89		43	—
1989–90		46	2
1990–91		41	—
1991–92	Crystal Palace	18	4
1992–93		38	5
1993–94		46	3
1994–95		35	1
1995–96		17	—
1995–96	Blackburn R	20	—

COLEMAN, Simon

Born Worksop 13.6.68 Ht 6 0 Wt 10 08
Defender.

Season	Club	Apps	Goals
1985–86	Mansfield T	—	—
1986–87		2	—
1987–88		44	2

Season	Club	Apps	Goals
1988–89		45	5
1989–90		5	—
1989–90	Middlesbrough	36	1
1990–91		19	1
1991–92	Derby Co	43	2
1992–93		25	—
1993–94		2	—
1993–94	Sheffield W	15	1
1994–95		1	—
1994–95	Bolton W	22	4
1995–96		12	1

COLGAN, Nick

Born Eire 19.9.73 Ht 6 1 Wt 13 06
Goalkeeper. From Drogheda. Eire Under-21.

Season	Club	Apps	Goals
1992–93	Chelsea	—	—
1993–94		—	—
1993–94	*Crewe Alex*	—	—
1994–95	Chelsea	—	—
1994–95	*Grimsby T*	—	—
1995–96	Chelsea	—	—
1995–96	*Millwall*	—	—

COLKIN, Lee

Born Nuneaton 15.7.74 Ht 5 11
Wt 12 04
Defender. From Trainee.

Season	Club	Apps	Goals
1991–92	Northampton T	3	—
1992–93		13	—
1993–94		20	1
1994–95		33	1
1995–96		24	1

COLL, Owen

Born Donegal 9.4.76 Ht 6 0 Wt 11 07
Defender. From Amateur.

Season	Club	Apps	Goals
1994–95	Tottenham H	—	—
1995–96		—	—
1995–96	Bournemouth	8	—

COLLETT, Andy

Born Middlesbrough 28.10.73 Ht 6 0
Wt 13 00
Goalkeeper. From Trainee.

Season	Club	Apps	Goals
1991–92	Middlesbrough	—	—
1992–93		2	—
1993–94		—	—
1994–95		—	—
1994–95	Bristol R	4	—
1995–96		26	—

COLLIER, Danny

Born Eccles 15.1.74 Ht 6 1 Wt 11 00
Defender. From Trainee.

Season	Club	Apps	Goals
1992–93	Wolverhampton W	—	—
1993–94		—	—
1994–95	Crewe Alex	5	—
1995–96		6	—

COLLINS, John

Born Galashiels 31.1.68 Ht 5 7 Wt 9 10
Midfield. From Hutchison Vale BC.
Scotland Youth, Under-21, 36 full caps.

Season	Club	Apps	Goals
1984–85	Hibernian	—	—
1985–86		19	1
1986–87		30	1
1987–88		44	6
1988–89		35	2
1989–90		35	6
1990–91	Celtic	35	1
1991–92		38	11
1992–93		43	8
1993–94		38	8
1994–95		34	8
1995–96		29	11

COLLINS, Lee

Born Bellshill 3.2.74 Ht 5 8 Wt 10 02
Midfield. From Possil U.

Season	Club	Apps	Goals
1993–94	Albion R	20	—
1994–95		17	—
1995–96		8	1
1995–96	Swindon T	5	—

COLLINS, Sam

Born Pontefract 5.6.77 Ht 6 2 Wt 13 07
Defender. From Trainee.

Season	Club	Apps	Goals
1994–95	Huddersfield T	—	—
1995–96		—	—

Season	Club	League Appearances/Goals	

COLLINS, Simon

Born Pontefract 16.12.73 Ht 6 0
Wt 13 02
Midfield. From Trainee.

Season	Club	Apps	Goals
1992–93	Huddersfield T	1	—
1993–94		1	—
1994–95		4	—
1995–96		30	3

COLLINS, Wayne

Born Manchester 4.3.69 Ht 6 0 Wt 12 00
Midfield. From Winsford U.

Season	Club	Apps	Goals
1993–94	Crewe Alex	35	2
1994–95		40	11
1995–96		42	1

COLLYMORE, Stan

Born Stone 22.1.71 Ht 6 3 Wt 14 10
Forward. From Stafford R. England 2 full caps.

Season	Club	Apps	Goals
1990–91	Crystal Palace	6	—
1991–92		12	1
1992–93		2	—
1992–93	Southend U	30	15
1993–94	Nottingham F	28	19
1994–95		37	22
1995–96	Liverpool	31	14

COLQUHOUN, John

Born Stirling 14.7.63 Ht 5 7 Wt 11 00
Forward. From Grangemouth Inter.

Season	Club	Apps	Goals
1980–81	Stirling Albion	13	—
1981–82		37	13
1982–83		39	21
1983–84		15	11
1983–84	Celtic	12	2
1984–85		20	2
1985–86	Hearts	36	8
1986–87		43	13
1987–88		44	15
1988–89		36	5
1989–90		36	6
1990–91		36	7
1991–92	Millwall	27	3
1992–93	Sunderland	20	—
1993–94	Hearts	41	4
1994–95		31	2
1995–96		31	4

COMYN, Andy

Born Manchester 2.6.68 Ht 6 1 Wt 11 12
Defender. From Alvechurch.

Season	Club	Apps	Goals
1989–90	Aston Villa	4	—
1990–91		11	—
1991–92	Derby Co	46	1
1992–93		17	—
1993–94	Plymouth Arg	46	5
1994–95		30	—
1995–96		—	—
1995–96	Preston NE	—	—
1995–96	WBA	3	—

CONLON, Paul

Born Sunderland 5.1.78 Ht 5 9 Wt 11 08
Forward. From Trainee.

Season	Club	Apps	Goals
1995–96	Hartlepool U	15	4

CONNELLY, Sean

Born Sheffield 26.6.70 Ht 5 10 Wt 11 10
Defender. From Hallam.

Season	Club	Apps	Goals
1991–92	Stockport Co	—	—
1992–93		7	—
1993–94		32	—
1994–95		39	—
1995–96		43	—

CONNOLLY, David

Born Willesden 6.6.77 Ht 5 8 Wt 10 09
Forward. From Trainee. Eire 4 full caps.

Season	Club	Apps	Goals
1994–95	Watford	2	—
1995–96		11	8

CONNOLLY, Karl

Born Prescot 9.2.70 Ht 5 9 Wt 11 00
Forward. From Napoli (Liverpool Sunday League).

Season	Club	Apps	Goals
1990–91	Wrexham	—	—
1991–92		36	8
1992–93		42	9
1993–94		39	2
1994–95		45	10
1995–96		46	18

CONNOLLY, Patrick

Born Glasgow 25.6.70 Ht 5 8 Wt 9 04
Forward. From 'S' Form. Scotland Under-21.

Season	Club	Apps	Goals
1986–87	Dundee U	—	—

Season	Club	League Appearances/Goals	
1987–88		—	—
1988–89		2	—
1989–90		15	5
1990–91		10	2
1991–92		5	—
1992–93		42	16
1993–94		28	5
1994–95		6	—
1995–96		6	1

CONNOR, James

Born Middlesbrough 22.8.74 Ht 6 0
Wt 13 00
Midfield. From Trainee.

Season	Club	Apps	Goals
1992–93	Millwall	—	—
1993–94		—	—
1994–95		1	—
1995–96		8	—

CONNOR, Robert

Born Kilmarnock 4.8.60 Ht 5 11
Wt 11 04
Midfield. From Ayr U BC. Scotland Youth, B, Under-21, 4 full caps.

Season	Club	Apps	Goals
1977–78	Ayr U	9	—
1978–79		29	—
1979–80		38	9
1980–81		39	8
1981–82		30	—
1982–83		39	4
1983–84		39	7
1984–85	Dundee	34	7
1985–86		35	2
1986–87		2	—
1986–87	Aberdeen	32	4
1987–88		34	1
1988–89		36	4
1989–90		34	1
1990–91		29	6
1991–92		11	—
1992–93		6	—
1993–94		25	1
1994–95	Kilmarnock	28	—
1995–96		23	—

CONROY, Mike

Born Glasgow 31.12.65 Ht 6 0 Wt 13 03
Forward. From Apprentice.

Season	Club	Apps	Goals
1983–84	Coventry C	—	—
1983–84	Clydebank	2	—
1984–85		26	11
1985–86		28	7
1986–87		36	9
1987–88		22	11
1987–88	St Mirren	10	1
1988–89	Reading	13	4
1989–90		34	2
1990–91		33	1
1991–92	Burnley	38	24
1992–93		39	6
1993–94	Preston NE	32	12
1994–95		25	10
1995–96	Fulham	40	9

CONWAY, Paul

Born London 17.4.70 Ht 6 1 Wt 12 10
Midfield. From Oldham Ath.

Season	Club	Apps	Goals
1993–94	Carlisle U	18	4
1994–95		24	6
1995–96		22	3

COOK, Andy

Born Romsey 10.8.69 Ht 5 9 Wt 12 00
Defender. From Apprentice.

Season	Club	Apps	Goals
1987–88	Southampton	2	—
1988–89		3	—
1989–90		4	1
1990–91		7	—
1991–92		—	—
1991–92	Exeter C	38	—
1992–93		32	1
1993–94	Swansea C	28	—
1994–95		1	—
1995–96		33	—

COOK, Anthony

Born Hemel Hempstead 17.9.76
Midfield. From Trainee.

Season	Club	Apps	Goals
1993–94	Colchester U	2	—
1994–95		—	—
1995–96		—	—

COOK, Mitch

Born Scarborough 15.10.61 Ht 6 0
Wt 12 00
Midfield. From Scarborough.

Season	Club	Apps	Goals
1984–85	Darlington	31	3

Season	Club	League Appearances/Goals	
1985–86	....	3	1
1985–86	Middlesbrough	6	—
1986–87	Scarborough	—	—
1987–88	....	38	5
1988–89	....	43	5
1989–90	Halifax T	37	2
1990–91	....	17	—
1990–91	*Scarborough*	9	1
1990–91	*Darlington*	9	—
1991–92	Darlington	27	3
1991–92	Blackpool	8	—
1992–93	....	9	—
1993–94	....	45	—
1994–95	....	6	—
1994–95	Hartlepool U	24	—
1995–96	Scarborough	2	—

COOK, Paul

Born Liverpool 22.2.67 Ht 5 11
Wt 10 10
Midfield. From Marine.

Season	Club	Apps	Goals
1984–85	Wigan Ath	2	—
1985–86	....	13	2
1986–87	....	27	4
1987–88	....	41	8
1988–89	Norwich C	4	—
1989–90	....	2	—
1989–90	Wolverhampton W	28	2
1990–91	....	42	6
1991–92	....	43	8
1992–93	....	44	1
1993–94	....	36	2
1994–95	Coventry C	34	3
1995–96	....	3	—
1995–96	Tranmere R	15	1

COOKE, Andy

Born Shrewsbury 2.1.74 Ht 5 11
Wt 12 08
Forward. From Newtown.

Season	Club	Apps	Goals
1994–95	Burnley	—	—
1995–96	....	23	5

COOKE, Jason

Born Birmingham 13.7.71
Forward. From Brierley Hill.

Season	Club	Apps	Goals
1994–95	Preston NE	—	—
1995–96	Torquay U	1	—

COOKE, Terry

Born Marston Green 5.8.76 Ht 5 7
Wt 9 09
Forward. From Trainee. England Youth, Under-21.

Season	Club	Apps	Goals
1994–95	Manchester U	—	—
1995–96	....	4	—
1995–96	*Sunderland*	6	—

COOPER, Colin

Born Durham 28.2.67 Ht 5 9 Wt 11 09
Defender. England Under-21, 2 full caps.

Season	Club	Apps	Goals
1984–85	Middlesbrough	—	—
1985–86	....	11	—
1986–87	....	46	—
1987–88	....	43	2
1988–89	....	35	2
1989–90	....	21	2
1990–91	....	32	—
1991–92	Millwall	36	2
1992–93	....	41	4
1993–94	Nottingham F	37	7
1994–95	....	35	1
1995–96	....	37	5

COOPER, Gary

Born Edgware 20.11.65 Ht 5 8 Wt 11 00
Defender. From Brentford, QPR, Fisher Ath.

Season	Club	Apps	Goals
1989–90	Maidstone U	33	4
1990–91	....	27	3
1990–91	Peterborough U	6	1
1991–92	....	33	4
1992–93	....	35	3
1993–94	....	14	2
1993–94	Birmingham C	18	1
1994–95	....	26	1
1995–96	....	18	—

COOPER, Kevin

Born Derby 8.2.75 Ht 5 7 Wt 10 07
Midfield. From Trainee.

Season	Club	Apps	Goals
1993–94	Derby Co	—	—
1994–95	....	1	—
1995–96	....	1	—

COOPER, Mark

Born Cambridge 5.4.67 Ht 6 4 Wt 14 00
Forward. From Apprentice.

Season	Club	Apps	Goals
1983–84	Cambridge U	2	—

Season	Club	League Appearances/Goals	
1984–85	....	18	3
1985–86	....	19	1
1986–87	....	32	13
1986–87	Tottenham H.............	—	—
1987–88	....	—	—
1987–88	Shrewsbury T.............	6	2
1987–88	Gillingham.................	31	8
1988–89	....	18	3
1988–89	Leyton Orient............	14	4
1989–90	....	39	11
1990–91	....	22	9
1991–92	....	18	6
1992–93	....	28	7
1993–94	....	29	8
1994–95	Barnet........................	34	11
1995–96	....	33	8

COOPER, Mark

Born Wakefield 18.12.68 Ht 5 8
Wt 10 10
Midfield. From Trainee.

Season	Club	Apps	Goals
1987–88	Bristol C....................	—	—
1988–89	....	—	—
1989–90	Exeter C.....................	5	—
1989–90	*Southend U*...............	5	—
1990–91	Exeter C.....................	42	11
1991–92	....	3	1
1991–92	Birmingham C............	33	4
1992–93	....	6	—
1992–93	Fulham.......................	9	—
1992–93	*Huddersfield T*..........	10	4
1993–94	Fulham.......................	5	—
1993–94	Wycombe W................	2	1
1993–94	Exeter C.....................	21	8
1994–95	....	40	6
1995–96	....	27	6

COOPER, Neale

Born Darjeeling 24.11.63 Ht 6 0
Wt 12 07
Defender. From King Street. Scotland Schools, Youth, Under-21.

Season	Club	Apps	Goals
1979–80	Aberdeen....................	—	—
1980–81	....	5	—
1981–82	....	27	3
1982–83	....	31	2
1983–84	....	26	—
1984–85	....	20	1
1985–86	....	23	—
1986–87	Aston Villa................	13	—
1987–88	....	7	—
1988–89	....	—	—
1988–89	Rangers......................	14	1
1989–90	....	3	—
1990–91	Aberdeen....................	—	—
1991–92	Reading......................	7	—
1991–92	Dunfermline Ath.......	21	—
1992–93	....	33	2
1993–94	....	30	2
1994–95	....	15	—
1995–96	....	4	—

COPE, James

Born Solihull 4.10.77
Midfield. From Trainee.

Season	Club	Apps	Goals
1995–96	Shrewsbury T.............	1	—

CORAZZIN, Carlo

Born Canada 25.12.71 Ht 5 11 Wt 12 07
Forward. From Vancouver 86ers. Canada full caps.

Season	Club	Apps	Goals
1993–94	Cambridge U..............	28	10
1994–95	....	46	19
1995–96	....	31	10
1995–96	Plymouth Arg............	6	1

CORDEN, Wayne

Born Leek 1.11.75 Ht 5 9 Wt 10 06
Midfield. From Trainee.

Season	Club	Apps	Goals
1994–95	Port Vale....................	1	—
1995–96	....	2	—

CORICA, Steve

Born Cairns 24.3.73 Ht 5 8 Wt 10 10
Forward. From Marconi. Australia full caps.

Season	Club	Apps	Goals
1995–96	Leicester C................	16	2
1995–96	Wolverhampton W....	17	—

CORNFORTH, John

Born Whitley Bay 7.10.67 Ht 6 1
Wt 12 08
Midfield. From Apprentice. Wales 2 full caps.

Season	Club	Apps	Goals
1984–85	Sunderland.................	1	—
1985–86	....	—	—
1986–87	....	—	—
1986–87	*Doncaster R*..............	7	3

Season	Club	League Appearances	Goals
1987–88	Sunderland	12	2
1988–89		15	—
1989–90		2	—
1989–90	*Shrewsbury T*	3	—
1989–90	*Lincoln C*	9	1
1990–91	Sunderland	2	—
1991–92	Swansea C	17	—
1992–93		44	5
1993–94		38	6
1994–95		33	3
1995–96		17	2
1995–96	Birmingham C	8	—

COSTELLO, Lorcan

Born Dublin 11.11.76 Ht 5 9 Wt 11 02
Defender. From Trainee.

Season	Club	League Appearances	Goals
1993–94	Coventry C	—	—
1994–95		—	—
1995–96		—	—

COTON, Tony

Born Tamworth 19.5.61 Ht 6 2 Wt 13 07
Goalkeeper. From Mile Oak. England B.

Season	Club	League Appearances	Goals
1978–79	Birmingham C	—	—
1979–80		—	—
1979–80	*Hereford U*	—	—
1980–81	Birmingham C	3	—
1981–82		15	—
1982–83		28	—
1983–84		41	—
1984–85		7	—
1984–85	Watford	33	—
1985–86		40	—
1986–87		31	—
1987–88		37	—
1988–89		46	—
1989–90		46	—
1990–91	Manchester C	33	—
1991–92		37	—
1992–93		40	—
1993–94		31	—
1994–95		23	—
1995–96		—	—
1995–96	Manchester U	—	—

COTTEE, Tony

Born West Ham 11.7.65 Ht 5 7
Wt 11 03
Forward. From Apprentice. England Youth, Under-21, 7 full caps.

Season	Club	League Appearances	Goals
1982–83	West Ham U	8	5
1983–84		39	15
1984–85		41	17
1985–86		42	20
1986–87		42	22
1987–88		40	13
1988–89	Everton	36	13
1989–90		27	13
1990–91		29	10
1991–92		24	8
1992–93		26	12
1993–94		39	16
1994–95		3	—
1994–95	West Ham U	31	13
1995–96		33	10

COTTERELL, Leo

Born Cambridge 2.9.74 Ht 5 9 Wt 10 00
Defender. From Trainee.

Season	Club	League Appearances	Goals
1993–94	Ipswich T	—	—
1994–95		2	—
1995–96		—	—

COTTERILL, Steve

Born Cheltenham 20.7.64 Ht 6 1
Wt 12 02
Forward. From Burton Alb.

Season	Club	League Appearances	Goals
1988–89	Wimbledon	4	1
1989–90		2	1
1990–91		4	1
1991–92		—	—
1992–93		7	3
1992–93	*Brighton & HA*	11	4
1993–94	Bournemouth	37	14
1994–95		8	1
1995–96		—	—

COUGHLAN, Derek

Born Cork 2.1.77 Ht 6 4 Wt 13 10
Defender. From Trainee.

Season	Club	League Appearances	Goals
1995–96	Brighton & HA	1	—

COUGHLAN, Graham

Born Dublin 18.11.74 Ht 6 2 Wt 13 04
Defender. From Bray Wanderers.

Season	Club	League Appearances	Goals
1995–96	Blackburn R	—	—

Season	Club	League Appearances/Goals	

COUGHLIN, Russell

Born Swansea 15.2.60 Ht 5 8 Wt 11 07
Midfield. From Apprentice.

1977–78	Manchester C	—	—
1978–79		—	—
1978–79	Blackburn R	11	—
1979–80		10	—
1980–81		3	—
1980–81	Carlisle U	25	3
1981–82		37	5
1982–83		38	2
1983–84		30	3
1984–85	Plymouth Arg	38	3
1985–86		45	10
1986–87		40	5
1987–88		8	—
1987–88	Blackpool	24	2
1988–89		43	5
1989–90		35	1
1990–91		—	—
1990–91	*Shrewsbury T*	5	—
1990–91	Swansea C	29	—
1991–92		33	1
1992–93		39	1
1993–94	Exeter C	35	—
1994–95		25	—
1995–96		8	—
1995–96	Torquay U	25	—

COUSINS, Jason

Born Hayes 14.10.70 Ht 5 10 Wt 12 05
Defender. From Trainee.

1989–90	Brentford	13	—
1990–91		8	—
From Wycombe W			
1993–94	Wycombe W	37	1
1994–95		41	2
1995–96		30	—

COUZENS, Andrew

Born Shipley 4.6.75 Ht 5 9 Wt 11 06
Defender. From Trainee. England Under-21.

1992–93	Leeds U	—	—
1993–94		—	—
1994–95		4	—
1995–96		14	—

COWAN, Tom

Born Bellshill 28.8.69 Ht 5 8 Wt 11 10
Defender. From Netherdale BC.

1988–89	Clyde	16	2
1988–89	Rangers	4	—
1989–90		3	—
1990–91		5	—
1991–92	Sheffield U	20	—
1992–93		21	—
1993–94		4	—
1993–94	*Stoke C*	14	—
1993–94	*Huddersfield T*	10	—
1994–95	Huddersfield T	37	2
1995–96		43	2

COWANS, Gordon

Born Durham 27.10.58 Ht 5 7 Wt 10 07
Midfield. From Apprentice. England Youth, Under-21, B, 10 full caps.

1975–76	Aston Villa	1	—
1976–77		18	3
1977–78		35	7
1978–79		34	4
1979–80		42	6
1980–81		42	5
1981–82		42	6
1982–83		42	10
1983–84		—	—
1984–85		30	1
1985–86	Bari	20	—
1986–87		38	3
1987–88		36	—
1988–89	Aston Villa	33	2
1989–90		34	4
1990–91		38	1
1991–92		12	—
1991–92	Blackburn R	26	1
1992–93		24	1
1993–94	Aston Villa	11	—
1993–94	Derby Co	19	—
1994–95		17	—
1994–95	Wolverhampton W	21	—
1995–96		16	—
1995–96	Sheffield U	20	—

COWE, Steve

Born Gloucester 29.9.74 Ht 5 7
Wt 10 02
Midfield. From Trainee.

1993–94	Aston Villa	—	—
1994–95		—	—

Season	Club	Apps	Goals
1995–96		—	—
1995–96	Swindon T	11	1

COWLING, Lee

Born Doncaster 22.9.77 Ht 5 8 Wt 9 04
Midfield. From Trainee.

Season	Club	Apps	Goals
1994–95	Nottingham F	—	—
1995–96		—	—

COX, Ian

Born Croydon 25.3.71 Ht 6 0 Wt 12 00
Midfield. From Carshalton Ath.

Season	Club	Apps	Goals
1993–94	Crystal Palace	—	—
1994–95		11	—
1995–96		4	—
1995–96	Bournemouth	8	—

COX, Neil

Born Scunthorpe 8.10.71 Ht 6 0 Wt 13 02
Defender. From Trainee. England Under-21.

Season	Club	Apps	Goals
1989–90	Scunthorpe U	—	—
1990–91		17	1
1990–91	Aston Villa	—	—
1991–92		7	—
1992–93		15	1
1993–94		20	2
1994–95	Middlesbrough	40	1
1995–96		35	2

COYLE, Owen

Born Paisley 14.7.66 Ht 5 9 Wt 9 12
Forward. From Renfrew YM. Eire Under-21, B, 1 full cap.

Season	Club	Apps	Goals
1984–85	Dumbarton	—	—
1985–86		16	5
1986–87		43	17
1987–88		41	14
1988–89		3	—
1988–89	Clydebank	36	16
1989–90		27	17
1989–90	Airdrieonians	10	10
1990–91		28	20
1991–92		43	11
1992–93		42	9
1993–94	Bolton W	30	7
1994–95		19	5
1995–96		5	—
1995–96	Dundee U	28	5

COYLE, Ronald

Born Glasgow 4.8.64 Ht 5 11 Wt 12 09
Midfield. From Celtic BC.

Season	Club	Apps	Goals
1983–84	Celtic	—	—
1984–85		1	—
1985–86		1	—
1986–87	Middlesbrough	3	—
1987–88	Rochdale	24	1
1987–88	Raith R	16	3
1988–89		36	1
1989–90		28	2
1990–91		35	1
1991–92		29	—
1992–93		35	1
1993–94		41	1
1994–95		9	—
1995–96		24	—

COYNE, Christopher

Born Brisbane 20.12.78 Ht 6 1 Wt 13 10
Defender. From Perth SC.

Season	Club	Apps	Goals
1995–96	West Ham U	—	—

COYNE, Danny

Born Prestatyn 27.8.73 Ht 5 11 Wt 13 00
Goalkeeper. From Trainee. Wales Under-21, 1 full cap.

Season	Club	Apps	Goals
1991–92	Tranmere R	—	—
1992–93		1	—
1993–94		5	—
1994–95		5	—
1995–96		46	—

COYNE, Tommy

Born Glasgow 14.11.62 Ht 5 11 Wt 12 00
Forward. From Hillwood BC. Eire B, 21 full caps.

Season	Club	Apps	Goals
1981–82	Clydebank	31	9
1982–83		38	18
1983–84		11	10
1983–84	Dundee U	18	3
1984–85		21	3
1985–86		13	2
1986–87	Dundee	20	9
1987–88		43	33
1988–89		26	9
1988–89	Celtic	7	—
1989–90		23	7
1990–91		26	18

Season	Club	League Appearances/Goals	
1991–92		39	15
1992–93		10	3
1992–93	Tranmere R	12	1
1993–94	Motherwell	26	12
1994–95		31	16
1995–96		14	4

CRABBE, Scott

Born Edinburgh 12.8.68 Ht 5 7 Wt 10 00
Midfield. From Tynecastle BC. Scotland Under-21.

Season	Club	Apps	Goals
1986–87	Hearts	5	—
1987–88		5	—
1988–89		1	—
1989–90		35	12
1990–91		21	3
1991–92		41	15
1992–93		8	1
1992–93	Dundee U	27	4
1993–94		21	2
1994–95		9	—
1995–96		2	—

CRADDOCK, Jody

Born Redditch 25.7.75 Ht 6 2 Wt 11 13
Defender. From Christchurch.

Season	Club	Apps	Goals
1993–94	Cambridge U	20	—
1994–95		38	—
1995–96		46	3

CRAGGS, Graham

Born Ashington 5.6.76 Ht 6 1 Wt 13 06
Defender. From Trainee.

Season	Club	Apps	Goals
1994–95	Blackpool	—	—
1995–96		—	—

CRAIG, Albert

Born Glasgow 3.1.62 Ht 5 8 Wt 11 03
Midfield. From Yoker Ath.

Season	Club	Apps	Goals
1981–82	Dumbarton	13	2
1982–83		32	7
1983–84		26	4
1984–85		35	4
1985–86		32	6
1986–87	Hamilton A	16	5
1986–87	Newcastle U	6	—
1987–88		3	—
1987–88	*Hamilton A*	6	1
1988–89	Newcastle U	1	—
1988–89	Northampton T	2	1
1988–89	Dundee	6	2
1989–90		20	2
1990–91		12	3
1991–92		25	7
1992–93	Partick T	29	1
1993–94		38	14
1994–95		30	2
1995–96		9	2
1995–96	Falkirk	14	3

CRAIG, Michael

Born Dundee 23.6.77 Ht 5 8 Wt 10 09
Midfield. From Banks o' Dee.

Season	Club	Apps	Goals
1994–95	Aberdeen	—	—
1995–96		1	—

CRAMB, Colin

Born Lanark 23.6.74 Ht 6 0 Wt 13 00
Forward. From Hamilton A BC.

Season	Club	Apps	Goals
1990–91	Hamilton A	3	2
1991–92		12	1
1992–93		33	7
1993–94	Southampton	1	—
1994–95	Falkirk	8	1
1994–95	Hearts	6	1
1995–96	Doncaster R	21	7

CRANSON, Ian

Born Easington 2.7.64 Ht 6 0 Wt 13 05
Defender. From Apprentice. England Under-21.

Season	Club	Apps	Goals
1982–83	Ipswich T	—	—
1983–84		8	—
1984–85		20	1
1985–86		42	1
1986–87		32	2
1987–88		29	1
1987–88	Sheffield W	4	—
1988–89		26	—
1989–90	Stoke C	17	2
1990–91		9	—
1991–92		41	2
1992–93		45	3
1993–94		44	—
1994–95		37	1
1995–96		24	1

Season Club League Appearances/Goals

Season Club League Appearances/Goals

CRAWFORD, Jimmy

Born USA 1.5.73 Ht 5 11 Wt 11 06
Midfield. From Bohemians.

Season	Club	Apps	Goals
1994–95	Newcastle U	—	—
1995–96		—	—

CRAWFORD, Keith

Born Dublin 31.10.78
Forward. From Belvedere, Trainee.

Season	Club	Apps	Goals
1995–96	Tranmere R	—	—

CRAWFORD, Stephen

Born Dunfermline 9.1.74 Ht 5 10
Wt 10 07
Midfield. From Rosyth Recreation.
Scotland Under-21, 1 full cap.

Season	Club	Apps	Goals
1992–93	Raith R	20	3
1993–94		36	5
1994–95		31	11
1995–96		28	3

CREANEY, Gerry

Born Coatbridge 13.4.70 Ht 5 11
Wt 13 06
Forward. From Celtic BC. Scotland Under-21.

Season	Club	Apps	Goals
1987–88	Celtic	—	—
1988–89		—	—
1989–90		6	1
1990–91		31	7
1991–92		32	14
1992–93		26	9
1993–94		18	5
1993–94	Portsmouth	18	11
1994–95		39	18
1995–96		3	3
1995–96	Manchester C	15	3
1995–96	*Oldham Ath*	9	2

CRESSWELL, Richard

Born Bridlington 20.9.77
Forward. From Trainee.

Season	Club	Apps	Goals
1995–96	York C	16	1

CRICHTON, Paul

Born Pontefract 3.10.68 Ht 6 0 Wt 12 05
Goalkeeper. From Apprentice.

Season	Club	Apps	Goals
1986–87	Nottingham F	—	—
1986–87	*Notts Co*	5	—
1986–87	*Darlington*	5	—
1986–87	*Peterborough U*	4	—
1987–88	Nottingham F	—	—
1987–88	*Darlington*	3	—
1987–88	*Swindon T*	4	—
1987–88	*Rotherham U*	6	—
1988–89	Nottingham F	—	—
1988–89	*Torquay U*	13	—
1988–89	Peterborough U	31	—
1989–90		16	—
1990–91	Doncaster R	20	—
1991–92		16	—
1992–93		41	—
1993–94	Grimsby T	46	—
1994–95		43	—
1995–96		44	—

CROFT, Brian

Born Chester 27.9.67 Ht 5 9 Wt 10 10
Midfield. From Trainee.

Season	Club	Apps	Goals
1984–85	Chester C	—	—
1985–86		1	—
1986–87		21	1
1987–88		37	2
1988–89	Cambridge U	17	2
1989–90	Chester C	44	3
1990–91		38	—
1991–92		32	—
1992–93	QPR	—	—
1993–94		—	—
1993–94	*Shrewsbury T*	4	—
1994–95	QPR	—	—
1995–96	Torquay U	1	—
1995–96	Stockport Co	3	—

CROFT, Gary

Born Stafford 17.2.74 Ht 5 9 Wt 11 08
Defender. From Trainee. England Under-21.

Season	Club	Apps	Goals
1990–91	Grimsby T	1	—
1991–92		—	—
1992–93		32	—
1993–94		36	1
1994–95		44	1
1995–96		36	1
1995–96	Blackburn R	—	—

CROOK, Ian

Born Romford 18.1.63 Ht 5 8 Wt 10 07
Midfield. From Apprentice. England B.

Season	Club	Apps	Goals
1980–81	Tottenham H	—	—

Season Club League Appearances/Goals

Season	Club	Apps	Goals
1981–82		4	—
1982–83		4	—
1983–84		3	—
1984–85		5	1
1985–86		4	—
1986–87	Norwich C	33	5
1987–88		23	1
1988–89		26	1
1989–90		35	—
1990–91		32	3
1991–92		21	1
1992–93		34	3
1993–94		38	—
1994–95		34	—
1995–96		28	2

CROOKS, Lee

Born Wakefield 14.1.78 Ht 5 11
Wt 12 01
Midfield. From Trainee. England Youth.

Season	Club	Apps	Goals
1994–95	Manchester C	—	—
1995–96		—	—

CROSBY, Andy

Born Rotherham 3.3.73 Ht 6 2 Wt 13 07
Defender. From Leeds U Trainee.

Season	Club	Apps	Goals
1991–92	Doncaster R	22	—
1992–93		29	—
1993–94		—	—
1993–94	Darlington	25	—
1994–95		35	—
1995–96		45	1

CROSBY, Gary

Born Sleaford 8.5.64 Ht 5 8 Wt 9 00
Forward. From Lincoln U.

Season	Club	Apps	Goals
1986–87	Lincoln C	7	—
From Grantham			
1987–88	Nottingham F	14	1
1988–89		13	—
1989–90		34	5
1990–91		29	2
1991–92		33	3
1992–93		23	1
1993–94		6	—
1993–94	*Grimsby T*	3	—
1994–95	Huddersfield T	19	4
1995–96		1	—

CROSS, John

Born Barking 6.4.76 Ht 5 9 Wt 12 03
Midfield. From Trainee.

Season	Club	Apps	Goals
1994–95	QPR	—	—
1995–96		—	—

CROSS, Jonathan

Born Wallasey 2.3.75 Ht 5 10 Wt 11 07
Midfield. From Trainee.

Season	Club	Apps	Goals
1991–92	Wrexham	6	—
1992–93		37	7
1993–94		25	2
1994–95		24	1
1995–96		7	—

CROSS, Nicky

Born Birmingham 7.2.61 Ht 5 10
Wt 12 09
Forward. From Apprentice.

Season	Club	Apps	Goals
1978–79	WBA	—	—
1979–80		—	—
1980–81		2	1
1981–82		22	2
1982–83		32	4
1983–84		25	3
1984–85		24	5
1985–86	Walsall	44	21
1986–87		39	16
1987–88		26	8
1987–88	Leicester C	17	6
1988–89		41	9
1989–90	Port Vale	42	13
1990–91		19	2
1991–92		8	—
1992–93		38	12
1993–94		37	12
1994–95	Hereford U	28	6
1995–96		37	8

CROSS, Ryan

Born Plymouth 11.10.72 Ht 6 0
Wt 13 08
Defender. From Trainee.

Season	Club	Apps	Goals
1990–91	Plymouth Arg	7	—
1991–92		12	—
1992–93	Hartlepool U	33	2
1993–94		17	—
1993–94	Bury	17	—
1994–95		12	—
1995–96		13	—

 Season Club League Appearances/Goals

CROSSLEY, Mark

Born Barnsley 16.6.69 Ht 6 0 Wt 16 00
Goalkeeper. From Trainee. England Under-21.

Season	Club	Apps	Goals
1987–88	Nottingham F	—	—
1988–89		2	—
1989–90		8	—
1989–90	*Manchester U*	—	—
1990–91	Nottingham F	38	—
1991–92		36	—
1992–93		37	—
1993–94		37	—
1994–95		42	—
1995–96		38	—

CROSSLEY, Matt

Born Basingstoke 18.3.68 Ht 6 1 Wt 13 12
Defender. From Overton U.

Season	Club	Apps	Goals
1993–94	Wycombe W	39	2
1994–95		36	—
1995–96		12	1

CROWE, Glen

Born Kent 30.9.78 Ht 5 10 Wt 13 01
Forward. From Trainee.

Season	Club	Apps	Goals
1995–96	Wolverhampton W	2	1

CROWE, Jason

Born Sidcup 30.9.78
Midfield. From Trainee. England Youth.

Season	Club	Apps	Goals
1995–96	Arsenal	—	—

CULKIN, Nick

Born York 6.7.78 Ht 6 2 Wt 12 13
Goalkeeper. From York C.

Season	Club	Apps	Goals
1995–96	Manchester U	—	—

CULLIP, Danny

Born Bracknell 17.9.76 Ht 6 1 Wt 12 07
Midfield. From Trainee.

Season	Club	Apps	Goals
1995–96	Oxford U	—	—

CULSHAW, Thomas

Born Liverpool 10.10.78 Ht 5 10 Wt 12 02
Midfield. From Trainee.

Season	Club	Apps	Goals
1995–96	Liverpool	—	—

CULVERHOUSE, Ian

Born Bishop's Stortford 22.9.64 Ht 5 10 Wt 11 02
Defender. From Apprentice. England Youth.

Season	Club	Apps	Goals
1982–83	Tottenham H	—	—
1983–84		2	—
1984–85		—	—
1985–86		—	—
1985–86	Norwich C	30	—
1986–87		25	—
1987–88		33	—
1988–89		38	—
1989–90		32	—
1990–91		34	—
1991–92		21	—
1992–93		41	—
1993–94		42	—
1994–95		—	1
1994–95	Swindon T	9	—
1995–96		46	—

CUMMINS, Michael

Born Dublin 1.6.78
Midfield. From Trainee.

Season	Club	Apps	Goals
1995–96	Middlesbrough	—	—

CUNDY, Jason

Born Wimbledon 12.11.69 Ht 6 1 Wt 13 13
Defender. From Trainee. England Under-21.

Season	Club	Apps	Goals
1988–89	Chelsea	—	—
1989–90		—	—
1990–91		29	—
1991–92		12	1
1991–92	*Tottenham H*	10	—
1992–93	Tottenham H	15	1
1993–94		—	—
1994–95		—	—
1995–96		1	—
1995–96	*Crystal Palace*	4	—

CUNNINGHAM, Carl

Born Derby 19.4.77 Ht 5 5 Wt 11 11
Midfield. From Trainee.

Season	Club	Apps	Goals
1995–96	Derby Co	—	—

CUNNINGHAM, Dean

Born Stoke 28.5.77 Ht 5 5 Wt 9 0
Forward. From Trainee.

Season	Club	Apps	Goals
1995–96	Port Vale	—	—

CUNNINGHAM, Kenny

Born Dublin 28.6.71 Ht 5 11 Wt 11 02
Defender. From Tolka R. Eire Under-21, B, 6 full caps.

Season	Club	Apps	Goals
1989–90	Millwall	5	—
1990–91		23	—
1991–92		17	—
1992–93		37	—
1993–94		39	1
1994–95		15	—
1994–95	Wimbledon	28	—
1995–96		33	—

CUNNINGTON, Shaun

Born Bourne 4.1.66 Ht 5 9 Wt 11 04
Midfield. From Bourne T.

Season	Club	Apps	Goals
1982–83	Wrexham	4	—
1983–84		42	—
1984–85		41	6
1985–86		42	2
1986–87		46	1
1987–88		24	3
1987–88	Grimsby T	15	2
1988–89		44	1
1989–90		44	3
1990–91		46	2
1991–92		33	5
1992–93	Sunderland	39	7
1993–94		11	1
1994–95		8	—
1995–96	WBA	9	—

CURBISHLEY, Alan

Born Forest Gate 8.11.57 Ht 5 10
Wt 11 07
Midfield. From Apprentice. England Schools, Youth, Under-21.

Season	Club	Apps	Goals
1974–75	West Ham U	2	—
1975–76		14	2
1976–77		10	1
1977–78		32	1
1978–79		27	1
1979–80	Birmingham C	42	3
1980–81		29	6
1981–82		29	1
1982–83		30	1
1982–83	Aston Villa	7	—
1983–84		26	1
1984–85		3	—
1984–85	Charlton Ath	23	2
1985–86		30	4
1986–87		10	—
1987–88	Brighton & HA	34	6
1988–89		37	6
1989–90		45	1
1990–91	Charlton Ath	25	—
1991–92		1	—
1992–93		1	—
1993–94		1	—
1994–95		—	—
1995–96		—	—

CURCIC, Sasa

Born Belgrade 14.2.72 Ht 5 9 Wt 10 07
Midfield. From Partizan Belgrade. Yugoslavia 5 full caps.

Season	Club	Apps	Goals
1995–96	Bolton W	28	4

CURETON, Jamie

Born Bristol 28.8.75 Ht 5 8 Wt 10 07
Forward. From Trainee. England Youth.

Season	Club	Apps	Goals
1992–93	Norwich C	—	—
1993–94		—	—
1994–95		17	4
1995–96		12	2
1995–96	*Bournemouth*	5	—

CURLE, Keith

Born Bristol 14.11.63 Ht 6 0 Wt 12 12
Defender. From Apprentice. England B, 3 full caps.

Season	Club	Apps	Goals
1981–82	Bristol R	20	2
1982–83		12	2
1983–84		—	—
1983–84	Torquay U	16	5
1983–84	Bristol C	6	—
1984–85		40	—
1985–86		44	1
1986–87		28	—
1987–88		3	—
1987–88	Reading	30	—
1988–89		10	—
1988–89	Wimbledon	18	—

Season Club League Appearances/Goals

Season	Club	Apps	Goals
1989–90		38	2
1990–91		37	1
1991–92	Manchester C	40	5
1992–93		39	3
1993–94		29	1
1994–95		31	2
1995–96		32	—

CURRAN, Chris

Born Birmingham 17.9.71 Ht 5 11
Wt 12 04
Defender. From Trainee.

Season	Club	Apps	Goals
1989–90	Torquay U	1	—
1990–91		13	—
1991–92		17	—
1992–93		34	—
1993–94		41	1
1994–95		27	2
1995–96		19	1
1995–96	Plymouth Arg	8	—

CURRAN, Henry

Born Glasgow 9.10.66 Ht 5 8
Wt 11 08
Midfield. From Eastercraigs.

Season	Club	Apps	Goals
1984–85	Dumbarton	—	—
1985–86		6	—
1986–87		8	—
1987–88	Dundee U	5	—
1988–89		6	—
1989–90	St Johnstone	31	3
1990–91		35	9
1991–92		39	8
1992–93		34	8
1993–94		39	3
1994–95		26	4
1995–96	Partick T	8	—

CURRIE, Darren

Born Hampstead 29.11.74 Ht 5 7
Wt 11 10
Midfield. From Trainee.

Season	Club	Apps	Goals
1993–94	West Ham U	—	—
1994–95		—	—
1994–95	*Shrewsbury T*	17	2
1995–96	West Ham U	—	—
1995–96	*Leyton Orient*	10	—
1995–96	Shrewsbury T	13	2

CURRIE, David

Born Stockton 27.11.62 Ht 5 11
Wt 12 13
Forward. From Local.

Season	Club	Apps	Goals
1981–82	Middlesbrough	1	—
1982–83		8	—
1983–84		39	15
1984–85		39	12
1985–86		26	4
1986–87	Darlington	45	12
1987–88		31	21
1987–88	Barnsley	15	7
1988–89		41	16
1989–90		24	7
1989–90	Nottingham F	8	1
1990–91	Oldham Ath	27	2
1991–92		4	1
1991–92	Barnsley	37	7
1992–93		35	4
1992–93	*Rotherham U*	5	2
1993–94	Barnsley	3	1
1993–94	*Huddersfield T*	7	1
1994–95	Carlisle U	38	4
1995–96		42	9

CURTIS, Andy

Born Doncaster 2.12.72 Ht 5 8 Wt 12 00
Forward. From Trainee.

Season	Club	Apps	Goals
1990–91	York C	5	—
1991–92		7	—
1992–93	Peterborough U	11	1
1993–94		—	—
1994–95		—	—
1995–96	York C	1	—
1995–96	Scarborough	5	—

CURTIS, John

Born Nuneaton 3.9.78 Ht 5 9 Wt 11 03
Defender. From Trainee. England Youth.

Season	Club	Apps	Goals
1995–96	Manchester U	—	—

CURTIS, Tom

Born Exeter 1.3.73 Ht 5 8 Wt 11 07
Midfield. From School.

Season	Club	Apps	Goals
1991–92	Derby Co	—	—
1992–93		—	—
1993–94	Chesterfield	36	3
1994–95		40	2
1995–96		46	—

Season	Club	League Appearances/Goals	

CUSACK, Nick

Born Rotherham 24.12.65 Ht 6 0 Wt 12 08
Forward. From Alvechurch.

1987–88	Leicester C	16	1
1988–89	Peterborough U	44	10
1989–90	Motherwell	31	11
1990–91		29	4
1991–92		17	2
1991–92	Darlington	21	6
1992–93	Oxford U	39	4
1993–94		20	6
1993–94	*Wycombe W*	4	—
1994–95	Oxford U	2	—
1994–95	Fulham	27	7
1995–96		42	5

CUTLER, Jason

Born Cleveland 8.9.76 Ht 5 7 Wt 9 06
Defender. From Trainee.

1995–96	York C	—	—

CUTLER, Neil

Born Birmingham 3.9.76 Ht 6 1 Wt 12 00
Goalkeeper. From Trainee. England Youth.

1993–94	WBA	—	—
1994–95		—	—
1995–96		—	—
1995–96	*Coventry C*	—	—
1995–96	*Chester C*	1	—

CYRUS, Andrew

Born Lambeth 30.9.76 Ht 5 8 Wt 10 07
Defender. From Trainee.

1995–96	Crystal Palace	—	—

D'ARCY, Ross

Born Balbriggan 21.3.78 Ht 6 0 Wt 12 00
Defender. From Trainee.

1995–96	Tottenham H	—	—

D'AURIA, David

Born Swansea 26.3.70 Ht 5 8 Wt 11 11
Midfield. From Trainee.

1987–88	Swansea C	4	—
1988–89		14	2
1989–90		7	—
1990–91		20	4
From Barry T			
1994–95	Scarborough	34	7
1995–96		18	1
1995–96	Scunthorpe U	27	5

DAILLY, Christian

Born Dundee 23.10.73 Ht 5 10 Wt 10 11
Forward. From 'S' Form. Scotland B, Under-21.

1990–91	Dundee U	18	5
1991–92		8	—
1992–93		14	4
1993–94		38	4
1994–95		33	4
1995–96		30	1

DAIR, Jason

Born Dunfermline 15.6.74 Ht 5 11 Wt 10 08
Forward. From Castlebridge. Scotland Under-21.

1991–92	Raith R	4	—
1992–93		15	1
1993–94		38	6
1994–95		18	1
1995–96		19	3

DAISH, Liam

Born Portsmouth 23.9.68 Ht 6 2 Wt 13 05
Defender. From Apprentice. Eire Under-21, B, 5 full caps.

1986–87	Portsmouth	1	—
1987–88		—	—
1988–89	Cambridge U	28	—
1989–90		42	1
1990–91		13	1

Season Club League Appearances/Goals

Season	Club	Apps	Goals
1991–92		22	—
1992–93		16	—
1993–94		18	2
1993–94	Birmingham C	19	—
1994–95		37	3
1995–96		17	—
1995–96	Coventry C	11	1

DAKIN, Simon

Born Nottingham 30.11.74 Ht 5 9
Wt 11 02
Defender. From Derby Co.

Season	Club	Apps	Goals
1993–94	Hull C	9	—
1994–95		21	1
1995–96		6	—

DALE, Carl

Born Colwyn Bay 29.4.66 Ht 5 8
Wt 10 07
Forward. From Bangor C.

Season	Club	Apps	Goals
1987–88	Chester C	—	—
1988–89		41	22
1989–90		31	9
1990–91		44	10
1991–92	Cardiff C	41	22
1992–93		20	8
1993–94		15	3
1994–95		35	5
1995–96		44	21

DALE, Geoff

Born Manchester 27.9.76 Ht 5 8
Wt 11 06
Defender. From Trainee.

Season	Club	Apps	Goals
1995–96	Bury	—	—

DALEY, Phil

Born Walton 12.4.67 Ht 6 2 Wt 12 09
Forward. From Newtown.

Season	Club	Apps	Goals
1989–90	Wigan Ath	33	6
1990–91		41	10
1991–92		38	14
1992–93		31	6
1993–94		18	3
1994–95	Lincoln C	20	4
1995–96		12	1

DALEY, Tony

Born Birmingham 18.10.67 Ht 5 8
Wt 10 08
Forward. From Apprentice. England Youth, 7 full caps.

Season	Club	Apps	Goals
1984–85	Aston Villa	5	—
1985–86		23	2
1986–87		33	3
1987–88		14	3
1988–89		29	5
1989–90		32	6
1990–91		23	2
1991–92		34	7
1992–93		13	2
1993–94		27	1
1994–95	Wolverhampton W	1	—
1995–96		18	3

DALLI, Jean

Born Enfield 13.8.76
Defender.

Season	Club	Apps	Goals
1994–95	Colchester U	1	—
1995–96		—	—

DALTON, Paul

Born Middlesbrough 25.4.67 Ht 5 11
Wt 12 06
Midfield. From Brandon.

Season	Club	Apps	Goals
1987–88	Manchester U	—	—
1988–89		—	—
1988–89	Hartlepool U	17	2
1989–90		45	11
1990–91		46	11
1991–92		43	13
1992–93	Plymouth Arg	32	9
1993–94		40	12
1994–95		26	4
1995–96	Huddersfield T	29	5

DALY, Matthew

Born Derby 8.10.76 Ht 6 3 Wt 13 07
Forward.

Season	Club	Apps	Goals
1995–96	Sheffield W	—	—

DANI

Born Lisbon 2.11.76
Midfield. From Sporting Lisbon. Portugal full caps.

Season	Club	Apps	Goals
1995–96	West Ham U	9	2

Season	Club	League Appearances/Goals	

DANIEL, Ray

Born Luton 10.12.64 Ht 5 8 Wt 12 05
Defender. From Apprentice.

1982–83	Luton T	3	—
1983–84		7	2
1983–84	*Gillingham*	5	—
1984–85	Luton T	7	1
1985–86		5	1
1986–87	Hull C	9	—
1987–88		26	2
1988–89		23	1
1989–90	Cardiff C	43	1
1990–91		13	—
1990–91	Portsmouth	14	—
1991–92		8	—
1992–93		40	4
1993–94		16	—
1994–95		22	—
1994–95	*Notts Co*	5	—
1995–96	Walsall	25	—

DARBY, Duane

Born Birmingham 17.10.73 Ht 5 11
Wt 11 02
Forward. From Trainee.

1991–92	Torquay U	14	2
1992–93		34	12
1993–94		36	8
1994–95		24	4
1995–96	Doncaster R	17	4
1995–96	Hull C	8	1

DARBY, Julian

Born Bolton 3.10.67 Ht 6 0 Wt 11 04
Midfield. From Trainee. England Schools.

1984–85	Bolton W	—	—
1985–86		2	—
1986–87		28	—
1987–88		35	2
1988–89		44	5
1989–90		46	10
1990–91		45	9
1991–92		44	6
1992–93		21	4
1993–94		5	—
1993–94	Coventry C	26	5
1994–95		29	—
1995–96		—	—
1995–96	WBA	22	1

Season	Club	League Appearances/Goals	

DARGO, Craig

Born Edinburgh 3.1.78 Ht 5 6 Wt 10 01
Midfield. From Links Utd.

1995–96	Raith R	1	—

DARNBROUGH, Lee

Born Ashton 15.9.77
Goalkeeper. From Trainee. England Youth.

1994–95	Oldham Ath	—	—
1995–96		—	—

DARTON, Scott

Born Ipswich 27.3.75 Ht 5 11 Wt 11 02
Defender. From Trainee.

1992–93	WBA	2	—
1993–94		6	—
1994–95		7	—
1994–95	Blackpool	18	—
1995–96		9	—

DAVENPORT, Peter

Born Birkenhead 24.3.61 Ht 5 10
Wt 11 06
Forward. From Everton, Cammell Laird. England B, 1 full cap.

1981–82	Nottingham F	5	4
1982–83		18	6
1983–84		33	15
1984–85		35	16
1985–86		27	13
1985–86	Manchester U	11	1
1986–87		39	14
1987–88		34	5
1988–89		8	2
1988–89	Middlesbrough	24	4
1989–90		35	3
1990–91	Sunderland	29	7
1991–92		36	4
1992–93		34	4
1993–94	Airdrie	38	9
1994–95	St Johnstone	22	4
1994–95	Stockport Co	6	1
1995–96		—	—

DAVEY, Simon

Born Swansea 1.10.70 Ht 5 9 Wt 11 08
Midfield. From Trainee.

1986–87	Swansea C	1	—
1987–88		4	—

Season	Club	League Appearances/Goals	
1988–89		3	—
1989–90		18	2
1990–91		18	2
1991–92		5	—
1992–93	Carlisle U	38	5
1993–94		42	9
1994–95		25	4
1994–95	Preston NE	13	3
1995–96		38	10

DAVIDSON, Ross

Born Chertsey 13.11.73 Ht 5 8 Wt 11 06
Defender. From Walton & Hersham.

Season	Club	Apps	Goals
1993–94	Sheffield U	—	—
1994–95		1	—
1995–96		1	—
1995–96	Chester C	19	1

DAVIES, Billy

Born Glasgow 31.5.64 Ht 5 6 Wt 10 09
Midfield. From School.

Season	Club	Apps	Goals
1980–81	Rangers	—	—
1981–82		4	—
1982–83		4	—
1983–84		3	1
1984–85		—	—
1985–86		—	—
From IF Elfsborg			
1987–88	St Mirren	18	—
1988–89		27	4
1989–90		29	1
1990–91	Lincoln C	6	—
1990–91	Dunfermline Ath	26	—
1991–92		33	—
1992–93		41	10
1993–94		4	—
1993–94	Motherwell	10	—
1994–95		31	4
1995–96		33	2

DAVIES, Darren

Born Port Talbot 13.8.78
Defender. From Trainee.

Season	Club	Apps	Goals
1995–96	Tottenham H	—	—

DAVIES, Gareth

Born Hereford 11.12.73 Ht 6 1 Wt 11 12
Defender. From Trainee. Wales Under-21.

Season	Club	Apps	Goals
1991–92	Hereford U	4	—
1992–93		32	1
1993–94		31	—
1994–95		28	—
1995–96	Crystal Palace	20	2

DAVIES, Glen

Born Brighton 20.2.76 Ht 6 1 Wt 12 10
Defender. From Trainee.

Season	Club	Apps	Goals
1994–95	Burnley	—	—
1995–96		—	—

DAVIES, Kevin

Born Sheffield 26.3.77 Ht 6 0 Wt 13 05
Forward. From Trainee. England Youth.

Season	Club	Apps	Goals
1993–94	Chesterfield	24	4
1994–95		41	11
1995–96		30	4

DAVIES, Martin

Born Swansea 28.6.74 Ht 6 2 Wt 13 04
Goalkeeper. From Trainee.

Season	Club	Apps	Goals
1993–94	Coventry C	—	—
1993–94		—	—
1994–95		—	—
1995–96	Cambridge U	15	—

DAVIES, Neil

Born Liverpool 9.11.76 Ht 6 2 Wt 14 02
Forward. From Fleetwood T.

Season	Club	Apps	Goals
1995–96	Lincoln C	—	—

DAVIES, Phil

Born Bangor 5.8.76 Ht 5 11 Wt 12 00
Midfield. From Trainee.

Season	Club	Apps	Goals
1995–96	Tranmere R	—	—

DAVIES, Simon

Born Middlewich 23.4.74 Ht 6 0
Wt 11 11
Midfield. From Trainee. Wales 1 full cap.

Season	Club	Apps	Goals
1992–93	Manchester U	—	—
1993–94		—	—
1993–94	*Exeter C*	6	1
1994–95	Manchester U	5	—
1995–96		6	—

DAVIES, Will

Born Derby 27.9.75 Ht 6 2 Wt 13 01
Forward. From Trainee.

Season	Club	Apps	Goals
1994–95	Derby Co	2	—
1995–96		—	—

DAVIS, Chris

Born Cardiff 17.10.76
Defender. From Trainee.

Season	Club	Apps	Goals
1995–96	Cardiff C	—	—

DAVIS, Darren

Born Sutton-in-Ashfield 5.2.67 Ht 6 0 Wt 11 00
Defender. From Apprentice. England Youth.

Season	Club	Apps	Goals
1983–84	Notts Co	1	—
1984–85		4	—
1985–86		22	1
1986–87		45	—
1987–88		20	—
1988–89	Lincoln C	38	2
1989–90		34	—
1990–91		30	2
1990–91	Maidstone U	11	—
1991–92		20	2
From Frickley Ath			
1993–94	Scarborough	25	1
1994–95		23	2
1995–96	Lincoln C	3	—

DAVIS, Kelvin

Born Bedford 29.9.76 Ht 6 0 Wt 14 00
Goalkeeper. From Trainee. England Youth, Under-21.

Season	Club	Apps	Goals
1993–94	Luton T	1	—
1994–95		9	—
1994–95	*Torquay U*	2	—
1995–96	Luton T	6	—

DAVIS, Mike

Born Bristol 19.10.74 Ht 6 0 Wt 12 00
Forward. From Yate T.

Season	Club	Apps	Goals
1992–93	Bristol R	1	1
1993–94		10	—
1994–95		2	—
1994–95	*Hereford U*	1	1
1995–96	Bristol R	4	—

DAVIS, Neil

Born Bloxwich 15.8.73 Ht 5 8 Wt 11 00
Forward. From Redditch U.

Season	Club	Apps	Goals
1991–92	Aston Villa	—	—
1992–93		—	—
1993–94		—	—
1994–95		—	—
1995–96		2	—

DAVIS, Paul

Born London 9.12.61 Ht 5 9 Wt 10 08
Midfield. From Apprentice. England Under-21, B.

Season	Club	Apps	Goals
1979–80	Arsenal	2	—
1980–81		10	1
1981–82		38	4
1982–83		41	4
1983–84		35	1
1984–85		24	1
1985–86		29	4
1986–87		39	4
1987–88		29	5
1988–89		12	1
1989–90		11	1
1990–91		37	3
1991–92		12	—
1992–93		6	—
1993–94		22	—
1994–95		4	1
1995–96	Brentford	5	—

DAVIS, Steve

Born Birmingham 26.7.65 Ht 5 11 Wt 12 12
Defender. From Stoke C Apprentice. England Youth.

Season	Club	Apps	Goals
1983–84	Crewe Alex	24	—
1984–85		40	—
1985–86		45	1
1986–87		33	—
1987–88		3	—
1987–88	Burnley	33	5
1988–89		37	—
1989–90		31	1
1990–91		46	5
1991–92	Barnsley	9	—
1992–93		11	—
1993–94		—	—
1994–95		36	2
1995–96		27	5

 Season Club League Appearances/Goals

DAVIS, Steve

Born Hexham 30.10.68 Ht 6 2 Wt 14 07
Defender. From Trainee.

Season	Club	Apps	Goals
1987–88	Southampton	—	—
1988–89		—	—
1989–90		4	—
1989–90	*Burnley*	9	—
1990–91	Southampton	3	—
1990–91	*Notts Co*	2	—
1991–92	Burnley	40	6
1992–93		37	2
1993–94		42	7
1994–95		43	7
1995–96	Luton T	36	2

DAVISON, Aidan

Born Sedgefield 11.5.68 Ht 6 1 Wt 13 12
Goalkeeper. From Billingham Synthonia. Northern Ireland 1 full cap.

Season	Club	Apps	Goals
1987–88	Notts Co	—	—
1988–89		1	—
1989–90		—	—
1989–90	*Leyton Orient*	—	—
1989–90	Bury	—	—
1989–90	*Chester C*	—	—
1990–91	Bury	—	—
1990–91	*Blackpool*	—	—
1991–92	Millwall	33	—
1992–93		1	—
1993–94	Bolton W	31	—
1994–95		4	—
1995–96		2	—

DAVISON, Bobby

Born South Shields 17.7.59 Ht 5 9
Wt 11 10
Forward. From Seaham CW.

Season	Club	Apps	Goals
1980–81	Huddersfield T	2	—
1981–82	Halifax T	46	20
1982–83		17	9
1982–83	Derby Co	26	8
1983–84		40	14
1984–85		46	24
1985–86		41	17
1986–87		40	19
1987–88		13	1
1987–88	Leeds U	16	5
1988–89		39	14
1989–90		29	11
1990–91		5	1
1991–92		2	—
1991–92	*Derby Co*	10	8
1991–92	*Sheffield U*	11	4
1992–93	Leicester C	25	6
1993–94		—	—
1993–94	Sheffield U	9	—
1994–95		3	1
1994–95	Rotherham U	21	4
1995–96		1	—
1995–96	*Hull C*	11	4

DAWE, Simon

Born Plymouth 16.3.77 Ht 5 10
Wt 11 06
Defender. From Trainee.

Season	Club	Apps	Goals
1994–95	Plymouth Arg	4	—
1995–96		—	—

DAWES, Ian

Born Croydon 22.2.63 Ht 5 7 Wt 11 10
Defender. From Apprentice. England Schools.

Season	Club	Apps	Goals
1980–81	QPR	—	—
1981–82		5	—
1982–83		42	—
1983–84		42	2
1984–85		42	—
1985–86		42	1
1986–87		23	—
1987–88		33	—
1988–89	Millwall	30	1
1989–90		38	4
1990–91		40	—
1991–92		36	—
1992–93		46	—
1993–94		21	—
1994–95		14	—
1995–96		—	—

DAWS, Nick

Born Manchester 15.3.70 Ht 5 11
Wt 13 03
Defender. From Altrincham.

Season	Club	Apps	Goals
1992–93	Bury	36	1
1993–94		37	1
1994–95		34	2
1995–96		37	1

DAWS, Tony

Born Sheffield 10.9.66 Ht 5 8 Wt 11 10
Forward. From Apprentice. England Youth.

Season	Club	Apps	Goals
1984–85	Notts Co	7	1
1985–86		1	—
1986–87	Sheffield U	11	3
1987–88	Scunthorpe U	10	3
1988–89		46	24
1989–90		33	11
1990–91		34	14
1991–92		36	7
1992–93		24	4
1992–93	Grimsby T	6	1
1993–94		10	—
1993–94	Lincoln C	14	3
1994–95		26	7
1995–96		11	3

DAWSON, Andrew

Born Northallerton 20.10.78 Ht 5 9
Wt 10 02
Midfield. From Trainee.

Season	Club	Apps	Goals
1995–96	Nottingham F	—	—

DAY, Chris

Born Whipps Cross 28.7.75 Ht 6 2
Wt 13 06
Goalkeeper. From Trainee. England Under-21.

Season	Club	Apps	Goals
1992–93	Tottenham H	—	—
1993–94		—	—
1994–95		—	—
1995–96		—	—

DAY, Mervyn

Born Chelmsford 26.6.55 Ht 6 2
Wt 14 13
Goalkeeper. From Apprentice. England Youth, Under-23.

Season	Club	Apps	Goals
1972–73	West Ham U	—	—
1973–74		33	—
1974–75		42	—
1975–76		41	—
1976–77		42	—
1977–78		23	—
1978–79		13	—
1979–80	Orient	42	—
1980–81		40	—
1981–82		42	—
1982–83		46	—
1983–84	Aston Villa	14	—
1984–85		16	—
1984–85	Leeds U	18	—
1985–86		40	—
1986–87		34	—
1987–88		44	—
1988–89		45	—
1989–90		44	—
1990–91		—	—
1990–91	*Coventry C*	—	—
1991–92	Leeds U	—	—
1991–92	*Luton T*	4	—
1991–92	*Sheffield U*	1	—
1992–93	Leeds U	2	—
1993–94	Carlisle U	16	—
1994–95		—	—
1995–96		—	—

DE FREITAS, Fabian

Born Paramaribo 28.7.72 Ht 6 1
Wt 12 09
Forward. From Volendam.

Season	Club	Apps	Goals
1994–95	Bolton W	13	2
1995–96		27	5

DE JONG, Davy

Born Rotterdam 26.4.75
Midfield. From Willem II.

Season	Club	Apps	Goals
1995–96	Wolverhampton W	—	—

DE SOUZA, Miguel

Born Newham 11.2.70 Ht 5 11 Wt 13 08
Forward. From Dagenham & Redbridge.

Season	Club	Apps	Goals
1993–94	Birmingham C	7	—
1994–95		8	—
1994–95	*Bury*	3	—
1994–95	Wycombe W	7	6
1995–96		43	18

DE WOLF, John

Born Schiedam 10.12.62 Ht 6 2
Wt 14 03
Defender. From Feyenoord. Holland 3 full caps.

Season	Club	Apps	Goals
1994–95	Wolverhampton W	13	4
1995–96		15	1

Season	Club	League Appearances/Goals	

DE ZEEUW, Arjan

Born Holland 16.4.70 Ht 6 2 Wt 12 12
Defender. From Telstar.

1995–96	Barnsley	31	1

DEAN, Michael

Born Weymouth 9.3.78
Defender. From Trainee.

1995–96	Bournemouth	5	—

DEANE, Brian

Born Leeds 7.2.68 Ht 6 3 Wt 12 07
Forward. From Apprentice. England B, 3 full caps.

1985–86	Doncaster R	3	—
1986–87		20	2
1987–88		43	10
1988–89	Sheffield U	43	22
1989–90		45	21
1990–91		38	13
1991–92		30	12
1992–93		41	14
1993–94	Leeds U	41	11
1994–95		35	9
1995–96		34	7

DEARDEN, Kevin

Born Luton 8.3.70 Ht 5 11 Wt 12 06
Goalkeeper. From Trainee.

1988–89	Tottenham H	—	—
1988–89	*Cambridge U*	15	—
1989–90	Tottenham H	—	—
1989–90	*Hartlepool U*	10	—
1989–90	*Oxford U*	—	—
1989–90	*Swindon T*	1	—
1990–91	Tottenham H	—	—
1990–91	*Peterborough U*	7	—
1990–91	*Hull C*	3	—
1991–92	Tottenham H	—	—
1991–92	*Rochdale*	2	—
1991–92	*Birmingham C*	12	—
1992–93	Tottenham H	1	—
1992–93	*Portsmouth*	—	—
1993–94	Tottenham H	—	—
1993–94	Brentford	35	—
1994–95		43	—
1995–96		41	—

Season	Club	League Appearances/Goals	

DEARY, John

Born Ormskirk 18.10.62 Ht 5 8
Wt 12 07
Midfield. From Apprentice.

1979–80	Blackpool	—	—
1980–81		10	—
1981–82		27	—
1982–83		45	6
1983–84		31	6
1984–85		32	13
1985–86		40	7
1986–87		44	3
1987–88		37	3
1988–89		37	5
1989–90	Burnley	41	2
1990–91		43	7
1991–92		40	6
1992–93		32	3
1993–94		43	4
1994–95		16	1
1994–95	Rochdale	17	1
1995–96		36	4

DEBONT, Andy

Born Wolverhampton 7.2.74 Ht 6 2
Wt 15 06
Goalkeeper. From Trainee.

1992–93	Wolverhampton W	—	—
1993–94		—	—
1994–95		—	—
1995–96		—	—
1995–96	*Hartlepool U*	1	—
1995–96	*Hereford U*	8	—

DEGRYSE, Marc

Born Belgium 4.9.65 Ht 5 8 Wt 10 13
Forward. From Ardooie. Belgium 59 full caps.

1983–84	FC Brugge	20	9
1984–85		34	18
1985–86		33	16
1986–87		33	16
1987–88		34	22
1988–89		28	12
1989–90	Anderlecht	31	18
1990–91		32	12
1991–92		28	4
1992–93		32	11
1993–94		19	9
1994–95		28	11
1995–96	Sheffield W	34	8

Season Club League Appearances/Goals

DELAP, Rory

Born Coldfield 6.7.76 Ht 6 0 Wt 12 03
Midfield. From Trainee.

Season	Club	Apps	Goals
1992–93	Carlisle U	1	—
1993–94		1	—
1994–95		3	—
1995–96		19	3

DEMPSEY, Mark

Born Dublin 10.12.72 Ht 5 6 Wt 12 05
Midfield. From Trainee. Eire Under-21.

Season	Club	Apps	Goals
1990–91	Gillingham	2	—
1991–92		30	2
1992–93		16	—
1993–94		—	—
1994–95	Leyton Orient	43	1
1995–96	Shrewsbury T	28	2

DEN BIEMAN, Ivo

Born Wamel 4.2.67 Ht 6 2 Wt 12 10
Midfield. From SV Leones.

Season	Club	Apps	Goals
1990–91	Montrose	36	5
1991–92		42	6
1992–93	Dundee	24	3
1993–94	Dunfermline Ath	41	3
1994–95		31	5
1995–96		26	1

DENHAM, Greig

Born Glasgow 5.10.76 Ht 6 0 Wt 12 02
Defender. From Cumbernauld Utd.

Season	Club	Apps	Goals
1994–95	Motherwell	—	—
1995–96		13	—

DENNIS, Shaun

Born Kirkcaldy 20.12.69 Ht 6 1
Wt 13 07
Defender. From Lochgelly Albert.
Scotland Under-21.

Season	Club	Apps	Goals
1988–89	Raith R	10	—
1989–90		18	—
1990–91		35	1
1991–92		42	—
1992–93		31	1
1993–94		43	3
1994–95		26	1
1995–96		25	—

DENNIS, Tony

Born Eton 1.12.63 Ht 5 7 Wt 10 02
Midfield. From Plymouth Arg, Bideford, Taunton, Slough.

Season	Club	Apps	Goals
1988–89	Cambridge U	18	3
1989–90		17	2
1990–91		20	2
1991–92		40	2
1992–93		16	1
1993–94	Chesterfield	10	—
1994–95	Colchester U	33	2
1995–96		32	3

DENNISON, Robbie

Born Banbridge 30.4.63 Ht 5 7 Wt 11 00
Forward. From Glenavon. Northern Ireland 17 full caps.

Season	Club	Apps	Goals
1985–86	WBA	12	1
1986–87		4	—
1986–87	Wolverhampton W	10	3
1987–88		43	3
1988–89		43	8
1989–90		46	8
1990–91		42	5
1991–92		22	1
1992–93		37	5
1993–94		14	2
1994–95		22	4
1995–96		—	—
1995–96	*Swansea C*	9	—

DERRY, Shaun

Born Nottingham 6.12.77 Ht 5 10
Wt 10 13
Defender. From Trainee.

Season	Club	Apps	Goals
1995–96	Notts Co	12	—

DEVINE, Sean

Born Lewisham 6.9.72 Ht 6 0 Wt 13 00
Forward. From Omonia.

Season	Club	Apps	Goals
1995–96	Barnet	35	19

DEVLIN, Mark

Born Irvine 18.1.73 Ht 5 10 Wt 11 05
Midfield. From Trainee.

Season	Club	Apps	Goals
1990–91	Stoke C	21	2
1991–92		—	—
1992–93		3	—

Season Club League Appearances/Goals

Season	Club	Apps	Goals
1993–94		—	—
1994–95		—	—
1995–96		10	—

DEVLIN, Paul

Born Birmingham 14.4.72 Ht 5 8
Wt 11 05
Forward. From Stafford R.

Season	Club	Apps	Goals
1991–92	Notts Co	2	—
1992–93		32	3
1993–94		41	7
1994–95		40	9
1995–96		26	6
1995–96	Birmingham C	16	7

DEWHURST, Rob

Born Keighley 10.9.71 Ht 6 3 Wt 12 02
Defender. From Trainee.

Season	Club	Apps	Goals
1990–91	Blackburn R	13	—
1991–92		—	—
1991–92	*Darlington*	11	1
1992–93	Blackburn R	—	—
1992–93	*Huddersfield T*	7	—
1993–94	Blackburn R	—	—
1993–94	Hull C	27	2
1994–95		41	8
1995–96		16	—

DIAZ, Isidro

Born Valencia 15.5.72 Ht 5 7 Wt 9 04
Midfield. From Balaguer.

Season	Club	Apps	Goals
1995–96	Wigan Ath	37	10

DIBBLE, Andy

Born Cwmbran 8.5.65 Ht 6 2 Wt 16 02
Goalkeeper. From Apprentice. Wales Schools, Youth, Under-21, 3 full caps.

Season	Club	Apps	Goals
1981–82	Cardiff C	1	—
1982–83		20	—
1983–84		41	—
1984–85	Luton T	13	—
1985–86		7	—
1985–86	*Sunderland*	12	—
1986–87	Luton T	1	—
1986–87	*Huddersfield T*	5	—
1987–88	Luton T	9	—
1988–89	Manchester C	38	—
1989–90		31	—
1990–91		3	—
1990–91	*Aberdeen*	5	—
1990–91	*Middlesbrough*	19	—
1991–92	Manchester C	2	—
1991–92	*Bolton W*	13	—
1991–92	*WBA*	9	—
1992–93	Manchester C	2	—
1992–93	*Oldham Ath*	—	—
1993–94	Manchester C	11	—
1994–95		15	—
1995–96		—	—

DICHIO, Daniele

Born Hammersmith 19.10.74 Ht 6 3
Wt 12 03
Forward. From Trainee. England Schools, Under-21.

Season	Club	Apps	Goals
1993–94	QPR	—	—
1993–94	*Barnet*	9	2
1994–95	QPR	9	3
1995–96		29	10

DICKINS, Matt

Born Sheffield 3.9.70 Ht 6 4 Wt 14 00
Goalkeeper. From Trainee.

Season	Club	Apps	Goals
1989–90	Sheffield U	—	—
1989–90	*Leyton Orient*	—	—
1990–91	Lincoln C	7	—
1991–92		20	—
1991–92	Blackburn R	1	—
1992–93		—	—
1992–93	*Blackpool*	19	—
1993–94	Blackburn R	—	—
1993–94	*Lincoln C*	—	—
1994–95	Blackburn R	—	—
1994–95	*Grimsby T*	—	—
1994–95	*Rochdale*	4	—
1994–95	Stockport Co	12	—
1995–96		1	—

DICKOV, Paul

Born Glasgow 1.11.72 Ht 5 5 Wt 11 09
Forward. From Trainee. Scotland Under-21.

Season	Club	Apps	Goals
1992–93	Arsenal	3	2
1993–94		1	—
1993–94	*Luton T*	15	1
1993–94	*Brighton & HA*	8	5
1994–95	Arsenal	9	—
1995–96		7	1

DICKS, Julian

Born Bristol 8.8.68 Ht 5 10 Wt 13 00
Defender. From Apprentice. England Under-21, B.

Season	Club	Apps	Goals
1985–86	Birmingham C	23	—
1986–87		34	—
1987–88		32	1
1987–88	West Ham U	8	—
1988–89		34	2
1989–90		40	9
1990–91		13	4
1991–92		23	3
1992–93		34	11
1993–94		7	—
1993–94	Liverpool	24	3
1994–95		—	—
1994–95	West Ham U	29	5
1995–96		34	10

DIGBY, Fraser

Born Sheffield 23.4.67 Ht 6 1 Wt 12 12
Goalkeeper. From Apprentice. England Youth, Under-21.

Season	Club	Apps	Goals
1984–85	Manchester U	—	—
1985–86		—	—
1985–86	*Oldham Ath*	—	—
1985–86	*Swindon T*	—	—
1986–87	Manchester U	—	—
1986–87	Swindon T	39	—
1987–88		31	—
1988–89		46	—
1989–90		45	—
1990–91		41	—
1991–92		21	—
1992–93		33	—
1992–93	*Manchester U*	—	—
1993–94	Swindon T	28	—
1994–95		39	—
1995–96		25	—

DINNIE, Alan

Born Glasgow 14.5.63 Ht 5 10 Wt 11 00
Defender. From Baillieston J.

Season	Club	Apps	Goals
1987–88	Partick T	37	1
1988–89		31	1
1989–90		14	2
1989–90	Dundee	22	—
1990–91		25	3
1991–92		29	—
1992–93		26	1
1993–94		7	—
1994–95		1	—
1994–95	Partick T	25	2
1995–96		31	—

DINNING, Tony

Born Wallsend 12.4.75 Ht 5 11 Wt 12 00
Defender. From Trainee.

Season	Club	Apps	Goals
1993–94	Newcastle U	—	—
1994–95	Stockport Co	40	1
1995–96		10	1

DIXON, Andy

Born Hartlepool 5.8.68 Ht 5 9 Wt 10 00
Forward. From Mons.

Season	Club	Apps	Goals
1995–96	Hartlepool U	3	—

DIXON, Ben

Born Lincoln 16.9.74 Ht 6 1 Wt 11 00
Forward. From Trainee.

Season	Club	Apps	Goals
1991–92	Lincoln C	3	—
1992–93		2	—
1993–94		8	—
1994–95		18	—
1995–96		12	—

DIXON, Ken

Born Knowsley 24.2.76 Ht 6 0 Wt 11 03
Goalkeeper. From Trainee.

Season	Club	Apps	Goals
1994–95	Wrexham	—	—
1995–96		—	—

DIXON, Kerry

Born Luton 24.7.61 Ht 6 0 Wt 13 10
Forward. From Tottenham H Apprentice, Dunstable. England Under-21, 8 full caps.

Season	Club	Apps	Goals
1980–81	Reading	39	13
1981–82		42	12
1982–83		35	26
1983–84	Chelsea	42	28
1984–85		41	24
1985–86		38	14
1986–87		36	10
1987–88		33	11
1988–89		39	25
1989–90		38	20
1990–91		33	10
1991–92		35	5
1992–93	Southampton	9	2
1992–93	*Luton T*	17	3

Season	Club	Apps	Goals
1993–94	Luton T	29	9
1994–95		29	7
1994–95	Millwall	9	4
1995–96		22	5
1995–96	Watford	11	—

DIXON, Lee

Born Manchester 17.3.64 Ht 5 8
Wt 11 08
Defender. From Local. England B, 21 full caps.

Season	Club	Apps	Goals
1982–83	Burnley	3	—
1983–84		1	—
1983–84	Chester	16	1
1984–85		41	—
1985–86	Bury	45	5
1986–87	Stoke C	42	3
1987–88		29	2
1987–88	Arsenal	6	—
1988–89		33	1
1989–90		38	5
1990–91		38	5
1991–92		38	4
1992–93		29	—
1993–94		33	—
1994–95		39	1
1995–96		38	2

DOBBIN, Jim

Born Dunfermline 17.9.63 Ht 5 10
Wt 10 07
Midfield. From Whitburn BC. Scotland Youth.

Season	Club	Apps	Goals
1980–81	Celtic	—	—
1981–82		—	—
1982–83		—	—
1983–84		2	—
1983–84	*Motherwell*	2	—
1983–84	Doncaster R	11	2
1984–85		17	1
1985–86		31	6
1986–87		5	4
1986–87	Barnsley	30	4
1987–88		16	2
1988–89		41	5
1989–90		28	1
1990–91		14	—
1991–92	Grimsby T	32	6
1992–93		39	6
1993–94		29	4
1994–95		38	2
1995–96		26	3

DOBBS, Gerald

Born Lambeth 24.1.71 Ht 5 8 Wt 11 07
Defender. From Trainee.

Season	Club	Apps	Goals
1990–91	Wimbledon	—	—
1991–92		4	—
1992–93		19	1
1993–94		10	—
1994–95		—	—
1995–96		—	—
1995–96	*Cardiff C*	3	—

DOBSON, Tony

Born Coventry 5.2.69 Ht 6 1 Wt 11 12
Defender. From Apprentice. England Under-21.

Season	Club	Apps	Goals
1986–87	Coventry C	1	—
1987–88		1	—
1988–89		16	—
1989–90		30	—
1990–91		6	1
1990–91	Blackburn R	17	—
1991–92		5	—
1992–93		19	—
1993–94		—	—
1993–94	Portsmouth	24	2
1994–95		14	—
1994–95	*Oxford U*	5	—
1995–96	Portsmouth	9	—
1995–96	*Peterborough U*	4	—

DOCHERTY, Stephen

Born Glasgow 18.2.76 Ht 5 8 Wt 10 10
Midfield. From St Roch's.

Season	Club	Apps	Goals
1992–93	Partick T	1	—
1993–94		—	—
1994–95		1	—
1995–96		24	3

DODD, Jason

Born Bath 2.11.70 Ht 5 11 Wt 12 03
Defender. From Bath C. England Under-21.

Season	Club	Apps	Goals
1988–89	Southampton	—	—
1989–90		22	—
1990–91		19	—
1991–92		28	—
1992–93		30	1
1993–94		10	—
1994–95		26	2
1995–96		37	2

DODDS, Billy

Born New Cumnock 5.2.69 Ht 5 8
Wt 10 10
Forward. From Apprentice.

Season	Club	Apps	Goals
1986–87	Chelsea	1	—
1987–88		—	—
1987–88	*Partick T*	30	9
1988–89	Chelsea	2	—
1989–90	Dundee	30	13
1990–91		37	15
1991–92		42	19
1992–93		41	16
1993–94		24	5
1993–94	St Johnstone	20	6
1994–95	Aberdeeen	35	15
1995–96		31	7

DODS, Darren

Born Edinburgh 7.6.75 Ht 6 1 Wt 12 13
Defender. From Hutchison Vale BC.

Season	Club	Apps	Goals
1994–95	Hibernian	1	—
1995–96		15	—

DOHERTY, James

Born Leicester 10.3.77
Midfield.

Season	Club	Apps	Goals
1995–96	Leicester C	—	—

DOHERTY, Neil

Born Barrow 21.2.69 Ht 5 8 Wt 10 09
Midfield. From Trainee.

Season	Club	Apps	Goals
1987–88	Watford	—	—
From Barrow			
1993–94	Birmingham C	13	1
1994–95		8	—
1995–96		2	1
1995–96	*Northampton T*	9	1

DOLAN, Jim

Born Salsburgh 22.2.69 Ht 5 10
Wt 10 07
Forward. From Motherwell BC.

Season	Club	Apps	Goals
1987–88	Motherwell	—	—
1988–89		5	—
1989–90		12	—
1990–91		8	1
1991–92		32	2
1992–93		25	2
1993–94		36	—
1994–95		31	—
1995–96		27	—

DOLBY, Chris

Born Dewsbury 4.9.74 Ht 5 8 Wt 10 03
Forward. From Trainee.

Season	Club	Apps	Goals
1993–94	Rotherham U	1	—
1994–95		2	—
1995–96	Bradford C	—	—

DOLBY, Tony

Born Greenwich 16.4.74 Ht 5 11
Wt 12 08
Forward. From Trainee.

Season	Club	Apps	Goals
1991–92	Millwall	—	—
1992–93		18	1
1993–94		17	—
1993–94	*Barnet*	16	2
1994–95	Millwall	—	—
1995–96		10	—

DOLING, Stuart

Born Newport, IOW 28.10.72 Ht 5 7
Wt 11 07
Midfield. From Trainee.

Season	Club	Apps	Goals
1990–91	Portsmouth	—	—
1991–92		13	2
1992–93		6	—
1993–94		13	1
1994–95		5	1
1995–96	Torquay U	—	—
1995–96	Doncaster R	1	—

DOMINGUEZ, Jose

Born Lisbon 16.2.74 Ht 5 3 Wt 10 00
Forward. From Benfica.

Season	Club	Apps	Goals
1993–94	Birmingham C	5	—
1994–95		30	3
1995–96		—	—

DONACHIE, Danny

Born Manchester 17.5.73 Ht 5 11
Wt 12 00
Midfield. From Radcliffe.

Season	Club	Apps	Goals
1995–96	Carlisle U	1	—

Season	Club	League Appearances/Goals	

DONALD, Graeme

Born Stirling 14.4.74 Ht 6 0 Wt 12 01
Forward. From Gairdoch Utd. Scotland Under-21.

1991–92	Hibernian	5	3
1992–93		4	—
1993–94		6	—
1994–95		—	—
1995–96		13	1

DONALDSON, O'Neill

Born Birmingham 24.11.69 Ht 5 11
Wt 11 07
Forward. From Hinckley.

1991–92	Shrewsbury T	19	2
1992–93		—	—
1993–94		9	2
1994–95	Doncaster R	9	2
1994–95	*Mansfield T*	4	6
1994–95	Sheffield W	1	—
1995–96		3	1

DONNELLY, Simon

Born Glasgow 1.12.74 Ht 5 9 Wt 10 12
Forward. From Celtic BC. Scotland Under-21.

1993–94	Celtic	12	5
1994–95		17	—
1995–96		35	6

DONOVAN, Kevin

Born Halifax 17.12.71 Ht 5 8 Wt 11 02
Forward. From Trainee.

1989–90	Huddersfield T	1	—
1990–91		6	1
1991–92		10	—
1991–92	*Halifax T*	6	—
1992–93	Huddersfield T	3	—
1992–93	WBA	32	6
1993–94		37	8
1994–95		33	5
1995–96		34	—

DONOWA, Lou

Born Ipswich 24.9.64 Ht 5 9 Wt 11 00
Forward. From Apprentice. England Under-21.

1982–83	Norwich C	1	—
1983–84		25	4
1984–85		34	7
1985–86		2	—
1985–86	*Stoke C*	4	1

From Coruna, Willem II

1989–90	Ipswich T	23	1
1990–91	Bristol C	24	3
1991–92	Birmingham C	26	2
1992–93		21	2
1992–93	*Crystal Palace*	—	—
1992–93	*Burnley*	4	—
1993–94	Birmingham C	21	5
1993–94	*Shrewsbury T*	4	—
1994–95	Birmingham C	31	9
1995–96		13	—

DOOLAN, John

Born Liverpool 7.5.74 Ht 6 0 Wt 13 00
Defender. From Trainee.

1992–93	Everton	—	—
1993–94		—	—
1994–95	Mansfield T	24	1
1995–96		42	2

DOOLAN, John

Born South Liverpool 10.11.68 Ht 5 9
Wt 11 05
Midfield. From Knowsley U.

1991–92	Wigan Ath	2	—
1992–93		17	—
1993–94		—	—
1994–95		16	1
1995–96		3	—

DORIGO, Tony

Born Melbourne 31.12.65 Ht 5 10
Wt 10 10
Defender. From Apprentice. England Under-21, B, 15 full caps.

1983–84	Aston Villa	1	—
1984–85		31	—
1985–86		38	1
1986–87		41	—
1987–88	Chelsea	40	—
1988–89		40	6
1989–90		35	3
1990–91		31	2
1991–92	Leeds U	38	3
1992–93		33	1
1993–94		37	—
1994–95		28	—
1995–96		17	1

Season Club League Appearances/Goals

DOUGLAS, Stuart

Born London 9.4.78 Ht 5 8 Wt 11 05
Forward. From Trainee.

Season	Club	Apps	Goals
1995–96	Luton T	8	1

DOW, Andrew

Born Dundee 7.2.73 Ht 5 9 Wt 11 00
Midfield. From Sporting Club 85, Scotland Under-21.

Season	Club	Apps	Goals
1990–91	Dundee	—	—
1991–92		4	—
1992–93		14	1
1993–94	Chelsea	14	—
1994–95		—	—
1994–95	*Bradford C*	5	—
1995–96	Chelsea	1	—
1995–96	Hibernian	8	1

DOWELL, Wayne

Born Co Durham 28.12.73 Ht 5 9 Wt 12 06
Defender. From Trainee.

Season	Club	Apps	Goals
1992–93	Burnley	—	—
1993–94		—	—
1994–95		5	—
1995–96		1	—
1995–96	*Carlisle U*	7	—

DOWIE, Iain

Born Hatfield 9.1.65 Ht 6 1 Wt 13 07
Forward. From Hendon. Northern Ireland Under-23, 36 full caps.

Season	Club	Apps	Goals
1988–89	Luton T	8	—
1989–90		29	9
1989–90	*Fulham*	5	1
1990–91	Luton T	29	7
1990–91	West Ham U	12	4
1991–92		—	—
1991–92	Southampton	30	9
1992–93		36	11
1993–94		39	5
1994–95		17	5
1994–95	Crystal Palace	15	4
1995–96		4	2
1995–96	West Ham U	33	8

DOWNING, Keith

Born Oldbury 23.7.65 Ht 5 9 Wt 11 05
Midfield. From Mile Oak R.

Season	Club	Apps	Goals
1984–85	Notts Co	12	—
1985–86		3	—
1986–87		8	1
1987–88	Wolverhampton W	34	1
1988–89		32	1
1989–90		31	3
1990–91		31	1
1991–92		32	—
1992–93		31	2
1993–94	Birmingham C	1	—
1994–95	Stoke C	16	—
1995–96	Cardiff C	4	—
1995–96	Hereford U	29	—

DOWSON, Keith

Born London 14.9.76
Forward. From Trainee.

Season	Club	Apps	Goals
1995–96	Charlton Ath	—	—

DOYLE, Maurice

Born Ellesmere Port 17.10.69 Ht 5 8 Wt 10 07
Forward. From Trainee.

Season	Club	Apps	Goals
1987–88	Crewe Alex	4	—
1988–89		4	2
1989–90	QPR	—	—
1990–91	*Crewe Alex*	7	2
1990–91	*Wolverhampton W*	—	—
1991–92	QPR	—	—
1992–93		5	—
1993–94		1	—
1994–95		—	—
1994–95	Millwall	—	—
1995–96		18	—

DOZZELL, Jason

Born Ipswich 9.12.67 Ht 6 1 Wt 13 08
Midfield. From School. England Youth, Under-21.

Season	Club	Apps	Goals
1983–84	Ipswich T	5	1
1984–85		14	2
1985–86		41	3
1986–87		42	2
1987–88		39	1
1988–89		29	11
1989–90		46	8
1990–91		30	6
1991–92		45	11
1992–93		41	7
1993–94	Tottenham H	32	8
1994–95		7	—
1995–96		28	3

DRAPER, Mark

Born Long Eaton 11.11.70 Ht 5 10
Wt 12 04
Forward. From Trainee. England Under-21.

Season	Club	Apps	Goals
1988–89	Notts Co	20	3
1989–90		34	3
1990–91		45	9
1991–92		35	1
1992–93		44	11
1993–94		44	13
1994–95	Leicester C	39	5
1995–96	Aston Villa	36	2

DREYER, John

Born Alnwick 11.6.63 Ht 6 1 Wt 12 13
Defender. From Wallingford T.

Season	Club	Apps	Goals
1984–85	Oxford U	—	—
1985–86		—	—
1985–86	*Torquay U*	5	—
1985–86	*Fulham*	12	2
1986–87	Oxford U	25	2
1987–88		35	—
1988–89	Luton T	18	1
1989–90		38	2
1990–91		38	3
1991–92		42	2
1992–93		38	2
1993–94		40	3
1994–95	Stoke C	18	2
1994–95	*Bolton W*	2	—
1995–96	Stoke C	19	—

DRUCE, Mark

Born Oxford 3.3.74 Ht 5 11 Wt 12 08
Forward. From Trainee.

Season	Club	Apps	Goals
1991–92	Oxford U	2	—
1992–93		4	1
1993–94		19	—
1994–95		19	3
1995–96		8	—

DRURY, Adam

Born Cambridge 29.8.78
Defender. From Trainee.

Season	Club	Apps	Goals
1995–96	Peterborough U	1	—

DRYDEN, Richard

Born Stroud 14.6.69 Ht 6 0 Wt 13 00
Defender. From Trainee.

Season	Club	Apps	Goals
1986–87	Bristol R	6	—
1987–88		6	—
1988–89		1	—
1988–89	Exeter C	21	—
1989–90		30	7
1990–91	*Manchester C*	—	—
1991–92	Notts Co	29	1
1992–93		2	—
1992–93	*Plymouth Arg*	5	—
1992–93	Birmingham C	11	—
1993–94		34	—
1994–95		3	—
1994–95	Bristol C	19	1
1995–96		18	1

DRYSDALE, Jason

Born Bristol 17.11.70 Ht 5 10 Wt 12 00
Defender. From Trainee. England Youth. Football League.

Season	Club	Apps	Goals
1988–89	Watford	—	—
1989–90		20	—
1990–91		30	—
1991–92		37	5
1992–93		39	6
1993–94		19	—
1994–95	Newcastle U	—	—
1994–95	Swindon T	1	—
1995–96		13	—

DUBERRY, Michael

Born Enfield 14.10.75 Ht 6 1 Wt 13 06
Defender. From Trainee.

Season	Club	Apps	Goals
1993–94	Chelsea	1	—
1994–95		—	—
1995–96		22	—
1995–96	*Bournemouth*	7	—

DUBLIN, Dion

Born Leicester 22.4.69 Ht 6 2 Wt 12 04
Forward.

Season	Club	Apps	Goals
1987–88	Norwich C	—	—
1988–89	Cambridge U	21	6
1989–90		46	15
1990–91		46	16
1991–92		43	15
1992–93	Manchester U	7	1
1993–94		5	1
1994–95	Coventry C	31	13
1995–96		34	14

DUBLIN, Keith

Born Wycombe 29.1.66 Ht 6 0
Wt 12 10
Defender. From Apprentice. England Youth.

Season	Club	Apps	Goals
1983–84	Chelsea	1	—
1984–85		11	—
1985–86		11	—
1986–87		28	—
1987–88	Brighton & HA	46	5
1988–89		43	—
1989–90		43	—
1990–91	Watford	43	—
1991–92		46	—
1992–93		46	1
1993–94		33	1
1994–95	Southend U	40	2
1995–96		43	3

DUCROS, Andrew

Born Evesham 16.9.77 Ht 5 4 Wt 9 08
Forward. From Trainee. England Youth.

Season	Club	Apps	Goals
1994–95	Coventry C	—	—
1995–96		—	—

DUFF, Damien

Born Ballyboden 2.3.79 Ht 5 10 Wt 9 07
Forward.

Season	Club	Apps	Goals
1995–96	Blackburn R	—	—

DUFFIELD, Peter

Born Middlesbrough 4.2.69 Ht 5 6
Wt 10 04
Forward.

Season	Club	Apps	Goals
1986–87	Middlesbrough	—	—
1987–88	Sheffield U	11	1
1987–88	*Halifax T*	12	6
1988–89	Sheffield U	38	11
1989–90		5	2
1990–91		2	—
1990–91	*Rotherham U*	17	4
1991–92	Sheffield U	2	—
1992–93		—	—
1992–93	*Blackpool*	5	1
1992–93	*Bournemouth*	—	—
1992–93	*Stockport Co*	7	4
1992–93	*Crewe Alex*	2	—
1993–94	Sheffield U	—	—
1993–94	Hamilton A	36	19
1994–95		36	20
1995–96	Airdrieonians	24	6
1995–96	Raith R	9	5

DUGUID, Karl

Born Hitchin 21.3.78 Ht 5 11 Wt 11 09
Forward. From Trainee.

Season	Club	Apps	Goals
1995–96	Colchester U	16	1

DUMITRESCU, Ilie

Born Bucharest 6.1.69 Ht 5 8 Wt 10 07
Midfield. From Steaua. Romania 54 full caps.

Season	Club	Apps	Goals
1987–88	FC Olt	32	1
1988–89	Steaua	29	8
1989–90		25	7
1990–91		25	6
1991–92		30	9
1992–93		29	24
1993–94		25	17
1994–95	Tottenham H	13	4
1995–96		5	—
1995–96	West Ham U	3	—

DUNCAN, Andrew

Born Hexham 20.10.77 Ht 5 11
Wt 13 04
Defender. From Trainee.

Season	Club	Apps	Goals
1995–96	Manchester U	—	—

DUNGEY, James

Born Plymouth 7.2.78 Ht 5 10 Wt 12 00
Goalkeeper. From Trainee. England Youth.

Season	Club	Apps	Goals
1994–95	Plymouth Arg	4	—
1995–96		—	—

DUNN, Iain

Born Derwent 1.4.70 Ht 5 10 Wt 12 00
Forward. From School. England Youth.

Season	Club	Apps	Goals
1988–89	York C	26	6
1989–90		18	2
1990–91		33	3
1991–92	Chesterfield	13	1
From Goole T			
1992–93	Huddersfield T	28	3
1993–94		34	6
1994–95		39	5
1995–96		14	—

Season Club League Appearances/Goals

DUNNE, Joe

Born Dublin 25.5.73 Ht 5 8 Wt 11 06
Defender. From Trainee. Eire Youth, Under-21.

Season	Club	App	Goals
1990–91	Gillingham	26	—
1991–92		11	—
1992–93		4	—
1993–94		37	—
1994–95		35	1
1995–96		2	—
1995–96	Colchester U	5	1

DUNPHY, Nick

Born Birmingham 3.8.74 Ht 5 11 Wt 12 06
Defender. From Hednesford.

Season	Club	App	Goals
1994–95	Peterborough U	2	—
1995–96		—	—

DUNWELL, Richard

Born Islington 17.6.71 Ht 6 0 Wt 13 00
Forward. From Collier Row.

Season	Club	App	Goals
1995–96	Barnet	13	1

DURIE, Gordon

Born Paisley 6.12.65 Ht 6 0 Wt 12 00
Forward. From Hill of Beath Hawthorn. Scotland B, Under-21, 31 full caps.

Season	Club	App	Goals
1981–82	East Fife	13	1
1982–83		25	2
1983–84		34	16
1984–85		9	7
1984–85	Hibernian	22	8
1985–86		25	6
1985–86	Chelsea	1	—
1986–87		25	5
1987–88		26	12
1988–89		32	17
1989–90		15	5
1990–91		24	12
1991–92	Tottenham H	31	7
1992–93		17	3
1993–94		10	1
1993–94	Rangers	24	12
1994–95		21	6
1995–96		27	17

DURKAN, Kieron

Born Chester 1.12.73 Ht 5 10 Wt 10 05
Midfield. From Trainee. Eire Under-21.

Season	Club	App	Goals
1991–92	Wrexham	1	—
1992–93		1	—
1993–94		10	1
1994–95		30	2
1995–96		8	—
1995–96	Stockport Co	16	—

DURNIN, John

Born Bootle 18.8.65 Ht 5 10 Wt 11 10
Forward. From Waterloo Dock.

Season	Club	App	Goals
1985–86	Liverpool	—	—
1986–87		—	—
1987–88		—	—
1988–89		—	—
1988–89	*WBA*	5	2
1988–89	Oxford U	19	3
1989–90		42	13
1990–91		26	9
1991–92		37	8
1992–93		37	11
1993–94	Portsmouth	28	6
1994–95		16	2
1995–96		41	3

DURRANT, Iain

Born Glasgow 29.10.66 Ht 5 8 Wt 9 07
Midfield. From Glasgow United. Scotland Youth, Under-21, 11 full caps.

Season	Club	App	Goals
1984–85	Rangers	5	—
1985–86		30	2
1986–87		39	4
1987–88		40	10
1988–89		8	2
1989–90		—	—
1990–91		4	1
1991–92		13	—
1992–93		30	3
1993–94		23	—
1994–95		25	4
1994–95	*Everton*	5	—
1995–96	Rangers	15	—

DURRANT, Lee

Born Gt Yarmouth 18.12.73 Ht 5 10 Wt 11 07
Midfield. From Trainee.

Season	Club	App	Goals
1992–93	Ipswich T	—	—
1993–94		7	—
1994–95		—	—
1995–96		—	—

Season	Club	League Appearances/Goals	

DUXBURY, Lee

Born Keighley 7.10.69 Ht 5 9 Wt 12 00
Midfield. From Trainee.

1988–89	Bradford C	1	—
1989–90		12	1
1989–90	*Rochdale*	10	—
1990–91	Bradford C	45	5
1991–92		46	5
1992–93		42	5
1993–94		43	9
1994–95		20	—
1994–95	Huddersfield T	26	2
1995–96		3	—
1995–96	Bradford C	30	4

DYCHE, Sean

Born Kettering 28.6.71 Ht 6 0 Wt 13 02
Defender. From Trainee.

1988–89	Nottingham F	—	—
1989–90		—	—
1989–90	Chesterfield	22	2
1990–91		28	2
1991–92		42	3
1992–93		20	1
1993–94		20	—
1994–95		22	—
1995–96		41	—

DYER, Alex

Born West Ham 14.11.65 Ht 6 0
Wt 13 04
Midfield. From Watford Apprentice.

1983–84	Blackpool	9	—
1984–85		36	8
1985–86		39	8
1986–87		24	3
1986–87	Hull C	17	4
1987–88		28	8
1988–89		15	2
1988–89	Crystal Palace	7	2
1989–90		10	—
1990–91	Charlton Ath	35	7
1991–92		13	—
1992–93		30	6
1993–94	Oxford U	38	5
1994–95		38	1
1995–96		—	—
1995–96	Lincoln C	1	—
1995–96	Barnet	35	2

DYER, Bruce

Born Ilford 13.4.75 Ht 5 11 Wt 11 03
Forward. From Trainee. England Under-21.

1992–93	Watford	2	—
1993–94		29	6
1993–94	Crystal Palace	11	—
1994–95		16	1
1995–96		35	13

DYER, Liam

Born Doncaster 2.5.78
Midfield. From Trainee.

1995–96	Sheffield U	—	—

DYKSTRA, Sieb

Born Kerkrade 20.10.66 Ht 6 5
Wt 14 10
Goalkeeper. From Roda JC.

1991–92	Motherwell	1	—
1992–93		35	—
1993–94		44	—
1994–95	QPR	11	—
1995–96		—	—
1995–96	*Bristol C*	8	—
1995–96	*Wycombe W*	13	—

DYSON, Jon

Born Mirfield 18.12.71 Ht 6 1 Wt 12 09
Defender. From School.

1991–92	Huddersfield T	—	—
1992–93		15	—
1993–94		22	—
1994–95		28	2
1995–96		17	—

Season Club League Appearances/Goals

EADEN, Nicky

Born Sheffield 12.12.72 Ht 5 8 Wt 11 09
Defender. From Trainee.

Season	Club	Apps	Goals
1991–92	Barnsley	—	—
1992–93		2	—
1993–94		37	2
1994–95		45	1
1995–96		46	2

EADIE, Darren

Born Chippenham 10.6.75 Ht 5 7
Wt 11 00
Forward. From Trainee. England Youth, Under-21.

Season	Club	Apps	Goals
1992–93	Norwich C	—	—
1993–94		15	3
1994–95		26	2
1995–96		31	6

EARLE, Robbie

Born Newcastle under Lyme 27.1.65
Ht 5 9 Wt 10 10
Forward. From Stoke C.

Season	Club	Apps	Goals
1981–82	Port Vale	—	—
1982–83		8	1
1983–84		12	—
1984–85		46	15
1985–86		46	15
1986–87		35	6
1987–88		25	4
1988–89		44	13
1989–90		43	12
1990–91		35	11
1991–92	Wimbledon	40	14
1992–93		42	7
1993–94		42	9
1994–95		9	—
1995–96		37	11

EATOCK, David

Born Blackrod 11.11.76 Ht 5 4 Wt 10 05
Forward. From Chorley.

Season	Club	Apps	Goals
1995–96	Newcastle U	—	—

EBBRELL, John

Born Bromborough 1.10.69 Ht 5 9
Wt 11 09
Midfield. FA Schools, England Youth, Under-21, B.

Season	Club	Apps	Goals
1986–87	Everton	—	—
1987–88		—	—
1988–89		4	—
1989–90		17	—
1990–91		36	3
1991–92		39	1
1992–93		24	1
1993–94		39	4
1994–95		26	—
1995–96		25	4

EBDON, Marcus

Born Pontypool 17.10.70 Ht 5 10
Wt 11 07
Midfield. From Trainee. Wales Under-21.

Season	Club	Apps	Goals
1988–89	Everton	—	—
1989–90		—	—
1990–91		—	—
1991–92	Peterborough U	15	2
1992–93		28	4
1993–94		10	—
1994–95		35	6
1995–96		39	2

ECKHARDT, Jeff

Born Sheffield 7.10.65 Ht 6 0 Wt 11 07
Defender.

Season	Club	Apps	Goals
1984–85	Sheffield U	7	—
1985–86		33	2
1986–87		22	—
1987–88		12	—
1987–88	Fulham	29	1
1988–89		43	2
1989–90		40	2
1990–91		29	2
1991–92		43	7
1992–93		30	6
1993–94		35	5
1994–95	Stockport Co	27	1
1995–96		35	6

EDGHILL, Richard

Born Oldham 23.9.74 Ht 5 9 Wt 11 03
Defender. From Trainee. England Under-21.

Season	Club	Apps	Goals
1992–93	Manchester C	—	—
1993–94		22	—
1994–95		14	—
1995–96		13	—

EDINBURGH, Justin

Born Brentwood 18.12.69 Ht 5 10
Wt 11 08
Defender. From Trainee.

Season	Club	App	Goals
1988–89	Southend U	15	—
1989–90		22	—
1989–90	*Tottenham H*	—	—
1990–91	Tottenham H	16	1
1991–92		23	—
1992–93		32	—
1993–94		25	—
1994–95		31	—
1995–96		22	—

EDMONDSON, Darren

Born Coniston 4.11.71 Ht 6 0 Wt 12 11
Midfield. From Trainee.

Season	Club	App	Goals
1990–91	Carlisle U	31	—
1991–92		27	2
1992–93		34	—
1993–94		22	3
1994–95		38	2
1995–96		42	1

EDWARDS, Alistair

Born Wyalla 21.6.68 Ht 6 1 Wt 12 06
Forward. From Sydney Olympic.

Season	Club	App	Goals
1989–90	Brighton & HA	1	—
From Selangor			
1994–95	Millwall	4	—
1995–96		—	—

EDWARDS, Andy

Born Epping 17.9.71 Ht 6 2 Wt 12 00
Defender. From Trainee.

Season	Club	App	Goals
1988–89	Southend U	1	—
1989–90		8	—
1990–91		2	1
1991–92		9	—
1992–93		41	—
1993–94		42	1
1994–95		44	3
1995–96	Birmingham C	37	1

EDWARDS, Christian

Born Caerphilly 23.11.75 Ht 6 2
Wt 11 09
Defender. From Trainee. Wales Under-21, 1 full cap.

Season	Club	App	Goals
1994–95	Swansea C	9	—
1995–96		38	2

EDWARDS, Mike

Born Bebbington 10.9.74 Ht 6 0
Wt 12 00
Midfield. From Trainee.

Season	Club	App	Goals
1993–94	Tranmere R	—	—
1994–95		3	—
1995–96		—	—

EDWARDS, Neil

Born Aberdare 5.12.70 Ht 5 8 Wt 11 02
Goalkeeper. From Trainee.

Season	Club	App	Goals
1988–89	Leeds U	—	—
1989–90		—	—
1990–91		—	—
1990–91	*Huddersfield T*	—	—
1991–92	Stockport Co	39	—
1992–93		35	—
1993–94		26	—
1994–95		19	—
1995–96		45	—

EDWARDS, Paul

Born Liverpool 22.2.65 Ht 6 0 Wt 13 02
Goalkeeper. From St. Helens T.

Season	Club	App	Goals
1988–89	Crewe Alex	10	—
1989–90		8	—
1990–91		9	—
1991–92		2	—
1992–93	Shrewsbury T	42	—
1993–94		42	—
1994–95		31	—
1995–96		31	—

EDWARDS, Paul R

Born Birkenhead 25.12.63 Ht 5 11
Wt 11 00
Defender. From Altrincham.

Season	Club	App	Goals
1987–88	Crewe Alex	13	1
1988–89		45	4
1989–90		28	1
1989–90	Coventry C	8	—
1990–91		23	—
1991–92		5	—
1992–93		—	—
1992–93	Wolverhampton W	35	—
1993–94		11	—
1993–94	WBA	15	—
1994–95		20	—
1995–96		16	—
1995–96	*Bury*	4	—

EDWARDS, Rob

Born Manchester 23.2.70 Ht 5 9
Wt 12 04
Forward. From Trainee.

1987–88	Crewe Alex	6	1
1988–89		4	—
1989–90		4	—
1990–91		29	11
1991–92		28	6
1992–93		23	7
1993–94		12	2
1994–95		17	2
1995–96		32	15
1995–96	Huddersfield T	13	7

EDWARDS, Robert

Born Kendal 1.7.73 Ht 6 0 Wt 12 02
Defender. From Trainee. Wales Youth, Under-21.

1989–90	Carlisle U	12	—
1990–91		36	5
1990–91	Bristol C	—	—
1991–92		20	1
1992–93		18	—
1993–94		38	2
1994–95		30	—
1995–96		19	—

EDWORTHY, Marc

Born Barnstaple 24.12.72 Ht 5 8
Wt 11 10
Defender. From Trainee.

1990–91	Plymouth Arg	—	—
1991–92		15	—
1992–93		15	—
1993–94		12	—
1994–95		27	1
1995–96	Crystal Palace	44	—

EHIOGU, Ugo

Born London 3.11.72 Ht 6 2 Wt 13 03
Defender. From Trainee. England Under-21, B, 1 full cap.

1990–91	WBA	2	—
1991–92	Aston Villa	8	—
1992–93		4	—
1993–94		17	—
1994–95		39	3
1995–96		36	1

EKELUND, Ronnie

Born Denmark 21.8.72 Ht 5 10
Wt 12 06
Midfield. From Barcelona. Denmark Under-21.

1994–95	Southampton	17	5
1995–96	Manchester C	4	—
1995–96	Coventry C	—	—

EKOKU, Efan

Born Manchester 8.6.67 Ht 6 1 Wt 12 00
Forward. From Sutton U. Nigeria full caps.

1990–91	Bournemouth	20	3
1991–92		28	11
1992–93		14	7
1992–93	Norwich C	4	3
1993–94		27	12
1994–95		6	—
1994–95	Wimbledon	24	9
1995–96		31	7

ELKINS, Gary

Born Wallingford 4.5.66 Ht 5 9
Wt 11 13
Midfield. From Apprentice. England Youth.

1983–84	Fulham	—	—
1984–85		21	—
1985–86		13	—
1986–87		9	—
1987–88		29	—
1988–89		22	1
1989–90		10	1
1989–90	*Exeter C*	5	—
1990–91	Wimbledon	10	—
1991–92		18	1
1992–93		18	—
1993–94		18	1
1994–95		36	1
1995–96		10	—

ELLIOT, David

Born Glasgow 13.11.69 Ht 5 9 Wt 11 00
Forward. From Celtic BC.

1987–88	Celtic	—	—
1988–89		4	—
1989–90		2	—
1990–91	Partick T	37	13
1991–92	St Mirren	28	1
1992–93		40	5

Season	Club	Appearances	Goals
1993–94		36	8
1994–95		28	3
1995–96	Falkirk	32	—

ELLIOTT, Matt

Born Epsom 1.11.68 Ht 6 3 Wt 14 10
Defender. From Epsom & Ewell.

Season	Club	Appearances	Goals
1988–89	Charlton Ath	—	—
1988–89	Torquay U	13	2
1989–90		33	2
1990–91		45	6
1991–92		33	5
1991–92	*Scunthorpe U*	8	1
1992–93	Scunthorpe U	39	6
1993–94		14	1
1993–94	Oxford U	32	5
1994–95		45	4
1995–96		45	8

ELLIOTT, Robbie

Born Newcastle 25.12.73 Ht 5 10
Wt 10 13
Defender. From Trainee. England Under-21.

Season	Club	Appearances	Goals
1990–91	Newcastle U	6	—
1991–92		9	—
1992–93		—	—
1993–94		15	—
1994–95		14	2
1995–96		6	—

ELLIOTT, Stuart

Born London 27.8.77 Ht 5 8 Wt 11 05
Defender. From Trainee.

Season	Club	Appearances	Goals
1995–96	Newcastle U	—	—

ELLIOTT, Tony

Born Nuneaton 30.11.69 Ht 6 0
Wt 13 04
Goalkeeper. England Youth.

Season	Club	Appearances	Goals
1986–87	Birmingham C	—	—
1987–88		—	—
1988–89		—	—
1988–89	Hereford U	23	—
1989–90		29	—
1990–91		5	—
1991–92		18	—
1992–93	Huddersfield T	15	—
1993–94	Carlisle U	6	—

Season Club League Appearances/Goals

Season	Club	Appearances	Goals
1994–95		3	—
1995–96		13	—

ELLIS, Kevin

Born Gt Yarmouth 12.5.77 Ht 6 2
Wt 12 07
Defender. From Trainee.

Season	Club	Appearances	Goals
1994–95	Ipswich T	1	—
1995–96		—	—

ELLIS, Tony

Born Salford 20.10.64 Ht 5 11 Wt 11 00
Forward. From Horwich RMI, Northwich Vic.

Season	Club	Appearances	Goals
1986–87	Oldham Ath	5	—
1987–88		3	—
1987–88	Preston NE	24	4
1988–89		45	19
1989–90		17	3
1989–90	Stoke C	24	6
1990–91		38	9
1991–92		15	4
1992–93	Preston NE	35	22
1993–94		37	26
1994–95	Blackpool	40	17
1995–96		43	14

ELLISON, Lee

Born Bishop Auckland 13.1.73 Ht 5 10
Wt 10 00
Forward. From Trainee.

Season	Club	Appearances	Goals
1990–91	Darlington	13	3
1991–92		27	10
1992–93		3	—
1992–93	*Hartlepool U*	4	1
1993–94	Darlington	29	4
1994–95	Leicester C	—	—
1995–96	Crewe Alex	1	—

EMBERSON, Carl

Born Epsom 13.7.73 Ht 6 1 Wt 14 09
Goalkeeper. From Trainee.

Season	Club	Appearances	Goals
1991–92	Millwall	—	—
1992–93		—	—
1992–93	*Colchester U*	13	—
1993–94	Millwall	—	—
1994–95	Colchester U	20	—
1995–96		41	—

Season	Club	League Appearances/Goals	

EMBLEN, Neil

Born Bromley 19.6.71 Ht 6 2 Wt 13 03
Defender. From Tonbridge, Sittingbourne.

1993–94	Millwall	12	—
1994–95	Wolverhampton W	27	7
1995–96		33	2

EMENALO, Michael

Born Nigeria 14.7.65 Ht 5 11 Wt 11 04
Defender. From Eintracht Trier.

1994–95	Notts Co	7	—
1995–96		—	—

ENGLISH, Tony

Born Luton 19.10.66 Ht 6 0 Wt 12 07
Defender. From Coventry C Apprentice. England Youth.

1984–85	Colchester U	22	3
1985–86		45	13
1986–87		32	7
1987–88		43	2
1988–89		36	8
1989–90		44	2
1990–91		—	—
1991–92		—	—
1992–93		33	1
1993–94		42	4
1994–95		33	2
1995–96		21	—

ENQVIST, Bjorn

Born Lund 12.10.77 Ht 5 10 Wt 10 09
Midfield. From Malmo.

1994–95	Crystal Palace	—	—
1995–96		—	—

ESKILSSON, Hans

Born Sweden 23.1.66 Ht 6 0 Wt 12 07
Forward. From Vasalund.

1995–96	Hearts	10	2

ESSANDOH, Roy

Born Belfast 17.2.76 Ht 6 0 Wt 12 03
Midfield. From Cumbernauld Jun.

1994–95	Motherwell	—	—
1995–96		4	—

EUELL, Jason

Born South London 6.2.77 Ht 5 11 Wt 11 02
Forward. From Trainee.

1995–96	Wimbledon	9	2

EUSTACE, Scott

Born Leicester 13.6.75 Ht 6 1 Wt 14 02
Defender. From Trainee.

1993–94	Leicester C	1	—
1994–95		—	—
1995–96	Mansfield T	27	1

EVANS, Andy

Born Aberystwyth 25.11.75 Ht 6 1 Wt 12 01
Forward. From Trainee.

1993–94	Cardiff C	1	—
1994–95		12	—
1995–96		2	—

EVANS, Darren

Born Wolverhampton 30.9.74 Ht 5 11 Wt 12 00
Defender. From Trainee.

1993–94	Aston Villa	—	—
1994–95		—	—
1995–96	Hereford U	24	—

EVANS, Gareth

Born Deeside 8.3.77 Ht 5 8 Wt 10 08
Midfield. From Trainee.

1995–96	Manchester C	—	—

EVANS, Gareth

Born Coventry 14.1.67 Ht 5 8 Wt 10 06
Forward. From Apprentice.

1984–85	Coventry C	—	—
1985–86		6	—
1986–87		1	—
1986–87	Rotherham U	34	9
1987–88		29	4
1987–88	Hibernian	12	2
1988–89		35	5
1989–90		28	3
1990–91		15	2
1990–91	*Northampton T*	2	—
1990–91	*Stoke C*	5	1
1991–92	Hibernian	41	6

Season	Club	League Appearances/Goals	
1992–93		39	6
1993–94		40	4
1994–95		24	—
1995–96		23	2

EVANS, Mike

Born Plymouth 1.1.73 Ht 6 0 Wt 13 04
Forward. From Trainee.

1990–91	Plymouth Arg	4	—
1991–92		13	—
1992–93		23	1
1992–93	*Blackburn R*	—	—
1993–94	Plymouth Arg	22	9
1994–95		23	4
1995–96		45	12

EVANS, Paul

Born Oswestry 1.9.74 Ht 5 6 Wt 12 00
Midfield. From Trainee. Wales Under-21.

1991–92	Shrewsbury T	2	—
1992–93		4	—
1993–94		13	—
1994–95		32	5
1995–96		34	3

EVANS, Paul

Born South Africa 28.12.73
Goalkeeper. From Witts Univ.

1995–96	Leeds U	—	—
1995–96	*Crystal Palace*	—	—

EVANS, Richard

Born Wrexham 24.9.76
Midfield. From Trainee.

1995–96	Oldham Ath	—	—

EVANS, Terry

Born Pontypridd 8.1.76 Ht 5 8 Wt 10 07
Defender. From Trainee. Wales Under-21.

1993–94	Cardiff C	5	—
1994–95		7	—
1995–96		2	—

EVANS, Terry

Born Hammersmith 12.4.65 Ht 6 4
Wt 15 04
Defender. From Hillingdon.

1985–86	Brentford	19	1
1986–87		1	—
1987–88		29	4
1988–89		45	5
1989–90		44	3
1990–91		36	2
1991–92		44	8
1992–93		11	—
1993–94		—	—
1993–94	Wycombe W	22	6
1994–95		44	4
1995–96		28	3

EVANS, Tom

Born Doncaster 31.12.76 Ht 6 0
Wt 12 10
Goalkeeper. From Trainee.

1995–96	Sheffield U	—	—

EVANS, Wayne

Born Abermule 25.8.71 Ht 5 10
Wt 12 05
Defender. From Welshpool.

1993–94	Walsall	41	—
1994–95		36	—
1995–96		24	—

EVEREST, Anthony

Born Maidstone 20.9.76 Ht 5 6 Wt 10 00
Midfield. From Trainee.

1995–96	Southampton	—	—

EVERITT, Dave

Born Chertsey 30.12.76
Midfield.

1995–96	Leyton Orient	—	—

EVERS, Sean

Born Hitchin 10.10.77 Ht 5 9 Wt 9 11
Midfield. From Trainee.

1995–96	Luton T	1	—

EYRE, John

Born Humberside 9.10.74 Ht 6 0
Wt 12 07
Forward. From Trainee.

1993–94	Oldham Ath	2	—
1994–95		8	1
1994–95	*Scunthorpe U*	9	8
1995–96	Scunthorpe U	39	10

Season	Club	League Appearances/Goals	

EYRE, Richard

Born Stockport 15.9.76 Ht 5 9 Wt 10 12
Forward. From Trainee.

1995–96	Port Vale	—	—

EYRES, David

Born Liverpool 26.2.64 Ht 5 9 Wt 11 10
Forward. From Rhyl.

1989–90	Blackpool	35	7
1990–91		36	6
1991–92		41	9
1992–93		46	16
1993–94	Burnley	45	19
1994–95		39	8
1995–96		42	6

FAIRCLOUGH, Chris

Born Nottingham 12.4.64 Ht 5 11
Wt 11 02
Defender. From Apprentice. England Under-21, B.

1981–82	Nottingham F	—	—
1982–83		15	—
1983–84		31	—
1984–85		35	—
1985–86		—	—
1986–87		26	1
1987–88	Tottenham H	40	4
1988–89		20	1
1988–89	Leeds U	11	—
1989–90		42	8
1990–91		34	4
1991–92		31	2
1992–93		30	3
1993–94		40	4
1994–95		5	—
1995–96	Bolton W	33	—

FAIRCLOUGH, Wayne

Born Nottingham 27.4.68 Ht 5 10
Wt 12 02
Defender. From Apprentice.

1985–86	Notts Co.	5	—
1986–87		9	—
1987–88		29	—
1988–89		20	—
1989–90		8	—
1989–90	Mansfield T	13	—
1990–91		41	6
1991–92		25	3
1992–93		33	1
1993–94		29	2
1994–95	Chesterfield	13	—
1995–96		2	—
1995–96	*Scarborough*	7	—

FALCONER, Willie

Born Aberdeen 5.4.66 Ht 6 1 Wt 11 09
Midfield. From Lewis United. Scotland Schools, Youth.

1982–83	Aberdeen	1	—
1983–84		8	1
1984–85		16	4
1985–86		8	—
1986–87		8	—
1987–88		36	8
1988–89	Watford	33	5

Season Club League Appearances/Goals

Season	Club	Apps	Goals
1989–90		30	3
1990–91		35	4
1991–92	Middlesbrough	25	5
1992–93		28	5
1993–94	Sheffield U	23	3
1993–94	Celtic	14	1
1994–95		26	4
1995–96		2	—
1995–96	Motherwell	15	5

FARNWORTH, Simon

Born Chorley 28.10.63 Ht 5 11 Wt 13 04
Goalkeeper. From Apprentice. England Schools.

Season	Club	Apps	Goals
1981–82	Bolton W	—	—
1982–83		—	—
1983–84		36	—
1984–85		46	—
1985–86		31	—
1986–87		—	—
1986–87	*Stockport Co*	10	—
1986–87	*Tranmere R*	7	—
1986–87	Bury	14	—
1987–88		39	—
1988–89		45	—
1989–90		7	—
1990–91	Preston NE	23	—
1991–92		23	—
1992–93		35	—
1993–94	Wigan Ath	42	—
1994–95		41	—
1995–96		43	—

FARRELL, Andy

Born Colchester 7.10.65 Ht 5 11 Wt 12 03
Defender. From School.

Season	Club	Apps	Goals
1983–84	Colchester U	15	—
1984–85		38	—
1985–86		24	1
1986–87		28	4
1987–88	Burnley	45	3
1988–89		36	4
1989–90		36	2
1990–91		37	2
1991–92		39	3
1992–93		42	3
1993–94		22	2
1994–95		—	—
1994–95	Wigan Ath	31	—
1995–96		23	1

FARRELL, Dave

Born Birmingham 11.11.71 Ht 5 10 Wt 11 07
Forward. From Redditch U.

Season	Club	Apps	Goals
1992–93	Aston Villa	2	—
1992–93	*Scunthorpe U*	5	1
1993–94	Aston Villa	4	—
1994–95		—	—
1995–96		—	—
1995–96	Wycombe W	33	7

FARRELL, David

Born Glasgow 29.10.69 Ht 5 9 Wt 10 12
Midfield. From Oxford U Apprentice.

Season	Club	Apps	Goals
1988–89	Hibernian	—	—
1989–90		—	—
1990–91		2	—
1991–92		6	—
1992–93		12	—
1993–94		35	2
1994–95		19	—
1995–96		8	—

FARRELL, Gerard

Born Glasgow 14.6.75 Ht 5 8 Wt 10 10
Defender. From Possil YM.

Season	Club	Apps	Goals
1995–96	Dunfermline Ath	6	—

FARRELL, Sean

Born Watford 28.2.69 Ht 6 1 Wt 13 03
Forward. From Apprentice.

Season	Club	Apps	Goals
1986–87	Luton T	—	—
1987–88		—	—
1987–88	*Colchester U*	9	1
1988–89	Luton T	—	—
1989–90		1	—
1990–91		20	1
1991–92		4	—
1991–92	*Northampton T*	4	1
1991–92	Fulham	25	10
1992–93		35	12
1993–94		34	9
1994–95	Peterborough U	33	8
1995–96		26	9

FARRELLY, Gareth

Born Dublin 28.8.75 Ht 6 0 Wt 12 07
Midfield. From Home Farm. Eire Under-21, 3 full caps.

Season	Club	Apps	Goals
1992–93	Aston Villa	—	—

Season Club League Appearances/Goals

Season	Club	Apps	Goals
1993–94		—	—
1994–95		—	—
1994–95	*Rotherham U*	10	2
1995–96	Aston Villa	5	—

FARRELLY, Stephen

Born Liverpool 27.3.65 Ht 6 5 Wt 15 07
Goalkeeper. From Macclesfield T.

Season	Club	Apps	Goals
1995–96	Rotherham U	—	—

FAULKNER, David

Born Sheffield 8.10.75 Ht 6 1 Wt 12 13
Defender. From Trainee. England Youth.

Season	Club	Apps	Goals
1992–93	Sheffield W	—	—
1993–94		—	—
1994–95		—	—
1995–96		—	—

FEAR, Peter

Born London 10.9.73 Ht 5 10 Wt 11 07
Defender. From Trainee. England Under-21.

Season	Club	Apps	Goals
1992–93	Wimbledon	4	—
1993–94		23	1
1994–95		14	1
1995–96		4	—

FEARON, Dean

Born Barnsley 9.1.76 Ht 6 1 Wt 13 12
Defender. From School.

Season	Club	Apps	Goals
1994–95	Barnsley	—	—
1995–96		—	—

FEARON, Ron

Born Romford 19.11.60 Ht 6 0 Wt 11 12
Goalkeeper. From QPR Apprentice.

Season	Club	Apps	Goals
1979–80	Reading	—	—
1980–81		6	—
1981–82		42	—
1982–83		13	—
From Sutton			
1987–88	Ipswich T	10	—
1988–89		18	—
1988–89	*Brighton & HA*	7	—
1989–90	Ipswich T	—	—
1990–91	Leyton Orient	—	—
1991–92	Ipswich T	—	—
1992–93		—	—
1992–93	*Walsall*	1	—
1993–94	Southend U	—	—
1994–95		—	—
1995–96	Leyton Orient	18	—

FEENEY, Gareth

Born Manchester 5.12.78
Midfield. From Trainee.

Season	Club	Apps	Goals
1995–96	Bolton W	—	—

FEENEY, Mark

Born Derry 26.7.74 Ht 5 7 Wt 11 00
Midfield. From Trainee.

Season	Club	Apps	Goals
1992–93	Barnsley	2	—
1993–94		—	—
1994–95		—	—
1995–96		—	—

FELGATE, David

Born Blaenau Ffestiniog 4.3.60 Ht 6 1 Wt 15 00
Goalkeeper. From Blaenau Ffestiniog. Wales Schools, Under-21, 1 full cap.

Season	Club	Apps	Goals
1978–79	Bolton W	—	—
1978–79	*Rochdale*	35	—
1979–80	Bolton W	—	—
1979–80	*Bradford C*	—	—
1979–80	*Crewe Alex*	14	—
1979–80	*Rochdale*	12	—
1980–81	Bolton W	—	—
1980–81	Lincoln C	42	—
1981–82		43	—
1982–83		46	—
1983–84		46	—
1984–85		21	—
1984–85	*Cardiff C*	4	—
1984–85	*Grimsby T*	12	—
1985–86	Grimsby T	12	—
1985–86	Bolton W	15	—
1986–87		20	—
1986–87	*Rotherham U*	—	—
1987–88	Bolton W	46	—
1988–89		46	—
1989–90		40	—
1990–91		46	—
1991–92		25	—
1992–93		—	—
1993–94	Bury	—	—
1993–94	Wolverhampton W	—	—
1993–94	Chester C	34	—
1994–95		38	—
1995–96	Wigan Ath	3	—

Season	Club	League Appearances/Goals	

FENN, Neale

Born Edmonton 18.1.77 Ht 5 10
Wt 11 06
Forward. From Trainee.

1995–96	Tottenham H	—	—

FENSOME, Andy

Born Northampton 18.2.69 Ht 5 8
Wt 11 02
Defender. From Trainee.

1986–87	Norwich C	—	—
1987–88		—	—
1988–89		—	—
1988–89	*Newcastle U*	—	—
1989–90	Cambridge U	24	—
1990–91		36	—
1991–92		34	1
1992–93		30	—
1993–94		2	—
1993–94	Preston NE	31	1
1994–95		42	—
1995–96		20	—

FENTON, Graham

Born Wallsend 22.5.74 Ht 5 10 Wt 12 10
Forward. From Trainee. England Under-21.

1991–92	Aston Villa	—	—
1992–93		—	—
1993–94		12	1
1993–94	*WBA*	7	3
1994–95	Aston Villa	17	2
1995–96		3	—
1995–96	Blackburn R	14	6

FENWICK, Paul

Born London 25.8.69 Ht 6 1 Wt 12 01
Defender. From Winnipeg Fury.

1992–93	Birmingham C	10	—
1993–94		9	—
1994–95		—	—
1995–96	Dunfermline Ath	1	—

FENWICK, Terry

Born Co. Durham 17.11.59 Ht 5 10
Wt 11 12
Defender. From Apprentice. England Youth, Under-21, 20 full caps.

1976–77	Crystal Palace	—	—
1977–78		10	—
1978–79		24	—
1979–80		15	—
1980–81		21	—
1980–81	QPR	19	2
1981–82		36	5
1982–83		39	3
1983–84		41	10
1984–85		41	2
1985–86		37	7
1986–87		21	1
1987–88		22	3
1987–88	Tottenham H	17	—
1988–89		34	8
1989–90		10	—
1990–91		4	—
1990–91	*Leicester C*	8	1
1991–92	Tottenham H	23	—
1992–93		5	—
1993–94	Swindon T	26	—
1994–95		2	—
1995–96		—	—
1995–96	Portsmouth	—	—

FERDINAND, Les

Born Acton 18.12.66 Ht 5 11 Wt 13 05
Forward. From Hayes. England 10 full caps.

1986–87	QPR	2	—
1987–88		1	—
1987–88	*Brentford*	3	—
1988–89	QPR	—	—
1988–89	*Besiktas*	—	—
1989–90	QPR	9	2
1990–91		18	8
1991–92		23	10
1992–93		37	20
1993–94		36	16
1994–95		37	24
1995–96	Newcastle U	37	25

FERDINAND, Rio

Born London 7.11.78 Ht 6 2 Wt 12 00
Defender. From Trainee. England Youth.

1995–96	West Ham U	1	—

FERGUSON, Darren

Born Glasgow 9.2.72 Ht 5 10 Wt 10 04
Midfield. From Trainee. Scotland Under-21.

1990–91	Manchester U	5	—
1991–92		4	—

Season	Club	League Appearances/Goals	
1992–93		15	—
1993–94		3	—
1993–94	Wolverhampton W	14	—
1994–95		24	—
1995–96		33	1

FERGUSON, Derek

Born Glasgow 31.7.67 Ht 5 8 Wt 11 12
Midfield. From Gartcosh United. Scotland Schools, Youth, Under-21, 2 full caps.

1983–84	Rangers	1	—
1984–85		8	—
1985–86		19	—
1986–87		30	1
1987–88		32	4
1988–89		16	2
1989–90		5	—
1989–90	*Dundee*	4	—
1990–91	Hearts	28	2
1991–92		38	1
1992–93		37	1
1993–94	Sunderland	41	—
1994–95		23	—
1995–96	Falkirk	26	—

FERGUSON, Duncan

Born Stirling 27.12.71 Ht 6 3 Wt 13 08
Forward. From Carse T. Scotland Under-21, 5 full caps.

1990–91	Dundee U	9	1
1991–92		38	15
1992–93		30	12
1993–94	Rangers	10	1
1994–95		4	1
1994–95	Everton	23	7
1995–96		18	5

FERGUSON, Ian

Born Glasgow 15.3.67 Ht 5 10 Wt 10 11
Midfield. From Clyde BC. Scotland B, Under-21, 8 full caps.

1984–85	Clyde	2	—
1985–86		19	4
1986–87		5	—
1986–87	St Mirren	35	4
1987–88		22	6
1987–88	Rangers	8	1
1988–89		30	6
1989–90		24	—
1990–91		11	1

Season	Club	League Appearances/Goals	
1991–92		16	1
1992–93		30	4
1993–94		35	5
1994–95		16	1
1995–96		18	2

FERGUSON, Paul

Born Dechmont 12.3.75 Ht 5 7 Wt 9 12
Midfield. From Stoneyburn Utd.

1994–95	Motherwell	—	—
1995–96		1	—
1995–96	East Fife	6	—

FERGUSON, Steven

Born Edinburgh 18.5.77 Ht 5 8 Wt 11 06
Midfield. From Rosyth Recreation.

1995–96	Dunfermline Ath	1	—

FERNANDES, Tamer

Born London 7.12.74 Ht 6 3 Wt 13 05
Goalkeeper. From Trainee.

1993–94	Brentford	1	—
1994–95		4	—
1995–96		5	—

FETTIS, Alan

Born Belfast 1.2.71 Ht 6 1 Wt 11 08
Goalkeeper. From Ards. Northern Ireland 15 full caps.

1991–92	Hull C	43	—
1992–93		20	—
1993–94		37	—
1994–95		28	2
1995–96		7	—
1995–96	*WBA*	3	—

FEUER, Tony

Born Las Vegas 20.5.71 Ht 6 6 Wt 15 06
Goalkeeper. From Los Angeles Salsa. USA full caps.

1993–94	West Ham U	—	—
1994–95		—	—
1994–95	*Peterborough U*	16	—
1995–96	West Ham U	—	—
1995–96	Luton T	38	—

FEWINGS, Paul

Born Hull 18.2.78 Ht 5 11 Wt 11 07
Forward. From Trainee.

Season	Club	Apps	Goals
1994–95	Hull C	2	—
1995–96		25	2

FICKLING, Ashley

Born Sheffield 15.11.72 Ht 5 10
Wt 11 06
Defender. From Trainee.

Season	Club	Apps	Goals
1991–92	Sheffield U	—	—
1992–93		—	—
1992–93	*Darlington*	14	—
1993–94		1	—
1994–95	Sheffield U	—	—
1994–95	Grimsby T	1	—
1995–96		11	—

FIDLER, Richard

Born Sheffield 26.10.76 Ht 5 9 Wt 10 09
Midfield. From Leeds U Trainee.

Season	Club	Apps	Goals
1995–96	Hull C	1	—

FILAN, John

Born Sydney 8.2.70 Ht 5 11 Wt 13 02
Goalkeeper. From Budapest St George.

Season	Club	Apps	Goals
1992–93	Cambridge U	6	—
1993–94		46	—
1994–95		16	—
1994–95	*Nottingham F*	—	—
1994–95	Coventry C	2	—
1995–96		13	—

FINDLAY, William

Born Kilmarnock 29.8.70 Ht 5 10
Wt 10 13
Midfield. From Kilmarnock BC. Scotland Under-21.

Season	Club	Apps	Goals
1987–88	Hibernian	—	—
1988–89		3	1
1989–90		10	—
1990–91		26	2
1991–92		9	—
1992–93		7	—
1993–94		20	3
1994–95		18	1
1994–95	Kilmarnock	9	—
1995–96		3	—

FINN, Neil

Born London 29.12.78
Goalkeeper. From Trainee.

Season	Club	Apps	Goals
1995–96	West Ham U	1	—

FINNAN, Steve

Born Chelmsford 20.4.76 Ht 5 9
Wt 10 09
Midfield. From Welling U.

Season	Club	Apps	Goals
1995–96	Birmingham C	12	1
1995–96	*Notts Co*	17	2

FINNEY, Stephen

Born Hexham 31.10.73 Ht 5 10
Wt 12 00
Forward. From Trainee.

Season	Club	Apps	Goals
1991–92	Preston NE	2	1
1992–93		4	—
1993–94	Manchester C	—	—
1994–95		—	—
1995–96	Swindon T	30	12

FINNIGAN, John

Born Wakefield 28.3.76 Ht 5 8 Wt 10 11
Midfield. From Trainee.

Season	Club	Apps	Goals
1992–93	Nottingham F	—	—
1993–94		—	—
1994–95		—	—
1995–96		—	—

FINNIGAN, Tony

Born Wimbledon 17.10.62 Ht 5 10
Wt 11 09
Midfield. From Crystal Palace Apprentice.

Season	Club	Apps	Goals
1980–81	Fulham	—	—
1981–82		—	—
1982–83		—	—
1983–84		—	—
1984–85	Crystal Palace	11	1
1985–86		36	3
1986–87		41	6
1987–88		17	—
1988–89	Blackburn R	17	—
1989–90		19	—
1990–91	Hull C	18	1
1990–91	Swindon T	3	—

Season	Club	League Appearances/Goals	
1991–92	Brentford	3	—
1992–93		—	—
1993–94	Barnet	6	1
1994–95	Fulham	11	—
1995–96		2	—
1995–96	Falkirk	9	1

FISHER, Neil

Born St Helens 7.11.70 Ht 5 10
Wt 11 00
Midfield. From Trainee.

1990–91	Bolton W	—	—
1991–92		7	1
1992–93		4	—
1993–94		2	—
1994–95		11	—
1995–96	Chester C	44	2

FISHLOCK, Murray

Born Marlborough 23.9.73 Ht 5 8
Wt 10 09
Defender. From Trowbridge T.

1994–95	Hereford U	14	—
1995–96		27	3

FITCHETT, Scott

Born Manchester 20.1.79 Ht 5 8 Wt 9 06
Midfield. From Trainee.

1995–96	Nottingham F	—	—

FITZGERALD, Gary

Born Hampstead 27.10.76 Ht 6 1
Wt 11 07
Defender. From Trainee.

1994–95	Watford	1	—
1995–96		—	—

FITZGERALD, Scott

Born London 13.8.69 Ht 6 0 Wt 12 02
Defender. From Trainee. Eire Under-21, B.

1988–89	Wimbledon	—	—
1989–90		1	—
1990–91		—	—

Season	Club	League Appearances/Goals	
1991–92		36	1
1992–93		20	—
1993–94		28	—
1994–95		17	—
1995–96		4	—
1995–96	*Sheffield U*	6	—

FJORTOFT, Jan-Aage

Born Aalesund 10.1.67 Ht 6 3 Wt 13 04
Forward. Norway 66 full caps.

1987	Hamar	22	10
1988	Lillestrom	24	14
1989		11	6
1989–90	Rapid Vienna	33	17
1990–91		33	16
1991–92		34	16
1992–93		28	13
1993–94	Swindon T	36	12
1994–95		36	16
1994–95	Middlesbrough	8	3
1995–96		28	6

FLACK, Steve

Born Cambridge 29.5.71 Ht 6 1
Wt 11 04
Forward. From Cambridge C.

1995–96	Cardiff C	10	1

FLAHAVAN, Aaron

Born Southampton 15.12.75 Ht 6 1
Wt 11 12
Goalkeeper. From Trainee.

1993–94	Portsmouth	—	—
1994–95		—	—
1995–96		—	—

FLASH, Richard

Born Birmingham 8.4.76 Ht 5 9
Wt 11 08
Midfield.

1994–95	Manchester U	—	—
1995–96		—	—
1995–96	Wolverhampton W	—	—

FLATTS, Mark

Born Haringey 14.10.72 Ht 5 6 Wt 9 08
Midfield. From Trainee.

1992–93	Arsenal	10	—
1993–94		3	—

Season	Club	League Appearances/Goals	
1993–94	*Cambridge U*	5	1
1993–94	*Brighton & HA*	10	1
1994–95	Arsenal	3	—
1994–95	*Bristol C*	6	—
1995–96	Arsenal	—	—
1995–96	*Grimsby T*	5	—

FLECK, Robert

Born Glasgow 11.8.65 Ht 5 8 Wt 11 09
Forward. From Possil YM. Scotland Youth, Under-21, 4 full caps.

Season	Club	League Appearances/Goals	
1983–84	Partick T	2	1
1983–84	Rangers	1	—
1984–85		8	—
1985–86		15	3
1986–87		40	19
1987–88		21	7
1987–88	Norwich C	18	7
1988–89		33	10
1989–90		27	7
1990–91		29	5
1991–92		36	11
1992–93	Chelsea	31	2
1993–94		9	1
1993–94	*Bolton W*	7	1
1994–95	Chelsea	—	—
1994–95	*Bristol C*	10	1
1995–96	Chelsea	—	—
1995–96	Norwich C	41	10

FLEMING, Craig

Born Calder 6.10.71 Ht 6 0 Wt 11 07
Defender. From Trainee.

Season	Club	League Appearances/Goals	
1988–89	Halifax T	1	—
1989–90		10	—
1990–91		46	—
1991–92	Oldham Ath	32	1
1992–93		24	—
1993–94		37	—
1994–95		5	—
1995–96		22	—

FLEMING, Curtis

Born Manchester 8.10.68 Ht 5 10
Wt 12 09
Defender. From St Patrick's Ath. Eire Youth, Under-21, B, 7 full caps.

Season	Club	League Appearances/Goals	
1988–89	Swindon T	—	—
From St Patrick's Ath			
1991–92	Middlesbrough	28	—
1992–93		24	—
1993–94		40	—
1994–95		21	—
1995–96		13	1

FLEMING, Derek

Born Falkirk 5.12.73 Ht 5 7 Wt 10 02
Defender. From Broxburn Ath.

Season	Club	League Appearances/Goals	
1992–93	Meadowbank T	4	—
1993–94		38	2
1994–95		7	1
1994–95	Dunfermline Ath	29	1
1995–96		33	3

FLEMING, Gary

Born Derry 17.2.67 Ht 5 7 Wt 11 09
Defender. From Apprentice. Northern Ireland 31 full caps.

Season	Club	League Appearances/Goals	
1984–85	Nottingham F	2	—
1985–86		16	—
1986–87		34	—
1987–88		22	—
1988–89		—	—
1989–90	Manchester C	14	—
1989–90	*Notts Co*	3	—
1989–90	Barnsley	12	—
1990–91		44	—
1991–92		42	—
1992–93		46	—
1993–94		46	—
1994–95		46	—
1995–96		3	—

FLEMING, Hayden

Born Islington 14.3.78
Defender. From Trainee.

Season	Club	League Appearances/Goals	
1995–96	Cardiff C	22	—

FLEMING, Terry

Born Marston Green 5.1.73 Ht 5 9
Wt 10 09
Defender. From Trainee.

Season	Club	League Appearances/Goals	
1990–91	Coventry C	2	—
1991–92		—	—
1992–93		11	—
1993–94	Northampton T	31	1
1994–95	Preston NE	27	2
1995–96		5	—
1995–96	Lincoln C	22	—

Season	Club	League Appearances/Goals	

FLETCHER, Steve

Born Hartlepool 26.7.72 Ht 6 2
Wt 14 09
Forward. From Trainee.

Season	Club	Apps	Goals
1990–91	Hartlepool U	14	2
1991–92		18	2
1992–93	Bournemouth	31	4
1993–94		36	6
1994–95		40	6
1995–96		7	1

FLITCROFT, David

Born Bolton 14.1.74 Ht 5 11 Wt 13 05
Midfield. From Trainee.

Season	Club	Apps	Goals
1991–92	Preston NE	—	—
1992–93		8	2
1993–94		—	—
1993–94	*Lincoln C*	2	—
1993–94	Chester C	8	1
1994–95		32	—
1995–96		9	1

FLITCROFT, Garry

Born Bolton 6.11.72 Ht 6 0 Wt 12 09
Midfield. From Trainee. England Under-21.

Season	Club	Apps	Goals
1991–92	Manchester C	—	—
1991–92	*Bury*	12	—
1992–93	Manchester C	32	5
1993–94		21	3
1994–95		37	5
1995–96		25	—
1995–96	Blackburn R	3	—

FLO, Jostein

Born Norway 3.10.64 Ht 6 4 Wt 15 03
Forward. From Sogndal. Norway 39 full caps.

Season	Club	Apps	Goals
1993–94	Sheffield U	33	9
1994–95		32	6
1995–96		19	4

FLOWERS, Tim

Born Kenilworth 3.2.67 Ht 6 3 Wt 14 04
Goalkeeper. From Apprentice. England Youth, Under-21, 8 full caps.

Season	Club	Apps	Goals
1984–85	Wolverhampton W	38	—
1985–86		25	—
1985–86	*Southampton*	—	—
1986–87	Southampton	9	—
1986–87	*Swindon T*	2	—
1987–88	Southampton	9	—
1987–88	*Swindon T*	5	—
1988–89	Southampton	7	—
1989–90		35	—
1990–91		37	—
1991–92		41	—
1992–93		42	—
1993–94		12	—
1993–94	Blackburn R	29	—
1994–95		39	—
1995–96		37	—

FLYNN, Mike

Born Oldham 23.2.69 Ht 6 0 Wt 11 02
Defender. From Trainee.

Season	Club	Apps	Goals
1986–87	Oldham Ath	—	—
1987–88		31	1
1988–89		9	—
1988–89	Norwich C	—	—
1989–90		—	—
1989–90	Preston NE	23	1
1990–91		35	1
1991–92		43	3
1992–93		35	2
1992–93	Stockport Co	10	—
1993–94		46	1
1994–95		43	2
1995–96		46	6

FLYNN, Sean

Born Birmingham 13.3.68 Ht 5 7
Wt 11 10
Midfield. From Halesowen T.

Season	Club	Apps	Goals
1991–92	Coventry C	22	2
1992–93		7	—
1993–94		36	3
1994–95		32	4
1995–96	Derby Co	42	2

FOLAN, Anthony

Born Lewisham 18.9.78 Ht 5 10
Wt 10 13
Midfield. From Trainee.

Season	Club	Apps	Goals
1995–96	Crystal Palace	—	—

FOLEY, Dominic

Born Dublin 7.7.76 Ht 6 1 Wt 12 08
Midfield. From St James Gate.

Season	Club	Apps	Goals
1995–96	Wolverhampton W	5	—

Season Club League Appearances/Goals

FOLEY, Steve

Born Liverpool 4.10.62 Ht 5 7 Wt 11 03
Midfield. From Apprentice.

Season	Club	Apps	Goals
1980–81	Liverpool	—	—
1981–82		—	—
1982–83		—	—
1983–84		—	—
1983–84	*Fulham*	3	—
1984–85	Grimsby T	31	2
1985–86	Sheffield U	28	5
1986–87		38	9
1987–88	Swindon T	35	4
1988–89		40	8
1989–90		23	4
1990–91		44	7
1991–92		9	—
1991–92	Stoke C	20	1
1992–93		44	7
1993–94		43	2
1994–95	Lincoln C	16	—
1995–96	Bradford C	1	—

FOOT, Danny

Born Edmonton 6.9.75 Ht 6 0 Wt 11 04
Defender. From Tottenham H Trainee.

Season	Club	Apps	Goals
1994–95	Southend U	3	—
1995–96		—	—

FORAN, Mark

Born Aldershot 30.10.73 Ht 6 4
Wt 14 03
Defender. From Trainee.

Season	Club	Apps	Goals
1991–92	Millwall	—	—
1992–93		—	—
1993–94		—	—
1993–94	Sheffield U	—	—
1994–95		4	1
1994–95	*Rotherham U*	3	—
1995–96	Sheffield U	7	—
1995–96	*Wycombe W*	5	—
1995–96	Peterborough U	17	1

FORBES, Steve

Born London 24.12.75 Ht 6 2 Wt 12 06
Midfield. From Sittingbourne.

Season	Club	Apps	Goals
1994–95	Millwall	1	—
1995–96		4	—

FORD, Bobby

Born Bristol 22.9.74 Ht 5 9 Wt 10 08
Midfield. From Trainee.

Season	Club	Apps	Goals
1992–93	Oxford U	—	—
1993–94		14	—
1994–95		23	2
1995–96		28	3

FORD, Gary

Born York 8.2.61 Ht 5 8 Wt 12 05
Midfield. From Apprentice.

Season	Club	Apps	Goals
1978–79	York C	33	4
1979–80		29	2
1980–81		43	4
1981–82		41	8
1982–83		45	11
1983–84		46	11
1984–85		44	5
1985–86		40	3
1986–87		45	4
1987–88	Leicester C	16	2
1987–88	Port Vale	23	3
1988–89		22	7
1989–90		—	—
1989–90	*Walsall*	13	2
1990–91	Port Vale	30	2
1990–91	Mansfield T	12	1
1991–92		39	4
1992–93		37	1
From Tromso, Harstad			
1995–96	Hartlepool U	3	—

FORD, John

Born Birmingham 12.4.68 Ht 6 2
Wt 13 04
Midfield. From Cradley T.

Season	Club	Apps	Goals
1991–92	Swansea C	44	—
1992–93		43	3
1993–94		27	1
1994–95		46	3
1995–96	Bradford C	19	—

FORD, Mark

Born Pontefract 10.10.75 Ht 5 7
Wt 10 08
Midfield. From Trainee. England Youth, Under-21.

Season	Club	Apps	Goals
1992–93	Leeds U	—	—

Season	Club	League Appearances/Goals	
1993–94		1	—
1994–95		—	—
1995–96		12	—

FORD, Mike

Born Bristol 9.2.66 Ht 6 0 Wt 12 06
Defender. From Apprentice.

Season	Club	Apps	Goals
1983–84	Leicester C	—	—
From Devizes			
1984–85	Cardiff C	20	1
1985–86		44	4
1986–87		36	1
1987–88		45	7
1988–89	Oxford U	10	1
1989–90		31	2
1990–91		28	1
1991–92		9	1
1992–93		44	4
1993–94		41	1
1994–95		18	—
1995–96		44	2

FORD, Tony

Born Grimsby 14.5.59 Ht 5 10 Wt 13 00
Defender. From Apprentice. England B.

Season	Club	Apps	Goals
1975–76	Grimsby T	14	—
1976–77		6	—
1977–78		34	2
1978–79		45	15
1979–80		37	5
1980–81		28	4
1981–82		35	7
1982–83		37	4
1983–84		42	8
1984–85		42	6
1985–86		34	3
1985–86	*Sunderland*	9	1
1986–87	Stoke C	41	6
1987–88		44	7
1988–89		27	—
1988–89	WBA	11	1
1989–90		42	8
1990–91		46	5
1991–92		15	—
1991–92	Grimsby T	22	1
1992–93		17	2
1993–94		29	—
1993–94	*Bradford C*	5	—
1994–95	Scunthorpe U	38	2
1995–96		38	7

FOREMAN, Matt

Born Gateshead 15.2.75 Ht 6 0
Wt 12 04
Defender. From Trainee.

Season	Club	Apps	Goals
1993–94	Sheffield U	—	—
1994–95		—	—
1995–96		—	—
1995–96	Scarborough	4	—

FORMBY, Kevin

Born Ormskirk 22.7.71 Ht 5 9 Wt 11 04
Defender. From Burscough.

Season	Club	Apps	Goals
1993–94	Rochdale	5	—
1994–95		28	—
1995–96		18	—

FORREST, Craig

Born Vancouver 20.9.67 Ht 6 5
Wt 14 00
Goalkeeper. From Apprentice. Canada full caps.

Season	Club	Apps	Goals
1985–86	Ipswich T	—	—
1986–87		—	—
1987–88		—	—
1987–88	*Colchester U*	11	—
1988–89	Ipswich T	28	—
1989–90		45	—
1990–91		43	—
1991–92		46	—
1992–93		11	—
1993–94		27	—
1994–95		36	—
1995–96		21	—

FORREST, Gordon

Born Dunfermline 14.1.77 Ht 5 6
Wt 8 02
Midfield. From Rosyth Recreation.

Season	Club	Apps	Goals
1994–95	Raith R	—	—
1995–96		1	—

FORRESTER, Jamie

Born Bradford 1.11.74 Ht 5 6 Wt 10 00
Forward. From Auxerre. England Youth.

Season	Club	Apps	Goals
1992–93	Leeds U	6	—
1993–94		3	—

Season	Club	League Appearances/Goals	
1994–95	....	—	—
1994–95	*Southend U*	5	—
1994–95	*Grimsby T*	9	1
1995–96	Leeds U	—	—
1995–96	Grimsby T	28	5

FORSTER, Nick

Born Oxted 8.9.73 Ht 5 9 Wt 10 12
Forward. From Horley T. England Under-21.

Season	Club	Apps	Goals
1992–93	Gillingham.................	26	6
1993–94	....	41	18
1994–95	Brentford..................	46	24
1995–96	....	38	5

FORSYTH, Mike

Born Liverpool 20.3.66 Ht 5 11
Wt 12 02
Defender. From Apprentice. England Youth, Under-21, B.

Season	Club	Apps	Goals
1983–84	WBA.........................	8	—
1984–85	....	10	—
1985–86	....	11	—
1985–86	*Northampton T*	—	—
1985–86	Derby Co..................	—	—
1986–87	....	41	1
1987–88	....	39	3
1988–89	....	38	—
1989–90	....	38	—
1990–91	....	35	—
1991–92	....	43	1
1992–93	....	41	1
1993–94	....	28	2
1994–95	....	22	—
1994–95	Notts Co....................	7	—
1995–96	....	—	—

FORSYTH, Richard

Born Dudley 3.10.70 Ht 5 10 Wt 12 04
Midfield. From Kidderminster H.

Season	Club	Apps	Goals
1995–96	Birmingham C...........	26	2

FORTUNE-WEST, Leo

Born Newham 9.4.71 Ht 6 3 Wt 13 10
Forward. From Stevenage Borough.

Season	Club	Apps	Goals
1995–96	Gillingham.................	40	12

FOSTER, Adrian

Born Kidderminster 19.3.71 Ht 5 9
Wt 11 00
Forward. From Trainee.

Season	Club	Apps	Goals
1989–90	WBA.........................	14	1
1990–91	....	5	—
1991–92	....	8	1
1992–93	Torquay U................	36	9
1993–94	....	39	15
1994–95	Gillingham.................	29	8
1995–96	....	11	1
1995–96	*Exeter C*	7	—

FOSTER, Colin

Born Chislehurst 16.7.64 Ht 6 4
Wt 14 01
Defender. From Apprentice.

Season	Club	Apps	Goals
1981–82	Orient........................	23	2
1982–83	....	43	2
1983–84	....	11	1
1984–85	....	42	1
1985–86	....	36	2
1986–87	....	19	2
1986–87	Nottingham F............	9	1
1987–88	....	39	2
1988–89	....	18	2
1989–90	....	6	—
1989–90	West Ham U	22	1
1990–91	....	36	3
1991–92	....	24	—
1992–93	....	6	1
1993–94	....	5	—
1993–94	*Notts Co*	9	—
1993–94	Watford....................	6	1
1994–95	....	34	2
1995–96	....	26	5

FOSTER, John

Born Manchester 19.9.73 Ht 5 11
Wt 13 02
Defender. From Trainee.

Season	Club	Apps	Goals
1992–93	Manchester C............	—	—
1993–94	....	1	—
1994–95	....	11	—
1995–96	....	4	—

FOSTER, Lee

Born Bishop Auckland 21.10.77
Forward. From Trainee.

Season	Club	Apps	Goals
1995–96	Hartlepool U............	1	—

FOSTER, Martin

Born Sheffield 29.10.77 Ht 5 5 Wt 9 10
Midfield. From Trainee.

1994–95	Leeds U	—	—
1995–96		—	—

FOSTER, Steve

Born Portsmouth 24.9.57 Ht 6 1
Wt 14 00
Defender. From Apprentice. England Under-21, 3 full caps.

1975–76	Portsmouth	11	—
1976–77		31	1
1977–78		31	3
1978–79		36	2
1979–80	Brighton & HA	38	1
1980–81		42	1
1981–82		40	2
1982–83		36	1
1983–84		16	1
1983–84	Aston Villa	7	1
1984–85		8	2
1984–85	Luton T	25	1
1985–86		35	3
1986–87		28	2
1987–88		39	2
1988–89		36	3
1989–90	Oxford U	35	4
1990–91		38	3
1991–92		22	2
1992–93	Brighton & HA	35	4
1993–94		34	2
1994–95		38	—
1995–96		8	1

FOSTER, Wayne

Born Leigh 11.9.63 Ht 5 8 Wt 11 00
Forward. From Apprentice. England Youth.

1981–82	Bolton W	23	2
1982–83		24	4
1983–84		30	3
1984–85		28	4
1985–86	Preston NE	31	3
1986–87	Hearts	31	4
1987–88		39	4
1988–89		9	1
1989–90		17	1
1990–91		28	1
1991–92		7	—
1992–93		11	—
1993–94		17	1
1994–95	Partick T	16	7
1994–95	*Hartlepool U*	4	1
1995–96	Partick T	19	1

FOWLER, Jason

Born Bristol 20.8.74 Ht 6 1 Wt 11 13
Midfield. From Trainee.

1992–93	Bristol C	1	—
1993–94		1	—
1994–95		13	—
1995–96		10	—

FOWLER, John

Born Preston 27.10.74 Ht 5 10 Wt 12 03
Midfield. From Trainee.

1991–92	Cambridge U	—	—
1992–93		3	—
1992–93	*Preston NE*	6	—
1993–94	Cambridge U	20	—
1994–95		16	—
1995–96		2	—

FOWLER, Robbie

Born Liverpool 9.4.75 Ht 5 11 Wt 11 10
Forward. From Trainee. England Youth, B, Under-21, 5 full caps.

1991–92	Liverpool	—	—
1992–93		—	—
1993–94		28	12
1994–95		42	25
1995–96		38	28

FOX, Mark

Born Basingstoke 17.11.75 Ht 5 11
Wt 10 05
Midfield. From Trainee.

1993–94	Brighton & HA	12	—
1994–95		9	1
1995–96		2	—

FOX, Peter

Born Scunthorpe 5.7.57 Ht 5 11
Wt 13 10
Goalkeeper. From Apprentice.

1972–73	Sheffield W	1	—
1973–74		—	—
1974–75		20	—
1975–76		27	—

Season	Club	League Appearances/Goals	
1976–77		1	—
1976–77	*West Ham U*	—	—
1977–78	Sheffield W	—	—
1977–78	*Barnsley*	1	—
1977–78	Stoke C	—	—
1978–79		1	—
1979–80		23	—
1980–81		42	—
1981–82		38	—
1982–83		35	—
1983–84		42	—
1984–85		14	—
1985–86		37	—
1986–87		39	—
1987–88		17	—
1988–89		29	—
1989–90		38	—
1990–91		44	—
1991–92		—	—
1992–93		10	—
1992–93	*Wrexham*	—	—
1993–94	Exeter C	26	—
1994–95		31	—
1995–96		46	—

FOX, Ruel

Born Ipswich 14.1.68 Ht 5 6 Wt 10 00
Midfield. From Apprentice. England B.

Season	Club	Apps	Goals
1985–86	Norwich C	—	—
1986–87		3	—
1987–88		34	2
1988–89		4	—
1989–90		7	3
1990–91		28	4
1991–92		37	2
1992–93		34	4
1993–94		25	7
1993–94	Newcastle U	14	2
1994–95		40	10
1995–96		4	—
1995–96	Tottenham H	26	6

FOX, Simon

Born Basingstoke 28.8.77 Ht 5 10
Wt 9 08
Forward. From Trainee.

Season	Club	Apps	Goals
1993–94	Brighton & HA	1	—
1994–95		2	—
1995–96		6	—

FOYLE, Martin

Born Salisbury 2.5.63 Ht 5 10 Wt 11 02
Forward. From Amateur.

Season	Club	Apps	Goals
1980–81	Southampton	—	—
1981–82		—	—
1982–83		7	1
1983–84		5	—
1983–84	*Blackburn R*	—	—
1984–85	Aldershot	44	15
1985–86		20	9
1986–87		34	11
1986–87	Oxford U	4	—
1987–88		33	10
1988–89		40	14
1989–90		13	2
1990–91		36	10
1991–92	Port Vale	43	11
1992–93		16	4
1993–94		37	18
1994–95		42	16
1995–96		25	8

FRAIL, Stephen

Born Glasgow 10.8.69 Ht 5 9 Wt 10 09
Midfield. From Possilpark YM.

Season	Club	Apps	Goals
1985–86	Dundee	—	—
1986–87		—	—
1987–88		4	—
1988–89		23	1
1989–90		6	—
1990–91		26	—
1991–92		3	—
1992–93		7	—
1993–94		32	—
1993–94	Hearts	9	2
1994–95		25	2
1995–96		—	—

FRAIN, John

Born Birmingham 8.10.68 Ht 5 7
Wt 11 00
Midfield. From Apprentice.

Season	Club	Apps	Goals
1985–86	Birmingham C	3	—
1986–87		3	1
1987–88		14	2
1988–89		28	3
1989–90		38	1
1990–91		42	3
1991–92		44	5
1992–93		45	6
1993–94		26	2

Season	Club	League Appearances/Goals	
1994–95		7	—
1995–96		23	—

FRANCIS, John

Born Dewsbury 12.11.63 Ht 5 8
Wt 12 13
Forward. From Emley.

Season	Club	Apps	Goals
1987–88	Halifax T	4	—
1988–89	Sheffield U	22	1
1989–90		20	5
1989–90	Burnley	19	4
1990–91		45	14
1991–92		37	8
1992–93	Cambridge U	29	3
1992–93	Burnley	9	1
1993–94		43	7
1994–95		2	—
1995–96		22	2

FRANCIS, Kevin

Born Moseley 6.12.67 Ht 6 7 Wt 15 00
Forward. From Mile Oak R.

Season	Club	Apps	Goals
1988–89	Derby Co	—	—
1989–90		8	—
1990–91		2	—
1990–91	Stockport Co	13	5
1991–92		35	15
1992–93		42	28
1993–94		45	28
1994–95		17	12
1994–95	Birmingham C	15	8
1995–96		19	3

FRANCIS, Steve

Born Billericay 29.5.64 Ht 6 1 Wt 14 00
Goalkeeper. From Apprentice. England Youth.

Season	Club	Apps	Goals
1981–82	Chelsea	29	—
1982–83		37	—
1983–84		—	—
1984–85		2	—
1985–86		3	—
1986–87		—	—
1986–87	Reading	14	—
1987–88		34	—
1988–89		22	—
1989–90		46	—
1990–91		34	—
1991–92		32	—
1992–93		34	—
1993–94	Huddersfield T	46	—
1994–95		43	—
1995–96		43	—

FRANKS, Michael

Born Edmonton 20.4.77 Ht 6 5
Wt 12 10
Goalkeeper.

Season	Club	Apps	Goals
1995–96	Bradford C	—	—

FRASER, James

Born Swindon 22.10.76
Forward.

Season	Club	Apps	Goals
1995–96	Portsmouth	—	—

FREEDMAN, Dougie

Born Glasgow 21.1.74 Ht 5 9 Wt 11 00
Forward. From Trainee. Scotland Under-21.

Season	Club	Apps	Goals
1991–92	QPR	—	—
1992–93		—	—
1993–94		—	—
1994–95	Barnet	42	24
1995–96		5	3
1995–96	Crystal Palace	39	2

FREEMAN, Andy

Born Reading 8.9.77
Forward. From Crystal Palace Trainee.

Season	Club	Apps	Goals
1995–96	Reading	1	—

FREEMAN, Darren

Born Brighton 22.8.73 Ht 5 10 Wt 13 01
Forward. From Horsham T.

Season	Club	Apps	Goals
1994–95	Gillingham	2	—
1995–96		10	—

FREEMAN, Nathan

Born Portsmouth 5.8.77
Goalkeeper. From Trainee.

Season	Club	Apps	Goals
1995–96	Manchester C	—	—

FREESTONE, Chris

Born Nottingham 4.9.71
Forward. From Arnold T.

Season	Club	Apps	Goals
1994–95	Middlesbrough	1	—
1995–96		3	1

FREESTONE, Roger

Born Newport 19.8.68 Ht 6 3 Wt 14 06
Goalkeeper. From Trainee. Wales Under-21.

Season	Club	Apps	Goals
1986–87	Newport Co	13	—
1986–87	Chelsea	6	—
1987–88		15	—
1988–89		21	—
1989–90		—	—
1989–90	*Swansea C*	14	—
1989–90	*Hereford U*	8	—
1990–91	Chelsea	—	—
1991–92	Swansea C	42	—
1992–93		46	—
1993–94		46	—
1994–95		45	1
1995–96		45	2

FRENCH, Hamish

Born Aberdeen 7.2.64 Ht 5 10 Wt 11 07
Midfield. From Keith.

Season	Club	Apps	Goals
1987–88	Dundee U	20	2
1988–89		18	3
1989–90		12	2
1990–91		19	3
1991–92		6	1
1991–92	Dunfermline Ath	31	2
1992–93		38	12
1993–94		36	15
1994–95		25	12
1995–96		23	4

FRENCH, John

Born Bristol 25.9.76 Ht 5 10 Wt 10 10
Forward. From Trainee.

Season	Club	Apps	Goals
1995–96	Bristol R	10	1

FRIARS, Sean

Born Derry 15.5.79
Midfield. From Trainee

Season	Club	Apps	Goals
1995–96	Liverpool		

FRIDGE, Les

Born Inverness 27.8.68 Ht 5 11
Wt 11 10
Goalkeeper. From Inverness Thistle. Scotland Under-21, Youths.

Season	Club	Apps	Goals
1985–86	Chelsea	1	—
1986–87		—	—
1986–87	St Mirren	1	—
1987–88		3	—
1988–89		15	—
1989–90		8	—
1990–91		11	—
1991–92		14	—
1992–93		18	—
1993–94	Clyde	42	—
1994–95		26	—
1995–96	Raith R	1	—

FROGGATT, Steve

Born Lincoln 9.3.73 Ht 5 10 Wt 11 00
Midfield. From Trainee England Under-21.

Season	Club	Apps	Goals
1990–91	Aston Villa	—	—
1991–92		9	—
1992–93		17	1
1993–94		9	1
1994–95	Wolverhampton W	20	2
1995–96		18	1

FRONTZECK, Michael

Born Germany 26.3.64 Ht 5 11 Wt 12 12
Defender. From Odenkirchen. Germany 19 full caps.

Season	Club	Apps	Goals
1983–84	Moenchengladbach	33	5
1984–85		31	3
1985–86		28	—
1986–87		34	5
1987–88		33	3
1988–89		31	1
1989–90	Stuttgart	31	4
1990–91		32	5
1991–92		38	5
1992–93		32	1
1993–94		30	1
1994–95	Bochum	28	2
1995–96	Moenchengladbach	8	—
1995–96	Manchester C	12	—

FRY, Chris

Born Cardiff 23.10.69 Ht 5 8 Wt 10 07
Forward. From Trainee.

Season	Club	App	Goals
1988–89	Cardiff C	9	—
1989–90		23	1
1990–91		23	—
1991–92	Hereford U	37	3
1992–93		37	4
1993–94		16	3
1993–94	Colchester U	17	—
1994–95		33	8
1995–96		38	2

FUCHS, Uwe

Born Germany 23.7.66 Ht 6 2 Wt 12 00
Forward. From Pirmasens.

Season	Club	App	Goals
1984–85	Homburg	21	1
1985–86		37	8
1986–87		2	—
1986–87	Stuttgart Kickers	10	2
1987–88	Fortuna Cologne	36	14
1988–89		31	22
1989–90	Fortuna Dusseldorf	25	7
1990–91	Cologne	—	—
1991–92		3	—
1992–93		16	4
1993–94	Kaiserslautern	19	3
1994–95	Middlesbrough	15	9
1995–96	Millwall	32	5

FULTON, Stephen

Born Greenock 10.8.70 Ht 5 10
Wt 11 00
Midfield. From Celtic BC. Scotland Under-21.

Season	Club	App	Goals
1986–87	Celtic	—	—
1987–88		—	—
1988–89		3	—
1989–90		16	—
1990–91		21	—
1991–92		30	2
1992–93		6	—
1993–94	Bolton W	4	—
1993–94	*Peterborough U*	3	—
1994–95	Falkirk	28	3
1995–96		5	—
1995–96	Hearts	26	2

FURLONG, Carl

Born Liverpool 18.10.76 Ht 5 11
Wt 12 06
Forward.

Season	Club	App	Goals
1993–94	Wigan Ath	2	1
1994–95		1	—
1995–96		—	—

FURLONG, Paul

Born London 1.10.68 Ht 6 0 Wt 13 08
Forward. From Enfield. England semi-pro.

Season	Club	App	Goals
1991–92	Coventry C	37	4
1992–93	Watford	41	19
1993–94		38	18
1994–95	Chelsea	36	10
1995–96		28	3

FURNELL, Andy

Born Peterborough 13.2.77 Ht 5 10
Wt 12 05
Forward. From Trainee. England Youth.

Season	Club	App	Goals
1993–94	Peterborough U	10	1
1994–95		8	—
1995–96		1	—

FUTCHER, Andy

Born Enfield 10.2.78 Ht 5 7 Wt 10 07
Defender. From Trainee. England Youth.

Season	Club	App	Goals
1994–95	Wimbledon	—	—
1995–96		—	—

FUTCHER, Paul

Born Chester 25.9.56 Ht 6 0 Wt 12 03
Defender. From Apprentice. England Under-21, Football League.

Season	Club	App	Goals
1972–73	Chester	2	—
1973–74		18	—
1974–75	Luton T	19	—
1975–76		41	—
1976–77		40	1
1977–78		31	—
1978–79	Manchester C	24	—
1979–80		13	—
1980–81	Oldham Ath	36	1
1981–82		37	—
1982–83		25	—
1982–83	Derby Co	17	—
1983–84		18	—
1983–84	Barnsley	10	—
1984–85		36	—

Season	Club	League Appearances/Goals	
1985–86		37	—
1986–87		36	—
1987–88		41	—
1988–89		41	—
1989–90		29	—
1990–91	Halifax T	15	—
1990–91	Grimsby T	22	—
1991–92		29	—
1992–93		35	—
1993–94		39	—
1994–95		7	—
1995–96		—	—

FUTCHER, Stephen

Born Chester 24.10.76
Midfield. From Trainee.

Season	Club	League Appearances/Goals	
1995–96	Wrexham	—	—

GABBIADINI, Marco

Born Nottingham 20.1.68 Ht 5 10
Wt 13 00
Forward. From Apprentice. England Under-21, B.

Season	Club	League Appearances/Goals	
1984–85	York C	1	—
1985–86		22	4
1986–87		29	9
1987–88		8	1
1987–88	Sunderland	35	21
1988–89		36	18
1989–90		46	21
1990–91		31	9
1991–92		9	5
1991–92	Crystal Palace	15	5
1991–92	Derby Co	20	6
1992–93		44	9
1993–94		39	13
1994–95		32	11
1995–96		39	11

GAGE, Kevin

Born Chiswick 21.4.64 Ht 5 9 Wt 11 07
Defender. From Apprentice. England Youth.

Season	Club	League Appearances/Goals	
1980–81	Wimbledon	1	—
1981–82		21	1
1982–83		26	4
1983–84		24	4
1984–85		37	2
1985–86		29	1
1986–87		30	3
1987–88	Aston Villa	44	2
1988–89		28	3
1989–90		22	3
1990–91		21	—
1991–92		—	—
1991–92	Sheffield U	22	2
1992–93		27	—
1993–94		21	—
1994–95		40	5
1995–96		2	—
1995–96	Preston NE	7	—

GAIN, Peter

Born Hammersmith 11.11.76 Ht 6 1
Wt 12 09
Midfield. From Trainee.

Season	Club	League Appearances/Goals	
1995–96	Tottenham H	—	—

Season Club League Appearances/Goals

GALE, Shaun

Born Reading 8.10.69 Ht 6 1 Wt 11 10
Defender. From Trainee.

Season	Club	Apps	Goals
1989–90	Portsmouth	—	—
1990–91		3	—
1991–92		—	—
1992–93		—	—
1993–94		—	—
1994–95	Barnet	27	2
1995–96		44	1

GALE, Tony

Born London 19.11.59 Ht 6 1 Wt 13 07
Defender. From Apprentice. England Youth, Under-21.

Season	Club	Apps	Goals
1977–78	Fulham	38	8
1978–79		36	2
1979–80		42	4
1980–81		40	1
1981–82		44	1
1982–83		42	2
1983–84		35	1
1984–85	West Ham U	37	—
1985–86		42	—
1986–87		32	2
1987–88		18	—
1988–89		31	—
1989–90		36	1
1990–91		24	1
1991–92		25	—
1992–93		23	1
1993–94		32	—
1994–95	Blackburn R	15	—
1995–96	Crystal Palace	2	—

GALLACHER, Kevin

Born Clydebank 23.11.66 Ht 5 8 Wt 11 03
Forward. From Duntocher BC. Scotland Youth, Under-21, B, 23 full caps.

Season	Club	Apps	Goals
1983–84	Dundee U	—	—
1984–85		—	—
1985–86		20	3
1986–87		37	10
1987–88		26	4
1988–89		31	9
1989–90		17	1
1989–90	Coventry C	15	3
1990–91		32	11
1991–92		33	8
1992–93		20	6
1992–93	Blackburn R	9	5
1993–94		30	7
1994–95		1	1
1995–96		16	2

GALLAGHER, Ian

Born Hartlepool 30.5.78
Midfield. From Trainee.

Season	Club	Apps	Goals
1995–96	Hartlepool U	1	—

GALLAGHER, Kieran

Born Barnet 23.12.76 Ht 5 8 Wt 10 03
Midfield. From Trainee.

Season	Club	Apps	Goals
1995–96	Barnet	—	—

GALLAGHER, Tommy

Born Nottingham 25.8.74 Ht 5 10 Wt 10 08
Defender. From Trainee.

Season	Club	Apps	Goals
1992–93	Notts Co.	—	—
1993–94		13	—
1994–95		7	—
1995–96		22	2

GALLEN, Kevin

Born Hammersmith 21.9.75 Ht 5 11 Wt 12 10
Forward. From Trainee. England Youth, Under-21.

Season	Club	Apps	Goals
1992–93	QPR	—	—
1993–94		—	—
1994–95		37	10
1995–96		30	8

GALLEN, Stephen

Born Acton 21.11.73 Ht 6 2 Wt 13 00
Defender. From Trainee. Eire Under-21.

Season	Club	Apps	Goals
1991–92	QPR	—	—
1992–93		—	—
1993–94		—	—
1994–95	Doncaster R	—	—
1995–96		—	—

GALLIMORE, Tony

Born Crewe 21.2.72 Ht 5 11 Wt 12 12
Defender. From Trainee.

Season	Club	Apps	Goals
1989–90	Stoke C	1	—
1990–91		7	—
1991–92		3	—

Season	Club	Apps	Goals
1991–92	*Carlisle U*	16	—
1992–93	Stoke C	—	—
1992–93	*Carlisle U*	8	1
1993–94	Carlisle U	40	1
1994–95		40	5
1995–96		36	2
1995–96	Grimsby T	10	1

GALLOWAY, Mick

Born Nottingham 13.10.74 Ht 5 11 Wt 11 05
Midfield. From Trainee.

Season	Club	Apps	Goals
1993–94	Notts Co	—	—
1994–95		7	—
1995–96		9	—

GAMBARO, Enzo

Born Genoa 23.2.66
Midfield. From Bolton W.

Season	Club	Apps	Goals
1995–96	Grimsby T	1	—

GANNON, Jim

Born Southwark 7.9.68 Ht 6 2 Wt 13 00
Defender. From Dundalk.

Season	Club	Apps	Goals
1988–89	Sheffield U	—	—
1989–90		—	—
1989–90	*Halifax T*	2	—
1989–90	Stockport Co	7	1
1990–91		41	6
1991–92		43	16
1992–93		46	12
1993–94		35	4
1993–94	*Notts Co*	2	—
1994–95	Stockport Co	45	7
1995–96		23	1

GANNON, John

Born Wimbledon 18.12.66 Ht 5 9 Wt 10 10
Midfield. From Apprentice.

Season	Club	Apps	Goals
1984–85	Wimbledon	—	—
1985–86		1	1
1986–87		2	—
1986–87	*Crewe Alex*	15	—
1987–88	Wimbledon	13	1
1988–89		—	—
1988–89	*Sheffield U*	16	1
1989–90	Sheffield U	39	3
1990–91		22	—
1991–92		32	1
1992–93		27	1
1993–94		14	—
1993–94	*Middlesbrough*	7	—
1994–95	Sheffield U	12	—
1995–96		12	—
1995–96	Oldham Ath	5	—

GARDNER, David

Born Salford 17.9.76 Ht 5 9 Wt 11 00
Midfield. From Manchester U Trainee.

Season	Club	Apps	Goals
1995–96	Manchester C	—	—

GARDNER, Jimmy

Born Dunfermline 27.9.67 Ht 5 10 Wt 10 02
Defender. From Ayresome North.

Season	Club	Apps	Goals
1986–87	Queen's Park	1	—
1987–88		1	—
1988–89	Motherwell	—	—
1989–90		1	—
1990–91		—	—
1991–92		12	—
1992–93		3	—
1993–94	St Mirren	21	1
1994–95		20	—
1995–96	Scarborough	6	1
1995–96	Cardiff C	35	4

GARLAND, Peter

Born Croydon 20.1.71 Ht 5 10 Wt 12 00
Midfield. From Trainee. England Youth.

Season	Club	Apps	Goals
1989–90	Tottenham H	—	—
1990–91		1	—
1991–92		—	—
1991–92	Newcastle U	2	—
1992–93		—	—
1992–93	Charlton Ath	13	1
1993–94		27	1
1994–95		10	—
1994–95	*Wycombe W*	5	—
1995–96	Charlton Ath	3	—

GARNER, Darren

Born Plymouth 10.12.71 Ht 5 9 Wt 12 07
Midfield. From Dorchester T.

Season	Club	Apps	Goals
1995–96	Rotherham U	31	1

Season	Club	League Appearances/Goals	

GARNER, Simon

Born Boston 23.11.59 Ht 5 8 Wt 13 00
Forward. From Apprentice.

1978–79	Blackburn R	25	8
1979–80		28	6
1980–81		33	7
1981–82		36	14
1982–83		41	22
1983–84		42	19
1984–85		37	12
1985–86		38	12
1986–87		40	10
1987–88		40	14
1988–89		44	20
1989–90		43	18
1990–91		12	1
1991–92		25	5
1992–93	WBA	25	8
1993–94		8	—
1993–94	Wycombe W	12	3
1994–95		41	9
1995–96		13	2
1995–96	*Torquay U*	11	1

GARNETT, Shaun

Born Wallasey 22.11.69 Ht 6 3 Wt 13 04
Defender. From Trainee.

1987–88	Tranmere R	1	—
1988–89		—	—
1989–90		4	—
1990–91		16	1
1991–92		8	—
1992–93		5	1
1992–93	*Chester C*	9	—
1992–93	*Preston NE*	10	2
1992–93	*Wigan Ath*	13	1
1993–94	Tranmere R	26	2
1994–95		34	1
1995–96		18	—
1995–96	Swansea C	9	—

GARVEY, Steve

Born Tameside 22.11.73 Ht 5 9
Wt 10 09
Forward. From Trainee.

1990–91	Crewe Alex	1	—
1991–92		11	—
1992–93		10	1
1993–94		—	—
1994–95		28	3
1995–96		29	2

GASCOIGNE, Paul

Born Gateshead 27.5.67 Ht 5 10
Wt 11 07
Midfield. From Apprentice. England, Under-21 B, 43 full caps.

1984–85	Newcastle U	2	—
1985–86		31	9
1986–87		24	5
1987–88		35	7
1988–89	Tottenham H	32	6
1989–90		34	6
1990–91		26	7
1991–92		—	—
1992–93	Lazio	22	4
1993–94		17	2
1994–95		2	—
1995–96	Rangers	28	14

GAUDINO, Maurizio

Born Brule 12.12.66 Ht 5 11 Wt 12 02
Midfield. From Eintracht Frankfurt.

1994–95	Manchester C	20	3
1995–96		—	—

GAUGHAN, Kevin

Born Glasgow 6.3.78
Defender.

1994–95	Ipswich T	—	—
1995–96		—	—

GAUGHAN, Steve

Born Doncaster 14.4.70 Ht 6 0 Wt 13 08
Midfield. From Hatfield Main.

1987–88	Doncaster R	4	—
1988–89		34	2
1989–90		29	1
1990–91	Sunderland	—	—
1991–92		—	—
1991–92	Darlington	20	—
1992–93		37	1
1993–94		32	3
1994–95		41	8
1995–96		41	3

GAVIN, Mark

Born Baillieston 10.12.63 Ht 5 9
Wt 11 01
Midfield. From Apprentice.

1981–82	Leeds U	—	—
1982–83		7	1

Season	Club	League Appearances/Goals	
1983–84	....	12	1
1984–85	....	11	1
1984–85	*Hartlepool U*	7	—
1985–86	Carlisle U..................	13	1
1985–86	Bolton W	8	1
1986–87	....	41	2
1987–88	Rochdale....................	23	6
1987–88	Hearts	7	—
1988–89	....	2	—
1988–89	Bristol C....................	29	3
1989–90	....	40	3
1990–91	Watford......................	13	—
1991–92	....	—	—
1991–92	Bristol C....................	14	1
1992–93	....	19	1
1993–94	....	8	—
1993–94	Exeter C....................	12	—
1994–95	....	37	2
1995–96	....	28	2

GAVIN, Pat

Born Hammersmith 5.6.67 Ht 6 0
Wt 12 00
Forward. From Hanwell T.

Season	Club	Apps	Goals
1988–89	Gillingham.................	13	7
1989–90	Leicester C	—	—
1989–90	*Gillingham*.................	34	1
1990–91	Leicester C	3	—
1990–91	Peterborough U.........	11	5
1991–92	....	11	—
1992–93	....	1	—
1992–93	Barnet	—	—
1992–93	Northampton T..........	14	4
1993–94	Wigan Ath..................	30	6
1994–95	....	12	2
1995–96	Crewe Alex	—	—

GAYLE, Brian

Born Kingston 6.3.65 Ht 6 2 Wt 13 12
Defender.

Season	Club	Apps	Goals
1984–85	Wimbledon.................	12	1
1985–86	....	13	—
1986–87	....	32	1
1987–88	....	26	1
1988–89	Manchester C............	41	3
1989–90	....	14	—
1989–90	Ipswich T	20	—
1990–91	....	33	4
1991–92	....	5	—
1991–92	Sheffield U.................	33	3
1992–93	....	31	2
1993–94	....	13	3
1994–95	....	35	1
1995–96	....	5	—

GAYLE, John

Born Birmingham 30.7.64 Ht 6 3
Wt 15 00
Forward. From Burton Alb.

Season	Club	Apps	Goals
1988–89	Wimbledon.................	2	—
1989–90	....	11	1
1990–91	....	7	1
1990–91	Birmingham C............	22	6
1991–92	....	3	1
1992–93	....	19	3
1993–94	....	—	—
1993–94	*Walsall*......................	4	1
1993–94	Coventry C	3	—
1994–95	....	—	—
1994–95	Burnley	14	3
1994–95	Stoke C	4	—
1995–96	....	10	3
1995–96	*Gillingham*................	9	3

GAYLE, Marcus

Born Hammersmith 27.9.70 Ht 6 1
Wt 12 09
Midfield. From Trainee. England Youth.

Season	Club	Apps	Goals
1988–89	Brentford..................	3	—
1989–90	....	9	—
1990–91	....	33	6
1991–92	....	38	6
1992–93	....	38	4
1993–94	....	35	6
1993–94	Wimbledon.................	10	—
1994–95	....	23	2
1995–96	....	34	5

GAYLE, Mark

Born Bromsgrove 21.10.69 Ht 6 2
Wt 12 03
Goalkeeper. From Trainee.

Season	Club	Apps	Goals
1988–89	Leicester C	—	—
1989–90	Blackpool	—	—
From Worcester C			
1991–92	Walsall	24	—
1992–93	....	41	—
1993–94	....	10	—
1993–94	Crewe Alex	8	—
1993–94	*Liverpool*....................	—	—
1994–95	Crewe Alex	25	—
1995–96	....	46	—

Season	Club	League Appearances/Goals	

GEDDES, Bobby

Born Inverness 12.8.60 Ht 6 0 Wt 11 04
Goalkeeper. From Ross County. Scotland Under-21.

1977–78	Dundee	—	—
1978–79		—	—
1979–80		—	—
1980–81		20	—
1981–82		28	—
1982–83		1	—
1983–84		24	—
1984–85		16	—
1985–86		36	—
1986–87		44	—
1987–88		38	—
1988–89		34	—
1989–90		12	—
1990–91	Kilmarnock	38	—
1991–92		33	—
1992–93		44	—
1993–94		44	—
1994–95		12	—
1995–96		2	—
1995–96	Raith R	9	—

GEE, Phil

Born Pelsall 19.12.64 Ht 5 11 Wt 12 06
Forward. From Riley Sports, Gresley R.

1985–86	Derby Co	4	2
1986–87		41	15
1987–88		38	6
1988–89		12	1
1989–90		8	1
1990–91		2	—
1991–92		19	1
1991–92	Leicester C	14	2
1992–93		18	4
1993–94		12	1
1994–95		7	2
1994–95	*Plymouth Arg*	6	—
1995–96	Leicester C	2	—

GEMMILL, Scot

Born Paisley 2.1.71 Ht 5 11 Wt 11 06
Midfield. From School. Scotland Under-21, 6 full caps.

1989–90	Nottingham F	—	—
1990–91		4	—
1991–92		39	8
1992–93		33	1
1993–94		31	8
1994–95		19	1
1995–96		31	1

GEORGE, Daniel

Born Lincoln 22.10.78 Ht 6 1 Wt 12 01
Defender. From Trainee.

1995–96	Nottingham F	—	—

GERMAINE, Gary

Born Birmingham 2.8.76 Ht 6 0
Wt 11 07
Goalkeeper. From Trainee.

1994–95	WBA	—	—
1995–96		—	—
1995–96	*Scunthorpe U*	11	—

GERRARD, Paul

Born Heywood 22.1.73 Ht 6 2 Wt 13 01
Goalkeeper. From Trainee. England Under-21.

1991–92	Oldham Ath	—	—
1992–93		25	—
1993–94		16	—
1994–95		42	—
1995–96		36	1

GIBB, Ali

Born Salisbury 17.2.76 Ht 5 9 Wt 11 07
Midfield. From Trainee.

1994–95	Norwich C	—	—
1995–96		—	—
1995–96	Northampton T	23	2

GIBBS, Nigel

Born St Albans 20.11.65 Ht 5 7
Wt 11 01
Defender. From Apprentice. England Youth, Under-21.

1983–84	Watford	3	—
1984–85		12	—
1985–86		40	1
1986–87		15	—
1987–88		30	—
1988–89		46	1
1989–90		41	—
1990–91		34	—
1991–92		43	1
1992–93		7	—
1993–94		—	—

Season	Club	League Appearances	Goals
1994–95		11	—
1995–96		9	—

GIBBS, Paul

Born Gorleston 26.10.72 Ht 5 10
Wt 11 03
Defender. From Diss T.

Season	Club	League Appearances	Goals
1994–95	Colchester U	9	—
1995–96		24	3

GIBSON, Andrew

Born Dechmont 2.2.69 Ht 5 8 Wt 11 04
Midfield. From Gairdoch U.

Season	Club	League Appearances	Goals
1987–88	Stirling Albion	5	—
1988–89		12	1
1988–89	Aberdeen	—	—
1989–90		—	—
1990–91		—	—
1991–92		5	—
1992–93		1	1
1993–94		2	—
1993–94	Partick T	11	—
1993–94	*Stockport Co*	—	—
1994–95	Partick T	11	1
1995–96		22	1

GIBSON, Colin

Born Bridport 6.4.60 Ht 5 8 Wt 11 04
Defender. From Apprentice. England Under-21, B.

Season	Club	League Appearances	Goals
1977–78	Aston Villa	—	—
1978–79		12	—
1979–80		31	2
1980–81		21	—
1981–82		23	—
1982–83		23	1
1983–84		28	1
1984–85		40	4
1985–86		7	2
1985–86	Manchester U	18	5
1986–87		24	1
1987–88		29	2
1988–89		2	—
1989–90		6	1
1990–91		—	—
1990–91	*Port Vale*	6	2
1990–91	Leicester C	18	1
1991–92		17	3
1992–93		9	—
1993–94		15	—
1994–95	Blackpool	2	—

Season	Club	League Appearances	Goals
1994–95	Walsall	33	—
1995–96		—	—

GIBSON, Paul

Born Sheffield 1.11.76 Ht 6 2 Wt 13 04
Goalkeeper. From Trainee.

Season	Club	League Appearances	Goals
1995–96	Manchester U	—	—

GIGGS, Ryan

Born Cardiff 29.11.73 Ht 5 11 Wt 10 07
Forward. From School. Wales Youth, Under-21, 16 full caps.

Season	Club	League Appearances	Goals
1990–91	Manchester U	2	1
1991–92		38	4
1992–93		41	9
1993–94		38	13
1994–95		29	1
1995–96		33	11

GILBERT, Dave

Born Lincoln 22.6.63 Ht 5 4 Wt 10 08
Midfield. From Apprentice.

Season	Club	League Appearances	Goals
1980–81	Lincoln C	1	—
1981–82		29	1
1982–83	Scunthorpe U	1	—
From Boston U			
1986–87	Northampton T	45	8
1987–88		41	6
1988–89		34	7
1988–89	Grimsby T	11	3
1989–90		45	10
1990–91		44	12
1991–92		41	2
1992–93		41	4
1993–94		37	4
1994–95		40	6
1995–96	WBA	40	5

GILBERT, Kenny

Born Aberdeen 8.3.75 Ht 5 8 Wt 10 11
Forward. From East End A.

Season	Club	League Appearances	Goals
1994–95	Aberdeen	—	—
1995–96	Hull C	13	—

GILCHRIST, Phil

Born Stockton 25.8.73 Ht 6 0 Wt 13 04
Defender. From Trainee.

Season	Club	League Appearances	Goals
1990–91	Nottingham F	—	—
1991–92	Middlesbrough	—	—

Season	Club	Apps	Goals
1992–93	Hartlepool U	24	—
1993–94		35	—
1994–95		23	—
1994–95	Oxford U	18	1
1995–96		42	3

GILKES, Michael

Born Hackney 20.7.65 Ht 5 8 Wt 10 10
Forward. From Leicester C.

Season	Club	Apps	Goals
1984–85	Reading	16	2
1985–86		9	2
1986–87		7	—
1987–88		39	4
1988–89		46	9
1989–90		42	2
1990–91		21	1
1991–92		20	—
1991–92	*Chelsea*	1	—
1991–92	*Southampton*	6	—
1992–93	Reading	38	12
1993–94		39	2
1994–95		40	8
1995–96		44	—

GILL, Wayne

Born Chorley 28.11.75 Ht 5 10 Wt 11 04
Midfield. From Trainee.

Season	Club	Apps	Goals
1994–95	Blackburn R	—	—
1995–96		—	—

GILLESPIE, Gary

Born Stirling 5.7.60 Ht 6 2 Wt 12 07
Defender. From Schools. Scotland Under-21, 13 full caps.

Season	Club	Apps	Goals
1977–78	Falkirk	22	—
1978–79	Coventry C	15	—
1979–80		38	1
1980–81		37	1
1981–82		40	2
1982–83		42	2
1983–84	Liverpool	—	—
1984–85		12	1
1985–86		14	3
1986–87		37	—
1987–88		35	4
1988–89		15	1
1989–90		13	4
1990–91		30	1
1991–92	Celtic	24	2
1992–93		18	—
1993–94		27	—
1994–95	Coventry C	3	—
1995–96		—	—

GILLESPIE, Keith

Born Larne 18.2.75 Ht 5 9 Wt 11 05
Forward. From Trainee. Northern Ireland Youth, 12 full caps.

Season	Club	Apps	Goals
1992–93	Manchester U	—	—
1993–94		—	—
1993–94	*Wigan Ath*	8	4
1994–95	Manchester U	9	1
1994–95	Newcastle U	17	2
1995–96		28	4

GINOLA, David

Born Gassin 25.1.67 Ht 6 0 Wt 11 10
Forward. France 16 full caps.

Season	Club	Apps	Goals
1985–86	Toulon	14	—
1986–87		34	—
1987–88		33	4
1988–89	Racing Paris	29	7
1989–90		32	1
1990–91	Brest	33	1
1991–92		17	9
1991–92	Paris St Germain	15	2
1992–93		34	6
1993–94		38	13
1994–95		28	11
1995–96	Newcastle U	34	5

GINTY, Rory

Born Galway 23.1.77 Ht 5 9 Wt 10 02
Forward. From Trainee.

Season	Club	Apps	Goals
1994–95	Crystal Palace	—	—
1995–96		—	—

GITTENS, Jon

Born Moseley 22.1.64 Ht 6 0 Wt 12 06
Defender. From Paget R.

Season	Club	Apps	Goals
1985–86	Southampton	4	—
1986–87		14	—
1987–88	Swindon T	29	—
1988–89		29	1
1989–90		40	4
1990–91		28	1
1990–91	Southampton	8	—
1991–92		11	—
1991–92	*Middlesbrough*	12	1
1992–93	Middlesbrough	13	—

Season	Club	Apps	Goals
1993–94	Portsmouth	30	1
1994–95		38	—
1995–96		15	1

GIVEN, Shay

Born Lifford 20.4.76 Ht 6 1 Wt 12 10
Goalkeeper. From Celtic. Eire Under-21, 7 full caps.

Season	Club	Apps	Goals
1994–95	Blackburn R	—	—
1994–95	*Swindon T*	—	—
1995–96	Blackburn R	—	—
1995–96	*Swindon T*	5	—
1995–96	*Sunderland*	17	—

GLASS, Jimmy

Born Epsom 1.8.73 Ht 6 1 Wt 13 04
Goalkeeper. From Trainee.

Season	Club	Apps	Goals
1991–92	Crystal Palace	—	—
1992–93		—	—
1993–94		—	—
1994–95		—	—
1994–95	*Portsmouth*	3	—
1995–96	Crystal Palace	—	—
1995–96	Bournemouth	13	—

GLASS, Stephen

Born Dundee 25.5.76 Ht 5 9 Wt 10 11
Midfield. From Crombie Sports. Scotland Under-21.

Season	Club	Apps	Goals
1994–95	Aberdeen	19	1
1995–96		32	3

GLEGHORN, Nigel

Born Seaham 12.8.62 Ht 6 0 Wt 13 07
Midfield. From Seaham Red Star.

Season	Club	Apps	Goals
1985–86	Ipswich T	21	2
1986–87		29	7
1987–88		16	2
1988–89	Manchester C	32	6
1989–90		2	1
1989–90	Birmingham C	43	9
1990–91		42	6
1991–92		46	17
1992–93		11	1
1992–93	Stoke C	34	7
1993–94		40	3
1994–95		46	7
1995–96		46	9

GLOVER, Dean

Born West Bromwich 29.12.63 Ht 5 11 Wt 11 02
Defender. From Apprentice.

Season	Club	Apps	Goals
1981–82	Aston Villa	—	—
1982–83		—	—
1983–84		—	—
1984–85		5	—
1985–86		18	—
1986–87		—	—
1986–87	*Sheffield U*	5	—
1987–88	Aston Villa	5	—
1987–88	Middlesbrough	38	4
1988–89		12	1
1988–89	Port Vale	22	—
1989–90		44	4
1990–91		41	1
1991–92		46	1
1992–93		39	3
1993–94		46	3
1994–95		29	—
1995–96		29	—

GLOVER, Lee

Born Kettering 24.4.70 Ht 5 10 Wt 12 01
Forward. From Trainee. Scotland Under-21.

Season	Club	Apps	Goals
1986–87	Nottingham F	—	—
1987–88		20	3
1988–89		—	—
1989–90		—	—
1989–90	*Leicester C*	5	1
1989–90	*Barnsley*	8	—
1990–91	Nottingham F	8	1
1991–92		16	—
1991–92	*Luton T*	1	—
1992–93	Nottingham F	14	—
1993–94		18	5
1994–95	Port Vale	28	4
1995–96		24	3

GOATER, Shaun

Born Bermuda 25.2.70 Ht 6 0 Wt 12 00
Forward. Bermuda full caps.

Season	Club	Apps	Goals
1988–89	Manchester U	—	—
1989–90		—	—
1989–90	Rotherham U	12	2
1990–91		22	2
1991–92		24	9
1992–93		23	7

Season	Club	Apps	Goals
1993–94		39	13
1993–94	*Notts Co*	1	—
1994–95	Rotherham U	45	19
1995–96		44	18

GOODALL, Danny

Born Bury 3.9.75 Ht 5 9 Wt 10 09
Defender. From Trainee.

Season	Club	Apps	Goals
1994–95	Blackburn R	—	—
1995–96		—	—

GOODEN, Ty

Born Canvey Island 23.10.72 Ht 5 8
Wt 12 06
Midfield. From Arsenal, Wycombe W.

Season	Club	Apps	Goals
1993–94	Swindon T	4	—
1994–95		16	2
1995–96		26	3

GOODING, Mick

Born Newcastle 12.4.59 Ht 5 9 Wt 10 07
Midfield. From Bishop Auckland.

Season	Club	Apps	Goals
1979–80	Rotherham U	34	3
1980–81		37	4
1981–82		22	2
1982–83		9	1
1982–83	Chesterfield	12	—
1983–84		—	—
1983–84	Rotherham U	26	7
1984–85		44	10
1985–86		40	8
1986–87		46	8
1987–88	Peterborough U	44	18
1988–89		3	3
1988–89	Wolverhampton W	31	4
1989–90		13	—
1989–90	Reading	27	3
1990–91		44	7
1991–92		40	3
1992–93		40	3
1993–94		41	7
1994–95		39	—
1995–96		40	3

GOODMAN, Don

Born Leeds 9.5.66 Ht 5 10 Wt 12 12
Forward. From School.

Season	Club	Apps	Goals
1983–84	Bradford C	2	—
1984–85		25	5
1985–86		20	4
1986–87		23	5
1986–87	WBA	10	2
1987–88		40	7
1988–89		36	15
1989–90		39	21
1990–91		22	8
1991–92		11	7
1991–92	Sunderland	22	11
1992–93		41	16
1993–94		35	10
1994–95		18	3
1994–95	Wolverhampton W	24	3
1995–96		44	16

GOODMAN, Jon

Born Walthamstow 2.6.71 Ht 6 0
Wt 12 03
Forward. From Bromley. Football League.

Season	Club	Apps	Goals
1990–91	Millwall	23	5
1991–92		17	3
1992–93		35	12
1993–94		19	7
1994–95		15	8
1994–95	Wimbledon	19	4
1995–96		27	6

GOODRIDGE, Greg

Born Barbados 10.7.71 Ht 5 6 Wt 10 00
Forward. From Lambada. Barbados full caps.

Season	Club	Apps	Goals
1993–94	Torquay U	8	1
1994–95		30	3
1995–96	QPR	7	1

GOODWIN, Scott

Born Hull 13.9.78 Ht 5 9 Wt 11 08
Defender. From Trainee.

Season	Club	Apps	Goals
1995–96	Coventry C	—	—

GOODWIN, Shaun

Born Rotherham 14.6.69 Ht 5 8
Wt 11 04
Midfield. From Trainee.

Season	Club	Apps	Goals
1987–88	Rotherham U	3	—
1988–89		41	4
1989–90		38	6
1990–91		34	3
1991–92		39	5
1992–93		30	1
1993–94		38	8

Season	Club	League Appearances/Goals	
1994–95		10	3
1995–96		26	4

GORAM, Andy

Born Bury 13.4.64 Ht 5 11 Wt 11 06
Goalkeeper. From West Bromwich Apprentice, Scotland Under-21, 39 full caps.

Season	Club	Apps	Goals
1981–82	Oldham Ath	3	—
1982–83		38	—
1983–84		22	—
1984–85		41	—
1985–86		41	—
1986–87		41	—
1987–88		9	—
1987–88	Hibernian	33	1
1988–89		36	—
1989–90		34	—
1990–91		35	—
1991–92	Rangers	44	—
1992–93		34	—
1993–94		8	—
1994–95		19	—
1995–96		30	—

GORDON, Alan

Born Glasgow 7.9.77
Midfield. From Rochedale R.

Season	Club	Apps	Goals
1995–96	Doncaster R	—	—
1995–96	Leicester C	—	—

GORDON, Dale

Born Gt Yarmouth 9.1.67 Ht 5 10 Wt 11 08
Forward. From Apprentice. England Schools, Youth, Under-21, B.

Season	Club	Apps	Goals
1983–84	Norwich C	—	—
1984–85		23	3
1985–86		6	1
1986–87		41	5
1987–88		21	3
1988–89		38	5
1989–90		26	3
1990–91		36	7
1991–92		15	4
1991–92	Rangers	23	5
1992–93		22	1
1993–94	West Ham U	8	1
1994–95		—	—
1994–95	*Peterborough U*	6	1
1995–96	West Ham U	1	—
1995–96	*Millwall*	6	—

GORDON, Dean

Born Thornton Heath 10.2.73 Ht 6 0 Wt 13 04
Defender. From Trainee. England Under-21.

Season	Club	Apps	Goals
1991–92	Crystal Palace	4	—
1992–93		10	—
1993–94		45	5
1994–95		41	2
1995–96		34	8

GORDON, Gavin

Born Manchester 24.6.79 Ht 6 1 Wt 11 05
Forward. From Trainee.

Season	Club	Apps	Goals
1995–96	Hull C	13	3

GORDON, Neville

Born Greenwich 15.11.75 Ht 5 10 Wt 11 00
Forward. From Trainee.

Season	Club	Apps	Goals
1994–95	Millwall	—	—
1995–96	Reading	1	—

GORE, Ian

Born Whiston 10.1.68 Ht 5 11 Wt 12 04
Midfield.

Season	Club	Apps	Goals
1986–87	Birmingham C	—	—
From Southport			
1987–88	Blackpool	—	—
1988–89		21	—
1989–90		34	—
1990–91		41	—
1991–92		41	—
1992–93		30	—
1993–94		29	—
1994–95		4	—
1995–96	Torquay U	25	2
1995–96	Doncaster R	5	—

GOSS, Jeremy

Born Oekolia 11.5.65 Ht 5 9 Wt 11 08
Midfield. From Amateur. England Youth, Wales 9 full caps.

Season	Club	Apps	Goals
1982–83	Norwich C	—	—
1983–84		1	—

Season	Club	League Appearances/Goals	
1984–85		5	—
1985–86		—	—
1986–87		1	—
1987–88		22	2
1988–89		—	—
1989–90		7	—
1990–91		19	1
1991–92		33	1
1992–93		25	1
1993–94		34	6
1994–95		25	2
1995–96		16	1

GOUCK, Andy

Born Blackpool 8.6.72 Ht 5 9 Wt 11 02
Midfield. From Trainee.

1989–90	Blackpool	8	1
1990–91		5	—
1991–92		24	2
1992–93		29	4
1993–94		27	2
1994–95		39	2
1995–96		16	1

GOUGH, Richard

Born Stockholm 5.4.62 Ht 6 0 Wt 12 00
Defender. From Wits University. Scotland Under-21, 61 full caps.

1980–81	Dundee U	4	—
1981–82		30	1
1982–83		34	8
1983–84		33	3
1984–85		33	6
1985–86		31	5
1986–87	Tottenham H	40	2
1987–88		9	—
1987–88	Rangers	31	5
1988–89		35	4
1989–90		26	—
1990–91		26	—
1991–92		33	2
1992–93		25	2
1993–94		37	3
1994–95		25	1
1995–96		29	3

GOULD, Jonathan

Born Paddington 18.7.68 Ht 6 1
Wt 12 07
Goalkeeper. From Clevedon T.

1990–91	Halifax T	23	—

Season	Club	League Appearances/Goals	
1991–92		9	—
1991–92	WBA	—	—
1992–93	Coventry C	9	—
1993–94		9	—
1994–95		7	—
1995–96		—	—
1995–96	*Bradford C*	9	—

GOWSHALL, Joby

Born Louth 7.8.75 Ht 5 11 Wt 13 00
Defender. From Trainee.

1993–94	Grimsby T	—	—
1994–95		—	—
1995–96		—	—

GRAHAM, Alastair

Born Glasgow 11.8.66 Ht 6 3 Wt 12 07
Forward. From Anniesland U.

1984–85	Clydebank	1	—
1985–86		2	—
1986–87		—	—
1987–88	Albion R	28	10
1988–89		39	15
1989–90		31	7
1990–91	Ayr U	38	8
1991–92		40	14
1992–93		30	9
1992–93	Motherwell	4	1
1993–94		5	—
1993–94	Raith R	36	5
1994–95		27	6
1995–96		25	5
1995–96	Falkirk	8	—

GRAHAM, Deniol

Born Cannock 4.10.69 Ht 5 10 Wt 10 05
Forward. From Trainee. Wales Under-21.

1987–88	Manchester U	1	—
1988–89		—	—
1989–90		1	—
1990–91		—	—
1991–92	Barnsley	21	1
1992–93		15	1
1992–93	*Preston NE*	8	—
1993–94	Barnsley	2	—
1993–94	*Carlisle U*	2	1
1994–95	Stockport Co	11	2
1995–96	Scunthorpe U	3	1

Season	Club	League Appearances/Goals	

GRAHAM, Jimmy

Born Glasgow 5.11.69 Ht 5 10 Wt 11 05
Defender. From Trainee.

1988–89	Bradford C	1	—
1989–90		6	—
1989–90	*Rochdale*	11	—
1990–91	Rochdale	28	1
1991–92		31	—
1992–93		38	—
1993–94		29	—
1994–95	Hull C	39	—
1995–96		24	1

GRAHAM, Mark

Born Newry 24.10.74 Ht 5 7 Wt 10 12
Forward. From Trainee.

1993–94	QPR	—	—
1994–95		—	—
1995–96		—	—

GRAHAM, Richard

Born Dewsbury 28.11.74 Ht 6 2
Wt 12 01
Midfield. From Trainee.

1993–94	Oldham Ath	5	—
1994–95		32	3
1995–96		32	1

GRAINGER, Martin

Born Enfield 23.8.72 Ht 5 10 Wt 11 07
Defender. From Trainee.

1989–90	Colchester U	7	2
1990–91		—	—
1991–92		—	—
1992–93		31	3
1993–94		8	2
1993–94	Brentford	31	2
1994–95		37	7
1995–96		33	3
1995–96	Birmingham C	8	—

GRANT, Brian

Born Bannockburn 19.6.64 Ht 5 9
Wt 10 07
Midfield. From Fallin Violet.

1981–82	Stirling Alb	1	—
1982–83		1	—
1983–84		24	3
1984–85	Aberdeen	—	—
1985–86		—	—
1986–87		15	4
1987–88		7	1
1988–89		26	1
1989–90		31	6
1990–91		32	2
1991–92		33	6
1992–93		29	3
1993–94		30	2
1994–95		32	2
1995–96		25	—

GRANT, Kim

Born Ghana 25.9.72 Ht 5 10 Wt 10 12
Forward. From Trainee.

1990–91	Charlton Ath	12	2
1991–92		4	—
1992–93		21	2
1993–94		30	1
1994–95		26	6
1995–96		30	7
1995–96	Luton T	10	3

GRANT, Peter

Born Bellshill 30.8.65 Ht 5 9 Wt 10 03
Midfield. From Celtic BC. Scotland Schools, Youth B, Under-21, 2 full caps.

1982–83	Celtic	—	—
1983–84		3	—
1984–85		20	4
1985–86		30	1
1986–87		37	1
1987–88		37	2
1988–89		21	—
1989–90		26	—
1990–91		27	—
1991–92		22	—
1992–93		31	2
1993–94		28	—
1994–95		28	2
1995–96		30	3

GRANT, Stephen

Born Birr 14.4.77 Ht 5 10 Wt 11 07
Forward. From Athlone T.

1995–96	Sunderland	—	—

GRANT, Tony

Born Liverpool 14.11.74 Ht 5 9
Wt 10 00
Midfield. From Trainee. England Under-21.

Season	Club	Apps	Goals
1993–94	Everton	—	—
1994–95		5	—
1995–96		13	1
1995–96	*Swindon T*	3	1

GRANT, Tony

Born Louth 20.8.76 Ht 5 9 Wt 11 04
Defender. From Trainee.

Season	Club	Apps	Goals
1994–95	Leeds U	—	—
1995–96		—	—
1995–96	Preston NE	1	—

GRANVILLE, Danny

Born Islington 19.1.75 Ht 6 0 Wt 12 01
Midfield. From Trainee.

Season	Club	Apps	Goals
1993–94	Cambridge U	11	5
1994–95		16	2
1995–96		35	—

GRAY, Andrew

Born Harrogate 15.11.77
Midfield. From Trainee.

Season	Club	Apps	Goals
1995–96	Leeds U	15	—

GRAY, Andy

Born Southampton 25.10.73 Ht 5 6
Wt 10 10
Forward. From Trainee.

Season	Club	Apps	Goals
1991–92	Reading	1	—
1992–93		11	3
1993–94		5	—
1994–95	Leyton Orient	25	3
1995–96		7	—

GRAY, Andy

Born Lambeth 22.2.64 Ht 5 11 Wt 13 03
Midfield. From Corinthian C, Dulwich H.
England Under-21, 1 full cap.

Season	Club	Apps	Goals
1984–85	Crystal Palace	21	5
1985–86		30	10
1986–87		30	6
1987–88		17	6
1987–88	Aston Villa	19	1
1988–89		18	3
1988–89	QPR	11	2
1989–90	Crystal Palace	35	6
1990–91		30	4
1991–92		25	2
1991–92	*Tottenham H*	14	1
1992–93	Tottenham H	17	1
1992–93	*Swindon T*	3	—
1993–94	Tottenham H	2	1

From Marbella

Season	Club	Apps	Goals
1995–96	Falkirk	16	—

GRAY, Ian

Born Manchester 25.2.75 Ht 6 2
Wt 12 00
Goalkeeper. From Trainee.

Season	Club	Apps	Goals
1993–94	Oldham Ath	—	—
1994–95		—	—
1994–95	*Rochdale*	12	—
1995–96	Rochdale	20	—

GRAY, Kevin

Born Sheffield 7.1.72 Ht 6 0 Wt 14 00
Defender. From Trainee.

Season	Club	Apps	Goals
1988–89	Mansfield T	1	—
1989–90		16	—
1990–91		31	1
1991–92		18	—
1992–93		33	—
1993–94		42	2
1994–95	Huddersfield T	5	—
1995–96		38	—

GRAY, Martin

Born Stockton 17.8.71 Ht 5 9 Wt 11 05
Midfield. From Trainee.

Season	Club	Apps	Goals
1989–90	Sunderland	—	—
1990–91		—	—
1990–91	*Aldershot*	5	—
1991–92	Sunderland	1	—
1992–93		12	1
1993–94		22	—
1994–95		22	—
1995–96		7	—
1995–96	*Fulham*	6	—
1995–96	Oxford U	7	—

GRAY, Michael

Born Sunderland 3.8.74 Ht 5 8 Wt 10 08
Defender. From Trainee.

Season	Club	Apps	Goals
1992–93	Sunderland	27	2

Season	Club	Apps	Goals
1993–94		22	1
1994–95		16	—
1995–96		46	4

GRAY, Phil

Born Belfast 2.10.68 Ht 5 9 Wt 12 09
Forward. From Apprentice. Northern Ireland Schools, Youth, Under-23, 17 full caps.

Season	Club	Apps	Goals
1986–87	Tottenham H	1	—
1987–88		1	—
1988–89		1	—
1989–90		—	—
1989–90	*Barnsley*	3	—
1990–91	Tottenham H	6	—
1990–91	*Fulham*	3	—
1991–92	Luton T	14	3
1992–93		45	19
1993–94	Sunderland	41	14
1994–95		42	12
1995–96		32	8

GRAY, Stuart

Born Harrogate 18.12.73 Ht 5 11
Wt 11 00
Midfield. From Giffnock N. Scotland Under-21.

Season	Club	Apps	Goals
1992–93	Celtic	1	—
1993–94		—	—
1994–95		11	—
1995–96		5	1

GRAYSON, Neil

Born York 1.11.64 Ht 5 10 Wt 12 09
Forward.

Season	Club	Apps	Goals
1989–90	Doncaster R	6	1
1990–91		23	5
1990–91	York C	1	—
1991–92	Chesterfield	15	—
From Boston U			
1994–95	Northampton T	38	8
1995–96		42	11

GRAYSON, Simon

Born Ripon 16.12.69 Ht 6 0 Wt 12 06
Defender. From Trainee.

Season	Club	Apps	Goals
1987–88	Leeds U	2	—
1988–89		—	—
1989–90		—	—
1990–91		—	—
1991–92		—	—
1991–92	Leicester C	13	—
1992–93		24	1
1993–94		40	1
1994–95		34	—
1995–96		41	2

GRAYSTON, Neil

Born Keighley 25.11.75 Ht 5 8 Wt 11 00
Defender. From Trainee.

Season	Club	Apps	Goals
1993–94	Bradford C	2	—
1994–95		3	—
1995–96		2	—

GRAZIOLI, Guiliano

Born London 23.3.75 Ht 5 11 Wt 12 00
Forward. From Wembley.

Season	Club	Apps	Goals
1995–96	Peterborough U	3	1

GREEN, Matt

Born Northampton 22.10.75 Ht 5 8
Wt 11 10
Midfield. From Trainee.

Season	Club	Apps	Goals
1994–95	Derby Co	—	—
1995–96		—	—

GREEN, Richard

Born Wolverhampton 22.11.67 Ht 6 1
Wt 13 07
Defender. From Apprentice.

Season	Club	Apps	Goals
1986–87	Shrewsbury T	15	—
1987–88		31	2
1988–89		39	3
1989–90		40	—
1990–91		—	—
1990–91	Swindon T	—	—
1991–92		—	—
1991–92	Gillingham	12	4
1992–93		39	3
1993–94		39	4
1994–95		37	1
1995–96		35	2

GREEN, Scott

Born Walsall 15.1.70 Ht 5 10 Wt 12 05
Midfield. From Trainee.

Season	Club	Apps	Goals
1988–89	Derby Co	—	—
1989–90		—	—
1989–90	Bolton W	5	2

Season	Club	League Appearances/Goals	
1990–91		41	6
1991–92		37	2
1992–93		41	6
1993–94		22	4
1994–95		31	1
1995–96		31	3

GREENACRE, Chris

Born Wakefield 23.12.77 Ht 5 11
Wt 12 08
Forward. From Trainee.

Season	Club	Apps	Goals
1995–96	Manchester C	—	—

GREENALL, Colin

Born Billinge 30.12.63 Ht 5 11 Wt 12 12
Defender. From Apprentice.

Season	Club	Apps	Goals
1980–81	Blackpool	12	—
1981–82		18	—
1982–83		24	1
1983–84		39	4
1984–85		44	3
1985–86		43	1
1986–87		3	—
1986–87	Gillingham	37	2
1987–88		25	2
1987–88	Oxford U	12	—
1988–89		40	2
1989–90		15	—
1989–90	*Bury*	3	—
1990–91	Bury	31	—
1991–92		37	5
1991–92	Preston NE	9	1
1992–93		20	—
1993–94	Chester C	42	1
1994–95	Lincoln C	39	3
1995–96		4	—
1995–96	Wigan Ath	37	2

GREENE, David

Born Luton 26.10.73 Ht 6 2 Wt 13 05
Defender. From Trainee. Eire Under-21.

Season	Club	Apps	Goals
1991–92	Luton T	—	—
1992–93		1	—
1993–94		10	—
1994–95		8	—
1995–96		—	—
1995–96	*Colchester U*	14	1
1995–96	*Brentford*	11	—

GREGAN, Sean

Born Cleveland 29.3.74 Ht 6 2 Wt 14 00
Defender. From Trainee.

Season	Club	Apps	Goals
1991–92	Darlington	17	—
1992–93		17	1
1993–94		23	1
1994–95		25	2
1995–96		38	—

GREGG, Matt

Born Cheltenham 30.11.78
Goalkeeper. From Trainee.

Season	Club	Apps	Goals
1995–96	Torquay U	1	—

GREGORY, Andrew

Born Barnsley 8.10.76 Ht 5 8 Wt 10 09
Midfield. From Trainee.

Season	Club	Apps	Goals
1995–96	Barnsley	—	—

GREGORY, David

Born Colchester 23.1.70 Ht 5 9
Wt 12 08
Midfield. From Trainee.

Season	Club	Apps	Goals
1987–88	Ipswich T	—	—
1988–89		2	—
1989–90		4	—
1990–91		21	1
1991–92		1	—
1992–93		3	1
1993–94		—	—
1994–95		1	—
1994–95	*Hereford U*	2	—
1995–96	Peterborough U	3	—
1995–96	Colchester U	10	—

GREGORY, John

Born Hounslow 16.5.77
Goalkeeper. From Trainee.

Season	Club	Apps	Goals
1994–95	Fulham	1	—
1995–96		—	—

GREGORY, Neil

Born Zambia 7.10.72 Ht 5 11 Wt 11 10
Forward. From Trainee.

Season	Club	Apps	Goals
1992–93	Ipswich T	—	—
1993–94		—	—
1993–94	*Chesterfield*	3	1

Season	Club	League Appearances/Goals	
1994–95	Ipswich T	3	—
1994–95	*Scunthorpe U*	10	7
1995–96	Ipswich T	17	2

GRENHAM, Tony

Born Brighton 22.6.77
Goalkeeper. From Trainee.

1995–96	Shrewsbury T	—	—

GRIDELET, Phil

Born Edgware 30.4.67 Ht 5 11 Wt 13 00
Midfield. From Watford, Hendon, Barnet.

1990–91	Barnsley	4	—
1991–92		—	—
1992–93		2	—
1992–93	*Rotherham U*	9	—
1993–94	Barnsley	—	—
1993–94	Southend U	29	—
1994–95		29	5
1995–96		40	2

GRIEMINK, Bart

Born Holland 29.3.72 Ht 6 4 Wt 15 04
Goalkeeper. From WKE.

1995–96	Birmingham C	20	—

GRIFFITHS, Carl

Born Oswestry 15.7.71 Ht 6 0 Wt 12 06
Forward. From Trainee. Wales Youth, Under-21.

1988–89	Shrewsbury T	28	6
1989–90		18	4
1990–91		19	4
1991–92		27	8
1992–93		42	27
1993–94		9	5
1993–94	Manchester C	16	4
1994–95		2	—
1995–96		—	—
1995–96	Portsmouth	14	2
1995–96	Peterborough U	4	1

GRIFFITHS, Gareth

Born Winsford 10.4.70 Ht 6 4 Wt 14 00
Defender. From Rhyl.

1992–93	Port Vale	—	—
1993–94		4	2
1994–95		20	—
1995–96		41	2

GRIGGS, Timmy

Born Bexley 9.11.76
Defender. From Trainee.

1995–96	Arsenal	—	—

GRIM, Robert

Born London 10.9.78 Ht 5 11 Wt 11 08
Midfield. From Trainee.

1995–96	Nottingham F	—	—

GRITT, Steve

Born Bournemouth 31.10.57 Ht 5 9 Wt 10 10
Defender. From Apprentice.

1976–77	Bournemouth	6	3
1977–78	Charlton Ath	34	3
1978–79		39	3
1979–80		31	7
1980–81		40	—
1981–82		34	3
1982–83		27	1
1983–84		33	1
1984–85		35	1
1985–86		11	2
1986–87		14	1
1987–88		27	—
1988–89		22	2
1989–90	Walsall	20	1
1989–90	Charlton Ath	2	—
1990–91		10	—
1991–92		14	1
1992–93		7	—
1993–94		—	—
1994–95		—	—
1995–96		—	—

GROBBELAAR, Bruce

Born Durban 6.10.57 Ht 6 1 Wt 14 02
Goalkeeper. From Vancouver Whitecaps. Zimbabwe full caps.

1979–80	Crewe Alex	24	1
1980–81	Liverpool	—	—
1981–82		42	—
1982–83		42	—
1983–84		42	—
1984–85		42	—
1985–86		42	—

Season	Club	League Appearances/Goals	
1986–87		31	—
1987–88		38	—
1988–89		21	—
1989–90		38	—
1990–91		31	—
1991–92		37	—
1992–93		5	—
1992–93	*Stoke C*	4	—
1993–94	Liverpool	29	—
1994–95	Southampton	30	—
1995–96		2	—

GROVES, Paul

Born Derby 28.2.66 Ht 5 11 Wt 11 05
Midfield. From Burton Alb.

1987–88	Leicester C	1	1
1988–89		15	—
1989–90		—	—
1989–90	*Lincoln C*	8	1
1989–90	Blackpool	19	1
1990–91		46	11
1991–92		42	9
1992–93	Grimsby T	46	12
1993–94		46	11
1994–95		46	5
1995–96		46	10

GRUGEL, Mark

Born Liverpool 9.3.76 Ht 5 8 Wt 10 00
Midfield. From Local.

1993–94	Everton	—	—
1994–95		—	—
1995–96		—	—

GUDMUNDSSON, Niklas

Born Sweden 29.2.72
Forward. From Halmstad. Sweden 7 full caps.

1995–96	Blackburn R	4	—

GUENTCHEV, Bontcho

Born Bulgaria 7.7.64 Ht 5 10 Wt 11 07
Forward. From Etur, Lokomotiv, Sporting Lisbon. Bulgaria 11 full caps.

1992–93	Ipswich T	21	3
1993–94		24	2
1994–95		16	1
1995–96	Luton T	35	9

GUEST, Mark

Born Mexborough 21.1.76 Ht 5 8 Wt 10 13
Forward. From Trainee.

1994–95	Sheffield W	—	—
1995–96		—	—

GUINAN, Stephen

Born Birmingham 24.12.75 Ht 6 1 Wt 13 07
Forward. From Trainee.

1992–93	Nottingham F	—	—
1993–94		—	—
1994–95		—	—
1995–96		2	—
1995–96	*Darlington*	3	1

GULLIT, Ruud

Born Surinam 1.9.62 Ht 6 2 Wt 12 00
Forward. From DWS Amsterdam. Holland Youth, Under-21, 65 full caps.

1979–80	Haarlem	24	4
1980–81		36	14
1981–82		31	14
1982–83	Feyenoord	33	8
1983–84		33	15
1984–85		19	7
1985–86	PSV Eindhoven	34	24
1986–87		34	22
1987–88	AC Milan	29	9
1988–89		19	5
1989–90		2	—
1990–91		26	7
1991–92		26	7
1992–93		15	7
1993–94	Sampdoria	31	15
1994–95	AC Milan	8	3
1994–95	Sampdoria	22	9
1995–96	Chelsea	31	3

GUNN, Bryan

Born Thurso 22.12.63 Ht 6 2 Wt 13 08
Goalkeeper. From Invergordon BC. Scotland Schools, Youth, Under-21, B, 6 full caps.

1980–81	Aberdeen	—	—
1981–82		—	—
1982–83		1	—
1983–84		—	—
1984–85		2	—

Season	Club	Apps	Goals
1985–86		10	—
1986–87		2	—
1986–87	Norwich C	29	—
1987–88		38	—
1988–89		37	—
1989–90		37	—
1990–91		34	—
1991–92		25	—
1992–93		42	—
1993–94		41	—
1994–95		21	—
1995–96		43	—

GUPPY, Steve

Born Winchester 29.3.69 Ht 5 11
Wt 10 10
Midfield. From Southampton.

Season	Club	Apps	Goals
1993–94	Wycombe W	41	8
1994–95	Newcastle U	—	—
1994–95	Port Vale	27	2
1995–96		44	4

GURNEY, Andy

Born Bristol 25.1.74 Ht 5 7 Wt 10 07
Defender. From Trainee.

Season	Club	Apps	Goals
1992–93	Bristol R	—	—
1993–94		3	—
1994–95		38	1
1995–96		43	6

GUTZMORE, Leon

Born London 30.10.76
Forward. From Trainee.

Season	Club	Apps	Goals
1995–96	Cambridge U	2	—

HAALAND, Alf-Inge

Born Stavanger 23.11.72 Ht 5 10
Wt 12 12
Midfield. From Bryne. Norway 13 full caps.

Season	Club	Apps	Goals
1993–94	Nottingham F	3	—
1994–95		20	1
1995–96		17	—

HACKETT, Warren

Born Newham 16.12.71 Ht 6 0 Wt 12 05
Defender. From Tottenham H Trainee.

Season	Club	Apps	Goals
1990–91	Leyton Orient	—	—
1991–92		22	—
1992–93		17	—
1993–94		33	3
1994–95	Doncaster R	39	2
1995–96		7	—
1995–96	Mansfield T	32	3

HADDAOUI, Riffi

Born Copenhagen 24.3.71
Forward. From Avarta.

Season	Club	Apps	Goals
1995–96	Torquay U	2	—

HADLEY, Stewart

Born Dudley 30.12.73 Ht 6 1 Wt 13 03
Forward. From Halesowen.

Season	Club	Apps	Goals
1992–93	Derby Co	—	—
1993–94		—	—
1993–94	Mansfield T	14	5
1994–95		39	14
1995–96		33	8

HAGEN, David

Born Edinburgh 5.5.73 Ht 5 11
Wt 13 00
Midfield. From Grahamston BC. Scotland Under-21.

Season	Club	Apps	Goals
1989–90	Rangers	—	—
1990–91		—	—
1991–92		—	—
1992–93		8	2
1993–94		6	1
1994–95		2	—
1994–95	Hearts	20	3
1995–96		7	1
1995–96	Falkirk	25	—

Season Club League Appearances/Goals

HAGUE, Paul

Born Consett 16.9.72 Ht 6 3 Wt 13 03
Defender. From Trainee.

Season	Club	Apps	Goals
1990–91	Gillingham	7	—
1991–92		—	—
1992–93		1	—
1993–94		1	—
1994–95	Leyton Orient	18	1
1995–96		—	—

HAIGH, Gavin

Born Doncaster 9.2.77 Ht 5 10 Wt 11 08
Midfield. From Trainee.

Season	Club	Apps	Goals
1995–96	Hull C	—	—

HAILS, Julian

Born Lincoln 20.11.67 Ht 5 10 Wt 11 02
Forward. From Hemel Hempstead.

Season	Club	Apps	Goals
1989–90	Fulham	—	—
1990–91		—	—
1991–92		18	1
1992–93		46	6
1993–94		37	4
1994–95		8	1
1994–95	Southend U	26	2
1995–96		42	4

HALEY, Martin

Born Salford 22.11.76 Ht 5 10 Wt 10 05
Goalkeeper. From Trainee.

Season	Club	Apps	Goals
1995–96	Wigan Ath	—	—

HALL, Danny

Born Bletchley 18.8.77 Ht 5 9 Wt 10 13
Defender. From Trainee.

Season	Club	Apps	Goals
1995–96	Manchester U	—	—

HALL, Derek

Born Manchester 5.1.65 Ht 5 8 Wt 11 12
Midfield. From Apprentice.

Season	Club	Apps	Goals
1982–83	Coventry C	1	—
1983–84		—	—
1983–84	*Torquay U*	10	2
1984–85	Torquay U	45	4
1985–86	Swindon T	10	—
1986–87	Southend U	43	9
1987–88		40	3
1988–89		40	3
1989–90	Halifax T	41	4
1990–91		8	—
1991–92	Hereford U	20	—
1992–93		41	9
1993–94		42	9
1994–95	Rochdale	9	1
1995–96		14	1

HALL, Gareth

Born Croydon 12.3.69 Ht 5 8 Wt 12 00
Defender. From Apprentice. England Schools, Wales Under-21, 9 full caps.

Season	Club	Apps	Goals
1986–87	Chelsea	1	—
1987–88		13	—
1988–89		22	—
1989–90		13	1
1990–91		24	—
1991–92		10	—
1992–93		37	2
1993–94		7	—
1994–95		6	—
1995–96		5	1
1995–96	Sunderland	14	—

HALL, Graeme

Born Stockton 22.11.75 Ht 6 3 Wt 13 12
Defender. From Trainee.

Season	Club	Apps	Goals
1994–95	Arsenal	—	—
1995–96	Barnet	—	—

HALL, Kevin

Born Edinburgh 7.2.76 Ht 5 10 Wt 11 00
Midfield. From Trainee.

Season	Club	Apps	Goals
1994–95	Crystal Palace	—	—
1995–96		—	—

HALL, Leigh

Born Hereford 10.6.75
Forward.

Season	Club	Apps	Goals
1994–95	Hereford U	1	—
1995–96		1	—

HALL, Marcus

Born Coventry 24.3.76 Ht 6 1 Wt 12 02
Defender. From Trainee.

Season	Club	Apps	Goals
1994–95	Coventry C	5	—
1995–96		25	—

HALL, Mark

Born Islington 13.1.73 Ht 5 7 Wt 10 09
Midfield. From Tottenham H Trainee.

Season	Club	Apps	Goals
1991–92	Southend U	3	—
1992–93		9	—
1993–94		—	—
1993–94	*Barnet*	3	—
1994–95	Southend U	—	—
1995–96	Torquay U	29	—

HALL, Paul

Born Manchester 3.7.72 Ht 5 9 Wt 10 02
Forward. From Trainee.

Season	Club	Apps	Goals
1989–90	Torquay U	10	—
1990–91		17	—
1991–92		38	1
1992–93		28	—
1992–93	Portsmouth	—	—
1993–94		28	4
1994–95		43	5
1995–96		46	10

HALL, Richard

Born Ipswich 14.3.72 Ht 6 2 Wt 13 11
Defender. From Trainee. England Under-21.

Season	Club	Apps	Goals
1989–90	Scunthorpe U	1	—
1990–91		21	3
1990–91	Southampton	1	—
1991–92		26	3
1992–93		28	4
1993–94		4	—
1994–95		37	4
1995–96		30	1

HALL, Wayne

Born Rotherham 25.10.68 Ht 5 9
Wt 10 06
Defender. From Darlington.

Season	Club	Apps	Goals
1988–89	York C	2	—
1989–90		27	3
1990–91		46	1
1991–92		37	3
1992–93		42	1
1993–94		45	—
1994–95		37	—
1995–96		23	—

HALLAM, Craig

Born Leicester 11.11.76 Ht 5 10
Wt 12 05
Forward. From Trainee.

Season	Club	Apps	Goals
1995–96	Leicester C	—	—

HALLE, Gunnar

Born Oslo 11.8.65 Ht 5 11 Wt 11 02
Defender. From Lillestrom. Norway 51 full caps.

Season	Club	Apps	Goals
1990–91	Oldham Ath	17	—
1991–92		10	—
1992–93		41	5
1993–94		23	1
1994–95		40	5
1995–96		37	3

HALLIDAY, Stephen

Born Sunderland 3.5.76 Ht 5 10
Wt 12 03
Forward. From Charlton Ath.

Season	Club	Apps	Goals
1993–94	Hartlepool U	11	—
1994–95		28	5
1995–96		39	7

HALLOWS, Marcus

Born Bolton 7.7.75 Ht 6 1 Wt 12 09
Midfield. From Leigh RMI.

Season	Club	Apps	Goals
1995–96	Bolton W	—	—

HALLWORTH, Jon

Born Stockport 26.10.65 Ht 6 2
Wt 13 10
Goalkeeper. From School.

Season	Club	Apps	Goals
1983–84	Ipswich T	—	—
1984–85		—	—
1984–85	*Swindon T*	—	—
1984–85	*Fulham*	—	—
1984–85	*Bristol R*	2	—
1985–86	Ipswich T	6	—
1986–87		6	—
1987–88		33	—
1988–89		—	—
1988–89	Oldham Ath	16	—
1989–90		15	—
1990–91		46	—
1991–92		41	—
1992–93		16	—

Season	Club	Apps	Goals
1993–94		19	—
1994–95		6	—
1995–96		11	—

HAMILL, Rory

Born Coleraine 4.5.76 Ht 5 10 Wt 12 02
Forward. From Portstewart.

Season	Club	Apps	Goals
1994–95	Fulham	23	5
1995–96		25	2

HAMILTON, Brian

Born Paisley 5.8.67 Ht 6 0 Wt 11 07
Midfield. From Pollok United BC.
Scotland Schools, Under-21.

Season	Club	Apps	Goals
1985–86	St Mirren	8	—
1986–87		28	3
1987–88		27	—
1988–89		23	1
1989–90	Hibernian	28	1
1990–91		26	2
1991–92		40	3
1992–93		41	1
1993–94		42	2
1994–95		18	—
1994–95	Hearts	13	2
1995–96		12	—

HAMILTON, Derrick

Born Bradford 15.8.76 Ht 5 10 Wt 12 13
Midfield. From Trainee.

Season	Club	Apps	Goals
1993–94	Bradford C	2	1
1994–95		30	1
1995–96		24	3

HAMILTON, Graeme

Born Stirling 22.1.74 Ht 5 10 Wt 10 10
Defender. From Gairdoch U.

Season	Club	Apps	Goals
1991–92	Falkirk	3	—
1992–93		—	—
1993–94		7	—
1994–95		3	—
1995–96		1	—

HAMILTON, Ian

Born Stevenage 14.12.67 Ht 5 9
Wt 11 03
Forward. From Apprentice.

Season	Club	Apps	Goals
1985–86	Southampton	—	—
1986–87		—	—
1987–88		—	—
1987–88	Cambridge U	9	1
1988–89		15	—
1988–89	Scunthorpe U	27	1
1989–90		43	6
1990–91		34	2
1991–92		41	9
1992–93	WBA	46	7
1993–94		42	3
1994–95		35	4
1995–96		41	3

HAMLET, Alan

Born Watford 30.9.77 Ht 6 0 Wt 11 03
Defender. From Trainee.

Season	Club	Apps	Goals
1994–95	Barnet	3	—
1995–96		—	—

HAMMOND, Nicky

Born Hornchurch 7.9.67 Ht 6 0
Wt 11 13
Goalkeeper. From Apprentice.

Season	Club	Apps	Goals
1985–86	Arsenal	—	—
1986–87		—	—
1986–87	*Bristol R*	3	—
1986–87	*Peterborough U*	—	—
1986–87	*Aberdeen*	—	—
1987–88	Swindon T	4	—
1988–89		—	—
1989–90		—	—
1990–91		5	—
1991–92		25	—
1992–93		13	—
1993–94		13	—
1994–95		7	—
1995–96	Plymouth Arg	4	—
1995–96	Reading	5	—

HAMON, Chris

Born Jersey 27.4.70 Ht 6 1 Wt 13 07
Forward. From St Peter.

Season	Club	Apps	Goals
1992–93	Swindon T	2	—
1993–94		1	—
1994–95		5	1
1995–96		—	—

HAMSHER, John

Born Lambeth 14.1.78
Defender. From Trainee.

Season	Club	Apps	Goals
1995–96	Fulham	3	—

Season Club League Appearances/Goals

HANBY, Robert

Born Pontefract 24.12.74 Ht 5 8
Wt 11 09
Defender. From Trainee.

Season	Club	Apps	Goals
1993–94	Barnsley	—	—
1994–95		—	—
1995–96		—	—

HANCOX, Richard

Born Stourbridge 4.10.70 Ht 5 10
Wt 13 00
Forward. From Stourbridge S.

Season	Club	Apps	Goals
1992–93	Torquay U	7	—
1993–94		3	—
1994–95		36	9
1995–96		25	1

HANDFORD, Paul

Born Chesterfield 24.3.77
Defender. From Trainee.

Season	Club	Apps	Goals
1995–96	Mansfield T	—	—

HANDYSIDE, Peter

Born Dumfries 31.7.74 Ht 6 1 Wt 12 03
Defender. From Trainee. Scotland Under-21.

Season	Club	Apps	Goals
1992–93	Grimsby T	11	—
1993–94		13	—
1994–95		35	—
1995–96		30	—

HANNAH, David

Born Coatbridge 4.8.74 Ht 5 11
Wt 11 01
Midfield. From Hamilton Th. Scotland Under-21.

Season	Club	Apps	Goals
1991–92	Dundee U	—	—
1992–93		5	—
1993–94		10	2
1994–95		32	2
1995–96		7	1

HANSEN, Glenn

Born Oslo 20.9.72
Midfield. From Drobak.

Season	Club	Apps	Goals
1995–96	Bradford C	—	—

HANSEN, Vergard

Born Drammen 8.8.69 Ht 6 2 Wt 12 07
Defender. From Stromsgodset.

Season	Club	Apps	Goals
1994–95	Bristol C	29	—
1995–96		8	—

HANSON, Dave

Born Huddersfield 19.11.68 Ht 6 1
Wt 13 01
Forward. From Farsley Celtic.

Season	Club	Apps	Goals
1993–94	Bury	1	—
From Hednesford			
1995–96	Leyton Orient	11	1

HARAN, Mark

Born Barnsley 21.1.77 Ht 6 1 Wt 12 00
Defender. From Trainee.

Season	Club	Apps	Goals
1995–96	Rotherham U	—	—

HARDING, Paul

Born Mitcham 6.3.64 Ht 5 10 Wt 12 05
Midfield. From Barnet.

Season	Club	Apps	Goals
1990–91	Notts Co	24	—
1991–92		29	1
1992–93		1	—
1993–94		—	—
1993–94	*Southend U*	5	—
1993–94	*Watford*	2	—
1993–94	Birmingham C	16	—
1994–95		6	—
1995–96	Cardiff C	36	—

HARDY, Jason

Born Burnley 14.12.69 Ht 5 9 Wt 11 07
Midfield. From Trainee.

Season	Club	Apps	Goals
1986–87	Burnley	1	—
1987–88		—	—
1988–89		17	1
1989–90		22	—
1990–91		—	—
1991–92		3	—
1991–92	*Halifax T*	4	—
1992–93	Halifax T	22	2
From Halifax T			
1995–96	Rochdale	7	—

HARDY, Paul

Born Plymouth 29.8.75 Ht 5 8 Wt 10 05
Midfield. From Trainee.

Season	Club	Apps	Goals
1993–94	Torquay U	1	—

Season	Club	Apps	Goals
1994–95		—	—
1995–96		—	—

HARDY, Phil

Born Chester 9.4.73 Ht 5 7 Wt 11 08
Defender. From Trainee. Eire Under-21.

Season	Club	Apps	Goals
1989–90	Wrexham	1	—
1990–91		32	—
1991–92		42	—
1992–93		32	—
1993–94		25	—
1994–95		44	—
1995–96		42	—

HARDYMAN, Paul

Born Portsmouth 11.3.64 Ht 5 8
Wt 11 04
Defender. From Fareham, Waterford.
England Under-21.

Season	Club	Apps	Goals
1983–84	Portsmouth	3	—
1984–85		15	—
1985–86		21	1
1986–87		33	—
1987–88		20	1
1988–89		25	1
1989–90	Sunderland	42	7
1990–91		32	—
1991–92		32	2
1992–93	Bristol R	37	4
1993–94		25	1
1994–95		5	—
1995–96	Wycombe W	15	—

HARE, Matthew

Born Barnstaple 26.12.76 Ht 6 2
Wt 13 00
Defender. From Trainee.

Season	Club	Apps	Goals
1995–96	Exeter C	13	—

HARFORD, Mick

Born Sunderland 12.2.59 Ht 6 3
Wt 14 05
Forward. From Lambton St BC. England B, 2 full caps.

Season	Club	Apps	Goals
1977–78	Lincoln C	27	9
1978–79		31	6
1979–80		36	16
1980–81		21	10
1980–81	Newcastle U	19	4
1981–82	Bristol C	30	11
1981–82	Birmingham C	12	9
1982–83		29	6
1983–84		39	8
1984–85		12	2
1984–85	Luton T	22	15
1985–86		37	22
1986–87		18	4
1987–88		25	9
1988–89		33	7
1989–90		4	—
1989–90	Derby Co	16	4
1990–91		36	8
1991–92		6	3
1991–92	Luton T	29	12
1992–93	Chelsea	28	9
1992–93	Sunderland	11	2
1993–94	Coventry C	1	1
1994–95	Wimbledon	27	6
1995–96		21	2

HARFORD, Paul

Born Kent 21.10.74 Ht 6 4 Wt 13 12
Forward. From Trainee.

Season	Club	Apps	Goals
1993–94	Blackburn R	—	—
1994–95		—	—
1994–95	*Wigan Ath*	3	—
1994–95	*Shrewsbury T*	6	—
1995–96	Blackburn R	—	—

HARGREAVES, Christian

Born Cleethorpes 12.5.72 Ht 5 11
Wt 12 02
Forward. From Trainee.

Season	Club	Apps	Goals
1989–90	Grimsby T	19	2
1990–91		18	3
1991–92		10	—
1992–93		4	—
1992–93	*Scarborough*	3	—
1993–94	Grimsby T	—	—
1993–94	Hull C	28	—
1994–95		21	—
1995–96	WBA	1	—
1995–96	*Hereford U*	17	2

HARKES, John

Born New Jersey 8.3.67 Ht 5 10
Wt 11 12
Midfield. From USSF. USA full caps.

Season	Club	Apps	Goals
1990–91	Sheffield W	23	2
1991–92		29	3

Season	Club	League Appearances/Goals	
1992–93		29	2
1993–94	Derby Co	33	2
1994–95		33	—
1995–96		8	—
1995–96	West Ham U	11	—

HARKIN, Joe

Born Derry 9.12.75 Ht 5 10 Wt 11 04
Defender. From Trainee.

Season	Club	League Appearances/Goals	
1992–93	Manchester C	—	—
1993–94		—	—
1994–95		—	—
1995–96		—	—

HARKNESS, Steve

Born Carlisle 27.8.71 Ht 5 10 Wt 11 02
Midfield. From Trainee. England Youth.

Season	Club	League Appearances/Goals	
1988–89	Carlisle U	13	—
1989–90	Liverpool	—	—
1990–91		—	—
1991–92		11	—
1992–93		10	—
1993–94		11	—
1993–94	*Huddersfield T*	5	—
1994–95	Liverpool	8	1
1994–95	*Southend U*	6	—
1995–96	Liverpool	24	1

HARLE, Mike

Born Lewisham 31.10.72 Ht 6 0
Wt 12 06
Defender. From Sittingbourne.

Season	Club	League Appearances/Goals	
1993–94	Millwall	—	—
1994–95		—	—
1995–96		—	—
1995–96	*Bury*	1	—

HARMER, Russell

Born Doncaster 29.10.76 Ht 5 10
Wt 11 09
Midfield. From Trainee.

Season	Club	League Appearances/Goals	
1995–96	Barnsley	—	—

HARMON, Darren

Born Northampton 30.1.73 Ht 5 5
Wt 9 12
Midfield. From Trainee.

Season	Club	League Appearances/Goals	
1991–92	Notts Co	—	—
1991–92	Shrewsbury T	5	2
1992–93		1	—
1992–93	Northampton T	25	1
1993–94		31	7
1994–95		33	4
1995–96		—	—
1995–96	*Cambridge U*	—	—

HARPER, Alan

Born Liverpool 1.11.60 Ht 5 9 Wt 11 09
Midfield. From Apprentice. England Youth.

Season	Club	League Appearances/Goals	
1977–78	Liverpool	—	—
1978–79		—	—
1979–80		—	—
1980–81		—	—
1981–82		—	—
1982–83		—	—
1983–84	Everton	29	1
1984–85		13	—
1985–86		21	—
1986–87		36	3
1987–88		28	—
1988–89	Sheffield W	24	—
1989–90		11	—
1989–90	Manchester C	21	—
1990–91		29	1
1991–92	Everton	33	—
1992–93		18	—
1993–94	Luton T	41	1
1994–95	Burnley	27	—
1995–96		4	—
1995–96	*Cardiff C*	5	—

HARPER, Kevin

Born Oldham 15.1.76 Ht 5 6 Wt 10 09
Midfield. From Hutcheson Vale BC. Scotland Under-21.

Season	Club	League Appearances/Goals	
1993–94	Hibernian	2	—
1994–95		23	5
1995–96		16	3

HARPER, Lee

Born London 30.10.71 Ht 6 1 Wt 13 11
Goalkeeper. From Sittingbourne.

Season	Club	League Appearances/Goals	
1994–95	Arsenal	—	—
1995–96		—	—

HARPER, Lee

Born Bridlington 24.3.75 Ht 5 11
Wt 12 05
Defender. From York C Trainee.

Season	Club	App	Gls
1993–94	Scarborough	2	—
1994–95		—	—
1995–96		—	—

HARPER, Steve

Born Stoke 3.2.69 Ht 5 10 Wt 11 12
Forward. From Trainee.

Season	Club	App	Gls
1987–88	Port Vale	21	2
1988–89		7	—
1988–89	Preston NE	5	—
1989–90		36	10
1990–91		36	—
1991–92	Burnley	35	3
1992–93		34	5
1993–94		—	—
1993–94	Doncaster R	31	2
1994–95		33	9
1995–96		1	—
1995–96	Mansfield T	29	5

HARPER, Steve

Born Easington 3.2.70 Ht 6 0 Wt 12 03
Goalkeeper. From Seaham Red Star.

Season	Club	App	Gls
1993–94	Newcastle U	—	—
1994–95		—	—
1995–96		—	—
1995–96	*Bradford C*	1	—

HARRINGTON, Justin

Born Truro 18.6.75 Ht 5 9 Wt 11 00
Forward. From Trainee.

Season	Club	App	Gls
1994–95	Norwich C	—	—
1995–96		—	—

HARRIS, Andrew

Born Springs 26.2.77 Ht 5 10 Wt 11 11
Defender. From Trainee.

Season	Club	App	Gls
1993–94	Liverpool	—	—
1994–95		—	—
1995–96		—	—

HARRIS, Jason

Born Sutton 24.11.76 Ht 6 1 Wt 11 07
Forward. From Trainee.

Season	Club	App	Gls
1995–96	Crystal Palace	—	—

Season Club League Appearances/Goals

HARRIS, Mark

Born Reading 15.7.63 Ht 6 2 Wt 14 07
Midfield. From Wokingham.

Season	Club	App	Gls
1987–88	Crystal Palace	—	—
1988–89		2	—
1989–90		—	—
1989–90	*Burnley*	4	—
1989–90	Swansea C	41	2
1990–91		41	1
1991–92		44	3
1992–93		42	5
1993–94		46	3
1994–95		14	—
1995–96		—	—
1995–96	Gillingham	44	2

HARRIS, Sammy

Born Stockport 2.4.78
Defender. From Trainee.

Season	Club	App	Gls
1995–96	Manchester C	—	—

HARRISON, Gary

Born Northampton 12.3.75 Ht 5 9
Wt 11 05
Forward. From Aston Villa Trainee.

Season	Club	App	Gls
1993–94	Northampton T	2	—
1994–95		5	—
1995–96		—	—

HARRISON, Gerry

Born Lambeth 15.4.72 Ht 5 9 Wt 12 03
Midfield. From Trainee.

Season	Club	App	Gls
1989–90	Watford	3	—
1990–91		6	—
1991–92	Bristol C	4	—
1991–92	*Cardiff C*	10	1
1992–93	Bristol C	33	1
1993–94		1	—
1993–94	*Hereford U*	6	—
1993–94	Huddersfield T	—	—
1994–95	Burnley	19	2
1995–96		35	1

HARRISON, Lee

Born Billericay 12.9.71 Ht 6 2 Wt 12 07
Goalkeeper. From Trainee.

Season	Club	App	Gls
1990–91	Charlton Ath	—	—
1991–92		—	—
1991–92	*Fulham*	—	—

Season Club League Appearances/Goals

Season	Club	Apps	Goals
1991–92	*Gillingham*	2	—
1992–93	Charlton Ath	—	—
1992–93	*Fulham*	—	—
1993–94	Fulham	—	—
1994–95		7	—
1995–96		5	—

HARTE, Ian

Born Drogheda 31.8.77
Defender. From Trainee. Eire 4 full caps.

Season	Club	Apps	Goals
1995–96	Leeds U	4	—

HARTFIELD, Charles

Born London 4.9.71 Ht 6 0 Wt 13 00
Defender. From Trainee.

Season	Club	Apps	Goals
1989–90	Arsenal	—	—
1990–91		—	—
1991–92	Sheffield U	7	—
1992–93		17	—
1993–94		5	—
1994–95		25	1
1995–96		—	—

HARTSON, John

Born Swansea 5.4.75 Ht 6 1 Wt 14 06
Forward. From Trainee. Wales Under-21, 5 full caps.

Season	Club	Apps	Goals
1992–93	Luton T	—	—
1993–94		34	6
1994–95		20	5
1994–95	Arsenal	15	7
1995–96		19	4

HARVEY, Lee

Born Harlow 21.12.66 Ht 5 11 Wt 11 07
Midfield. From Harrow. England Youth.

Season	Club	Apps	Goals
1983–84	Leyton Orient	4	—
1984–85		4	—
1985–86		12	2
1986–87		15	1
1987–88		23	1
1988–89		29	6
1989–90		37	6
1990–91		26	3
1991–92		13	—
1992–93		21	4
1993–94	Nottingham F	2	—
1993–94	Brentford	26	4
1994–95		25	2
1995–96		40	—

HARVEY, Richard

Born Letchworth 17.4.69 Ht 5 10 Wt 11 12
Defender. From Apprentice. England Schools, Youth.

Season	Club	Apps	Goals
1986–87	Luton T	5	—
1987–88		—	—
1988–89		12	—
1989–90		26	—
1990–91		29	—
1991–92		32	2
1992–93		1	—
1992–93	*Blackpool*	5	—
1993–94	Luton T	—	—
1994–95		12	1
1995–96		36	1

HATELEY, Mark

Born Liverpool 7.11.61 Ht 6 1 Wt 11 07
Forward. From Apprentice. England Youth, Under-21, 32 full caps.

Season	Club	Apps	Goals
1978–79	Coventry C	1	—
1979–80		4	—
1980–81		19	3
1981–82		34	13
1982–83		35	9
1983–84	Portsmouth	38	22
1984–85	AC Milan	21	7
1985–86		22	8
1986–87		23	2
1987–88	Monaco	28	14
1988–89		18	6
1989–90		13	2
1990–91	Rangers	33	10
1991–92		30	21
1992–93		37	19
1993–94		42	22
1994–95		23	13
1995–96	QPR	14	2

HATHAWAY, Ian

Born Wordsley 22.8.68 Ht 5 6 Wt 10 10
Midfield. From WBA Apprentice, Bedworth U.

Season	Club	Apps	Goals
1988–89	Mansfield T	12	1
1989–90		22	1
1990–91		10	—
1990–91	Rotherham U	5	1
1991–92		8	—
1992–93		—	—
1993–94	Torquay U	41	7

Season Club League Appearances/Goals

Season	Club	Apps	Goals
1994–95		38	5
1995–96		26	1

HATTON, Paul

Born Kidderminster 2.11.78
Midfield. From Trainee.

Season	Club	Apps	Goals
1995–96	Birmingham C	—	—

HAWES, Steve

Born Wycombe 17.7.78 Ht 5 8 Wt 11 04
Midfield. From Trainee.

Season	Club	Apps	Goals
1995–96	Sheffield U	2	—

HAWKES, Marc

Born Stoke 22.9.76 Ht 6 0 Wt 11 05
Forward. From Trainee.

Season	Club	Apps	Goals
1995–96	Stoke C	—	—

HAWKINS, Colin

Born Galway 17.8.77 Ht 6 1 Wt 12 06
Goalkeeper.

Season	Club	Apps	Goals
1995–96	Coventry C	—	—

HAWORTH, Robert

Born Edgware 21.11.75 Ht 6 2 Wt 13 04
Forward. From Trainee.

Season	Club	Apps	Goals
1993–94	Fulham	11	1
1994–95		10	—
1995–96	Millwall	—	—

HAWORTH, Simon

Born Cardiff 30.3.77 Ht 6 3 Wt 11 05
Forward. From Trainee.

Season	Club	Apps	Goals
1995–96	Cardiff C	13	—

HAWTHORNE, Mark

Born Glasgow 31.10.73 Ht 5 8 Wt 11 09
Midfield. From Trainee.

Season	Club	Apps	Goals
1992–93	Crystal Palace	—	—
1993–94		—	—
1994–95	Sheffield U	—	—
1994–95	Walsall	—	—
1994–95	Torquay U	2	—
1995–96		22	—

HAWTIN, Dale

Born Crewe 28.12.75 Ht 5 11 Wt 11 00
Defender. From Trainee.

Season	Club	Apps	Goals
1995–96	Crewe Alex	—	—

HAY, Christopher

Born Glasgow 28.8.74 Ht 5 11 Wt 11 07
Midfield. From Giffnock N.

Season	Club	Apps	Goals
1993–94	Celtic	2	—
1994–95		5	—
1995–96		4	—

HAYDON, Nicky

Born Barking 10.8.78 Ht 5 9 Wt 11 07
Midfield. From Trainee.

Season	Club	Apps	Goals
1995–96	Colchester U	—	—

HAYES, Adi

Born Norwich 22.5.78 Ht 6 1 Wt 11 10
Midfield. From Trainee.

Season	Club	Apps	Goals
1995–96	Cambridge U	1	—

HAYES, Martin

Born Walthamstow 21.3.66 Ht 6 0
Wt 12 04
Forward. From Apprentice. England Under-21, B.

Season	Club	Apps	Goals
1983–84	Arsenal	—	—
1984–85		—	—
1985–86		11	2
1986–87		35	19
1987–88		27	1
1988–89		17	1
1989–90		12	3
1990–91	Celtic	7	—
1991–92		—	—
1991–92	*Wimbledon*	2	—
1992–93	Swansea C	15	—
1993–94		22	4
1994–95		24	4
1995–96	Southend U	—	—

HAYFIELD, Matthew

Born Bristol 8.8.75 Ht 5 10 Wt 11 07
Midfield. From Trainee.

Season	Club	Apps	Goals
1995–96	Bristol R	6	—

HAYRETTIN, Hakan

Born London 4.2.70 Ht 5 9 Wt 12 04
Midfield. From Trainee.

Season	Club	Apps	Goals
1988–89	Leyton Orient	—	—

Season	Club	League Appearances/Goals	
From Barnet			
1991–92	Barnet	4	—
1992–93		2	—
1992–93	*Torquay U*	4	—
1993–94	Wycombe W	19	1
1994–95	Cambridge U	17	—
1995–96	Doncaster R	—	—

HAYTER, Robert

Born London 20.4.77
Defender. From Trainee.

1995–96	WBA	—	—

HAYWARD, Andy

Born Barnsley 21.6.70 Ht 6 0 Wt 11 00
Forward. From Frickley Ath.

1994–95	Rotherham U	37	6
1995–96		36	2

HAYWARD, Steve

Born Walsall 8.9.71 Ht 5 11 Wt 12 03
Midfield. From Trainee. England Youth.

1988–89	Derby Co	—	—
1989–90		3	—
1990–91		1	—
1991–92		7	—
1992–93		7	1
1993–94		5	—
1994–95		3	—
1994–95	Carlisle U	9	2
1995–96		38	4

HAYWOOD, Paul

Born Barnsley 4.10.75 Ht 5 11 Wt 10 02
Defender. From Trainee.

1992–93	Nottingham F	—	—
1993–94		—	—
1994–95		—	—
1995–96		—	—
1995–96	Doncaster R	—	—

HAZARD, Mickey

Born Sunderland 5.2.60 Ht 5 8 Wt 11 08
Midfield. From Apprentice.

1977–78	Tottenham H	—	—
1978–79		—	—
1979–80		3	—
1980–81		4	—
1981–82		28	5
1982–83		18	1
1983–84		11	2
1984–85		23	4
1985–86		4	1
1985–86	Chelsea	18	1
1986–87		18	6
1987–88		28	2
1988–89		4	—
1989–90		13	—
1989–90	Portsmouth	8	1
1990–91		—	—
1990–91	Swindon T	34	8
1991–92		44	6
1992–93		32	3
1993–94		9	—
1993–94	Tottenham H	17	2
1994–95		11	—
1995–96		—	—

HAZEL, Des

Born Bradford 15.7.67 Ht 5 10 Wt 11 10
Midfield. From Apprentice.

1985–86	Sheffield W	—	—
1986–87		—	—
1986–87	*Grimsby T*	9	2
1987–88	Sheffield W	6	—
1988–89	Rotherham U	42	6
1989–90		33	2
1990–91		39	3
1991–92		38	8
1992–93		36	7
1993–94		29	3
1994–95		21	1
1994–95	Chesterfield	—	—
1995–96		21	—

HEALD, Greg

Born London 26.9.71 Ht 6 2 Wt 13 01
Defender. From Enfield.

1994–95	Peterborough U	29	—
1995–96		40	4

HEALD, Oliver

Born Vancouver 13.3.75 Ht 6 0
Wt 11 13
Forward.

1993–94	Port Vale	—	—
1994–95		—	—
1995–96	Scarborough	9	1

HEALD, Paul

Born Wath-on-Dearne 20.9.68 Ht 6 2
Wt 12 05
Goalkeeper. From Trainee.

Season	Club	Apps	Goals
1987–88	Sheffield U	—	—
1988–89		—	—
1988–89	Leyton Orient	28	—
1989–90		37	—
1990–91		38	—
1991–92		2	—
1991–92	*Coventry C*	2	—
1992–93	Leyton Orient	26	—
1992–93	*Crystal Palace*	—	—
1993–94	Leyton Orient	—	—
1993–94	*Swindon T*	2	—
1994–95	Leyton Orient	45	—
1995–96	Wimbledon	18	—

HEALY, Brett

Born Coventry 6.10.77 Ht 5 8 Wt 10 08
Midfield. From Trainee.

Season	Club	Apps	Goals
1994–95	Coventry C	—	—
1995–96		—	—

HEANEY, Neil

Born Middlesbrough 3.11.71 Ht 5 9
Wt 11 07
Forward. From Trainee. England Youth, Under-21.

Season	Club	Apps	Goals
1989–90	Arsenal	—	—
1990–91		—	—
1990–91	*Hartlepool U*	3	—
1991–92	Arsenal	1	—
1991–92	*Cambridge U*	13	4
1992–93	Arsenal	5	—
1993–94		1	—
1993–94	Southampton	2	—
1994–95		34	2
1995–96		17	2

HEARY, Thomas

Born Dublin 14.2.79 Ht 5 9 Wt 11 03
Midfield. From Trainee.

Season	Club	Apps	Goals
1995–96	Huddersfield T	—	—

HEATH, Adrian

Born Newcastle under Lyme 11.1.61
Ht 5 6 Wt 11 00
Forward. From Apprentice. England Under-21, B.

Season	Club	Apps	Goals
1978–79	Stoke C	2	—
1979–80		38	5
1980–81		38	6
1981–82		17	5
1981–82	Everton	22	6
1982–83		38	10
1983–84		36	12
1984–85		17	11
1985–86		36	10
1986–87		41	11
1987–88		29	9
1988–89		7	2
From Espanol			
1989–90	Aston Villa	9	—
1989–90	Manchester C	12	2
1990–91		35	1
1991–92		28	1
1991–92	Stoke C	6	—
1992–93	Burnley	43	20
1993–94		41	9
1994–95		27	—
1995–96		4	—
1995–96	Sheffield U	4	—
1995–96	Burnley	3	—

HEATH, Stephen

Born Hull 15.11.77
Defender. From Trainee. England Youth.

Season	Club	Apps	Goals
1994–95	Leeds U	—	—
1995–96		—	—

HEATHCOTE, Mike

Born Durham 10.9.65 Ht 6 2 Wt 12 06
Defender. From Middlesbrough, Spennymoor U.

Season	Club	Apps	Goals
1987–88	Sunderland	1	—
1987–88	*Halifax T*	7	1
1988–89	Sunderland	—	—
1989–90		8	—
1989–90	*York C*	3	—
1990–91	Shrewsbury T	39	6
1991–92		5	—
1991–92	Cambridge U	22	5
1992–93		42	2
1993–94		40	5
1994–95		24	1
1995–96	Plymouth Arg	44	4

HECKINGBOTTOM, Paul

Born Barnsley 17.7.77 Ht 5 11 Wt 12 00
Midfield.

1995–96	Sunderland	—	—

HEGARTY, Ryan

Born Edinburgh 8.3.76 Ht 5 11
Wt 10 00
Midfield. From Dundee U BC.

1994–95	Dundee U	—	—
1995–96	Dunfermline Ath	9	1

HEGGS, Carl

Born Leicester 11.10.70 Ht 6 1 Wt 12 10
Forward. From Doncaster R Trainee, Paget R.

1991–92	WBA	3	—
1992–93		17	2
1993–94		6	—
1994–95		14	1
1994–95	*Bristol R*	5	1
1995–96	Swansea C	32	5

HELDER, Glenn

Born Leiden 28.10.68 Ht 5 11 Wt 11 07
Forward. Holland 4 full caps.

1989–90	Sparta	22	2
1990–91		29	4
1991–92		24	2
1992–93		18	1
1993–94	Vitesse	34	5
1994–95		18	7
1994–95	Arsenal	13	—
1995–96		24	1

HELLIWELL, Ian

Born Rotherham 7.11.62 Ht 6 4
Wt 14 08
Forward. From Matlock T.

1987–88	York C	32	8
1988–89		41	11
1989–90		46	14
1990–91		41	7
1991–92	Scunthorpe U	39	9
1992–93		41	13
1993–94	Rotherham U	40	3
1994–95		12	1
1994–95	Stockport Co	17	4
1995–96		22	9
1995–96	Burnley	4	—

HEMMINGS, Tony

Born Burton 21.9.67 Ht 5 10 Wt 12 09
Forward. From Northwich Vic.

1993–94	Wycombe W	26	7
1994–95		20	5
1995–96		3	—

HENDERSON, Damian

Born Leeds 12.5.73 Ht 6 2 Wt 13 12
Forward. From Trainee.

1991–92	Leeds U	—	—
1992–93		—	—
1993–94	Scarborough	17	5
1993–94	Scunthorpe U	20	1
1994–95		17	3
1994–95	*Hereford U*	5	—
1994–95	*Hartlepool U*	12	3
1995–96	Hartlepool U	36	3

HENDERSON, Nicholas

Born Edinburgh 8.2.69 Ht 5 10
Wt 11 01
Forward. From Broxburn.

1990–91	Raith R	1	—
1991–92		—	—
1992–93		—	—
1992–93	Cowdenbeath	32	5
1993–94		22	9
1993–94	Falkirk	10	2
1994–95		21	5
1995–96		9	—
1995–96	Partick T	16	1

HENDON, Ian

Born Ilford 5.12.71 Ht 6 0 Wt 12 10
Defender. From Trainee. England Youth, Under-21.

1989–90	Tottenham H	—	—
1990–91		2	—
1991–92		2	—
1991–92	*Portsmouth*	4	—
1991–92	*Leyton Orient*	6	—
1992–93	Tottenham H	—	—
1992–93	*Barnsley*	6	—
1993–94	Leyton Orient	36	2

Season	Club	League Appearances/Goals	
1994–95		29	—
1994–95	*Birmingham C*	4	—
1995–96	Leyton Orient	38	2

HENDRIE, John

Born Lennoxtown 24.10.63 Ht 5 8
Wt 12 05
Forward. From Apprentice. Scotland Youth.

1981–82	Coventry C	6	—
1982–83		12	2
1983–84		3	—
1983–84	*Hereford U*	6	—
1984–85	Bradford C	46	9
1985–86		42	10
1986–87		42	14
1987–88		43	13
1988–89	Newcastle U	34	4
1989–90	Leeds U	27	5
1990–91	Middlesbrough	41	3
1991–92		38	3
1992–93		32	9
1993–94		29	13
1994–95		39	15
1995–96		13	1

HENDRIE, Lee

Born Birmingham 18.5.77 Ht 5 9
Wt 10 03
Forward. From Trainee. England Youth, Under-21.

1993–94	Aston Villa	—	—
1994–95		—	—
1995–96		3	—

HENDRY, Colin

Born Keith 7.12.65 Ht 6 1 Wt 12 07
Defender. From Islavale. Scotland B, 21 full caps.

1983–84	Dundee	4	—
1984–85		4	—
1985–86		20	—
1986–87		13	2
1986–87	Blackburn R	13	3
1987–88		44	12
1988–89		38	7
1989–90		7	—
1989–90	Manchester C	25	3
1990–91		32	1
1991–92		6	1
1991–92	Blackburn R	30	4
1992–93		41	1
1993–94		23	—
1994–95		38	4
1995–96		33	1

HENDRY, John

Born Glasgow 6.1.70 Ht 5 11 Wt 10 12
Forward. From Hillington YC. Scotland Under-21.

1988–89	Dundee	2	—
1989–90		—	—
1989–90	*Forfar Ath*	10	6
1990–91	Tottenham H	4	2
1991–92		5	1
1991–92	*Charlton Ath*	5	1
1992–93	Tottenham H	5	2
1993–94		3	—
1994–95		—	—
1994–95	*Swansea C*	8	2
1995–96	Motherwell	16	2

HENNIGAN, Gerard

Born Liverpool 2.8.77
Midfield. From Trainee.

1995–96	Everton	—	—

HENRY, David

Born Nottingham 12.9.77
Goalkeeper.

1995–96	Nottingham F	—	—

HENRY, John

Born Vale of Leven 31.12.71 Ht 5 9
Wt 10 00
Forward. From Clydebank BC.

1990–91	Clydebank	3	1
1991–92		35	8
1992–93		32	12
1993–94		44	7
1994–95	Kilmarnock	30	4
1995–96		28	3

Season Club League Appearances/Goals

HENRY, Nick

Born Liverpool 21.2.69 Ht 5 6
Wt 10 08
Midfield. From Trainee.

Season	Club	Apps	Goals
1987–88	Oldham Ath	5	—
1988–89		18	—
1989–90		41	—
1990–91		43	4
1991–92		42	6
1992–93		32	6
1993–94		22	—
1994–95		34	2
1995–96		14	—

HERBERT, Craig

Born Coventry 9.11.75 Ht 5 10
Wt 11 00
Defender. From Torquay U.

Season	Club	Apps	Goals
1993–94	WBA	—	—
1994–95		8	—
1995–96		—	—

HERRERA, Robbie

Born Torbay 12.6.70 Ht 5 6 Wt 10 07
Defender. From Trainee.

Season	Club	Apps	Goals
1987–88	QPR	—	—
1988–89		2	—
1989–90		1	—
1990–91		3	—
1991–92		—	—
1991–92	*Torquay U*	11	—
1992–93	QPR	—	—
1992–93	*Torquay U*	5	—
1993–94	QPR	—	—
1993–94	Fulham	23	1
1994–95		27	—
1995–96		43	—

HESKEY, Emile

Born Leicester 11.1.78 Ht 6 2 Wt 13 02
Midfield. From Trainee. England Youth.

Season	Club	Apps	Goals
1994–95	Leicester C	1	—
1995–96		30	7

HESSENTHALER, Andy

Born Gravesend 17.8.65 Ht 5 7
Wt 11 05
Midfield. From Dartford, Redbridge
Forest.

Season	Club	Apps	Goals
1991–92	Watford	35	1
1992–93		45	3
1993–94		42	5
1994–95		43	2
1995–96		30	—

HETHERSTON, Peter

Born Bellshill 6.11.64 Ht 5 9 Wt 10 07
Midfield. From Bargeddie Ams.

Season	Club	Apps	Goals
1984–85	Falkirk	12	2
1985–86		22	2
1986–87		36	3
1987–88	Watford	5	—
1987–88	Sheffield U	11	—
1988–89	Falkirk	31	3
1989–90		22	2
1990–91		26	4
1991–92	Raith R	31	1
1992–93		44	4
1993–94		34	5
1994–95	Aberdeen	22	—
1995–96		11	—

HEWITT, Jamie

Born Chesterfield 17.5.68 Ht 5 10
Wt 11 04
Midfield. From School.

Season	Club	Apps	Goals
1984–85	Chesterfield	—	—
1985–86		17	—
1986–87		42	2
1987–88		28	2
1988–89		40	1
1989–90		42	6
1990–91		43	—
1991–92		37	3
1992–93	Doncaster R	27	—
1993–94		6	—
1993–94	Chesterfield	29	3
1994–95		38	3
1995–96		28	2

HEWLETT, Matthew

Born Bristol 25.2.76 Ht 6 1 Wt 11 03
Midfield. From Trainee. England Youth.

Season	Club	Apps	Goals
1993–94	Bristol C	12	—
1994–95		1	—
1995–96		27	2

HICKS, Stuart

Born Peterborough 30.5.67 Ht 6 1 Wt 13 03
Defender. From Peterborough U Apprentice, Wisbech.

Season	Club	App	Goals
1987–88	Colchester U	7	—
1988–89		37	—
1989–90		20	—
1990–91	Scunthorpe U	46	1
1991–92		21	—
1992–93	Doncaster R	36	—
1993–94		—	—
1993–94	Huddersfield T	22	1
1993–94	Preston NE	4	—
1994–95		8	—
1994–95	Scarborough	6	—
1995–96		41	1

HIGGINS, Dave

Born Liverpool 19.8.61 Ht 6 0 Wt 11 07
Defender. From Eagle.

Season	Club	App	Goals
1983–84	Tranmere R	20	—
1984–85		8	—
From S. Liverpool, Caernarfon			
1987–88		33	1
1988–89		43	1
1989–90		45	1
1990–91		33	2
1991–92		33	1
1992–93		40	4
1993–94		37	—
1994–95		16	—
1995–96		17	—

HIGGS, Shane

Born Oxford 13.5.77 Ht 6 2 Wt 12 12
Goalkeeper. From Trainee.

Season	Club	App	Goals
1994–95	Bristol R	—	—
1995–96		—	—

HIGNETT, Craig

Born Whiston 12.1.70 Ht 5 9 Wt 11 10
Midfield. From Liverpool Trainee.

Season	Club	App	Goals
1987–88	Crewe Alex	—	—
1988–89		1	—
1989–90		35	8
1990–91		38	13
1991–92		33	13
1992–93		14	8
1992–93	Middlesbrough	21	4
1993–94		29	5
1994–95		26	8
1995–96		22	5

HILES, Paul

Born Bristol 27.9.76 Ht 6 0 Wt 11 06
Defender. From Trainee.

Season	Club	App	Goals
1995–96	Birmingham C	—	—

HILEY, Scott

Born Plymouth 27.9.68 Ht 5 9 Wt 11 05
Midfield. From Trainee.

Season	Club	App	Goals
1986–87	Exeter C	—	—
1987–88		15	1
1988–89		37	5
1989–90		46	—
1990–91		46	2
1991–92		33	1
1992–93		33	3
1992–93	Birmingham C	7	—
1993–94		28	—
1994–95		9	—
1995–96		5	—
1995–96	Manchester C	6	—

HILL, Andy

Born Maltby 20.1.65 Ht 5 11 Wt 12 00
Defender. From Apprentice. England Youth.

Season	Club	App	Goals
1982–83	Manchester U	—	—
1983–84		—	—
1984–85	Bury	43	3
1985–86		35	2
1986–87		42	1
1987–88		43	2
1988–89		43	—
1989–90		46	2
1990–91		12	—
1990–91	Manchester C	8	1
1991–92		36	4
1992–93		24	1
1993–94		17	—
1994–95		13	—
1995–96	Port Vale	35	—

Season	Club	League Appearances/Goals	

HILL, Colin

Born Hillingdon 12.11.63 Ht 6 0
Wt 12 07
Defender. From Apprentice. Northern Ireland 14 full caps.

1981–82	Arsenal	—	—
1982–83		7	—
1983–84		37	1
1984–85		2	—
1985–86		—	—
1985–86	*Brighton & HA*	—	—
From Maritimo			
1987–88	Colchester U	25	—
1988–89		44	—
1989–90	Sheffield U	43	—
1990–91		24	—
1991–92		15	1
1991–92	*Leicester C*	10	—
1992–93	Leicester C	46	—
1993–94		31	—
1994–95		24	—
1995–96		27	—

HILL, Danny

Born Edmonton 1.10.74 Ht 5 9
Wt 11 03
Midfield. From Trainee. England Under-21.

1992–93	Tottenham H	4	—
1993–94		3	—
1994–95		3	—
1995–96		—	—
1995–96	*Birmingham C*	5	—
1995–96	*Watford*	1	—

HILL, Keith

Born Bolton 17.5.69 Ht 6 0 Wt 12 06
Defender. From Apprentice.

1986–87	Blackburn R	—	—
1987–88		1	—
1988–89		15	1
1989–90		25	—
1990–91		22	2
1991–92		32	—
1992–93		1	—
1992–93	Plymouth Arg	36	—
1993–94		29	1
1994–95		34	1
1995–96		24	—

HILLIER, David

Born Blackheath 19.12.69 Ht 5 10
Wt 12 05
Midfield. From Trainee. England Under-21.

1987–88	Arsenal	—	—
1988–89		—	—
1989–90		—	—
1990–91		16	—
1991–92		27	1
1992–93		30	1
1993–94		15	—
1994–95		9	—
1995–96		5	—

HILLS, John

Born Blackpool 21.4.78 Ht 5 8 Wt 10 08
Midfield. From Trainee.

1995–96	Blackpool	—	—
1995–96	Everton	—	—

HILTON, David

Born Barnsley 10.11.77 Ht 5 11
Wt 10 10
Defender. From Trainee. England Youth.

1994–95	Manchester U	—	—
1995–96		—	—

HIMSWORTH, Gary

Born Appleton 19.12.69 Ht 5 8
Wt 11 00
Defender. From Trainee.

1987–88	York C	31	2
1988–89		32	2
1989–90		23	4
1990–91		2	—
1990–91	Scarborough	23	1
1991–92		36	4
1992–93		33	1
1993–94	Darlington	28	3
1994–95		38	2
1995–96		28	3
1995–96	York C	8	1

HINCHCLIFFE, Andy

Born Manchester 5.2.69 Ht 5 10
Wt 13 07
Defender. From Apprentice. England Youth, Under-21.

1986–87	Manchester C	—	—

Season	Club	League Appearances/Goals		
1987–88		....	42	1
1988–89		....	39	5
1989–90		....	31	2
1990–91	Everton	....	21	1
1991–92		....	18	—
1992–93		....	25	1
1993–94		....	26	—
1994–95		....	29	2
1995–96		....	28	2

HINES, Leslie

Born Germany 7.1.77 Ht 6 5 Wt 9 08
Midfield. From Trainee.

1994–95	Aston Villa	....	—	—
1995–96		....	—	—

HINSHELWOOD, Danny

Born Bromley 4.12.75 Ht 5 9 Wt 11 14
Defender. From Trainee. England Youth.

1992–93	Nottingham F	....	—	—
1993–94		....	—	—
1994–95		....	—	—
1995–96		....	—	—
1995–96	Portsmouth	....	5	—

HIRST, David

Born Barnsley 7.12.67 Ht 6 0 Wt 13 08
Forward. From Apprentice. England Youth, Under-21, B, 3 full caps.

1985–86	Barnsley	....	28	9
1986–87	Sheffield W	....	21	6
1987–88		....	24	3
1988–89		....	32	7
1989–90		....	38	14
1990–91		....	41	24
1991–92		....	33	18
1992–93		....	22	11
1993–94		....	7	1
1994–95		....	15	3
1995–96		....	30	13

HISLOP, Shaka

Born London 22.2.69 Ht 6 3 Wt 14 04
Goalkeeper. From Howard Univ, USA.

1992–93	Reading	....	12	—
1993–94		....	46	—
1994–95		....	46	—
1995–96	Newcastle U	....	24	—

HITCHCOCK, Kevin

Born Custom House 5.10.62 Ht 6 1 Wt 13 04
Goalkeeper. From Barking.

1983–84	Nottingham F	....	—	—
1983–84	*Mansfield T*	....	14	—
1984–85	Mansfield T	....	43	—
1985–86		....	46	—
1986–87		....	46	—
1987–88		....	33	—
1987–88	Chelsea	....	8	—
1988–89		....	3	—
1989–90		....	—	—
1990–91		....	3	—
1990–91	*Northampton T*	....	17	—
1991–92	Chelsea	....	21	—
1992–93		....	20	—
1992–93	*West Ham U*	....	—	—
1993–94	Chelsea	....	2	—
1994–95		....	12	—
1995–96		....	12	—

HITCHEN, Steve

Born Salford 28.11.76 Ht 5 10 Wt 11 04
Defender. From Trainee.

1995–96	Blackburn R	....	—	—

HOBSON, Gary

Born North Ferriby 12.11.71 Ht 6 1 Wt 13 03
Defender. From Trainee.

1990–91	Hull C	....	4	—
1991–92		....	16	—
1992–93		....	21	—
1993–94		....	36	—
1994–95		....	36	—
1995–96		....	29	—
1995–96	Brighton & HA	....	9	—

HOCKING, Matthew

Born Boston 30.1.78
Midfield. From Trainee.

1995–96	Sheffield U	....	—	—

HODDLE, Glenn

Born Hayes 27.10.57 Ht 6 0 Wt 11 06
Midfield. From Apprentice. England Youth, Under-21, B, 53 full caps.

Season	Club	Apps	Goals
1974–75	Tottenham H	—	—
1975–76		7	1
1976–77		39	4
1977–78		41	12
1978–79		35	7
1979–80		41	19
1980–81		38	12
1981–82		34	10
1982–83		24	1
1983–84		24	4
1984–85		28	8
1985–86		31	7
1986–87		35	3
From Monaco			
1990–91	Chelsea	—	—
1991–92	Swindon T	22	—
1992–93		42	1
1993–94	Chelsea	19	1
1994–95		12	—
1995–96		—	—

HODGE, John

Born Ormskirk 1.4.69 Ht 5 7 Wt 11 03
Forward. From Exmouth.

Season	Club	Apps	Goals
1991–92	Exeter C	23	1
1992–93		42	9
1993–94	Swansea C	27	2
1994–95		44	7
1995–96		41	1

HODGE, Martin

Born Southport 4.2.59 Ht 6 2 Wt 15 03
Goalkeeper. From Apprentice.

Season	Club	Apps	Goals
1976–77	Plymouth Arg	—	—
1977–78		5	—
1978–79		38	—
1979–80	Everton	23	—
1980–81		2	—
1981–82	*Preston NE*	28	—
1982–83	*Oldham Ath*	4	—
1982–83	*Gillingham*	4	—
1982–83	*Preston NE*	16	—
1983–84	Sheffield W	42	—
1984–85		42	—
1985–86		42	—
1986–87		42	—
1987–88		29	—
1988–89	Leicester C	19	—
1989–90		46	—
1990–91		10	—
1991–92	Hartlepool U	40	—
1992–93		29	—
1993–94	Rochdale	42	—
1994–95	Plymouth Arg	17	—
1995–96		—	—

HODGE, Steve

Born Nottingham 25.10.62 Ht 5 8
Wt 11 03
Midfield. From Apprentice. England Under-21, B, 24 full caps.

Season	Club	Apps	Goals
1980–81	Nottingham F	—	—
1981–82		1	—
1982–83		39	8
1983–84		39	10
1984–85		42	12
1985–86		2	—
1985–86	Aston Villa	36	8
1986–87		17	4
1986–87	Tottenham H	19	4
1987–88		26	3
1988–89	Nottingham F	34	7
1989–90		34	10
1990–91		14	3
1991–92	Leeds U	23	7
1992–93		23	2
1993–94		8	1
1994–95		—	—
1994–95	*Derby Co*	10	2
1994–95	QPR	15	—
1995–96		—	—
1995–96	Watford	2	—

HODGES, Danny

Born Greenwich 14.9.76 Ht 6 0
Wt 12 07
Defender. From Trainee. England Youth.

Season	Club	Apps	Goals
1995–96	Wimbledon	—	—

HODGES, Glyn

Born Streatham 30.4.63 Ht 6 1 Wt 12 03
Midfield. From Apprentice. Wales Youth, Under-21, B, 18 full caps.

Season	Club	Apps	Goals
1980–81	Wimbledon	30	5
1981–82		34	2
1982–83		37	9
1983–84		42	15
1984–85		22	3

Season	Club	Apps	Goals
1985–86		30	6
1986–87		37	9
1987–88	Newcastle U	7	—
1987–88	Watford	24	3
1988–89		27	5
1989–90		35	7
1990–91	Crystal Palace	7	—
1990–91	Sheffield U	12	4
1991–92		26	2
1992–93		31	4
1993–94		31	2
1994–95		25	4
1995–96		22	3
1995–96	Derby Co	9	—

HODGES, Kevin

Born Bridport 12.6.60 Ht 5 7 Wt 11 01
Midfield. From Apprentice.

Season	Club	Apps	Goals
1977–78	Plymouth Arg	—	—
1978–79		12	—
1979–80		44	5
1980–81		41	5
1981–82		46	11
1982–83		46	11
1983–84		43	4
1984–85		45	10
1985–86		46	16
1986–87		35	5
1987–88		37	6
1988–89		31	1
1989–90		44	4
1990–91		42	3
1991–92		14	—
1991–92	*Torquay U*	3	—
1992–93	Plymouth Arg	4	—
1992–93	Torquay U	8	1
1993–94		29	2
1994–95		28	1
1995–96		2	—

HODGES, Lee

Born Epping 4.9.73 Ht 6 0 Wt 12 01
Forward. From Trainee.

Season	Club	Apps	Goals
1991–92	Tottenham H	—	—
1992–93		4	—
1992–93	*Plymouth Arg*	7	2
1993–94	Tottenham H	—	—
1993–94	*Wycombe W*	4	—
1994–95	Barnet	34	4
1995–96		40	17

HODGES, Lee

Born Newham 2.3.78 Ht 5 5 Wt 10 02
Forward. From Trainee.

Season	Club	Apps	Goals
1994–95	West Ham U	—	—
1995–96		—	—

HODGSON, Doug

Born Frankston 27.2.69 Ht 6 2 Wt 13 09
Midfield. From Heidelberg.

Season	Club	Apps	Goals
1994–95	Sheffield U	1	—
From Heidelberg			
1995–96		16	—
1995–96	*Plymouth Arg*	5	—

HOGARTH, Myles

Born Falkirk 30.3.75 Ht 6 1 Wt 11 11
Goalkeeper. From Newtongrange Star.

Season	Club	Apps	Goals
1995–96	Hearts	1	—

HOGG, Graeme

Born Aberdeen 17.6.64 Ht 6 1 Wt 12 04
Defender. From Apprentice. Scotland Under-21.

Season	Club	Apps	Goals
1982–83	Manchester U	—	—
1983–84		16	1
1984–85		29	—
1985–86		17	—
1986–87		11	—
1987–88		10	—
1987–88	*WBA*	7	—
1988–89	Portsmouth	41	1
1989–90		39	1
1990–91		20	—
1991–92	Hearts	18	1
1992–93		22	2
1993–94		17	—
1994–95		1	—
1994–95	Notts Co	17	—
1995–96		10	—

HOLCROFT, Peter

Born Liverpool 3.1.76 Ht 5 9 Wt 11 00
Midfield. From Trainee.

Season	Club	Apps	Goals
1994–95	Everton	—	—
1995–96		—	—

Season Club League Appearances/Goals

HOLDEN, Andy

Born Flint 14.9.62 Ht 6 1 Wt 13 02
Defender. From Rhyl.

Season	Club	Apps	Goals
1983–84	Chester C	44	7
1984–85		38	6
1985–86		10	2
1986–87		8	2
1986–87	Wigan Ath	11	1
1987–88		15	2
1988–89		23	1
1988–89	Oldham Ath	13	4
1989–90		6	—
1990–91		2	—
1991–92		—	—
1992–93		—	—
1993–94		—	—
1994–95		1	—
1995–96		—	—

HOLDEN, Mark

Born Tamworth 2.4.76 Ht 5 7 Wt 11 06
Defender. From Trainee.

Season	Club	Apps	Goals
1994–95	Stoke C	—	—
1995–96		—	—

HOLDEN, Rick

Born Skipton 9.9.64 Ht 5 11 Wt 12 07
Forward.

Season	Club	Apps	Goals
1985–86	Burnley	1	—
1986–87	Halifax T	32	2
1987–88		35	10
1987–88	Watford	10	2
1988–89		32	6
1989–90	Oldham Ath	45	9
1990–91		42	5
1991–92		42	5
1992–93	Manchester C	41	3
1993–94		9	—
1993–94	Oldham Ath	29	6
1994–95		31	3
1995–96	Blackpool	22	2

HOLDSWORTH, David

Born Walthamstow 8.11.68 Ht 6 1
Wt 12 04
Defender. From Trainee. England Youth, Under-21.

Season	Club	Apps	Goals
1986–87	Watford	—	—
1987–88		—	—
1988–89		33	1
1989–90		44	3
1990–91		15	2
1991–92		33	2
1992–93		39	—
1993–94		28	—
1994–95		39	1
1995–96		27	1

HOLDSWORTH, Dean

Born Walthamstow 8.11.68 Ht 5 11
Wt 11 13
Forward. From Trainee.

Season	Club	Apps	Goals
1986–87	Watford	2	—
1987–88	*Carlisle U*	4	1
1987–88	*Port Vale*	6	2
1988–89	Watford	10	2
1988–89	*Swansea C*	5	1
1988–89	*Brentford*	7	1
1989–90	Watford	4	1
1989–90	Brentford	39	24
1990–91		30	5
1991–92		41	24
1992–93	Wimbledon	36	19
1993–94		42	17
1994–95		28	7
1995–96		33	10

HOLLAND, Chris

Born Whalley 11.9.75 Ht 5 9 Wt 11 05
Midfield. From Trainee. England Youth, Under-21.

Season	Club	Apps	Goals
1993–94	Preston NE	1	—
1993–94	Newcastle U	3	—
1994–95		—	—
1995–96		—	—

HOLLAND, Matthew

Born Bury 11.4.74 Ht 5 9 Wt 11 12
Midfield. From Trainee.

Season	Club	Apps	Goals
1992–93	West Ham U	—	—
1993–94		—	—
1994–95		—	—
1994–95	Bournemouth	16	1
1995–96		43	10

HOLLAND, Paul

Born Lincoln 8.7.73 Ht 5 10 Wt 12 03
Midfield. From School. England Under-21.

Season	Club	Apps	Goals
1990–91	Mansfield T	1	—
1991–92		38	6

Season Club League Appearances/Goals

Season	Club	Apps	Goals
1992–93	....	39	3
1993–94	....	38	7
1994–95	....	33	9
1995–96	Sheffield U	18	1
1995–96	Chesterfield	17	2

HOLLMAN, James

Born Canterbury 22.3.78
Midfield. From Trainee.

Season	Club	Apps	Goals
1995–96	Ipswich T	—	—

HOLLOWAY, Darren

Born Bishop Auckland 3.10.77
Defender. From Trainee.

Season	Club	Apps	Goals
1995–96	Sunderland	—	—

HOLLOWAY, Ian

Born Kingswood 12.3.63 Ht 5 7
Wt 10 10
Midfield. From Apprentice.

Season	Club	Apps	Goals
1980–81	Bristol R	1	—
1981–82	....	1	—
1982–83	....	31	7
1983–84	....	36	1
1984–85	....	42	6
1985–86	Wimbledon	19	2
1985–86	*Brentford*	13	2
1986–87	Brentford	16	—
1986–87	*Torquay U*	5	—
1987–88	Brentford	1	—
1987–88	Bristol R	43	5
1988–89	....	44	6
1989–90	....	46	8
1990–91	....	46	7
1991–92	QPR	40	—
1992–93	....	24	2
1993–94	....	25	—
1994–95	....	31	1
1995–96	....	27	1

HOLLOWAY, Jonathan

Born Swindon 11.2.77 Ht 5 10 Wt 12 04
Defender. From Trainee.

Season	Club	Apps	Goals
1995–96	Swindon T	—	—

HOLMES, Darren

Born Sheffield 30.1.75 Ht 5 10 Wt 11 07
Midfield. From Trainee.

Season	Club	Apps	Goals
1993–94	Sheffield W	—	—
1994–95	....	—	—
1995–96	....	—	—

HOLMES, Matt

Born Luton 1.8.69 Ht 5 7 Wt 11 00
Forward. From Trainee.

Season	Club	Apps	Goals
1988–89	Bournemouth	4	1
1988–89	*Cardiff C*	1	—
1989–90	Bournemouth	22	2
1990–91	....	42	2
1991–92	....	46	3
1992–93	West Ham U	18	—
1993–94	....	34	3
1994–95	....	24	1
1995–96	Blackburn R	9	1

HOLMES, Paul

Born Wortley 18.2.68 Ht 5 10 Wt 11 00
Defender. From Apprentice.

Season	Club	Apps	Goals
1985–86	Doncaster R	5	1
1986–87	....	16	—
1987–88	....	26	—
1988–89	Torquay U	25	—
1989–90	....	44	2
1990–91	....	33	1
1991–92	....	36	1
1992–93	Birmingham C	12	—
1992–93	Everton	4	—
1993–94	....	15	—
1994–95	....	1	—
1995–96	....	1	—
1995–96	WBA	18	—

HOLMES, Steve

Born Middlesbrough 13.1.71 Ht 6 2
Wt 13 00
Defender. From Guisborough T.

Season	Club	Apps	Goals
1993–94	Preston NE	—	—
1994–95	....	5	1
1994–95	*Hartlepool U*	5	2
From Guisborough T			
1995–96	Preston NE	8	—
1995–96	Lincoln C	23	2

Season Club League Appearances/Goals

HOLSGROVE, Paul

Born Wellington 26.8.69 Ht 6 1
Wt 11 10
Forward. From Trainee.

Season	Club	Apps	Goals
1986–87	Aldershot	—	—
1987–88		2	—
1988–89		1	—
1988–89	*Wimbledon*	—	—
1989–90	Aldershot	—	—
1989–90	*WBA*	—	—
From Wokingham			
1990–91	Luton T	1	—
1991–92		1	—
From Heracles			
1992–93	Millwall	11	—
1993–94		—	—
1994–95	Reading	24	3
1995–96		30	1

HOLT, Gary

Born Irvine 9.3.73 Ht 6 1 Wt 11 11
Midfield. From Celtic.

Season	Club	Apps	Goals
1994–95	Stoke C	—	—
1995–96	Kilmarnock	26	—

HOLT, Michael

Born Burnley 28.7.77 Ht 5 9 Wt 10 09
Forward. From Trainee.

Season	Club	Apps	Goals
1995–96	Blackburn R	—	—

HOLWYN, Jermaine

Born Amsterdam 16.4.73 Ht 5 10
Wt 11 08
Defender. From Ajax.

Season	Club	Apps	Goals
1995–96	Port Vale	—	—

HOMER, Chris

Born Stockton 16.4.77 Ht 5 9 Wt 10 05
Midfield. From Trainee.

Season	Club	Apps	Goals
1994–95	Hartlepool U	1	—
1995–96		5	—

HONE, Mark

Born Croydon 31.3.68 Ht 6 1 Wt 13 01
Defender. From Trainee.

Season	Club	Apps	Goals
1985–86	Crystal Palace	—	—
1986–87		—	—
1987–88		3	—
1988–89		1	—
1989–90		—	—
From Welling			
1994–95	Southend U	40	—
1995–96		16	—

HONEYMAN, Ben

Born Adelaide 14.2.77 Ht 5 9 Wt 10 03
Midfield. From Dundee U BC.

Season	Club	Apps	Goals
1994–95	Dundee U	—	—
1995–96		1	—

HOOKER, Jon

Born London 31.3.72 Ht 5 6 Wt 11 00
Midfield. From Hertford T.

Season	Club	Apps	Goals
1994–95	Gillingham	—	—
1994–95	Brentford	1	—
1995–96		4	—

HOOKS, John

Born Armagh 10.2.77 Ht 5 8 Wt 11 07
Defender. From Southampton.

Season	Club	Apps	Goals
1995–96	Blackpool	—	—

HOOPER, Dean

Born Harefield 13.4.71 Ht 5 10 Wt 12 08
Midfield. From Hayes.

Season	Club	Apps	Goals
1994–95	Swindon T	4	—
From Hayes			
1995–96		—	—
1995–96	*Peterborough U*	4	—

HOOPER, Mike

Born Bristol 10.2.64 Ht 6 3 Wt 13 05
Goalkeeper. From Mangotsfield.

Season	Club	Apps	Goals
1983–84	Bristol C	—	—
1984–85		1	—
1984–85	*Wrexham*	20	—
1985–86	Wrexham	14	—
1985–86	Liverpool	—	—
1986–87		11	—
1987–88		2	—
1988–89		17	—
1989–90		—	—
1990–91		7	—
1990–91	*Leicester C*	14	—
1991–92	Liverpool	5	—
1992–93		9	—

Season	Club	Apps	Goals
1993–94		—	—
1993–94	Newcastle U	19	—
1994–95		6	—
1995–96		—	—
1995–96	*Sunderland*	—	—

HOPE, Chris

Born Sheffield 14.11.72 Ht 6 0 Wt 12 02
Defender. From Darlington.

Season	Club	Apps	Goals
1991–92	Nottingham F	—	—
1992–93		—	—
1993–94	Scunthorpe U	41	—
1994–95		24	—
1995–96		40	3

HOPE, Richard

Born Stockton 22.6.78 Ht 6 2 Wt 12 06
Defender. From Trainee.

Season	Club	Apps	Goals
1995–96	Blackburn R	—	—

HOPKIN, David

Born Greenock 21.8.70 Ht 5 9 Wt 10 03
Midfield. From Pt Glasgow R BC.

Season	Club	Apps	Goals
1989–90	Morton	8	—
1990–91		10	—
1991–92		—	—
1992–93	Chelsea	4	—
1993–94		21	—
1994–95		15	1
1995–96	Crystal Palace	42	8

HOPKINS, Jeff

Born Swansea 14.4.64 Ht 6 0 Wt 12 11
Defender. From Apprentice. Wales Youth, Under-21, 16 full caps.

Season	Club	Apps	Goals
1980–81	Fulham	1	—
1981–82		35	—
1982–83		41	1
1983–84		33	—
1984–85		40	2
1985–86		23	—
1986–87		20	1
1987–88		26	—
1988–89	Crystal Palace	43	—
1989–90		27	2
1990–91		—	—
1991–92		—	—
1991–92	*Plymouth Arg*	8	—
1991–92	Bristol R	6	—
1992–93	Reading	36	1
1993–94		42	2
1994–95		21	—
1995–96		14	—

HOPPER, Neil

Born Southampton 27.1.76 Ht 6 1
Wt 12 08
Goalkeeper. From Trainee.

Season	Club	Apps	Goals
1994–95	Southampton	—	—
1995–96	Blackpool	—	—
1995–96	Crewe Alex	—	—

HOPPER, Tony

Born Carlisle 31.5.76 Ht 5 10 Wt 11 13
Midfield. From Trainee.

Season	Club	Apps	Goals
1992–93	Carlisle U	1	—
1993–94		—	—
1994–95		5	—
1995–96		5	—

HORLOCK, Kevin

Born Plumstead 1.11.72 Ht 6 0 Wt 12 00
Defender. From Trainee. Northern Ireland 2 full caps.

Season	Club	Apps	Goals
1991–92	West Ham U	—	—
1992–93		—	—
1992–93	Swindon T	14	1
1993–94		38	—
1994–95		38	1
1995–96		45	12

HORNE, Barry

Born St Asaph 18.5.62 Ht 5 10 Wt 12 01
Midfield. From Rhyl. Wales 54 full caps.

Season	Club	Apps	Goals
1984–85	Wrexham	44	6
1985–86		46	3
1986–87		46	8
1987–88	Portsmouth	39	3
1988–89		31	4
1988–89	Southampton	11	—
1989–90		29	4
1990–91		38	1
1991–92		34	1
1992–93	Everton	34	1
1993–94		32	1
1994–95		31	—
1995–96		26	1

Season	Club	League Appearances/Goals	

HORNE, Brian

Born Billericay 5.10.67 Ht 5 10
Wt 14 00
Goalkeeper. From Apprentice. England Youth, Under-21.

Season	Club	Apps	Goals
1985–86	Millwall	—	—
1986–87		32	—
1987–88		43	—
1988–89		38	—
1989–90		22	—
1990–91		28	—
1991–92		—	—
1991–92	*Watford*	—	—
1992–93	Millwall	—	—
1992–93	*Middlesbrough*	4	—
1992–93	*Stoke C*	1	—
1992–93	Portsmouth	—	—
1993–94		3	—
1994–95	Hartlepool U	41	—
1995–96		32	—

HORNER, Philip

Born Leeds 10.11.66 Ht 6 1 Wt 12 07
Forward. From Lincoln C Schools.

Season	Club	Apps	Goals
1984–85	Leicester C	—	—
1985–86		—	—
1985–86	*Rotherham U*	4	—
1986–87	Leicester C	3	—
1987–88		7	—
1988–89	Halifax T	38	3
1989–90		34	1
1990–91	Blackpool	39	7
1991–92		27	4
1992–93		46	7
1993–94		41	2
1994–95		34	2
1995–96		—	—

HOTTIGER, Marc

Born Lausanne 7.11.67 Ht 5 9 Wt 11 00
Defender. Switzerland 61 full caps.

Season	Club	Apps	Goals
1988–89	Lausanne	20	3
1989–90		35	1
1990–91		33	1
1991–92		35	—
1992–93	Sion	32	7
1993–94		35	6
1994–95	Newcastle U	38	1
1995–96		1	—
1995–96	Everton	9	1

HOUCHEN, Keith

Born Middlesbrough 25.7.60 Ht 6 2
Wt 13 04
Forward. From Chesterfield Amateur.

Season	Club	Apps	Goals
1977–78	Hartlepool U	13	4
1978–79		39	12
1979–80		41	14
1980–81		45	17
1981–82		32	18
1981–82	Orient	14	1
1982–83		32	10
1983–84		30	9
1983–84	York C	7	1
1984–85		35	12
1985–86		25	6
1985–86	Scunthorpe U	9	3
1986–87	Coventry C	20	2
1987–88		21	3
1988–89		13	2
1988–89	Hibernian	7	2
1989–90		29	8
1990–91		21	1
1991–92	Port Vale	21	4
1992–93		28	6
1993–94	Hartlepool U	34	8
1994–95		32	13
1995–96		38	6

HOUGHTON, Ray

Born Glasgow 9.1.62 Ht 5 7 Wt 10 10
Midfield. From Amateur. Eire 66 full caps.

Season	Club	Apps	Goals
1979–80	West Ham U	—	—
1980–81		—	—
1981–82		1	—
1982–83	Fulham	42	5
1983–84		40	3
1984–85		42	8
1985–86		5	—
1985–86	Oxford U	35	4
1986–87		37	5
1987–88		11	1
1987–88	Liverpool	28	5
1988–89		38	7
1989–90		19	1
1990–91		32	7
1991–92		36	8
1992–93	Aston Villa	39	3
1993–94		30	2
1994–95		26	1
1994–95	Crystal Palace	10	2
1995–96		41	4

HOUGHTON, Scott

Born Hitchin 22.10.71 Ht 5 6
Wt 12 01
Forward. From Trainee. England Schools, Youth.

Season	Club	Apps	Goals
1990–91	Tottenham H	—	—
1990–91	*Ipswich T*	8	1
1991–92	Tottenham H	10	2
1992–93		—	—
1992–93	*Cambridge U*	—	—
1992–93	*Gillingham*	3	—
1992–93	*Charlton Ath*	6	—
1993–94	Luton T	15	1
1994–95		1	—
1994–95	Walsall	38	8
1995–96		40	6

HOULT, Russell

Born Leicester 22.11.72 Ht 6 4
Wt 14 05
Goalkeeper. From Trainee.

Season	Club	Apps	Goals
1990–91	Leicester C	—	—
1991–92		—	—
1991–92	*Lincoln C*	2	—
1991–92	*Blackpool*	—	—
1992–93	Leicester C	10	—
1993–94		—	—
1993–94	*Bolton W*	4	—
1994–95	Leicester C	—	—
1994–95	*Lincoln C*	15	—
1994–95	*Derby Co*	15	—
1995–96	Derby Co	41	—

HOUNSELL, Daniel

Born Southampton 11.10.76
Defender. From Trainee.

Season	Club	Apps	Goals
1995–96	Portsmouth	—	—

HOUSHAM, Steven

Born Gainsborough T 24.2.76 Ht 5 10
Wt 11 00
Defender. From Trainee.

Season	Club	Apps	Goals
1993–94	Scunthorpe U	—	—
1994–95		4	—
1995–96		28	—

HOWARD, Jonathan

Born Sheffield 7.10.71 Ht 5 10 Wt 12 00
Forward. From Trainee.

Season	Club	Apps	Goals
1990–91	Rotherham U	1	—
1991–92		10	3
1992–93		17	2
1993–94		8	—
1994–95		—	—
1994–95	Chesterfield	12	1
1995–96		30	2

HOWARD, Steve

Born Durham 10.5.76 Ht 6 1 Wt 13 08
Midfield. From Tow Law T.

Season	Club	Apps	Goals
1995–96	Hartlepool U	39	7

HOWARD, Terry

Born Stepney 26.2.66 Ht 6 1 Wt 14 00
Defender. From Apprentice. England Youth.

Season	Club	Apps	Goals
1983–84	Chelsea	—	—
1984–85		4	—
1985–86		1	—
1985–86	*Crystal Palace*	4	—
1986–87	Chelsea	1	—
1986–87	*Chester C*	2	—
1986–87	Leyton Orient	12	2
1987–88		41	2
1988–89		46	5
1989–90		45	7
1990–91		46	3
1991–92		45	4
1992–93		41	5
1993–94		25	2
1994–95		27	1
1994–95	Wycombe W	20	—
1995–96		39	2

HOWARTH, Lee

Born Bolton 3.1.68 Ht 6 3 Wt 13 08
Defender. From Chorley.

Season	Club	Apps	Goals
1991–92	Peterborough U	7	—
1992–93		30	—
1993–94		25	—
1994–95	Mansfield T	40	2
1995–96		17	—
1995–96	Barnet	19	—

Season	Club	League Appearances/Goals

HOWE, Eddie
Born Amersham 29.11.77
Defender. From Trainee.

1995–96	Bournemouth	5	—

HOWE, Stephen
Born Annitsford 6.1.73 Ht 5 7 Wt 10 06
Midfield. From Trainee.

1991–92	Nottingham F	—	—
1992–93		—	—
1993–94		4	—
1994–95		—	—
1995–96		9	2

HOWELL, David
Born London 10.10.58 Ht 6 0 Wt 12 00
Defender. From Fulham, Hillingdon, Hounslow, Harrow Borough, Enfield.

1991–92	Barnet	34	3
1992–93		23	—
1993–94	Southend U	6	—
1994–95		—	—
1994–95	Birmingham C	2	—
1995–96		—	—

HOWELL, Jamie
Born Rustington 19.2.77
Midfield. From Trainee. England Youth.

1995–96	Arsenal	—	—

HOWELLS, David
Born Guildford 15.12.67 Ht 5 11
Wt 12 04
Midfield. From Trainee. England Youth.

1984–85	Tottenham H	—	—
1985–86		1	1
1986–87		1	—
1987–88		11	—
1988–89		27	3
1989–90		34	5
1990–91		29	4
1991–92		31	1
1992–93		18	1
1993–94		18	1
1994–95		26	1
1995–96		29	3

HOWES, Shaun
Born Norwich 7.11.77 Ht 5 10 Wt 11 02
Midfield. From Trainee.

1995–96	Cambridge U	1	—

HOWEY, Lee
Born Sunderland 1.4.69 Ht 6 2 Wt 13 08
Forward. From AC Hemptinne Eghezee.

1992–93	Sunderland	1	—
1993–94		14	3
1994–95		15	2
1995–96		27	3

HOWEY, Steve
Born Sunderland 26.10.71 Ht 6 1
Wt 11 12
Midfield. From Trainee. England 4 full caps.

1988–89	Newcastle U	1	—
1989–90		—	—
1990–91		11	—
1991–92		21	1
1992–93		41	2
1993–94		14	—
1994–95		30	1
1995–96		28	1

HOWIE, Scott
Born Glasgow 4.1.72 Ht 6 2 Wt 13 07
Goalkeeper. From Ferguslie U. Scotland Under-21.

1991–92	Clyde	15	—
1992–93		39	—
1993–94		1	—
1993–94	Norwich C	2	—
1994–95	Motherwell	3	—
1995–96		36	—

HOY, Kristian
Born Doncaster 27.4.76 Ht 5 11
Wt 12 00
Forward.

1994–95	Doncaster R	1	—
1995–96		—	—

HOYLAND, Jamie

Born Sheffield 23.1.66 Ht 6 0 Wt 14 00
Midfield. From Apprentice. England Youth.

Season	Club	Apps	Goals
1983–84	Manchester C	1	—
1984–85		1	—
1985–86		—	—
1986–87	Bury	36	2
1987–88		44	8
1988–89		46	9
1989–90		46	16
1990–91	Sheffield U	21	—
1991–92		26	4
1992–93		22	2
1993–94		18	—
1993–94	*Bristol C*	6	—
1994–95	Sheffield U	2	—
1994–95	Burnley	30	2
1995–96		23	—

HOYLE, Colin

Born Derby 15.1.72 Ht 5 11 Wt 12 03
Defender. From Trainee.

Season	Club	Apps	Goals
1989–90	Arsenal	—	—
1989–90	*Chesterfield*	3	—
1990–91	Barnsley	—	—
1991–92		—	—
1992–93		—	—
1992–93	Bradford C	33	1
1993–94		29	—
1994–95	Notts Co	3	—
1994–95	*Mansfield T*	5	—
1995–96	Notts Co	2	—

HUCKERBY, Darren

Born Nottingham 23.4.76 Ht 5 10
Wt 11 11
Midfield. From Trainee.

Season	Club	Apps	Goals
1993–94	Lincoln C	6	1
1994–95		6	2
1995–96		16	2
1995–96	Newcastle U	1	—

HUGGINS, Dean

Born Cardiff 21.11.76 Ht 5 10 Wt 11 00
Defender. From Trainee. Wales Under-21.

Season	Club	Apps	Goals
1995–96	Bristol C	—	—

HUGHES, Andrew

Born Manchester 2.1.78
Midfield. From Trainee.

Season	Club	Apps	Goals
1995–96	Oldham Ath	15	1

HUGHES, Anthony

Born Liverpool 3.10.73 Ht 6 0 Wt 12 05
Defender. From Trainee. England Youth.

Season	Club	Apps	Goals
1992–93	Crewe Alex	17	1
1993–94		6	—
1994–95		—	—
1995–96		—	—

HUGHES, Bryan

Born Liverpool 19.6.76 Ht 5 11
Wt 11 02
Midfield. From Trainee.

Season	Club	Apps	Goals
1993–94	Wrexham	11	—
1994–95		38	9
1995–96		22	—

HUGHES, Ceri

Born Pontypridd 26.2.71 Ht 5 10
Wt 12 07
Midfield. From Trainee. Wales Youth, Under-21, 5 full caps.

Season	Club	Apps	Goals
1989–90	Luton T	1	—
1990–91		17	1
1991–92		18	—
1992–93		29	2
1993–94		42	7
1994–95		9	2
1995–96		23	1

HUGHES, Darren

Born Prescot 6.10.65 Ht 5 11 Wt 13 01
Defender. From Apprentice.

Season	Club	Apps	Goals
1983–84	Everton	1	—
1984–85		2	—
1985–86	Shrewsbury T	31	1
1986–87		6	—
1986–87	Brighton & HA	26	2
1987–88		—	—
1987–88	Port Vale	43	1
1988–89		44	—
1989–90		38	1
1990–91		17	—
1991–92		42	2
1992–93		—	—
1993–94		—	—

Season	Club	Apps	Goals
1994–95	Northampton T.........	13	—
1995–96	....	8	—
1995–96	Exeter C....................	26	—

HUGHES, David

Born St Albans 30.12.72 Ht 5 10
Wt 11 08
Midfield. From Trainee.

Season	Club	Apps	Goals
1991–92	Southampton.............	—	—
1992–93	....	—	—
1993–94	....	2	—
1994–95	....	12	2
1995–96	....	11	1

HUGHES, Ian

Born Bangor 2.8.74 Ht 5 11 Wt 12 08
Midfield. From Trainee. Wales Under-21.

Season	Club	Apps	Goals
1991–92	Bury..........................	17	—
1992–93	....	15	—
1993–94	....	38	—
1994–95	....	23	1
1995–96	....	32	—

HUGHES, Jamie

Born Liverpool 5.4.77 Ht 6 0 Wt 11 00
Forward. From Trainee.

Season	Club	Apps	Goals
1995–96	Tranmere R...............	—	—

HUGHES, John

Born Edinburgh 9.9.64 Ht 6 0 Wt 13 07
Defender. From Newtongrange Star.

Season	Club	Apps	Goals
1988–89	Berwick R.................	27	10
1989–90	....	14	4
1989–90	Swansea C	24	4
1990–91	Falkirk.......................	32	2
1991–92	....	38	2
1992–93	....	15	—
1993–94	....	29	3
1994–95	....	20	—
1995–96	Celtic.........................	26	2

HUGHES, Lee

Born Walsall 19.6.77
Midfield. From Trainee.

Season	Club	Apps	Goals
1995–96	Birmingham C...........	—	—

Season Club League Appearances/Goals

HUGHES, Mark

Born Wrexham 1.11.63 Ht 6 0 Wt 12 04
Forward. From Apprentice. Wales Youth, Under-21, 60 full caps.

Season	Club	Apps	Goals
1980–81	Manchester U	—	—
1981–82	....	—	—
1982–83	....	—	—
1983–84	....	11	4
1984–85	....	38	16
1985–86	....	40	17
1986–87	Barcelona	28	4
1987–88	*Bayern Munich*	18	6
1988–89	Manchester U	38	14
1989–90	....	37	13
1990–91	....	31	10
1991–92	....	39	11
1992–93	....	41	15
1993–94	....	36	11
1994–95	....	34	8
1995–96	Chelsea	31	8

HUGHES, Mark

Born Port Talbot 3.2.62 Ht 6 0 Wt 13 00
Defender. From Apprentice. Wales Youth.

Season	Club	Apps	Goals
1979–80	Bristol R	1	—
1980–81	....	38	1
1981–82	....	22	2
1982–83	....	4	—
1982–83	*Torquay U*	9	1
1983–84	Bristol R	9	—
1984–85	Swansea C	12	—
1984–85	Bristol C....................	20	—
1985–86	....	2	—
1985–86	Tranmere R...............	32	—
1986–87	....	38	1
1987–88	....	20	—
1988–89	....	37	1
1989–90	....	45	4
1990–91	....	42	2
1991–92	....	33	1
1992–93	....	11	—
1993–94	....	8	—
1994–95	Shrewsbury T	20	—
1995–96	....	2	—

HUGHES, Michael

Born Larne 2.8.71 Ht 5 7 Wt 10 13
Forward. From Carrick R. Northern Ireland Under-23, 31 full caps.

Season	Club	Apps	Goals
1988–89	Manchester C............	1	—
1989–90	....	—	—

Season	Club	League Appearances	Goals
1990–91		1	—
1991–92		24	1
1992–93	Strasbourg	36	2
1993–94		34	7
1994–95		13	—
1994–95	*West Ham U*	17	2
1995–96	*West Ham U*	28	—

HUGHES, Paul

Born Hammersmith 19.4.76 Ht 6 0
Wt 11 07
Midfield. From Trainee. England Schools.

Season	Club	League Appearances	Goals
1994–95	Chelsea	—	—
1995–96		—	—

HUGHES, Stephen

Born Wokingham 18.9.76 Ht 6 0
Wt 12 08
Midfield. From Trainee. England Youth.

Season	Club	League Appearances	Goals
1994–95	Arsenal	1	—
1995–96		1	—

HULME, Kevin

Born Farnworth 7.12.67 Ht 5 10
Wt 13 07
Forward. From Radcliffe Borough.

Season	Club	League Appearances	Goals
1988–89	Bury	5	—
1989–90		19	1
1989–90	*Chester C*	4	—
1990–91	Bury	24	7
1991–92		30	4
1992–93		32	9
1993–94	Doncaster R	34	8
1994–95	Bury	28	—
1995–96		1	—
1995–96	Lincoln C	5	—

HUMES, Tony

Born Blyth 19.3.66 Ht 6 0 Wt 12 00
Defender. From Apprentice.

Season	Club	League Appearances	Goals
1983–84	Ipswich T	—	—
1984–85		—	—
1985–86		—	—
1986–87		22	2
1987–88		27	—
1988–89		26	3
1989–90		24	3
1990–91		16	2
1991–92		5	—
1991–92	Wrexham	8	—

Season	Club	League Appearances	Goals
1992–93		38	—
1993–94		27	1
1994–95		29	—
1995–96		27	3

HUMPHREY, John

Born Paddington 31.1.61 Ht 5 10
Wt 11 04
Defender. From Apprentice.

Season	Club	League Appearances	Goals
1978–79	Wolverhampton W	—	—
1979–80		2	—
1980–81		12	—
1981–82		23	—
1982–83		42	3
1983–84		28	—
1984–85		42	—
1985–86	Charlton Ath	39	2
1986–87		39	—
1987–88		40	—
1988–89		38	1
1989–90		38	—
1990–91	Crystal Palace	38	1
1991–92		37	—
1992–93		32	—
1993–94		32	1
1993–94	*Reading*	8	—
1994–95	Crystal Palace	21	—
1995–96	Charlton Ath	28	—

HUMPHREYS, Richie

Born Sheffield 30.11.77
Midfield. From Trainee.

Season	Club	League Appearances	Goals
1995–96	Sheffield W	5	—

HUMPHRIES, Glenn

Born Hull 11.8.64 Ht 6 0 Wt 12 00
Defender. From Apprentice. England Youth.

Season	Club	League Appearances	Goals
1980–81	Doncaster R	1	—
1981–82		14	—
1982–83		40	5
1983–84		44	2
1984–85		27	—
1985–86		29	—
1986–87		17	1
1986–87	*Lincoln C*	9	—
1987–88	Doncaster R	8	—
1987–88	Bristol C	24	—

Season Club League Appearances/Goals

Season	Club	Apps	Goals
1988–89		22	—
1989–90		37	—
1990–91		2	—
1990–91	Scunthorpe U	10	1
1991–92		32	3
1992–93		30	1
From Golden			
1995–96	Hull C	12	—

HUMPHRIES, Mark

Born Glasgow 23.12.71 Ht 5 10
Wt 12 12
Defender. From Cove R.

Season	Club	Apps	Goals
1990–91	Aberdeen	—	—
1991–92		2	—
1992–93		—	—
1993–94	Leeds U	—	—
1994–95	Bristol C	4	—
1995–96		—	—
1995–96	Raith R	9	—

HUNT, Andy

Born Thurrock 9.6.70 Ht 6 0 Wt 11 12
Forward. From Kettering T.

Season	Club	Apps	Goals
1990–91	Newcastle U	16	2
1991–92		27	9
1992–93		—	—
1992–93	*WBA*	10	9
1993–94	WBA	35	12
1994–95		39	13
1995–96		45	14

HUNT, James

Born Nottingham 17.12.76 Ht 5 8
Wt 10 03
Midfield. From Trainee.

Season	Club	Apps	Goals
1994–95	Notts Co	—	—
1995–96		10	1

HUNT, Jonathan

Born London 2.11.71 Ht 5 10 Wt 11 00
Midfield. From Barnet, Slough T.

Season	Club	Apps	Goals
1991–92	Barnet	14	—
1992–93		19	—
1993–94	Southend U	42	6
1994–95		7	—
1994–95	Birmingham C	20	5
1995–96		45	11

HUNT, Kevin

Born Chatham 4.7.75 Ht 5 10 Wt 11 00
Midfield.

Season	Club	Apps	Goals
1994–95	Gillingham	—	—
1995–96		—	—

HUNTER, Barry

Born Coleraine 18.11.68 Ht 6 3
Wt 12 09
Defender. From Crusaders. Northern Ireland 6 full caps.

Season	Club	Apps	Goals
1993–94	Wrexham	23	1
1994–95		37	—
1995–96		31	3

HUNTER, Gordon

Born Wallyford 3.5.67 Ht 5 10 Wt 10 05
Defender. From Musselburgh Windsor. Scotland Youth, Under-21.

Season	Club	Apps	Goals
1983–84	Hibernian	1	—
1984–85		6	—
1985–86		25	—
1986–87		29	—
1987–88		35	—
1988–89		33	1
1989–90		34	—
1990–91		20	1
1991–92		37	2
1992–93		23	—
1993–94		29	1
1994–95		29	2
1995–96		22	—

HUNTER, Roy

Born Cleveland 29.10.73 Ht 5 10
Wt 12 08
Midfield. From Trainee.

Season	Club	Apps	Goals
1991–92	WBA	6	1
1992–93		1	—
1993–94		2	—
1994–95		—	—
1995–96	Northampton T	34	—

HURDLE, Gus

Born London 14.10.73 Ht 5 7 Wt 11 01
Defender. From Fulham.

Season	Club	Apps	Goals
1994–95	Brentford	9	—
1995–96		14	—

HURLOCK, Terry

Born Hackney 22.9.58 Ht 5 9 Wt 14 01
Midfield. From Leytonstone/Ilford.
England B.

Season	Club	Apps	Goals
1980–81	Brentford	42	4
1981–82		40	2
1982–83		39	3
1983–84		32	4
1984–85		40	3
1985–86		27	2
1985–86	Reading	16	—
1986–87		13	—
1986–87	Millwall	13	1
1987–88		28	4
1988–89		34	3
1989–90		29	—
1990–91	Rangers	29	2
1991–92		—	—
1991–92	Southampton	29	—
1992–93		30	—
1993–94		2	—
1993–94	Millwall	13	—
1994–95	Fulham	27	1
1995–96		—	—

HURST, Glynn

Born Barnsley 17.1.76 Ht 5 10 Wt 11 06
Defender. From Tottenham H Trainee.

Season	Club	Apps	Goals
1994–95	Barnsley	2	—
1995–96		5	—
1995–96	*Swansea C*	2	1

HURST, Lee

Born Nuneaton 21.9.70 Ht 6 0 Wt 11 09
Midfield. From Trainee.

Season	Club	Apps	Goals
1989–90	Coventry C	—	—
1990–91		4	—
1991–92		10	—
1992–93		35	2
1993–94		—	—
1994–95		—	—
1995–96		—	—

HURST, Matthew

Born Farnborough 3.11.77 Ht 5 7
Wt 10 03
Forward. From Trainee.

Season	Club	Apps	Goals
1994–95	Nottingham F	—	—
1995–96		—	—

HURST, Paul

Born Sheffield 25.9.74 Ht 5 4 Wt 9 00
Defender. From Trainee.

Season	Club	Apps	Goals
1993–94	Rotherham U	4	—
1994–95		13	—
1995–96		40	1

HURST, Richard

Born Hammersmith 23.12.76 Ht 6 0
Wt 13 00
Goalkeeper. From Trainee.

Season	Club	Apps	Goals
1994–95	QPR	—	—
1995–96		—	—

HUTCHINGS, Carl

Born London 24.9.74 Ht 5 11 Wt 11 00
Midfield. From Trainee.

Season	Club	Apps	Goals
1993–94	Brentford	29	—
1994–95		39	—
1995–96		23	—

HUTCHISON, Don

Born Gateshead 9.5.71 Ht 6 2 Wt 11 04
Forward. From Trainee.

Season	Club	Apps	Goals
1989–90	Hartlepool U	13	2
1990–91		11	—
1990–91	Liverpool	—	—
1991–92		3	—
1992–93		31	7
1993–94		11	—
1994–95	West Ham U	23	9
1995–96		12	2
1995–96	Sheffield U	19	2

HUTT, Stephen

Born Middlesbrough 19.2.79
Forward. From Trainee.

Season	Club	Apps	Goals
1995–96	Hartlepool U	1	—

HUXFORD, Richard

Born Scunthorpe 25.7.69 Ht 6 0
Wt 12 02
Defender. From Kettering T.

Season	Club	Apps	Goals
1992–93	Barnet	33	1
1993–94	Millwall	31	—
1993–94	*Birmingham C*	5	—
1994–95	Millwall	1	—
1994–95	Bradford C	33	1
1995–96		26	1

Season Club League Appearances/Goals

HYDE, Graham

Born Doncaster 10.11.70 Ht 5 8
Wt 11 11
Midfield. From Trainee.

Season	Club	Apps	Goals
1988–89	Sheffield W	—	—
1989–90		—	—
1990–91		—	—
1991–92		13	—
1992–93		20	1
1993–94		36	1
1994–95		35	5
1995–96		26	1

HYDE, Micah

Born Newham 10.11.74 Ht 5 10
Wt 11 07
Midfield. From Trainee.

Season	Club	Apps	Goals
1993–94	Cambridge U	18	2
1994–95		27	—
1995–96		24	4

HYDE, Paul

Born Hayes 7.4.63 Ht 6 1 Wt 14 00
Goalkeeper. From Hayes.

Season	Club	Apps	Goals
1993–94	Wycombe W	42	—
1994–95		46	—
1995–96		17	—
1995–96	Leicester C	—	—

IGA, Andrew

Born Kampala 9.12.77
Goalkeeper. From Trainee.

Season	Club	Apps	Goals
1995–96	Millwall	—	—

IGOE, Sammy

Born Spelthorne 30.9.75 Ht 5 6
Wt 10 08
Midfield. From Trainee.

Season	Club	Apps	Goals
1993–94	Portsmouth	—	—
1994–95		1	—
1995–96		22	—

ILLINGWORTH, Jeremy

Born Huddersfield 20.5.77 Ht 5 10
Wt 11 11
Midfield. From Trainee.

Season	Club	Apps	Goals
1995–96	Huddersfield T	—	—

ILLMAN, Neil

Born Doncaster 29.4.75 Ht 5 9 Wt 11 00
Forward. From Eastwood T.

Season	Club	Apps	Goals
1995–96	Plymouth Arg	—	—
1995–96	*Cambridge U*	5	—

IMBER, Noel

Born London 4.12.76
Goalkeeper. From Trainee.

Season	Club	Apps	Goals
1995–96	Arsenal	—	—

IMMEL, Eike

Born Marburg/Lahn 27.11.60 Ht 6 2
Wt 13 05
Goalkeeper. From Stadtallendorf.

Season	Club	Apps	Goals
1978–79	Borussia Dortmund	10	—
1979–80		34	—
1980–81		34	—
1981–82		34	—
1982–83		34	—
1983–84		33	—
1984–85		34	—
1985–86		34	—
1986–87	Stuttgart	33	—
1987–88		29	—
1988–89		29	—
1989–90		27	—
1990–91		34	—
1991–92		38	—

Season Club League Appearances/Goals

Season	Club	Apps	Goals
1992–93		30	—
1993–94		34	—
1994–95		33	—
1995–96	Manchester C	38	—

IMPEY, Andrew

Born Hammersmith 13.9.71 Ht 5 8
Wt 11 02
Forward. From Yeading. England Under-21.

Season	Club	Apps	Goals
1990–91	QPR	—	—
1991–92		13	—
1992–93		40	2
1993–94		33	3
1994–95		40	3
1995–96		29	3

IMPEY, Jamie

Born Bournemouth 28.7.77 Ht 6 3
Wt 11 11
Midfield. From Trainee.

Season	Club	Apps	Goals
1994–95	Aston Villa	—	—
1995–96		—	—

INCE, Paul

Born Ilford 21.10.67 Ht 5 10 Wt 12 02
Midfield. From Trainee. England Youth, Under-21, B, 23 full caps.

Season	Club	Apps	Goals
1985–86	West Ham U	—	—
1986–87		10	1
1987–88		28	3
1988–89		33	3
1989–90		1	—
1989–90	Manchester U	26	—
1990–91		31	3
1991–92		33	3
1992–93		41	5
1993–94		39	8
1994–95		36	5
1995–96	Internazionale	30	3

INGESSON, Klas

Born Odeshog 20.8.68 Ht 6 3 Wt 14 00
Midfield. From IFK Gothenburg, Mechelen, PSV Eindhoven. Sweden full caps.

Season	Club	Apps	Goals
1994–95	Sheffield W	13	2
1995–96		5	—

INGLETHORPE, Alex

Born Epsom 14.11.71 Ht 5 11 Wt 11 07
Forward. From School.

Season	Club	Apps	Goals
1990–91	Watford	1	—
1991–92		2	—
1992–93		—	—
1993–94		9	2
1994–95		—	—
1994–95	*Barnet*	6	3
1994–95	Leyton Orient	—	—
1995–96		30	9

INGLIS, John

Born Edinburgh 16.10.66 Ht 6 0
Wt 13 00
Defender. From Hutchison Vale.

Season	Club	Apps	Goals
1983–84	East Fife	4	1
1984–85		9	—
1985–86		30	—
1986–87		13	—
1986–87	Brechin C	15	—
1987–88		26	3
1988–89		12	1
1988–89	Meadowbank T	12	1
1989–90		38	3
1990–91	St Johnstone	31	1
1991–92		40	—
1992–93		39	—
1993–94		25	1
1994–95		5	—
1994–95	Aberdeen	17	1
1995–96		24	1

INGLIS, Neil

Born Glasgow 10.9.74 Ht 6 1 Wt 12 02
Goalkeeper. From Rangers BC.

Season	Club	Apps	Goals
1991–92	Rangers	—	—
1992–93		—	—
1993–94		—	—
1994–95		—	—
1995–96	Falkirk	1	—

INGRAM, Chris

Born Cardiff 5.12.76
Forward. From Trainee.

Season	Club	Apps	Goals
1995–96	Cardiff C	8	1

INGRAM, Denny

Born Sunderland 27.6.76 Ht 5 10
Wt 12 01
Defender. From Trainee.

1993–94	Hartlepool U	13	—
1994–95		35	—
1995–96		33	2

INGRAM, Rae

Born Manchester 6.12.74 Ht 5 11
Wt 12 08
Defender. From Trainee.

1993–94	Manchester C	—	—
1994–95		—	—
1995–96		5	—

INMAN, Niall

Born Wakefield 6.2.78
Midfield. From Trainee.

1995–96	Peterborough U	1	—

INNES, Lee

Born Co Durham 28.2.76 Ht 6 2
Wt 11 10
Forward. From Trainee.

1994–95	Sheffield U	—	—
1995–96		—	—
1995–96	Darlington	—	—

INNES, Mark

Born Bellshill 27.9.78
Defender. From Trainee.

1995–96	Oldham Ath	—	—

IORFA, Dominic

Born Lagos 1.10.68 Ht 6 0 Wt 12 12
Forward. From Antwerp. Nigeria full caps.

1989–90	QPR	1	—
1990–91		6	—
1991–92		1	—
1992–93		—	—
1992–93	Peterborough U	26	1
1993–94		34	8
1994–95	Southend U	8	1
1995–96		2	—
1995–96	Falkirk	4	1

IRELAND, Craig

Born Aberdeen 29.11.75 Ht 6 3
Wt 13 09
Defender. From Aberdeen Lads.

1994–95	Aberdeen	—	—
1995–96	Dunfermline Ath	10	—

IRELAND, Simon

Born Barnstaple 23.11.71 Ht 5 10
Wt 10 10
Midfield. From School.

1990–91	Huddersfield T	6	—
1991–92		9	—
1991–92	*Wrexham*	5	—
1992–93	Huddersfield T	4	—
1992–93	Blackburn R	1	—
1993–94		—	—
1993–94	*Mansfield T*	9	1
1994–95	Mansfield T	40	5
1995–96		39	5

IRONS, Kenny

Born Liverpool 4.11.70 Ht 5 10
Wt 12 02
Midfield. From Trainee.

1989–90	Tranmere R	3	—
1990–91		32	6
1991–92		43	7
1992–93		42	7
1993–94		34	3
1994–95		38	4
1995–96		32	3

IRONSIDE, Ian

Born Sheffield 8.3.64 Ht 6 2 Wt 13 10
Goalkeeper. From Barnsley Apprentice, N Ferriby U.

1987–88	Scarborough	6	—
1988–89		28	—
1989–90		14	—
1990–91		40	—
1991–92	Middlesbrough	1	—
1991–92	*Scarborough*	7	—
1992–93	Middlesbrough	12	—
1993–94		—	—
1993–94	Stockport Co	11	—
1994–95		8	—
1994–95	Scarborough	9	—
1995–96		40	—

IRVINE, Brian

Born Bellshill 24.5.65 Ht 6 2 Wt 13 00
Defender. From Victoria Park. Scotland 9 full caps.

Season	Club	Apps	Goals
1983–84	Falkirk	3	—
1984–85		35	—
1985–86	Aberdeen	1	—
1986–87		20	1
1987–88		16	1
1988–89		27	2
1989–90		31	1
1990–91		29	2
1991–92		41	4
1992–93		39	5
1993–94		42	7
1994–95		17	1
1995–96		18	3

IRVING, Richard

Born Halifax 10.9.75 Ht 5 8 Wt 10 07
Forward. From Trainee. England Youth.

Season	Club	Apps	Goals
1992–93	Manchester U	—	—
1993–94		—	—
1994–95		—	—
1995–96	Nottingham F	1	—

IRWIN, Denis

Born Cork 31.10.65 Ht 5 8 Wt 10 08
Defender. From Apprentice. Eire Schools, Youth, Under-21, B, 40 full caps.

Season	Club	Apps	Goals
1983–84	Leeds U	12	—
1984–85		41	1
1985–86		19	—
1986–87	Oldham Ath	41	1
1987–88		43	—
1988–89		41	2
1989–90		42	1
1990–91	Manchester U	34	—
1991–92		38	4
1992–93		40	5
1993–94		42	2
1994–95		40	2
1995–96		31	1

ISAIAS

Born Brazil 0.0.0 Ht 5 10 Wt 12 10
Midfield. From Benfica.

Season	Club	Apps	Goals
1995–96	Coventry C	11	2

IZZET, Muzzy

Born Mile End 31.10.74 Ht 5 10 Wt 10 12
Midfield. From Trainee.

Season	Club	Apps	Goals
1993–94	Chelsea	—	—
1994–95		—	—
1995–96		—	—
1995–96	*Leicester C*	9	1

JACK, Rodney

Born Kingston, Ja 28.9.72 Ht 5 6
Wt 10 08
Forward. From Lambada. St Vincent full caps.

1995–96	Torquay U	14	2

JACKSON, Chris

Born Barnsley 16.1.76 Ht 5 9 Wt 11 06
Forward. From Trainee. England Youth.

1992–93	Barnsley	3	—
1993–94		4	1
1994–95		8	1
1995–96		8	—

JACKSON, Christopher

Born Edinburgh 29.10.73 Ht 5 7
Wt 10 11
Midfield. From Salvesen BC.

1992–93	Hibernian	1	—
1993–94		11	—
1994–95		—	—
1995–96		23	2

JACKSON, Darren

Born Edinburgh 25.7.66 Ht 5 10
Wt 10 10
Forward. From Broxburn Am. Scotland 12 full caps.

1985–86	Meadowbank T	39	17
1986–87		9	5
1986–87	Newcastle U	23	3
1987–88		31	2
1988–89		15	2
1988–89	Dundee U	1	—
1989–90		25	7
1990–91		33	12
1991–92		28	11
1992–93	Hibernian	36	13
1993–94		40	7
1994–95		31	10
1995–96		36	9

JACKSON, David

Born Solihull 22.8.78
Defender. From Trainee.

1995–96	Shrewsbury T	1	—

JACKSON, Kirk

Born Barnsley 16.10.76 Ht 5 11
Wt 11 06
Forward. From Trainee.

1994–95	Sheffield W	—	—
1995–96		—	—

JACKSON, Mark

Born Leeds 30.9.77
Defender. From Trainee. England Youth.

1995–96	Leeds U	1	—

JACKSON, Matthew

Born Leeds 19.10.71 Ht 6 1 Wt 12 09
Defender. From Schools. England Schools, Under-21.

1990–91	Luton T	—	—
1990–91	*Preston NE*	4	—
1991–92	Luton T	9	—
1991–92	Everton	30	1
1992–93		27	3
1993–94		38	—
1994–95		29	—
1995–96		14	—
1995–96	*Charlton Ath*	8	—

JACKSON, Michael

Born West Cheshire 4.12.73 Ht 6 0
Wt 13 10
Defender. From Trainee.

1991–92	Crewe Alex	1	—
1992–93		4	—
1993–94	Bury	39	—
1994–95		24	2
1995–96		31	4

JACKSON, Peter

Born Bradford 6.4.61 Ht 6 0 Wt 13 06
Defender. From Apprentice.

1978–79	Bradford C	9	1
1979–80		12	—
1980–81		45	1
1981–82		32	8
1982–83		41	3
1983–84		42	3
1984–85		45	8
1985–86		42	—
1986–87		10	—
1986–87	Newcastle U	31	1

Season	Club	League Appearances/Goals	
1987–88		28	2
1988–89		1	—
1988–89	Bradford C	32	3
1989–90		26	2
1990–91	Huddersfield T	38	1
1991–92		45	1
1992–93		39	1
1993–94		33	—
1994–95		—	—
1994–95	Chester C	32	1
1995–96		36	1

JACKSON, Scott

Born Leeds 6.1.77 Ht 6 1 Wt 11 08
Midfield. From Trainee.

1995–96	Bradford C	—	—

JACOBS, Wayne

Born Sheffield 3.2.69 Ht 5 10 Wt 11 02
Defender. From Apprentice.

1986–87	Sheffield W	—	—
1987–88		6	—
1987–88	Hull C	6	—
1988–89		33	—
1989–90		46	3
1990–91		19	1
1991–92		25	—
1992–93		—	—
1993–94	Rotherham U	42	2
1994–95	Bradford C	38	1
1995–96		28	—

JAKUB, Joe

Born Falkirk 7.12.56 Ht 5 6 Wt 9 06
Midfield. From Apprentice.

1973–74	Burnley	—	—
1974–75		—	—
1975–76		1	—
1976–77		5	—
1977–78		—	—
1978–79		13	—
1979–80		23	—
1980–81		—	—
1981–82	Bury	33	1
1982–83		46	2
1983–84		46	3
1984–85		46	11
1985–86		40	3
1986–87		44	6
1987–88		10	1

From AZ Alkmaar

Season	Club	League Appearances/Goals	
1988–89	Chester C	42	1
1989–90	Burnley	46	5
1990–91		46	3
1991–92		39	—
1992–93		32	—
1993–94	Chester C	36	—
1994–95	Wigan Ath	16	—
1995–96	Preston NE	—	—

JAMES, David

Born Welwyn 1.8.70 Ht 6 5 Wt 14 02
Goalkeeper. From Trainee. England Youth, Under-21, B.

1988–89	Watford	—	—
1989–90		—	—
1990–91		46	—
1991–92		43	—
1992–93	Liverpool	29	—
1993–94		14	—
1994–95		42	—
1995–96		38	—

JAMES, Julian

Born Tring 22.3.70 Ht 5 10 Wt 12 04
Midfield. From Trainee. England Under-21.

1987–88	Luton T	3	—
1988–89		1	—
1989–90		20	1
1990–91		17	1
1991–92		28	2
1991–92	*Preston NE*	6	—
1992–93	Luton T	43	2
1993–94		33	3
1994–95		42	3
1995–96		27	—

JAMES, Kevin

Born Edinburgh 3.12.75 Ht 6 0
Wt 12 00
Defender. From Musselburgh Ath.

1994–95	Falkirk	1	—
1995–96		13	2

JAMES, Martin

Born Formby 18.5.71 Ht 5 10 Wt 11 10
Midfield. From Trainee.

1989–90	Preston NE	—	—
1990–91		37	2
1991–92		36	4

Season	Club	League Appearances/Goals	
1992–93		25	5
1992–93	Stockport Co	8	—
1993–94		24	—
1994–95	Rotherham U	40	—
1995–96		1	—

JAMES, Tony

Born Sheffield 27.6.67 Ht 6 3 Wt 14 05
Defender. From Gainsborough T.

Season	Club	League Appearances/Goals	
1988–89	Lincoln C	28	—
1989–90		1	—
1989–90	Leicester C	31	2
1990–91		38	8
1991–92		13	—
1992–93		16	—
1993–94		9	1
1994–95	Hereford U	18	2
1995–96		17	2

JAMIESON, Willie

Born Barnsley 27.4.63 Ht 5 11 Wt 12 00
Defender. From Tynecastle BC.

Season	Club	League Appearances/Goals	
1980–81	Hibernian	28	12
1981–82		12	5
1982–83		19	2
1983–84		33	4
1984–85		25	2
1985–86	Hamilton A	39	2
1986–87		15	—
1987–88		41	4
1988–89		34	1
1989–90	Dundee	14	—
1990–91		38	2
1991–92		38	4
1992–93	Partick T	28	3
1993–94		43	1
1994–95		15	—
1994–95	Hearts	15	3
1995–96		5	—

JANNEY, Mark

Born Romford 2.12.77
Forward. From Trainee.

Season	Club	League Appearances/Goals	
1995–96	Tottenham H	—	—

JANSEN, Matthew

Born Carlisle 20.10.77
Midfield. From Trainee.

Season	Club	League Appearances/Goals	
1995–96	Carlisle U	—	—

JAQUES, Daniel

Born North Ormesby 18.1.78
Midfield. From Trainee.

Season	Club	League Appearances/Goals	
1994–95	Leeds U	—	—
1995–96		—	—

JARDINE, Jamie

Born Liverpool 1.2.77 Ht 5 10 Wt 12 00
Midfield.

Season	Club	League Appearances/Goals	
1995–96	Tranmere R	—	—

JARMAN, Lee

Born Cardiff 16.12.77 Ht 6 1 Wt 10 10
Defender. From Trainee. Wales Under-21.

Season	Club	League Appearances/Goals	
1995–96	Cardiff C	32	—

JEFFERIS, Martin

Born Shrewsbury 22.8.76
Defender. From Trainee.

Season	Club	League Appearances/Goals	
1995–96	Shrewsbury T	—	—

JEFFERS, John

Born Liverpool 5.10.68 Ht 5 10
Wt 11 10
Forward. From Trainee. England Schools.

Season	Club	League Appearances/Goals	
1986–87	Liverpool	—	—
1987–88		—	—
1988–89		—	—
1988–89	Port Vale	15	—
1989–90		40	1
1990–91		31	2
1991–92		33	3
1992–93		26	2
1993–94		25	1
1994–95		10	1
1994–95	*Shrewsbury T*	3	1
1995–96	Port Vale	—	—
1995–96	Stockport Co	23	3

JEFFREY, Andrew

Born Bellshill 15.1.72 Ht 5 10 Wt 12 08
Defender. From Cambridge C.

Season	Club	League Appearances/Goals	
1993–94	Cambridge U	40	—
1994–95		28	2
1995–96		27	—

Season Club League Appearances/Goals

JEFFREY, Mike

Born Liverpool 11.8.71 Ht 6 1 Wt 11 09
Forward. From Trainee.

Season	Club	Apps	Goals
1988–89	Bolton W	9	—
1989–90		4	—
1990–91		—	—
1991–92		2	—
1991–92	*Doncaster R*	11	6
1992–93	Doncaster R	30	12
1993–94		8	1
1993–94	Newcastle U	2	—
1994–95		—	—
1995–96	Rotherham U	22	5

JEMSON, Nigel

Born Hutton 10.8.69 Ht 5 10 Wt 12 10
Forward. From Trainee. England Under-21.

Season	Club	Apps	Goals
1985–86	Preston NE	1	—
1986–87		4	3
1987–88		27	5
1987–88	Nottingham F	—	—
1988–89		—	—
1988–89	*Bolton W*	5	—
1988–89	*Preston NE*	9	2
1989–90	Nottingham F	18	4
1990–91		23	8
1991–92		6	1
1991–92	Sheffield W	20	4
1992–93		13	—
1993–94		18	5
1993–94	*Grimsby T*	6	2
1994–95	Notts Co	11	1
1994–95	*Watford*	4	—
1994–95	*Coventry C*	—	—
1995–96	Notts Co	3	—
1995–96	*Rotherham U*	16	5

JENKINS, Iain

Born Whiston 24.11.72 Ht 5 9 Wt 11 10
Defender. From Trainee.

Season	Club	Apps	Goals
1990–91	Everton	1	—
1991–92		3	—
1992–93		1	—
1992–93	*Bradford C*	6	—
1993–94	Chester C	34	—
1994–95		40	—
1995–96		13	—

Season Club League Appearances/Goals

JENKINS, Steve

Born Merthyr 16.7.72 Ht 5 11 Wt 12 03
Defender. From Trainee. Wales Under-21, 3 full caps.

Season	Club	Apps	Goals
1990–91	Swansea C	1	—
1991–92		34	—
1992–93		33	—
1993–94		40	1
1994–95		42	—
1995–96		15	—
1995–96	Huddersfield T	31	1

JENKINSON, Leigh

Born Thorne 9.7.69 Ht 6 0 Wt 12 02
Forward. From Trainee.

Season	Club	Apps	Goals
1987–88	Hull C	3	1
1988–89		11	—
1989–90		22	—
1990–91		26	—
1990–91	*Rotherham U*	7	—
1991–92	Hull C	42	8
1992–93		26	4
1992–93	Coventry C	5	—
1993–94		16	—
1993–94	*Birmingham C*	3	—
1994–95	Coventry C	11	1
1995–96		—	—

JENSEN, John

Born Denmark 3.5.65 Ht 5 10 Wt 12 06
Midfield. From Brondby. Denmark full caps.

Season	Club	Apps	Goals
1992–93	Arsenal	32	—
1993–94		27	—
1994–95		24	1
1995–96		15	—

JEPSON, Ronnie

Born Stoke 12.5.63 Ht 6 0 Wt 13 07
Forward. From Nantwich.

Season	Club	Apps	Goals
1988–89	Port Vale	2	—
1989–90		5	—
1989–90	*Peterborough U*	18	5
1990–91	Port Vale	15	—
1990–91	Preston NE	14	3
1991–92		24	5
1992–93	Exeter C	38	8
1993–94		16	13
1993–94	Huddersfield T	23	5

Season	Club	Apps	Goals
1994–95		41	19
1995–96		43	12

JESS, Eoin

Born Aberdeen 13.12.70 Ht 5 10 Wt 11 07
Forward. From Rangers S Form. Scotland Under-21, 13 full caps.

Season	Club	Apps	Goals
1987–88	Aberdeen	—	—
1988–89		2	—
1989–90		11	3
1990–91		27	13
1991–92		39	12
1992–93		31	12
1993–94		41	6
1994–95		25	1
1995–96		25	3
1995–96	Coventry C	12	1

JEWELL, Paul

Born Liverpool 28.9.64 Ht 5 8 Wt 12 01
Forward. From Apprentice.

Season	Club	Apps	Goals
1982–83	Liverpool	—	—
1983–84		—	—
1984–85	Wigan Ath	26	9
1985–86		29	6
1986–87		39	9
1987–88		43	11
1988–89	Bradford C	39	4
1989–90		30	4
1990–91		38	4
1991–92		30	6
1992–93		46	16
1993–94		30	5
1994–95		38	14
1995–96		18	3
1995–96	*Grimsby T*	5	1

JOACHIM, Julian

Born Peterborough 20.9.74 Ht 5 6 Wt 12 11
Forward. From Trainee. England Youth, Under-21.

Season	Club	Apps	Goals
1992–93	Leicester C	26	10
1993–94		36	11
1994–95		15	3
1995–96		22	1
1995–96	Aston Villa	11	1

JOBLING, Kevin

Born Sunderland 1.1.68 Ht 5 9 Wt 10 11
Midfield. From Apprentice.

Season	Club	Apps	Goals
1985–86	Leicester C	—	—
1986–87		3	—
1987–88		6	—
1987–88	Grimsby T	15	1
1988–89		32	4
1989–90		33	1
1990–91		45	—
1991–92		36	2
1992–93		14	—
1993–94		11	—
1993–94	*Scunthorpe U*	—	—
1994–95	Grimsby T	38	1
1995–96		3	—

JOBSON, Richard

Born Hull 9.5.63 Ht 6 1 Wt 12 10
Defender. From Burton Alb. England B.

Season	Club	Apps	Goals
1982–83	Watford	13	1
1983–84		13	2
1984–85		2	1
1984–85	Hull C	8	—
1985–86		36	7
1986–87		40	5
1987–88		44	2
1988–89		46	1
1989–90		45	2
1990–91		2	—
1990–91	Oldham Ath	44	1
1991–92		36	2
1992–93		40	2
1993–94		37	5
1994–95		20	—
1995–96		12	—
1995–96	Leeds U	12	1

JOHNROSE, Lenny

Born Preston 29.11.69 Ht 5 10 Wt 12 04
Forward. From Trainee.

Season	Club	Apps	Goals
1987–88	Blackburn R	1	—
1988–89		—	—
1989–90		8	3
1990–91		26	7
1991–92		7	1
1991–92	*Preston NE*	3	1
1991–92	Hartlepool U	15	2
1992–93		38	6
1993–94		13	3
1993–94	Bury	14	—

Season Club League Appearances/Goals

Season	Club	Apps	Goals
1994–95		26	4
1995–96		34	6

JOHNSEN, Erland

Born Fredrikstad 5.4.67 Ht 6 1 Wt 14 04
Defender. From Bayern Munich. Norway Youth, Under-21, 22 full caps.

Season	Club	Apps	Goals
1989–90	Chelsea	18	—
1990–91		6	—
1991–92		7	—
1992–93		13	—
1993–94		28	1
1994–95		33	—
1995–96		22	—

JOHNSON, Alan

Born Ince 19.2.71 Ht 6 0 Wt 12 00
Defender. From Trainee.

Season	Club	Apps	Goals
1988–89	Wigan Ath	8	1
1989–90		33	1
1990–91		43	5
1991–92		44	4
1992–93		36	1
1993–94		16	1
1993–94	Lincoln C	16	—
1994–95		25	—
1995–96		22	—
1995–96	*Preston NE*	2	—

JOHNSON, Andy

Born Bristol 2.5.74 Ht 6 1 Wt 12 02
Midfield. From Trainee.

Season	Club	Apps	Goals
1991–92	Norwich C	2	—
1992–93		2	1
1993–94		2	—
1994–95		7	—
1995–96		26	7

JOHNSON, Damien

Born Blackburn 18.11.78 Ht 5 9
Wt 10 00
Midfield. From Trainee.

Season	Club	Apps	Goals
1995–96	Blackburn R	—	—

JOHNSON, David

Born Rother Valley 29.10.70 Ht 6 2
Wt 13 08
Forward. From Trainee.

Season	Club	Apps	Goals
1989–90	Sheffield W	—	—
1990–91		—	—
1991–92		6	—
1991–92	*Hartlepool U*	7	2
1992–93	Sheffield W	—	—
1992–93	*Hartlepool U*	3	—
1993–94	Lincoln C	41	8
1994–95		24	4
1995–96		24	1

JOHNSON, David

Born Kingston 15.8.76 Ht 5 6 Wt 12 05
Forward. From Trainee.

Season	Club	Apps	Goals
1994–95	Manchester U	—	—
1995–96	Bury	36	5

JOHNSON, Frank

Born South Shields 24.2.77 Ht 6 3
Wt 13 00
Goalkeeper.

Season	Club	Apps	Goals
1995–96	Darlington	—	—

JOHNSON, Gavin

Born Eye 10.10.70 Ht 5 11 Wt 11 07
Defender. From Trainee.

Season	Club	Apps	Goals
1988–89	Ipswich T	4	—
1989–90		6	—
1990–91		7	—
1991–92		42	5
1992–93		40	5
1993–94		16	1
1994–95		17	—
1995–96	Luton T	5	—
1995–96	Wigan Ath	27	3

JOHNSON, Glenn

Born Sydney 16.7.72 Ht 5 10 Wt 11 10
Forward. From Blacktown City.

Season	Club	Apps	Goals
1995–96	Cardiff C	5	—

JOHNSON, Grant

Born Dundee 24.3.72 Ht 5 11 Wt 10 00
Midfield. From Broughty Ferry. Scotland Under-21.

Season	Club	Apps	Goals
1990–91	Dundee U	—	—
1991–92		10	1
1992–93		17	1
1993–94		10	—
1994–95		13	1
1995–96		28	4

JOHNSON, Marvin

Born Wembley 29.10.68 Ht 6 1
Wt 13 06
Defender. From Apprentice.

Season	Club	App	Goals
1986–87	Luton T	—	—
1987–88		9	—
1988–89		16	—
1989–90		12	—
1990–91		26	—
1991–92		—	—
1992–93		40	3
1993–94		17	—
1994–95		46	1
1995–96		36	—

JOHNSON, Michael

Born Nottingham 7.7.73 Ht 5 10
Wt 11 12
Defender. From Trainee.

Season	Club	App	Goals
1991–92	Notts Co	5	—
1992–93		37	—
1993–94		34	—
1994–95		31	—
1995–96		—	—
1995–96	Birmingham C	33	—

JOHNSON, Phil

Born Liverpool 7.4.75 Ht 5 7 Wt 10 06
Defender. From Trainee.

Season	Club	App	Goals
1994–95	Tranmere R	—	—
1995–96	Stockport Co	—	—

JOHNSON, Richard

Born Kurri Kurri 27.4.74 Ht 5 10
Wt 11 13
Midfield. From Trainee.

Season	Club	App	Goals
1991–92	Watford	2	—
1992–93		1	—
1993–94		27	—
1994–95		35	3
1995–96		20	1

JOHNSON, Ross

Born Brighton 2.1.76 Ht 6 0 Wt 12 04
Defender. From Trainee.

Season	Club	App	Goals
1993–94	Brighton & HA	2	—
1994–95		—	—
1995–96		20	—

JOHNSON, Tommy

Born Newcastle 15.1.71 Ht 5 11
Wt 12 04
Forward. From Trainee. England Under-21.

Season	Club	App	Goals
1988–89	Notts Co	10	4
1989–90		40	18
1990–91		37	16
1991–92		31	9
1991–92	Derby Co	12	2
1992–93		35	8
1993–94		37	13
1994–95		14	7
1994–95	Aston Villa	14	4
1995–96		23	5

JOHNSTON, Alan

Born Glasgow 14.12.73 Ht 5 7 Wt 9 07
Forward. From Tynecastle BC. Scotland Under-21.

Season	Club	App	Goals
1991–92	Hearts	—	—
1992–93		2	1
1993–94		28	1
1994–95		21	1
1995–96		33	9

JOHNSTON, Forbes

Born Aberdeen 3.8.71 Ht 5 10 Wt 9 12
Defender. From Musselburgh Ath.
Scotland Under-21.

Season	Club	App	Goals
1990–91	Falkirk	—	—
1991–92		12	—
1992–93		22	1
1993–94		15	1
1994–95		3	—
1995–96		6	—

JOHNSTON, Mo

Born Glasgow 30.4.63 Ht 5 9 Wt 10 06
Forward. From Milton Battlefield.
Scotland Under-21, 38 full caps.

Season	Club	App	Goals
1980–81	Partick T	—	—
1981–82		32	9
1982–83		39	22
1983–84		14	10
1983–84	Watford	29	20
1984–85		9	3
1984–85	Celtic	27	14
1985–86		32	15
1986–87		40	23

Season	Club	League Appearances	Goals
1987–88	Nantes	32	13
1988–89		34	9
1989–90	Rangers	36	15
1990–91		29	11
1991–92		11	5
1991–92	Everton	21	7
1992–93		13	3
1993–94		—	—
1993–94	Hearts	31	4
1994–95		4	1
1994–95	Falkirk	10	1
1995–96		31	5

JONES, Barry

Born Prescot 20.6.70 Ht 5 11 Wt 11 12
Defender. From Prescot T.

Season	Club	League Appearances	Goals
1988–89	Liverpool	—	—
1989–90		—	—
1990–91		—	—
1991–92		—	—
1992–93	Wrexham	42	2
1993–94		33	2
1994–95		44	—
1995–96		40	—

JONES, Gary

Born Huddersfield 6.4.69 Ht 6 1
Wt 12 09
Forward. From Rossington Main.

Season	Club	League Appearances	Goals
1988–89	Doncaster R	17	2
1989–90		3	—
From Boston U			
1993–94	Southend U	22	3
1993–94	*Lincoln C*	4	2
1994–95	Southend U	25	11
1995–96		23	2
1995–96	Notts Co	18	5

JONES, Gary

Born Chester 10.5.75 Ht 6 3 Wt 13 12
Forward. From Trainee.

Season	Club	League Appearances	Goals
1993–94	Tranmere R	6	2
1994–95		19	3
1995–96		23	1

JONES, Graeme

Born Gateshead 13.3.70 Ht 6 0
Wt 12 12
Forward. From Bridlington T.

Season	Club	League Appearances	Goals
1993–94	Doncaster R	28	4
1994–95		32	12
1995–96		32	10

JONES, Ian

Born Germany 26.8.76
Defender. From Trainee.

Season	Club	League Appearances	Goals
1993–94	Cardiff C	2	—
1994–95		—	—
1995–96		1	—

JONES, Ian

Born Birmingham 25.10.76 Ht 5 7
Wt 10 02
Midfield. From Trainee.

Season	Club	League Appearances	Goals
1995–96	Birmingham C	—	—

JONES, Keith

Born Dulwich 14.10.65 Ht 5 9 Wt 10 11
Midfield. From Apprentice. England Schools, Youth.

Season	Club	League Appearances	Goals
1982–83	Chelsea	2	—
1983–84		—	—
1984–85		19	2
1985–86		14	2
1986–87		17	3
1987–88		—	—
1987–88	Brentford	36	1
1988–89		40	3
1989–90		42	2
1990–91		45	6
1991–92		6	1
1991–92	Southend U	34	5
1992–93		29	1
1993–94		20	5
1994–95		7	—
1994–95	Charlton Ath	31	1
1995–96		25	—

JONES, Lee

Born Wrexham 29.5.73 Ht 5 8 Wt 10 08
Forward. From Trainee. Wales Under-21.

Season	Club	League Appearances	Goals
1990–91	Wrexham	18	5
1991–92		21	5
1991–92	Liverpool	—	—
1992–93		—	—
1993–94		—	—
1993–94	*Crewe Alex*	8	1
1994–95	Liverpool	1	—
1995–96		—	—
1995–96	*Wrexham*	20	9

JONES, Lee

Born Pontypridd 9.8.70 Ht 6 3 Wt 14 04
Goalkeeper. From Porth.

1993–94	Swansea C	—	—
1994–95		2	—
1995–96		1	—
1995–96	*Crewe Alex*	—	—

JONES, Martin

Born Liverpool 27.3.75 Ht 6 1 Wt 13 03
Goalkeeper. From Trainee.

1993–94	Tranmere R	—	—
1994–95		—	—
1995–96		—	—

JONES, Nathan

Born Rhondda 28.5.73
Midfield. From Merthyr T.

1995–96	Luton T	—	—

JONES, Paul

Born Chirk 18.4.67 Ht 6 3 Wt 14 00
Goalkeeper. From Kidderminster H.

1991–92	Wolverhampton W	—	—
1992–93		16	—
1993–94		—	—
1994–95		9	—
1995–96		8	—

JONES, Paul

Born Liverpool 3.6.78
Defender. From Trainee.

1995–96	Tranmere R	—	—

JONES, Rob

Born Wrexham 5.11.71 Ht 5 8 Wt 11 00
Defender. From Trainee. England Under-21, 8 full caps.

1987–88	Crewe Alex	5	—
1988–89		19	1
1989–90		11	—
1990–91		32	1
1991–92		8	—
1991–92	Liverpool	28	—
1992–93		30	—
1993–94		38	—
1994–95		31	—
1995–96		33	—

JONES, Ryan

Born Sheffield 23.7.73 Ht 6 3 Wt 13 08
Midfield. From Trainee. Wales Under-21, 1 full cap.

1991–92	Sheffield W	—	—
1992–93		9	—
1993–94		27	6
1994–95		5	—
1995–96		—	—
1995–96	*Scunthorpe U*	11	3

JONES, Scott

Born Sheffield 1.5.75 Ht 5 10 Wt 11 06
Defender. From Trainee.

1993–94	Barnsley	—	—
1994–95		—	—
1995–96		4	—

JONES, Stephen

Born Derry 25.10.76
Midfield.

1995–96	Blackpool	—	—

JONES, Steve

Born Cambridge 17.3.70 Ht 5 11
Wt 12 00
Forward. From Billericay.

1992–93	West Ham U	6	2
1993–94		8	2
1994–95		2	—
1994–95	Bournemouth	30	9
1995–96		44	17
1995–96	West Ham U	—	—

JONES, Steve

Born Teeside 31.1.74 Ht 5 11 Wt 13 04
Goalkeeper. From Trainee.

1991–92	Hartlepool U	6	—
1992–93		3	—
1993–94		28	—
1994–95		2	—
1995–96		9	—

JONES, Steve

Born Bristol 25.12.70 Ht 5 10 Wt 12 02
Defender. From Cheltenham T.

1995–96	Swansea C	17	—

JONES, Tom

Born Aldershot 7.10.64 Ht 5 10
Wt 11 07
Midfield. From Chelsea Apprentice, Farnborough, Weymouth.

Season	Club	Apps	Goals
1987–88	Aberdeen	28	3
1988–89		—	—
1988–89	Swindon T	40	6
1989–90		44	2
1990–91		43	—
1991–92		41	4
1992–93	Reading	21	1
1993–94		17	—
1994–95		20	1
1995–96		21	—

JONES, Vinnie

Born Watford 5.1.65 Ht 6 0 Wt 11 12
Midfield. From Wealdstone. Wales 5 full caps.

Season	Club	Apps	Goals
1986–87	Wimbledon	22	4
1987–88		24	2
1988–89		31	3
1989–90	Leeds U	45	5
1990–91		1	—
1990–91	Sheffield U	31	2
1991–92		4	—
1991–92	Chelsea	35	3
1992–93		7	1
1992–93	Wimbledon	27	1
1993–94		33	2
1994–95		33	3
1995–96		31	3

JORDAN, Scott

Born Newcastle 19.7.75 Ht 5 10
Wt 11 05
Midfield. From Trainee.

Season	Club	Apps	Goals
1992–93	York C	1	—
1993–94		—	—
1994–95		37	3
1995–96		26	1

JOSEPH, Marc

Born Leicester 10.11.76 Ht 6 1 Wt 12 05
Defender. From Trainee.

Season	Club	Apps	Goals
1995–96	Cambridge U	12	—
1995–96		—	—

JOSEPH, Matthew

Born Bethnal Green 30.9.72 Ht 5 8
Wt 10 05
Defender. From Trainee.

Season	Club	Apps	Goals
1991–92	Arsenal	—	—
1992–93	Gillingham	—	—
1993–94	Cambridge U	27	2
1994–95		39	2
1995–96		42	2

JOSEPH, Roger

Born Paddington 24.12.65 Ht 5 11
Wt 11 10
Defender. From Juniors. England B.

Season	Club	Apps	Goals
1984–85	Brentford	1	—
1985–86		28	1
1986–87		32	1
1987–88		43	—
1988–89	Wimbledon	31	—
1989–90		19	—
1990–91		38	—
1991–92		26	—
1992–93		32	—
1993–94		13	—
1994–95		3	—
1994–95	*Millwall*	5	—
1995–96	Wimbledon	—	—

JOYCE, Joe

Born Consett 18.3.61 Ht 5 9 Wt 11 01
Defender. From School.

Season	Club	Apps	Goals
1979–80	Barnsley	8	—
1980–81		33	—
1981–82		20	—
1982–83		32	1
1983–84		40	1
1984–85		41	—
1985–86		40	—
1986–87		34	—
1987–88		38	2
1988–89		45	—
1989–90		—	—
1990–91		3	—
1990–91	Scunthorpe U	21	—
1991–92		40	2
1992–93		30	—
1993–94	Carlisle U	29	—
1993–94	*Darlington*	4	—
1994–95	Carlisle U	21	—
1995–96		—	—

JOYCE, Warren

Born Oldham 20.1.65 Ht 5 8 Wt 12 04
Midfield. From Local.

Season	Club	Apps	Goals
1982–83	Bolton W	8	—
1983–84		45	3
1984–85		45	5
1985–86		31	4
1986–87		44	5
1987–88		11	—
1987–88	Preston NE	22	—
1988–89		40	9
1989–90		44	11
1990–91		42	9
1991–92		29	5
1992–93	Plymouth Arg	30	3
1993–94	Burnley	22	4
1994–95		5	—
1994–95	*Hull C*	9	3
1995–96	Burnley	43	5

JULES, Mark

Born Bradford 5.9.71 Ht 5 9 Wt 11 00
Forward. From Trainee.

Season	Club	Apps	Goals
1990–91	Bradford C	—	—
1991–92	Scarborough	41	8
1992–93		36	8
1993–94	Chesterfield	33	1
1994–95		23	—
1995–96		32	2

JUNINHO

Born Sao Paulo 22.2.73 Ht 5 5 Wt 9 10
Forward. From Sao Paulo. Brazil full caps.

Season	Club	Apps	Goals
1995–96	Middlesbrough	21	2

JUPP, Duncan

Born Guildford 25.1.75 Ht 6 0 Wt 12 11
Defender. From Trainee. Scotland Under-21.

Season	Club	Apps	Goals
1992–93	Fulham	3	—
1993–94		30	—
1994–95		36	2
1995–96		36	—

KALAC, Zeljko

Born Camperdown 16.12.72 Ht 6 7
Wt 14 03
Goalkeeper. From Sydney United.
Australia full caps.

Season	Club	Apps	Goals
1995–96	Leicester C	1	—

KAMARA, Chris

Born Middlesbrough 25.12.57 Ht 6 1
Wt 12 10
Midfield. From Apprentice.

Season	Club	Apps	Goals
1975–76	Portsmouth	24	4
1976–77		39	3
1977–78	Swindon T	40	10
1978–79		28	2
1979–80		34	5
1980–81		45	4
1981–82	Portsmouth	11	—
1981–82	Brentford	31	5
1982–83		44	11
1983–84		38	6
1984–85		39	6
1985–86	Swindon T	20	1
1986–87		42	3
1987–88		25	2
1988–89	Stoke C	38	4
1989–90		22	1
1989–90	Leeds U	11	1
1990–91		7	—
1991–92		2	—
1991–92	Luton T	28	—
1992–93		21	—
1992–93	*Sheffield U*	8	—
1992–93	*Middlesbrough*	5	—
1993–94	Sheffield U	16	—
1994–95	Bradford C	23	3
1995–96		—	—

KAMARK, Pontus

Born Sweden 5.4.69 Ht 5 10 Wt 12 03
Defender. From IFK Gothenburg. Sweden 27 full caps.

Season	Club	Apps	Goals
1995–96	Leicester C	1	—

KANCHELSKIS, Andrei

Born Kirovograd 23.1.69 Ht 5 10
Wt 12 12
Forward. USSR, CIS, Russia 43 full caps.

Season	Club	Apps	Goals
1988	Dynamo Kiev	7	1
1989		15	—

Season	Club	League Appearances	Goals
1990	Donetsk	16	2
1991		5	1
1990–91	Manchester U	1	—
1991–92		34	5
1992–93		27	3
1993–94		31	6
1994–95		30	14
1995–96	Everton	32	16

KANE, Paul

Born Edinburgh 20.6.65 Ht 5 8 Wt 9 09
Midfield. From Salvesen BC. Scotland Youth.

Season	Club	League Appearances	Goals
1982–83	Hibernian	—	—
1983–84		13	1
1984–85		34	8
1985–86		32	5
1986–87		37	1
1987–88		44	10
1988–89		35	5
1989–90		31	3
1990–91		21	—
1990–91	Oldham Ath	17	—
1991–92		4	—
1991–92	Aberdeen	25	2
1992–93		27	4
1993–94		39	3
1994–95		27	2
1995–96	*Barnsley*	4	—

KAVANAGH, Graham

Born Dublin 2.12.73 Ht 5 10 Wt 12 08
Midfield. From Home Farm. Eire Under-21.

Season	Club	League Appearances	Goals
1991–92	Middlesbrough	—	—
1992–93		10	—
1993–94		11	2
1993–94	*Darlington*	5	—
1994–95	Middlesbrough	7	—
1995–96		7	1

KAVANAGH, Jason

Born Birmingham 23.11.71 Ht 5 9 Wt 12 07
Defender. From Birmingham C Schoolboy. FA Schools, England Youth.

Season	Club	League Appearances	Goals
1988–89	Derby Co	—	—
1989–90		—	—
1990–91		11	—
1991–92		25	—
1992–93		10	—
1993–94		19	—
1994–95		25	1
1995–96		9	—

KAVELASHVILI, Mikhail

Born Tbilisi 22.7.71 Ht 5 11 Wt 12 01
Midfield. From Spartak Vladikavkaz. Georgia full caps.

Season	Club	League Appearances	Goals
1995–96	Manchester C	4	1

KAY, John

Born Sunderland 29.1.64 Ht 5 9 Wt 11 08
Defender. From Apprentice.

Season	Club	League Appearances	Goals
1981–82	Arsenal	—	—
1982–83		7	—
1983–84		7	—
1984–85	Wimbledon	21	1
1984–85	*Middlesbrough*	8	—
1985–86	Wimbledon	26	1
1986–87		16	—
1987–88	Sunderland	46	—
1988–89		11	—
1989–90		32	—
1990–91		30	—
1991–92		41	—
1992–93		36	—
1993–94		3	—
1994–95		—	—
1995–96		—	—
1995–96	*Shrewsbury T*	7	—

KAY, Simon

Born Rochdale 10.6.77
Defender. From Trainee.

Season	Club	League Appearances	Goals
1995–96	Oldham Ath	—	—

KEAN, Robert

Born Luton 3.6.78
Midfield. From Trainee.

Season	Club	League Appearances	Goals
1995–96	Luton T	—	—

KEANE, Roy

Born Cork 10.8.71 Ht 5 10 Wt 12 10
Midfield. From Cobh Ramblers. Eire Youth, Under-21, 30 full caps.

Season	Club	League Appearances	Goals
1990–91	Nottingham F	35	8
1991–92		39	8

Season	Club	League Appearances	Goals
1992–93		40	6
1993–94	Manchester U	37	5
1994–95		25	2
1995–96		29	6

KEARN, Stewart

Born Salisbury 1.12.75
Goalkeeper.

Season	Club	League Appearances	Goals
1993–94	Sheffield W	—	—
1994–95		—	—
1995–96		—	—
1995–96	Bournemouth	—	—

KEARTON, Jason

Born Ipswich (Aus) 9.7.69 Ht 5 11
Wt 12 00
Goalkeeper. From Brisbane Lions.

Season	Club	League Appearances	Goals
1988–89	Everton	—	—
1989–90		—	—
1990–91		—	—
1991–92		—	—
1991–92	*Stoke C*	16	—
1991–92	*Blackpool*	14	—
1992–93	Everton	5	—
1993–94		—	—
1994–95		1	—
1994–95	*Notts Co*	10	—
1995–96	Everton	—	—
1995–96	*Preston NE*	—	—

KEEN, Kevin

Born Amersham 25.2.67 Ht 5 7
Wt 10 10
Midfield. From Wycombe W and Apprentice, England Schools, Youth.

Season	Club	League Appearances	Goals
1983–84	West Ham U	—	—
1984–85		—	—
1985–86		—	—
1986–87		13	—
1987–88		23	1
1988–89		24	3
1989–90		44	10
1990–91		40	—
1991–92		29	—
1992–93		46	7
1993–94	Wolverhampton W	41	7
1994–95		1	—
1994–95	Stoke C	21	2
1995–96		33	3

KEEN, Peter

Born Middlesbrough 16.11.76 Ht 6 0
Wt 11 09
Goalkeeper. From Trainee.

Season	Club	League Appearances	Goals
1995–96	Newcastle U	—	—

KEISTER, John

Born Manchester 11.11.70 Ht 5 8
Wt 10 06
Midfield. From Fawah FC.

Season	Club	League Appearances	Goals
1993–94	Walsall	22	1
1994–95		11	—
1995–96		21	—

KEITH, Marino

Born Peterhead 16.12.74
Forward. From Fraserburgh.

Season	Club	League Appearances	Goals
1995–96	Dundee U	4	—

KELLER, Kasey

Born Washington 27.1.69 Ht 6 1
Wt 12 07
Goalkeeper. From Portland University. USA full caps.

Season	Club	League Appearances	Goals
1991–92	Millwall	1	—
1992–93		45	—
1993–94		44	—
1994–95		44	—
1995–96		42	—

KELLY, Alan

Born Preston 11.8.68 Ht 6 3 Wt 14 03
Goalkeeper. From Trainee. Eire Youth, Under-21, Under-23, 14 full caps.

Season	Club	League Appearances	Goals
1985–86	Preston NE	13	—
1986–87		22	—
1987–88		19	—
1988–89		—	—
1989–90		42	—
1990–91		23	—
1991–92		23	—
1992–93	Sheffield U	33	—
1993–94		30	—
1994–95		38	—
1995–96		35	—

Season Club League Appearances/Goals

KELLY, David

Born Birmingham 25.11.65 Ht 5 11
Wt 12 01
Forward. From Alvechurch. Eire Under-21, Under-23, B, 20 full caps.

Season	Club	Apps	Goals
1983–84	Walsall	6	3
1984–85		32	7
1985–86		28	10
1986–87		42	23
1987–88		39	20
1988–89	West Ham U	25	6
1989–90		16	1
1989–90	Leicester C	10	7
1990–91		44	14
1991–92		12	1
1991–92	Newcastle U	25	11
1992–93		45	24
1993–94	Wolverhampton W	36	11
1994–95		42	15
1995–96		5	—
1995–96	Sunderland	10	2

KELLY, Gary

Born Fulwood 3.8.66 Ht 5 10 Wt 13 06
Goalkeeper. From Apprentice. Eire Under-21, B.

Season	Club	Apps	Goals
1984–85	Newcastle U	—	—
1985–86		—	—
1986–87		3	—
1987–88		37	—
1988–89		9	—
1988–89	*Blackpool*	5	—
1989–90	Newcastle U	4	—
1989–90	Bury	38	—
1990–91		46	—
1991–92		46	—
1992–93		42	—
1993–94		1	—
1993–94	*West Ham U*	—	—
1994–95	Bury	38	—
1995–96		25	—

KELLY, Gary

Born Drogheda 9.7.74 Ht 5 8 Wt 13 03
Defender. From Home Farm. Eire Youth, 18 full caps.

Season	Club	Apps	Goals
1991–92	Leeds U	2	—
1992–93		—	—
1993–94		42	—
1994–95		42	—
1995–96		34	—

KELLY, Gavin

Born Beverley 29.9.68 Ht 6 0 Wt 13 13
Goalkeeper. From Trainee.

Season	Club	Apps	Goals
1987–88	Hull C	—	—
1988–89		3	—
1989–90		8	—
1989–90	*Bristol R*	—	—
1990–91	Bristol R	7	—
1991–92		3	—
1992–93		19	—
1993–94		1	—
1994–95	Scarborough	24	—
1995–96		6	—

KELLY, Jimmy

Born Liverpool 14.2.73 Ht 5 7 Wt 11 10
Midfield. From Trainee.

Season	Club	Apps	Goals
1990–91	Wrexham	12	—
1991–92		9	—
1991–92	Wolverhampton W	3	—
1992–93		—	—
1992–93	*Walsall*	10	2
1993–94	Wolverhampton W	4	—
1993–94	*Wrexham*	9	—
1994–95	Wolverhampton W	—	—
1995–96		—	—

KELLY, Mark

Born Gibraltar 5.10.76 Ht 6 0 Wt 11 10
Midfield. From Trainee.

Season	Club	Apps	Goals
1995–96	Huddersfield T	—	—

KELLY, Ray

Born Athlone 29.12.76 Ht 5 11 Wt 12 00
Forward. From Athlone T.

Season	Club	Apps	Goals
1994–95	Manchester C	—	—
1995–96		—	—

KELLY, Russell

Born Ballymoney 10.8.76 Ht 5 10
Wt 11 00
Midfield. From Trainee.

Season	Club	Apps	Goals
1995–96	*Leyton Orient*	6	—

KELLY, Tom

Born Bellshill 28.3.64 Ht 5 9 Wt 12 07
Defender. From Hibs.

Season	Club	Apps	Goals
1985–86	Hartlepool U	15	—
1986–87	Torquay U	38	—

Season Club League Appearances/Goals

Season Club League Appearances/Goals

Season	Club	Apps	Goals
1987–88		38	—
1988–89		44	—
1989–90	York C	35	2
1989–90	Exeter C	12	2
1990–91		22	1
1991–92		32	5
1992–93		22	1
1992–93	Torquay U	18	3
1993–94		35	2
1994–95		33	3
1995–96		31	—

KELLY, Tony

Born Meridan 14.2.66 Ht 5 11 Wt 11 08
Forward.

Season	Club	Apps	Goals
1982–83	Bristol C	6	1
From St Albans C			
1989–90	Stoke C	9	—
1990–91		29	3
1991–92		13	2
1991–92	*Hull C*	6	1
1992–93	Stoke C	7	—
1992–93	*Cardiff C*	5	1
1993–94	Stoke C	—	—
1993–94	Bury	35	7
1994–95		22	3
1995–96	Leyton Orient	34	3

KELLY, Tony

Born Prescot 1.10.64 Ht 5 10 Wt 14 07
Midfield. From Liverpool Apprentice.

Season	Club	Apps	Goals
1983–84	Derby Co	—	—
1983–84	Wigan Ath	29	2
1984–85		40	4
1985–86		32	9
1985–86	Stoke C	1	—
1986–87		35	4
1987–88	WBA	26	1
1988–89		—	—
1988–89	*Chester C*	5	—
1988–89	*Colchester U*	13	2
1988–89	Shrewsbury T	20	5
1989–90		43	5
1990–91		38	5
1991–92	Bolton W	31	2
1992–93		36	2
1993–94		35	1
1994–95		4	—
1994–95	Port Vale	4	1
1994–95	Millwall	2	—
1994–95	Wigan Ath	—	—
1994–95	Peterborough U	13	2
1995–96	Wigan Ath	2	—

KENNA, Jeff

Born Dublin 28.8.70 Ht 5 11 Wt 12 03
Defender. From Trainee. Eire Youth, Under-21, B, 12 full caps.

Season	Club	Apps	Goals
1988–89	Southampton	—	—
1989–90		—	—
1990–91		2	—
1991–92		14	—
1992–93		29	2
1993–94		41	2
1994–95		28	—
1994–95	Blackburn R	9	1
1995–96		32	—

KENNEDY, Mark

Born Dublin 15.5.76 Ht 5 11 Wt 11 00
Forward. From Belvedere, Trainee. Eire Under-21, 10 full caps.

Season	Club	Apps	Goals
1992–93	Millwall	1	—
1993–94		12	4
1994–95		30	5
1994–95	Liverpool	6	—
1995–96		4	—

KENNY, Billy

Born Liverpool 19.9.73 Ht 5 8 Wt 11 00
Midfield. From Trainee. England Under-21.

Season	Club	Apps	Goals
1992–93	Everton	17	1
1993–94		—	—
1994–95		—	—
1994–95	Oldham Ath	4	—
1995–96		—	—

KENT, Kevin

Born Stoke 19.3.65 Ht 5 8 Wt 11 00
Forward. From Apprentice.

Season	Club	Apps	Goals
1982–83	WBA	—	—
1983–84		2	—
1984–85	Newport Co	33	1
1985–86	Mansfield T	34	8
1986–87		46	6
1987–88		45	10
1988–89		39	5
1989–90		38	3
1990–91		27	4
1990–91	Port Vale	11	—

Season Club League Appearances/Goals

Season Club League Appearances/Goals

Season	Club	Apps	Goals
1991–92		23	—
1992–93		27	1
1993–94		30	4
1994–95		23	2
1995–96		1	—

KENWORTHY, Jon

Born St Asaph 18.8.74 Ht 5 8 Wt 11 00
Forward. From Trainee. Wales Under-21.

Season	Club	Apps	Goals
1993–94	Tranmere R	16	2
1994–95		6	—
1995–96		4	—
1995–96	*Chester C*	7	1

KEOWN, Darren

Born Chertsey 28.2.78
Forward. From Trainee.

Season	Club	Apps	Goals
1995–96	Millwall	—	—

KEOWN, Martin

Born Oxford 24.7.66 Ht 6 1 Wt 12 04
Defender. From Apprentice. England Youth, Under-21, B, 11 full caps.

Season	Club	Apps	Goals
1983–84	Arsenal	—	—
1984–85		—	—
1984–85	*Brighton & HA*	16	—
1985–86	Arsenal	22	—
1985–86	*Brighton & HA*	7	1
1986–87	Aston Villa	36	—
1987–88		42	3
1988–89		34	—
1989–90	Everton	20	—
1990–91		24	—
1991–92		39	—
1992–93		13	—
1992–93	Arsenal	16	—
1993–94		33	—
1994–95		31	1
1995–96		34	—

KERNAGHAN, Alan

Born Otley 25.4.67 Ht 6 2 Wt 14 01
Defender. From Apprentice. Eire 22 full caps.

Season	Club	Apps	Goals
1984–85	Middlesbrough	8	1
1985–86		6	—
1986–87		13	—
1987–88		35	6
1988–89		23	—
1989–90		37	4
1990–91		24	—
1990–91	*Charlton Ath*	13	—
1991–92	Middlesbrough	38	2
1992–93		22	2
1993–94		6	1
1993–94	Manchester C	24	—
1994–95		22	1
1994–95	*Bolton W*	11	—
1995–96	Manchester C	6	—
1995–96	*Bradford C*	5	—

KERR, David

Born Dumfries 6.9.74 Ht 5 10 Wt 12 07
Midfield. From Trainee.

Season	Club	Apps	Goals
1991–92	Manchester C	—	—
1992–93		1	—
1993–94		2	—
1994–95		2	—
1995–96		1	—
1995–96	*Mansfield T*	5	—

KERR, Dylan

Born Valetta 14.1.67 Ht 5 9 Wt 11 04
Defender. From Arcadia Shepherds.

Season	Club	Apps	Goals
1988–89	Leeds U	3	—
1989–90		5	—
1990–91		—	—
1991–92		—	—
1991–92	*Doncaster R*	7	1
1991–92	*Blackpool*	12	1
1992–93	Leeds U	5	—
1993–94	Reading	45	2
1994–95		36	1
1995–96		8	2

KERR, John

Born Toronto 6.3.65 Ht 5 8 Wt 11 05
Forward. From Harrow Borough. USA full caps.

Season	Club	Apps	Goals
1987–88	Portsmouth	4	—
1987–88	*Peterborough U*	10	1
From San Diego Sockers			
1992–93	Millwall	6	1
1993–94		23	4
1994–95		14	3
1995–96	Walsall	1	—

Season Club League Appearances/Goals

KERSLAKE, David

Born Stepney 19.6.66 Ht 5 9 Wt 12 03
Defender. From Apprentice. England Schools, Youth, Under-21. Football League.

Season	Club	Apps	Goals
1983–84	QPR	—	—
1984–85		1	—
1985–86		14	1
1986–87		3	—
1987–88		18	5
1988–89		21	—
1989–90		1	—
1989–90	Swindon T	28	—
1990–91		37	—
1991–92		39	1
1992–93		31	—
1992–93	Leeds U	8	—
1993–94	Tottenham H	17	—
1994–95		18	—
1995–96		2	—

KEWELL, Harry

Born Australia 22.9.78
Midfield.

Season	Club	Apps	Goals
1995–96	Leeds U	2	—

KEY, Lance

Born Kettering 13.5.68 Ht 6 3 Wt 14 13
Goalkeeper. From Histon.

Season	Club	Apps	Goals
1991–92	Sheffield W	—	—
1991–92	*York C*	—	—
1992–93	Sheffield W	—	—
1993–94		—	—
1993–94	*Oldham Ath*	2	—
1993–94	*Portsmouth*	—	—
1994–95	Sheffield W	—	—
1994–95	*Oxford U*	6	—
From Histon			
1995–96	Sheffield W	—	—
1995–96	*Lincoln C*	5	—
1995–96	*Hartlepool U*	1	—
1995–96	*Rochdale*	14	—

KHARINE, Dmitri

Born Moscow 16.8.68 Ht 6 2 Wt 13 09
Goalkeeper. USSR Youth, Under-21, full caps, Russia 34 full caps.

Season	Club	Apps	Goals
1984	Torpedo Moscow	1	—
1985		10	—
1986		25	—
1987		27	—
1988	Dynamo Moscow	19	—
1989		20	—
1990		1	—
1991	CSKA Moscow	11	—
1992		23	—
1992–93	Chelsea	5	—
1993–94		40	—
1994–95		31	—
1995–96		26	—

KIDD, Ryan

Born Radcliffe 6.10.71 Ht 6 1 Wt 13 03
Defender. From Trainee.

Season	Club	Apps	Goals
1990–91	Port Vale	—	—
1991–92		1	—
1992–93	Preston NE	15	—
1993–94		36	1
1994–95		32	3
1995–96		30	—

KIELTY, Ged

Born Manchester 1.9.76 Ht 5 8 Wt 10 11
Midfield. From Trainee.

Season	Club	Apps	Goals
1995–96	Manchester C	—	—

KIELY, Dean

Born Salford 10.10.70 Ht 6 0 Wt 13 05
Goalkeeper. From WBA Schools, FA Schools, England Youth.

Season	Club	Apps	Goals
1987–88	Coventry C	—	—
1988–89		—	—
1989–90		—	—
1989–90	*Ipswich T*	—	—
1989–90	*York C*	—	—
1990–91	York C	17	—
1991–92		21	—
1992–93		40	—
1993–94		46	—
1994–95		46	—
1995–96		40	—

KILBANE, Kevin

Born Preston 1.2.77 Ht 5 11 Wt 12 10
Midfield. From Trainee.

Season	Club	Apps	Goals
1993–94	Preston NE	1	—
1994–95		—	—
1995–96		11	1

KILCLINE, Brian

Born Nottingham 7.5.62 Ht 6 2
Wt 12 10
Defender. From Apprentice. England Under-21.

Season	Club	Apps	Goals
1979–80	Notts Co.	16	1
1980–81		42	1
1981–82		36	3
1982–83		40	3
1983–84		24	1
1984–85	Coventry C	26	2
1985–86		32	7
1986–87		29	3
1987–88		28	8
1988–89		33	4
1989–90		11	1
1990–91		14	3
1991–92	Oldham Ath	8	—
1991–92	Newcastle U	12	—
1992–93		19	—
1993–94		1	—
1993–94	Swindon T	10	—
1994–95		7	—
1995–96		—	—
1995–96	Mansfield T	19	—

KILFORD, Ian

Born Bristol 6.10.73 Ht 5 10 Wt 11 00
Midfield. From Trainee.

Season	Club	Apps	Goals
1991–92	Nottingham F	—	—
1992–93		—	—
1993–94		1	—
1993–94	*Wigan Ath*	8	3
1994–95	Wigan Ath	35	5
1995–96		25	3

KIMBLE, Alan

Born Poole 6.8.66 Ht 5 10 Wt 12 04
Defender.

Season	Club	Apps	Goals
1984–85	Charlton Ath	6	—
1985–86		—	—
1985–86	*Exeter C*	1	—
1986–87	Cambridge U	35	—
1987–88		41	2
1988–89		45	6
1989–90		44	8
1990–91		43	4
1991–92		45	—
1992–93		46	4
1993–94	Wimbledon	14	—
1994–95		26	—
1995–96		31	—

KING, Nathan

Born West Bromwich 1.8.75 Ht 6 0
Wt 12 06
Defender. From Trainee.

Season	Club	Apps	Goals
1994–95	Shrewsbury T	—	—
1995–96		—	—

KING, Phil

Born Bristol 28.12.67 Ht 5 8 Wt 11 09
Defender. From Apprentice. England B.

Season	Club	Apps	Goals
1984–85	Exeter C	16	—
1985–86		11	—
1986–87	Torquay U	24	3
1986–87	Swindon T	21	—
1987–88		44	1
1988–89		37	2
1989–90		14	1
1989–90	Sheffield W	25	—
1990–91		43	—
1991–92		39	1
1992–93		12	1
1993–94		10	—
1993–94	*Notts Co*	6	—
1994–95	Aston Villa	16	—
1995–96		—	—
1995–96	*WBA*	4	—

KINKLADZE, Georgiou

Born Tbilisi 6.7.73 Ht 5 8 Wt 10 09
Midfield. From Dynamo Tbilisi. Georgia full caps.

Season	Club	Apps	Goals
1995–96	Manchester C	37	4

KINNAIRD, Paul

Born Glasgow 11.11.66 Ht 5 8 Wt 10 10
Forward. From Apprentice.

Season	Club	Apps	Goals
1984–85	Norwich C	—	—
1985–86	Dundee U	—	—
1986–87		7	—
1987–88		11	—
1987–88	Motherwell	10	—
1988–89		24	—
1988–89	St Mirren	6	—
1989–90		25	—
1990–91		23	4
1991–92		3	—
1991–92	Partick T	13	2
1992–93		20	1

Season	Club	League Appearances/Goals	
1992–93	Shrewsbury T	4	1
1992–93	St Johnstone	8	—
1993–94	Partick T	3	—
1994–95		—	—
1995–96	Dunfermline Ath	9	—
1995–96	Ayr U	18	2
1995–96	Scarborough	3	—

KINSELLA, Mark

Born Dublin 12.8.72 Ht 5 9 Wt 11 05
Midfield. From Home Farm.

Season	Club	Apps	Goals
1989–90	Colchester U	6	—
1990–91		—	—
1991–92		—	—
1992–93		38	6
1993–94		42	8
1994–95		42	6
1995–96		45	5

KIRBY, Alan

Born Waterford 8.9.77 Ht 5 7 Wt 9 11
Midfield. From Trainee.

Season	Club	Apps	Goals
1995–96	Aston Villa	—	—

KIRBY, Ryan

Born Chingford 6.9.74 Ht 6 0 Wt 12 00
Defender. From Trainee.

Season	Club	Apps	Goals
1993–94	Arsenal	—	—
1994–95	Doncaster R	42	—
1995–96		36	—

KIRK, Steve

Born Kirkcaldy 3.1.63 Ht 5 11 Wt 11 04
Midfield. From Buckhaven Hibs.

Season	Club	Apps	Goals
1979–80	East Fife	25	2
1980–81	Stoke C	—	—
1981–82		12	—
1982–83	Partick T	—	—
1982–83	East Fife	25	8
1983–84		33	5
1984–85		38	8
1985–86		39	14
1986–87	Motherwell	35	10
1987–88		38	4
1988–89		33	14
1989–90		34	8
1990–91		29	2
1991–92		38	6
1992–93		40	10
1993–94		36	7
1994–95		18	2
1994–95	Falkirk	11	5
1995–96		20	4
1995–96	Raith R	7	1

KIRKHAM, Peter

Born Newcastle 28.10.74 Ht 5 11
Wt 11 07
Midfield. From Newcastle U Trainee.

Season	Club	Apps	Goals
1993–94	Darlington	9	—
1994–95		4	—
1995–96		—	—

KIRKWOOD, David

Born St Andrews 27.8.67 Ht 5 10
Wt 11 07
Midfield. From Leven Royal Colts.
Scotland Under-21.

Season	Club	Apps	Goals
1983–84	East Fife	14	2
1984–85		17	4
1985–86		34	2
1986–87		35	2
1987–88	Rangers	4	—
1988–89		2	—
1989–90	Hearts	19	—
1990–91		9	1
1991–92	Airdrieonians	36	9
1992–93		27	2
1993–94		29	10
1994–95	Raith R	19	1
1995–96		28	2

KIROVSKI, Jovan

Born Escondido 18.3.76
Forward. USA full caps.

Season	Club	Apps	Goals
1995–96	Manchester U	—	—

KITE, Phil

Born Bristol 26.10.62 Ht 6 2 Wt 15 04
Goalkeeper. From Apprentice. England Youth.

Season	Club	Apps	Goals
1980–81	Bristol R	4	—
1981–82		27	—
1982–83		46	—
1983–84		19	—
1983–84	*Tottenham H*	—	—
1984–85	Southampton	1	—
1985–86		3	—
1985–86	*Middlesbrough*	2	—
1986–87	Gillingham	17	—

Season	Club	League Appearances	Goals
1987–88		26	—
1988–89		27	—
1989–90	Bournemouth	7	—
1990–91	Sheffield U	7	—
1991–92		4	—
1991–92	*Mansfield T*	11	—
1992–93	Sheffield U	—	—
1992–93	*Plymouth Arg*	2	—
1992–93	*Rotherham U*	1	—
1992–93	*Crewe Alex*	5	—
1992–93	*Stockport Co*	5	—
1993–94	Cardiff C	18	—
1994–95	Bristol C	2	—
1995–96		4	—

KITSON, Paul

Born Murton 9.1.71 Ht 5 10 Wt 10 12
Forward. From Trainee. England Under-21.

Season	Club	League Appearances	Goals
1988–89	Leicester C	—	—
1989–90		13	—
1990–91		7	—
1991–92		30	6
1991–92	Derby Co	12	4
1992–93		44	17
1993–94		41	13
1994–95		8	2
1994–95	Newcastle U	26	8
1995–96		7	2

KIWOMYA, Andrew

Born Huddersfield 1.10.67 Ht 5 11
Wt 10 10
Forward. From Trainee. England Youth.

Season	Club	League Appearances	Goals
1985–86	Barnsley	1	—
1986–87	Sheffield W	—	—
1987–88		—	—
1988–89		—	—
From Retired injury.			
1992–93	Dundee	21	1
1993–94	Rotherham U	7	—
From Halifax T			
1994–95	Scunthorpe U	9	3
1995–96	Bradford C	16	2

KIWOMYA, Chris

Born Huddersfield 2.12.69 Ht 5 9
Wt 10 07
Forward. From Trainee.

Season	Club	League Appearances	Goals
1986–87	Ipswich T	—	—
1987–88		—	—
1988–89		26	2
1989–90		29	5
1990–91		37	10
1991–92		43	16
1992–93		38	10
1993–94		37	5
1994–95		15	3
1994–95	Arsenal	14	3
1995–96		—	—

KJELDBJERG, Jakob

Born Frederiks 21.10.69 Ht 6 3
Wt 13 08
Defender. From Silkeborg. Denmark Youth, Under-21, 14 full caps.

Season	Club	League Appearances	Goals
1993–94	Chelsea	29	1
1994–95		23	1
1995–96		—	—

KNIGHT, Alan

Born Balham 3.6.61 Ht 6 1 Wt 13 11
Goalkeeper. From Apprentice. England Youth, Under-21.

Season	Club	League Appearances	Goals
1977–78	Portsmouth	1	—
1978–79		—	—
1979–80		8	—
1980–81		1	—
1981–82		45	—
1982–83		46	—
1983–84		42	—
1984–85		42	—
1985–86		38	—
1986–87		42	—
1987–88		36	—
1988–89		32	—
1989–90		46	—
1990–91		22	—
1991–92		45	—
1992–93		46	—
1993–94		43	—
1994–95		43	—
1995–96		42	—

KNIGHT, Jason

Born Australia 16.9.74 Ht 6 1 Wt 11 09
Midfield. From West Ham U Trainee.

Season	Club	League Appearances	Goals
1995–96	Doncaster R	4	—

Season Club League Appearances/Goals

KNILL, Alan

Born Slough 8.10.64 Ht 6 4 Wt 13 02
Defender. From Apprentice. Wales Youth, 1 full cap.

Season	Club	Apps	Goals
1982–83	Southampton	—	—
1983–84		—	—
1984–85	Halifax T	44	1
1985–86		33	2
1986–87		41	3
1987–88	Swansea C	46	1
1988–89		43	2
1989–90	Bury	43	1
1990–91		20	1
1991–92		35	1
1992–93		38	5
1993–94		8	—
1993–94	*Cardiff C*	4	—
1993–94	Scunthorpe U	25	1
1994–95		39	4
1995–96		38	3

KNOTT, Gareth

Born Blackwood 19.1.76 Ht 5 8
Wt 11 04
Forward. From Trainee. Wales Under-21.

Season	Club	Apps	Goals
1994–95	Tottenham H	—	—
1994–95	*Gillingham*	5	—
1995–96	Tottenham H	—	—

KNOWLES, Darren

Born Sheffield 8.10.70 Ht 5 6 Wt 11 01
Defender. From Trainee.

Season	Club	Apps	Goals
1989–90	Sheffield U	—	—
1989–90	Stockport Co	9	—
1990–91		12	—
1991–92		31	—
1992–93		11	—
1993–94	Scarborough	42	1
1994–95		39	—
1995–96		46	1

KOVACEVIC, Darko

Born Yugoslavia 18.11.73 Ht 6 2
Wt 12 06
Forward. From Red Star Belgrade.
Yugoslavia 6 full caps.

Season	Club	Apps	Goals
1995–96	Sheffield W	16	4

KOZLUK, Robert

Born Mansfield 5.8.77
Midfield. From Trainee.

Season	Club	Apps	Goals
1995–96	Derby Co	—	—

KPEDEKPO, Malcolm

Born Aberdeen 27.8.76 Ht 6 0 Wt 12 11
Midfield. From Hermes BC.

Season	Club	Apps	Goals
1994–95	Aberdeen	1	—
1995–96		5	—

KREFT, Stacey

Born Southampton 2.2.76 Ht 5 9
Wt 11 00
Defender. From Trainee.

Season	Club	Apps	Goals
1994–95	Norwich C	—	—
1995–96		—	—

KRIVOKAPIC, Miodrag

Born Niksic 6.9.59 Ht 6 1 Wt 12 12
Defender. From Red Star Belgrade.
Yugoslavia full caps.

Season	Club	Apps	Goals
1988–89	Dundee U	24	1
1989–90		26	—
1990–91		24	—
1991–92		—	—
1992–93		8	—
1993–94	Motherwell	42	1
1994–95		16	—
1995–96		13	—
1995–96	Raith R	5	—

KUBICKI, Dariusz

Born Kozuchow 6.6.63 Ht 5 11 Wt 11 12
Defender. From Legia Warsaw. Poland 46 full caps.

Season	Club	Apps	Goals
1991–92	Aston Villa	23	—
1992–93		—	—
1993–94		2	—
1993–94	*Sunderland*	15	—
1994–95	Sunderland	46	—
1995–96		46	—

KUHL, Martin

Born Frimley 10.1.65 Ht 5 10 Wt 12 08
Midfield. From Apprentice.

Season	Club	Apps	Goals
1982–83	Birmingham C	2	—
1983–84		22	1
1984–85		27	2

Season	Club	League Appearances/Goals	
1985–86		37	1
1986–87		23	1
1986–87	Sheffield U	10	1
1987–88		28	3
1987–88	Watford	4	—
1988–89		—	—
1988–89	Portsmouth	32	1
1989–90		40	9
1990–91		41	13
1991–92		41	3
1992–93		3	1
1992–93	Derby Co	32	1
1993–94		27	—
1994–95		9	—
1994–95	*Notts Co*	2	—
1994–95	Bristol C	17	1
1995–96		46	6

KULKOV, Vasili

Born Moscow 11.6.66
Midfield. From Porto. Russia full caps.

1995–96	Millwall	6	—

KYD, Michael

Born Hackney 21.5.77 Ht 5 9 Wt 12 08
Midfield. From Trainee.

1994–95	Cambridge U	19	1
1995–96		9	1

KYDD, Peter

Born Bournemouth 20.1.78 Ht 5 8
Wt 10 00
Midfield. From Trainee.

1994–95	West Ham U	—	—
1995–96		—	—

KYTE, Jamie

Born Erith 17.9.77 Ht 5 7 Wt 10 00
Midfield. From Trainee.

1994–95	Charlton Ath	—	—
1995–96		—	—

LAIDLAW, Iain

Born Newcastle 10.12.76 Ht 6 2
Wt 12 07
Defender. From Trainee.

1995–96	Wimbledon	—	—

LAIDLAW, Jamie

Born Irvine 14.11.75 Ht 5 10 Wt 12 03
Midfield. From Trainee.

1995–96	Swindon T	—	—

LAIGHT, Ellis

Born Birmingham 30.6.76 Ht 5 10
Wt 11 02
Forward. From Trainee.

1993–94	Torquay U	1	—
1994–95		10	—
1995–96		20	2

LAISTER, Jamie

Born Newport 9.2.79
Midfield.

1995–96	Hull C	—	—

LAKE, Paul

Born Manchester 28.10.68 Ht 6 0
Wt 12 02
Midfield. From Trainee. England Under-21.

1986–87	Manchester C	3	1
1987–88		33	3
1988–89		38	3
1989–90		31	—
1990–91		3	—
1991–92		—	—
1992–93		2	—
1993–94		—	—
1994–95		—	—
1995–96		—	—

LAKIN, Barry

Born Dartford 19.9.73 Ht 5 9 Wt 12 02
Midfield. From Trainee.

1992–93	Leyton Orient	9	2
1993–94		15	—
1994–95		22	—
1995–96		8	—

LAMBERT, James

Born Henley 14.9.73 Ht 5 7 Wt 10 04
Forward. From School.

Season	Club	Apps	Goals
1992–93	Reading	27	3
1993–94		6	—
1994–95		11	1
1995–96		15	4

LAMBERT, Paul

Born Glasgow 7.8.69 Ht 5 11 Wt 9 10
Midfield. From Linwood Rangers BC. Scotland Under-21, 2 full caps.

Season	Club	Apps	Goals
1985–86	St Mirren	1	—
1986–87		36	2
1987–88		36	2
1988–89		16	2
1989–90		25	3
1990–91		31	2
1991–92		40	2
1992–93		39	1
1993–94		3	—
1993–94	Motherwell	32	3
1994–95		36	1
1995–96		35	2

LAMONT, William

Born Falkirk 24.7.66 Ht 5 11 Wt 13 12
Goalkeeper. From Armadale Th.

Season	Club	Apps	Goals
1989–90	Cowdenbeath	35	—
1990–91		32	—
1991–92		26	—
1992–93		25	—
From Whitburn Juniors			
1994–95	Falkirk	8	—
1995–96		7	—
1995–96	Ayr U	4	—
1995–96	Alloa	1	—

LAMPARD, Frank

Born Romford 21.6.78 Ht 6 0 Wt 13 07
Midfield. From Trainee. England Youth.

Season	Club	Apps	Goals
1994–95	West Ham U	—	—
1995–96		2	—
1995–96	*Swansea C*	9	1

LAMPKIN, Kevin

Born Liverpool 20.12.72 Ht 6 0
Wt 12 02
Midfield. From Trainee.

Season	Club	Apps	Goals
1991–92	Liverpool	—	—
1992–93	Huddersfield T	13	—
1993–94		—	—
1993–94	Mansfield T	13	1
1994–95		23	2
1995–96		6	—

LAMPTEY, Nii

Born Accra 10.12.74 Ht 5 8 Wt 11 04
Forward. Ghana full caps.

Season	Club	Apps	Goals
1990–91	Anderlecht	14	7
1991–92		15	2
1992–93		1	—
1993–94	PSV Eindhoven	22	9
1994–95	Aston Villa	6	—
1995–96		—	—
1995–96	Coventry C	6	—

LANCASHIRE, Graham

Born Blackpool 19.10.72 Ht 5 10
Wt 11 12
Forward. From Trainee.

Season	Club	Apps	Goals
1990–91	Burnley	1	—
1991–92		25	8
1992–93		3	—
1992–93	*Halifax T*	2	—
1993–94	Burnley	1	—
1993–94	*Chester C*	11	7
1994–95	Burnley	1	—
1994–95	Preston NE	17	—
1995–96		6	2
1995–96	Wigan Ath	5	3

LANCASTER, David

Born Preston 8.9.61 Ht 6 3 Wt 15 00
Forward. From Colne Dynamoes.

Season	Club	Apps	Goals
1990–91	Blackpool	8	1
1990–91	*Chesterfield*	12	4
1991–92	Chesterfield	29	7
1992–93		40	9
1993–94	Rochdale	40	14
1994–95	Bury	5	1
1995–96		5	—
1995–96	*Rochdale*	14	2

LANDELS, Graeme

Born Broxburn 27.3.78 Ht 5 11
Wt 12 05
Midfield. From ICI Juv.

Season	Club	Apps	Goals
1995–96	Raith R	1	—

LANDON, Richard

Born Worthing 22.3.70 Ht 6 3 Wt 13 05
Forward. From Bedworth U.

Season	Club	Apps	Goals
1993–94	Plymouth Arg	6	5
1994–95		24	7
1995–96	Stockport Co	11	5

LANGE, Tony

Born London 10.12.64 Ht 6 0 Wt 14 06
Goalkeeper. From Apprentice.

Season	Club	Apps	Goals
1982–83	Charlton Ath	—	—
1983–84		6	—
1984–85		2	—
1985–86		4	—
1985–86	*Aldershot*	7	—
1986–87	Aldershot	45	—
1987–88		35	—
1988–89		45	—
1989–90	Wolverhampton W	5	—
1990–91		3	—
1990–91	*Aldershot*	2	—
1991–92	Wolverhampton W	—	—
1991–92	*Torquay U*	1	—
1991–92	*Portsmouth*	—	—
1992–93	WBA	14	—
1993–94		29	—
1994–95		5	—
1995–96	Fulham	41	—

LAPPER, Mike

Born California 28.8.70 Ht 6 0 Wt 12 02
Defender. From USSF. USA full caps.

Season	Club	Apps	Goals
1995–96	Southend U	24	—

LARKIN, Andy

Born Kent 24.9.77 Ht 6 1 Wt 11 09
Defender. From Trainee.

Season	Club	Apps	Goals
1994–95	Charlton Ath	—	—
1995–96		—	—

LAUCHLAN, James

Born Glasgow 2.2.77 Ht 6 1 Wt 10 13
Midfield. From Highbury BC.

Season	Club	Apps	Goals
1993–94	Kilmarnock	1	—
1994–95		2	—
1995–96		5	—

LAUDRUP, Brian

Born Vienna 22.2.69 Ht 6 0 Wt 13 02
Forward. From Fiorentina. Denmark 63 full caps.

Season	Club	Apps	Goals
1994–95	Rangers	33	10
1995–96		22	2

LAUNDERS, Brian

Born Dublin 8.1.76 Ht 5 10 Wt 11 10
Midfield. From Trainee. Eire Under-21.

Season	Club	Apps	Goals
1993–94	Crystal Palace	—	—
1994–95		2	—
1995–96		2	—
1995–96	*Oldham Ath*	—	—

LAVIN, Gerard

Born Corby 5.2.74 Ht 5 10 Wt 11 00
Midfield. From Trainee. Scotland Under-21.

Season	Club	Apps	Goals
1991–92	Watford	1	—
1992–93		28	—
1993–94		46	3
1994–95		35	—
1995–96		16	—
1995–96	Millwall	20	—

LAW, Brian

Born Merthyr 1.1.70 Ht 6 2 Wt 14 00
Defender. From Apprentice. Wales Under-21, 1 full cap.

Season	Club	Apps	Goals
1987–88	QPR	1	—
1988–89		6	—
1989–90		10	—
1990–91		3	—
1991–92		—	—
1992–93		—	—
1993–94		—	—
1994–95	Wolverhampton W	17	—
1995–96		7	1

LAW, Nicky

Born London 8.9.61 Ht 6 0 Wt 13 07
Defender. From Apprentice.

Season	Club	Apps	Goals
1979–80	Arsenal	—	—
1980–81		—	—
1981–82	Barnsley	19	—
1982–83		28	—
1983–84		31	1
1984–85		35	—
1985–86		1	—

Season	Club	Apps	Goals
1985–86	Blackpool	39	1
1986–87		27	—
1986–87	Plymouth Arg	12	2
1987–88		26	3
1988–89	Notts Co	44	4
1989–90		3	—
1989–90	*Scarborough*	12	—
1990–91	Rotherham U	32	2
1991–92		42	—
1992–93		44	2
1993–94		10	—
1993–94	Chesterfield	31	2
1994–95		35	1
1995–96		38	7

LAWFORD, Craig

Born Dewsbury 25.11.72 Ht 5 10
Wt 11 00
Midfield. From Trainee.

Season	Club	Apps	Goals
1989–90	Bradford C	1	—
1990–91		—	—
1991–92		—	—
1992–93		8	1
1993–94		11	—
1994–95	Hull C	31	3
1995–96		31	—

LAWLESS, Chris

Born Dublin 4.10.74 Ht 5 8 Wt 11 01
Midfield. From Home Farm.

Season	Club	Apps	Goals
1993–94	Sunderland	—	—
1994–95		—	—
1995–96		—	—

LAWRENCE, Alan

Born Edinburgh 19.8.62 Ht 5 7
Wt 10 00
Forward. From Easthouses BC.

Season	Club	Apps	Goals
1984–85	Meadowbank T	35	—
1985–86		38	17
1986–87		29	6
1986–87	Dundee	4	1
1987–88		22	1
1988–89		10	—
1988–89	Airdrieonians	7	2
1989–90		34	9
1990–91		38	13
1991–92		31	7
1992–93		35	2
1993–94		27	5
1994–95		32	11
1995–96	Hearts	26	5

LAWRENCE, Jamie

Born Balham 8.3.70 Ht 6 0 Wt 12 06
Forward. From Cowes.

Season	Club	Apps	Goals
1993–94	Sunderland	4	—
1993–94	Doncaster R	9	1
1994–95		16	2
1994–95	Leicester C	17	1
1995–96		15	—

LAWRENCE, Matthew

Born Northampton 19.6.74 Ht 5 10
Wt 11 04
Midfield. From Grays Ath.

Season	Club	Apps	Goals
1995–96	Wycombe W	3	—

LAWRIE, Andrew

Born Galashiels 24.11.78
Midfield. From Falkirk Under-16.

Season	Club	Apps	Goals
1995–96	Falkirk	1	—

LAWS, Brian

Born Wallsend 14.10.61 Ht 5 8 Wt 11 05
Defender. From Apprentice. England B.

Season	Club	Apps	Goals
1979–80	Burnley	1	—
1980–81		42	2
1981–82		44	6
1982–83		38	4
1983–84	Huddersfield T	31	—
1984–85		25	1
1984–85	Middlesbrough	11	1
1985–86		42	2
1986–87		26	8
1987–88		28	1
1988–89	Nottingham F	22	1
1989–90		38	3
1990–91		32	—
1991–92		15	—
1992–93		33	—
1993–94		7	—
1994–95		—	—
1994–95	Grimsby T	16	1
1995–96		27	1

LAWSON, Ian

Born Huddersfield 4.11.77 Ht 5 11
Wt 11 05
Forward. From Trainee.

Season	Club	Apps	Goals
1994–95	Huddersfield T	—	—
1995–96		—	—

Season	Club	League Appearances/Goals	

LAWTON, Craig

Born Mancot 5.1.72 Ht 5 7 Wt 10 03
Midfield. From Trainee.

Season	Club	Apps	Goals
1991–92	Manchester U	—	—
1992–93		—	—
1993–94		—	—
1994–95	Port Vale	1	—
1995–96		2	—

LAZARIDIS, Stan

Born Perth 16.8.72 Ht 5 9 Wt 11 12
Midfield. From West Adelaide. Australia full caps.

Season	Club	Apps	Goals
1995–96	West Ham U	4	—

LE BIHAN, Neil

Born London 14.3.76 Ht 6 0 Wt 12 03
Midfield. From Tottenham H Trainee.

Season	Club	Apps	Goals
1994–95	Peterborough U	4	—
1995–96		25	—

LE SAUX, Graeme

Born Jersey 17.10.68 Ht 5 10 Wt 12 02
Defender. From St Pauls. England Under-21, B, 12 full caps.

Season	Club	Apps	Goals
1987–88	Chelsea	—	—
1988–89		1	—
1989–90		7	1
1990–91		28	4
1991–92		40	3
1992–93		14	—
1992–93	Blackburn R	9	—
1993–94		41	2
1994–95		39	3
1995–96		14	1

LE TISSIER, Matthew

Born Guernsey 14.10.68 Ht 6 1
Wt 13 08
Forward. From Trainee. England Youth, B, 6 full caps.

Season	Club	Apps	Goals
1986–87	Southampton	24	6
1987–88		19	—
1988–89		28	9
1989–90		35	20
1990–91		35	19
1991–92		32	6
1992–93		40	15
1993–94		38	25
1994–95		41	20
1995–96		34	7

LEABURN, Carl

Born Lewisham 30.3.69 Ht 6 3 Wt 13 00
Forward. From Apprentice. England Youth.

Season	Club	Apps	Goals
1986–87	Charlton Ath	3	1
1987–88		12	—
1988–89		32	2
1989–90		13	—
1989–90	*Northampton T*	9	—
1990–91	Charlton Ath	20	1
1991–92		39	11
1992–93		39	5
1993–94		39	10
1994–95		27	3
1995–96		40	9

LEACH, Gavin

Born Middlesbrough 9.8.77 Ht 6 1
Wt 13 06
Midfield. From Stockton.

Season	Club	Apps	Goals
1995–96	Doncaster R	—	—

LEADBITTER, Chris

Born Middlesbrough 17.10.67 Ht 5 9
Wt 10 07
Forward. From Apprentice.

Season	Club	Apps	Goals
1985–86	Grimsby T	—	—
1986–87	Hereford U	6	—
1987–88		30	1
1988–89	Cambridge U	31	6
1989–90		43	4
1990–91		39	1
1991–92		25	1
1992–93		38	6
1993–94	Bournemouth	27	—
1994–95		27	3
1995–96	Plymouth Arg	33	1

LEANING, Andy

Born York 18.5.63 Ht 6 0 Wt 13 00
Goalkeeper. From Rowntree Mackintosh.

Season	Club	Apps	Goals
1984–85	York C	—	—
1985–86		30	—
1986–87		39	—
1987–88	Sheffield U	21	—
1988–89		—	—
1988–89	Bristol C	6	—
1989–90		19	—

Season	Club	League Appearances/Goals	
1990–91		29	—
1991–92		20	—
1992–93		1	—
1993–94		—	—
1993–94	Lincoln C	8	—
1994–95		21	—
1995–96		7	—

LEE, Alan

Born Galway 21.8.78 Ht 6 2 Wt 13 04
Forward. From Trainee.

Season	Club	Apps	Goals
1995–96	Aston Villa	—	—

LEE, Chris

Born Halifax 18.6.71 Ht 5 9 Wt 11 05
Midfield. From Trainee.

Season	Club	Apps	Goals
1989–90	Bradford C	—	—
1990–91	Rochdale	26	2
1990–91	Scarborough	9	—
1991–92		41	2
1992–93		28	1
1993–94	Hull C	43	3
1994–95		45	1
1995–96		28	1

LEE, Christian

Born Aylesbury 8.10.76 Ht 6 1 Wt 11 07
Forward. From Doncaster R.

Season	Club	Apps	Goals
1995–96	Northampton T	5	—

LEE, David

Born Whitefield 5.11.67 Ht 5 7 Wt 11 00
Midfield. From Blackburn Schools.

Season	Club	Apps	Goals
1984–85	Bury	—	—
1985–86		1	—
1986–87		30	4
1987–88		40	3
1988–89		45	4
1989–90		45	8
1990–91		45	15
1991–92		2	1
1991–92	Southampton	19	—
1992–93		1	—
1992–93	Bolton W	32	5
1993–94		41	5
1994–95		39	4
1995–96		18	1

LEE, David

Born Kingswood 26.11.69 Ht 6 3
Wt 15 01
Defender. From Trainee. England Youth, Under-21.

Season	Club	Apps	Goals
1988–89	Chelsea	20	4
1989–90		30	1
1990–91		21	1
1991–92		1	—
1991–92	*Reading*	5	5
1991–92	*Plymouth Arg*	9	1
1992–93	Chelsea	25	2
1993–94		7	1
1994–95		14	—
1994–95	*Portsmouth*	5	—
1995–96	Chelsea	31	1

LEE, Graeme

Born Middlesbrough 31.5.78 Ht 6 2
Wt 12 07
Midfield. From Trainee.

Season	Club	Apps	Goals
1995–96	Hartlepool U	6	—

LEE, Jason

Born Newham 9.5.71 Ht 6 3 Wt 13 03
Forward. From Trainee.

Season	Club	Apps	Goals
1989–90	Charlton Ath	1	—
1990–91		—	—
1990–91	*Stockport Co*	2	—
1990–91	Lincoln C	17	3
1991–92		35	6
1992–93		41	12
1993–94	Southend U	24	3
1993–94	Nottingham F	13	2
1994–95		22	3
1995–96		28	8

LEE, Paddy

Born Dublin 2.8.77
Midfield. From Manchester U.

Season	Club	Apps	Goals
1995–96	Middlesbrough	—	—

LEE, Robert

Born West Ham 1.2.66 Ht 5 10
Wt 11 13
Forward. From Hornchurch. England Under-21, 7 full caps.

Season	Club	Apps	Goals
1983–84	Charlton Ath	11	4
1984–85		39	10
1985–86		35	8

Season	Club	League Appearances/Goals	
1986–87		33	3
1987–88		23	2
1988–89		31	5
1989–90		37	1
1990–91		43	13
1991–92		39	12
1992–93		7	1
1992–93	Newcastle U	36	10
1993–94		41	7
1994–95		35	9
1995–96		36	8

LEGG, Andy

Born Neath 28.7.66 Ht 5 8 Wt 10 07
Midfield. From Briton Ferry. Wales 2 full caps.

Season	Club	League Appearances/Goals	
1988–89	Swansea C	6	—
1989–90		26	3
1990–91		39	5
1991–92		46	9
1992–93		46	12
1993–94	Notts Co	30	2
1994–95		34	3
1995–96		25	4
1995–96	Birmingham C	12	1

LEIGHTON, Jim

Born Johnstone 24.7.58 Ht 6 1 Wt 12 09
Goalkeeper. From Dalry Thistle. Scotland Under-21, 74 full caps.

Season	Club	League Appearances/Goals	
1978–79	Aberdeen	11	—
1979–80		1	—
1980–81		35	—
1981–82		36	—
1982–83		35	—
1983–84		36	—
1984–85		34	—
1985–86		26	—
1986–87		42	—
1987–88		44	—
1988–89	Manchester U	38	—
1989–90		35	—
1990–91		—	—
1990–91	*Arsenal*	—	—
1991–92	Manchester U	—	—
1991–92	*Reading*	8	—
1991–92	Dundee	13	—
1992–93		8	—
1992–93	*Sheffield U*	—	—
1993–94	Hibernian	44	—
1994–95		36	—
1995–96		36	—

LEITCH, Scott

Born Motherwell 6.10.69 Ht 5 9 Wt 11 08
Defender.

Season	Club	League Appearances/Goals	
1990–91	Dunfermline Ath	14	3
1991–92		33	4
1992–93		42	9
1993–94	Hearts	28	2
1994–95		21	—
1995–96		6	—
1995–96	Swindon T	7	—

LEKOVIC, Dragote

Born Sivac, Montenegro 21.11.67 Ht 6 2 Wt 12 09
Goalkeeper. From Buducnost Podogorica.

Season	Club	League Appearances/Goals	
1994–95	Kilmarnock	20	—
1995–96		33	—

LENNON, Daniel

Born Whitburn 6.4.69 Ht 5 5 Wt 9 05
Midfield. From Hutchison Vale BC.

Season	Club	League Appearances/Goals	
1987–88	Hibernian	1	—
1988–89		1	—
1989–90		—	—
1990–91		6	—
1991–92		11	1
1992–93		13	—
1993–94		5	1
1993–94	Raith R	7	—
1994–95		20	—
1995–96		34	5

LENNON, Neil

Born Lurgan 25.6.71 Ht 5 10 Wt 12 12
Defender. From Trainee. Northern Ireland Under-23, 6 full caps.

Season	Club	League Appearances/Goals	
1987–88	Manchester C	1	—
1988–89		—	—
1989–90		—	—
1990–91	Crewe Alex	34	3
1991–92		—	—
1992–93		24	—
1993–94		33	4
1994–95		31	6
1995–96		25	2
1995–96	Leicester C	15	1

LEONARD, Mark

Born St Helens 27.9.62 Ht 5 11
Wt 13 03
Forward. From Witton Alb.

Season	Club	App	Gls
1981–82	Everton	—	—
1982–83		—	—
1982–83	*Tranmere R*	7	—
1983–84	Crewe Alex	38	10
1984–85		16	5
1984–85	Stockport Co	23	4
1985–86		44	20
1986–87		6	—
1986–87	Bradford C	24	3
1987–88		28	10
1988–89		44	7
1989–90		24	5
1990–91		18	4
1991–92		19	—
1991–92	Rochdale	9	1
1992–93	Preston NE	22	1
1993–94	Chester C	32	8
1994–95		—	—
1994–95	Wigan Ath	29	5
1995–96		35	7

LEONHARDSEN, Oyvind

Born Norway 17.8.70 Ht 5 10 Wt 11 02
Midfield. From Rosenborg. Norway 42 full caps.

Season	Club	App	Gls
1994–95	Wimbledon	20	4
1995–96		29	4

LESLIE, Steven

Born Dumfries 6.2.76 Ht 5 6 Wt 10 00
Midfield. From Trainee.

Season	Club	App	Gls
1992–93	Stoke C	—	—
1993–94		—	—
1994–95		1	—
1995–96		—	—

LESTER, Jack

Born Sheffield 8.10.75 Ht 5 10 Wt 11 00
Forward. From Trainee.

Season	Club	App	Gls
1994–95	Grimsby T	7	—
1995–96		5	—

LEVEIN, Craig

Born Dunfermline 22.10.64 Ht 6 0
Wt 11 04
Defender. From Lochore Welfare.
Scotland Youth, Under-21, 16 full caps.

Season	Club	App	Gls
1981–82	Cowdenbeath	15	—
1982–83		30	—
1983–84		15	—
1983–84	Hearts	22	—
1984–85		36	1
1985–86		33	2
1986–87		12	—
1987–88		21	—
1988–89		9	—
1989–90		35	—
1990–91		33	4
1991–92		36	2
1992–93		37	3
1993–94		30	3
1994–95		24	—
1995–96		1	—

LEVER, Mark

Born Beverley 29.3.70 Ht 6 3 Wt 12 08
Defender. From Trainee.

Season	Club	App	Gls
1987–88	Grimsby T	1	—
1988–89		37	2
1989–90		38	2
1990–91		40	2
1991–92		36	—
1992–93		14	1
1993–94		22	—
1994–95		31	—
1995–96		24	1

LEWIS, Ben

Born Chelmsford 22.6.77 Ht 5 10
Wt 12 04
Defender. From Trainee.

Season	Club	App	Gls
1995–96	Colchester U	2	—

LEWIS, Mickey

Born Birmingham 15.2.65 Ht 5 7
Wt 12 06
Midfield. From School. England Youth.

Season	Club	App	Gls
1981–82	WBA	4	—
1982–83		5	—
1983–84		14	—
1984–85		1	—
1984–85	Derby Co	22	—

Season	Club	League Appearances/Goals	
1985–86		5	1
1986–87		—	—
1987–88		16	—
1988–89	Oxford U	36	—
1989–90		45	1
1990–91		34	1
1991–92		40	4
1992–93		41	—
1993–94		46	—
1994–95		39	1
1995–96		19	—

LEWIS, Neil

Born Wolverhampton 28.6.74 Ht 5 8 Wt 10 05
Midfield. From Trainee.

1992–93	Leicester C	7	—
1993–94		24	—
1994–95		16	—
1995–96		14	1

LIBURD, Richard

Born Nottingham 26.9.73 Ht 5 10 Wt 11 01
Defender. From Forest Athletic.

1992–93	Middlesbrough	—	—
1993–94		41	1
1994–95	Bradford C	9	1
1995–96		33	1

LIDDELL, Andrew

Born Leeds 28.6.73 Ht 5 6 Wt 10 09
Forward. From Trainee. Scotland Under-21.

1990–91	Barnsley	—	—
1991–92		1	—
1992–93		21	2
1993–94		22	1
1994–95		39	13
1995–96		43	9

LIDDLE, Craig

Born Chester-le-Street 21.10.71 Ht 5 11 Wt 12 03
Midfield. From Blyth Spartans.

1994–95	Middlesbrough	1	—
1995–96		13	—

LIGHTBOURNE, Kyle

Born Bermuda 29.9.68 Ht 6 2 Wt 12 04
Forward. Bermuda full caps.

1992–93	Scarborough	19	3
1993–94		—	—
1993–94	Walsall	35	7
1994–95		42	23
1995–96		43	15

LIGHTFOOT, Chris

Born Warrington 1.4.70 Ht 6 1 Wt 13 03
Midfield. From Trainee.

1987–88	Chester C	16	1
1988–89		36	7
1989–90		40	1
1990–91		37	2
1991–92		44	5
1992–93		39	2
1993–94		37	11
1994–95		28	3
1995–96	Wigan Ath	14	1
1995–96	Crewe Alex	6	—

LIMPAR, Anders

Born Solna 24.9.65 Ht 5 8 Wt 11 02
Forward. Sweden full caps.

1981	Brommapojkarna	1	—
1982		17	—
1983		15	2
1984		20	7
1985		24	3
1986	Orgryte	19	5
1987		22	4
1988		6	—
1988–89	Young Boys	15	6
1989–90		2	—
1989–90	Cremonese	24	3
1990–91	Arsenal	34	11
1991–92		29	4
1992–93		23	2
1993–94		10	—
1993–94	Everton	9	—
1994–95		27	2
1995–96		28	3

LINDSEY, Scott

Born Walsall 4.5.72 Ht 5 9 Wt 11 10
Defender. From Bridlington T.

1994–95	Gillingham	12	—
1995–96		—	—

LINEY, Andrew

Born Frimley 18.7.77 Ht 5 11 Wt 13 02
Midfield. From Trainee.

Season	Club	Apps	Goals
1995–96	Southampton	—	—

LING, Martin

Born West Ham 15.7.66 Ht 5 7
Wt 10 08
Midfield. From Apprentice.

Season	Club	Apps	Goals
1983–84	Exeter C	29	—
1984–85		42	6
1985–86		45	8
1986–87	Swindon T	2	—
1986–87	Southend U	24	8
1987–88		42	7
1988–89		44	6
1989–90		25	10
1990–91		3	—
1990–91	*Mansfield T*	3	—
1990–91	*Swindon T*	1	—
1991–92	Swindon T	21	3
1992–93		43	3
1993–94		33	1
1994–95		36	3
1995–96		16	—

LINGER, Paul

Born Stepney 20.12.74 Ht 5 6 Wt 10 03
Midfield. From Trainee.

Season	Club	Apps	Goals
1992–93	Charlton Ath	2	—
1993–94		5	—
1994–95		8	—
1995–96		8	1

LINIGHAN, Andy

Born Hartlepool 18.6.62 Ht 6 4
Wt 13 10
Defender. From Smiths BC. England B.

Season	Club	Apps	Goals
1980–81	Hartlepool U	6	—
1981–82		17	—
1982–83		45	3
1983–84		42	1
1984–85	Leeds U	42	2
1985–86		24	1
1985–86	Oldham Ath	15	1
1986–87		40	3
1987–88		32	2
1987–88	Norwich C	12	2
1988–89		37	4
1989–90		37	2
1990–91	Arsenal	10	—
1991–92		17	—
1992–93		21	2
1993–94		21	—
1994–95		20	2
1995–96		18	—

LINIGHAN, Brian

Born Hartlepool 2.11.73 Ht 6 3
Wt 12 10
Defender. From Trainee.

Season	Club	Apps	Goals
1992–93	Sheffield W	—	—
1993–94		1	—
1994–95		—	—
1995–96		—	—

LINIGHAN, David

Born Hartlepool 9.1.65 Ht 6 2 Wt 12 06
Defender. From Local.

Season	Club	Apps	Goals
1981–82	Hartlepool U	6	—
1982–83		6	1
1983–84		23	1
1984–85		17	2
1984–85	*Leeds U*	—	—
1985–86	Hartlepool U	39	1
1986–87	Derby Co	—	—
1986–87	Shrewsbury T	24	—
1987–88		41	1
1988–89	Ipswich T	41	2
1989–90		41	—
1990–91		45	3
1991–92		36	3
1992–93		42	1
1993–94		38	3
1994–95		32	—
1995–96		2	—
1995–96	Blackpool	29	4

LINTON, Des

Born Birmingham 5.9.71 Ht 6 1
Wt 13 10
Defender. From Trainee.

Season	Club	Apps	Goals
1989–90	Leicester C	2	—
1990–91		8	—
1991–92		1	—
1991–92	Luton T	3	—
1992–93		20	1
1993–94		33	—
1994–95		10	—
1995–96		10	—

Season Club League Appearances/Goals

LINYARD, Paul

Born Keighley 18.7.77 Ht 6 1 Wt 12 00
Goalkeeper. From Trainee.

Season	Club	Apps	Goals
1993–94	Hartlepool U	—	—
1994–95		—	—
1995–96		—	—

LITTLE, Colin

Born Wythenshaw 4.11.72 Ht 5 8
Wt 10 00
Forward. From Hyde U.

Season	Club	Apps	Goals
1995–96	Crewe Alex	12	1

LITTLEJOHN, Adrian

Born Wolverhampton 26.9.70 Ht 5 9
Wt 10 04
Forward. From WBA Trainee.

Season	Club	Apps	Goals
1989–90	Walsall	11	—
1990–91		33	1
1991–92	Sheffield U	7	—
1992–93		27	8
1993–94		19	3
1994–95		16	1
1995–96	Plymouth Arg	42	17

LIVINGSTONE, Steve

Born Middlesbrough 8.9.69 Ht 6 1
Wt 11 04
Forward. From Trainee.

Season	Club	Apps	Goals
1986–87	Coventry C	3	—
1987–88		4	—
1988–89		1	—
1989–90		13	3
1990–91		10	2
1990–91	Blackburn R	18	9
1991–92		10	1
1992–93		2	—
1992–93	Chelsea	1	—
1993–94		—	—
1993–94	*Port Vale*	5	—
1993–94	Grimsby T	27	3
1994–95		34	8
1995–96		38	11

LLOYD, Kevin

Born Llanidloes 26.9.70 Ht 6 0 Wt 12 04
Defender. From Caersws.

Season	Club	Apps	Goals
1994–95	Hereford U	24	3
1995–96		27	—

LOCK, Tony

Born Harlow 3.9.76 Ht 5 10 Wt 13 00
Midfield. From Trainee.

Season	Club	Apps	Goals
1994–95	Colchester U	3	1
1995–96		—	—

LOCKE, Adam

Born Croydon 20.8.70 Ht 5 11 Wt 12 07
Midfield. From Trainee.

Season	Club	Apps	Goals
1988–89	Crystal Palace	—	—
1989–90		—	—
1990–91	Southend U	28	4
1991–92		10	—
1992–93		27	—
1993–94		8	—
1993–94	*Colchester U*	4	—
1994–95	Colchester U	22	1
1995–96		25	3

LOCKE, Gary

Born Edinburgh 16.6.75 Ht 5 8
Wt 10 07
Midfield. From Whitehill Welfare.
Scotland Under-21.

Season	Club	Apps	Goals
1992–93	Hearts	1	—
1993–94		33	—
1994–95		9	—
1995–96		29	4

LOCKWOOD, Matthew

Born Rochford 17.10.76 Ht 5 9
Wt 10 12
Midfield. From Trainee.

Season	Club	Apps	Goals
1994–95	QPR	—	—
1995–96		—	—

LOGAN, Richard

Born Barnsley 24.5.69 Ht 6 0 Wt 13 03
Midfield. From Gainsborough T.

Season	Club	Apps	Goals
1993–94	Huddersfield T	16	—
1994–95		27	1
1995–96		2	—
1995–96	Plymouth Arg	31	4

LOMAS, Andrew

Born Hartlepool 26.4.65
Goalkeeper. From Baldock T, Barnet, Chesham, Stevenage.

Season	Club	Apps	Goals
1994–95	*Cambridge U*	2	—
1995–96	Cambridge U	—	—

Season	Club	League Appearances/Goals

LOMAS, Steve

Born Hanover 18.1.74 Ht 6 0 Wt 11 09
Midfield. From Trainee. Northern Ireland 12 full caps.

1991–92	Manchester C	—	—
1992–93		—	—
1993–94		23	—
1994–95		20	2
1995–96		33	3

LONERGAN, Darren

Born Cork 28.1.74
Defender. From Waterford.

1994–95	Oldham Ath	—	—
1995–96		2	—

LORMOR, Tony

Born Ashington 29.10.70 Ht 6 0 Wt 12 10
Forward. From Trainee.

1987–88	Newcastle U	5	2
1988–89		3	1
1988–89	*Norwich C*	—	—
1989–90	Newcastle U	—	—
1989–90	Lincoln C	21	8
1990–91		34	12
1991–92		35	9
1992–93		—	—
1993–94		10	1
1994–95	Peterborough U	5	—
1994–95	Chesterfield	23	10
1995–96		41	13

LOVE, Graeme

Born Bathgate 7.12.73 Ht 5 10 Wt 11 08
Midfield. From Salvesen BC. Scotland Under-21.

1991–92	Hibernian	1	—
1992–93		1	—
1993–94		4	—
1994–95		12	—
1995–96		13	—

LOVE, Michael

Born Stockport 27.11.73 Ht 5 11 Wt 12 04
Midfield. From Hinckley Ath.

1995–96	Wigan Ath	—	—

LOVELL, Stuart

Born Sydney 9.1.72 Ht 5 10 Wt 11 00
Midfield. From Trainee.

1990–91	Reading	30	2
1991–92		24	4
1992–93		22	8
1993–94		45	20
1994–95		30	11
1995–96		35	7

LOVELOCK, Andrew

Born Swindon 20.12.76 Ht 5 9 Wt 10 12
Forward. From Trainee.

1993–94	Coventry C	—	—
1994–95		—	—
1995–96		—	—

LOW, Joshua

Born Bristol 15.2.79
Midfield. From Trainee.

1995–96	Bristol R	1	—

LOWE, David

Born Liverpool 30.8.65 Ht 5 10 Wt 11 04
Forward. From Apprentice. England Youth, Under-21.

1982–83	Wigan Ath	28	6
1983–84		40	8
1984–85		29	5
1985–86		46	5
1986–87		45	16
1987–88	Ipswich T	41	17
1988–89		32	6
1989–90		34	13
1990–91		13	—
1991–92		14	1
1991–92	*Port Vale*	9	2
1992–93	Leicester C	32	11
1993–94		5	—
1993–94	*Port Vale*	19	5
1994–95	Leicester C	29	8
1995–96		28	3
1995–96	Wigan Ath	7	3

LOWE, Kenny

Born Sedgefield 6.11.64 Ht 6 1 Wt 11 13
Midfield. From Apprentice.

1981–82	Hartlepool U	4	—
1982–83		22	1

Season Club League Appearances/Goals

Season	Club	Apps	Goals
1983–84		28	2
From Barrow			
1987–88	Scarborough	4	—
1988–89		—	—
From Barrow			
1991–92	Barnet	36	3
1992–93		36	2
1993–94	Stoke C	9	—
1993–94	Birmingham C	12	1
1994–95		7	2
1994–95	*Carlisle U*	2	—
1995–96	Birmingham C	2	—
1995–96	*Hartlepool U*	13	3

LOWNDES, Nathan

Born Salford 2.6.77 Ht 5 11 Wt 10 04
Forward. From Trainee.

Season	Club	Apps	Goals
1994–95	Leeds U	—	—
1995–96		—	—
1995–96	Watford	—	—

LOWTHORPE, Adam

Born Hull 7.8.75 Ht 5 7 Wt 10 06
Defender. From Trainee.

Season	Club	Apps	Goals
1993–94	Hull C	3	—
1994–95		22	—
1995–96		19	—

LUCAS, David

Born Preston 23.11.77 Ht 6 1 Wt 12 04
Goalkeeper. From Trainee. England Youth.

Season	Club	Apps	Goals
1989–90	Sheffield U	—	—
1990–91		9	—
1991–92		1	—
1992–93		—	—
1992–93	Preston NE	26	—
1993–94		24	—
1994–95		—	—
1994–95	*Lincon C*	4	—
1995–96	Preston NE	1	—
1995–96	*Darlington*	6	—

LUCAS, Richard

Born Sheffield 22.9.70 Ht 5 10 Wt 12 06
Midfield. From Trainee.

Season	Club	Apps	Goals
1994–95	Preston NE	—	—
1995–96	Scarborough	44	—

LUCKETTI, Chris

Born Littleborough 28.9.71 Ht 6 0 Wt 13 04
Defender. From Trainee.

Season	Club	Apps	Goals
1988–89	Rochdale	1	—
1989–90		—	—
1990–91	Stockport Co	—	—
1991–92	Halifax T	36	—
1992–93		42	2
1993–94	Bury	27	1
1994–95		39	3
1995–96		42	1

LUDDEN, Dominic

Born Basildon 30.3.74 Ht 5 7 Wt 10 09
Defender. From Trainee.

Season	Club	Apps	Goals
1992–93	Leyton Orient	24	1
1993–94		34	—
1994–95	Watford	1	—
1995–96		12	—

LUDLAM, Craig

Born Sheffield 8.11.76 Ht 5 11 Wt 11 05
Midfield. From Trainee.

Season	Club	Apps	Goals
1994–95	Sheffield W	—	—
1995–96		—	—

LUKIC, John

Born Chesterfield 11.12.60 Ht 6 4 Wt 13 12
Goalkeeper. From Apprentice. England Youth, Under-21, B.

Season	Club	Apps	Goals
1978–79	Leeds U	—	—
1979–80		33	—
1980–81		42	—
1981–82		42	—
1982–83		29	—
1983–84	Arsenal	4	—
1984–85		27	—
1985–86		40	—
1986–87		36	—
1987–88		40	—
1988–89		38	—
1989–90		38	—
1990–91	Leeds U	38	—
1991–92		42	—
1992–93		39	—
1993–94		20	—
1994–95		42	—
1995–96		28	—

Season Club League Appearances/Goals

LUND, Gary

Born Grimsby 13.9.64 Ht 6 1 Wt 12 08
Forward. From School. England Youth, Under-21.

Season	Club	Apps	Goals
1983–84	Grimsby T	7	4
1984–85		24	12
1985–86		29	8
1986–87	Lincoln C	44	13
1987–88	Notts Co	40	20
1988–89		42	8
1989–90		40	9
1990–91		16	3
1991–92		13	2
1992–93		28	4
1992–93	*Hull C*	11	3
1993–94	Notts Co	46	11
1994–95		23	5
1994–95	*Hull C*	11	3
1995–96	Notts Co	—	—
1995–96	Chesterfield	8	1

LYDIATE, Jason

Born Manchester 29.10.71 Ht 5 11
Wt 12 04
Defender. From Trainee.

Season	Club	Apps	Goals
1989–90	Manchester U	—	—
1990–91		—	—
1991–92		—	—
1991–92	Bolton W	1	—
1992–93		6	—
1993–94		5	—
1994–95		18	—
1994–95	Blackpool	11	—
1995–96		32	1

LYNCH, Chris

Born Middlesbrough 18.11.74 Ht 6 0
Wt 11 07
Forward. From Halifax T Trainee.

Season	Club	Apps	Goals
1992–93	Hartlepool U	1	—
1993–94		19	—
1994–95		11	1
1995–96		19	1

LYNCH, Tom

Born Limerick 10.10.64 Ht 6 0 Wt 13 03
Defender. From Limerick.

Season	Club	Apps	Goals
1988–89	Sunderland	4	—
1989–90		—	—
1989–90	Shrewsbury T	22	—
1990–91		39	2
1991–92		40	2
1992–93		39	2
1993–94		35	4
1994–95		34	1
1995–96		25	3

LYNE, Neil

Born Leicester 4.4.70 Ht 6 1 Wt 13 01
Forward. From Leicester U.

Season	Club	Apps	Goals
1989–90	Nottingham F	—	—
1989–90	*Walsall*	7	—
1990–91	Nottingham F	—	—
1990–91	*Shrewsbury T*	16	6
1991–92	Shrewsbury T	44	8
1992–93		20	3
1992–93	Cambridge U	14	—
1993–94		3	—
1993–94	*Chesterfield*	6	1
1994–95	Hereford U	31	1
1995–96		32	1

LYONS, Andy

Born Blackpool 19.10.66 Ht 5 10
Wt 12 07
Midfield. From Fleetwood.

Season	Club	Apps	Goals
1992–93	Crewe Alex	9	2
1993–94		2	—
1993–94	Wigan Ath	33	11
1994–95		32	15
1995–96		22	1
1995–96	Partick T	9	5

LYONS, Paul

Born Leigh 24.6.77 Ht 5 6 Wt 10 11
Midfield.

Season	Club	Apps	Goals
1995–96	Rochdale	3	—

LYTTLE, Des

Born Wolverhampton 26.9.71 Ht 5 8
Wt 12 13
Defender. From Worcester C.

Season	Club	Apps	Goals
1992–93	Swansea C	46	1
1993–94	Nottingham F	37	1
1994–95		38	—
1995–96		33	1

Season Club League Appearances/Goals

MABBUTT, Gary

Born Bristol 23.8.61 Ht 5 9 Wt 12 09
Defender. From Apprentice. England Youth, Under-21, B, 16 full caps.

1978–79 Bristol R 11 —
1979–80 33 —
1980–81 42 5
1981–82 45 5
1982–83 Tottenham H 38 10
1983–84 21 2
1984–85 25 2
1985–86 32 3
1986–87 37 1
1987–88 37 2
1988–89 38 1
1989–90 36 —
1990–91 35 2
1991–92 40 2
1992–93 29 2
1993–94 29 —
1994–95 36 —
1995–96 32 —

MACDONALD, Billy

Born Irvine 17.9.76 Ht 5 7 Wt 11 00
Forward. From Rangers 'S' Form.

1994–95 WBA — —
1995–96 Partick T 17 1

MACKAY, Malcolm

Born Bellshill 19.2.72 Ht 6 1 Wt 11 07
Defender. From Queen's Park Youth.

1990–91 Queen's Park 10 —
1991–92 27 3
1992–93 33 3
1993–94 Celtic — —
1994–95 1 —
1995–96 11 1

MACKENZIE, Chris

Born Northampton 14.5.72 Ht 6 0
Wt 12 06
Goalkeeper. From Corby T.

1994–95 Hereford U 22 —
1995–96 38 1

MACLEOD, Murdo

Born Glasgow 24.9.58 Ht 5 9 Wt 12 04
Midfield. From Glasgow Amateurs. Scotland Under-21, 20 caps.

1974–75 Dumbarton — —
1975–76 7 —
1976–77 27 7
1977–78 39 1
1978–79 14 1
1978–79 Celtic 23 3
1979–80 36 7
1980–81 18 8
1981–82 36 10
1982–83 35 11
1983–84 34 7
1984–85 31 3
1985–86 30 3
1986–87 38 4
From Borussia Dortmund
1990–91 Hibernian 25 2
1991–92 22 —
1992–93 31 —
1993–94 Dumbarton 42 1
1994–95 24 —
1995–96 Partick T 1 —

MACPHERSON, Angus

Born Glasgow 11.10.68 Ht 5 11
Wt 10 04
Defender. From 'S' Form.

1988–89 Rangers — —
1989–90 — —
1989–90 *Exeter C* 11 1
1990–91 Kilmarnock 11 —
1991–92 43 3
1992–93 40 5
1993–94 43 2
1994–95 33 1
1995–96 35 1

MACARI, Michael

Born Kilwinning 4.2.73 Ht 5 7 Wt 10 10
Forward. From Trainee.

1991–92 West Ham U — —
1991–92 Stoke C — —
1992–93 — —
1993–94 — —
1994–95 — —
1995–96 — —

MACARI, Paul

Born Manchester 23.8.76 Ht 5 8
Wt 11 03
Forward. From Trainee.

1993–94 Stoke C — —
1994–95 — —
1995–96 — —

Season	Club	Apps	Goals
1984–85		42	6
1985–86	Derby Co	46	4
1986–87		42	—
1987–88		34	—
1988–89	Swindon T	37	4
1989–90		46	3
1990–91		45	1
1991–92		32	1
1992–93		22	—
1993–94		12	—
1994–95		3	—
1995–96		—	—

MACAULEY, Steve

Born Lytham 4.3.69 Ht 6 1 Wt 12 00
Defender. From Fleetwood.

Season	Club	Apps	Goals
1991–92	Crewe Alex	9	1
1992–93		25	3
1993–94		17	3
1994–95		43	4
1995–96		29	7

MACDONALD, James

Born Inverness 21.2.79 Ht 6 0 Wt 12 05
Midfield. From Trainee.

Season	Club	Apps	Goals
1995–96	Arsenal	—	—

MACKAY, Gary

Born Edinburgh 23.1.64 Ht 5 9
Wt 10 05
Midfield. From Salvesen BC. Scotland Schools, Youth, 4 full caps.

Season	Club	Apps	Goals
1980–81	Hearts	12	—
1981–82		17	2
1982–83		34	6
1983–84		31	4
1984–85		17	2
1985–86		32	4
1986–87		37	7
1987–88		41	5
1988–89		29	2
1989–90		33	1
1990–91		30	3
1991–92		43	1
1992–93		37	2
1993–94		36	1
1994–95		34	2
1995–96		26	2

MACKEN, Jonathan

Born Manchester 7.9.77 Ht 5 10
Wt 12 10
Forward. From Trainee.

Season	Club	Apps	Goals
1995–96	Manchester U	—	—

MACLAREN, Ross

Born Edinburgh 14.4.62 Ht 5 10
Wt 12 12
Midfield. From Rangers.

Season	Club	Apps	Goals
1980–81	Shrewsbury T	4	—
1981–82		35	—
1982–83		40	5
1983–84		40	7

Season Club League Appearances/Goals

MADDEN, Lawrie

Born Hackney 28.9.55 Ht 5 10 Wt 13 00
Defender. From Arsenal Amateur.

Season	Club	Apps	Goals
1974–75	Mansfield T	7	—
1975–76		3	—
From Manchester Univ			
1977–78	Charlton Ath	4	—
1978–79		38	3
1979–80		36	1
1980–81		28	1
1981–82		7	2
1981–82	Millwall	10	—
1982–83		37	2
1983–84	Sheffield W	38	1
1984–85		19	—
1985–86		25	—
1986–87		35	1
1987–88		38	—
1988–89		27	—
1989–90		25	—
1990–91		5	—
1990–91	*Leicester C*	3	—
1991–92	Wolverhampton W	43	1
1992–93		24	—
1993–94	Darlington	5	—
1993–94	Chesterfield	26	—
1994–95		10	1
1995–96		1	—

MADDISON, Lee

Born Bristol 5.10.72 Ht 5 11 Wt 12 04
Defender. From Trainee.

Season	Club	Apps	Goals
1991–92	Bristol R	10	—
1992–93		12	—
1993–94		37	—
1994–95		14	—
1995–96		—	—
1995–96	Northampton T	21	—

Season	Club	League Appearances/Goals	

MADDISON, Neil

Born Darlington 2.10.69 Ht 5 11 Wt 11 06
Midfield. From Trainee.

1987–88	Southampton	—	—
1988–89		5	2
1989–90		2	—
1990–91		4	—
1991–92		6	—
1992–93		37	4
1993–94		41	7
1994–95		35	3
1995–96		15	1

MADDIX, Danny

Born Ashford 11.10.67 Ht 5 11 Wt 11 07
Defender. From Apprentice.

1985–86	Tottenham H	—	—
1986–87		—	—
1986–87	*Southend U*	2	—
1987–88	QPR	9	—
1988–89		33	2
1989–90		32	3
1990–91		32	1
1991–92		19	—
1992–93		14	—
1993–94		—	—
1994–95		27	1
1995–96		22	—

MAGEE, Kevin

Born Edinburgh 10.4.71 Ht 5 10 Wt 11 05
Forward. From Armadale T.

1991–92	Partick T	6	—
1992–93		5	—
1993–94	Preston NE	7	—
1994–95		14	1
1995–96		5	—
1995–96	Plymouth Arg	4	—
1995–96	Scarborough	28	1

MAGILTON, Jim

Born Belfast 6.5.69 Ht 6 1 Wt 14 02
Midfield. From Apprentice. Northern Ireland Under-23, 32 full caps. Football League.

1986–87	Liverpool	—	—
1987–88		—	—
1988–89		—	—
1989–90		—	—
1990–91		—	—
1990–91	Oxford U	37	6
1991–92		44	12
1992–93		40	11
1993–94		29	5
1993–94	Southampton	15	—
1994–95		42	6
1995–96		31	3

MAHER, Kevin

Born Ilford 17.10.76 Ht 6 0 Wt 13 06
Defender. From Trainee.

1995–96	Tottenham H	—	—

MAHON, Alan

Born Dublin 4.4.78 Ht 5 10 Wt 10 09
Midfield.

1994–95	Tranmere R	—	—
1995–96		2	—

MAHON, Gavin

Born Birmingham 2.1.77 Ht 6 0 Wt 13 02
Midfield. From Trainee.

1995–96	Wolverhampton W	—	—

MAHONEY-JOHNSON, Michael

Born Paddington 6.11.76 Ht 5 10 Wt 12 00
Forward. From Trainee.

1994–95	QPR	—	—
1995–96		—	—

MAHORN, Paul

Born Whipps Cross 13.8.73 Ht 5 8 Wt 11 06
Forward. From Trainee.

1991–92	Tottenham H	—	—
1992–93		—	—
1993–94		1	—
1993–94	*Fulham*	3	—
1994–95	Tottenham H	—	—
1995–96		—	—
1995–96	*Burnley*	8	1

MAKEL, Lee

Born Sunderland 11.1.73 Ht 5 9
Wt 11 05
Midfield. From Trainee.

Season	Club	Apps	Goals
1990–91	Newcastle U	3	—
1991–92		9	1
1992–93	Blackburn R	1	—
1993–94		2	—
1994–95		—	—
1995–96		3	—
1995–96	Huddersfield T	33	2

MAKIN, Chris

Born Manchester 8.5.73 Ht 5 10
Wt 10 06
Defender. From Trainee. England Under-21.

Season	Club	Apps	Goals
1991–92	Oldham Ath	—	—
1992–93		—	—
1992–93	*Wigan Ath*	15	2
1993–94	Oldham Ath	27	1
1994–95		28	1
1995–96		39	2

MALKIN, Chris

Born Bebington 4.6.67 Ht 6 3 Wt 12 07
Forward. From Stork, Overpool.

Season	Club	Apps	Goals
1987–88	Tranmere R	5	—
1988–89		20	4
1989–90		40	18
1990–91		25	4
1991–92		35	3
1992–93		36	7
1993–94		28	8
1994–95		43	16
1995–96	Millwall	43	11

MALONE, Chris

Born Drogheda 29.12.75 Ht 5 11
Wt 10 02
Forward.

Season	Club	Apps	Goals
1993–94	Blackburn R	—	—
1994–95		—	—
1995–96		—	—

MALPAS, Maurice

Born Dunfermline 3.8.62 Ht 5 8
Wt 10 11
Defender. From 'S' Form. Scotland Schools, Youth, Under-21, 55 full caps.

Season Club League Appearances/Goals

Season	Club	Apps	Goals
1979–80	Dundee U	—	—
1980–81		—	—
1981–82		19	—
1982–83		34	1
1983–84		34	2
1984–85		35	2
1985–86		36	2
1986–87		36	—
1987–88		44	—
1988–89		36	1
1989–90		30	2
1990–91		36	1
1991–92		44	3
1992–93		37	—
1993–94		35	—
1994–95		31	2
1995–96		30	2

MANN, Neil

Born Nottingham 19.11.72 Ht 5 10
Wt 12 01
Midfield. From Notts Co, Spalding U, Grantham T.

Season	Club	Apps	Goals
1993–94	Hull C	5	—
1994–95		31	2
1995–96		38	1

MANNIX, Alan

Born Castle Knock 23.10.77 Ht 5 8
Wt 10 09
Midfield. From Trainee.

Season	Club	Apps	Goals
1995–96	Tottenham H	—	—

MANUEL, Billy

Born Hackney 28.6.69 Ht 5 8 Wt 12 04
Defender. From Apprentice.

Season	Club	Apps	Goals
1987–88	Tottenham H	—	—
1988–89		—	—
1988–89	Gillingham	17	1
1989–90		32	4
1990–91		38	—
1991–92	Brentford	35	—
1992–93		41	1
1993–94		18	—
1994–95	Cambridge U	10	—
1994–95	Peterborough U	14	1
1995–96		13	1
1995–96	Gillingham	10	—

MARDENBOROUGH, Steve

Born Birmingham 11.9.64 Ht 5 8
Wt 11 09
Forward. From Apprentice.

Season	Club	Apps	Goals
1982–83	Coventry C	—	—
1983–84	Wolverhampton W	9	1
1983–84	*Cambridge C*	6	—
1984–85	Swansea C	36	7
1985–86	Newport Co	39	7
1986–87		25	4
1986–87	Cardiff C	11	1
1987–88		21	—
1988–89	Hereford U	27	—
1989–90	Darlington	—	—
1990–91		35	1
1991–92		29	6
1992–93		42	11
1993–94	Lincoln C	21	2
1994–95	Scarborough	1	—
1995–96	Colchester U	12	2
1995–96	Swansea C	1	—

MARDON, Paul

Born Bristol 14.9.69 Ht 6 0 Wt 12 00
Defender. From Trainee. Wales 1 full cap.

Season	Club	Apps	Goals
1987–88	Bristol C	8	—
1988–89		20	—
1989–90		7	—
1990–91		7	—
1990–91	*Doncaster R*	3	—
1991–92	Birmingham C	35	—
1992–93		21	—
1993–94		8	—
1993–94	WBA	22	1
1994–95		28	1
1995–96		39	—

MARGETSON, Martyn

Born West Neath 8.9.71 Ht 6 0
Wt 14 00
Goalkeeper. From Trainee. Wales Under-21.

Season	Club	Apps	Goals
1990–91	Manchester C	2	—
1991–92		3	—
1992–93		1	—
1993–94		—	—
1993–94	*Bristol R*	3	—
1993–94	*Bolton W*	—	—
1994–95	Manchester C	—	—
1994–95	*Luton T*	—	—
1995–96	Manchester C	—	—

MARKER, Nicky

Born Exeter 3.5.65 Ht 6 0 Wt 13 00
Defender. From Apprentice.

Season	Club	Apps	Goals
1981–82	Exeter C	14	1
1982–83		18	1
1983–84		31	—
1984–85		45	—
1985–86		40	—
1986–87		43	1
1987–88		11	—
1987–88	Plymouth Arg	26	1
1988–89		43	6
1989–90		43	1
1990–91		39	2
1991–92		44	1
1992–93		7	2
1992–93	Blackburn R	15	—
1993–94		23	—
1994–95		—	—
1995–96		9	1

MARKEY, Brendan

Born Ireland 19.5.76
Forward. From Bohemians.

Season	Club	Apps	Goals
1995–96	Millwall	—	—

MARKMAN, Damien

Born Ascot 7.1.78
Forward.

Season	Club	Apps	Goals
1995–96	Wycombe W	2	—

MARKS, Jamie

Born Belfast 18.3.77 Ht 5 10 Wt 10 13
Defender. From Trainee.

Season	Club	Apps	Goals
1994–95	Leeds U	—	—
1995–96		—	—
1995–96	Hull C	5	—

MARPLES, Chris

Born Chesterfield 3.8.64 Ht 6 0
Wt 13 10
Goalkeeper. From Sutton T, Goole.

Season	Club	Apps	Goals
1984–85	Chesterfield	38	—
1985–86		32	—
1986–87		14	—
1986–87	Stockport Co	13	—

Season Club League Appearances/Goals

Season	Club	Apps	Goals
1987–88		44	—
1988–89	York C	45	—
1989–90		46	—
1990–91		29	—
1991–92		16	—
1991–92	*Scunthorpe U*	1	—
1992–93	York C	2	—
1992–93	Chesterfield	25	—
1993–94		11	—
1994–95		21	—
1995–96		—	—

MARQUIS, Paul

Born Enfield 29.8.72 Ht 6 2 Wt 12 04
Defender. From Trainee.

Season	Club	Apps	Goals
1991–92	West Ham U	—	—
1992–93		—	—
1993–94		1	—
1993–94	Doncaster R	9	—
1994–95		2	—
1995–96		15	1

MARRIOTT, Andy

Born Nottingham 11.10.70 Ht 6 1 Wt 12 08
Goalkeeper. From Trainee. FA Schools, England Youth, Under-21, Wales 1 full cap.

Season	Club	Apps	Goals
1988–89	Arsenal	—	—
1989–90	Nottingham F	—	—
1989–90	*WBA*	3	—
1989–90	*Blackburn R*	2	—
1989–90	*Colchester U*	10	—
1990–91	Nottingham F	—	—
1991–92		6	—
1991–92	*Burnley*	15	—
1992–93	Nottingham F	5	—
1993–94		—	—
1993–94	Wrexham	36	—
1994–95		46	—
1995–96		46	—

MARSDEN, Chris

Born Sheffield 3.1.69 Ht 6 0 Wt 10 12
Midfield. From Trainee.

Season	Club	Apps	Goals
1986–87	Sheffield U	—	—
1987–88		16	1
1988–89	Huddersfield T	14	1
1989–90		32	2
1990–91		43	5
1991–92		23	1
1992–93		7	—
1993–94		2	—
1993–94	*Coventry C*	7	—
1993–94	Wolverhampton W	8	—
1994–95		—	—
1994–95	Notts Co	7	—
1995–96		3	—
1995–96	Stockport Co	20	1

MARSH, Chris

Born Dudley 14.1.70 Ht 5 10 Wt 13 04
Midfield. From Trainee.

Season	Club	Apps	Goals
1987–88	Walsall	3	—
1988–89		13	—
1989–90		9	—
1990–91		23	2
1991–92		37	1
1992–93		33	3
1993–94		39	4
1994–95		38	9
1995–96		41	2

MARSH, Mike

Born Liverpool 21.7.69 Ht 5 8 Wt 11 00
Forward. From Kirkby T.

Season	Club	Apps	Goals
1987–88	Liverpool	—	—
1988–89		1	—
1989–90		2	—
1990–91		2	—
1991–92		34	—
1992–93		28	1
1993–94		2	1
1993–94	West Ham U	33	1
1994–95		16	—
1994–95	Coventry C	15	2
From Galatasaray			
1995–96	Southend U	40	5

MARSH, Simon

Born Ealing 29.1.77 Ht 5 11 Wt 11 06
Defender. From Trainee.

Season	Club	Apps	Goals
1994–95	Oxford U	8	—
1995–96		5	—

MARSHALL, Andy

Born Bury 14.4.75 Ht 6 2 Wt 13 00
Goalkeeper. From Trainee. England Under-21.

Season	Club	Apps	Goals
1993–94	Norwich C	—	—
1994–95		21	—
1995–96		3	—

Season Club League Appearances/Goals

MARSHALL, Dwight

Born Jamaica 3.10.65 Ht 5 7 Wt 11 02
Forward. From Grays Ath.

Season	Club	Apps	Goals
1991–92	Plymouth Arg	44	14
1992–93		24	1
1992–93	*Middlesbrough*	3	—
1993–94	Plymouth Arg	31	12
1994–95	Luton T	45	11
1995–96		26	9

MARSHALL, Gordon

Born Edinburgh 19.4.64 Ht 6 2
Wt 12 00
Goalkeeper. From School. Scotland 1 full cap.

Season	Club	Apps	Goals
1982–83	East Stirling	15	—
1982–83	East Fife	10	—
1983–84		34	—
1984–85		39	—
1985–86		39	—
1986–87		36	—
1986–87	Falkirk	10	—
1987–88		44	—
1988–89		39	—
1989–90		39	—
1990–91		39	—
1991–92	Celtic	25	—
1992–93		11	—
1993–94		1	—
1993–94	*Stoke C*	10	—
1994–95	Celtic	16	—
1995–96		36	—

MARSHALL, Ian

Born Liverpool 20.3.66 Ht 6 1 Wt 12 12
Forward. From Apprentice.

Season	Club	Apps	Goals
1983–84	Everton	—	—
1984–85		—	—
1985–86		9	—
1986–87		2	1
1987–88		4	—
1987–88	Oldham Ath	10	—
1988–89		41	4
1989–90		25	3
1990–91		26	17
1991–92		41	10
1992–93		27	2
1993–94	Ipswich T	29	10
1994–95		18	3
1995–96		35	19

MARSHALL, John

Born Surrey 18.8.64 Ht 5 10 Wt 12 04
Midfield. From Apprentice.

Season	Club	Apps	Goals
1982–83	Fulham	—	—
1983–84		25	—
1984–85		32	1
1985–86		42	3
1986–87		29	4
1987–88		25	2
1988–89		41	7
1989–90		36	4
1990–91		35	2
1991–92		41	—
1992–93		41	2
1993–94		21	1
1994–95		27	2
1995–96		16	—

MARSHALL, Lee

Born Nottingham 1.8.75 Ht 5 9 Wt 9 12
Forward. From Trainee.

Season	Club	Apps	Goals
1992–93	Nottingham F	—	—
1993–94		—	—

From Grantham

Season	Club	Apps	Goals
1994–95	Stockport Co	1	—
1995–96		—	—

MARSHALL, Scott

Born Edinburgh 1.5.73 Ht 6 1 Wt 12 05
Defender. From Trainee. Scotland Under-21.

Season	Club	Apps	Goals
1992–93	Arsenal	2	—
1993–94		—	—
1993–94	*Rotherham U*	10	1
1993–94	*Oxford U*	—	—
1994–95	Arsenal	—	—
1994–95	*Sheffield U*	17	—
1995–96	Arsenal	11	1

MARSTON, Marvin

Born London 27.8.76 Ht 6 5 Wt 13 02
Defender. From Notts Co Schoolboy.

Season	Club	Apps	Goals
1994–95	Sheffield U	—	—
1995–96		—	—

MARTIN, Alvin

Born Bootle 29.7.58 Ht 6 1 Wt 13 07
Defender. From Apprentice. England Youth, B, 17 full caps.

Season	Club	Apps	Goals
1976–77	West Ham U	—	—

Season	Club	League Appearances	Goals
1977–78		7	1
1978–79		22	1
1979–80		40	2
1980–81		41	1
1981–82		28	4
1982–83		38	3
1983–84		29	3
1984–85		40	1
1985–86		40	4
1986–87		16	2
1987–88		15	—
1988–89		27	1
1989–90		31	—
1990–91		20	1
1991–92		7	—
1992–93		23	1
1993–94		7	2
1994–95		24	—
1995–96		14	—

MARTIN, Brian

Born Bellshill 24.2.63 Ht 6 0 Wt 13 00
Midfield. From Shotts Bon-Accord.
Scotland 2 full caps.

Season	Club	League Appearances	Goals
1985–86	Falkirk	25	1
1986–87		34	1
1986–87	Hamilton A	7	—
1987–88		23	—
1987–88	St Mirren	12	1
1988–89		34	2
1989–90		35	2
1990–91		31	2
1991–92		17	2
1991–92	Motherwell	25	—
1992–93		44	3
1993–94		43	2
1994–95		32	2
1995–96		33	2

MARTIN, Dave

Born East Ham 25.4.63 Ht 6 1 Wt 13 02
Midfield. From Apprentice. England Youth.

Season	Club	League Appearances	Goals
1979–80	Millwall	3	—
1980–81		33	1
1981–82		38	1
1982–83		33	1
1983–84		31	3
1984–85		2	—
1984–85	Wimbledon	20	2
1985–86		15	1
1986–87	Southend U	32	2
1987–88		41	—
1988–89		37	1
1989–90		39	3
1990–91		41	11
1991–92		5	1
1992–93		26	1
1993–94	Bristol C	34	1
1994–95		4	—
1994–95	*Northampton T*	7	1
1995–96	Gillingham	31	1

MARTIN, Dean

Born Halifax 9.9.67 Ht 5 11 Wt 11 09
Midfield. From Apprentice.

Season	Club	League Appearances	Goals
1984–85	Halifax T	—	—
1985–86		—	—
1986–87		16	1
1987–88		40	3
1988–89		32	2
1989–90		37	—
1990–91		28	1
1991–92	Scunthorpe U	37	2
1992–93		38	3
1993–94		26	2
1994–95		5	—
1994–95	Rochdale	15	—
1995–96		37	—

MARTIN, Dean

Born Islington 31.8.72 Ht 5 7 Wt 10 06
Forward. From Fisher Ath.

Season	Club	League Appearances	Goals
1991–92	West Ham U	2	—
1992–93		—	—
1992–93	*Colchester U*	8	2
From Iceland			
1995–96	Brentford	19	1

MARTIN, Eliot

Born Plumstead 27.9.72 Ht 5 6 Wt 10 00
Defender. From Trainee.

Season	Club	League Appearances	Goals
1990–91	Gillingham	—	—
1991–92		22	—
1992–93		22	1
1993–94		9	—
1994–95		7	—
1995–96		—	—

MARTIN, Jae

Born London 5.2.76 Ht 5 10 Wt 12 04
Forward. From Trainee.

Season	Club	League Appearances	Goals
1992–93	Southend U	—	—

Season	Club	League Appearances/Goals	
1993–94		4	—
1994–95		4	—
1994–95	*Leyton Orient*	4	—
1995–96	Birmingham C	7	—

MARTIN, Kevin

Born Bromsgrove 22.6.76 Ht 6 1 Wt 12 09
Goalkeeper. From Trainee.

Season	Club	Apps	Goals
1994–95	Scarborough	3	—
1995–96		—	—

MARTIN, Lee

Born Huddersfield 9.9.68 Ht 6 0 Wt 13 00
Goalkeeper. From Trainee. England Schools.

Season	Club	Apps	Goals
1987–88	Huddersfield T	18	—
1988–89		—	—
1989–90		25	—
1990–91		4	—
1991–92		7	—
1992–93	Blackpool	24	—
1993–94		43	—
1994–95		31	—
1995–96		—	—
1995–96	*Bradford C*	—	—

MARTIN, Lee

Born Birmingham 3.10.76 Ht 5 10 Wt 12 00
Midfield. From Trainee.

Season	Club	Apps	Goals
1995–96	Shrewsbury T	—	—

MARTINDALE, Gary

Born Liverpool 24.6.71 Ht 6 0 Wt 12 00
Forward. From Burscough.

Season	Club	Apps	Goals
1993–94	Bolton W	—	—
1994–95		—	—
1995–96	Peterborough U	31	15
1995–96	Notts Co	16	6

MARTINEZ, Roberto

Born Balaguer 13.7.73 Ht 5 11 Wt 11 12
Midfield. From Balaguer.

Season	Club	Apps	Goals
1995–96	Wigan Ath	42	9

MARTYN, Nigel

Born St Austell 11.8.66 Ht 6 2 Wt 14 07
Goalkeeper. From St Blazey. England Under-21, B, 3 full caps.

Season	Club	Apps	Goals
1987–88	Bristol R	39	—
1988–89		46	—
1989–90		16	—
1989–90	Crystal Palace	25	—
1990–91		38	—
1991–92		38	—
1992–93		42	—
1993–94		46	—
1994–95		37	—
1995–96		46	—

MASINGA, Phil

Born Johannesburg 28.6.69 Ht 6 2 Wt 12 07
Forward. From Mamelodi Sundowns. South Africa full caps.

Season	Club	Apps	Goals
1994–95	Leeds U	22	5
1995–96		9	—

MASKELL, Craig

Born Aldershot 10.4.68 Ht 5 10 Wt 11 10
Forward. From Apprentice. Football League.

Season	Club	Apps	Goals
1985–86	Southampton	2	1
1986–87		4	—
1986–87	*Swindon T*	—	—
1987–88	Southampton	—	—
1988–89	Huddersfield T	46	28
1989–90		41	15
1990–91	Reading	38	10
1991–92		34	16
1992–93	Swindon T	33	19
1993–94		14	3
1993–94	Southampton	10	1
1994–95		6	—
1995–96		1	—
1995–96	*Bristol C*	5	1
1995–96	Brighton & HA	15	4

MASKREY, Steve

Born Edinburgh 16.8.62 Ht 5 6 Wt 10 00
Forward. From Strathbrock Jun.

Season	Club	Apps	Goals
1984–85	East Stirling	37	12
1985–86		21	12
1985–86	Q of S	12	2
1986–87		31	2
1987–88	St Johnstone	33	5

Season	Club	League Appearances/Goals	
1988–89		31	12
1989–90		29	11
1990–91		34	7
1991–92		24	2
1992–93		19	2
1993–94		4	—
1994–95	Kilmarnock	30	4
1995–96		22	1

MASON, Andy

Born Bolton 22.11.74 Ht 5 11 Wt 11 11
Forward. From Trainee.

1993–94	Bolton W	—	—
1994–95		—	—
1995–96	Hull C	20	1

MASON, Paul

Born Liverpool 3.9.63 Ht 5 9 Wt 12 01
Midfield. From Groningen.

1988–89	Aberdeen	28	4
1989–90		34	9
1990–91		26	3
1991–92		31	7
1992–93		39	4
1993–94	Ipswich T	22	3
1994–95		21	3
1995–96		26	7

MASON, Richard

Born Sheffield 5.6.77 Ht 5 11 Wt 11 11
Defender. From Trainee.

1994–95	Sheffield W	—	—
1995–96		—	—

MASSEY, Stuart

Born Crawley 17.11.64 Ht 5 10 Wt 12 07
Midfield. From Sutton U.

1992–93	Crystal Palace	1	—
1993–94		1	—
1994–95	Oxford U	22	—
1995–96		35	4

MASTERS, Neil

Born Lisburn 25.5.72 Ht 6 1 Wt 13 00
Defender. From Trainee.

1992–93	Bournemouth	20	—
1993–94		18	2
1993–94	Wolverhampton W	4	—
1994–95		5	—
1995–96		3	—

MATEU, Jose-Luis

Born Castellon 15.1.66 Ht 5 11 Wt 11 06
Forward. From Castellon.

1995–96	Torquay U	10	1

MATHIE, Alex

Born Bathgate 20.12.68 Ht 5 10
Wt 11 07
Forward. From Celtic BC.

1987–88	Celtic	—	—
1988–89		1	—
1989–90		6	—
1990–91		4	—
1991–92	Morton	42	18
1992–93		32	13
1992–93	*Port Vale*	3	—
1993–94	Newcastle U	16	3
1994–95		9	1
1994–95	Ipswich T	13	2
1995–96		39	18

MATTEO, Dominic

Born Dumfries 24.4.74 Ht 6 1 Wt 11 10
Defender. From Trainee. England Youth, Under-21.

1992–93	Liverpool	—	—
1993–94		11	—
1994–95		7	—
1994–95	*Sunderland*	1	—
1995–96	Liverpool	5	—

MATTHEW, Damian

Born Islington 23.9.70 Ht 5 11 Wt 10 10
Midfield. From Trainee. England Under-21.

1989–90	Chelsea	2	—
1990–91		8	—
1991–92		7	—
1992–93		4	—
1992–93	*Luton T*	5	—
1993–94	Chelsea	—	—
1993–94	Crystal Palace	12	1
1994–95		4	—
1995–96		8	—
1995–96	*Bristol R*	8	—

MATTHEWS, Lee

Born Middlesbrough 16.1.79
Midfield. From Trainee.

1995–96	Leeds U	—	—

Season Club League Appearances/Goals

MATTHEWS, Martin

Born Peterborough 22.12.75 Ht 5 10
Wt 11 03
Defender. From Trainee.

Season	Club	Apps	Goals
1994–95	Derby Co	—	—
1995–96	Northampton T	—	—

MATTHEWS, Rob

Born Slough 14.10.70 Ht 5 11 Wt 13 00
Forward. From Loughborough Univ.

Season	Club	Apps	Goals
1991–92	Notts Co	5	3
1992–93		8	2
1993–94		12	3
1994–95		18	3
1994–95	Luton T	11	—
1995–96		—	—
1995–96	York C	17	1
1995–96	Bury	16	4

MATTHEWSON, Trevor

Born Sheffield 12.2.63 Ht 6 4 Wt 13 06
Defender. From Apprentice.

Season	Club	Apps	Goals
1980–81	Sheffield W	1	—
1981–82		1	—
1982–83		1	—
1983–84		—	—
1983–84	Newport Co	32	—
1984–85		43	—
1985–86	Stockport Co	35	—
1986–87		45	—
1987–88	Lincoln C	—	—
1988–89		43	2
1989–90	Birmingham C	46	1
1990–91		46	3
1991–92		36	6
1992–93		40	2
1993–94	Preston NE	12	1
1994–95		—	—
1994–95	Bury	18	—
1995–96		16	—

MATTISON, Paul

Born Wakefield 24.4.73 Ht 5 8 Wt 11 00
Midfield. From North Ferriby U.

Season	Club	Apps	Goals
1994–95	Darlington	10	—
1995–96		7	—

MAUGE, Ron

Born Islington 10.3.69 Ht 5 10 Wt 11 10
Midfield. From Trainee.

Season	Club	Apps	Goals
1987–88	Charlton Ath	—	—
1988–89	Fulham	13	—
1989–90		37	2
1990–91	Bury	29	6
1991–92		22	—
1991–92	*Manchester C*	—	—
1992–93	Bury	13	1
1993–94		26	3
1994–95		18	—
1995–96	Plymouth Arg	37	7

MAUTONE, Steve

Born Myrtleford 10.8.70 Ht 6 1
Wt 12 00
Goalkeeper. From Canberra Cosmos.

Season	Club	Apps	Goals
1995–96	West Ham U	—	—

MAWSON, David

Born Sunderland 4.3.77 Ht 5 11
Wt 12 05
Forward. From Trainee.

Season	Club	Apps	Goals
1995–96	Sunderland	—	—

MAXFIELD, Scott

Born Doncaster 13.7.76 Ht 5 9 Wt 10 09
Defender. From Trainee.

Season	Club	Apps	Goals
1994–95	Doncaster R	10	—
1995–96		19	1
1995–96	Hull C	4	—

MAXWELL, Ally

Born Hamilton 16.2.65 Ht 6 1 Wt 12 07
Goalkeeper. From Fir Park BC.

Season	Club	Apps	Goals
1981–82	Motherwell	—	—
1982–83		—	—
1983–84		4	—
1984–85		15	—
1985–86		4	—
1986–87		21	—
1987–88		1	—
1987–88	*Clydebank*	1	—
1988–89	Motherwell	17	—
1989–90		36	—
1990–91		36	—
1991–92		—	—
1991–92	*Liverpool*	—	—
1991–92	*Bolton W*	3	—
1992–93	Rangers	10	—
1993–94		32	—
1994–95		11	—
1995–96	Dundee U	35	—

MAY, David

Born Oldham 24.6.70 Ht 6 0 Wt 12 10
Defender. From Trainee.

Season	Club	Apps	Goals
1988–89	Blackburn R	1	—
1989–90		17	—
1990–91		19	1
1991–92		12	—
1992–93		34	1
1993–94		40	1
1994–95	Manchester U	19	2
1995–96		16	1

MAY, Edward

Born Edinburgh 30.8.67 Ht 5 7
Wt 10 03
Forward. From Hutchison Vale BC.
Scotland Youth, Under-21.

Season	Club	Apps	Goals
1983–84	Dundee U	—	—
1984–85		—	—
1984–85	Hibernian	—	—
1985–86		19	1
1986–87		30	5
1987–88		35	2
1988–89		25	2
1989–90	Brentford	30	8
1990–91		17	2
1990–91	Falkirk	13	6
1991–92		36	9
1992–93		42	6
1993–94		38	9
1994–95		24	2
1994–95	Motherwell	10	2
1995–96		28	1

MAYBURY, Alan

Born Dublin 8.8.78
Midfield. From Trainee.

Season	Club	Apps	Goals
1995–96	Leeds U	1	—

MAZZARELLI, Guiseppe

Born Switzerland 14.8.72
Midfield. Switzerland full caps.

Season	Club	Apps	Goals
1995–96	Manchester C	2	—

McALINDON, Gareth

Born Hexham 6.4.77 Ht 5 9 Wt 12 09
Forward. From Newcastle U Trainee.

Season	Club	Apps	Goals
1995–96	Carlisle U	3	—

McALLISTER, Brian

Born Glasgow 30.11.70 Ht 5 11
Wt 12 05
Defender. From Trainee.

Season	Club	Apps	Goals
1988–89	Wimbledon	—	—
1989–90		3	—
1990–91		—	—
1990–91	*Plymouth Arg*	8	—
1991–92	Wimbledon	10	—
1992–93		27	—
1993–94		13	—
1994–95		—	—
1995–96		2	—
1995–96	*Crewe Alex*	13	1

McALLISTER, Gary

Born Motherwell 25.12.64 Ht 5 10
Wt 10 11
Midfield. From Fir Park BC. Scotland
Under-21, B, 44 full caps.

Season	Club	Apps	Goals
1981–82	Motherwell	1	—
1982–83		1	—
1983–84		21	—
1984–85		35	6
1985–86		1	—
1985–86	Leicester C	31	7
1986–87		39	10
1987–88		42	9
1988–89		46	11
1989–90		43	10
1990–91	Leeds U	38	2
1991–92		42	5
1992–93		32	5
1993–94		42	8
1994–95		41	6
1995–96		36	5

McALLISTER, Kevin

Born Falkirk 8.11.62 Ht 5 5 Wt 11 00
Forward.

Season	Club	Apps	Goals
1983–84	Falkirk	35	11
1984–85		29	7
1985–86	Chelsea	20	—
1986–87		8	—
1987–88		5	—
1987–88	*Falkirk*	6	3
1988–89	Chelsea	36	6
1989–90		24	1
1990–91		13	—
1991–92	Falkirk	42	9
1992–93		41	3

Season Club League Appearances/Goals

1993–94 Hibernian 36 6
1994–95 23 1
1995–96 31 4

McANESPIE, Steve

Born Kilmarnock 1.2.72 Ht 5 9 Wt 10 07
Defender. From Vasterhauringe.

1993–94 Raith R 3 —
1994–95 34 —
1995–96 3 —
1995–96 Bolton W 9 —

McAREE, Rod

Born Dungannon 19.8.74 Ht 5 7 Wt 10 02
Defender. From Trainee.

1991–92 Liverpool — —
1992–93 — —
1993–94 — —
1994–95 Bristol C 6 —
1995–96 — —
1995–96 Fulham 17 2

McATEER, Jason

Born Birkenhead 18.6.71 Ht 5 11
Wt 11 10
Midfield. From Marine. Eire B, 18 full caps.

1991–92 Bolton W — —
1992–93 21 —
1993–94 46 3
1994–95 43 5
1995–96 4 —
1995–96 Liverpool 29 —

McAULEY, Sean

Born Sheffield 23.6.72 Ht 5 10 Wt 11 03
Defender. From Trainee. Scotland Under-21.

1991–92 Manchester U — —
1992–93 St Johnstone 26 —
1993–94 28 —
1994–95 8 —
1994–95 *Chesterfield* 1 1
1995–96 Hartlepool U 46 —

McCALL, Steve

Born Carlisle 15.10.60 Ht 5 10 Wt 12 06
Midfield. From Apprentice. England Youth, Under-21, B.

1978–79 Ipswich T — —

Season Club League Appearances/Goals

1979–80 10 —
1980–81 31 1
1981–82 42 1
1982–83 42 4
1983–84 42 1
1984–85 31 —
1985–86 33 —
1986–87 26 —
1987–88 Sheffield W 5 —
1988–89 2 —
1989–90 3 —
1989–90 *Carlisle U* 6 —
1990–91 Sheffield W 19 2
1991–92 — —
1991–92 Plymouth Arg 9 1
1992–93 35 1
1993–94 45 2
1994–95 7 1
1995–96 4 —

McCALL, Stuart

Born Leeds 10.6.64 Ht 5 6 Wt 10 01
Midfield. From Apprentice. Scotland Under-21, 37 full caps.

1982–83 Bradford C 28 4
1983–84 46 5
1984–85 46 8
1985–86 38 4
1986–87 36 7
1987–88 44 9
1988–89 Everton 33 —
1989–90 37 3
1990–91 33 3
1991–92 Rangers 36 1
1992–93 36 5
1993–94 34 3
1994–95 30 2
1995–96 21 3

McCANN, Chris

Born Plaistow 28.11.76 Ht 5 8 Wt 10 05
Defender. From Trainee.

1995–96 Chelsea — —

McCANN, Gavin

Born Blackpool 10.1.78 Ht 5 11
Wt 11 00
Midfield. From Trainee.

1995–96 Everton — —

Season	Club	League Appearances/Goals	

McCART, Chris

Born Motherwell 17.4.67 Ht 5 9
Wt 10 05
Midfield. From Fir Park BC.

1984–85	Motherwell	—	—
1985–86		13	—
1986–87		—	—
1987–88		1	—
1988–89		26	—
1989–90		34	1
1990–91		36	—
1991–92		22	2
1992–93		29	3
1993–94		36	—
1994–95		24	—
1995–96		20	—

McCARTHY, Alan

Born London 11.1.72 Ht 5 11 Wt 12 10
Defender. From Trainee.

1989–90	QPR	—	—
1990–91		2	—
1991–92		3	—
1992–93		—	—
1993–94		4	—
1993–94	*Watford*	9	—
1993–94	*Plymouth Arg*	2	—
1994–95	QPR	2	—
1995–96	Leyton Orient	43	—

McCARTHY, Jon

Born Middlesbrough 18.8.70 Ht 5 9
Wt 11 05
Midfield. Northern Ireland 1 full cap.

1987–88	Hartlepool U	1	—
From Shepshed			
1990–91	York C	27	2
1991–92		42	6
1992–93		42	7
1993–94		44	7
1994–95		44	9
1995–96	Port Vale	45	7

McCARTHY, Mick

Born Barnsley 7.2.59 Ht 6 2 Wt 13 12
Defender. From Apprentice. Eire 57 full caps.

1977–78	Barnsley	46	1
1978–79		46	2
1979–80		44	1
1980–81		43	1
1981–82		42	1
1982–83		39	1
1983–84		12	—
1983–84	Manchester C	24	1
1984–85		39	—
1985–86		38	—
1986–87		39	1
1987–88	Celtic	22	—
1988–89		26	—
From Lyon			
1989–90	Millwall	6	—
1990–91		12	—
1991–92		17	2
1992–93		—	—
1993–94		—	—
1994–95		—	—
1995–96		—	—

McCARTHY, Paul

Born Cork 4.8.71 Ht 6 0 Wt 13 06
Defender. From Trainee. Eire Youth, Under-21.

1989–90	Brighton & HA	3	—
1990–91		21	—
1991–92		20	—
1992–93		30	—
1993–94		37	3
1994–95		37	2
1995–96		33	1

McCARTHY, Sean

Born Bridgend 12.9.67 Ht 6 1 Wt 11 07
Forward. From Bridgend. Wales B.

1985–86	Swansea C	22	3
1986–87		44	14
1987–88		25	8
1988–89	Plymouth Arg	38	8
1989–90		32	11
1990–91	Bradford C	42	13
1991–92		29	16
1992–93		42	17
1993–94		18	14
1993–94	Oldham Ath	20	4
1994–95		39	18
1995–96		35	10

McCARTHY, Tony

Born Dublin 9.11.69 Ht 6 1 Wt 12 06
Defender. From Shelbourne.

1992–93	Millwall	7	1

Season	Club	Apps	Goals
1993–94		2	—
1994–95		12	—
1994–95	*Crewe Alex*	2	—
1994–95	Colchester U	10	1
1995–96		44	—

McCATHIE, Norrie (Deceased)

Born Edinburgh 23.3.61 Ht 6 0
Wt 12 10
Midfield. From Edina Hibs.

Season	Club	Apps	Goals
1980–81	Cowdenbeath	11	—
1981–82	Dunfermline Ath	19	4
1982–83		24	3
1983–84		38	5
1984–85		37	8
1985–86		37	8
1986–87		44	6
1987–88		39	1
1988–89		20	1
1988–89	*Ayr U*	2	—
1989–90	Dunfermline Ath	36	—
1990–91		36	1
1991–92		40	1
1992–93		32	2
1993–94		43	8
1994–95		32	4
1995–96		18	3

McCLAIR, Brian

Born Airdrie 8.12.63 Ht 5 10 Wt 12 12
Forward. From Apprentice. Scotland Youth, Under-21, B, 30 full caps.

Season	Club	Apps	Goals
1980–81	Aston Villa	—	—
1981–82	Motherwell	11	4
1982–83		28	11
1983–84	Celtic	35	23
1984–85		32	19
1985–86		34	22
1986–87		44	35
1987–88	Manchester U	40	24
1988–89		38	10
1989–90		37	5
1990–91		36	13
1991–92		42	18
1992–93		42	9
1993–94		26	1
1994–95		40	5
1995–96		22	3

McCLUSKIE, Mark

Born Ogar 23.10.76 Ht 5 11 Wt 11 03
Forward.

Season	Club	Apps	Goals
1995–96	Doncaster R	—	—

McCOIST, Ally

Born Bellshill 24.9.62 Ht 5 10 Wt 12 00
Forward. From Fir Park BC. Scotland Youth, Under-21, 54 caps.

Season	Club	Apps	Goals
1978–79	St Johnstone	4	—
1979–80		15	—
1980–81		38	22
1981–82	Sunderland	28	2
1982–83		28	6
1983–84	Rangers	30	9
1984–85		25	12
1985–86		33	24
1986–87		44	33
1987–88		40	31
1988–89		19	9
1989–90		34	14
1990–91		26	11
1991–92		38	34
1992–93		34	34
1993–94		21	7
1994–95		9	1
1995–96		25	16

McCONNELL, Barry

Born Exeter 1.1.77 Ht 5 11 Wt 10 03
Forward. From Trainee.

Season	Club	Apps	Goals
1995–96	Exeter C	8	—

McCRINDLE, Scott

Born Stranraer 30.9.77
Midfield. From Trainee.

Season	Club	Apps	Goals
1995–96	Ipswich T	—	—

McCRONE, Chris

Born Preston 5.2.77 Ht 6 1 Wt 12 07
Goalkeeper. From Trainee.

Season	Club	Apps	Goals
1995–96	Blackburn R	—	—

McCUE, James

Born Glasgow 29.6.75 Ht 5 8 Wt 10 00
Forward. From Trainee.

Season	Club	Apps	Goals
1992–93	WBA	—	—
1993–94		—	—
1994–95		—	—

Season	Club	League Appearances/Goals	
1995–96		—	—
1995–96	Partick T	3	—

McCULLOCH, Greig

Born Girvan 18.4.76 Ht 5 8 Wt 10 07
Defender. From Banchory St Ternans.

Season	Club	Apps	Goals
1994–95	Aberdeen	—	—
1995–96	Raith R	7	1

McCULLOCH, Lee

Born Bellshill 14.5.78 Ht 5 11 Wt 12 05
Midfield. From Cumbernauld Utd. Scotland Under-18.

Season	Club	Apps	Goals
1995–96	Motherwell	1	—

McCULLOCH, Mark

Born Inverness 19.5.75 Ht 5 11 Wt 12 00
Midfield. From Clachnacuddin.

Season	Club	Apps	Goals
1994–95	Dunfermline Ath	9	—
1995–96		10	—

McDERMOTT, Andrew

Born Sydney 20.3.77 Ht 5 9 Wt 11 03
Midfield. From Australian Institute of Sport.

Season	Club	Apps	Goals
1995–96	QPR	—	—

McDERMOTT, John

Born Middlesbrough 3.1.69 Ht 5 7 Wt 10 00
Defender. From Trainee.

Season	Club	Apps	Goals
1986–87	Grimsby T	13	—
1987–88		28	—
1988–89		38	1
1989–90		39	—
1990–91		43	—
1991–92		39	1
1992–93		38	2
1993–94		26	—
1994–95		12	—
1995–96		28	1

McDONALD, Alan

Born Belfast 12.10.63 Ht 6 2 Wt 13 11
Defender. From Apprentice. Northern Ireland Youth, 52 full caps.

Season	Club	Apps	Goals
1981–82	QPR	—	—
1982–83		—	—
1982–83	*Charlton Ath*	9	—
1983–84	QPR	5	—
1984–85		16	1
1985–86		42	—
1986–87		39	4
1987–88		36	3
1988–89		30	—
1989–90		34	—
1990–91		17	—
1991–92		28	—
1992–93		39	—
1993–94		12	1
1994–95		39	1
1995–96		26	1

McDONALD, Colin

Born Edinburgh 10.4.74 Ht 5 7 Wt 11 04
Forward. Scotland Under-21.

Season	Club	Apps	Goals
1991–92	Hibernian	—	—
1992–93		—	—
1993–94	Falkirk	16	1
1994–95		31	9
1995–96		9	1
1995–96	Swansea C	8	—

McDONALD, David

Born Dublin 2.1.71 Ht 5 10 Wt 12 05
Defender. From Trainee. Eire Youth, Under-21, B.

Season	Club	Apps	Goals
1989–90	Tottenham H	—	—
1990–91		—	—
1990–91	*Gillingham*	10	—
1991–92	Tottenham H	—	—
1992–93		2	—
1992–93	*Bradford C*	7	—
1992–93	*Reading*	11	—
1993–94	Peterborough U	29	—
1993–94	Barnet	10	—
1994–95		35	—
1995–96		32	—

McDONALD, Neil

Born Wallsend 2.11.65 Ht 5 11 Wt 12 08
Defender. From Wallsend BC. England Schools, Youth, Under-21.

Season	Club	Apps	Goals
1982–83	Newcastle U	24	4
1983–84		12	—
1984–85		36	6
1985–86		28	4
1986–87		40	7
1987–88		40	3

Season	Club	League Appearances/Goals	
1988–89	Everton	25	1
1989–90		31	1
1990–91		29	2
1991–92		5	—
1991–92	Oldham Ath	17	1
1992–93		4	—
1993–94		3	—
1994–95	Bolton W	4	—
1995–96		—	—
1995–96	Preston NE	11	—

McDONALD, Paul

Born Motherwell 20.4.68 Ht 5 6
Wt 10 00
Forward. From Merry Street BC.

Season	Club	Apps	Goals
1986–87	Hamilton A	5	—
1987–88		18	—
1988–89		34	—
1989–90		38	3
1990–91		38	7
1991–92		38	5
1992–93		44	11
1993–94	Southampton	—	—
1994–95		2	—
1995–96		1	—
1995–96	*Burnley*	9	1
1995–96	Brighton & HA	5	—

McDONALD, Rod

Born London 20.3.67 Ht 5 10 Wt 12 07
Forward. From South Liverpool, Colne Dynamoes.

Season	Club	Apps	Goals
1990–91	Walsall	36	5
1991–92		39	18
1992–93		39	12
1993–94		35	6
1994–95	Partick T	25	5
1995–96		16	5

McDOUGALD, Junior

Born Big Spring 12.1.75 Ht 5 11
Wt 12 06
Forward. From Trainee.

Season	Club	Apps	Goals
1993–94	Tottenham H	—	—
1994–95	Brighton & HA	41	10
1995–96		37	4
1995–96	*Chesterfield*	9	3

McELHATTON, Mike

Born Co. Kerry 16.4.75 Ht 6 1 Wt 12 08
Defender. From Trainee.

Season	Club	Apps	Goals
1992–93	Bournemouth	1	—
1993–94		10	—
1994–95		27	2
1995–96		4	—

McFARLANE, Andy

Born Wolverhampton 30.11.66 Ht 6 3
Wt 13 07
Forward. From Cradley T.

Season	Club	Apps	Goals
1990–91	Portsmouth	—	—
1991–92		2	—
1992–93	Swansea C	24	5
1993–94		28	3
1994–95		3	—
1995–96	Scunthorpe U	46	16

McGARGLE, Stephen

Born Gateshead 24.10.75 Ht 5 9
Wt 11 00
Forward. From Trainee.

Season	Club	Apps	Goals
1993–94	Middlesbrough	—	—
1994–95		—	—
1995–96		—	—

McGARRIGLE, Kevin

Born Newcastle 9.4.77 Ht 5 11 Wt 11 00
Defender. From Trainee.

Season	Club	Apps	Goals
1993–94	Brighton & HA	1	—
1994–95		17	—
1995–96		14	1

McGAVIN, Steve

Born North Walsham 24.1.69 Ht 5 9
Wt 12 08
Forward. From Sudbury.

Season	Club	Apps	Goals
1990–91	Colchester U	—	—
1991–92		—	—
1992–93		37	9
1993–94		21	8
1993–94	Birmingham C	8	1
1994–95		15	1
1994–95	Wycombe W	12	2
1995–96		31	2

McGHEE, David

Born Sussex 19.6.76 Ht 5 9 Wt 11 04
Forward. From Trainee.

Season	Club	Apps	Goals
1994–95	Brentford	7	1
1995–96		36	5

McGIBBON, Patrick

Born Lurgan 6.9.73 Ht 6 1 Wt 13 02
Defender. From Portadown. Northern Ireland 4 full caps.

Season	Club	App	Gls
1992–93	Manchester U	—	—
1993–94		—	—
1994–95		—	—
1995–96		—	—

McGINLAY, John

Born Inverness 8.4.64 Ht 5 9 Wt 11 04
Forward. From Elgin C. Scotland 9 full caps.

Season	Club	App	Gls
1988–89	Shrewsbury T	16	5
1989–90		44	22
1990–91	Bury	25	9
1990–91	Millwall	2	—
1991–92		25	8
1992–93		7	2
1992–93	Bolton W	34	16
1993–94		39	25
1994–95		37	16
1995–96		32	6

McGINLAY, Pat

Born Glasgow 30.5.67 Ht 5 10 Wt 10 10
Midfield. From Scottish Junior.

Season	Club	App	Gls
1985–86	Blackpool	—	—
1986–87		12	1
1987–88	Hibernian	—	—
1988–89		2	—
1989–90		28	3
1990–91		32	1
1991–92		43	9
1992–93		40	10
1993–94	Celtic	41	10
1994–95		8	1
1994–95	Hibernian	24	7
1995–96		31	5

McGINTY, Brian

Born East Kilbride 10.12.76 Ht 6 1
Wt 11 04
Midfield. From Rangers BC.

Season	Club	App	Gls
1993–94	Rangers	—	—
1994–95		1	—
1995–96		2	—

McGIVEN, Joseph

Born Newcastle 8.6.77
Midfield. From Watford.

Season	Club	App	Gls
1995–96	Sunderland	—	—

McGLASHAN, John

Born Dundee 3.6.67 Ht 6 2 Wt 13 00
Forward. From Dundee Violet.

Season	Club	App	Gls
1988–89	Montrose	35	2
1989–90		33	9
1990–91	Millwall	8	—
1991–92		8	—
1992–93		—	—
1992–93	*Cambridge U*	1	—
1992–93	*Fulham*	5	1
1992–93	Peterborough U	18	—
1993–94		28	3
1994–95		—	—
1994–95	Rotherham U	27	3
1995–96		16	2

McGLEISH, Scott

Born London 10.2.74 Ht 5 9 Wt 11 04
Forward. From Edgware T.

Season	Club	App	Gls
1994–95	Charlton Ath	6	—
1994–95	*Leyton Orient*	6	1
1995–96	Peterborough U	12	—
1995–96	*Colchester U*	15	6

McGLINCHEY, Brian

Born Derry 26.10.77
Midfield. From Trainee.

Season	Club	App	Gls
1995–96	Manchester C	—	—

McGOLDRICK, Eddie

Born London 30.4.65 Ht 5 10 Wt 11 07
Forward. From Nuneaton, Kettering T. Eire 15 full caps.

Season	Club	App	Gls
1986–87	Northampton T	39	5
1987–88		46	2
1988–89		22	2
1988–89	Crystal Palace	21	—
1989–90		22	—
1990–91		26	—
1991–92		36	3
1992–93		42	8
1993–94	Arsenal	26	—
1994–95		11	—
1995–96		1	—

McGORRY, Brian

Born Liverpool 16.4.70 Ht 5 10
Wt 12 05
Midfield. From Weymouth.

Season	Club	Apps	Goals
1991–92	Bournemouth	8	—
1992–93		37	8
1993–94		16	3
1993–94	Peterborough U	18	3
1994–95		34	3
1995–96		—	—
1995–96	Wycombe W	4	—
1995–96	*Cardiff C*	7	—

McGOWAN, Gavin

Born Blackheath 16.1.76 Ht 5 8
Wt 11 07
Midfield. From Trainee. England Youth.

Season	Club	Apps	Goals
1992–93	Arsenal	2	—
1993–94		—	—
1994–95		1	—
1995–96		1	—

McGOWAN, Jamie

Born Morecambe 5.12.70 Ht 6 0
Wt 11 01
Defender. From Morecambe.

Season	Club	Apps	Goals
1992–93	Dundee	21	1
1993–94		14	—
1993–94	Falkirk	9	2
1994–95		31	1
1995–96		29	1

McGRATH, Lloyd

Born Birmingham 24.2.65 Ht 5 8
Wt 12 05
Midfield. From Apprentice. England Youth, Under-21.

Season	Club	Apps	Goals
1982–83	Coventry C	—	—
1983–84		1	—
1984–85		23	—
1985–86		32	—
1986–87		30	3
1987–88		17	—
1988–89		8	—
1989–90		13	—
1990–91		14	—
1991–92		40	1
1992–93		25	—
1993–94		11	—
1994–95	Portsmouth	18	—
1995–96		—	—

McGRATH, Paul

Born Ealing 4.12.59 Ht 6 2 Wt 14 00
Defender. From St Patrick's Ath. Eire 82 full caps. Football League.

Season	Club	Apps	Goals
1981–82	Manchester U	—	—
1982–83		14	3
1983–84		9	1
1984–85		23	—
1985–86		40	3
1986–87		35	2
1987–88		22	2
1988–89		20	1
1989–90	Aston Villa	35	1
1990–91		35	—
1991–92		41	1
1992–93		42	4
1993–94		30	1
1994–95		40	—
1995–96		30	2

McGRAW, Mark

Born Rutherglen 5.1.71 Ht 5 11
Wt 10 07
Forward. From Port Glasgow R.

Season	Club	Apps	Goals
1988–89	Morton	1	—
1989–90		11	3
1990–91	Hibernian	13	—
1991–92		24	1
1992–93		2	—
1993–94		2	—
1994–95		8	2
1995–96	Falkirk	9	—

McGREAL, John

Born Birkenhead 2.6.72 Ht 5 11
Wt 12 08
Defender. From Trainee.

Season	Club	Apps	Goals
1990–91	Tranmere R	3	—
1991–92		—	—
1992–93		—	—
1993–94		15	1
1994–95		43	—
1995–96		32	—

McGREGOR, Mark

Born Chester 16.2.77 Ht 5 11 Wt 11 05
Defender. From Trainee.

Season	Club	Apps	Goals
1994–95	Wrexham	1	—
1995–96		32	1

Season	Club	League Appearances/Goals	

McGREGOR, Paul

Born Liverpool 17.12.74 Ht 5 10 Wt 11 06
Forward. From Trainee.

1991–92	Nottingham F	—	—
1992–93		—	—
1993–94		—	—
1994–95		11	1
1995–96		14	2

McGRILLEN, Paul

Born Glasgow 19.8.71 Ht 5 8 Wt 10 05
Forward. From Motherwell BC. Scotland Under-21.

1990–91	Motherwell	2	—
1991–92		16	—
1992–93		22	6
1993–94		40	5
1994–95		7	2
1994–95	Falkirk	6	1
1995–96		30	6

McGUCKIN, Ian

Born Middlesbrough 24.4.73 Ht 6 2 Wt 14 00
Defender. From Trainee.

1991–92	Hartlepool U	7	—
1992–93		14	1
1993–94		35	2
1994–95		34	3
1995–96		40	2

McINALLY, Jim

Born Glasgow 19.2.64 Ht 6 0 Wt 12 00
Midfield. From Celtic BC. Scottish Youth, Under-21. 10 full caps.

1982–83	Celtic	1	—
1983–84		—	—
1983–84	*Dundee*	11	2
1984–85	Nottingham F	24	—
1985–86		12	—
1985–86	Coventry C	5	—
1986–87	Dundee U	32	1
1987–88		36	2
1988–89		29	1
1989–90		35	3
1990–91		33	1
1991–92		32	4
1992–93		32	—
1993–94		31	—
1994–95		24	—
1995–96	Raith R	25	—

McINNES, Derek

Born Paisley 5.7.71 Ht 5 7 Wt 11 04
Midfield. From Gleniffer Thistle.

1987–88	Greenock Morton	2	—
1988–89		29	1
1989–90		23	1
1990–91		31	3
1991–92		42	7
1992–93		40	2
1993–94		16	1
1994–95		26	3
1995–96		12	1
1995–96	Rangers	6	—

McINTYRE, James

Born Dumbarton 24.5.72 Ht 5 11 Wt 11 05
Forward. From Duntocher Boys.

1991–92	Bristol C	1	—
1992–93		—	—
1992–93	*Exeter C*	15	3
1993–94	Airdrieonians	13	—
1994–95		12	1
1995–96		29	9
1995–96	Kilmarnock	7	2

McKAY, Andrew

Born Bolton 16.1.75 Ht 5 10 Wt 11 10
Defender. From Trainee.

1993–94	Bolton W	—	—
1994–95		—	—
1995–96		—	—

McKEE, Colin

Born Glasgow 22.8.73 Ht 5 10 Wt 11 00
Forward. From Trainee.

1991–92	Manchester U	—	—
1992–93		—	—
1992–93	*Bury*	2	—
1993–94	Manchester U	1	—
1994–95	Kilmarnock	25	6
1995–96		28	4

McKEE, Kevin

Born Edinburgh 10.6.66 Ht 5 8 Wt 11 11
Defender. From Whitburn BC.

1982–83	Hibernian	4	—

Season	Club	League Appearances/Goals	
1983–84		16	—
1984–85		17	—
1985–86		2	—
1986–87	Hamilton A	29	4
1987–88		40	—
1988–89		36	—
1989–90		39	1
1990–91		38	—
1991–92		34	1
1992–93		20	1
1993–94	Partick T	23	—
1994–95		17	—
1995–96		11	—

McKENNA, Paul

Born Chorley 20.10.77
Midfield. From Trainee.

Season	Club	Apps	Goals
1995–96	Preston NE	—	—

McKENZIE, Leon

Born Croydon 17.5.78 Ht 5 10 Wt 11 02
Midfield. From Trainee.

Season	Club	Apps	Goals
1995–96	Crystal Palace	12	—

McKENZIE, Scott

Born Glasgow 7.7.70 Ht 5 9 Wt 10 05
Forward. From Musselburgh Ath.

Season	Club	Apps	Goals
1990–91	Falkirk	—	—
1991–92		2	—
1992–93		3	—
1993–94		19	—
1994–95		36	1
1995–96		30	1

McKILLIGAN, Neil

Born Falkirk 2.1.74 Ht 5 10 Wt 11 00
Defender. From Southampton Trainee.

Season	Club	Apps	Goals
1992–93	Partick T	5	—
1993–94		—	—
1993–94	Ayr U	8	1
1994–95		34	—
1995–96		10	—
1995–96	Raith R	3	—

McKIMMIE, Stuart

Born Aberdeen 27.10.62 Ht 5 8
Wt 10 07
Defender. From Banks o' Dee. Scotland Under-21, 40 full caps.

Season	Club	Apps	Goals
1980–81	Dundee	17	—
1981–82		16	—
1982–83		31	—
1983–84		16	—
1983–84	Aberdeen	18	1
1984–85		34	3
1985–86		34	3
1986–87		37	—
1987–88		42	—
1988–89		35	—
1989–90		33	—
1990–91		26	1
1991–92		39	—
1992–93		14	—
1993–94		40	—
1994–95		34	1
1995–96		29	—

McKINLAY, Billy

Born Glasgow 22.4.69 Ht 5 8 Wt 11 04
Midfield. From Hamilton T. Scotland Under-21, B, 18 full caps.

Season	Club	Apps	Goals
1986–87	Dundee U	3	—
1987–88		12	1
1988–89		30	1
1989–90		13	—
1990–91		34	2
1991–92		22	1
1992–93		37	1
1993–94		39	9
1994–95		27	4
1995–96		5	4
1995–96	Blackburn R	19	2

McKINLAY, Tosh

Born Glasgow 3.12.64 Ht 5 7 Wt 10 03
Defender. From Celtic BC. Scotland Youth, Under-21, 6 full caps.

Season	Club	Apps	Goals
1981–82	Dundee	—	—
1982–83		1	—
1983–84		36	3
1984–85		34	3
1985–86		22	—
1986–87		32	2
1987–88		19	—
1988–89		18	—
1988–89	Hearts	17	1
1989–90		29	1
1990–91		33	2
1991–92		39	2
1992–93		34	—
1993–94		43	—
1994–95		11	—
1994–95	Celtic	17	—
1995–96		32	—

Season Club League Appearances/Goals

McKINNON, Ray

Born Dundee 5.8.70 Ht 5 8 Wt 9 11
Defender. From 'S' Form. Scotland Under-21.

Season	Club	Apps	Goals
1987–88	Dundee U	—	—
1988–89		1	—
1989–90		10	—
1990–91		17	2
1991–92		25	4
1992–93	Nottingham F	6	1
1993–94		—	—
1993–94	Aberdeen	5	—
1994–95		20	—
1995–96		1	—
1995–96	Dundee U	9	—

McKINNON, Rob

Born Glasgow 31.7.66 Ht 5 11 Wt 11 01
Defender. From Rutherglen Glencairn. Scotland 3 full caps.

Season	Club	Apps	Goals
1984–85	Newcastle U	—	—
1985–86		1	—
1986–87	Hartlepool	45	—
1987–88		42	2
1988–89		46	2
1989–90		46	1
1990–91		45	1
1990–91	*Manchester U*	—	—
1991–92	Hartlepool U	23	1
1991–92	Motherwell	16	1
1992–93		35	—
1993–94		42	4
1994–95		32	3
1995–96		27	—

McKOP, Henry

Born Zimbabwe 8.7.67 Ht 5 11
Wt 12 00
Defender. From Bonner Sport Club.

Season	Club	Apps	Goals
1993–94	Bristol C	4	—
1994–95		1	—
1995–96		—	—

McLAREN, Alan

Born Edinburgh 4.1.71 Ht 5 11
Wt 11 06
Defender. From Cavalry Bank. Scotland Under-21, 24 full caps.

Season	Club	Apps	Goals
1987–88	Hearts	1	—
1988–89		12	1
1989–90		27	1
1990–91		23	1
1991–92		38	1
1992–93		34	—
1993–94		37	1
1994–95		10	1
1994–95	Rangers	24	2
1995–96		36	3

McLAREN, Andrew

Born Glasgow 5.6.73 Ht 5 10 Wt 10 06
Forward. From Rangers Amateur BC. Scotland Under-21.

Season	Club	Apps	Goals
1989–90	Dundee U	—	—
1990–91		—	—
1991–92		13	—
1992–93		5	—
1993–94		27	1
1994–95		20	—
1995–96		31	3

McLAREN, Paul

Born High Wycombe 17.11.76 Ht 6 1
Wt 13 04
Defender. From Trainee.

Season	Club	Apps	Goals
1993–94	Luton T	1	—
1994–95		—	—
1995–96		12	1

McLAUGHLIN, Brian

Born Bellshill 14.5.74 Ht 5 4 Wt 8 07
Midfield. From Giffnock N. Scotland Under-21.

Season	Club	Apps	Goals
1992–93	Celtic	—	—
1993–94		8	—
1994–95		21	—
1995–96		26	4

McLAUGHLIN, Joe

Born Greenock 2.6.60 Ht 6 1 Wt 12 00
Defender. From School. Scotland Under-21.

Season	Club	Apps	Goals
1977–78	Morton	—	—
1978–79		—	—
1979–80		30	2
1980–81		34	1
1981–82		36	—
1982–83		34	—
1983–84	Chelsea	41	—
1984–85		36	1

Season	Club	League Appearances/Goals	
1985–86		40	1
1986–87		36	2
1987–88		36	1
1988–89		31	—
1989–90	Charlton Ath	31	—
1990–91	Watford	24	1
1991–92		22	1
1992–93		—	—
1992–93	Falkirk	8	1
1993–94		38	2
1994–95		28	2
1995–96		16	1
1995–96	Hibernian	9	—

McLEAN, Ian

Born Paisley 13.8.66 Ht 6 2 Wt 13 02
Defender. From Metroford. Canada full caps.

Season	Club	Apps	Goals
1993–94	Bristol R	27	2
1994–95		1	—
1994–95	*Cardiff C*	4	—
From Metroford			
1995–96	Bristol R	7	—
1995–96	*Rotherham U*	9	—

McLEARY, Alan

Born Lambeth 6.10.64 Ht 5 10 Wt 10 06
Defender. From Apprentice. England Youth, Under-21, B.

Season	Club	Apps	Goals
1981–82	Millwall	—	—
1982–83		3	1
1983–84		30	—
1984–85		21	—
1985–86		35	3
1986–87		42	—
1987–88		31	—
1988–89		38	1
1989–90		31	—
1990–91		42	—
1991–92		28	—
1992–93		6	—
1992–93	*Sheffield U*	3	—
1992–93	*Wimbledon*	4	—
1993–94	Charlton Ath	44	3
1994–95		22	—
1995–96	Bristol C	31	—

McLEISH, Alex

Born Glasgow 21.1.59 Ht 6 1 Wt 12 04
Defender. From Glasgow United. Scotland Under-21, 77 full caps.

Season	Club	Apps	Goals
1977–78	Aberdeen	1	—
1978–79		19	1
1979–80		35	2
1980–81		32	3
1981–82		32	5
1982–83		34	2
1983–84		32	2
1984–85		30	1
1985–86		34	3
1986–87		40	3
1987–88		36	1
1988–89		34	—
1989–90		32	2
1990–91		33	—
1991–92		7	—
1992–93		27	—
1993–94		35	—
1994–95	Motherwell	2	—
1995–96		1	—

McLOUGHLIN, Alan

Born Manchester 20.4.67 Ht 5 8 Wt 10 10
Midfield. From Local. Eire B, 23 full caps.

Season	Club	Apps	Goals
1984–85	Manchester U	—	—
1985–86		—	—
1986–87	Swindon T	9	—
1986–87	Torquay U	16	1
1987–88		8	3
1987–88	Swindon T	8	—
1988–89		26	3
1989–90		46	12
1990–91		17	4
1990–91	Southampton	22	1
1991–92		2	—
1991–92	*Aston Villa*	—	—
1991–92	Portsmouth	14	2
1992–93		46	9
1993–94		38	6
1994–95		38	6
1995–96		40	10

McMAHON, Gerard

Born Belfast 29.12.73 Ht 5 11 Wt 11 00
Forward. From Glenavon. Northern Ireland 7 full caps.

Season	Club	Apps	Goals
1992–93	Tottenham H	—	—
1993–94		—	—
1994–95		2	—
1994–95	*Barnet*	10	2
1995–96	Tottenham H	14	—

Season	Club	League Appearances/Goals	

McMAHON, Sam

Born Newark 10.2.76 Ht 5 10 Wt 11 06
Midfield. From Trainee.

1994–95	Leicester C	1	—
1995–96		3	1

McMAHON, Steve

Born Liverpool 20.8.61 Ht 5 9 Wt 11 08
Midfield. From Apprentice. England Under-21, B, 17 full caps.

1979–80	Everton	—	—
1980–81		34	5
1981–82		32	2
1982–83		34	4
1983–84	Aston Villa	37	5
1984–85		35	2
1985–86		3	—
1985–86	Liverpool	23	6
1986–87		37	5
1987–88		40	9
1988–89		29	3
1989–90		38	5
1990–91		22	—
1991–92		15	1
1991–92	Manchester C	18	—
1992–93		27	1
1993–94		35	—
1994–95		7	—
1994–95	Swindon T	17	—
1995–96		21	—

McMAHON, Steve

Born Glasgow 22.4.70 Ht 6 4 Wt 14 07
Defender. From Foshan.

1995–96	Partick T	1	—
1995–96	Darlington	10	1

McMANAMAN, Steve

Born Liverpool 11.2.72 Ht 6 0 Wt 10 06
Forward. From School. England Youth, Under-21, 15 full caps.

1989–90	Liverpool	—	—
1990–91		2	—
1991–92		30	5
1992–93		31	4
1993–94		30	2
1994–95		40	7
1995–96		38	6

McMANUS, Allan

Born Paisley 17.11.74 Ht 6 0 Wt 12 00
Defender. From Links Utd.

1992–93	Hearts	—	—
1993–94		—	—
1994–95		—	—
1995–96		18	2

McMILLAN, Andy

Born Bloemfontein 22.6.68 Ht 5 11
Wt 11 02
Defender.

1987–88	York C	22	—
1988–89		2	—
1989–90		25	—
1990–91		45	1
1991–92		41	1
1992–93		42	—
1993–94		46	—
1994–95		43	1
1995–96		46	1

McMILLAN, Ian

Born Broxburn 9.6.76 Ht 5 10 Wt 11 04
Defender. From Armadale Th.

1993–94	Raith R	—	—
1994–95		1	—
1995–96		8	—

McMILLAN, Stephen

Born Edinburgh 19.1.76 Ht 5 10
Wt 11 00
Midfield. From Troon Juniors.

1993–94	Motherwell	1	—
1994–95		3	—
1995–96		12	—

McMINN, Ted

Born Castle Douglas 28.9.62 Ht 6 0
Wt 13 08
Forward. From Glenafton Athletic.

1982–83	Q of S	22	1
1983–84	Queen of the S	32	3
1984–85		8	1
1984–85	Rangers	20	1
1985–86		28	2
1986–87		15	1
From Seville			
1987–88	Derby Co	7	1
1988–89		32	4

Season	Club	League Appearances/Goals	
1989–90		15	—
1990–91		13	—
1991–92		37	2
1992–93		19	2
1993–94	Birmingham C	22	—
1993–94	Burnley	14	3
1994–95		22	—
1995–96		10	—

McNALLY, Mark

Born Bellshill 10.3.71 Ht 5 10 Wt 12 02
Defender. From Celtic BC. Scotland Under-21.

Season	Club	League Appearances/Goals	
1987–88	Celtic	—	—
1988–89		—	—
1989–90		—	—
1990–91		19	—
1991–92		25	1
1992–93		27	—
1993–94		32	2
1994–95		20	—
1995–96	Southend U	20	2

McNAMARA, Jackie

Born Glasgow 24.10.73 Ht 5 8 Wt 9 07
Midfield. From Gairdoch Utd. Scotland B, Under-21.

Season	Club	League Appearances/Goals	
1991–92	Dunfermline Ath	—	—
1992–93		3	—
1993–94		39	—
1994–95		30	2
1995–96		7	1
1995–96	Celtic	26	1

McNIVEN, David

Born Leeds 27.5.78
Forward. From Trainee.

Season	Club	League Appearances/Goals	
1995–96	Oldham Ath	—	—

McNIVEN, Scott

Born Leeds 27.5.78
Defender. From Trainee. Scotland Under-21.

Season	Club	League Appearances/Goals	
1994–95	Oldham Ath	1	—
1995–96		15	—

McPHERSON, David

Born Paisley 28.1.64 Ht 6 3 Wt 11 11
Defender. From Gartcosh United. Scotland Youth, Under-21 B, 27 full caps.

Season	Club	League Appearances/Goals	
1980–81	Rangers	—	—
1981–82		—	—
1982–83		18	1
1983–84		36	2
1984–85		31	—
1985–86		34	5
1986–87		42	7
1987–88		44	4
1988–89	Hearts	32	4
1989–90		35	4
1990–91		34	2
1991–92		44	2
1992–93	Rangers	34	2
1993–94		28	1
1994–95		9	—
1994–95	Hearts	23	2
1995–96		26	1

McPHERSON, Keith

Born Greenwich 11.9.63 Ht 5 11 Wt 11 00
Defender. From Apprentice.

Season	Club	League Appearances/Goals	
1981–82	West Ham U	—	—
1982–83		—	—
1983–84		—	—
1984–85		1	—
1985–86		—	—
1985–86	*Cambridge U*	11	1
1985–86	Northampton T	20	—
1986–87		46	5
1987–88		32	—
1988–89		41	2
1989–90		43	1
1990–91	Reading	46	3
1991–92		44	1
1992–93		44	1
1993–94		20	1
1994–95		23	—
1995–96		16	—

McPHERSON, Malcolm

Born Glasgow 9.12.74 Ht 5 10 Wt 12 00
Forward. From Yeovil.

Season	Club	League Appearances/Goals	
1993–94	West Ham U	—	—
1994–95		—	—
1995–96		—	—

McQUILKEN, James

Born Glasgow 3.10.74 Ht 5 9 Wt 10 07
Defender. From Giffnock North.

Season	Club	League Appearances/Goals	
1992–93	Celtic	1	—
1993–94		—	—

Season	Club	League Appearances/Goals	
1994–95		—	—
1995–96		4	—
1995–96	Dundee U	9	—

McROBERT, Lee

Born Bromley 4.10.72 Ht 5 9 Wt 10 12
Midfield. From Sittingbourne.

1994–95	Millwall	7	1
1995–96		7	—

McSKIMMING, Shaun

Born Stranraer 29.5.70 Ht 5 11 Wt 10 08
Defender. From School.

1986–87	Stranraer	—	—
1987–88	Dundee	—	—
1988–89		—	—
1989–90		7	—
1990–91		16	3
1991–92	Kilmarnock	30	1
1992–93		35	5
1993–94		40	3
1994–95		8	—
1994–95	Motherwell	14	2
1995–96		15	1

McSTAY, Paul

Born Hamilton 22.10.64 Ht 5 10
Wt 10 07
Midfield. From Celtic BC. Scotland Schools, Youth, Under-21, 73 full caps.

1981–82	Celtic	10	1
1982–83		36	6
1983–84		34	3
1984–85		32	4
1985–86		34	8
1986–87		43	3
1987–88		44	5
1988–89		33	5
1989–90		35	3
1990–91		30	2
1991–92		31	7
1992–93		43	4
1993–94		35	2
1994–95		29	1
1995–96		30	2

McSWEGAN, Gary

Born Glasgow 24.9.70 Ht 5 8 Wt 10 09
Forward. From Rangers Amateur BC.

Season	Club	League Appearances/Goals	
1986–87	Rangers	—	—
1987–88		1	—
1988–89		1	—
1989–90		—	—
1990–91		3	—
1991–92		4	—
1992–93		9	4
1993–94	Notts Co	37	15
1994–95		22	6
1995–96		3	—
1995–96	Dundee U	25	17

McVEIGH, Paul

Born Belfast 6.12.77
Midfield. From Trainee.

1995–96	Tottenham H	—	—

McWILLIAMS, Derek

Born Broxburn 16.1.66 Ht 5 10
Wt 11 07
Forward. From Broxburn J.

1984–85	Dundee	16	2
1985–86		11	1
1986–87		1	—
1986–87	*Stirling Albion*	4	—
1986–87	Dundee	5	—
1987–88	Falkirk	31	4
1988–89		28	11
1989–90		33	17
1990–91		29	10
1991–92	Dunfermline Ath	24	3
1992–93		25	3
1993–94		20	3
1994–95	Partick T	29	3
1995–96		27	3

MEAKER, Michael

Born Greenford 18.8.71 Ht 5 11
Wt 11 00
Midfield. From Trainee. Wales Under-21.

1989–90	QPR	—	—
1990–91		8	—
1991–92		1	—
1991–92	*Plymouth Arg*	4	—
1992–93	QPR	3	—
1993–94		14	1
1994–95		8	—
1995–96	Reading	21	—

Season	Club	League Appearances/Goals	

MEAN, Scott

Born Crawley 13.12.73 Ht 5 11 Wt 13 08
Midfield. From Trainee.

1992–93	Bournemouth	15	1
1993–94		5	—
1994–95		40	6
1995–96		14	1

MEARA, Jim

Born London 7.10.72 Ht 5 9 Wt 11 02
Midfield. From Trainee.

1991–92	Watford	—	—
1992–93		2	—
1993–94		—	—
1994–95	Doncaster R	15	1
1995–96		1	—

MEASHAM, Ian

Born Barnsley 14.12.64 Ht 5 11
Wt 11 09
Defender. From Apprentice.

1982–83	Huddersfield T	—	—
1983–84		—	—
1984–85		17	—
1985–86		—	—
1985–86	*Lincoln C*	6	—
1985–86	*Rochdale*	12	—
1986–87	Cambridge U	46	—
1987–88		—	—
1988–89		—	—
1988–89	Burnley	30	1
1989–90		35	—
1990–91		45	1
1991–92		27	—
1992–93		39	—
1993–94		6	—
1993–94	Doncaster R	21	—
1994–95		1	—
1995–96		10	—

MEDLIN, Nicky

Born Camborne 23.11.76 Ht 5 7
Wt 10 01
Midfield. From Trainee.

1995–96	Exeter C	6	—

MEGSON, Gary

Born Manchester 2.5.59 Ht 5 10
Wt 12 00
Midfield. From Apprentice.

1977–78	Plymouth Arg	24	2
1978–79		42	8
1979–80		12	—
1979–80	Everton	12	1
1980–81		10	1
1981–82	Sheffield W	40	5
1982–83		41	4
1983–84		42	4
1984–85	Nottingham F	—	—
1984–85	Newcastle U	20	1
1985–86		4	—
1985–86	Sheffield W	20	3
1986–87		35	6
1987–88		37	2
1988–89		18	1
1988–89	Manchester C	22	1
1989–90		19	—
1990–91		19	1
1991–92		22	—
1992–93	Norwich C	23	1
1993–94		22	—
1994–95		1	—
1995–96	Lincoln C	2	—
1995–96	Shrewsbury T	2	—
1995–96	Bradford C	—	—

MEHEW, David

Born Camberley 29.10.67 Ht 5 10
Wt 12 06
Midfield. From Trainee.

1984–85	Leeds U	—	—
1985–86	Bristol R	4	—
1986–87		21	10
1987–88		18	8
1988–89		31	7
1989–90		46	18
1990–91		41	8
1991–92		37	9
1992–93		24	3
1993–94		—	—
1993–94	*Exeter C*	7	—
1994–95	Walsall	13	—
1995–96	Northampton T	—	—

MELDRUM, Colin

Born Kilmarnock 26.11.75 Ht 5 10
Wt 13 04
Goalkeeper. From Kilwinning Rangers.
Scotland Under-21.

1993–94	Kilmarnock	—	—
1994–95		40	—
1995–96		1	—

MELLON, Michael

Born Paisley 18.3.72 Ht 5 9 Wt 11 03
Midfield. From Trainee.

Season	Club	Apps	Goals
1989–90	Bristol C	9	—
1990–91		—	—
1991–92		16	—
1992–93		10	1
1992–93	WBA	17	3
1993–94		21	2
1994–95		7	1
1994–95	Blackpool	26	4
1995–96		45	6

MELTON, Stephen

Born Lincoln 3.10.78 Ht 5 11 Wt 10 11
Midfield. From Trainee.

Season	Club	Apps	Goals
1995–96	Nottingham F	—	—

MELVILLE, Andy

Born Swansea 29.11.68 Ht 6 0 Wt 13 10
Defender. From School. Wales Under-21, B, 27 full caps.

Season	Club	Apps	Goals
1985–86	Swansea C	5	—
1986–87		42	3
1987–88		37	4
1988–89		45	10
1989–90		46	5
1990–91	Oxford U	46	3
1991–92		45	4
1992–93		44	6
1993–94	Sunderland	44	2
1994–95		36	3
1995–96		40	4

MENDES, Junior

Born Balham 15.9.76 Ht 5 8 Wt 10 00
Midfield. From Trainee.

Season	Club	Apps	Goals
1995–96	Chelsea	—	—

MENDONCA, Clive

Born Islington 9.9.68 Ht 5 10 Wt 10 07
Forward. From Apprentice.

Season	Club	Apps	Goals
1986–87	Sheffield U	2	—
1987–88		11	4
1987–88	*Doncaster R*	2	—
1987–88	Rotherham U	8	2
1988–89		10	1
1989–90		32	14
1990–91		34	10
1991–92	Sheffield U	10	1
1991–92	*Grimsby T*	10	3
1992–93	Grimsby T	42	10
1993–94		39	14
1994–95		22	11
1995–96		8	4

MERCER, Billy

Born Liverpool 22.5.69 Ht 6 2 Wt 13 03
Goalkeeper. From Trainee.

Season	Club	Apps	Goals
1987–88	Liverpool	—	—
1988–89		—	—
1988–89	Rotherham U	—	—
1989–90		2	—
1990–91		13	—
1991–92		35	—
1992–93		36	—
1993–94		17	—
1994–95		1	—
1994–95	Sheffield U	3	—
1994–95	*Nottingham F*	—	—
1995–96	Sheffield U	1	—
1995–96	Chesterfield	34	—

MEREDITH, Tom

Born Enfield 27.10.77
Defender. From Trainee.

Season	Club	Apps	Goals
1995–96	Peterborough U	2	—

MERSON, Paul

Born London 20.3.68 Ht 6 0 Wt 13 02
Forward. From Apprentice. England Youth, Under-21, B, 14 full caps.

Season	Club	Apps	Goals
1985–86	Arsenal	—	—
1986–87		7	3
1986–87	*Brentford*	7	—
1987–88	Arsenal	15	5
1988–89		37	10
1989–90		29	7
1990–91		37	13
1991–92		42	12
1992–93		33	6
1993–94		33	7
1994–95		24	4
1995–96		38	5

MICKLEWHITE, Gary

Born Southwark 21.3.61 Ht 5 7
Wt 10 04
Midfield. From Apprentice.

Season	Club	Apps	Goals
1977–78	Manchester U	—	—

Season	Club	League Appearances/Goals	
1978–79		—	—
1979–80	QPR	—	—
1980–81		1	—
1981–82		26	2
1982–83		34	6
1983–84		30	2
1984–85		15	1
1984–85	Derby Co	19	4
1985–86		46	11
1986–87		42	6
1987–88		16	1
1988–89		26	3
1989–90		18	2
1990–91		35	2
1991–92		32	2
1992–93		6	—
1993–94	Gillingham	29	1
1994–95		35	2
1995–96		31	—

MIDDLETON, Craig

Born Nuneaton 10.9.70 Ht 5 10
Wt 11 02
Midfield. From Trainee.

Season	Club	Apps	Goals
1989–90	Coventry C	1	—
1990–91		—	—
1991–92		1	—
1992–93		1	—
1993–94	Cambridge U	19	2
1994–95		—	—
1995–96		40	8

MIDDLETON, Darren

Born Lichfield 28.12.78
Midfield. From Trainee.

Season	Club	Apps	Goals
1995–96	Aston Villa	—	—

MIDDLETON, Lee

Born Nuneaton 10.9.70 Ht 5 9 Wt 11 09
Midfield. From Trainee.

Season	Club	Apps	Goals
1991–92	Coventry C	2	—
1992–93	Swindon T	—	—
1993–94		—	—
1994–95		—	—
1995–96		—	—
1995–96	Cambridge U	3	—

MIDGLEY, Craig

Born Bradford 24.5.76 Ht 5 8 Wt 10 11
Forward. From Trainee.

Season	Club	Apps	Goals
1994–95	Bradford C	3	—
1995–96		5	1
1995–96	*Scarborough*	16	1

MIKE, Adie

Born Manchester 16.11.73 Ht 6 0
Wt 11 06
Forward. From Trainee. England Youth.

Season	Club	Apps	Goals
1991–92	Manchester C	2	1
1992–93		3	—
1992–93	*Bury*	7	1
1993–94	Manchester C	9	1
1994–95		2	—
1995–96		—	—
1995–96	Stockport Co	8	—

MIKHAILICHENKO, Alexei

Born Kiev 30.3.63 Ht 6 2 Wt 13 03
Midfield. From Sampdoria. USSR, CIS full caps.

Season	Club	Apps	Goals
1991–92	Rangers	27	10
1992–93		29	5
1993–94		34	5
1994–95		9	2
1995–96		11	—

MIKHAILOV, Bobby

Born Bulgaria 12.2.63 Ht 6 1 Wt 12 04
Goalkeeper. From Botev Plovdiv. Bulgaria 96 full caps.

Season	Club	Apps	Goals
1995–96	Reading	16	—

MIKLOSKO, Ludek

Born Ostrava 9.12.61 Ht 6 5 Wt 14 00
Goalkeeper. From Banik Ostrava. Czechoslovakia 40 full caps.

Season	Club	Apps	Goals
1989–90	West Ham U	18	—
1990–91		46	—
1991–92		36	—
1992–93		46	—
1993–94		42	—
1994–95		42	—
1995–96		36	—

MILES, Ben

Born Middlesex 13.4.76 Ht 6 1 Wt 11 07
Goalkeeper. From Trainee.

Season	Club	Apps	Goals
1994–95	Swansea C	—	—
1995–96		—	—

MILLAR, John

Born Lanark 8.12.66 Ht 5 10
Wt 10 00
Midfield.

Season	Club	Apps	Goals
1984–85	Chelsea	—	—
1985–86		7	—
1986–87		4	—
1986–87	*Hamilton A*	10	—
1986–87	*Northampton T*	1	—
1987–88	Blackburn R	15	—
1988–89		38	—
1989–90		39	1
1990–91		34	—
1991–92	Hearts	41	7
1992–93		24	—
1993–94		20	4
1994–95		28	6
1995–96		20	4
1995–96	Raith R	3	1

MILLAR, Marc

Born Dundee 10.4.69 Ht 5 9
Wt 10 12
Forward. From Riverside Ath.

Season	Club	Apps	Goals
1991–92	Brechin C	17	1
1992–93		31	11
1993–94		39	10
1994–95		8	1
1994–95	Dunfermline Ath	24	2
1995–96		24	5

MILLEN, Andrew

Born Glasgow 10.6.65 Ht 5 11
Wt 11 04
Defender. From Pollok Juniors.

Season	Club	Apps	Goals
1983–84	St Johnstone	—	—
1984–85		4	—
1985–86		36	1
1986–87		31	1
1987–88	Alloa	36	4
1988–89		38	3
1989–90		37	2
1990–91	Hamilton A	39	—
1991–92		39	1
1992–93		41	3
1993–94	Kilmarnock	44	—
1994–95		13	—
1994–95	Hibernian	8	—
1995–96		25	—

MILLEN, Keith

Born Croydon 26.9.66 Ht 6 2 Wt 12 04
Defender. From Juniors.

Season	Club	Apps	Goals
1984–85	Brentford	17	—
1985–86		32	2
1986–87		39	2
1987–88		40	3
1988–89		36	3
1989–90		32	—
1990–91		32	2
1991–92		34	1
1992–93		43	4
1993–94		—	—
1993–94	Watford	10	—
1994–95		31	1
1995–96		33	—

MILLER, Alan

Born Epping 29.3.70 Ht 6 3 Wt 14 08
Goalkeeper. From Trainee. FA Schools, England Under-21.

Season	Club	Apps	Goals
1987–88	Arsenal	—	—
1988–89		—	—
1988–89	*Plymouth Arg*	13	—
1989–90	Arsenal	—	—
1990–91		—	—
1991–92		—	—
1991–92	*WBA*	3	—
1991–92	*Birmingham C*	15	—
1992–93	Arsenal	4	—
1993–94		4	—
1994–95	Middlesbrough	41	—
1995–96		6	—

MILLER, Charles

Born Glasgow 18.3.76 Ht 5 9 Wt 10 08
Forward. From Rangers BC. Scotland Under-21.

Season	Club	Apps	Goals
1992–93	Rangers	—	—
1993–94		3	—
1994–95		21	3
1995–96		23	3

MILLER, Colin

Born Lanark 4.10.64 Ht 5 7 Wt 12 02
Defender. From Toronto Blizzard. Canada 51 full caps.

Season	Club	Apps	Goals
1985–86	Rangers	2	—

Season Club League Appearances/Goals

Season	Club	Apps	Goals
1986–87	Doncaster R	20	2
1987–88		41	1
From Hamilton Steelers			
1988–89	Hamilton A	21	—
1989–90		37	1
1990–91		37	—
1991–92		43	1
1992–93		29	3
1993–94		31	—
1993–94	St Johnstone	12	—
1994–95		12	—
1994–95	Hearts	16	1
1995–96		3	—
1995–96	Dunfermline Ath	25	—

MILLER, David

Born Burnley 8.1.64 Ht 5 11
Wt 11 13
Midfield. From Apprentice.

Season	Club	Apps	Goals
1981–82	Burnley	—	—
1982–83		1	—
1982–83	*Crewe Alex*	3	—
1983–84	Burnley	17	2
1984–85		14	1
1985–86	Tranmere R	29	1
1986–87	Preston NE	15	—
1987–88		28	2
1988–89		12	—
1988–89	*Burnley*	4	—
1989–90	Preston NE	3	—
1989–90	Carlisle U	42	3
1990–91		41	4
1991–92		26	—
1991–92	Stockport Co	3	—
1992–93		37	1
1993–94		38	—
1994–95		3	—
1994–95	Wigan Ath	31	3
1995–96		7	—

MILLER, Graeme

Born Glasgow 21.2.73 Ht 5 7
Wt 10 03
Midfield. From Tynecastle BC.

Season	Club	Apps	Goals
1992–93	Hibernian	1	—
1993–94		1	—
1994–95		—	—
1995–96		4	—

MILLER, Joe

Born Glasgow 8.12.67 Ht 5 8
Wt 9 12
Forward. From 'S' Form. Scotland Schools, Youth, Under-21.

Season	Club	Apps	Goals
1984–85	Aberdeen	1	—
1985–86		18	3
1986–87		27	6
1987–88		14	4
1987–88	Celtic	27	3
1988–89		22	8
1989–90		24	5
1990–91		30	8
1991–92		26	2
1992–93		23	2
1993–94	Aberdeen	27	4
1994–95		27	—
1995–96		31	9

MILLER, Kevin

Born Falmouth 15.3.69 Ht 6 1
Wt 13 00
Goalkeeper. From Newquay.

Season	Club	Apps	Goals
1988–89	Exeter C	3	—
1989–90		28	—
1990–91		46	—
1991–92		42	—
1992–93		44	—
1993–94	Birmingham C	24	—
1994–95	Watford	44	—
1995–96		42	—

MILLER, Paul

Born Bisley 31.1.68 Ht 6 0
Wt 11 07
Forward. From Trainee.

Season	Club	Apps	Goals
1987–88	Wimbledon	5	—
1987–88	*Newport Co*	6	2
1988–89	Wimbledon	18	5
1989–90		15	2
1989–90	*Bristol C*	3	—
1990–91	Wimbledon	1	—
1991–92		22	2
1992–93		19	1
1993–94		—	—
1994–95	Bristol R	42	16
1995–96		38	4

Season	Club	League Appearances/Goals		Season	Club	League Appearances/Goals

MILLER, William

Born Edinburgh 1.11.69 Ht 5 8
Wt 10 06
Defender. From Edina Hibs BC. Scotland Under-21.

Season	Club	Apps	Goals
1989–90	Hibernian	11	—
1990–91		25	1
1991–92		30	—
1992–93		34	—
1993–94		37	—
1994–95		34	—
1995–96		13	—

MILLETT, Mike (Deceased)

Born Wigan 22.9.77 Ht 5 10 Wt 11 07
Defender. From Trainee. England Youth.

Season	Club	Apps	Goals
1994–95	Wigan Ath	3	—
1995–96		—	—

MILLIGAN, Mike

Born Manchester 20.2.67 Ht 5 8
Wt 11 00
Midfield. From Trainee. Eire Under-21, B, 1 full cap.

Season	Club	Apps	Goals
1984–85	Oldham Ath	—	—
1985–86		5	1
1986–87		38	2
1987–88		39	1
1988–89		39	6
1989–90		41	7
1990–91	Everton	17	1
1991–92	Oldham Ath	36	3
1992–93		42	3
1993–94		39	—
1994–95	Norwich C	26	2
1995–96		28	2

MILLS, Danny

Born Sidcup 13.2.75 Ht 5 11 Wt 11 06
Midfield. From Trainee.

Season	Club	Apps	Goals
1993–94	Charlton Ath	—	—
1994–95		—	—
1995–96	Barnet	19	—

MILLS, Danny

Born Norwich 18.5.77 Ht 5 11 Wt 11 11
Defender. From Trainee. England Youth.

Season	Club	Apps	Goals
1994–95	Norwich C	—	—
1995–96		14	—

MILLS, Gary

Born Northampton 11.11.61 Ht 5 9
Wt 11 10
Defender. From Apprentice. England Schools, Youth, Under-21.

Season	Club	Apps	Goals
1978–79	Nottingham F	4	1
1979–80		13	1
1980–81		27	5
1981–82		14	1
From Seattle S			
1982–83	Derby Co	18	1
From Seattle S			
1983–84	Nottingham F	7	—
1984–85		26	4
1985–86		14	—
1986–87		32	—
1987–88	Notts Co	46	5
1988–89		29	3
1988–89	Leicester C	13	—
1989–90		29	4
1990–91		45	5
1991–92		46	6
1992–93		43	—
1993–94		23	—
1994–95		1	—
1994–95	Notts Co	34	—
1995–96		13	—

MILLS, Lee

Born Mexborough 10.7.70 Ht 6 1
Wt 12 11
Forward. From Stocksbridge.

Season	Club	Apps	Goals
1992–93	Wolverhampton W	—	—
1993–94		14	1
1994–95		11	1
1994–95	Derby Co	16	7
1995–96	Port Vale	32	8

MILNE, Callum

Born Edinburgh 27.8.65 Ht 5 8
Wt 10 07
Defender. From Salvesen BC.

Season	Club	Apps	Goals
1983–84	Hibernian	—	—
1984–85		1	—

Season	Club	League Appearances/Goals	
1985–86		7	—
1986–87		2	—
1987–88		3	—
1988–89		19	—
1989–90		3	—
1990–91		21	—
1991–92		8	—
1992–93		15	—
1993–94	Partick T	31	1
1994–95		4	—
1995–96		22	—

MILNER, Andy

Born Kendal 10.2.67 Ht 6 0 Wt 11 00
Forward. From Netherfield.

Season	Club	Apps	Goals
1988–89	Manchester C	—	—
1989–90		—	—
1989–90	Rochdale	16	4
1990–91		35	5
1991–92		33	10
1992–93		18	4
1993–94		25	2
1994–95	Chester C	36	8
1995–96		42	4

MILOSEVIC, Savo

Born Bijelina 2.9.73 Ht 6 1 Wt 13 05
Forward. Yugoslavia 7 full caps.

Season	Club	Apps	Goals
1993–94	Partizan Belgrade	32	20
1994–95		35	30
1995–96	Aston Villa	37	12

MILSOM, Paul

Born Bristol 5.10.74 Ht 6 1 Wt 13 01
Forward. From Trainee.

Season	Club	Apps	Goals
1993–94	Bristol C	3	—
1994–95		—	—
1994–95	Cardiff C	3	—
1995–96	Oxford U	—	—

MILTON, Simon

Born Fulham 23.8.63 Ht 5 10 Wt 11 05
Midfield. From Bury St Edmunds.

Season	Club	Apps	Goals
1987–88	Ipswich T	8	1
1987–88	*Exeter C*	2	3
1987–88	*Torquay U*	4	1
1988–89	Ipswich T	35	10
1989–90		41	10
1990–91		31	6
1991–92		34	7
1992–93		12	2
1993–94		15	1
1994–95		25	2
1995–96		37	9

MIMMS, Bobby

Born York 12.10.63 Ht 6 4 Wt 14 04
Goalkeeper. From Halifax T Apprentice. England Under-21.

Season	Club	Apps	Goals
1981–82	Rotherham U	2	—
1982–83		13	—
1983–84		22	—
1984–85		46	—
1985–86	Everton	10	—
1985–86	*Notts Co*	2	—
1986–87	Everton	11	—
1986–87	*Sunderland*	4	—
1986–87	*Blackburn R*	6	—
1987–88	Everton	8	—
1987–88	*Manchester C*	3	—
1987–88	Tottenham H	13	—
1988–89		20	—
1989–90		4	—
1989–90	*Aberdeen*	6	—
1990–91	Tottenham H	—	—
1990–91	Blackburn R	22	—
1991–92		45	—
1992–93		42	—
1993–94		13	—
1994–95		4	—
1995–96		2	—

MINETT, Jason

Born Peterborough 12.8.71 Ht 5 10 Wt 10 02
Midfield. From Trainee.

Season	Club	Apps	Goals
1989–90	Norwich C	—	—
1990–91		2	—
1991–92		—	—
1992–93		1	—
1992–93	*Exeter C*	12	—
1993–94	Exeter C	38	1
1994–95		38	2
1995–96	Lincoln C	42	5

MINTO, Scott

Born Cheshire 6.8.71 Ht 5 10 Wt 12 07
Defender. From Trainee. England Youth, Under-21.

Season	Club	Apps	Goals
1988–89	Charlton Ath	3	—
1989–90		23	2
1990–91		43	1

Season	Club	League Appearances/Goals	
1991–92		33	1
1992–93		36	1
1993–94		42	2
1994–95	Chelsea	19	—
1995–96		10	—

MINTON, Jeffrey

Born Hackney 28.12.73 Ht 5 6 Wt 10 13
Midfield. From Trainee.

1991–92	Tottenham H	2	1
1992–93		—	—
1993–94		—	—
1994–95	Brighton & HA	39	5
1995–96		39	8

MISON, Michael

Born London 8.11.75 Ht 6 3 Wt 14 00
Midfield. From Trainee.

1993–94	Fulham	4	—
1994–95		24	1
1995–96		23	4

MITCHELL, Alistair

Born Kirkcaldy 3.12.68 Ht 5 7 Wt 11 00
Forward. From Ballingry Rovers.

1988–89	East Fife	18	4
1989–90		35	12
1990–91		34	7
1991–92	Kilmarnock	42	10
1992–93		32	6
1993–94		34	5
1994–95		35	4
1995–96		30	3

MITCHELL, Andrew

Born Rotherham 12.9.76 Ht 6 0
Wt 12 00
Defender. From Trainee.

1993–94	Aston Villa	—	—
1994–95		—	—
1995–96		—	—

MITCHELL, Graham

Born Shipley 16.2.68 Ht 6 2 Wt 12 13
Defender. From Apprentice.

1986–87	Huddersfield T	17	—
1987–88		29	1
1988–89		34	—
1989–90		37	1
1990–91		46	—
1991–92		43	—
1992–93		4	—
1993–94		22	—
1993–94	*Bournemouth*	4	—
1994–95	Huddersfield T	12	—
1994–95	Bradford C	26	—
1995–96		33	1

MITCHELL, Graham

Born Glasgow 2.11.62 Ht 5 10 Wt 11 08
Defender. From Auchengill BC.

1980–81	Hamilton A	4	—
1981–82		37	—
1982–83		32	1
1983–84		21	1
1984–85		30	—
1985–86		32	6
1986–87		23	1
1986–87	Hibernian	17	1
1987–88		41	1
1988–89		20	—
1989–90		31	—
1990–91		28	—
1991–92		27	—
1992–93		41	—
1993–94		36	1
1994–95		18	—
1995–96		6	—

MITCHELL, Jamie

Born Glasgow 6.11.76 Ht 5 6 Wt 9 10
Midfield. From Trainee.

1995–96	Norwich C	—	—

MITCHELL, Neil

Born Lytham 7.11.74 Ht 5 6 Wt 10 00
Midfield. From Trainee.

1991–92	Blackpool	1	—
1992–93		12	1
1993–94		24	3
1994–95		30	4
1995–96		—	—
1995–96	*Rochdale*	4	—

MITCHELL, Paul

Born Bournemouth 20.10.71 Ht 5 10
Wt 12 00
Defender. From Trainee.

1990–91	Bournemouth	2	—

Season Club League Appearances/Goals

Season Club League Appearances/Goals

Season	Club	Apps	Goals
1991–92		5	—
1992–93		5	—
1993–94	West Ham U	1	—
1994–95		—	—
1995–96		—	—
1995–96	Bournemouth	4	—

MITTEN, Paul

Born Stockport 22.12.75 Ht 5 8
Wt 10 12
Forward. From Manchester U Trainee.

Season	Club	Apps	Goals
1995–96	Stockport Co	—	—
1995–96	Coventry C	—	—

MOHAN, Nicky

Born Middlesbrough 6.10.70 Ht 6 2
Wt 14 00
Defender. From Trainee.

Season	Club	Apps	Goals
1987–88	Middlesbrough	—	—
1988–89		6	—
1989–90		22	—
1990–91		—	—
1991–92		27	2
1992–93		18	2
1992–93	*Hull C*	5	1
1993–94	Middlesbrough	26	—
1994–95	Leicester C	23	—
1995–96	Bradford C	39	4

MOILANEN, Teuvo

Born Oulu 12.12.73 Ht 6 3 Wt 12 05
Goalkeeper.

Season	Club	Apps	Goals
1995–96	Preston NE	2	—

MOLBY, Jan

Born Kolding 4.7.63 Ht 6 1 Wt 14 07
Midfield. From Kolding, Ajax. Denmark Youth, Under-21, 33 full caps.

Season	Club	Apps	Goals
1984–85	Liverpool	22	1
1985–86		39	14
1986–87		34	7
1987–88		7	—
1988–89		13	2
1989–90		17	1
1990–91		25	9
1991–92		26	3
1992–93		10	3
1993–94		11	2
1994–95		14	2
1995–96		—	—
1995–96	*Barnsley*	5	—
1995–96	*Norwich C*	3	—
1995–96	Swansea C	12	2

MONCUR, John

Born Stepney 22.9.66 Ht 5 7 Wt 9 10
Midfield. From Apprentice.

Season	Club	Apps	Goals
1984–85	Tottenham H	—	—
1985–86		—	—
1986–87		1	—
1986–87	*Cambridge U*	4	—
1986–87	*Doncaster R*	4	—
1987–88	Tottenham H	5	—
1988–89		1	—
1988–89	*Portsmouth*	7	—
1989–90	Tottenham H	5	1
1989–90	*Brentford*	5	1
1990–91	Tottenham H	9	—
1991–92	*Ipswich T*	6	—
1991–92	*Nottingham F*	—	—
1991–92	Swindon T	3	—
1992–93		14	1
1993–94		41	4
1994–95	West Ham U	30	2
1995–96		20	—

MONINGTON, Mark

Born Bilsthorpe 21.10.70 Ht 6 1
Wt 14 02
Defender. From School.

Season	Club	Apps	Goals
1988–89	Burnley	8	1
1989–90		13	—
1990–91		—	—
1991–92		12	1
1992–93		31	2
1993–94		20	1
1994–95		—	—
1994–95	Rotherham U	25	2
1995–96		11	—

MONK, Garry

Born Bedford 6.3.79 Ht 5 11 Wt 11 13
Defender. From Trainee.

Season	Club	Apps	Goals
1995–96	Torquay U	5	—

MONKOU, Ken

Born Surinam 29.11.64 Ht 6 3 Wt 14 05
Defender. From Feyenoord. Holland Under-21.

Season	Club	Apps	Goals
1988–89	Chelsea	2	—
1989–90		34	1

Season	Club	League Appearances/Goals	
1990–91		27	1
1991–92		31	—
1992–93		—	—
1992–93	Southampton	33	1
1993–94		35	4
1994–95		31	1
1995–96		32	2

MONTGOMERIE, Ray

Born Irvine 17.4.61 Ht 5 8 Wt 11 07
Defender. From Saltcoats Vic.

Season	Club	Apps	Goals
1980–81	Newcastle U	—	—
1981–82	Dumbarton	20	5
1982–83		25	2
1983–84		39	1
1984–85		6	—
1985–86		24	—
1986–87		35	—
1987–88		31	—
1988–89	Kilmarnock	31	2
1989–90		35	3
1990–91		37	—
1991–92		30	1
1992–93		42	—
1993–94		42	—
1994–95		12	—
1995–96		14	—

MOODY, Jimmy

Born Hull 16.11.77 Ht 5 10 Wt 11 02
Defender. From Trainee.

Season	Club	Apps	Goals
1994–95	Leeds U	—	—
1995–96		—	—

MOODY, Paul

Born Portsmouth 13.6.67 Ht 6 3
Wt 14 07
Forward. From Waterlooville.

Season	Club	Apps	Goals
1991–92	Southampton	4	—
1992–93		3	—
1992–93	*Reading*	5	1
1993–94	Southampton	5	—
1993–94	Oxford U	15	8
1994–95		41	20
1995–96		42	17

MOONEY, Tommy

Born Teesside North 11.8.71 Ht 5 11
Wt 12 06
Forward. From Trainee.

Season	Club	Apps	Goals
1989–90	Aston Villa	—	—
1990–91	Scarborough	27	13
1991–92		40	8
1992–93		40	9
1993–94	Southend U	14	5
1993–94	*Watford*	10	2
1994–95	Watford	29	3
1995–96		42	6

MOORE, Alan

Born Dublin 25.11.74 Ht 5 9 Wt 10 08
Forward. From Rivermount. Eire Under-21, 5 full caps.

Season	Club	Apps	Goals
1991–92	Middlesbrough	—	—
1992–93		2	—
1993–94		42	10
1994–95		37	4
1995–96		12	—

MOORE, Allan

Born Glasgow 25.12.64 Ht 5 7 Wt 10 00
Forward. From Possil YM.

Season	Club	Apps	Goals
1983–84	Dumbarton	4	—
1984–85		4	—
1985–86		33	4
1986–87		18	3
1986–87	Hearts	10	—
1987–88		7	1
1988–89		12	2
1989–90	St Johnstone	33	13
1990–91		31	5
1991–92		21	1
1992–93		26	3
1993–94		13	1
1993–94	Dunfermline Ath	8	—
1994–95		12	1
1995–96		28	5

MOORE, Craig

Born Canterbury, Australia 12.12.75
Ht 6 1 Wt 12 00
Defender. From Australian Institute of Sport.

Season	Club	Apps	Goals
1993–94	Rangers	1	—
1994–95		21	2
1995–96		11	1

MOORE, Darren

Born Birmingham 22.4.74 Ht 6 2
Wt 15 00
Defender. From Trainee.

Season	Club	Apps	Goals
1991–92	Torquay U	5	1

Season	Club	League Appearances/Goals	
1992–93		31	2
1993–94		37	2
1994–95		30	3
1995–96	Doncaster R	35	2

MOORE, David

Born Birmingham 23.11.76 Ht 6 0
Wt 14 00
Midfield. From Trainee.

Season	Club	League Appearances/Goals	
1994–95	Aston Villa	—	—
1995–96		—	—

MOORE, Ian

Born Birkenhead 26.8.76 Ht 6 0
Wt 11 10
Forward. From Trainee. England Youth, Under-21.

Season	Club	League Appearances/Goals	
1994–95	Tranmere R	1	—
1995–96		36	9

MOORE, Jason

Born Dover 16.2.79 Ht 5 8 Wt 11 04
Defender. From Trainee.

Season	Club	League Appearances/Goals	
1995–96	West Ham U	—	—

MOORE, Kevin

Born Grimsby 29.4.58 Ht 5 11 Wt 12 12
Defender. From Local. England Schools.

Season	Club	League Appearances/Goals	
1976–77	Grimsby T	28	—
1977–78		42	—
1978–79		46	6
1979–80		41	4
1980–81		41	1
1981–82		36	4
1982–83		38	—
1983–84		41	1
1984–85		31	4
1985–86		31	2
1986–87		25	5
1986–87	Oldham Ath	13	1
1987–88	Southampton	35	3
1988–89		25	3
1989–90		21	1
1990–91		19	1
1991–92		16	—
1991–92	*Bristol R*	7	—
1992–93	Southampton	18	2
1992–93	*Bristol R*	4	1
1993–94	Southampton	14	—
1994–95	Fulham	31	3
1995–96		20	1

MOORE, Neil

Born Liverpool 21.9.72 Ht 6 1 Wt 12 07
Defender. From Trainee.

Season	Club	League Appearances/Goals	
1991–92	Everton	—	—
1992–93		1	—
1993–94		4	—
1994–95		—	—
1994–95	*Blackpool*	7	—
1994–95	*Oldham Ath*	5	—
1995–96	Everton	—	—
1995–96	*Carlisle U*	13	—
1995–96	*Rotherham U*	11	—

MOORE, Richard

Born Scunthorpe 2.9.77 Ht 6 2 Wt 13 07
Goalkeeper. From Trainee. England Youth.

Season	Club	League Appearances/Goals	
1994–95	Everton	—	—
1995–96		—	—

MOORS, Christopher

Born Yeovil 18.8.76
Defender. From West Ham U Trainee.

Season	Club	League Appearances/Goals	
1995–96	Torquay U	1	—

MORAH, Ollie

Born Islington 30.9.72 Ht 6 1 Wt 13 04
Forward. From Trainee.

Season	Club	League Appearances/Goals	
1991–92	Tottenham H	—	—
1991–92	*Hereford U*	2	—
1992–93	Tottenham H	—	—
1992–93	Swindon T	—	—
From Sutton U			
1994–95	Cambridge U	14	2
1994–95	*Torquay U*	2	—
1995–96	Cambridge U	—	—

MORALEE, Jamie

Born Wandsworth 2.12.71 Ht 5 11
Wt 11 00
Forward. From Trainee.

Season	Club	League Appearances/Goals	
1989–90	Crystal Palace	—	—
1990–91		—	—
1991–92		6	—
1992–93		—	—
1992–93	Millwall	37	15

Season Club League Appearances/Goals

Season	Club	Apps	Goals
1993–94		30	4
1994–95	Watford	24	4
1995–96		25	3

MORAN, Paul

Born Enfield 22.5.68 Ht 5 10 Wt 12 07
Forward. From Trainee.

Season	Club	Apps	Goals
1984–85	Tottenham H	—	—
1985–86		—	—
1986–87		1	—
1987–88		13	1
1988–89		8	—
1988–89	*Portsmouth*	3	—
1989–90	Tottenham H	5	1
1989–90	*Leicester C*	10	1
1990–91	Tottenham H	1	—
1990–91	*Newcastle U*	1	—
1990–91	*Southend U*	1	—
1991–92	Tottenham H	—	—
1992–93		3	—
1992–93	*Cambridge U*	—	—
1993–94	Tottenham H	5	—
1994–95	Peterborough U	7	—
1995–96		—	—

MORENO, Jaime

Born Bolivia 19.1.74 Ht 5 9 Wt 11 09
Forward. From Blooming. Bolivia full caps.

Season	Club	Apps	Goals
1994–95	Middlesbrough	14	1
1995–96		7	—

MORGAN, Alan

Born Aberystwyth 2.11.73 Ht 5 10
Wt 11 02
Defender. From Trainee. Wales Under-21.

Season	Club	Apps	Goals
1991–92	Tranmere R	—	—
1992–93		—	—
1993–94		—	—
1994–95		—	—
1995–96		4	1

MORGAN, Ian

Born Birmingham 11.10.77 Ht 6 2
Wt 12 10
Defender. From Trainee.

Season	Club	Apps	Goals
1994–95	Nottingham F	—	—
1995–96		—	—

MORGAN, Jamie

Born Plymouth 1.10.75 Ht 5 11
Wt 12 00
Midfield. From Trainee.

Season	Club	Apps	Goals
1992–93	Plymouth Arg	3	—
1993–94		—	—
1994–95		8	—
1995–96	Exeter C	6	—

MORGAN, Matthew

Born Swansea 24.2.77
Defender.

Season	Club	Apps	Goals
1995–96	Swansea C	—	—

MORGAN, Philip

Born Stoke 18.12.74 Ht 6 1 Wt 13 00
Goalkeeper. From Trainee.

Season	Club	Apps	Goals
1993–94	Ipswich T	—	—
1994–95		1	—
1995–96		—	—
1995–96	Stoke C	—	—

MORGAN, Simon

Born Birmingham 5.9.66 Ht 5 10
Wt 12 05
Midfield. From Trainee. England Under-21.

Season	Club	Apps	Goals
1984–85	Leicester C	—	—
1985–86		30	—
1986–87		41	1
1987–88		40	—
1988–89		32	—
1989–90		17	2
1990–91		—	—
1990–91	Fulham	32	—
1991–92		36	3
1992–93		39	8
1993–94		37	6
1994–95		42	11
1995–96		41	6

MORGAN, Steve

Born Oldham 19.9.68 Ht 5 9 Wt 11 00
Defender. From Apprentice. England Youth.

Season	Club	Apps	Goals
1985–86	Blackpool	5	—
1986–87		11	—
1987–88		46	6
1988–89		44	3
1989–90		38	1

Season Club League Appearances/Goals

Season Club League Appearances/Goals

1990–91 Plymouth Arg 40 3
1991–92 .... 45 2
1992–93 .... 36 1
1993–94 Coventry C 40 2
1994–95 .... 28 —
1995–96 .... — —
1995–96 *Bristol R* .... 5 —

MORGAN, Thomas

Born Dublin 30.3.77 Ht 5 8 Wt 10 08
Midfield. From Belvedere, Trainee.

1993–94 Blackburn R .... — —
1994–95 .... — —
1995–96 .... — —

MORLEY, David

Born St Helens 25.9.77
Defender. From Trainee.

1995–96 Manchester C .... — —

MORLEY, Trevor

Born Nottingham 20.3.61 Ht 5 11
Wt 12 01
Forward. From Derby Co, Corby T, Nuneaton.

1985–86 Northampton T 43 13
1986–87 .... 37 16
1987–88 .... 27 10
1987–88 Manchester C 15 4
1988–89 .... 40 12
1989–90 .... 17 2
1989–90 West Ham U 19 10
1990–91 .... 38 12
1991–92 .... 24 2
1992–93 .... 41 20
1993–94 .... 42 13
1994–95 .... 14 —
1995–96 Reading 17 4

MORRIS, Andy

Born Sheffield 17.11.67 Ht 6 4 Wt 15 10
Forward.

1984–85 Rotherham U .... 1 —
1985–86 .... — —
1986–87 .... 6 —
1987–88 .... — —
1987–88 Chesterfield .... 10 —
1988–89 .... 42 9
1989–90 .... 43 4
1990–91 .... 15 4
1991–92 .... 8 2
1991–92 *Exeter C* 7 2
1992–93 Chesterfield 40 10
1993–94 .... 34 11
1994–95 .... 26 6
1995–96 .... 16 5

MORRIS, Chris

Born Newquay 24.12.63 Ht 5 11
Wt 11 11
Defender. From England Schools. Eire 35 full caps.

1982–83 Sheffield W .... — —
1983–84 .... 13 1
1984–85 .... 14 —
1985–86 .... 30 —
1986–87 .... 17 —
1987–88 Celtic 44 3
1988–89 .... 33 3
1989–90 .... 32 1
1990–91 .... 19 —
1991–92 .... 32 1
1992–93 .... 3 —
1992–93 Middlesbrough 25 1
1993–94 .... 15 —
1994–95 .... 15 —
1995–96 .... 23 2

MORRIS, Jody

Born London 22.12.78 Ht 5 5 Wt 9 00
Midfield. From Trainee.

1995–96 Chelsea .... 1 —

MORRIS, Mark

Born Morden 26.9.62 Ht 6 1 Wt 14 02
Defender. From Apprentice.

1980–81 Wimbledon .... — —
1981–82 .... 33 1
1982–83 .... 26 3
1983–84 .... 39 3
1984–85 .... 29 1
1985–86 .... 20 1
1985–86 *Aldershot* .... 14 —
1986–87 Wimbledon .... 21 —
1987–88 Watford 39 1
1988–89 .... 2 —
1989–90 Sheffield U 42 3
1990–91 .... 14 —
1991–92 Bournemouth 43 3
1992–93 .... 43 1
1993–94 .... 38 —

Season	Club	League Appearances	Goals
1994–95		38	3
1995–96		31	1

MORRIS, Steve

Born Liverpool 13.5.76 Ht 5 10
Wt 12 00
Forward. From Liverpool Trainee.

Season	Club	League Appearances	Goals
1994–95	Wrexham	12	2
1995–96		13	3

MORRISH, Luke

Born Greenwich 14.11.77 Ht 6 1
Wt 11 00
Defender. From Trainee.

Season	Club	League Appearances	Goals
1995–96	Southend U	—	—

MORRISON, Andy

Born Inverness 30.7.70 Ht 5 11
Wt 13 10
Defender. From Trainee.

Season	Club	League Appearances	Goals
1987–88	Plymouth Arg	1	—
1988–89		2	—
1989–90		19	1
1990–91		32	2
1991–92		30	3
1992–93		29	—
1993–94	Blackburn R	5	—
1994–95		—	—
1994–95	Blackpool	18	—
1995–96		29	3

MORRISON, David

Born Waltham Forest 30.11.74 Ht 5 11
Wt 12 10
Forward. From Chelmsford C.

Season	Club	League Appearances	Goals
1993–94	Peterborough U	—	—
1994–95		42	8
1995–96		24	2

MORRISSEY, John

Born Liverpool 8.3.65 Ht 5 8 Wt 11 10
Forward. From Apprentice. England Youth.

Season	Club	League Appearances	Goals
1982–83	Everton	—	—
1983–84		—	—
1984–85		1	—
1985–86	Wolverhampton W	10	1
1985–86	Tranmere R	32	5
1986–87		38	7
1987–88		39	4
1988–89		42	4
1989–90		27	4
1990–91		40	9
1991–92		40	5
1992–93		43	5
1993–94		25	1
1994–95		36	3
1995–96		16	—

MORROW, Steve

Born Belfast 2.7.70 Ht 5 11 Wt 12 02
Defender. From Trainee. Northern Ireland Youth, Under-23, 19 full caps.

Season	Club	League Appearances	Goals
1987–88	Arsenal	—	—
1988–89		—	—
1989–90		—	—
1990–91	*Reading*	10	—
1991–92	Arsenal	2	—
1991–92	*Watford*	8	—
1991–92	*Reading*	3	—
1991–92	*Barnet*	1	—
1992–93	Arsenal	16	—
1993–94		11	—
1994–95		15	1
1995–96		4	—

MORTIMER, Paul

Born Kensington 8.5.68 Ht 5 11
Wt 11 03
Midfield. From Fulham Apprentice. England Under-21.

Season	Club	League Appearances	Goals
1987–88	Charlton Ath	12	—
1988–89		33	5
1989–90		36	5
1990–91		32	7
1991–92	Aston Villa	12	1
1991–92	Crystal Palace	21	2
1992–93		1	—
1992–93	*Brentford*	6	—
1993–94	Crystal Palace	—	—
1994–95	Charlton Ath	26	4
1995–96		19	5

MOSES, Adrian

Born Doncaster 4.5.75 Ht 5 8 Wt 12 08
Defender. From School.

Season	Club	League Appearances	Goals
1993–94	Barnsley	—	—
1994–95		4	—
1995–96		24	1

Season Club League Appearances/Goals

MOSS, David

Born Doncaster 15.11.68 Ht 6 2
Wt 13 03
Forward. From Boston U.

Season	Club	Apps	Goals
1992–93	Doncaster R	9	3
1993–94		9	2
1993–94	Chesterfield	26	6
1994–95		32	10
1995–96		13	—

MOSS, Neil

Born New Milton 10.5.75 Ht 6 2
Wt 12 13
Goalkeeper. From Trainee.

Season	Club	Apps	Goals
1992–93	Bournemouth	1	—
1993–94		6	—
1994–95		8	—
1995–96		7	—
1995–96	Southampton	—	—

MOULDEN, Paul

Born Farnworth 6.9.67 Ht 5 8 Wt 11 03
Forward. From Apprentice. England Youth.

Season	Club	Apps	Goals
1984–85	Manchester C	—	—
1985–86		2	—
1986–87		20	5
1987–88		6	—
1988–89		36	13
1989–90	Bournemouth	32	13
1989–90	Oldham Ath	8	—
1990–91		24	3
1991–92		2	1
1992–93		4	—
1992–93	*Brighton & HA*	11	5
1992–93	Birmingham C	13	6
1993–94		7	—
1994–95		—	—
1994–95	Huddersfield T	2	—
1995–96	Rochdale	16	1

MOUNTFIELD, Derek

Born Liverpool 2.11.62 Ht 6 0 Wt 13 06
Defender. From Apprentice. England Under-21, B.

Season	Club	Apps	Goals
1980–81	Tranmere R	5	—
1981–82		21	1
1982–83	Everton	1	—
1983–84		31	3
1984–85		37	10
1985–86		15	3
1986–87		13	3
1987–88		9	—
1988–89	Aston Villa	24	1
1989–90		32	4
1990–91		32	4
1991–92		2	—
1991–92	Wolverhampton W	28	1
1992–93		36	2
1993–94		19	1
1994–95	Carlisle U	31	3
1995–96		—	—
1995–96	Northampton T	4	—
1995–96	Walsall	28	1

MOUSSADDIK, Chuck

Born Morocco 23.2.70 Ht 6 0 Wt 13 00
Goalkeeper. From Wimbledon.

Season	Club	Apps	Goals
1993–94	Wycombe W	—	—
1994–95		—	—
1995–96		1	—
1995–96	Barnet	—	—

MOWBRAY, Tony

Born Saltburn 22.11.63 Ht 6 1 Wt 13 00
Defender. From Apprentice. England B.

Season	Club	Apps	Goals
1981–82	Middlesbrough	—	—
1982–83		26	—
1983–84		35	1
1984–85		40	2
1985–86		35	4
1986–87		46	7
1987–88		44	3
1988–89		37	3
1989–90		28	2
1990–91		40	3
1991–92		17	—
1991–92	Celtic	15	2
1992–93		26	2
1993–94		22	1
1994–95		15	1
1995–96	Ipswich T	19	2

MOYES, David

Born Glasgow 25.4.63 Ht 6 1 Wt 12 09
Defender. From Drumchapel A.

Season	Club	Apps	Goals
1980–81	Celtic	—	—
1981–82		19	—
1982–83		5	—
1983–84		—	—
1983–84	Cambridge U	30	—

Season	Club	League Appearances/Goals	
1984–85		40	1
1985–86		9	—
1985–86	Bristol C	27	2
1986–87		41	3
1987–88		15	1
1987–88	Shrewsbury T	17	2
1988–89		33	1
1989–90		46	8
1990–91	Dunfermline Ath	35	7
1991–92		39	5
1992–93		30	1
1993–94		1	—
1993–94	Hamilton A	5	—
1993–94	Preston NE	29	4
1994–95		38	4
1995–96		41	3

MUDD, Paul

Born Hull 13.11.70 Ht 5 9 Wt 11 04
Defender. From Trainee.

Season	Club	Apps	Goals
1988–89	Hull C	1	—
1989–90		—	—
1990–91	Scarborough	24	—
1991–92		36	1
1992–93		38	1
1993–94	Scunthorpe U	33	3
1994–95		35	1
1995–96	Lincoln C	4	—

MUGGLETON, Carl

Born Leicester 13.9.68 Ht 6 1 Wt 12 13
Goalkeeper. From Apprentice. England Under-21.

Season	Club	Apps	Goals
1986–87	Leicester C	—	—
1987–88		—	—
1987–88	*Chesterfield*	17	—
1987–88	*Blackpool*	2	—
1988–89	Leicester C	3	—
1988–89	*Hartlepool U*	8	—
1989–90	Leicester C	—	—
1989–90	*Stockport Co*	4	—
1990–91	Leicester C	22	—
1990–91	*Liverpool*	—	—
1991–92	Leicester C	4	—
1992–93		17	—
1993–94		—	—
1993–94	*Stoke C*	6	—
1993–94	*Sheffield U*	—	—
1993–94	Celtic	12	—
1994–95	Stoke C	24	—
1995–96		6	—
1995–96	*Rotherham U*	6	—
1995–96	*Sheffield U*	1	—

MUIR, Ian

Born Coventry 5.5.63 Ht 5 8 Wt 11 00
Forward. From Apprentice. England Youth.

Season	Club	Apps	Goals
1980–81	QPR	2	2
1981–82		—	—
1982–83		—	—
1982–83	*Burnley*	2	1
1983–84	Birmingham C	1	—
1983–84	Brighton & HA	2	—
1984–85		2	—
1984–85	*Swindon T*	2	—
1985–86	Tranmere R	32	14
1986–87		46	20
1987–88		43	27
1988–89		46	21
1989–90		46	23
1990–91		35	13
1991–92		20	5
1992–93		11	2
1993–94		16	9
1994–95		19	7
1995–96	Birmingham C	1	—
1995–96	*Darlington*	4	1

MULLIGAN, James

Born Dublin 21.4.74 Ht 5 6 Wt 11 07
Forward. From Trainee.

Season	Club	Apps	Goals
1992–93	Stoke C	—	—
1993–94		—	—
1993–94	*Bury*	3	1
1994–95	Bury	15	2
1995–96		2	—

MULLIN, John

Born Bury 11.8.75 Ht 6 0 Wt 11 08
Forward. From School.

Season	Club	Apps	Goals
1992–93	Burnley	—	—
1993–94		6	1
1994–95		12	1
1995–96	Sunderland	10	1

MULRYNE, Philip

Born Belfast 1.1.78 Ht 5 8 Wt 10 04
Forward. From Trainee.

Season	Club	Apps	Goals
1994–95	Manchester U	—	—
1995–96		—	—

Season Club League Appearances/Goals

MUNDAY, Stuart

Born Newham 28.9.72 Ht 5 11 Wt 11 00
Defender. From Trainee.

Season	Club	Apps	Goals
1990–91	Brighton & HA	—	—
1991–92		14	1
1992–93		7	—
1993–94		34	1
1994–95		31	2
1995–96		9	—

MUNDEE, Denny

Born Swindon 10.10.68 Ht 5 10
Wt 13 00
Forward. From Apprentice.

Season	Club	Apps	Goals
1986–87	QPR	—	—
1986–87	Swindon T	—	—
1987–88	Bournemouth	—	—
1988–89		2	—
1989–90		10	—
1989–90	*Torquay U*	9	—
1990–91	Bournemouth	21	2
1991–92		41	2
1992–93		26	2
1993–94	Brentford	39	11
1994–95		39	5
1995–96		6	—
1995–96	Brighton & HA	32	3

MUNGALL, Steve

Born Bellshill 22.5.58 Ht 5 8 Wt 11 12
Defender.

Season	Club	Apps	Goals
1976–77	Motherwell	3	—
1977–78		13	—
1978–79		4	—
1979–80	Tranmere R	24	—
1980–81		38	3
1981–82		44	1
1982–83		31	1
1983–84		26	—
1984–85		23	—
1985–86		46	1
1986–87		46	—
1987–88		45	—
1988–89		42	1
1989–90		17	1
1990–91		33	1
1991–92		18	—
1992–93		35	3
1993–94		12	—
1994–95		26	1
1995–96		6	—

MUNRO, Stuart

Born Falkirk 15.9.62 Ht 5 8 Wt 10 05
Defender. From Bo'ness U. Scotland B.

Season	Club	Apps	Goals
1980–81	St Mirren	1	—
1981–82		—	—
1982–83	Alloa	39	5
1983–84		21	1
1983–84	Rangers	5	—
1984–85		13	—
1985–86		29	—
1986–87		43	—
1987–88		17	—
1988–89		22	2
1989–90		36	1
1990–91		14	—
1991–92	Blackburn R	1	—
1992–93		—	—
1992–93	Bristol C	16	—
1993–94		44	—
1994–95		31	—
1995–96		3	—
1995–96	Falkirk	13	—

MURDOCK, Colin

Born Ballymena 2.7.75 Ht 6 3 Wt 12 13
Defender. From Trainee.

Season	Club	Apps	Goals
1992–93	Manchester U	—	—
1993–94		—	—
1994–95		—	—
1995–96		—	—

MURFIN, Andrew

Born Doncaster 26.11.77
Midfield.

Season	Club	Apps	Goals
1995–96	Scunthorpe U	1	—

MURPHY, Brendan

Born Wexford 19.8.75 Ht 5 11 Wt 11 12
Goalkeeper. From Bradford C Trainee.

Season	Club	Apps	Goals
1994–95	Wimbledon	—	—
1995–96		—	—

MURPHY, Danny

Born Chester 18.3.77 Ht 5 9 Wt 10 08
Midfield. From Trainee. England Youth.

Season	Club	Apps	Goals
1993–94	Crewe Alex	12	2
1994–95		35	5
1995–96		42	10

Season Club League Appearances/Goals

MURPHY, Jamie

Born Manchester 25.2.73 Ht 6 1
Wt 13 00
Defender. From Trainee.

Season	Club	Apps	Goals
1991–92	Blackpool	—	—
1992–93		33	—
1993–94		16	—
1994–95		6	1
1995–96		—	—
1995–96	Doncaster R	23	—

MURPHY, John

Born Whiston 18.10.76 Ht 6 1 Wt 14 00
Forward. From Trainee.

Season	Club	Apps	Goals
1994–95	Chester C	5	—
1995–96		18	3

MURPHY, Matt

Born Northampton 20.8.71 Ht 6 0
Wt 12 02
Forward. From Corby.
From Corby

Season	Club	Apps	Goals
1992–93	Oxford U	2	—
1993–94		—	—
1994–95		22	7
1995–96		34	5

MURPHY, Shaun

Born Sydney 5.11.70 Ht 6 1 Wt 12 00
Defender. From Perth Italia.

Season	Club	Apps	Goals
1992–93	Notts Co	8	1
1993–94		11	1
1994–95		35	—
1995–96		39	3

MURPHY, Stephen

Born Dublin 5.4.78 Ht 5 11 Wt 12 00
Midfield. From Belvedere.

Season	Club	Apps	Goals
1994–95	Huddersfield T	—	—
1995–96		—	—

MURRAY, Edwin

Born Redbridge 31.8.73 Ht 5 11
Wt 12 00
Defender. From Trainee.

Season	Club	Apps	Goals
1990–91	Swindon T	1	—
1991–92		—	—
1992–93		—	—
1993–94		—	—
1994–95		6	—
1995–96		5	1

MURRAY, Nathan

Born South Shields 10.9.75 Ht 6 1
Wt 12 07
Defender. From Trainee. England Schools, Youth.

Season	Club	Apps	Goals
1992–93	Newcastle U	—	—
1993–94		—	—
1994–95		—	—
1995–96		—	—
1995–96	Carlisle U	—	—

MURRAY, Neil

Born Bellshill 21.2.73 Ht 5 9 Wt 10 10
Midfield. From Rangers Ams. Scotland Under-21.

Season	Club	Apps	Goals
1989–90	Rangers	—	—
1990–91		—	—
1991–92		—	—
1992–93		16	—
1993–94		22	—
1994–95		20	1
1995–96		5	—

MURRAY, Paul

Born Carlisle 31.8.76 Ht 5 9 Wt 10 03
Midfield. From Trainee. England Youth.

Season	Club	Apps	Goals
1993–94	Carlisle U	8	—
1994–95		5	—
1995–96		28	1
1995–96	QPR	1	—

MURRAY, Robert

Born Hammersmith 31.10.74 Ht 5 11
Wt 12 07
Forward. From Trainee. Scotland Under-21.

Season	Club	Apps	Goals
1992–93	Bournemouth	25	4
1993–94		20	4
1994–95		31	—
1995–96		35	2

MURRAY, Scott

Born Aberdeen 26.5.74 Ht 5 10
Wt 11 00
Forward. From Fraserburgh.

Season	Club	Apps	Goals
1993–94	Aston Villa	—	—

Season	Club	Apps	Goals
1994–95		—	—
1995–96		3	—

MURRAY, Shaun

Born Newcastle 7.2.70 Ht 5 8 Wt 10 11
Midfield. From Trainee. England Youth.

Season	Club	Apps	Goals
1987–88	Tottenham H	—	—
1988–89		—	—
1989–90	Portsmouth	—	—
1990–91		25	1
1991–92		2	—
1992–93		7	—
1993–94		—	—
1993–94	*Millwall*	—	—
1993–94	Scarborough	29	5
1994–95	Bradford C	41	5
1995–96		34	2

MURTY, Graeme

Born Middlesbrough 13.11.74 Ht 5 10
Wt 11 12
Midfield. From Trainee.

Season	Club	Apps	Goals
1992–93	York C	—	—
1993–94		1	—
1994–95		20	2
1995–96		35	2

MUSSELWHITE, Paul

Born Portsmouth 22.12.68 Ht 6 2
Wt 12 09
Goalkeeper.

Season	Club	Apps	Goals
1987–88	Portsmouth	—	—
1988–89	Scunthorpe U	41	—
1989–90		29	—
1990–91		38	—
1991–92		24	—
1992–93	Port Vale	41	—
1993–94		46	—
1994–95		44	—
1995–96		39	—

MUSTOE, Neil

Born Gloucester 5.11.76 Ht 5 8
Wt 12 00
Forward. From Trainee.

Season	Club	Apps	Goals
1995–96	Manchester U	—	—

MUSTOE, Robbie

Born Oxford 28.8.68 Ht 5 10 Wt 11 10
Midfield.

Season	Club	Apps	Goals
1986–87	Oxford U	3	—
1987–88		17	—
1988–89		33	3
1989–90		38	7
1990–91	Middlesbrough	41	4
1991–92		30	2
1992–93		23	1
1993–94		38	2
1994–95		27	3
1995–96		21	1

MUTCH, Andy

Born Liverpool 28.12.63 Ht 5 10
Wt 11 00
Forward. From Southport. England Under-21, B.

Season	Club	Apps	Goals
1985–86	Wolverhampton W	15	7
1986–87		41	11
1987–88		46	19
1988–89		45	21
1989–90		37	11
1990–91		29	8
1991–92		37	10
1992–93		39	9
1993–94	Swindon T	30	6
1994–95		20	—
1995–96		—	—
1995–96	*Wigan Ath*	7	1
1995–96	Stockport Co	11	4

MYALL, Stuart

Born Eastbourne 12.11.74 Ht 5 10
Wt 12 12
Midfield. From Trainee.

Season	Club	Apps	Goals
1992–93	Brighton & HA	7	—
1993–94		13	—
1994–95		27	2
1995–96		33	2

MYERS, Andy

Born Hounslow 3.11.73 Ht 5 10
Wt 12 11
Midfield. From Trainee. England Schools, Youth, Under-21.

Season	Club	Apps	Goals
1990–91	Chelsea	3	—
1991–92		11	1
1992–93		3	—

Season	Club	League Appearances/Goals	
1993–94		6	—
1994–95		10	—
1995–96		20	—

MYERS, Chris

Born Yeovil 1.4.69 Ht 5 10 Wt 11 10
Midfield. From Apprentice.

Season	Club	Apps	Goals
1986–87	Torquay U	9	—
From Local			
1990–91		29	2
1991–92		39	4
1992–93		28	1
1993–94	Dundee U	5	—
1993–94	*Torquay U*	6	—
1994–95	Dundee U	1	—
1995–96	Wrexham	—	—
1995–96	Scarborough	9	—
1995–96	Exeter C	8	—

NAPIER, Craig

Born East Kilbride 14.11.65 Ht 5 9
Wt 10 10
Midfield. From Kirkton Utd.

Season	Club	Apps	Goals
1984–85	Clyde	—	—
1985–86		8	—
1986–87		42	—
1987–88		42	1
1988–89		14	—
1988–89	Hamilton A	20	—
1989–90		39	6
1990–91		39	6
1991–92		22	2
1992–93		29	1
1993–94		27	2
1993–94	Kilmarnock	15	—
1994–95		3	—
1995–96	Falkirk	4	—
1995–96	Ayr U	10	—

NARBETT, Jon

Born Birmingham 21.11.68 Ht 5 10
Wt 12 02
Midfield. From Apprentice.

Season	Club	Apps	Goals
1986–87	Shrewsbury T	1	—
1987–88		25	3
1988–89		—	—
1988–89	Hereford U	36	7
1989–90		36	5
1990–91		44	11
1991–92		33	8
1991–92	*Leicester C*	—	—
1992–93	Oxford U	14	—
1993–94		1	—
1994–95	Chesterfield	3	—
1995–96		17	1

NAYLOR, Dominic

Born Watford 12.8.70 Ht 5 9 Wt 12 12
Defender. From Trainee.

Season	Club	Apps	Goals
1988–89	Watford	—	—
1989–90		—	—
1989–90	Halifax T	6	1
From Barnet			
1991–92	Barnet	26	—
1992–93		25	—
1993–94	Plymouth Arg	43	—
1994–95		42	—
1995–96	Gillingham	31	1

Season	Club	League Appearances/Goals	

NAYLOR, Glenn

Born York 11.8.72 Ht 5 11 Wt 11 00
Forward. From Trainee.

1989–90	York C	1	—
1990–91		20	5
1991–92		21	8
1992–93		4	—
1993–94		10	1
1994–95		29	9
1995–96		25	7
1995–96	*Darlington*	4	1

NAYLOR, Richard

Born Leeds 28.2.77 Ht 6 1 Wt 13 07
Forward. From Trainee.

1995–96	Ipswich T	—	—

NAYLOR, Stuart

Born Wetherby 6.12.62 Ht 6 4 Wt 12 02
Goalkeeper. From Yorkshire A. England Youth, B.

1980–81	Lincoln C	—	—
1981–82		3	—
1982–83		1	—
1982–83	*Peterborough U*	8	—
1983–84	Lincoln C	—	—
1983–84	*Crewe Alex*	38	—
1984–85		17	—
1984–85	Lincoln C	25	—
1985–86		20	—
1985–86	WBA	12	—
1986–87		42	—
1987–88		35	—
1988–89		44	—
1989–90		39	—
1990–91		28	—
1991–92		34	—
1992–93		32	—
1993–94		20	—
1994–95		42	—
1995–96		27	—

NAYLOR, Tony

Born Manchester 29.3.67 Ht 5 6 Wt 9 00
Forward. From Droylsden.

1989–90	Crewe Alex	2	—
1990–91		14	1
1991–92		34	15
1992–93		35	16
1993–94		37	13
1994–95	Port Vale	33	9
1995–96		39	11

NAYSMITH, Gary

Born Edinburgh 16.11.78
Forward. From Whitehill Welfare Colts. Scotland Under-18.

1995–96	Hearts	1	—

NDAH, George

Born Camberwell 23.12.74 Ht 6 1 Wt 11 04
Midfield. From Trainee.

1992–93	Crystal Palace	13	—
1993–94		1	—
1994–95		12	1
1995–96		23	4
1995–96	*Bournemouth*	12	2

NDAH, Jamie

Born East Dulwich 5.8.71 Ht 6 2 Wt 11 13
Forward. From Kingstonian.

1995–96	Torquay U	16	3

NDLOVU, Peter

Born Zimbabwe 25.2.73 Ht 5 8 Wt 10 2
Forward. From Highlanders. Zimbabwe 37 full caps.

1991–92	Coventry C	23	2
1992–93		32	7
1993–94		40	11
1994–95		30	11
1995–96		32	5

NEAL, Ashley

Born Liverpool 16.12.74 Ht 6 0 Wt 11 10
Midfield. From Trainee.

1992–93	Liverpool	—	—
1993–94		—	—
1994–95		—	—
1995–96		—	—

NEIL, James

Born Bury St Edmunds 28.2.76 Ht 5 9 Wt 10 05
Defender. From Trainee.

1994–95	Grimsby T	—	—
1995–96		1	—

NEILL, Lucas

Born Australia 9.3.78 Ht 6 1 Wt 12 00
Midfield.

1995–96	Millwall	13	—

Season	Club	League Appearances/Goals	

NEILL, Warren

Born Acton 21.11.62 Ht 5 9 Wt 11 05
Midfield. From Apprentice. England Schools.

Season	Club	Apps	Goals
1980–81	QPR	4	—
1981–82		11	—
1982–83		39	2
1983–84		41	1
1984–85		18	—
1985–86		16	—
1986–87		29	—
1987–88		23	—
1988–89	Portsmouth	43	—
1989–90		37	—
1990–91		30	—
1991–92		38	—
1992–93		28	—
1993–94		35	2
1994–95		7	—
1995–96	Watford	1	—

NEILSON, Alan

Born Wegburg 26.9.72 Ht 5 11 Wt 12 09
Defender. From Trainee. Wales Under-21, 4 full caps.

Season	Club	Apps	Goals
1990–91	Newcastle U	3	—
1991–92		16	1
1992–93		3	—
1993–94		14	—
1994–95		6	—
1995–96	Southampton	18	—

NELSON, Craig

Born Coatbridge 28.5.71 Ht 6 1
Wt 13 00
Goalkeeper. From Ashfield.

Season	Club	Apps	Goals
1990–91	Partick T	1	—
1991–92		11	—
1992–93		27	—
1993–94		39	—
1994–95		13	—
1994–95	Hearts	20	—
1995–96		4	—

NELSON, Garry

Born Braintree 16.1.61 Ht 5 10
Wt 11 10
Forward. From Amateur.

Season	Club	Apps	Goals
1979–80	Southend U	22	2
1980–81		22	3
1981–82		40	4
1982–83		45	8
1983–84	Swindon T	36	4
1984–85		43	3
1985–86	Plymouth Arg	42	13
1986–87		32	7
1987–88	Brighton & HA	42	22
1988–89		46	15
1989–90		33	4
1990–91		23	5
1990–91	*Notts Co*	2	—
1991–92	Charlton Ath	41	6
1992–93		44	6
1993–94		43	15
1994–95		27	7
1995–96		30	3

NETHERCOTT, Stuart

Born Chadwell Heath 21.3.73 Ht 5 11
Wt 13 08
Defender. From Trainee. England Under-21.

Season	Club	Apps	Goals
1991–92	Tottenham H	—	—
1991–92	*Maidstone U*	13	1
1991–92	*Barnet*	3	—
1992–93	Tottenham H	5	—
1993–94		10	—
1994–95		17	—
1995–96		13	—

NEVES, Rui

Born Portugal 10.3.65
Forward. From Famalicao.

Season	Club	Apps	Goals
1995–96	Darlington	5	—

NEVILLE, Gary

Born Bury 18.2.75 Ht 5 10 Wt 11 11
Defender. From Trainee. England Youth, 14 full caps.

Season	Club	Apps	Goals
1992–93	Manchester U	—	—
1993–94		1	—
1994–95		18	—
1995–96		31	—

NEVILLE, Philip

Born Bury 21.1.77 Ht 5 10 Wt 11 10
Defender. From Trainee. England Youth, Under-21, 1 full cap.

Season	Club	Apps	Goals
1994–95	Manchester U	2	—
1995–96		24	—

NEVIN, Pat

Born Glasgow 6.9.63 Ht 5 6 Wt 10 07
Forward. From Gartcosh U. Scotland Youth, Under-21, B, 28 full caps.

Season	Club	Apps	Goals
1981–82	Clyde	34	12
1982–83		39	5
1983–84	Chelsea	38	14
1984–85		41	4
1985–86		40	7
1986–87		37	5
1987–88		37	6
1988–89	Everton	25	2
1989–90		30	4
1990–91		37	8
1991–92		17	2
1991–92	*Tranmere R*	8	—
1992–93	Tranmere R	43	13
1993–94		45	8
1994–95		44	4
1995–96		40	3

NEWELL, Mike

Born Liverpool 27.1.65 Ht 6 2 Wt 12 00
Forward. From Liverpool Amateur. England Under-21, B.

Season	Club	Apps	Goals
1983–84	Crewe Alex	3	—
1983–84	Wigan Ath	9	—
1984–85		39	9
1985–86		24	16
1985–86	Luton T	16	6
1986–87		42	12
1987–88		5	—
1987–88	Leicester C	36	8
1988–89		45	13
1989–90	Everton	26	7
1990–91		29	7
1991–92		13	1
1991–92	Blackburn R	20	6
1992–93		40	13
1993–94		28	6
1994–95		12	—
1995–96		30	3

NEWELL, Paul

Born Greenwich 23.2.69 Ht 6 2 Wt 14 07
Goalkeeper. From Trainee.

Season	Club	Apps	Goals
1987–88	Southend U	13	—
1988–89		2	—
1989–90		—	—
1990–91	Leyton Orient	8	—
1991–92		10	—
1992–93		3	—
1992–93	*Colchester U*	14	—
1993–94	Leyton Orient	40	—
1994–95	Barnet	15	—
1995–96		1	—
1995–96	Darlington	21	—

NEWHOUSE, Aidan

Born Wallasey 23.5.72 Ht 6 2 Wt 13 05
Midfield. From Trainee. England Youth.

Season	Club	Apps	Goals
1987–88	Chester C	1	—
1988–89		25	2
1989–90		18	4
1989–90	Wimbledon	2	—
1990–91		8	1
1991–92		12	1
1992–93		1	—
1993–94		—	—
1993–94	*Tranmere R*	—	—
1993–94	*Port Vale*	2	—
1994–95	Wimbledon	—	—
1994–95	*Portsmouth*	6	1
1995–96	Wimbledon	—	—
1995–96	*Torquay U*	4	2

NEWLAND, Ray

Born Liverpool 19.7.71 Ht 6 2 Wt 12 02
Goalkeeper. From Everton Trainee.

Season	Club	Apps	Goals
1992–93	Plymouth Arg	21	—
1993–94		5	—
1994–95	Chester C	10	—
1995–96		—	—
1995–96	Torquay U	17	—

NEWMAN, Ricky

Born Guildford 5.8.70 Ht 5 10 Wt 12 06
Midfield. From Trainee.

Season	Club	Apps	Goals
1987–88	Crystal Palace	—	—
1988–89		—	—
1989–90		—	—
1990–91		—	—
1991–92		—	—
1991–92	*Maidstone U*	10	1
1992–93	Crystal Palace	2	—
1993–94		11	—
1994–95		35	3
1995–96	Millwall	36	1

NEWMAN, Rob

Born Bradford-on-Avon 13.12.63 Ht 6 2 Wt 13 02
Defender. From Apprentice.

Season	Club	Apps	Goals
1981–82	Bristol C	21	3
1982–83		43	3

Season	Club	League Appearances	Goals
1983–84		30	1
1984–85		34	3
1985–86		39	3
1986–87		45	6
1987–88		44	11
1988–89		46	6
1989–90		46	8
1990–91		46	8
1991–92	Norwich C	41	7
1992–93		18	2
1993–94		32	2
1994–95		32	1
1995–96		23	1

NEWSOME, Jon

Born Sheffield 6.9.70 Ht 6 3 Wt 13 10
Defender. From Trainee.

Season	Club	League Appearances	Goals
1989–90	Sheffield W	6	—
1990–91		1	—
1991–92	Leeds U	10	2
1992–93		37	—
1993–94		29	1
1994–95	Norwich C	35	3
1995–96		27	4
1995–96	Sheffield W	8	1

NEWTON, Eddie

Born Hammersmith 13.12.71 Ht 6 0
Wt 12 08
Forward. From Trainee. England Under-21.

Season	Club	League Appearances	Goals
1990–91	Chelsea	—	—
1991–92		1	1
1991–92	*Cardiff C*	18	4
1992–93	Chelsea	34	5
1993–94		36	—
1994–95		30	1
1995–96		24	1

NEWTON, Shaun

Born Camberwell 20.8.75 Ht 5 8 Wt 11 00
Midfield. From Trainee.

Season	Club	League Appearances	Goals
1992–93	Charlton Ath	2	—
1993–94		19	2
1994–95		26	—
1995–96		41	5

NICHOLL, Jimmy

Born Hamilton, Canada 20.12.56 Ht 5 10
Wt 11 10
Defender. From Apprentice. Northern Ireland Under-21, 73 full caps.

Season	Club	League Appearances	Goals
1973–74	Manchester U	—	—
1974–75		1	—
1975–76		20	—
1976–77		30	—
1977–78		37	2
1978–79		21	—
1979–80		42	—
1980–81		36	1
1981–82		1	—
1981–82	Sunderland	3	—
From Toronto Blizzard.			
1982–83		29	—
From Toronto Blizzard.			
1983–84	Rangers	17	—
1984–85	WBA	27	—
1985–86		29	—
1986–87	Rangers	42	—
1987–88		22	—
1988–89		1	—
1989–90	Dunfermline Ath	17	—
1990–91		7	—
1990–91	Raith R	10	—
1991–92		32	1
1992–93		38	5
1993–94		34	1
1994–95		13	—
1995–96		1	—

NICHOLLS, Kevin

Born Newham 2.1.79
Midfield. From Trainee.

Season	Club	League Appearances	Goals
1995–96	Charlton Ath	—	—

NICHOLLS, Mark

Born Hillingdon 30.5.77 Ht 5 9 Wt 9 10
Forward. From Trainee.

Season	Club	League Appearances	Goals
1995–96	Chelsea	—	—

NICHOLSON, Max

Born Leeds 3.10.71 Ht 5 11 Wt 12 07
Forward. From Trainee.

Season	Club	League Appearances	Goals
1989–90	Doncaster R	2	—
1990–91		1	—
1991–92		24	2
1992–93	Hereford U	36	3
1993–94		27	4
1994–95	Torquay U	1	—
1994–95	Scunthorpe U	15	4
1995–96		36	1

NICHOLSON, Shane

Born Newark 3.6.70 Ht 5 10 Wt 11 00
Defender. From Trainee.

Season	Club	League Appearances	Goals
1986–87	Lincoln C	7	—

Season Club League Appearances/Goals

Season	Club	Apps	Goals
1987–88		—	—
1988–89		34	1
1989–90		23	—
1990–91		40	4
1991–92		29	1
1991–92	Derby Co	—	—
1992–93		17	—
1993–94		22	1
1994–95		15	—
1995–96		20	—
1995–96	WBA	18	—

NICOL, Steve

Born Irvine 11.12.61 Ht 5 10 Wt 12 06
Defender. From Ayr U BC. Scotland Under-21, 27 full caps.

Season	Club	Apps	Goals
1979–80	Ayr U	20	2
1980–81		39	3
1981–82		11	2
1981–82	Liverpool	—	—
1982–83		4	—
1983–84		23	5
1984–85		31	5
1985–86		34	4
1986–87		14	3
1987–88		40	6
1988–89		38	2
1989–90		23	6
1990–91		35	3
1991–92		34	1
1992–93		32	—
1993–94		31	1
1994–95		4	—
1994–95	Notts Co	19	—
1995–96		13	2
1995–96	Sheffield W	19	—

NIELSEN, Jimmi

Born Aalborg 6.8.77 Ht 6 3 Wt 12 11
Goalkeeper. From Aalborg.

Season	Club	Apps	Goals
1994–95	Millwall	—	—
1995–96		—	—

NIGHTINGALE, Lewis

Born Greenwich 25.3.79
Midfield. From Trainee.

Season	Club	Apps	Goals
1995–96	Millwall	—	—

NILSEN, Roger

Born Norway 8.8.69 Ht 5 11 Wt 12 02
Defender. From Viking Stavanger. Norway 25 full caps.

Season	Club	Apps	Goals
1993–94	Sheffield U	22	—
1994–95		33	—
1995–96		39	—

NIXON, Eric

Born Manchester 4.10.62 Ht 6 4 Wt 15 07
Goalkeeper. From Curzon Ashton.

Season	Club	Apps	Goals
1983–84	Manchester C	—	—
1984–85		—	—
1985–86		28	—
1986–87		5	—
1986–87	*Wolverhampton W*	16	—
1986–87	*Bradford C*	3	—
1986–87	*Southampton*	4	—
1986–87	*Carlisle U*	16	—
1987–88	Manchester C	25	—
1987–88	*Tranmere R*	8	—
1988–89	Tranmere R	45	—
1989–90		46	—
1990–91		43	—
1991–92		46	—
1992–93		45	—
1993–94		42	—
1994–95		41	—
1995–96		—	—
1995–96	*Blackpool*	20	—

NOGAN, Kurt

Born Cardiff 9.9.70 Ht 5 11 Wt 11 11
Forward. From Trainee. Wales Under-21.

Season	Club	Apps	Goals
1989–90	Luton T	10	2
1990–91		9	—
1991–92		14	1
1992–93	Peterborough U	—	—
1992–93	Brighton & HA	30	20
1993–94		41	22
1994–95		26	7
1994–95	Burnley	15	3
1995–96		46	20

NOGAN, Lee

Born Cardiff 21.5.69 Ht 5 10 Wt 10 08
Forward. From Apprentice. Wales Under-21, B, 2 full caps.

Season	Club	Apps	Goals
1986–87	Oxford U	—	—
1986–87	*Brentford*	11	2

Season Club League Appearances/Goals

Season	Club	Apps	Goals
1987–88	Oxford U	3	—
1987–88	*Southend U*	6	1
1988–89	Oxford U	3	—
1989–90		4	—
1990–91		32	5
1991–92		22	5
1991–92	Watford	23	5
1992–93		42	11
1993–94		26	3
1993–94	*Southend U*	5	—
1994–95	Watford	14	7
1994–95	Reading	20	10
1995–96		39	10

NOLAN, Ian

Born Liverpool 9.7.70 Ht 5 11 Wt 11 11
Defender. From Preston NE Trainee, Northwich Vic, Marine.

Season	Club	Apps	Goals
1991–92	Tranmere R	34	1
1992–93		14	—
1993–94		40	—
1994–95	Sheffield W	42	3
1995–96		29	—

NORBURY, Mike

Born Hemsworth 22.1.69 Ht 6 1 Wt 11 10
Forward. From Ossett, Scarborough, Bridlington.

Season	Club	Apps	Goals
1991–92	Cambridge U	14	2
1992–93		12	1
1992–93	Preston NE	21	8
1993–94		21	5
1994–95		—	—
1994–95	Doncaster R	22	5
1995–96		5	—

NORFOLK, Lee

Born Dunedin NZ 17.10.75 Ht 5 10 Wt 11 03
Midfield. From Trainee.

Season	Club	Apps	Goals
1994–95	Ipswich T	3	—
1995–96		—	—

NORMAN, Craig

Born Perivale 21.3.75 Ht 5 11 Wt 11 11
Defender. From Trainee.

Season	Club	Apps	Goals
1993–94	Chelsea	—	—
1994–95		—	—
1995–96		—	—

NORMAN, Tony

Born Mancot 24.2.58 Ht 6 1 Wt 13 08
Goalkeeper. From Amateur. Wales B, 5 full caps.

Season	Club	Apps	Goals
1976–77	Burnley	—	—
1977–78		—	—
1978–79		—	—
1979–80		—	—
1979–80	Hull C	17	—
1980–81		42	—
1981–82		36	—
1982–83		36	—
1983–84		46	—
1984–85		46	—
1985–86		42	—
1986–87		42	—
1987–88		44	—
1988–89		21	—
1988–89	Sunderland	24	—
1989–90		28	—
1990–91		37	—
1991–92		44	—
1992–93		33	—
1993–94		3	—
1994–95		29	—
1995–96	Huddersfield T	3	—

NORTON, David

Born Cannock 3.3.65 Ht 5 8 Wt 11 12
Midfield. From Apprentice. England Youth.

Season	Club	Apps	Goals
1982–83	Aston Villa	—	—
1983–84		—	—
1984–85		2	—
1985–86		20	—
1986–87		20	2
1987–88		2	—
1988–89	Notts Co	8	—
1989–90		15	1
1990–91		4	—
1990–91	*Rochdale*	9	—
1990–91	*Hull C*	15	—
1991–92	Hull C	45	2
1992–93		45	1
1993–94		44	2
1994–95		—	—
1994–95	Northampton T	38	—
1995–96		44	—

 Season Club League Appearances/Goals

NOTEMAN, Kevin

Born Preston 15.10.69 Ht 5 10 Wt 12 02
Forward. From Trainee.

Season	Club	Apps	Goals
1987–88	Leeds U	1	—
1988–89		—	—
1989–90		—	—
1989–90	Doncaster R	30	3
1990–91		42	7
1991–92		34	10
1991–92	Mansfield T	6	—
1992–93		24	4
1993–94		33	5
1994–95		32	6
1995–96	Doncaster R	4	1
1995–96	Chester C	33	9

NTAMARK, Charlie

Born Paddington 22.7.64 Ht 5 9
Wt 11 09
Midfield. From Boreham Wood.
Cameroon full caps.

Season	Club	Apps	Goals
1990–91	Walsall	42	3
1991–92		41	3
1992–93		41	4
1993–94		37	—
1994–95		35	1
1995–96		42	—

NUGENT, Kevin

Born Edmonton 10.4.69 Ht 6 1
Wt 12 04
Forward. From Trainee. Eire Youth.

Season	Club	Apps	Goals
1987–88	Leyton Orient	11	3
1988–89		3	—
1988–89	*Cork C*	—	—
1989–90	Leyton Orient	11	—
1990–91		33	5
1991–92		36	12
1991–92	Plymouth Arg	4	—
1992–93		45	11
1993–94		39	14
1994–95		37	7
1995–96		6	—
1995–96	Bristol C	34	8

NURSE, David

Born Kings Lynn 12.10.76
Goalkeeper. From Trainee.

Season	Club	Apps	Goals
1995–96	Manchester C	—	—

O'BRIEN, Liam

Born Dublin 5.9.64 Ht 6 1 Wt 13 07
Midfield. From Shamrock R. Eire Youth, 15 full caps.

Season	Club	Apps	Goals
1986–87	Manchester U	11	—
1987–88		17	2
1988–89		3	—
1988–89	Newcastle U	20	4
1989–90		19	2
1990–91		33	3
1991–92		40	4
1992–93		33	6
1993–94		6	—
1993–94	Tranmere R	17	1
1994–95		38	1
1995–96		22	4

O'BRIEN, Roy

Born Cork 27.11.74 Ht 6 1 Wt 12 00
Defender. From Trainee.

Season	Club	Apps	Goals
1993–94	Arsenal	—	—
1994–95		—	—
1995–96		—	—

O'CONNELL, Brendan

Born London 12.11.66 Ht 5 9 Wt 12 01
Forward.

Season	Club	Apps	Goals
1984–85	Portsmouth	—	—
1985–86		—	—
1986–87	Exeter C	42	8
1987–88		39	11
1988–89	Burnley	43	13
1989–90		21	4
1989–90	*Huddersfield T*	11	1
1989–90	Barnsley	11	2
1990–91		45	9
1991–92		36	4
1992–93		40	6
1993–94		38	6
1994–95		45	7
1995–96		25	1

O'CONNOR, Derek

Born Dublin 9.3.78 Ht 5 11 Wt 12 01
Goalkeeper. From Crumplin U.

Season	Club	Apps	Goals
1994–95	Huddersfield T	—	—
1995–96		—	—

O'CONNOR, Gary

Born Newtongrange 7.4.74 Ht 6 3 Wt 13 00
Goalkeeper. From Dalkeith T.

Season	Club	Apps	Goals
1991–92	Hearts	—	—

Season	Club	League Appearances/Goals	
1992–93	Berwick R	13	—
1993–94		26	—
1993–94	Hearts	—	—
1994–95		—	—
1995–96		3	—
1995–96	Doncaster R	8	—

O'CONNOR, Jonathan

Born Darlington 29.10.76 Ht 6 0 Wt 11 00
Midfield. From Trainee. England Youth, Under-21.

Season	Club	Apps	Goals
1993–94	Everton	—	—
1994–95		—	—
1995–96		4	—

O'CONNOR, Mark

Born Rochdale 10.3.63 Ht 5 7 Wt 10 11
Midfield. From Apprentice. Eire Under-21.

Season	Club	Apps	Goals
1980–81	QPR	—	—
1981–82		1	—
1982–83		2	—
1983–84		—	—
1983–84	*Exeter C*	38	1
1984–85	Bristol R	46	8
1985–86		34	2
1985–86	Bournemouth	9	1
1986–87		43	7
1987–88		37	2
1988–89		33	2
1989–90		6	—
1989–90	Gillingham	15	1
1990–91		41	3
1991–92		39	3
1992–93		21	1
1993–94	Bournemouth	45	3
1994–95		13	—
1995–96	Gillingham	18	1

O'CONNOR, Martin

Born Walsall 10.12.67 Ht 5 10 Wt 12 10
Midfield. From Bromsgrove R.

Season	Club	Apps	Goals
1992–93	Crystal Palace	—	—
1992–93	*Walsall*	10	1
1993–94	Crystal Palace	2	—
1993–94	Walsall	14	2
1994–95		39	10
1995–96		41	9

O'CONNOR, Paul

Born Easington 17.8.71
Goalkeeper. From Blyth Spartans.

Season	Club	Apps	Goals
1995–96	Hartlepool U	1	—

O'DONNELL, Phillip

Born Bellshill 25.3.72 Ht 5 10 Wt 10 05
Midfield. From X Form. Scotland Under-21, 1 full cap.

Season	Club	Apps	Goals
1990–91	Motherwell	12	—
1991–92		42	4
1992–93		32	4
1993–94		35	7
1994–95		3	—
1994–95	Celtic	27	6
1995–96		15	3

O'HAGAN, Danny

Born Padstow 24.4.76 Ht 6 1 Wt 13 08
Forward. From Trainee.

Season	Club	Apps	Goals
1994–95	Plymouth Arg	3	1
1995–96		6	—

O'HALLORAN, Keith

Born Ireland 10.11.75 Ht 5 9 Wt 11 06
Defender. From Cherry Orchard.

Season	Club	Apps	Goals
1994–95	Middlesbrough	1	—
1995–96		3	—
1995–96	*Scunthorpe U*	7	—

O'HANLON, Kelham

Born Saltburn 16.5.62 Ht 6 1 Wt 13 01
Goalkeeper. From Apprentice. Eire Under-21, 1 full cap.

Season	Club	Apps	Goals
1980–81	Middlesbrough	—	—
1981–82		—	—
1982–83		19	—
1983–84		30	—
1984–85		38	—
1985–86	Rotherham U	46	—
1986–87		40	—
1987–88		40	—
1988–89		46	—
1989–90		43	—
1990–91		33	—
1991–92	Carlisle U	42	—
1992–93		41	—
1993–94	Preston NE	23	—
1994–95	Dundee U	29	—
1995–96		1	—

Season Club League Appearances/Goals

O'KANE, John

Born Nottingham 15.11.74 Ht 5 10
Wt 12 02
Defender. From Trainee.

Season	Club	Apps	Goals
1992–93	Manchester U	—	—
1993–94		—	—
1994–95		—	—
1994–95	*Wimbledon*	—	—
1995–96	Manchester U	1	—

O'KEEFFE, Darren

Born Dublin 29.8.78
Midfield. From Trainee.

Season	Club	Apps	Goals
1995–96	Huddersfield T	—	—

O'LEARY, David

Born London 2.5.58 Ht 6 1 Wt 13 09
Defender. From Apprentice. Eire Youth, 67 full caps.

Season	Club	Apps	Goals
1975–76	Arsenal	27	—
1976–77		33	2
1977–78		41	1
1978–79		37	2
1979–80		34	1
1980–81		24	1
1981–82		40	1
1982–83		36	1
1983–84		36	—
1984–85		36	—
1985–86		35	—
1986–87		39	—
1987–88		23	—
1988–89		26	—
1989–90		34	—
1990–91		21	1
1991–92		25	—
1992–93		11	—
1993–94	Leeds U	10	—
1994–95		—	—
1995–96		—	—

O'LEARY, Kristian

Born Neath 30.8.77
Defender. From Trainee.

Season	Club	Apps	Goals
1995–96	Swansea C	1	—

O'NEIL, Brian

Born Paisley 6.9.72 Ht 6 1 Wt 12 04
Midfield. From X Form. Scotland Under-21, 1 full cap.

Season Club League Appearances/Goals

Season	Club	Apps	Goals
1991–92	Celtic	28	1
1992–93		17	3
1993–94		28	2
1994–95		26	—
1995–96		5	—

O'NEIL, Phil

Born Sidcup 22.10.77 Ht 5 10 Wt 12 00
Midfield. From Trainee.

Season	Club	Apps	Goals
1994–95	Millwall	—	—
1995–96		—	—

O'NEILL, Jon

Born Glasgow 2.1.74 Ht 5 11 Wt 12 00
Forward. From Queen's Park BC.

Season	Club	Apps	Goals
1991–92	Queen's Park	25	6
1992–93		27	6
1993–94		39	18
1994–95	Celtic	1	—
1995–96	Bournemouth	6	—

O'NEILL, Keith

Born Dublin 16.2.76 Ht 6 1 Wt 11 09
Midfield. From Trainee. Eire 6 full caps.

Season	Club	Apps	Goals
1994–95	Norwich C	1	—
1995–96		19	1

O'NEILL, Michael

Born Portadown 5.7.69 Ht 5 11
Wt 10 10
Forward. From Coleraine. Northern Ireland 29 full caps.

Season	Club	Apps	Goals
1987–88	Newcastle U	21	12
1988–89		27	3
1989–90	Dundee U	18	5
1990–91		13	—
1991–92		8	4
1992–93		25	2
1993–94	Hibernian	36	3
1994–95		33	10
1995–96		29	6

O'NEILL, Shane

Born Limavady 20.6.78 Ht 5 10
Wt 12 00
Midfield. From Trainee.

Season	Club	Apps	Goals
1994–95	Nottingham F	—	—
1995–96		—	—

Season Club League Appearances/Goals

O'REILLY, Justin

Born Derby 29.6.73
Midfield. From Gresley R.

Season	Club	Apps	Goals
1995–96	Port Vale	—	—

O'RIORDAN, Don

Born Dublin 14.5.57 Ht 6 0 Wt 12 07
Defender. From Apprentice. Eire Youth, Under-21.

Season	Club	Apps	Goals
1975–76	Derby Co	—	—
1976–77		1	—
1977–78		5	1
1977–78	*Doncaster R*	2	—
From Tulsa			
1978–79	Preston NE	32	—
1979–80		18	—
1980–81		21	—
1981–82		46	4
1982–83		41	4
1983–84	Carlisle U	42	8
1984–85		42	10
1985–86	Middlesbrough	41	2
1986–87	Grimsby T	40	6
1987–88		46	8
1988–89	Notts Co	43	3
1989–90		17	—
1989–90	*Mansfield T*	6	—
1990–91	Notts Co	31	1
1991–92		1	—
1992–93		17	1
1992–93	Torquay U	16	—
1993–94		31	2
1994–95		24	1
1995–96		8	—
1995–96	Scarborough	1	—

O'SHEA, Alan

Born Dublin 21.7.77 Ht 5 10 Wt 10 12
Defender. From Trainee.

Season	Club	Apps	Goals
1994–95	Leeds U	—	—
1995–96		—	—

O'SHEA, Danny

Born Kennington 26.3.63 Ht 6 0
Wt 13 02
Defender. From Apprentice.

Season	Club	Apps	Goals
1980–81	Arsenal	—	—
1981–82		—	—
1982–83		6	—
1983–84		—	—
1983–84	*Charlton Ath*	9	—
1984–85	Exeter C	45	2
1985–86	Southend U	35	9
1986–87		41	2
1987–88		22	—
1988–89		20	1
1989–90	Cambridge U	26	—
1990–91		40	—
1991–92		31	1
1992–93		37	—
1993–94		38	—
1994–95		31	—
1994–95	Northampton T	7	1
1995–96		38	—

O'SULLIVAN, Wayne

Born Akrotiri 25.2.74 Ht 5 8 Wt 10 06
Defender. From Trainee.

Season	Club	Apps	Goals
1992–93	Swindon T	—	—
1993–94		—	—
1994–95		30	—
1995–96		34	3

O'TOOLE, Gavin

Born Dublin 19.9.75 Ht 5 9 Wt 11 00
Midfield. From Trainee.

Season	Club	Apps	Goals
1993–94	Coventry C	—	—
1994–95		—	—
1995–96		—	—

OAKES, Andrew

Born Crewe 11.1.77
Goalkeeper.

Season	Club	Apps	Goals
1995–96	Bury	—	—

OAKES, Michael

Born Northwich 30.10.73 Ht 6 1
Wt 12 07
Goalkeeper. From Trainee. England Under-21.

Season	Club	Apps	Goals
1991–92	Aston Villa	—	—
1992–93		—	—
1993–94		—	—
1993–94	*Scarborough*	1	—
1993–94	*Tranmere R*	—	—
1994–95	Aston Villa	—	—
1995–96		—	—

OAKES, Scott

Born Leicester 5.8.72 Ht 5 11 Wt 11 11
Forward. From Trainee.

Season	Club	Apps	Goals
1989–90	Leicester C	2	—
1990–91		—	—
1991–92		1	—
1991–92	Luton T	21	2
1992–93		44	5
1993–94		36	8
1994–95		43	9
1995–96		29	3

OAKLEY, Matthew

Born Peterborough 17.8.77 Ht 5 10
Wt 12 01
Forward. From Trainee.

Season	Club	Apps	Goals
1994–95	Southampton	1	—
1995–96		10	—

OATWAY, Charlie

Born Hammersmith 28.11.73 Ht 5 6
Wt 10 04
Midfield. From Yeading.

Season	Club	Apps	Goals
1994–95	Cardiff C	30	—
1995–96		2	—
1995–96	Torquay U	24	—

OGDEN, Neil

Born Billinge 29.11.75 Ht 5 10 Wt 11 07
Midfield. From Trainee.

Season	Club	Apps	Goals
1992–93	Wigan Ath	2	—
1993–94		2	—
1994–95		1	—
1995–96		10	—

OGRIZOVIC, Steve

Born Mansfield 12.9.57 Ht 6 5 Wt 15 00
Goalkeeper. From ONRYC.

Season	Club	Apps	Goals
1977–78	Chesterfield	16	—
1977–78	Liverpool	2	—
1978–79		—	—
1979–80		1	—
1980–81		1	—
1981–82		—	—
1982–83	Shrewsbury T	42	—
1983–84		42	—
1984–85	Coventry C	42	—
1985–86		42	—
1986–87		42	1
1987–88		40	—
1988–89		38	—
1989–90		37	—
1990–91		37	—
1991–92		38	—
1992–93		33	—
1993–94		33	—
1994–95		33	—
1995–96		25	—

OLDBURY, Marcus

Born Bournemouth 29.3.76 Ht 5 7
Wt 11 13
Midfield. From Trainee.

Season	Club	Apps	Goals
1994–95	Norwich C	—	—
1995–96	Bournemouth	13	—

OLDFIELD, David

Born Perth, Australia 30.5.68 Ht 6 0
Wt 13 04
Midfield. From Apprentice. England Under-21.

Season	Club	Apps	Goals
1986–87	Luton T	—	—
1987–88		8	3
1988–89		21	1
1988–89	Manchester C	11	3
1989–90		15	3
1989–90	Leicester C	20	5
1990–91		42	7
1991–92		41	4
1992–93		44	5
1993–94		27	4
1994–95		14	1
1994–95	*Millwall*	17	6
1995–96	Luton T	34	2

OLIVER, Keith

Born South Shields 15.1.76 Ht 5 8
Wt 11 00
Midfield. From Trainee.

Season	Club	Apps	Goals
1993–94	Hartlepool U	1	—
1994–95		18	—
1995–96		13	—

OLIVER, Michael

Born Cleveland 2.8.75 Ht 5 10 Wt 12 04
Midfield. From Trainee.

Season	Club	Apps	Goals
1992–93	Middlesbrough	—	—
1993–94		—	—
1994–95	Stockport Co	13	—
1995–96		9	1

Season	Club	League Appearances/Goals	

OLIVER, Neil

Born Berwick 11.4.67 Ht 5 11 Wt 11 10
Defender. From Coldstream.

Season	Club	Apps	Goals
1985–86	Berwick R	5	—
1986–87		37	—
1987–88		12	—
1988–89		39	—
1989–90	Blackburn R	3	—
1990–91		3	—
1991–92	Falkirk	35	—
1992–93		25	—
1993–94		32	2
1994–95		27	—
1995–96		3	—

OLNEY, Ian

Born Luton 17.12.69 Ht 6 1 Wt 12 04
Forward. From Trainee. England Under-21.

Season	Club	Apps	Goals
1988–89	Aston Villa	15	2
1989–90		35	9
1990–91		18	3
1991–92		20	2
1992–93	Oldham Ath	34	12
1993–94		10	1
1994–95		—	—
1995–96		1	—

OLSSON, Paul

Born Hull 24.12.65 Ht 6 0 Wt 12 10
Midfield. From Apprentice.

Season	Club	Apps	Goals
1983–84	Hull C	—	—
1984–85		—	—
1985–86		—	—
1986–87		—	—
1986–87	*Exeter C*	8	—
1987–88	Exeter C	35	2
1988–89	Scarborough	32	4
1989–90		16	1
1989–90	Hartlepool U	23	2
1990–91		31	1
1991–92		46	6
1992–93		39	2
1993–94		32	2
1994–95	Darlington	42	4
1995–96		34	4

OMIGIE, Joe

Born Hammersmith 13.6.72 Ht 6 2 Wt 13 00
Forward. From Donna.

Season	Club	Apps	Goals
1994–95	Brentford	—	—
1995–96		10	—

OMOYIMNI, Emmanuel

Born Nigeria 28.12.77 Ht 5 6 Wt 10 07
Midfield. From Trainee.

Season	Club	Apps	Goals
1994–95	West Ham U	—	—
1995–96		—	—

ONUORA, Iffy

Born Glasgow 28.7.67 Ht 6 1 Wt 13 10
Forward. From British Univ.

Season	Club	Apps	Goals
1989–90	Huddersfield T	20	3
1990–91		43	7
1991–92		41	8
1992–93		39	6
1993–94		22	6
1994–95	Mansfield T	14	7
1995–96		14	1

ONWERE, Udo

Born Hammersmith 9.11.71 Ht 6 0
Wt 11 03
Midfield. From Trainee.

Season	Club	Apps	Goals
1990–91	Fulham	7	1
1991–92		27	3
1992–93		29	3
1993–94		22	—
1994–95	Lincoln C	8	—
1995–96		35	4

ORD, Richard

Born Easington 3.3.69 Ht 6 2 Wt 13 03
Defender. From Trainee. England Under-21.

Season	Club	Apps	Goals
1987–88	Sunderland	8	—
1988–89		34	1
1989–90		7	1
1989–90	*York C*	3	—
1990–91	Sunderland	14	—
1991–92		6	—
1992–93		24	—
1993–94		28	2
1994–95		33	—
1995–96		42	1

ORLYGSSON, Thorvaldur

Born Odense 2.8.66 Ht 5 11 Wt 11 03
Midfield. From FC Akureyi. Iceland 38 full caps.

Season	Club	Apps	Goals
1989–90	Nottingham F	12	1

Season Club League Appearances/Goals

Season	Club	Apps	Goals
1990–91		—	—
1991–92		5	—
1992–93		20	1
1993–94	Stoke C	45	9
1994–95		38	7
1995–96		7	—
1995–96	Oldham Ath	16	—

ORMEROD, Anthony

Born Middlesbrough 31.3.79
Midfield. From Trainee.

Season	Club	Apps	Goals
1995–96	Middlesbrough	—	—

ORMEROD, Mark

Born Bournemouth 5.2.76 Ht 6 0
Wt 12 11
Goalkeeper. From Trainee.

Season	Club	Apps	Goals
1994–95	Brighton & HA	—	—
1995–96		—	—

ORMONDROYD, Ian

Born Bradford 22.9.64 Ht 6 5 Wt 13 07
Forward. From Thackley.

Season	Club	Apps	Goals
1985–86	Bradford C	12	3
1986–87		13	4
1986–87	*Oldham Ath*	10	1
1987–88	Bradford C	37	9
1988–89		25	4
1988–89	Aston Villa	12	1
1989–90		25	4
1990–91		18	1
1991–92		1	—
1991–92	Derby Co	25	8
1991–92	Leicester C	14	1
1992–93		26	2
1993–94		31	4
1994–95		6	—
1994–95	*Hull C*	10	6
1995–96	Bradford C	37	6

ORR, Stephen

Born Belper 19.1.78 Ht 5 7 Wt 10 00
Forward. From Trainee.

Season	Club	Apps	Goals
1994–95	Nottingham F	—	—
1995–96		—	—

OSBORN, Simon

Born New Addington 19.1.72 Ht 5 10
Wt 11 04
Midfield. From Apprentice.

Season	Club	Apps	Goals
1989–90	Crystal Palace	—	—
1990–91		4	—
1991–92		14	2
1992–93		31	2
1993–94		6	1
1994–95	Reading	32	5
1995–96	QPR	9	1
1995–96	Wolverhampton W	21	2

OSBORNE, Wayne

Born Stockton 14.1.77 Ht 5 10 Wt 11 07
Defender. From Trainee.

Season	Club	Apps	Goals
1995–96	York C	6	—

OSMAN, Russell

Born Repton 14.2.59 Ht 5 11 Wt 12 01
Defender. From Apprentice. England Under-21, B, 11 full caps.

Season	Club	Apps	Goals
1975–76	Ipswich T	—	—
1976–77		—	—
1977–78		28	—
1978–79		39	2
1979–80		42	2
1980–81		42	1
1981–82		39	2
1982–83		38	4
1983–84		37	3
1984–85		29	3
1985–86	Leicester C	40	—
1986–87		31	3
1987–88		37	5
1988–89	Southampton	36	—
1989–90		35	5
1990–91		20	1
1991–92		5	—
1991–92	Bristol C	31	2
1992–93		34	—
1993–94		5	1
1994–95		—	—
1994–95	Plymouth Arg	—	—
1995–96		—	—
1995–96	Brighton & HA	12	—
1995–96	Cardiff C	15	—

Season	Club	League Appearances/Goals	

OTTO, Ricky

Born Hackney 9.11.67 Ht 5 10 Wt 11 00
Midfield. From Dartford.

1990–91	Leyton Orient	1	—
1991–92		32	5
1992–93		23	8
1993–94	Southend U	45	13
1994–95		19	4
1994–95	Birmingham C	24	4
1995–96		18	2

OVERSON, Vince

Born Kettering 15.5.62 Ht 6 2 Wt 14 13
Defender. From Apprentice.

1979–80	Burnley	22	—
1980–81		39	1
1981–82		36	4
1982–83		6	—
1983–84		38	—
1984–85		42	1
1985–86		28	—
1986–87	Birmingham C	34	1
1987–88		37	—
1988–89		41	—
1989–90		30	—
1990–91		40	2
1991–92	Stoke C	35	3
1992–93		43	1
1993–94		39	2
1994–95		35	—
1995–96		18	—

OWEN, Dafydd

Born Bangor 3.6.77
Defender. From Trainee.

1995–96	Arsenal	—	—

OWEN, Gareth

Born Chester 21.10.71 Ht 5 7 Wt 12 00
Midfield. From Trainee. Wales Under-21.

1989–90	Wrexham	13	—
1990–91		27	2
1991–92		36	7
1992–93		41	3
1993–94		27	3
1994–95		28	3
1995–96		19	2

Season	Club	League Appearances/Goals	

OWERS, Gary

Born Newcastle 3.10.68 Ht 6 0 Wt 12 07
Midfield. From Apprentice.

1986–87	Sunderland	—	—
1987–88		37	4
1988–89		38	3
1989–90		43	9
1990–91		38	1
1991–92		30	4
1992–93		33	1
1993–94		30	2
1994–95		19	1
1994–95	Bristol C	21	2
1995–96		37	2

OXLEY, Scott

Born Sheffield 22.11.77 Ht 5 9 Wt 12 00
Midfield. From Trainee.

1995–96	York C	2	—

Season Club League Appearances/Goals

PAATELAINEN, Mixu

Born Helsinki 3.2.67 Ht 6 0 Wt 13 11
Forward. From Valkeakosken Haka. Finland 48 full caps.

Season	Club	Apps	Goals
1987–88	Dundee U	19	9
1988–89		33	10
1989–90		31	7
1990–91		20	1
1991–92		30	6
1991–92	Aberdeen	6	1
1992–93		33	16
1993–94		36	6
1994–95	Bolton W	44	12
1995–96		15	1

PACK, Lenny

Born Salisbury 27.9.76 Ht 5 9 Wt 12 08
Midfield. From Trainee.

Season	Club	Apps	Goals
1994–95	Cambridge U	3	—
1995–96		11	—

PAGE, Don

Born Manchester 18.1.64 Ht 5 10 Wt 11 03
Forward. From Runcorn.

Season	Club	Apps	Goals
1988–89	Wigan Ath	15	2
1989–90		25	—
1990–91		34	13
1991–92	Rotherham U	31	11
1992–93		24	2
1992–93	*Rochdale*	4	1
1993–94	Rotherham U	—	—
1993–94	Doncaster R	22	4
1994–95	Chester C	30	5
1995–96	Scarborough	37	5

PAGE, Robert

Born Llwynpia 3.9.74 Ht 6 0 Wt 12 05
Defender. From Trainee. Wales Under-21.

Season	Club	Apps	Goals
1992–93	Watford	—	—
1993–94		4	—
1994–95		5	—
1995–96		19	—

PAINTER, Robbie

Born Ince 26.1.71 Ht 5 10 Wt 12 02
Midfield. From Trainee.

Season	Club	Apps	Goals
1987–88	Chester C	2	—
1988–89		8	1
1989–90		32	4
1990–91		42	3
1991–92	Maidstone U	30	5
1991–92	Burnley	9	2
1992–93		17	—
1993–94		—	—
1993–94	Darlington	36	11
1994–95		38	9
1995–96		35	8

PALLISTER, Gary

Born Ramsgate 30.6.65 Ht 6 4 Wt 14 13
Defender. From Billingham. England B, 20 full caps.

Season	Club	Apps	Goals
1984–85	Middlesbrough	—	—
1985–86		28	—
1985–86	*Darlington*	7	—
1986–87	Middlesbrough	44	1
1987–88		44	3
1988–89		37	1
1989–90		3	—
1989–90	Manchester U	35	3
1990–91		36	—
1991–92		40	1
1992–93		42	1
1993–94		41	1
1994–95		42	2
1995–96		21	1

PALMER, Carlton

Born Oldbury 5.12.65 Ht 6 2 Wt 12 04
Defender. From Trainee. England Under-21, B, 18 full caps.

Season	Club	Apps	Goals
1984–85	WBA	—	—
1985–86		20	—
1986–87		37	1
1987–88		38	3
1988–89		26	—
1988–89	Sheffield W	13	1
1989–90		34	—
1990–91		45	2
1991–92		42	5
1992–93		34	1
1993–94		37	5
1994–95	Leeds U	39	3
1995–96		35	2

PALMER, Charlie

Born Aylesbury 10.7.63 Ht 5 11 Wt 13 01
Defender. From Apprentice.

Season	Club	Apps	Goals
1981–82	Watford	—	—

Season	Club	League Appearances/Goals	
1982–83		—	—
1983–84		10	1
1984–85	Derby Co	33	2
1985–86		18	—
1986–87		—	—
1986–87	Hull C	17	—
1987–88		35	—
1988–89		18	1
1988–89	Notts Co	11	—
1989–90		37	5
1990–91		40	1
1991–92		41	—
1992–93		31	—
1993–94		22	1
1994–95	Walsall	39	2
1995–96		15	—

PALMER, Lee

Born Croydon 19.9.70 Ht 6 0 Wt 12 07
Defender. From Trainee.

Season	Club	Apps	Goals
1987–88	Gillingham	1	—
1988–89		—	—
1989–90		39	3
1990–91		21	1
1991–92		11	—
1992–93		10	—
1993–94		28	—
1994–95		10	1
1995–96	Cambridge U	30	1

PALMER, Steve

Born Brighton 31.3.68 Ht 6 1 Wt 12 13
Midfield. From Cambridge University.

Season	Club	Apps	Goals
1989–90	Ipswich T	5	—
1990–91		23	1
1991–92		23	—
1992–93		7	—
1993–94		36	1
1994–95		12	—
1995–96		5	—
1995–96	Watford	35	1

PARDEW, Alan

Born Wimbledon 18.7.61 Ht 6 1
Wt 12 04
Midfield. From Yeovil.

Season	Club	Apps	Goals
1986–87	Crystal Palace	—	—
1987–88		20	—
1988–89		45	1
1989–90		36	6
1990–91		19	1
1991–92		8	—
1991–92	Charlton Ath	24	2
1992–93		30	9
1993–94		26	10
1994–95		24	3
1995–96	Barnet	41	—

PARKER, Garry

Born Oxford 7.9.65 Ht 6 0 Wt 13 02
Midfield. From Apprentice. England Youth, Under-21, B.

Season	Club	Apps	Goals
1982–83	Luton T	1	—
1983–84		13	2
1984–85		20	1
1985–86		8	—
1985–86	Hull C	12	—
1986–87		38	—
1987–88		34	8
1987–88	Nottingham F	2	—
1988–89		22	7
1989–90		37	6
1990–91		36	3
1991–92		6	1
1991–92	Aston Villa	25	1
1992–93		37	9
1993–94		19	2
1994–95		14	1
1994–95	Leicester C	14	2
1995–96		40	3

PARKER, Justin

Born Stoke 11.11.76
Defender. From Trainee.

Season	Club	Apps	Goals
1994–95	Crewe Alex	—	—
1995–96		—	—

PARKER, Paul

Born West Ham 4.4.64 Ht 5 7 Wt 11 07
Defender. From Apprentice. England Youth, Under-21, B, 19 full caps.

Season	Club	Apps	Goals
1980–81	Fulham	1	—
1981–82		5	—
1982–83		16	—
1983–84		34	—
1984–85		36	—
1985–86		30	—
1986–87		31	2
1987–88	QPR	40	—
1988–89		36	—
1989–90		32	—
1990–91		17	1

Season	Club	League Appearances/Goals	
1991–92	Manchester U	26	—
1992–93		31	1
1993–94		40	—
1994–95		2	—
1995–96		6	—

PARKIN, Brian

Born Birkenhead 12.10.65 Ht 6 2
Wt 13 00
Goalkeeper. From Local.

Season	Club	League Appearances/Goals	
1982–83	Oldham Ath	—	—
1983–84		5	—
1984–85		1	—
1984–85	*Crewe Alex*	12	—
1985–86	Crewe Alex	39	—
1986–87		44	—
1987–88		3	—
1987–88	*Crystal Palace*	—	—
1988–89	Crystal Palace	19	—
1989–90		1	—
1989–90	Bristol R	30	—
1990–91		39	—
1991–92		43	—
1992–93		26	—
1993–94		43	—
1994–95		40	—
1995–96		20	—

PARKIN, Steve

Born Mansfield 7.11.65 Ht 5 6 Wt 11 01
Midfield. From Apprentice. England Schools, Youth, Under-21.

Season	Club	League Appearances/Goals	
1982–83	Stoke C	2	—
1983–84		1	—
1984–85		13	1
1985–86		12	1
1986–87		38	—
1987–88		43	3
1988–89		4	—
1989–90	WBA	14	1
1990–91		25	1
1991–92		9	—
1992–93	Mansfield T	16	—
1993–94		23	1
1994–95		22	1
1995–96		26	1

PARKINSON, Gary

Born Thornaby 10.1.68 Ht 5 11
Wt 13 00
Defender. From Everton Amateur.

Season	Club	League Appearances/Goals	
1985–86	Middlesbrough	—	—
1986–87		46	—
1987–88		38	—
1988–89		36	2
1989–90		41	2
1990–91		10	1
1991–92		27	—
1992–93		4	—
1992–93	*Southend U*	6	—
1992–93	Bolton W	2	—
1993–94		1	—
1993–94	Burnley	20	1
1994–95		43	2
1995–96		29	—

PARKINSON, Joe

Born Eccles 11.6.71 Ht 6 1 Wt 13 00
Defender. From Trainee.

Season	Club	League Appearances/Goals	
1988–89	Wigan Ath	12	1
1989–90		33	2
1990–91		25	—
1991–92		36	3
1992–93		13	—
1993–94	Bournemouth	30	1
1993–94	Everton	—	—
1994–95		34	—
1995–96		28	3

PARKINSON, Phil

Born Chorley 1.12.67 Ht 6 0 Wt 11 06
Midfield. From Apprentice.

Season	Club	League Appearances/Goals	
1985–86	Southampton	—	—
1986–87		—	—
1987–88		—	—
1987–88	Bury	8	1
1988–89		39	—
1989–90		22	2
1990–91		44	2
1991–92		32	—
1992–93	Reading	39	4
1993–94		42	3
1994–95		31	—
1995–96		42	—

PARKINSON, Stuart

Born Blackpool 18.2.76 Ht 5 8 Wt 10 04
Forward. From Trainee.

Season	Club	League Appearances/Goals	
1994–95	Blackpool	1	—
1995–96		—	—

Season	Club	League Appearances/Goals	

PARKS, Tony

Born Hackney 26.1.63 Ht 5 11 Wt 10 08
Goalkeeper. From Apprentice.

1980–81	Tottenham H.	—	—
1981–82		2	—
1982–83		1	—
1983–84		16	—
1984–85		—	—
1985–86		—	—
1986–87		2	—
1986–87	*Oxford U*	5	—
1987–88	Tottenham H.	16	—
1987–88	*Gillingham*	2	—
1988–89	Brentford	33	—
1989–90		37	—
1990–91		1	—
1990–91	*QPR*	—	—
1990–91	Fulham	2	—
1991–92	West Ham U	6	—
1992–93	Stoke C	2	—
1992–93	Falkirk	15	—
1993–94		41	—
1994–95		28	—
1995–96		28	—

PARLOUR, Ray

Born Romford 7.3.73 Ht 5 10 Wt 11 12
Midfield. From Trainee. England Under-21.

1990–91	Arsenal	—	—
1991–92		6	1
1992–93		21	1
1993–94		27	2
1994–95		30	—
1995–96		22	—

PARMENTER, Steven

Born Chelmsford 22.1.77 Ht 5 9
Wt 11 00
Midfield. From Trainee.

1994–95	QPR	—	—
1995–96		—	—

PARRIS, George

Born Ilford 11.9.64 Ht 5 9 Wt 13 00
Defender. From Apprentice. England Schools.

1982–83	West Ham U	—	—
1983–84		—	—
1984–85		1	—
1985–86		26	1
1986–87		36	2
1987–88		30	1
1988–89		27	1
1989–90		38	2
1990–91		44	5
1991–92		21	—
1992–93		16	—
1992–93	Birmingham C.	13	—
1993–94		24	—
1994–95		2	1
1994–95	*Brentford*	5	—
1994–95	*Bristol C*	6	—
1994–95	*Brighton & HA*	18	2
1995–96	Brighton & HA	38	2

PARRISH, Sean

Born Wrexham 14.3.72 Ht 5 10 Wt 10 00
Midfield. From Trainee.

1989–90	Shrewsbury T	2	—
1990–91		1	—
From Telford U			
1994–95	Doncaster R	25	3
1995–96		41	5

PARRY, David

Born Belfast 12.3.78 Ht 5 10 Wt 11 02
Midfield. From Trainee.

1995–96	Crystal Palace	—	—

PARSLEY, Neil

Born Liverpool 25.4.66 Ht 5 10
Wt 11 08
Defender. From Witton Alb.

1988–89	Leeds U	—	—
1989–90		—	—
1989–90	*Chester C*	6	—
1990–91	Huddersfield T	8	—
1990–91	*Doncaster R*	3	—
1991–92	Huddersfield T	5	—
1992–93		44	—
1993–94		—	—
1993–94	WBA	20	—
1994–95		23	—
1995–96	Exeter C	32	—

PARTRIDGE, Scott

Born Leicester 13.10.74 Ht 5 8 Wt 11 01
Forward. From Trainee.

1992–93	Bradford C	4	—

Season	Club	Apps	Goals
1993–94		1	—
1993–94	Bristol C	9	4
1994–95		33	2
1995–96		9	1
1995–96	*Torquay U*	5	2
1995–96	*Plymouth Arg*	7	2
1995–96	*Scarborough*	7	—

PASCOE, Colin

Born Bridgend 9.4.65 Ht 5 10 Wt 12 00
Forward. From Apprentice. Wales Youth, Under-21, 10 full caps.

Season	Club	Apps	Goals
1982–83	Swansea C	7	1
1983–84		32	2
1984–85		41	9
1985–86		19	3
1986–87		41	11
1987–88		34	13
1987–88	Sunderland	9	4
1988–89		39	10
1989–90		33	1
1990–91		25	5
1991–92		20	2
1992–93		—	—
1992–93	*Swansea C*	15	4
1993–94	Swansea C	33	5
1994–95		35	5
1995–96		13	1
1995–96	Blackpool	1	—

PASKIN, John

Born Capetown 1.2.62 Ht 6 1 Wt 13 08
Forward. From Seiko.

Season	Club	Apps	Goals
1988–89	WBA	25	5
1989–90	Wolverhampton W	17	2
1990–91		15	1
1991–92		2	—
1991–92	*Stockport Co*	5	1
1991–92	*Birmingham C*	10	3
1991–92	*Shrewsbury T*	1	—
1991–92	Wrexham	17	3
1992–93		19	8
1993–94		15	—
1994–95	Bury	26	8
1995–96		12	—

PASS, Steven

Born Leigh 15.9.76 Ht 5 11 Wt 11 06
Forward. From Trainee.

Season	Club	Apps	Goals
1994–95	Sheffield W	—	—
1995–96		—	—

PATERSON, Jamie

Born Dumfries 26.4.73 Ht 5 4 Wt 10 04
Forward. From Trainee.

Season	Club	Apps	Goals
1990–91	Halifax T	6	1
1991–92		15	2
1992–93		23	2
1993–94		42	13
1994–95	Falkirk	4	—
1995–96	Scunthorpe U	26	2

PATERSON, Scott

Born Aberdeen 13.5.72 Ht 6 2 Wt 12 08
Midfield. From Cove Rangers.

Season	Club	Apps	Goals
1991–92	Liverpool	—	—
1992–93		—	—
1993–94		—	—
1994–95	Bristol C	3	—
1995–96		18	1

PATTERSON, Darren

Born Belfast 15.10.69 Ht 6 1 Wt 12 10
Defender. From Trainee. Northern Ireland 10 full caps.

Season	Club	Apps	Goals
1988–89	WBA	—	—
1989–90	Wigan Ath	29	1
1990–91		28	4
1991–92		40	1
1992–93	Crystal Palace	—	—
1993–94		—	—
1994–95		22	1
1995–96	Luton T	23	—

PATTERSON, Gary

Born Newcastle 27.11.72 Ht 6 0
Wt 12 05
Midfield. From Trainee.

Season	Club	Apps	Goals
1991–92	Notts Co	—	—
1992–93		—	—
1993–94	Shrewsbury T	39	1
1994–95		18	1
1994–95	Wycombe W	13	1
1995–96		37	1

PATTERSON, Mark

Born Darwen 24.5.65 Ht 5 6 Wt 11 04
Midfield. From Apprentice.

Season	Club	Apps	Goals
1983–84	Blackburn R	29	7
1984–85		9	—
1985–86		26	10
1986–87		24	1

Season	Club	Apps	Goals
1987–88		13	2
1988–89	Preston NE	42	15
1989–90		13	4
1989–90	Bury	20	4
1990–91		22	6
1990–91	Bolton W	19	2
1991–92		36	2
1992–93		37	2
1993–94		35	1
1994–95		26	3
1995–96		16	1
1995–96	Sheffield U	21	2

PATTERSON, Mark

Born Leeds 13.9.68 Ht 5 10 Wt 12 04
Defender. From Trainee.

Season	Club	Apps	Goals
1986–87	Carlisle U	6	—
1987–88		16	—
1987–88	Derby Co	—	—
1988–89		1	—
1989–90		9	—
1990–91		11	1
1991–92		12	2
1992–93		18	—
1993–94	Plymouth Arg	41	—
1994–95		38	3
1995–96		43	—

PAUL, Martin

Born Whalley 2.2.75 Ht 5 8 Wt 9 07
Forward. From Trainee.

Season	Club	Apps	Goals
1993–94	Bristol R	4	—
1994–95		5	—
1995–96		13	1

PAULO, Pedro

Born Portugal 21.11.73
Midfield.

Season	Club	Apps	Goals
1995–96	Darlington	6	—

PAYNE, Derek

Born Edgware 26.4.67 Ht 5 6 Wt 10 08
Midfield. From Kingsbury T, Burnham, Hayes.

Season	Club	Apps	Goals
1991–92	Barnet	14	1
1992–93		37	5
1993–94	Southend U	35	—
1994–95	Watford	24	—
1995–96		12	1

PAYNE, Grant

Born Woking 25.12.75 Ht 5 9 Wt 11 04
Forward. From Trainee.

Season	Club	Apps	Goals
1992–93	Wimbledon	—	—
1993–94		—	—
1994–95		—	—
1995–96		—	—

PAYNE, Ian

Born Crawley 19.1.77 Ht 5 9 Wt 11 00
Defender. From Trainee.

Season	Club	Apps	Goals
1994–95	Plymouth Arg	1	—
1995–96		—	—

PAYTON, Andy

Born Burnley 23.10.67 Ht 5 7 Wt 11 13
Forward. From Apprentice.

Season	Club	Apps	Goals
1985–86	Hull C	—	—
1986–87		2	—
1987–88		22	2
1988–89		28	4
1989–90		39	17
1990–91		43	25
1991–92		10	7
1991–92	Middlesbrough	19	3
1992–93	Celtic	29	13
1993–94		7	2
1993–94	Barnsley	25	12
1994–95		43	12
1995–96		40	17

PEACOCK, Darren

Born Bristol 3.2.68 Ht 6 2 Wt 12 12
Defender. From Apprentice.

Season	Club	Apps	Goals
1984–85	Newport Co	—	—
1985–86		18	—
1986–87		5	—
1987–88		5	—
1988–89	Hereford U	8	—
1989–90		36	3
1990–91		15	1
1990–91	QPR	19	—
1991–92		39	1
1992–93		38	2
1993–94		30	3
1993–94	Newcastle U	9	—
1994–95		35	1
1995–96		34	—

Season	Club	League Appearances/Goals	

PEACOCK, Gavin

Born Welling 18.11.67 Ht 5 9 Wt 11 09
Midfield. From Apprentice. England Schools, Youth, Football League.

1984–85	QPR	—	—
1985–86		—	—
1986–87		12	1
1987–88		5	—
1987–88	Gillingham	26	2
1988–89		44	9
1989–90	Bournemouth	41	4
1990–91		15	4
1990–91	Newcastle U	27	7
1991–92		46	16
1992–93		32	12
1993–94	Chelsea	37	8
1994–95		38	4
1995–96		28	5

PEACOCK, Lee

Born Paisley 9.10.76 Ht 6 0 Wt 12 05
Forward. From Trainee.

1993–94	Carlisle U	1	—
1994–95		7	—
1995–96		22	2

PEACOCK, Richard

Born Sheffield 29.10.72 Ht 5 10
Wt 11 00
Forward. From Sheffield FC.

1993–94	Hull C	11	1
1994–95		37	5
1995–96		45	7

PEAKE, Jason

Born Leicester 29.9.71 Ht 5 11 Wt 12 08
Midfield. From Trainee. England Youth.

1989–90	Leicester C	—	—
1990–91		8	1
1991–92		—	—
1991–92	*Hartlepool U*	6	1
1992–93	Halifax T	33	1
1993–94	Rochdale	10	—
1994–95		39	2
1995–96		46	4

PEAKE, Trevor

Born Nuneaton 10.2.57 Ht 6 0 Wt 12 09
Defender. From Nuneaton.

1979–80	Lincoln C	45	1
1980–81		43	1
1981–82		37	4
1982–83		46	1
1983–84	Coventry C	33	3
1984–85		35	1
1985–86		37	1
1986–87		39	—
1987–88		31	—
1988–89		32	—
1989–90		33	—
1990–91		36	1
1991–92		2	—
1991–92	Luton T	38	—
1992–93		40	—
1993–94		36	—
1994–95		46	—
1995–96		18	—

PEARCE, Andy

Born Bradford on Avon 20.4.66 Ht 6 4
Wt 14 11
Defender. From Halesowen.

1990–91	Coventry C	11	1
1991–92		36	2
1992–93		24	1
1993–94	Sheffield W	32	3
1994–95		34	—
1995–96		3	—
1995–96	Wimbledon	7	—

PEARCE, Dennis

Born Wolverhampton 10.9.74 Ht 5 9
Wt 11 00
Forward. From Trainee.

1993–94	Aston Villa	—	—
1994–95		—	—
1995–96	Wolverhampton W	5	—

PEARCE, Ian

Born Bury St Edmunds 7.5.74 Ht 6 4
Wt 14 04
Defender. From Schools. England Youth, Under-21.

1990–91	Chelsea	1	—
1991–92		2	—
1992–93		1	—
1993–94		—	—
1993–94	Blackburn R	5	1
1994–95		28	—
1995–96		12	1

PEARCE, Stuart

Born London 24.4.62 Ht 5 10 Wt 12 12
Defender. From Wealdstone. England Under-21, 70 full caps.

Season	Club	Apps	Goals
1983–84	Coventry C	23	—
1984–85		28	4
1985–86	Nottingham F	30	1
1986–87		39	6
1987–88		34	5
1988–89		36	6
1989–90		34	5
1990–91		33	11
1991–92		30	5
1992–93		23	2
1993–94		42	6
1994–95		36	8
1995–96		31	3

PEARCEY, Jason

Born Leamington Spa 23.7.71 Ht 6 1
Wt 13 12
Goalkeeper. From Trainee.

Season	Club	Apps	Goals
1988–89	Mansfield T	1	—
1989–90		5	—
1990–91		4	—
1991–92		22	—
1992–93		33	—
1993–94		9	—
1994–95		3	—
1994–95	Grimsby T	3	—
1995–96		2	—

PEARS, Richard

Born Exeter 16.7.76 Ht 5 10 Wt 12 07
Forward. From Trainee.

Season	Club	Apps	Goals
1993–94	Exeter C	11	1
1994–95		19	1
1995–96		22	5

PEARS, Steve

Born Brandon 22.1.62 Ht 6 0 Wt 13 07
Goalkeeper. From Apprentice.

Season	Club	Apps	Goals
1978–79	Manchester U	—	—
1979–80		—	—
1980–81		—	—
1981–82		—	—
1982–83		—	—
1983–84		—	—
1983–84	*Middlesbrough*	12	—
1984–85	Manchester U	4	—
1985–86	Middlesbrough	38	—
1986–87		46	—
1987–88		43	—
1988–89		26	—
1989–90		25	—
1990–91		27	—
1991–92		45	—
1992–93		26	—
1993–94		46	—
1994–95		5	—
1995–96	Liverpool	—	—

PEARSON, Chris

Born Leicester 5.1.76 Ht 5 6 Wt 10 06
Forward. From Trainee.

Season	Club	Apps	Goals
1994–95	Notts Co	—	—
1995–96		—	—

PEARSON, Gary

Born Co Durham 7.12.76 Ht 5 10
Wt 12 05
Midfield. From Trainee.

Season	Club	Apps	Goals
1995–96	Sheffield U	—	—

PEARSON, Nigel

Born Nottingham 21.8.63 Ht 6 1
Wt 14 03
Defender. From Heanor T.

Season	Club	Apps	Goals
1981–82	Shrewsbury T	—	—
1982–83		39	1
1983–84		26	—
1984–85		—	—
1985–86		35	1
1986–87		42	3
1987–88		11	—
1987–88	Sheffield W	19	2
1988–89		37	2
1989–90		33	1
1990–91		39	6
1991–92		31	2
1992–93		16	1
1993–94		5	—
1994–95	Middlesbrough	33	3
1995–96		36	—

PEEL, Nathan

Born Blackburn 17.5.72 Ht 6 1 Wt 13 03
Forward. From Trainee.

Season	Club	Apps	Goals
1990–91	Preston NE	10	1
1991–92	Sheffield U	1	—

Season	Club	Apps	Goals
1992–93		—	—
1992–93	*Halifax T*	3	—
1993–94	Sheffield U	—	—
1993–94	Burnley	13	2
1994–95		3	—
1994–95	*Rotherham U*	9	4
1995–96	Burnley	—	—
1995–96	*Mansfield T*	2	—
1995–96	*Doncaster R*	2	—

PEER, Dean

Born Dudley 8.8.69 Ht 6 2 Wt 12 05
Midfield. From Trainee.

Season	Club	Apps	Goals
1986–87	Birmingham C	2	—
1987–88		—	—
1988–89		17	1
1989–90		27	3
1990–91		40	2
1991–92		21	1
1992–93		13	1
1992–93	*Mansfield T*	10	—
1993–94	Birmingham C	—	—
1993–94	Walsall	33	8
1994–95		12	—
1995–96	Northampton T	42	1

PEJIC, Mel

Born Chesterton 27.4.59 Ht 5 9
Wt 11 05
Defender. From Local.

Season	Club	Apps	Goals
1977–78	Stoke C	—	—
1978–79		—	—
1979–80		1	—
1980–81	Hereford U	13	—
1981–82		27	—
1982–83		45	1
1983–84		44	—
1984–85		46	1
1985–86		45	1
1986–87		31	—
1987–88		44	1
1988–89		18	3
1989–90		38	5
1990–91		46	1
1991–92		15	1
1991–92	Wrexham	7	—
1992–93		39	2
1993–94		40	—
1994–95		20	1
1995–96		—	—

PEMBERTON, John

Born Oldham 18.11.64 Ht 5 11 Wt 12 12
Defender. From Chadderton.

Season	Club	Apps	Goals
1984–85	Rochdale	1	—
1984–85	Crewe Alex	6	—
1985–86		41	—
1986–87		43	—
1987–88		31	1
1987–88	Crystal Palace	2	—
1988–89		42	1
1989–90		34	1
1990–91	Sheffield U	21	—
1991–92		20	—
1992–93		19	—
1993–94		8	—
1993–94	Leeds U	9	—
1994–95		27	—
1995–96		17	—

PEMBERTON, Martin

Born Bradford 1.2.76
Midfield. From Trainee.

Season	Club	Apps	Goals
1994–95	Oldham Ath	—	—
1995–96		2	—

PEMBRIDGE, Mark

Born Merthyr Tydfil 29.11.70 Ht 5 7
Wt 11 11
Midfield. From Trainee. Wales Under-21, B, 16 full caps.

Season	Club	Apps	Goals
1989–90	Luton T	—	—
1990–91		18	1
1991–92		42	5
1992–93	Derby Co	42	8
1993–94		41	11
1994–95		27	9
1995–96	Sheffield W	25	1

PENDER, John

Born Luton 19.11.63 Ht 6 0 Wt 13 09
Defender. From Apprentice. Eire Youth, Under-21.

Season	Club	Apps	Goals
1981–82	Wolverhampton W	8	—
1982–83		39	1
1983–84		34	1
1984–85		36	1
1985–86	Charlton Ath	38	—
1986–87		1	—
1987–88		2	—
1987–88	Bristol C	28	2

Season Club League Appearances/Goals

Season	Club	Apps	Goals
1988–89		45	1
1989–90		10	—
1990–91		—	—
1990–91	Burnley	40	—
1991–92		39	3
1992–93		44	4
1993–94		42	1
1994–95		5	—
1995–96		1	—
1995–96	Wigan Ath	41	1

PENNEY, David

Born Wakefield 17.8.64 Ht 5 10 Wt 12 00
Midfield. From Pontefract.

Season	Club	Apps	Goals
1985–86	Derby Co	—	—
1986–87		1	—
1987–88		9	—
1988–89		9	—
1989–90	Oxford U	29	2
1990–91		9	1
1990–91	*Swansea C*	12	3
1991–92	Oxford U	23	4
1992–93		33	6
1993–94		16	2
1993–94	*Swansea C*	11	2
1994–95	Swansea C	35	5
1995–96		29	—

PENNOCK, Adrian

Born Ipswich 27.3.71 Ht 5 11 Wt 13 06
Defender. From Trainee.

Season	Club	Apps	Goals
1989–90	Norwich C	1	—
1990–91		—	—
1991–92		—	—
1992–93	Bournemouth	43	1
1993–94		40	3
1994–95		31	5
1995–96		17	—

PENRICE, Gary

Born Bristol 23.3.64 Ht 5 8 Wt 10 06
Forward. From Bristol C Apprentice.

Season	Club	Apps	Goals
1984–85	Bristol R	5	1
1985–86		39	5
1986–87		43	7
1987–88		46	18
1988–89		43	20
1989–90		12	3
1989–90	Watford	29	13
1990–91		14	5
1990–91	Aston Villa	12	—
1991–92		8	1
1991–92	QPR	19	3
1992–93		15	6
1993–94		26	8
1994–95		19	3
1995–96		3	—
1995–96	Watford	7	1

PEPPER, Graham

Born Darlington 19.8.77 Ht 5 7
Wt 11 00
Midfield. From Newcastle U Trainee.

Season	Club	Apps	Goals
1995–96	Darlington	—	—

PEPPER, Nigel

Born Rotherham 25.4.68 Ht 5 10
Wt 12 04
Midfield. From Apprentice.

Season	Club	Apps	Goals
1985–86	Rotherham U	7	—
1986–87		2	—
1987–88		15	—
1988–89		2	—
1989–90		19	1
1990–91	York C	39	3
1991–92		35	4
1992–93		34	8
1993–94		23	—
1994–95		35	4
1995–96		40	8

PERIFIMOU, Chris

Born Enfield 27.11.75 Ht 5 8 Wt 11 07
Midfield. From Trainee.

Season	Club	Apps	Goals
1994–95	Leyton Orient	4	—
1995–96		—	—
1995–96	Barnet	—	—

PERKINS, Chris

Born Nottingham 9.1.74 Ht 5 11 Wt 11 00
Midfield. From Trainee.

Season	Club	Apps	Goals
1992–93	Mansfield T	5	—
1993–94		3	—
1994–95	Chesterfield	18	—
1995–96		22	—

PERKINS, Declan

Born Ilford 17.10.75 Ht 5 11 Wt 12 04
Forward. From Trainee. Eire Under-21.

Season	Club	Apps	Goals
1994–95	Southend U	6	—

Season	Club	League Appearances/Goals	
1995–96		—	—
1995–96	*Cambridge U*	2	1

PERRETT, Darren

Born Cardiff 29.12.69 Ht 5 8 Wt 11 06
Forward. From Cheltenham T.

1992–93	Swansea C	—	—
1993–94		11	1
1994–95		15	—
1995–96		4	—

PERRETT, Russell

Born Barton on Sea 18.6.73 Ht 6 2
Wt 13 00
Defender. From AFC Lymington.

1995–96	Portsmouth	9	—

PERRY, Chris

Born London 26.4.73 Ht 5 8 Wt 10 08
Defender. From Trainee.

1991–92	Wimbledon	—	—
1992–93		—	—
1993–94		2	—
1994–95		22	—
1995–96		37	—

PERRY, Jason

Born Caerphilly 2.4.70 Ht 5 11 Wt 10 09
Defender. From Trainee. Wales Under-21, B, 1 full cap.

1986–87	Cardiff C	1	—
1987–88		3	—
1988–89		—	—
1989–90		36	—
1990–91		43	—
1991–92		36	—
1992–93		39	3
1993–94		40	1
1994–95		34	1
1995–96		14	—

PERRY, Jonathan

Born Hamilton 22.11.76 Ht 6 0 Wt 11 11
Defender. From Trainee.

1995–96	Barnsley	—	—

PERRY, Mark

Born London 19.10.78 Ht 5 10 Wt 11 03
Midfield. From Trainee.

1995–96	QPR	—	—

PERRY, Mark

Born Aberdeen 7.2.71 Ht 6 1 Wt 11 00
Defender. From Cove R.

1988–89	Dundee U	—	—
1989–90		—	—
1990–91		—	—
1991–92		—	—
1992–93		18	1
1993–94		9	—
1994–95		9	—
1995–96		20	2

PESCHISOLIDO, Paul

Born Canada 25.5.71 Ht 5 7 Wt 10 12
Forward. From Toronto Blizzard. Canada full caps.

1992–93	Birmingham C	19	7
1993–94		24	9
1994–95	Stoke C	40	13
1995–96		26	6
1995–96	Birmingham C	9	1

PETCHEY, Stewart

Born Grimsby 22.1.77
Defender. From Trainee.

1995–96	Grimsby T	—	—

PETERS, Mark

Born St Asaph 6.7.72 Ht 6 1 Wt 13 00
Defender. From Trainee. Wales Under-21.

1991–92	Manchester C	—	—
1992–93	Norwich C	—	—
1993–94	Peterborough U	19	—
1994–95		—	—
1994–95	Mansfield T	26	4
1995–96		21	2

PETHICK, Robbie

Born Tavistock 8.9.70 Ht 5 10 Wt 11 11
Midfield. From Weymouth.

1993–94	Portsmouth	18	—
1994–95		44	1
1995–96		38	—

PETRESCU, Dan

Born Bucharest 22.12.67 Ht 5 8 Wt 9 05
Midfield. From Steaua, Foggia, Genoa. Romania 54 full caps.

1994–95	Sheffield W	29	3

Season	Club	League Appearances/Goals	
1995–96		8	—
1995–96	Chelsea	24	2

PETRIC, Gordan

Born Belgrade 30.7.69 Ht 6 2 Wt 13 09
Defender. From Partizan Belgrade.
Yugoslavia full caps.

1993–94	Dundee U	27	1
1994–95		33	2
1995–96	Rangers	33	1

PETRIE, Stewart

Born Dundee 27.2.70 Ht 5 10 Wt 11 11
Forward. From East Craigie.

1988–89	Forfar Ath	—	—
1989–90		—	—
1990–91		36	6
1991–92		41	7
1992–93		37	21
1993–94		3	—
1993–94	Dunfermline Ath	37	6
1994–95		33	14
1995–96		34	13

PETTERSON, Andy

Born Fremantle 26.9.69 Ht 6 2 Wt 14 12
Goalkeeper.

1988–89	Luton T	—	—
1988–89	*Swindon T*	—	—
1989–90	Luton T	—	—
1990–91		—	—
1991–92		—	—
1991–92	*Ipswich T*	—	—
1992–93	Luton T	14	—
1992–93	*Ipswich T*	1	—
1993–94	Luton T	5	—
1994–95	Charlton Ath	9	—
1994–95	*Bradford C*	3	—
1995–96	Charlton Ath	9	—
1995–96	*Ipswich T*	1	—
1995–96	*Plymouth Arg*	6	—
1995–96	*Colchester U*	5	—

PETTINGER, Paul

Born Sheffield 1.10.75 Ht 6 0 Wt 13 07
Goalkeeper. From Barnsley. England Youth.

1992–93	Leeds U	—	—
1993–94		—	—
1994–95		—	—
1994–95	*Torquay U*	3	—
1995–96	Leeds U	—	—
1995–96	*Rotherham U*	1	—
1995–96	Gillingham	—	—

PETTY, Ben

Born Solihull 22.3.77 Ht 6 0 Wt 12 06
Defender. From Trainee.

1994–95	Aston Villa	—	—
1995–96		—	—

PEVERELL, Nick

Born Middlesbrough 28.4.73 Ht 5 10
Wt 11 02
Forward. From Trainee.

1991–92	Middlesbrough	—	—
1992–93	Hartlepool U	19	1
1993–94		16	2
1994–95		1	—
1994–95	York C	9	1
1995–96		20	1

PHELAN, Mike

Born Nelson 24.9.62 Ht 5 11 Wt 11 01
Defender. From Apprentice. England Youth, 1 full cap.

1980–81	Burnley	16	2
1981–82		23	1
1982–83		42	3
1983–84		44	2
1984–85		43	1
1985–86	Norwich C	42	3
1986–87		40	4
1987–88		37	—
1988–89		37	2
1989–90	Manchester U	38	1
1990–91		33	1
1991–92		18	—
1992–93		11	—
1993–94		2	—
1994–95	WBA	20	—
1995–96		1	—

PHELAN, Terry

Born Manchester 16.3.67 Ht 5 7 Wt 9 00
Defender. From Trainee. Eire Youth, Under-21, Under-23, B, 35 full caps.

1984–85	Leeds U	—	—
1985–86		14	—
1986–87	Swansea C	45	—

Season	Club	League Appearances/Goals	
1987–88	Wimbledon	30	—
1988–89		29	—
1989–90		34	—
1990–91		29	—
1991–92		37	1
1992–93		—	—
1992–93	Manchester C	37	—
1993–94		30	1
1994–95		27	—
1995–96		9	—
1995–96	Chelsea	12	—

PHILLIBEN, John

Born Stirling 14.3.64 Ht 5 10 Wt 11 00
Defender. From Gairdoch U. Scotland Youth.

Season	Club	League Appearances/Goals	
1980–81	Stirling A	15	—
1981–82		37	1
1982–83		34	—
1983–84		23	—
1983–84	Doncaster R	12	—
1984–85		36	1
1985–86		22	—
1985–86	*Cambridge U*	6	—
1986–87	Doncaster R	1	—
1986–87	Motherwell	37	—
1987–88		35	2
1988–89		19	—
1989–90		24	—
1990–91		11	1
1991–92		32	1
1992–93		31	—
1993–94		28	2
1994–95		31	—
1995–96		24	—

PHILLIPS, David

Born Wegberg 29.7.63 Ht 5 9 Wt 12 05
Midfield. From Apprentice. Wales Under-21, 62 full caps.

Season	Club	League Appearances/Goals	
1981–82	Plymouth Arg	8	1
1982–83		23	8
1983–84		42	6
1984–85	Manchester C	42	12
1985–86		39	1
1986–87	Coventry C	39	4
1987–88		35	2
1988–89		26	2
1989–90	Norwich C	38	4
1990–91		38	4
1991–92		34	1
1992–93		42	9
1993–94	Nottingham F	43	4
1994–95		38	1
1995–96		18	—

PHILLIPS, Jimmy

Born Bolton 8.2.66 Ht 6 0 Wt 12 07
Defender. From Apprentice.

Season	Club	League Appearances/Goals	
1983–84	Bolton W	1	—
1984–85		40	1
1985–86		33	1
1986–87		34	—
1986–87	Rangers	6	—
1987–88		19	—
1988–89	Oxford U	45	5
1989–90		34	3
1989–90	Middlesbrough	12	—
1990–91		44	2
1991–92		43	2
1992–93		40	2
1993–94	Bolton W	42	—
1994–95		46	1
1995–96		37	—

PHILLIPS, Kevin

Born Hitchin 25.7.73 Ht 5 7 Wt 11 00
Forward. From Baldock T.

Season	Club	League Appearances/Goals	
1994–95	Watford	16	9
1995–96		27	11

PHILLIPS, Martin

Born Exeter 13.3.76 Ht 5 9 Wt 10 03
Forward. From Trainee.

Season	Club	League Appearances/Goals	
1992–93	Exeter C	6	—
1993–94		9	—
1994–95		24	2
1995–96		13	3
1995–96	Manchester C	11	—

PHILLIPS, Wayne

Born Bangor 15.12.70 Ht 5 10 Wt 11 02
Midfield. From Trainee.

Season	Club	League Appearances/Goals	
1989–90	Wrexham	5	—
1990–91		28	—
1991–92		30	3
1992–93		15	—
1993–94		21	1
1994–95		18	1
1995–96		44	5

Season	Club	League Appearances/Goals	

PHILLISKIRK, Tony

Born Sunderland 10.2.65 Ht 6 1 Wt 13 02
Forward. From Amateur. England Schools.

1983–84	Sheffield U	21	8
1984–85		23	2
1985–86		4	—
1986–87		6	1
1986–87	*Rotherham U*	6	1
1987–88	Sheffield U	26	9
1988–89	Oldham Ath	10	1
1988–89	Preston NE	14	6
1989–90	Bolton W	45	18
1990–91		43	19
1991–92		43	12
1992–93		10	2
1992–93	Peterborough U	32	11
1993–94		11	4
1993–94	Burnley	19	7
1994–95		13	1
1995–96		8	1
1995–96	*Carlisle U*	3	1
1995–96	Cardiff C	28	4

PHILPOTT, Lee

Born Hackney 21.2.70 Ht 5 9 Wt 11 08
Forward. From Trainee.

1987–88	Peterborough U	1	—
1988–89		3	—
1989–90	Cambridge U	42	5
1990–91		45	5
1991–92		31	5
1992–93		16	2
1992–93	Leicester C	27	3
1993–94		19	—
1994–95		23	—
1995–96		6	—
1995–96	Blackpool	10	—

PHILSON, Graeme

Born Ireland 24.3.75 Ht 5 10 Wt 11 00
Defender. From Coleraine.

1995–96	West Ham U	—	—

PICK, Gary

Born Leicester 9.7.71 Ht 5 9 Wt 11 10
Midfield. From Leicester U.

1992–93	Stoke C	—	—
1993–94		—	—
1994–95	Hereford U	29	2
1995–96		14	—
1995–96	Cambridge U	4	—

PICKERING, Ally

Born Manchester 22.6.67 Ht 5 11
Wt 11 00
Defender. From Buxton.

1989–90	Rotherham U	10	—
1990–91		1	—
1991–92		27	—
1992–93		38	1
1993–94		12	1
1993–94	Coventry C	4	—
1994–95		31	—
1995–96		30	—

PICKERING, Steven

Born Sunderland 25.9.76 Ht 5 10
Wt 9 13
Midfield. From Trainee.

1995–96	Sunderland	—	—

PIEARCE, Stephen

Born Sutton Coldfield 29.9.74 Ht 5 11
Wt 10 10
Forward. From Trainee.

1993–94	Wolverhampton W	—	—
1994–95		—	—
1995–96		—	—

PIERCE, David

Born Manchester 4.10.75
Goalkeeper. From Rotherham U.

1995–96	Chesterfield	1	—

PIKE, Chris

Born Cardiff 19.10.61 Ht 6 2 Wt 13 07
Forward. From Barry T.

1984–85	Fulham	—	—
1985–86		26	4
1986–87		13	—
1986–87	*Cardiff C*	6	2
1987–88	Fulham	3	—
1988–89		—	—
1989–90	Cardiff C	41	18
1990–91		39	14
1991–92		40	21
1992–93		28	12
1993–94	Hereford U	34	18
1994–95		4	—
1994–95	Gillingham	27	13
1995–96		—	—

Season	Club	League Appearances/Goals	

PIKE, Martin

Born South Shields 21.10.64 Ht 5 11 Wt 12 09
Defender. From Apprentice.

Season	Club	Apps	Goals
1982–83	WBA	—	—
1983–84	Peterborough U	35	2
1984–85		45	4
1985–86		46	2
1986–87	Sheffield U	42	—
1987–88		39	—
1988–89		45	5
1989–90		3	—
1989–90	*Tranmere R*	2	—
1989–90	*Bolton W*	5	1
1989–90	Fulham	20	2
1990–91		46	3
1991–92		45	2
1992–93		46	6
1993–94		33	1
1994–95	Rotherham U	7	—
1995–96		2	—

PILKINGTON, Kevin

Born Hitchin 8.3.74 Ht 6 0 Wt 13 00
Goalkeeper. From Trainee.

Season	Club	Apps	Goals
1992–93	Manchester U	—	—
1993–94		—	—
1994–95		1	—
1995–96		3	—
1995–96	*Rochdale*	6	—

PIPER, Len

Born London 8.8.77 Ht 5 6 Wt 9 09
Midfield. From Trainee. England Youth.

Season	Club	Apps	Goals
1995–96	Wimbledon	—	—

PITCHER, Darren

Born London 12.10.69 Ht 5 9 Wt 12 02
Midfield. From Trainee.

Season	Club	Apps	Goals
1987–88	Charlton Ath	—	—
1988–89		—	—
1988–89	*Galway*	—	—
1989–90	Charlton Ath	—	—
1990–91		44	3
1991–92		46	2
1992–93		41	2
1993–94		42	1
1994–95	Crystal Palace	25	—
1995–96		36	—

PITCHER, Geoffrey

Born Sutton 15.8.75 Ht 5 6 Wt 10 13
Midfield. From Trainee.

Season	Club	Apps	Goals
1992–93	Millwall	—	—
1993–94		—	—
1994–95	Watford	4	1
1995–96		9	1

PITMAN, Jamie

Born Warminster 6.1.76 Ht 5 8 Wt 10 12
Midfield. From Trainee.

Season	Club	Apps	Goals
1994–95	Swindon T	3	—
1995–96		—	—
1995–96	Hereford U	13	—

PITTMAN, Stephen

Born N Carolina 18.7.67 Ht 5 10 Wt 12 05
Defender. From Broxburn J.

Season	Club	Apps	Goals
1986–87	East Fife	11	—
1987–88		31	2
1988–89		25	8
1988–89	Shrewsbury T	12	—
1989–90		20	2
1990–91		—	—
1991–92		—	—
1992–93	Dundee	20	1
1993–94		36	3
1994–95		3	1
1994–95	Partick T	27	4
1995–96		14	—

PLANT, Ian

Born Hull 15.5.77 Ht 5 11 Wt 12 02
Defender. From Trainee.

Season	Club	Apps	Goals
1995–96	Hull C	—	—

PLATNAUER, Nicky

Born Leicester 10.6.61 Ht 5 11 Wt 12 10
Defender. From Northampton T Amateur, Bedford T.

Season	Club	Apps	Goals
1982–83	Bristol R	24	7
1983–84	Coventry C	34	6
1984–85		10	—
1984–85	Birmingham C	11	1
1985–86		17	1
1985–86	*Reading*	7	—
1986–87	Cardiff C	38	3
1987–88		38	1

Season	Club	League Appearances/Goals	
1988–89	....	39	2
1989–90	Notts Co........................	44	—
1990–91	....	13	1
1990–91	*Port Vale*.....................	14	—
1991–92	Leicester C	29	—
1992–93	....	6	—
1992–93	Scunthorpe U.............	14	2
1993–94	Mansfield T	25	—
1993–94	Lincoln C.....................	13	—
1994–95	....	13	—
1995–96	....	1	—

PLATT, Clive

Born Wolverhampton 27.10.77
Forward. From Trainee.

Season	Club	Apps	Goals
1995–96	Walsall	4	2

PLATT, David

Born Chadderton 10.6.66 Ht 5 10
Wt 11 12
Forward. From Chadderton. England Under-21, B, 62 full caps.

Season	Club	Apps	Goals
1984–85	Manchester U	—	—
1984–85	Crewe Alex	22	5
1985–86	....	43	8
1986–87	....	43	23
1987–88	....	26	19
1987–88	Aston Villa	11	5
1988–89	....	38	7
1989–90	....	37	19
1990–91	....	35	19
1991–92	Bari................................	29	11
1992–93	Juventus........................	16	3
1993–94	Sampdoria	29	9
1994–95	....	26	8
1995–96	Arsenal	29	6

PLATTS, Mark

Born Sheffield 23.5.79
Midfield. From Trainee.

Season	Club	Apps	Goals
1995–96	Sheffield W	2	—

PLUMMER, Chris

Born Isleworth 12.10.76 Ht 6 2 Wt 12 09
Defender. From Trainee. England Youth, Under-21.

Season	Club	Apps	Goals
1994–95	QPR	—	—
1995–96	....	1	—

Season Club League Appearances/Goals

PLUMMER, Dwayne

Born Bristol 12.5.78 Ht 5 10 Wt 10 09
Forward. From Trainee.

Season	Club	Apps	Goals
1995–96	Bristol C......................	11	—

POINTON, Neil

Born Church Warsop 28.11.64 Ht 5 10
Wt 12 10
Defender. From Apprentice.

Season	Club	Apps	Goals
1981–82	Scunthorpe U.............	5	—
1982–83	....	46	1
1983–84	....	45	1
1984–85	....	46	—
1985–86	....	17	—
1985–86	Everton.........................	15	—
1986–87	....	12	1
1987–88	....	33	3
1988–89	....	23	—
1989–90	....	19	1
1990–91	Manchester C.............	35	1
1991–92	....	39	1
1992–93	Oldham Ath	34	3
1993–94	....	24	—
1994–95	....	32	—
1995–96	....	4	—
1995–96	Hearts	22	3

POLLITT, Michael

Born Bolton 29.2.72 Ht 6 4 Wt 14 00
Goalkeeper. From Trainee.

Season	Club	Apps	Goals
1990–91	Manchester U	—	—
1990–91	*Oldham Ath*................	—	—
1991–92	Bury...............................	—	—
1992–93	Lincoln C.....................	27	—
1993–94	....	30	—
1994–95	Darlington	40	—
1995–96	....	15	—
1995–96	Notts Co........................	—	—

POLLOCK, Jamie

Born Stockton 16.2.74 Ht 5 10 Wt 14 01
Midfield. From Trainee. England Youth, Under-21.

Season	Club	Apps	Goals
1990–91	Middlesbrough...........	1	—
1991–92	....	26	1
1992–93	....	22	1
1993–94	....	34	9
1994–95	....	41	5
1995–96	....	31	1

POLSTON, John

Born Walthamstow 10.6.68 Ht 5 11
Wt 11 12
Defender. From Apprentice. England Youth.

Season	Club	Apps	Goals
1985–86	Tottenham H	—	—
1986–87		6	—
1987–88		2	—
1988–89		3	—
1989–90		13	1
1990–91	Norwich C	27	4
1991–92		19	1
1992–93		34	1
1993–94		24	—
1994–95		38	—
1995–96		30	—

POOLE, Darren

Born Northampton 9.11.77 Ht 5 8
Wt 10 03
Forward. From Trainee.

Season	Club	Apps	Goals
1994–95	Nottingham F	—	—
1995–96		—	—

POOLE, Gary

Born Stratford 11.9.67 Ht 6 0 Wt 11 00
Defender. From Arsenal Schoolboys.

Season	Club	Apps	Goals
1984–85	Tottenham H	—	—
1985–86		—	—
1986–87		—	—
1987–88	Cambridge U	42	—
1988–89		1	—
From Barnet			
1991–92	Barnet	40	2
1992–93	Plymouth Arg	39	5
1993–94	Southend U	38	2
1994–95		6	—
1994–95	Birmingham C	34	—
1995–96		28	—

POOLE, Kevin

Born Bromsgrove 21.7.63 Ht 5 10
Wt 12 06
Goalkeeper. From Apprentice.

Season	Club	Apps	Goals
1981–82	Aston Villa	—	—
1982–83		—	—
1983–84		—	—
1984–85		7	—
1984–85	*Northampton T*	3	—
1985–86	Aston Villa	11	—
1986–87		10	—
1987–88	Middlesbrough	1	—
1988–89		12	—
1989–90		21	—
1990–91		—	—
1990–91	*Hartlepool U*	12	—
1991–92	Leicester C	42	—
1992–93		19	—
1993–94		14	—
1994–95		36	—
1995–96		45	—

POOM, Mart

Born Tallinn 3.2.72 Ht 6 4 Wt 13 07
Goalkeeper. From FC Wil. Estonia 31 full caps.

Season	Club	Apps	Goals
1994–95	Portsmouth	—	—
1995–96		4	—

POPE, Steven

Born Mow Cop 8.9.76 Ht 5 11 Wt 11 00
Defender. From Trainee.

Season	Club	Apps	Goals
1995–96	Crewe Alex	—	—

PORIC, Adem

Born London 22.4.73 Ht 5 10 Wt 12 06
Midfield. From St George's Budapest. Australia full caps.

Season	Club	Apps	Goals
1993–94	Sheffield W	6	—
1994–95		4	—
1995–96		—	—

PORTER, Andy

Born Holmes Chapel 17.9.68 Ht 5 9
Wt 11 02
Midfield. From Trainee.

Season	Club	Apps	Goals
1986–87	Port Vale	1	—
1987–88		6	—
1988–89		14	1
1989–90		36	1
1990–91		40	—
1991–92		32	1
1992–93		17	1
1993–94		37	—
1994–95		44	3
1995–96		45	10

PORTER, Gary

Born Sunderland 6.3.66 Ht 5 6 Wt 11 00
Midfield. From Apprentice. England Youth, Under-21.

Season	Club	Apps	Goals
1983–84	Watford	2	—
1984–85		9	—

Season	Club	League Appearances/Goals	
1985–86		8	1
1986–87		26	4
1987–88		40	3
1988–89		42	10
1989–90		32	4
1990–91		45	4
1991–92		44	8
1992–93		33	—
1993–94		43	9
1994–95		41	3
1995–96		29	1

PORTREY, Simon

Born Wakefield 2.11.76 Ht 6 2 Wt 12 07
Midfield. From Trainee.

1995–96	Ipswich T	—	—

POTTER, Graham

Born Solihull 20.5.75 Ht 6 1 Wt 11 08
Defender. From Trainee. England Youth.

1992–93	Birmingham C	18	2
1993–94		7	—
1993–94	*Wycombe W*	3	—
1993–94	Stoke C	3	—
1994–95		1	—
1995–96		41	1

POTTS, Steve

Born Hartford (USA) 7.5.67 Ht 5 7
Wt 10 11
Defender. From Apprentice. England Youth.

1984–85	West Ham U	1	—
1985–86		1	—
1986–87		8	—
1987–88		8	—
1988–89		28	—
1989–90		32	—
1990–91		37	1
1991–92		34	—
1992–93		46	—
1993–94		41	—
1994–95		42	—
1995–96		34	—

POUNDER, Tony

Born Yeovil 11.3.66 Ht 5 9 Wt 11 01
Midfield. From Westland Sports, Weymouth.

1990–91	Bristol R	45	3
1991–92		40	4
1992–93		18	1
1993–94		10	2
From Weymouth			
1994–95	Hereford U	28	2
1995–96		34	2

POUTON, Alan

Born Newcastle 1.2.77 Ht 6 0 Wt 12 02
Midfield. From Newcastle U Trainee.

1995–96	Oxford U	—	—
1995–96	York C	—	—

POVEY, Neil

Born Birmingham 26.6.77 Ht 5 8
Wt 10 00
Midfield. From Trainee.

1994–95	Torquay U	8	—
1995–96		3	—

POWELL, Chris

Born Lambeth 8.9.69 Ht 5 10 Wt 11 07
Defender. From Trainee.

1987–88	Crystal Palace	—	—
1988–89		3	—
1989–90		—	—
1989–90	*Aldershot*	11	—
1990–91	Southend U	45	1
1991–92		44	—
1992–93		42	2
1993–94		46	—
1994–95		44	—
1995–96		27	—
1995–96	Derby Co	19	—

POWELL, Craig

Born Doncaster 10.6.77 Ht 5 10
Wt 12 04
Forward. From Trainee.

1995–96	Sheffield U	—	—

POWELL, Darryl

Born Lambeth 15.1.71 Ht 6 1 Wt 10 13
Forward. From Trainee.

1988–89	Portsmouth	3	—
1989–90		—	—
1990–91		8	—
1991–92		36	6
1992–93		23	—

Season	Club	League Appearances/Goals	
1993–94		28	5
1994–95		34	5
1995–96	Derby Co	37	5

POWELL, Francis

Born Burnley 17.6.77 Ht 6 1 Wt 12 00
Forward. From Burnley Trainee.

1995–96	Rochdale	2	—

POWELL, Paul

Born Wallingford 30.6.78 Ht 5 8
Wt 11 00
Defender. From Trainee.

1995–96	Oxford U	3	—

POWELL, Stephen

Born Derby 14.12.76 Ht 5 9 Wt 11 05
Midfield. From Trainee.

1993–94	Derby Co	—	—
1994–95		—	—
1995–96		—	—

POWER, Danny

Born Haverfordwest 24.11.76 Ht 5 10
Wt 12 00
Defender. From Trainee.

1995–96	Luton T	—	—

POWER, Graeme

Born Northwick Park 7.3.77 Ht 5 9
Wt 10 10
Defender. From Trainee. England Youth.

1994–95	QPR	—	—
1995–96		—	—

POWER, Lee

Born Lewisham 30.6.72 Ht 5 10
Wt 12 00
Forward. From Trainee. Eire Youth, Under-21, B.

1989–90	Norwich C	1	—
1990–91		16	3
1991–92		4	1
1992–93		18	6
1992–93	*Charlton Ath*	5	—
1993–94	Norwich C	5	—
1993–94	*Sunderland*	3	—
1993–94	*Portsmouth*	2	—
1993–94	Bradford C	3	2
1994–95		27	3
1994–95	*Millwall*	—	—
1995–96	Peterborough U	38	6

PREECE, Andy

Born Evesham 27.3.67 Ht 6 1 Wt 12 00
Midfield. From Evesham.

1988–89	Northampton T	1	—
From Worcester C			
1989–90	Wrexham	7	1
1990–91		34	4
1991–92		10	2
1991–92	Stockport Co	25	13
1992–93		29	8
1993–94		43	21
1994–95	Crystal Palace	20	4
1995–96	Blackpool	41	14

PREECE, David

Born Bridgnorth 28.5.63 Ht 5 5
Wt 10 12
Midfield. From Apprentice. England B.

1980–81	Walsall	8	—
1981–82		8	—
1982–83		42	2
1983–84		41	3
1984–85		12	—
1984–85	Luton T	21	2
1985–86		41	2
1986–87		14	—
1987–88		13	—
1988–89		26	—
1989–90		32	1
1990–91		37	1
1991–92		38	3
1992–93		43	3
1993–94		29	5
1994–95		42	4
1995–96	Derby Co	13	1
1995–96	*Birmingham C*	6	—
1995–96	*Swindon T*	7	1

PREECE, David

Born Sunderland 28.8.76 Ht 6 2
Wt 12 03
Goalkeeper. From Trainee.

1994–95	Sunderland	—	—
1995–96		—	—

Season	Club	League Appearances/Goals	

PREECE, Roger

Born Much Wenlock 9.6.69 Ht 5 8
Wt 10 11
Midfield. From Coventry C Apprentice.

1986–87	Wrexham	7	2
1987–88		40	4
1988–89		31	5
1989–90		32	1
1990–91	Chester C	35	—
1991–92		29	—
1992–93		23	—
1993–94		39	2
1994–95		43	2
1995–96		1	—

PREEDY, Phil

Born Hereford 20.11.75 Ht 5 10 Wt 11 02
Midfield. From Trainee.

1993–94	Hereford U	13	—
1994–95		16	1
1995–96		13	1

PRENDERGAST, Rory

Born Pontefract 6.4.78 Ht 5 9 Wt 12 00
Midfield. From Rochdale.

1995–96	Barnsley	—	—

PRENDERVILLE, Barry

Born Dublin 16.10.76 Ht 6 0 Wt 12 08
Defender. From Trainee.

1994–95	Coventry C	—	—
1995–96		—	—

PRESSLEY, Steven

Born Elgin 11.10.73 Ht 6 0 Wt 11 00
Defender.

1991–92	Rangers	1	—
1992–93		8	—
1993–94		23	—
1994–95		2	1
1994–95	Coventry C	19	1
1995–96		—	—
1995–96	Dundee U	35	2

PRESSMAN, Kevin

Born Fareham 6.11.67 Ht 6 1 Wt 14 13
Goalkeeper. From Apprentice. England Schools, Youth, Under-21, B.

1985–86	Sheffield W	—	—
1986–87		—	—
1987–88		11	—
1988–89		9	—
1989–90		15	—
1990–91		23	—
1991–92		1	—
1991–92	*Stoke C*	4	—
1992–93	Sheffield W	3	—
1993–94		32	—
1994–95		34	—
1995–96		30	—

PRESTON, Michael

Born Plymouth 22.11.77 Ht 5 7
Wt 10 02
Midfield. From Trainee.

1995–96	Torquay U	8	—

PRICE, Chris

Born Liverpool 24.10.75 Ht 5 9
Wt 11 09
Midfield. From Trainee.

1994–95	Everton	—	—
1995–96		—	—

PRICE, James

Born Preston 1.2.78
Defender. From Trainee.

1995–96	Rochdale	3	—

PRICE, Jason

Born Pontypridd 12.4.77 Ht 6 2
Wt 11 05
Midfield. From Aberaman.

1995–96	Swansea C	—	—

PRICE, Ryan

Born Stafford 13.3.70 Ht 6 4
Wt 14 00
Goalkeeper. From Stafford R.

1994–95	Birmingham C	—	—
1995–96		—	—

PRIEST, Chris

Born Leigh 18.10.73 Ht 5 10 Wt 10 10
Midfield. From Trainee.

1992–93	Everton	—	—
1993–94		—	—
1994–95		—	—

Season	Club	Apps	Goals
1994–95	Chester C	24	1
1995–96		39	13

PRIMUS, Linvoy

Born Stratford 14.9.73 Ht 6 0 Wt 13 08
Defender. From Trainee.

Season	Club	Apps	Goals
1992–93	Charlton Ath	4	—
1993–94		—	—
1994–95	Barnet	39	—
1995–96		42	4

PRIOR, Lee

Born Liverpool 30.10.77
Defender. From Trainee.

Season	Club	Apps	Goals
1995–96	Liverpool	—	—

PRIOR, Spencer

Born Rochford 22.4.71 Ht 6 3 Wt 12 12
Defender. From Trainee.

Season	Club	Apps	Goals
1988–89	Southend U	14	1
1989–90		15	1
1990–91		19	—
1991–92		42	1
1992–93		45	—
1993–94	Norwich C	13	—
1994–95		17	—
1995–96		44	1

PRITCHARD, David

Born Wolverhampton 27.5.72 Ht 5 7
Wt 11 04
Defender. From Telford U.

Season	Club	Apps	Goals
1990–91	WBA	—	—
1991–92		5	—
1993–94	Bristol R	11	—
1994–95		43	—
1995–96		12	—

PROCTOR, James

Born Doncaster 25.10.76 Ht 5 8
Wt 11 07
Midfield. From Bradford C Trainee.

Season	Club	Apps	Goals
1995–96	Rochdale	3	—

PROKAS, Richard

Born Penrith 22.1.76 Ht 5 9 Wt 11 04
Midfield. From Trainee.

Season	Club	Apps	Goals
1994–95	Carlisle U	39	1
1995–96		20	—

Season Club League Appearances/Goals

PRUDHOE, Mark

Born Washington 8.11.63 Ht 6 0
Wt 14 00
Goalkeeper. From Apprentice.

Season	Club	Apps	Goals
1981–82	Sunderland	—	—
1982–83		7	—
1983–84		—	—
1983–84	*Hartlepool U*	3	—
1984–85	Sunderland	—	—
1984–85	Birmingham C	1	—
1985–86	Walsall	16	—
1986–87		10	—
1986–87	*Doncaster R*	5	—
1986–87	*Sheffield W*	—	—
1986–87	*Grimsby T*	8	—
1987–88	Walsall	—	—
1987–88	*Hartlepool U*	13	—
1987–88	*Bristol C*	3	—
1987–88	Carlisle U	22	—
1988–89		12	—
1988–89	Darlington	12	—
1989–90		—	—
1990–91		46	—
1991–92		46	—
1992–93		42	—
1993–94	Stoke C	30	—
1994–95		—	—
1994–95	*Peterborough U*	6	—
1994–95	*Liverpool*	—	—
1995–96	Stoke C	39	—

PRUNIER, William

Born Montreuil 14.8.67 Ht 6 0 Wt 12 08
Defender.

Season	Club	Apps	Goals
1984–85	Auxerre	1	—
1985–86		2	—
1986–87		36	3
1987–88		38	1
1988–89		35	3
1989–90		5	—
1990–91		36	2
1991–92		35	4
1992–93		33	7
1993–94	Marseille	35	4
1994–95	Bordeaux	20	—
1995–96	Manchester U	2	—

PUGH, David

Born Liverpool 19.9.64 Ht 6 2 Wt 13 02
Forward. From Runcorn.

Season	Club	Apps	Goals
1989–90	Chester C	35	3

Season	Club	League Appearances/Goals	
1990–91		37	3
1991–92		35	—
1992–93		35	5
1993–94		37	12
1994–95	Bury	42	16
1995–96		42	10

PUGH, Michael

Born Stockton 27.3.77 Ht 5 7 Wt 11 07
Midfield. From Trainee.

1995–96	Darlington	—	—

PURSE, Darren

Born London 14.2.77 Ht 6 2 Wt 12 08
Defender. From Trainee.

1993–94	Leyton Orient	5	—
1994–95		38	3
1995–96		12	—

PUTTNAM, Dave

Born Leicester 3.2.67 Ht 5 10 Wt 12 02
Midfield. From Leicester U.

1988–89	Leicester C	3	—
1989–90		4	—
1989–90	Lincoln C	23	1
1990–91		43	6
1991–92		39	6
1992–93		37	2
1993–94		13	1
1994–95		17	4
1995–96		5	1
1995–96	Gillingham	26	1

QUASHIE, Nigel

Born Nunhead 20.7.78 Ht 5 9 Wt 11 00
Forward. From Trainee. England Youth.

1995–96	QPR	11	—

QUAYLE, Mark

Born Liverpool 2.10.78 Ht 5 9 Wt 10 02
Forward. From Trainee.

1995–96	Everton	—	—

QUIGLEY, Michael

Born Manchester 2.10.70 Ht 5 7
Wt 10 00
Midfield. From Trainee.

1990–91	Manchester C	—	—
1991–92		5	—
1992–93		5	—
1993–94		2	—
1994–95		—	—
1994–95	*Wrexham*	4	—
1995–96	Hull C	13	1

QUINN, James

Born Coventry 15.12.74 Ht 6 1 Wt 12 10
Forward. From Trainee. Northern Ireland 1 full cap.

1992–93	Birmingham C	4	—
1993–94	Blackpool	14	2
1993–94	*Stockport Co*	1	—
1994–95	Blackpool	41	9
1995–96		44	9

QUINN, Jimmy

Born Belfast 18.11.59 Ht 6 0 Wt 11 06
Forward. From Oswestry T. Northern Ireland 46 full caps.

1981–82	Swindon T	4	—
1982–83		13	3
1983–84		32	7
1984–85	Blackburn R	25	10
1985–86		31	4
1986–87		15	3
1986–87	Swindon T	22	9
1987–88		42	21
1988–89	Leicester C	31	6
1988–89	Bradford C	12	8
1989–90		23	6
1989–90	West Ham U	21	12
1990–91		26	6
1991–92	Bournemouth	43	19

Season	Club	League Appearances/Goals	
1992–93	Reading	42	17
1993–94		46	35
1994–95		35	5
1995–96		35	11

QUINN, Mark

Born Warrington 7.10.77
Midfield. From Trainee.

Season	Club	Apps	Goals
1995–96	Liverpool	—	—

QUINN, Niall

Born Dublin 6.10.66 Ht 6 4 Wt 15 10
Forward. From Eire Youth, Under-21, Under-23, B, 60 full caps.

Season	Club	Apps	Goals
1983–84	Arsenal	—	—
1984–85		—	—
1985–86		12	1
1986–87		35	8
1987–88		11	2
1988–89		3	1
1989–90		6	2
1989–90	Manchester C	9	4
1990–91		38	20
1991–92		35	12
1992–93		39	9
1993–94		15	5
1994–95		35	8
1995–96		32	8

QUINN, Robert

Born Sidcup 8.11.76 Ht 5 11 Wt 11 02
Defender. From Trainee.

Season	Club	Apps	Goals
1994–95	Crystal Palace	—	—
1995–96		1	—

QUINN, Stuart

Born Whiston 11.12.77
Midfield. From Trainee.

Season	Club	Apps	Goals
1995–96	Liverpool	—	—

QUINN, Wayne

Born Cornwall 19.11.76 Ht 5 10
Wt 11 08
Midfield.

Season	Club	Apps	Goals
1994–95	Sheffield U	—	—
1995–96		—	—

QUITONGO, Jose

Born Angola 18.11.74
Forward.

Season	Club	Apps	Goals
1995–96	Darlington	1	—

QUY, Andy

Born Harlow 4.7.76 Ht 5 11 Wt 13 02
Goalkeeper. From Tottenham H Trainee.

Season	Club	Apps	Goals
1994–95	Derby Co	—	—
1995–96		—	—

RACHEL, Adam

Born Birmingham 10.12.76 Ht 5 11
Wt 12 00
Goalkeeper. From Trainee.

1994–95	Aston Villa	—	—
1995–96		—	—

RADEBE, Lucas

Born Johannesburg 12.4.69 Ht 6 1
Wt 11 09
Midfield. From Kaiser Chiefs. South Africa full caps.

1994–95	Leeds U	12	—
1995–96		13	—

RADZKI, Lee

Born Mansfield 14.11.78
Midfield. From Trainee.

1995–96	Derby Co	—	—

RAE, Alex

Born Glasgow 30.9.69 Ht 5 9 Wt 11 11
Midfield. From Bishopbriggs. Scotland Under-21.

1987–88	Falkirk	12	—
1988–89		37	12
1989–90		34	8
1990–91	Millwall	39	10
1991–92		38	11
1992–93		30	6
1993–94		36	13
1994–95		38	10
1995–96		37	13

RAESIDE, Robert

Born South Africa 7.7.72 Ht 6 0
Wt 11 10
Defender. From St Andrews University.

1990–91	Raith R	14	—
1991–92		13	—
1992–93		10	—
1993–94		—	—
1994–95		10	—
1995–96		8	1

RAMAGE, Craig

Born Derby 30.3.70 Ht 5 9 Wt 11 08
Midfield. From Trainee. England Under-21.

1988–89	Derby Co	—	—
1988–89	*Wigan Ath*	10	2
1989–90	Derby Co	12	1
1990–91		17	1
1991–92		7	2
1992–93		1	—
1993–94		5	—
1993–94	Watford	13	—
1994–95		44	9
1995–96		36	15

RAMASUT, Tom

Born Cardiff 30.8.77 Ht 5 9 Wt 10 07
Midfield.

1995–96	Norwich C	—	—

RAMMELL, Andy

Born Nuneaton 10.2.67 Ht 6 2 Wt 13 10
Forward. From Atherstone U.

1989–90	Manchester U	—	—
1990–91	Barnsley	40	12
1991–92		37	8
1992–93		30	7
1993–94		34	6
1994–95		24	7
1995–96		20	4
1995–96	Southend U	7	2

RAMSEY, Paul

Born Londonderry 3.9.62 Ht 5 10
Wt 12 00
Defender. From Apprentice. Northern Ireland 14 full caps.

1979–80	Leicester C	—	—
1980–81		3	—
1981–82		10	—
1982–83		40	1
1983–84		33	1
1984–85		39	—
1985–86		13	1
1986–87		29	6
1987–88		42	1
1988–89		22	—
1989–90		35	3
1990–91		24	—
1991–92	Cardiff C	39	3
1992–93		30	4
1993–94	St Johnstone	22	—
1994–95		11	—
1994–95	*Cardiff C*	11	—
1995–96	Torquay U	18	—

Season	Club	League Appearances/Goals	

RANDALL, Adrian

Born Amesbury 10.11.68 Ht 5 10
Wt 12 05
Midfield. From Apprentice. England Youth.

1985–86	Bournemouth	2	—
1986–87		—	—
1987–88		1	—
1988–89		—	—
1988–89	Aldershot	37	2
1989–90		34	2
1990–91		36	8
1991–92		—	—
1991–92	Burnley	18	2
1992–93		23	1
1993–94		37	4
1994–95		32	1
1995–96		15	—
1995–96	York C	16	—

RANDELL, Gareth

Born Salisbury 11.8.77 Ht 5 5 Wt 9 07
Forward. From Trainee.

1995–96	Reading	—	—

RANKIN, Isiah

Born London 22.5.78 Ht 5 10 Wt 11 00
Forward. From Trainee.

1995–96	Arsenal	—	—

RANKINE, Mark

Born Doncaster 30.9.69 Ht 5 10
Wt 11 01
Midfield. From Trainee.

1987–88	Doncaster R	18	2
1988–89		46	11
1989–90		36	2
1990–91		40	2
1991–92		24	3
1991–92	Wolverhampton W	15	1
1992–93		27	—
1993–94		31	—
1994–95		27	—
1995–96		32	—

RATCLIFFE, Kevin

Born Mancot 12.11.60 Ht 6 1 Wt 13 06
Defender. From Apprentice. Wales Schools, Youth, Under-21, 59 full caps.

1978–79	Everton	—	—
1979–80		2	—
1980–81		21	—
1981–82		25	—
1982–83		29	1
1983–84		38	—
1984–85		40	—
1985–86		39	1
1986–87		42	—
1987–88		24	—
1988–89		30	—
1989–90		24	—
1990–91		36	—
1991–92		9	—
1992–93	Dundee	4	—
1992–93	Everton	—	—
1992–93	Cardiff C	19	1
1993–94		6	—
1993–94	Nottingham F	—	—
1993–94	Derby Co	6	—
1994–95	Chester C	23	—
1995–96		—	—

RATCLIFFE, Simon

Born Davyhulme 8.2.67 Ht 5 11
Wt 13 08
Midfield. From Apprentice. England Schools, Youth.

1984–85	Manchester U	—	—
1985–86		—	—
1986–87		—	—
1987–88	Norwich C	9	—
1988–89		—	—
1988–89	Brentford	9	1
1989–90		35	2
1990–91		38	2
1991–92		34	2
1992–93		30	2
1993–94		43	4
1994–95		25	1
1995–96	Gillingham	41	3

RATTLE, Jon

Born Melton 22.7.76 Ht 5 8 Wt 12 09
Defender. From Trainee.

1994–95	Cambridge U	6	—
1995–96		9	—

RATTRAY, Kevin

Born London 6.10.68 Ht 5 9 Wt 11 05
Midfield. From Woking.

1995–96	Gillingham	26	3

Season	Club	League Appearances/Goals	

RAVEN, Paul

Born Salisbury 28.7.70 Ht 6 1 Wt 12 11
Defender. From School. England Schools, Youth.

1987–88	Doncaster R	17	3
1988–89		35	1
1988–89	WBA	3	—
1989–90		7	—
1990–91		13	—
1991–92		7	1
1991–92	*Doncaster R*	7	—
1992–93	WBA	44	7
1993–94		34	1
1994–95		31	—
1995–96		40	4

RAVENSCROFT, Craig

Born London 20.12.74 Ht 5 6 Wt 9 04
Forward. From Trainee.

1993–94	Brentford	7	1
1994–95		1	—
1995–96		1	—

RAWLINSON, Mark

Born Bolton 9.6.75 Ht 5 10 Wt 11 04
Midfield. From Trainee.

1993–94	Manchester U	—	—
1994–95		—	—
1995–96	Bournemouth	19	—

RAYNOR, Paul

Born Nottingham 29.4.66 Ht 5 11
Wt 12 08
Midfield. From Apprentice.

1983–84	Nottingham F	—	—
1984–85		3	—
1984–85	*Bristol R*	8	—
1985–86	Huddersfield T	30	5
1986–87		20	4
1986–87	Swansea C	12	1
1987–88		44	8
1988–89		26	5
1988–89	*Wrexham*	6	—
1989–90	Swansea C	40	6
1990–91		43	5
1991–92		26	2
1991–92	Cambridge U	8	—
1992–93		41	2
1993–94	Preston NE	39	6
1994–95		38	3
1995–96		3	—
1995–96	Cambridge U	35	3

REA, Simon

Born Coventry 20.9.76 Ht 6 1 Wt 13 00
Defender. From Trainee.

1994–95	Birmingham C	—	—
1995–96		1	—

READ, Paul

Born Harlow 25.9.73 Ht 5 11 Wt 12 06
Forward. From Trainee.

1991–92	Arsenal	—	—
1992–93		—	—
1993–94		—	—
1994–95		—	—
1994–95	*Leyton Orient*	11	—
1995–96	Arsenal	—	—
1995–96	*Southend U*	4	1

READY, Karl

Born Neath 14.8.72 Ht 6 1 Wt 13 03
Defender. From Trainee. Wales Under-21, B.

1990–91	QPR	—	—
1991–92		1	—
1992–93		3	—
1993–94		22	1
1994–95		13	1
1995–96		22	1

REDDISH, Shane

Born Bolsover 5.5.71 Ht 5 10 Wt 11 10
Midfield. From Mansfield T Trainee, Doncaster R Trainee.

1989–90	Doncaster R	1	—
1990–91		11	—
1991–92		17	2
1992–93		31	1
1993–94	Carlisle U	35	1
1994–95		2	—
1994–95	*Chesterfield*	3	—
1994–95	Hartlepool U	23	—
1995–96		20	—

REDFEARN, Neil

Born Dewsbury 20.6.65 Ht 5 8 Wt 12 00
Midfield. From Nottingham F Apprentice.

1982–83	Bolton W	10	—
1983–84		25	1
1983–84	*Lincoln C*	10	1
1984–85	Lincoln C	45	4
1985–86		45	8

Season	Club	League Appearances/Goals	
1986–87	Doncaster R	46	14
1987–88	Crystal Palace	42	8
1988–89		15	2
1988–89	Watford	12	2
1989–90		12	1
1989–90	Oldham Ath	17	2
1990–91		45	14
1991–92	Barnsley	36	4
1992–93		46	3
1993–94		46	12
1994–95		39	11
1995–96		45	14

REDKNAPP, Jamie

Born Barton on Sea 25.6.73 Ht 6 0 Wt 12 10
Midfield. From Tottenham H Schoolboy, Bournemouth Trainee. England Youth, B, Under-21, 5 full caps.

Season	Club	Apps	Goals
1989–90	Bournemouth	4	—
1990–91		9	—
1990–91	Liverpool	—	—
1991–92		6	1
1992–93		29	2
1993–94		35	4
1994–95		41	3
1995–96		23	3

REDMILE, Matthew

Born Nottingham 12.11.76 Ht 6 0 Wt 14 01
Defender. From Trainee.

Season	Club	Apps	Goals
1995–96	Notts Co	—	—

REDMOND, Steven

Born Liverpool 2.11.67 Ht 5 10 Wt 11 02
Defender. From Apprentice. England Youth, Under-21.

Season	Club	Apps	Goals
1984–85	Manchester C	—	—
1985–86		9	—
1986–87		30	2
1987–88		44	—
1988–89		46	1
1989–90		38	—
1990–91		37	3
1991–92		31	1
1992–93	Oldham Ath	31	—
1993–94		33	1
1994–95		43	—
1995–96		40	1

REECE, Andy

Born Shrewsbury 5.9.62 Ht 5 10 Wt 12 02
Midfield. From Walsall, Worcester C, Willenhall.

Season	Club	Apps	Goals
1987–88	Bristol R	40	1
1988–89		42	7
1989–90		43	2
1990–91		46	1
1991–92		42	4
1992–93		26	2
1992–93	*Walsall*	9	1
1993–94	Bristol R	—	—
1993–94	*Walsall*	6	—
1993–94	Hereford U	28	1
1994–95		37	4
1995–96		6	—

REECE, Paul

Born Nottingham 16.7.68 Ht 5 10 Wt 12 08
Goalkeeper. From Kettering T.

Season	Club	Apps	Goals
1988–89	Grimsby T	14	—
1989–90		15	—
1990–91		—	—
1991–92		25	—
1992–93	Doncaster R	1	—
1992–93	Oxford U	35	—
1993–94		4	—
1994–95	Notts Co	11	—
1995–96	WBA	1	—

REED, Adam

Born Bishop Auckland 18.2.75 Ht 6 0 Wt 11 00
Defender. From Trainee.

Season	Club	Apps	Goals
1991–92	Darlington	1	—
1992–93		—	—
1993–94		13	—
1994–95		38	1
1995–96	Blackburn R	—	—

REED, Ian

Born Lichfield 4.9.75 Ht 5 8 Wt 11 04
Midfield. From Trainee.

Season	Club	Apps	Goals
1994–95	Shrewsbury T	4	—
1995–96		11	2

REED, John

Born Rotherham 27.8.72 Ht 5 8 Wt 11 07
Forward. From Trainee.

Season	Club	Apps	Goals
1990–91	Sheffield U	—	—

Season	Club	League Appearances/Goals	
1990–91	*Scarborough*	14	6
1991–92	Sheffield U	1	—
1991–92	*Scarborough*	6	—
1992–93	Sheffield U	—	—
1992–93	*Darlington*	10	2
1993–94	Sheffield U	—	—
1993–94	*Mansfield T*	13	2
1994–95	Sheffield U	12	2
1995–96		2	—

REES, Jason

Born Pontypridd 22.12.69 Ht 5 5 Wt 9 10
Forward. From Trainee. Wales Schools, Youth, Under-21, B, 1 full cap.

1988–89	Luton T	—	—
1989–90		14	—
1990–91		21	—
1991–92		5	—
1992–93		32	—
1993–94		10	—
1993–94	*Mansfield T*	15	1
1994–95	Portsmouth	19	1
1995–96		21	1

REES, Tony

Born Merthyr Tydfil 1.8.64 Ht 5 10
Wt 12 02
Forward. From Apprentice. Wales Youth, Under-21, 1 full cap.

1982–83	Aston Villa	—	—
1983–84	Birmingham C	25	2
1984–85		9	2
1985–86		8	—
1985–86	*Peterborough U*	5	2
1985–86	*Shrewsbury T*	2	—
1986–87	Birmingham C	30	4
1987–88		23	4
1987–88	Barnsley	14	2
1988–89		17	1
1989–90	Grimsby T	35	13
1990–91		36	10
1991–92		23	5
1992–93		31	5
1993–94		16	—
1994–95		—	—
1994–95	WBA	14	2
1995–96		9	—

REEVES, Alan

Born Birkenhead 19.11.67 Ht 6 0 Wt 12 00
Defender. From Heswall.

1988–89	Norwich C	—	—
1988–89	*Gillingham*	18	—
1989–90	Chester C	30	2
1990–91		10	—
1991–92	Rochdale	34	3
1992–93		41	3
1993–94		41	3
1994–95		5	—
1994–95	Wimbledon	31	3
1995–96		24	1

REEVES, David

Born Birkenhead 19.11.67 Ht 6 0
Wt 12 08
Forward. From Heswall.

1986–87	Sheffield W	—	—
1986–87	*Scunthorpe U*	4	2
1987–88	Sheffield W	—	—
1987–88	*Scunthorpe U*	6	4
1987–88	*Burnley*	16	8
1988–89	Sheffield W	17	2
1989–90	Bolton W	41	10
1990–91		44	10
1991–92		35	8
1992–93		14	1
1992–93	Notts Co	9	2
1993–94		4	—
1993–94	Carlisle U	34	11
1994–95		42	21
1995–96		43	13

REEVES, Steve

Born Dagenham 24.9.74 Ht 5 11
Wt 13 00
Goalkeeper. From Trainee.

1993–94	Everton	—	—
1994–95		—	—
1995–96		—	—
1995–96	Chelsea	—	—
1995–96	Oxford U	—	—

REGIS, Cyrille

Born French Guyana 9.2.58 Ht 6 0
Wt 13 04
Forward. From Moseley, Hayes. England Under-21, B, 5 full caps.

1977–78	WBA	34	10
1978–79		39	13
1979–80		26	8
1980–81		38	14
1981–82		37	17
1982–83		26	9

Season	Club	League Appearances/Goals	
1983–84	....	30	10
1984–85	....	7	1
1984–85	Coventry C.................	31	5
1985–86	....	34	5
1986–87	....	40	12
1987–88	....	31	10
1988–89	....	34	7
1989–90	....	34	4
1990–91	....	34	4
1991–92	Aston Villa................	39	11
1992–93	....	13	1
1993–94	Wolverhampton W....	19	2
1994–95	Wycombe W...............	35	9
1995–96	Chester C..................	29	7

REGIS, Dave

Born Paddington 3.3.64 Ht 6 1 Wt 13 06
Forward. From Barnet.

Season	Club	League Appearances/Goals	
1990–91	Notts Co......................	37	15
1991–92	....	9	—
1991–92	Plymouth Arg	24	2
1992–93	....	7	2
1992–93	*Bournemouth*	6	2
1992–93	Stoke C	25	5
1993–94	....	38	10
1994–95	Birmingham C............	6	2
1994–95	Southend U	9	1
1995–96	....	29	8
1995–96	Barnsley.....................	12	1

REID, Nicky

Born Ormston 30.10.60 Ht 5 10
Wt 12 04
Defender. From Apprentice. England Under-21.

Season	Club	League Appearances/Goals	
1978–79	Manchester C............	8	—
1979–80	....	23	—
1980–81	....	37	—
1981–82	....	36	—
1982–83	....	25	—
1983–84	....	19	2
1984–85	....	32	—
1985–86	....	30	—
1986–87	....	7	—
1987–88	Blackburn R...............	44	1
1988–89	....	37	1
1989–90	....	42	4
1990–91	....	30	2
1991–92	....	21	1
1992–93	....	—	—
1992–93	*Bristol C*	4	—
1992–93	WBA..........................	15	—
1993–94	....	5	—
1993–94	Wycombe W...............	5	—
1994–95	....	3	—

From Woking.

Season	Club	League Appearances/Goals	
1995–96	Bury..........................	18	—

REID, Paul

Born Oldbury 19.1.68 Ht 5 8 Wt 11 08
Midfield. From Apprentice.

Season	Club	League Appearances/Goals	
1985–86	Leicester C	—	—
1986–87	....	6	—
1987–88	....	26	5
1988–89	....	45	6
1989–90	....	40	8
1990–91	....	33	2
1991–92	....	12	—
1991–92	*Bradford C*	7	—
1992–93	Bradford C	44	6
1993–94	....	38	9
1994–95	Huddersfield T..........	42	6
1995–96	....	13	—

REID, Shaun

Born Huyton 13.10.65 Ht 5 8 Wt 12 00
Midfield. From Local.

Season	Club	League Appearances/Goals	
1983–84	Rochdale....................	17	—
1984–85	....	21	1
1985–86	....	8	—
1985–86	*Preston NE*	3	—
1986–87	Rochdale....................	41	1
1987–88	....	28	—
1988–89	....	18	2
1988–89	York C	24	2
1989–90	....	25	4
1990–91	....	29	—
1991–92	....	28	1
1992–93	Rochdale....................	40	4
1993–94	....	39	3
1994–95	....	28	3
1995–96	Bury..........................	21	—

REILLY, Mark

Born Bellshill 30.3.69 Ht 5 8 Wt 10 00
Defender. From Wishaw J.

Season	Club	League Appearances/Goals	
1988–89	Motherwell.................	—	—
1989–90	....	4	—
1990–91	....	—	—
1991–92	Kilmarnock.................	19	—
1992–93	....	19	3
1993–94	....	38	—
1994–95	....	32	—
1995–96	....	28	—

Season	Club	League Appearances/Goals	

REINELT, Robbie

Born Epping 11.3.74 Ht 5 10 Wt 12 07
Midfield. From Trainee.

1990–91	Aldershot	5	—
1991–92		—	—
1992–93	Gillingham	—	—
1993–94		25	1
1994–95		27	4
1994–95	Colchester U	5	—
1995–96		22	7

RENNIE, David

Born Edinburgh 29.8.64 Ht 6 0
Wt 12 00
Defender. From Apprentice. Scotland Youth.

1982–83	Leicester C	—	—
1983–84		15	—
1984–85		3	1
1985–86		3	—
1985–86	Leeds U	16	2
1986–87		24	—
1987–88		28	2
1988–89		33	1
1989–90	Bristol C	45	4
1990–91		32	2
1991–92		27	2
1991–92	Birmingham C	17	2
1992–93		18	2
1992–93	Coventry C	9	—
1993–94		34	1
1994–95		28	—
1995–96		11	2

RENWICK, Michael

Born Edinburgh 29.2.76 Ht 5 9
Wt 11 00
Defender. From Hutchison Vale BC.

1994–95	Hibernian	1	—
1995–96		2	—

RHODES, Andy

Born Doncaster 23.8.64 Ht 6 1 Wt 13 06
Goalkeeper. From Apprentice.

1982–83	Barnsley	—	—
1983–84		31	—
1984–85		5	—
1985–86		—	—
1985–86	Doncaster R	30	—
1986–87		41	—
1987–88		35	—
1987–88	Oldham Ath	11	—
1988–89		27	—
1989–90		31	—
1990–91	Dunfermline Ath	35	—
1991–92		44	—
1992–93	St Johnstone	44	—
1993–94		44	—
1994–95		19	—
1994–95	*Bolton W*	—	—
1995–96	Bolton W	—	—

RICE, Brian

Born Glasgow 11.10.63 Ht 6 0 Wt 12 04
Midfield. From Whitburn Central. Scotland Youth, Under-21.

1980–81	Hibernian	1	—
1981–82		1	—
1982–83		22	2
1983–84		25	5
1984–85		35	4
1985–86	Nottingham F	19	3
1986–87		3	1
1986–87	*Grimsby T*	4	—
1987–88		30	2
1988–89		20	1
1988–89	*WBA*	3	—
1989–90	Nottingham F	18	2
1990–91		1	—
1990–91	*Stoke C*	18	—
1991–92	Falkirk	16	1
1992–93		17	2
1993–94		37	3
1994–95		26	2
1995–96		5	—
1996–97	Dunfermline Ath	6	—

RICE, Gary

Born Zambia 29.9.75 Ht 5 9 Wt 11 10
Defender. From Trainee.

1994–95	Exeter C	10	—
1995–96		19	—

RICHARDS, Dave

Born Birmingham 31.12.76 Ht 6 0
Wt 12 02
Midfield. From Trainee.

1994–95	Walsall	—	—
1995–96		—	—

RICHARDS, Dean

Born Bradford 9.6.74 Ht 6 2 Wt 13 07
Defender. From Trainee. England Under-21.

Season	Club	Apps	Goals
1991–92	Bradford C	7	1
1992–93		3	—
1993–94		46	2
1994–95		30	1
1994–95	*Wolverhampton W*	10	2
1995–96	Wolverhampton W	37	1

RICHARDS, Tony

Born Newham 17.9.73 Ht 6 1 Wt 13 01
Forward. From West Ham U Trainee, Sudbury T.

Season	Club	Apps	Goals
1995–96	Cambridge U	19	1

RICHARDSON, Barry

Born Wallsend 5.8.69 Ht 6 1 Wt 12 01
Goalkeeper. From Trainee.

Season	Club	Apps	Goals
1987–88	Sunderland	—	—
1988–89	Scunthorpe U	—	—
1989–90	Scarborough	24	—
1990–91		6	—
1991–92	Northampton T	27	—
1992–93		42	—
1993–94		27	—
1994–95	Preston NE	17	—
1995–96		3	—
1995–96	Lincoln C	34	—

RICHARDSON, Ian

Born Barking 22.10.70 Ht 5 10 Wt 11 01
Midfield. From Dagenham & Redbridge.

Season	Club	Apps	Goals
1995–96	Birmingham C	7	—
1995–96	Notts Co	15	—

RICHARDSON, Jon

Born Nottingham 29.8.75 Ht 6 1 Wt 12 05
Midfield. From Trainee.

Season	Club	Apps	Goals
1993–94	Exeter C	7	—
1994–95		38	1
1995–96		43	1

RICHARDSON, Kevin

Born Newcastle 4.12.62 Ht 5 7 Wt 11 07
Midfield. From Apprentice. England 1 full cap.

Season	Club	Apps	Goals
1980–81	Everton	—	—
1981–82		18	2
1982–83		29	3
1983–84		28	4
1984–85		15	4
1985–86		18	3
1986–87		1	—
1986–87	Watford	39	2
1987–88	Arsenal	29	4
1988–89		34	1
1989–90		33	—
From Real Sociedad			
1991–92	Aston Villa	42	6
1992–93		42	2
1993–94		40	5
1994–95		19	—
1994–95	Coventry C	14	—
1995–96		33	—

RICHARDSON, Lee

Born Halifax 12.3.69 Ht 5 11 Wt 11 00
Midfield.

Season	Club	Apps	Goals
1986–87	Halifax T	1	—
1987–88		30	1
1988–89		25	1
1988–89	Watford	9	—
1989–90		32	1
1990–91	Blackburn R	38	2
1991–92		24	1
1992–93		—	—
1992–93	Aberdeen	29	2
1993–94		35	4
1994–95	Oldham Ath	30	6
1995–96		27	11

RICHARDSON, Lloyd

Born Dewsbury 7.10.77
Midfield. From Trainee. England Youth.

Season	Club	Apps	Goals
1994–95	Oldham Ath	—	—
1995–96		—	—

RICHARDSON, Neil

Born Sunderland 3.3.68 Ht 6 0 Wt 13 00
Defender. From Brandon U.

Season	Club	Apps	Goals
1989–90	Rotherham U	2	—
1990–91		16	2
1991–92		18	2
1992–93		14	—
1993–94		27	—
1994–95		25	—
1995–96		25	2

Season	Club	League Appearances/Goals	

RICHARDSON, Nick

Born Halifax 11.4.67 Ht 6 1 Wt 12 06
Midfield. From Local.

1988–89	Halifax T	7	—
1989–90		27	6
1990–91		26	3
1991–92		41	8
1992–93	Cardiff C	39	4
1993–94		39	5
1994–95		33	4
1994–95	*Wrexham*	4	2
1994–95	*Chester C*	6	1
1995–96	Bury	5	—
1995–96	Chester C	37	4

RICHARDSON, Paul

Born Durham 22.7.77 Ht 6 0 Wt 13 00
Forward. From Trainee.

1995–96	Middlesbrough	—	—

RICKERS, Paul

Born Pontefract 9.5.75 Ht 5 10 Wt 11 00
Midfield. From Trainee.

1993–94	Oldham Ath	—	—
1994–95		4	1
1995–96		23	—

RICKETTS, Michael

Born Birmingham 4.12.78
Forward. From Trainee.

1995–96	Walsall	1	1

RIDEOUT, Paul

Born Bournemouth 14.8.64 Ht 5 11
Wt 12 00
Forward. From Apprentice. England Schools, Youth, Under-21.

1980–81	Swindon T	16	4
1981–82		35	14
1982–83		44	20
1983–84	Aston Villa	25	5
1984–85		29	14
1985–86	Bari	28	6
1986–87		34	10
1987–88		37	7
1988–89	Southampton	24	6
1989–90		31	7
1990–91		16	6
1990–91	*Swindon T*	9	1
1991–92	Southampton	4	—
1991–92	Notts Co	11	3
1991–92	Rangers	11	1
1992–93		1	—
1992–93	Everton	24	3
1993–94		24	6
1994–95		29	14
1995–96		25	6

RIDGEWAY, Ian

Born Nottingham 28.12.75 Ht 5 8
Wt 10 06
Midfield. From Trainee.

1994–95	Notts Co	1	—
1995–96		—	—

RIDINGS, Dave

Born Farnworth 27.2.70 Ht 6 1 Wt 11 08
Forward. From Curzon Ashton.

1992–93	Halifax T	21	4
1993–94	Lincoln C	10	—
From Curzon Ashton			
1995–96	Rochdale	—	—
1995–96	Crewe Alex	1	—

RIEPER, Marc

Born Denmark 5.6.68 Ht 6 3 Wt 14 00
Defender. From Brondby. Denmark 40 full caps.

1994–95	West Ham U	21	1
1995–96		36	2

RIGBY, Malcolm

Born Nottingham 13.3.76 Ht 6 1 Wt 12 03
Goalkeeper. From Notts Co.

1994–95	Nottingham F	—	—
1995–96		—	—

RIGBY, Tony

Born Ormskirk 10.8.72 Ht 5 10
Wt 12 12
Midfield. From Barrow.

1992–93	Bury	21	2
1993–94		33	7
1994–95		30	2
1995–96		41	7

RIMMER, Neill

Born Liverpool 13.11.67 Ht 5 6 Wt 10 05
Midfield. From Apprentice. England Schools, Youth.

1984–85	Everton	1	—

Season	Club	League Appearances/Goals	
1985–86	Ipswich T	2	—
1986–87		1	—
1987–88		19	3
1988–89	Wigan Ath	25	3
1989–90		38	1
1990–91		34	2
1991–92		9	—
1992–93		1	—
1993–94		20	—
1994–95		33	4
1995–96		30	—

RIMMER, Stuart

Born Southport 12.10.64 Ht 5 7
Wt 11 00
Forward. From Apprentice. England Youth.

Season	Club	Apps	Goals
1981–82	Everton	2	—
1982–83		—	—
1983–84		1	—
1984–85		—	—
1984–85	Chester C	24	14
1985–86		18	16
1986–87		38	13
1987–88		34	24
1987–88	Watford	9	1
1988–89		1	—
1988–89	Notts Co	4	2
1988–89	Walsall	20	8
1989–90		41	10
1990–91		27	13
1990–91	Barnsley	15	1
1991–92	Chester C	44	13
1992–93		43	20
1993–94		35	8
1994–95		25	2
1994–95	*Rochdale*	3	—
1994–95	*Preston NE*	2	—
1995–96	Chester C	41	13

RIOCH, Greg

Born Sutton Coldfield 24.6.75 Ht 5 10
Wt 12 12
Defender. From Trainee.

Season	Club	Apps	Goals
1993–94	Luton T	—	—
1993–94	*Barnet*	3	—
1994–95	Luton T	—	—
1995–96	Peterborough U	18	—

RIPLEY, Stuart

Born Middlesbrough 20.11.67 Ht 6 0
Wt 13 00
Forward. From Apprentice. England Youth, Under-21, 1 full cap.

Season	Club	Apps	Goals
1984–85	Middlesbrough	1	—
1985–86		8	—
1985–86	*Bolton W*	5	1
1986–87	Middlesbrough	44	4
1987–88		43	8
1988–89		36	4
1989–90		39	1
1990–91		39	6
1991–92		39	3
1992–93	Blackburn R	40	7
1993–94		40	4
1994–95		37	—
1995–96		28	—

RISETH, Vidar

Born Levanger 21.4.72 Ht 6 2 Wt 12 07
Forward.

Season	Club	Apps	Goals
1995–96	Luton T	11	—

RISSANEN, Kari

Born 29.8.66
Defender.

Season	Club	Apps	Goals
1995–96	Dunfermline Ath	2	—

RITCHIE, Andy

Born Manchester 28.11.60 Ht 5 10
Wt 12 09
Forward. From Apprentice. England Schools, Youth, Under-21.

Season	Club	Apps	Goals
1977–78	Manchester U	4	—
1978–79		17	10
1979–80		8	3
1980–81		4	—
1980–81	Brighton & HA	26	5
1981–82		39	13
1982–83		24	5
1982–83	Leeds U	10	3
1983–84		38	7
1984–85		28	12
1985–86		29	11
1986–87		31	7
1987–88	Oldham Ath	36	19
1988–89		31	14
1989–90		38	15
1990–91		31	15

Season	Club	League Appearances/Goals	
1991–92		14	3
1992–93		12	3
1993–94		22	1
1994–95		33	12
1995–96	Scarborough	37	8

RITCHIE, Innes

Born Edinburgh 24.8.73 Ht 6 0
Wt 12 07
Forward. From Bathgate Th.

Season	Club	Apps	Goals
1994–95	Motherwell	1	—
1995–96		10	—

RITCHIE, Paul

Born Kirkcaldy 21.8.75 Ht 5 11
Wt 12 00
Defender. From Links Utd. Scotland Under-21.

Season	Club	Apps	Goals
1992–93	Hearts	—	—
1993–94		—	—
1994–95		—	—
1995–96		28	1

RIVERS, Mark

Born Crewe 26.11.75 Ht 5 11 Wt 10 08
Defender. From Trainee.

Season	Club	Apps	Goals
1993–94	Crewe Alex	—	—
1994–95		—	—
1995–96		33	10

RIX, Graham

Born Doncaster 23.10.57 Ht 5 9
Wt 11 00
Forward. From Apprentice. England Under-21, 17 full caps.

Season	Club	Apps	Goals
1974–75	Arsenal	—	—
1975–76		—	—
1976–77		7	1
1977–78		39	2
1978–79		39	3
1979–80		38	4
1980–81		35	5
1981–82		39	9
1982–83		36	6
1983–84		34	4
1984–85		18	2
1985–86		38	3
1986–87		18	2
1987–88		10	—
1987–88	*Brentford*	6	—

From Caen, Le Havre

Season	Club	Apps	Goals
1992–93	Dundee	14	2
1993–94	Chelsea	—	—
1994–95		1	—
1995–96		—	—

ROBBINS, Terry

Born London 18.7.65 Ht 5 7 Wt 10 08
Forward. From Welling U.

Season	Club	Apps	Goals
1995–96	Barnet	15	1

ROBERTS, Andy

Born Dartford 20.3.74 Ht 5 10 Wt 13 00
Midfield. From Trainee. England Under-21.

Season	Club	Apps	Goals
1991–92	Millwall	7	—
1992–93		45	—
1993–94		42	2
1994–95		44	3
1995–96	Crystal Palace	38	—

ROBERTS, Ben

Born Bishop Auckland 22.6.75 Ht 6 1
Wt 12 11
Goalkeeper. From Trainee.

Season	Club	Apps	Goals
1992–93	Middlesbrough	—	—
1993–94		—	—
1994–95		—	—
1995–96		—	—
1995–96	*Hartlepool U*	4	—
1995–96	*Wycombe W*	15	—

ROBERTS, Darren

Born Birmingham 12.10.69 Ht 6 0
Wt 12 04
Forward. From Burton Alb.

Season	Club	Apps	Goals
1991–92	Wolverhampton W	—	—
1992–93		21	5
1993–94		—	—
1993–94	*Hereford U*	6	5
1994–95	Doncaster R	—	—
1994–95	Chesterfield	11	1
1995–96		14	—

ROBERTS, Gareth

Born Wrexham 6.2.78
Defender. From Trainee.

Season	Club	Apps	Goals
1995–96	Liverpool	—	—

Season	Club	League Appearances/Goals	

ROBERTS, Iwan

Born Bangor 26.6.68 Ht 6 2 Wt 14 04
Forward. From Trainee. Wales Youth, 7 full caps.

Season	Club	Apps	Goals
1985–86	Watford	4	—
1986–87		3	1
1987–88		25	2
1988–89		22	6
1989–90		9	—
1990–91	Huddersfield T	44	13
1991–92		46	24
1992–93		37	9
1993–94		15	4
1993–94	Leicester C	26	13
1994–95		37	9
1995–96		37	19

ROBERTS, Mark

Born Irvine 29.10.75 Ht 5 9 Wt 9 10
Forward. From Bellfield BC.

Season	Club	Apps	Goals
1991–92	Kilmarnock	1	—
1992–93		5	—
1993–94		13	2
1994–95		4	1
1995–96		11	—

ROBERTS, Tony

Born Bangor 4.8.69 Ht 6 0 Wt 13 11
Goalkeeper. From Trainee. Wales Under-21, 1 full cap.

Season	Club	Apps	Goals
1987–88	QPR	1	—
1988–89		—	—
1989–90		5	—
1990–91		12	—
1991–92		1	—
1992–93		28	—
1993–94		16	—
1994–95		31	—
1995–96		5	—

ROBERTSON, Craig

Born Dunfermline 22.4.63 Ht 5 10
Wt 12 00
Midfield. From 'S' Form.

Season	Club	Apps	Goals
1979–80	Hearts	—	—
1980–81	Raith R	—	—
1981–82		11	—
1982–83		22	—
1983–84		38	3
1984–85		39	11
1985–86		25	2
1986–87		35	3
1987–88	Dunfermline Ath	42	13
1988–89		13	5
1988–89	Aberdeen	4	1
1989–90		22	2
1990–91		8	1
1991–92	Dunfermline Ath	33	1
1992–93		34	3
1993–94		40	3
1994–95		35	6
1995–96		28	5

ROBERTSON, David

Born Aberdeen 17.10.68 Ht 5 11
Wt 11 00
Defender. From Deeside BC. Scotland Under-21, 3 full caps.

Season	Club	Apps	Goals
1986–87	Aberdeen	34	—
1987–88		23	—
1988–89		23	—
1989–90		20	1
1990–91		35	1
1991–92	Rangers	42	1
1992–93		39	3
1993–94		32	1
1994–95		23	3
1995–96		25	3

ROBERTSON, Hugh

Born Aberdeen 19.3.75 Ht 5 9
Wt 12 07
Defender. From Lewis United. Scotland Under-21.

Season	Club	Apps	Goals
1993–94	Aberdeen	8	—
1994–95		3	2
1995–96		11	—

ROBERTSON, John

Born Liverpool 8.1.74 Ht 6 2
Wt 12 08
Defender. From Trainee.

Season	Club	Apps	Goals
1992–93	Wigan Ath	24	1
1993–94		34	1
1994–95		40	1
1995–96		14	1
1995–96	Lincoln C	22	—

Season	Club	League Appearances/Goals	

ROBERTSON, John

Born Edinburgh 2.10.64 Ht 5 7
Wt 11 06
Forward. From Edina Hibs. Scotland, Under-21 B, 16 full caps.

Season	Club	App	Gls
1980–81	Hearts	—	—
1981–82		1	—
1982–83		23	19
1983–84		35	15
1984–85		33	8
1985–86		35	20
1986–87		37	16
1987–88		39	26
1987–88	Newcastle U	—	—
1988–89		12	—
1988–89	Hearts	15	4
1989–90		32	17
1990–91		31	12
1991–92		42	14
1992–93		42	11
1993–94		36	10
1994–95		31	10
1995–96		33	11

ROBERTSON, Paul

Born Stockport 5.2.72 Ht 5 7 Wt 11 08
Defender. From York C Trainee.

Season	Club	App	Gls
1989–90	Stockport Co	9	—
1990–91		1	—
1991–92	Bury	5	—
1992–93		3	—
From Runcorn			
1995–96	Doncaster R	16	—

ROBERTSON, Sandy

Born Edinburgh 26.4.71 Ht 5 9
Wt 10 07
Midfield. From 'S' Form. Scotland Under-21.

Season	Club	App	Gls
1987–88	Rangers	—	—
1988–89		2	—
1989–90		1	—
1990–91		15	1
1991–92		6	—
1992–93		2	—
1993–94		—	—
1993–94	Coventry C	—	—
1994–95		1	—
1995–96		—	—
1995–96	Dundee U	4	—

ROBINS, Mark

Born Ashton-U-Lyme 22.12.69 Ht 5 8
Wt 11 08
Forward. From Apprentice. England Under-21.

Season	Club	App	Gls
1986–87	Manchester U	—	—
1987–88		—	—
1988–89		10	—
1989–90		17	7
1990–91		19	4
1991–92		2	—
1992–93	Norwich C	37	15
1993–94		13	1
1994–95		17	4
1994–95	Leicester C	17	5
1995–96		31	6

ROBINSON, Carl

Born Llandrudod 13.10.76 Ht 6 3
Wt 12 05
Midfield. From Trainee. Wales Under-21.

Season	Club	App	Gls
1995–96	Wolverhampton W	—	—
1995–96	*Shrewsbury T*	4	—

ROBINSON, David

Born Newcastle 27.11.69 Ht 6 0
Wt 13 02
Forward. From Gateshead.

Season	Club	App	Gls
1995–96	Cambridge U	17	1

ROBINSON, Earl

Born Birmingham 8.10.78 Ht 6 3
Wt 12 05
Midfield.

Season	Club	App	Gls
1995–96	Doncaster R	—	—
1995–96		—	—

ROBINSON, Ian

Born Nottingham 25.8.78 Ht 5 10
Wt 11 10
Midfield. From Trainee.

Season	Club	App	Gls
1995–96	Mansfield T	9	1

Season	Club	League Appearances/Goals	

ROBINSON, Jamie

Born Liverpool 22.2.72 Ht 6 1 Wt 12 08
Defender. From Trainee.

1991–92	Liverpool	—	—
1992–93	Barnsley	8	—
1993–94		1	—
1993–94	Carlisle U	16	1
1994–95		14	1
1995–96		20	2

ROBINSON, John

Born Bulawayo 29.8.71 Ht 5 10
Wt 11 02
Midfield. From Apprentice. Wales Under-21, 3 full caps.

1989–90	Brighton & HA	5	—
1990–91		15	—
1991–92		36	6
1992–93		6	—
1992–93	Charlton Ath	15	2
1993–94		27	1
1994–95		21	3
1995–96		44	6

ROBINSON, Les

Born Shirerook 1.3.67 Ht 5 10 Wt 12 04
Defender. From Local.

1984–85	Mansfield T	6	—
1985–86		7	—
1986–87		2	—
1986–87	Stockport Co	30	1
1987–88		37	2
1987–88	Doncaster R	7	1
1988–89		43	3
1989–90		32	8
1989–90	Oxford U	1	—
1990–91		43	—
1991–92		27	—
1992–93		16	—
1993–94		36	2
1994–95		46	—
1995–96		41	—

ROBINSON, Liam

Born Bradford 20.12.65 Ht 5 7 Wt 12 07
Forward. From Nottingham F Schoolboy.

1983–84	Huddersfield T	5	1
1984–85		15	1

Season	Club	League Appearances/Goals	
1985–86		1	—
1985–86	*Tranmere R*	4	3
1986–87	Bury	33	13
1987–88		43	19
1988–89		43	20
1989–90		45	17
1990–91		43	4
1991–92		41	10
1992–93		14	6
1993–94	Bristol C	41	4
1994–95	Burnley	39	7
1995–96		16	2

ROBINSON, Mark

Born Rochdale 21.11.68 Ht 5 9
Wt 11 08
Defender. From Trainee.

1985–86	WBA	1	—
1986–87		1	—
1987–88	Barnsley	3	—
1988–89		18	2
1989–90		24	—
1990–91		22	1
1991–92		41	2
1992–93		29	1
1992–93	Newcastle U	9	—
1993–94		16	—
1994–95	Swindon T	40	—
1995–96		46	1

ROBINSON, Matthew

Born Exeter 23.12.74 Ht 5 10 Wt 11 03
Midfield. From Trainee.

1993–94	Southampton	—	—
1994–95		1	—
1995–96		5	—

ROBINSON, Paul

Born Sunderland 20.11.78
Forward. From Trainee.

1995–96	Darlington	4	—

ROBINSON, Philip

Born Stafford 6.1.67 Ht 5 9 Wt 11 07
Midfield. From Apprentice.

1984–85	Aston Villa	—	—

Season	Club	League Appearances/Goals	
1985–86	....	—	—
1986–87	....	3	1
1987–88	Wolverhampton W....	41	5
1988–89	....	30	3
1989–90	Notts Co....................	46	2
1990–91	....	19	3
1990–91	*Birmingham C*...........	9	—
1991–92	Notts Co....................	1	—
1992–93	....	—	—
1992–93	Huddersfield T..........	36	4
1993–94	....	39	1
1994–95	....	—	—
1994–95	*Northampton T*..........	14	—
1994–95	Chesterfield..............	22	8
1995–96	....	39	9

ROBINSON, Ronnie

Born Sunderland 22.10.66 Ht 5 9
Wt 13 06
Defender. From SC Vaux.

Season	Club	Apps	Goals
1984–85	Ipswich T..................	—	—
From Vaux Breweries			
1985–86	Leeds U....................	16	—
1986–87	....	11	—
1986–87	Doncaster R..............	12	—
1987–88	....	37	1
1988–89	....	29	4
1988–89	WBA.........................	1	—
1989–90	Rotherham U.............	43	1
1990–91	....	38	—
1991–92	....	5	1
1991–92	Peterborough U.........	27	—
1992–93	....	20	—
1993–94	Exeter C....................	22	1
1993–94	*Huddersfield T*..........	2	—
1994–95	Exeter C....................	17	—
1995–96	Scarborough..............	1	—

ROBINSON, Steve

Born Lisburn 10.12.74 Ht 5 9
Wt 11 03
Forward. From Trainee.

Season	Club	Apps	Goals
1992–93	Tottenham H.............	—	—
1993–94	....	2	—
1994–95	....	—	—
1994–95	*Leyton Orient*............	—	—
1994–95	Bournemouth.............	32	5
1995–96	....	41	7

ROBINSON, Steve

Born Nottingham 17.1.75 Ht 5 9
Wt 11 03
Midfield. From Trainee.

Season	Club	Apps	Goals
1993–94	Birmingham C...........	—	—
1994–95	....	6	—
1995–96	....	—	—
1995–96	*Peterborough U*..........	5	—

ROBSON, Bryan

Born Witton Gilbert 11.1.57 Ht 5 9
Wt 12 05
Midfield. From Apprentice. England Schools, Youth, Under-21, B, 90 full caps.

Season	Club	Apps	Goals
1974–75	WBA.........................	3	2
1975–76	....	16	1
1976–77	....	23	8
1977–78	....	35	3
1978–79	....	41	7
1979–80	....	34	8
1980–81	....	40	10
1981–82	....	5	—
1981–82	Manchester U...........	32	5
1982–83	....	33	10
1983–84	....	33	12
1984–85	....	33	9
1985–86	....	21	7
1986–87	....	30	7
1987–88	....	36	11
1988–89	....	34	4
1989–90	....	20	2
1990–91	....	17	1
1991–92	....	27	4
1992–93	....	14	1
1993–94	....	15	1
1994–95	Middlesbrough...........	22	1
1995–96	....	2	—

ROBSON, Gary

Born Durham 6.7.65 Ht 5 9 Wt 11 10
Midfield. From Apprentice.

Season	Club	Apps	Goals
1982–83	WBA.........................	2	—
1983–84	....	7	—
1984–85	....	11	—
1985–86	....	14	—
1986–87	....	5	1
1987–88	....	31	1
1988–89	....	38	8
1989–90	....	25	5
1990–91	....	31	2
1991–92	....	32	9

Season	Club	League Appearances	Goals
1992–93		22	2
1993–94	Bradford C	46	2
1994–95		23	1
1995–96		6	—

ROBSON, Mark

Born Newham 22.5.69 Ht 5 7 Wt 10 02
Midfield. From Trainee.

Season	Club	League Appearances	Goals
1986–87	Exeter C	26	7
1987–88	Tottenham H	—	—
1987–88	*Reading*	7	—
1988–89	Tottenham H	5	—
1989–90		3	—
1989–90	*Watford*	1	—
1989–90	*Plymouth Arg*	7	—
1990–91	Tottenham H	—	—
1991–92		—	—
1991–92	*Exeter C*	8	1
1992–93	West Ham U	44	8
1993–94		3	—
1993–94	Charlton Ath	23	2
1994–95		40	3
1995–96		27	1

ROCASTLE, David

Born Lewisham 2.5.67 Ht 5 9 Wt 12 10
Forward. From Apprentice. England Under-21, B, 14 full caps.

Season	Club	League Appearances	Goals
1984–85	Arsenal	—	—
1985–86		16	1
1986–87		36	2
1987–88		40	7
1988–89		38	6
1989–90		33	2
1990–91		16	2
1991–92		39	4
1992–93	Leeds U	18	1
1993–94		7	1
1993–94	Manchester C	21	2
1994–95	Chelsea	28	—
1995–96		1	—

ROCHE, David

Born Newcastle 13.12.70 Ht 6 0
Wt 13 02
Midfield. From Trainee.

Season	Club	League Appearances	Goals
1988–89	Newcastle U	2	—
1989–90		—	—
1990–91		8	—
1991–92		26	—
1992–93		—	—
1992–93	*Peterborough U*	4	—
1993–94	Newcastle U	—	—
1993–94	Doncaster R	30	5
1994–95		20	3
1994–95	Southend U	4	—
1995–96		—	—

ROCHE, Stephen

Born Dublin 2.10.78
Midfield. From Belvedere.

Season	Club	League Appearances	Goals
1995–96	Millwall	—	—

ROCKETT, Jason

Born London 26.9.69 Ht 6 1 Wt 13 04
Defender.

Season	Club	League Appearances	Goals
1992–93	Rotherham U	—	—
1992–93		—	—
1993–94	Scarborough	34	—
1994–95		27	—
1995–96		39	4

RODDIE, Andrew

Born Glasgow 4.11.71 Ht 5 9 Wt 11 00
Midfield. From 'S' Form. Scotland Under-21.

Season	Club	League Appearances	Goals
1988–89	Aberdeen	—	—
1989–90		—	—
1990–91		—	—
1991–92		10	2
1992–93		11	2
1993–94		6	1
1994–95	Motherwell	19	—
1995–96		24	—

RODGER, Graham

Born Glasgow 1.4.67 Ht 6 2 Wt 11 13
Defender. From Apprentice. England Under-21.

Season	Club	League Appearances	Goals
1983–84	Wolverhampton W	1	—
1984–85	Coventry C	—	—
1985–86		10	—
1986–87		6	—
1987–88		12	1
1988–89		8	1
1989–90	Luton T	2	—
1990–91		14	2
1991–92		12	—
1991–92	Grimsby T	16	—
1992–93		30	7
1993–94		24	1

Season	Club	Apps	Goals
1994–95		21	1
1995–96		16	—

RODGER, Simon

Born Shoreham 3.10.71 Ht 5 9 Wt 11 09
Midfield. From Trainee.

Season	Club	Apps	Goals
1989–90	Crystal Palace	—	—
1990–91		—	—
1991–92		22	—
1992–93		23	2
1993–94		42	3
1994–95		4	—
1995–96		24	—

RODGERSON, Ian

Born Hereford 9.4.66 Ht 5 8 Wt 10 07
Midfield. From Pegasus Juniors.

Season	Club	Apps	Goals
1984–85	Hereford U	—	—
1985–86		19	2
1986–87		44	1
1987–88		37	3
1988–89	Cardiff C	40	—
1989–90		45	4
1990–91		14	—
1990–91	Birmingham C	25	2
1991–92		39	9
1992–93		31	2
1993–94	Sunderland	4	—
1994–95		6	—
1995–96	Cardiff C	34	1

RODOSTHENOUS, Michael

Born Islington 25.8.76 Ht 5 11 Wt 11 02
Forward. From Trainee.

Season	Club	Apps	Goals
1995–96	WBA	—	—

ROGAN, Anton

Born Belfast 25.3.66 Ht 6 1 Wt 13 00
Defender. From Distillery. Northern Ireland 17 full caps.

Season	Club	Apps	Goals
1986–87	Celtic	10	1
1987–88		33	1
1988–89		34	1
1989–90		18	—
1990–91		27	1
1991–92		5	—
1991–92	Sunderland	33	1
1992–93		13	—
1993–94	Oxford U	29	2

Season Club League Appearances/Goals

Season	Club	Apps	Goals
1994–95		29	1
1995–96	Millwall	8	—

ROGERS, Alan

Born Liverpool 3.1.77 Ht 5 10 Wt 11 09
Defender. From Trainee.

Season	Club	Apps	Goals
1995–96	Tranmere R	26	2

ROGERS, Darren

Born Birmingham 9.4.70 Ht 5 11 Wt 12 11
Defender. From Trainee.

Season	Club	Apps	Goals
1988–89	WBA	—	—
1989–90		—	—
1990–91		4	—
1991–92		10	1
1992–93	Birmingham C	17	—
1993–94		1	—
1993–94	*Wycombe W*	1	—
1994–95	Walsall	27	—
1995–96		25	—

ROGERS, Dave

Born Liverpool 25.8.75 Ht 6 1 Wt 12 00
Midfield. From Trainee.

Season	Club	Apps	Goals
1994–95	Tranmere R	—	—
1995–96	Chester C	20	1

ROGERS, Lee

Born Doncaster 28.10.66 Ht 5 11 Wt 12 00
Defender. From Doncaster R.

Season	Club	Apps	Goals
1986–87	Chesterfield	36	—
1987–88		43	—
1988–89		24	—
1989–90		32	—
1990–91		34	—
1991–92		18	—
1992–93		35	1
1993–94		32	—
1994–95		39	—
1995–96		21	—

ROGERS, Paul

Born Portsmouth 21.3.65 Ht 6 0 Wt 11 13
Midfield. From Sutton U.

Season	Club	Apps	Goals
1991–92	Sheffield U	13	—
1992–93		27	3

Season	Club	League Appearances/Goals	
1993–94		25	3
1994–95		44	4
From Sutton U			
1995–96		16	—
1995–96	Notts Co	21	2

ROGET, Leo

Born Ilford 1.8.77 Ht 6 1 Wt 12 02
Defender. From Trainee.

1995–96	Southend U	8	1

ROLLING, Frank

Born Colnar 23.8.68 Ht 6 1 Wt 13 00
Defender. From FC Pau.

1994–95	Ayr U	33	2
1995–96		2	—
1995–96	Leicester C	17	—

ROLLO, James

Born Wisbech 22.5.76 Ht 5 11 Wt 10 10
Midfield. From Trainee.

1995–96	Walsall	—	—

ROPER, Ian

Born Nuneaton 20.6.77 Ht 6 2 Wt 13 04
Defender. From Trainee.

1994–95	Walsall	—	—
1995–96		5	—

ROSARIO, Robert

Born Hammersmith 4.3.66 Ht 6 4
Wt 14 10
Forward. From Hillingdon. England Youth.

1983–84	Norwich C	8	1
1984–85		4	1
1985–86		8	2
1985–86	*Wolverhampton W*	2	1
1986–87	Norwich C	25	3
1987–88		14	2
1988–89		27	4
1989–90		31	5
1990–91		9	—
1990–91	Coventry C	2	—
1991–92		29	4
1992–93		28	4
1992–93	Nottingham F	10	1
1993–94		16	2
1994–95		1	—
1995–96		—	—

ROSCOE, Andy

Born Liverpool 4.6.73 Ht 5 10 Wt 11 08
Midfield. From Trainee.

1991–92	Liverpool	—	—
1992–93	Bolton W	—	—
1993–94		3	—
1994–95		—	—
1994–95	Rotherham U	31	4
1995–96		45	2

ROSE, Karl

Born Barnsley 12.10.78 Ht 5 10
Wt 11 00
Midfield.

1995–96	Barnsley	—	—

ROSE, Matthew

Born Dartford 24.9.75 Ht 5 11 Wt 11 01
Defender. From Trainee.

1994–95	Arsenal	—	—
1995–96		4	—

ROSENTHAL, Ronny

Born Haifa 11.10.63 Ht 5 11 Wt 12 13
Forward. From Maccabi Haifa, FC Brugge, Standard Liege. Israel full caps.

1989–90	*Luton T*	—	—
1989–90	*Liverpool*	8	7
1990–91	Liverpool	16	5
1991–92		20	3
1992–93		27	6
1993–94		3	—
1993–94	Tottenham H	15	2
1994–95		20	—
1995–96		33	1

ROSLER, Uwe

Born Attenburg 15.11.68 Ht 6 1
Wt 12 06
Forward. From Chemie Leipzig. East Germany full caps.

1988–89	Magdeburg	12	3
1989–90		24	10
1990–91		26	9
1991–92	Dynamo Dresden	33	4
1992–93	Nuremberg	28	—
1993–94	Dynamo Dresden	7	—
1993–94	Manchester C	12	5
1994–95		31	15
1995–96		36	9

Season Club League Appearances/Goals

ROSS, Ian

Born Broxburn 27.8.74 Ht 5 10
Wt 10 07
Midfield. From Bathgate Thistle.

Season	Club	Apps	Goals
1993–94	Motherwell	—	—
1994–95		—	—
1995–96		1	—

ROSS, Mike

Born Southampton 2.9.71 Ht 5 6 Wt 9 13
Forward. From Trainee.

Season	Club	Apps	Goals
1988–89	Portsmouth	1	—
1989–90		—	—
1990–91		—	—
1991–92		3	—
1992–93		—	—
1993–94	Exeter C	27	9
1994–95		1	—
1994–95	Plymouth Arg	17	—
1995–96		—	—
1995–96	*Exeter C*	7	2

ROUGIER, Anthony

Born Trinidad & Tobago 17.7.71 Ht 6 00
Wt 14 01
Midfield. From Trinity Pros.

Season	Club	Apps	Goals
1994–95	Raith R	4	—
1995–96		22	1

ROUND, Steve

Born Buxton 9.11.70 Ht 5 10 Wt 10 12
Defender. From Trainee.

Season	Club	Apps	Goals
1990–91	Derby Co	—	—
1991–92		3	—
1992–93		6	—
1993–94		—	—
1994–95		—	—
1995–96		—	—

ROUND, Steven

Born Wolverhampton 8.10.76 Ht 5 9
Wt 11 00
Midfield. From Trainee.

Season	Club	Apps	Goals
1995–96	Birmingham C	—	—

ROUSSET, Gilles

Born Hyeres 22.8.63 Ht 6 5 Wt 14 07
Goalkeeper. From Rennes.

Season	Club	Apps	Goals
1995–96	Hearts	25	—

ROWBOTHAM, Darren

Born Cardiff 22.10.66 Ht 5 10 Wt 12 13
Midfield. From Trainee.

Season	Club	Apps	Goals
1984–85	Plymouth Arg	7	—
1985–86		14	1
1986–87		16	1
1987–88		9	—
1987–88	Exeter C	23	2
1988–89		45	20
1989–90		32	21
1990–91		13	3
1991–92		5	1
1991–92	Torquay U	14	3
1991–92	Birmingham C	22	4
1992–93		14	2
1992–93	*Hereford U*	8	2
1992–93	*Mansfield T*	4	—
1993–94	Crewe Alex	40	15
1994–95		21	6
1995–96	Shrewsbury T	26	8

ROWBOTHAM, Jason

Born Cardiff 3.1.69 Ht 5 8 Wt 11 05
Defender. From Trainee.

Season	Club	Apps	Goals
1987–88	Plymouth Arg	4	—
1988–89		5	—
1989–90		—	—
1990–91		—	—
1991–92	Shrewsbury T	—	—
1992–93	Hereford U	5	1
1993–94	Raith R	36	1
1994–95		20	—
1995–96	Wycombe W	27	—

ROWE, Rodney

Born Huddersfield 30.7.75 Ht 5 9
Wt 12 04
Forward. From Trainee.

Season	Club	Apps	Goals
1993–94	Huddersfield T	13	1
1994–95		—	—
1994–95	*Scarborough*	14	1
1994–95	*Bury*	3	—
1995–96	Huddersfield T	14	1

ROWE, Zeke

Born Stoke Newington 30.10.73 Ht 5 10
Wt 11 08
Midfield. From Trainee.

Season	Club	Apps	Goals
1992–93	Chelsea	—	—
1993–94		—	—

Season Club League Appearances/Goals

Season	Club	Apps	Goals
1993–94	*Barnet*	10	2
1994–95	Chelsea	—	—
1995–96		—	—
1995–96	*Brighton & HA*	9	3

ROWETT, Gary

Born Bromsgrove 6.3.74 Ht 6 1
Wt 12 06
Forward. From Trainee.

Season	Club	Apps	Goals
1991–92	Cambridge U	13	2
1992–93		21	2
1993–94		29	5
1993–94	Everton	2	—
1994–95		2	—
1994–95	*Blackpool*	17	—
1995–96	Derby Co	35	—

ROWLAND, Keith

Born Portadown 1.9.71 Ht 5 10
Wt 10 00
Midfield. From Trainee. Northern Ireland 8 full caps.

Season	Club	Apps	Goals
1990–91	Bournemouth	—	—
1991–92		37	—
1992–93		35	2
1992–93	*Coventry C*	2	—
1993–94	West Ham U	23	—
1994–95		12	—
1995–96		23	—

ROWLANDS, Aled

Born Anglesey 9.6.78 Ht 5 8 Wt 10 13
Midfield. From Trainee. Wales Under-21.

Season	Club	Apps	Goals
1995–96	Manchester C	—	—

ROWSON, David

Born Aberdeen 14.9.76 Ht 5 10
Wt 11 10
Midfield. From FC Stoneywood.

Season	Club	Apps	Goals
1994–95	Aberdeen	—	—
1995–96		9	—

ROY, Bryan

Born Amsterdam 12.2.69 Ht 5 10
Wt 10 10
Midfield. From Foggia. Holland 32 full caps.

Season	Club	Apps	Goals
1987–88	Ajax	13	2
1988–89		29	5
1989–90		29	3
1990–91		29	4
1991–92		21	3
1992–93		5	—
1992–93	Foggia	20	3
1993–94		30	11
1994–95	Nottingham F	37	13
1995–96		28	8

ROYCE, Simon

Born Forest Gate 9.9.71 Ht 6 2
Wt 12 10
Goalkeeper. From Heybridge Swifts.

Season	Club	Apps	Goals
1991–92	Southend U	1	—
1992–93		3	—
1993–94		6	—
1994–95		13	—
1995–96		46	—

RUDDOCK, Neil

Born London 9.5.68 Ht 6 2 Wt 12 12
Defender. From Apprentice. England Youth, Under-21, B, 1 full cap.

Season	Club	Apps	Goals
1985–86	Millwall	—	—
1985–86	Tottenham H	—	—
1986–87		4	—
1987–88		5	—
1988–89	Millwall	2	1
1988–89	Southampton	13	3
1989–90		29	3
1990–91		35	3
1991–92		30	—
1992–93	Tottenham H	38	3
1993–94	Liverpool	39	3
1994–95		37	2
1995–96		20	5

RUFUS, Marvin

Born Lewisham 11.9.76
Midfield. From Charlton Ath Trainee.

Season	Club	Apps	Goals
1994–95	Leyton Orient	7	—
1995–96		—	—

RUFUS, Richard

Born Lewisham 12.1.75 Ht 6 1 Wt 10 05
Defender. From Trainee. England Under-21.

Season	Club	Apps	Goals
1993–94	Charlton Ath	—	—
1994–95		28	—
1995–96		41	—

Season Club League Appearances/Goals

RUSH, David

Born Sunderland 15.5.71 Ht 5 10
Wt 11 02
Forward. From Trainee.

Season	Club	Apps	Goals
1989–90	Sunderland	—	—
1990–91		11	2
1991–92		25	4
1991–92	*Hartlepool U*	8	2
1992–93	Sunderland	18	6
1993–94		5	—
1993–94	*Peterborough U*	4	1
1994–95	Sunderland	—	—
1994–95	*Cambridge U*	2	—
1994–95	Oxford U	34	9
1995–96		43	11

RUSH, Ian

Born St Asaph 20.10.61 Ht 6 0 Wt 12 06
Forward. From Apprentice. Wales Schools, Under-21, 73 full caps.

Season	Club	Apps	Goals
1978–79	Chester C	1	—
1979–80	Chester	33	14
1979–80	Liverpool	—	—
1980–81		7	—
1981–82		32	17
1982–83		34	24
1983–84		41	32
1984–85		28	14
1985–86		40	22
1986–87		42	30
1987–88	Juventus	29	7
1988–89	Liverpool	24	7
1989–90		36	18
1990–91		37	16
1991–92		18	4
1992–93		32	14
1993–94		42	14
1994–95		36	12
1995–96		20	5
1995–96	Leeds U	—	—

RUSH, Matthew

Born Dalston 6.8.71 Ht 5 11 Wt 12 06
Midfield. From Trainee. Eire Under-21.

Season	Club	Apps	Goals
1990–91	West Ham U	5	—
1991–92		10	2
1992–93		—	—
1992–93	*Cambridge U*	10	—
1993–94	West Ham U	10	1
1993–94	*Swansea C*	13	—
1994–95	West Ham U	23	2
1995–96	Norwich C	1	—

RUSHFELDT, Sigurd

Born Tromso 11.12.72 Ht 6 3 Wt 13 00
Forward. Norway 6 full caps.

Season	Club	Apps	Goals
1995–96	Birmingham C	7	—

RUSSELL, Alex

Born Crosby 17.3.73 Ht 5 8 Wt 11 07
Midfield. From Burscough.

Season	Club	Apps	Goals
1994–95	Rochdale	7	1
1995–96		25	—

RUSSELL, Craig

Born Jarrow 4.2.74 Ht 5 10 Wt 12 06
Forward. From Trainee.

Season	Club	Apps	Goals
1991–92	Sunderland	4	—
1992–93		—	—
1993–94		35	9
1994–95		38	5
1995–96		41	13

RUSSELL, Kevin

Born Portsmouth 6.12.66 Ht 5 9
Wt 10 12
Forward. From Brighton Apprentice. England Youth.

Season	Club	Apps	Goals
1984–85	Portsmouth	—	—
1985–86		1	—
1986–87		3	1
1987–88	Wrexham	38	21
1988–89		46	22
1989–90	Leicester C	10	—
1990–91		13	5
1990–91	*Peterborough U*	7	3
1990–91	*Cardiff C*	3	—
1991–92	Leicester C	20	5
1991–92	*Hereford U*	3	1
1991–92	*Stoke C*	5	1
1992–93	Stoke C	40	5
1993–94	Burnley	28	6
1993–94	Bournemouth	17	1
1994–95		13	—
1994–95	Notts Co	11	—
1995–96	Wrexham	40	7

RUSSELL, Lee

Born Southampton 3.9.69 Ht 5 10
Wt 11 09
Defender. From Trainee.

Season	Club	Apps	Goals
1988–89	Portsmouth	2	—
1989–90		3	—

Season	Club	League Appearances/Goals	
1990–91		19	1
1991–92		9	—
1992–93		14	—
1993–94		10	—
1994–95		19	—
1994–95	*Bournemouth*	3	—
1995–96	Portsmouth	19	—

RUSSELL, Wayne

Born Cardiff 29.11.67 Ht 6 2 Wt 12 12
Goalkeeper. From Ebbw Vale.

1993–94	Burnley	—	—
1994–95		8	—
1995–96		10	—

RUST, Nicky

Born Ely 25.9.74 Ht 6 0 Wt 13 01
Goalkeeper. From Arsenal Trainee.

1993–94	Brighton & HA	46	—
1994–95		44	—
1995–96		46	—

RYAN, Darren

Born Oswestry 3.7.72 Ht 5 9 Wt 11 00
Midfield. From Trainee.

1990–91	Shrewsbury T	2	—
1991–92		2	—
1992–93	Chester C	17	2
1992–93	Stockport Co	4	—
1993–94		32	6
1994–95	Rochdale	25	2
1995–96		7	—
1995–96	Chester C	4	1

RYAN, John

Born Cork 7.12.75 Ht 5 8 Wt 11 06
Forward. From Cork C.

1993–94	Brighton & HA	—	—
1994–95		—	—
1995–96		—	—

RYAN, Keith

Born Northampton 25.6.70 Ht 5 11
Wt 12 07
Midfield. From Berkhamsted T.

1993–94	Wycombe W	42	1
1994–95		24	4
1995–96		23	4

RYAN, Robbie

Born Dublin 11.8.76 Ht 5 10 Wt 12 00
Defender. From Belvedere.

1994–95	Huddersfield T	—	—
1995–96		—	—

RYDER, Stuart

Born Sutton Coldfield 6.11.73 Ht 6 0
Wt 12 05
Defender. From Trainee. England Under-21.

1992–93	Walsall	22	—
1993–94		26	—
1994–95		36	5
1995–96		3	—

Season	Club	League Appearances/Goals	

SAHLIN, Dan

Born Falun 18.4.67
Forward. From Hammarby.

1995–96	Birmingham C	1	—

SALAKO, John

Born Nigeria 11.2.69 Ht 5 9 Wt 12 03
Forward. From Trainee. England 5 full caps.

1986–87	Crystal Palace	4	—
1987–88		31	—
1988–89		28	—
1989–90		17	2
1989–90	*Swansea C*	13	3
1990–91	Crystal Palace	35	6
1991–92		10	2
1992–93		13	—
1993–94		38	8
1994–95		39	4
1995–96	Coventry C	37	3

SALE, Mark

Born Burton-on-Trent 27.2.72 Ht 6 5
Wt 14 04
Forward. From Trainee.

1989–90	Stoke C	2	—
1990–91		—	—
1991–92	Cambridge U	—	—
1991–92	Birmingham C	6	—
1992–93		15	—
1992–93	Torquay U	11	2
1993–94		33	6
1994–95	Preston NE	13	7
1995–96	Mansfield T	27	7

SALENKO, Oleg

Born St Pietroburg 25.10.69 Ht 5 11
Wt 12 09
Forward. From Valencia. Russia 8 full caps.

1995–96	Rangers	16	7

SALMON, Marc

Born Edmonton 10.2.73
Midfield. From Harlow T.

1995–96	Charlton Ath	—	—

Season	Club	League Appearances/Goals	

SALMON, Mike

Born Leyland 14.7.64 Ht 6 2 Wt 12 12
Goalkeeper. From Local.

1981–82	Blackburn R	1	—
1982–83		—	—
1982–83	*Chester C*	16	—
1983–84	Stockport Co	46	—
1984–85		46	—
1985–86		26	—
1986–87	Bolton W	26	—
1986–87	*Wrexham*	17	—
1987–88	Wrexham	40	—
1988–89		43	—
1989–90	Charlton Ath	—	—
1990–91		7	—
1991–92		—	—
1992–93		19	—
1993–94		41	—
1994–95		20	—
1995–96		27	—

SAMPSON, Ian

Born Wakefield 14.11.68 Ht 6 2
Wt 13 03
Defender. From Goole T.

1990–91	Sunderland	—	—
1991–92		8	—
1992–93		5	1
1993–94		4	—
1993–94	*Northampton T*	8	—
1994–95	Northampton T	42	2
1995–96		33	4

SAMUEL, Randy

Born Trinidad 23.12.63
Defender. From Fortuna Sittard. Canada full caps.

1995–96	Port Vale	9	1

SAMWAYS, Mark

Born Doncaster 11.11.68 Ht 6 3
Wt 13 07
Goalkeeper. From Trainee.

1987–88	Doncaster R	11	—
1988–89		12	—
1989–90		46	—
1990–91		26	—
1991–92		26	—
1991–92	*Scunthorpe U*	8	—
1992–93	Scunthorpe U	31	—

Season	Club	League Appearances/Goals	
1993–94		41	—
1994–95		42	—
1995–96		33	—

SAMWAYS, Vinny

Born Bethnal Green 27.10.68 Ht 5 8
Wt 11 02
Midfield. From Apprentice. England Youth, Under-21.

Season	Club	Apps	Goals
1985–86	Tottenham H	—	—
1986–87		2	—
1987–88		26	—
1988–89		19	3
1989–90		23	3
1990–91		23	1
1991–92		27	1
1992–93		34	—
1993–94		39	3
1994–95	Everton	19	1
1995–96		4	1
1995–96	*Wolverhampton W*	3	—
1995–96	*Birmingham C*	12	—

SANDEMAN, Bradley

Born Northampton 24.2.70 Ht 5 10
Wt 10 08
Midfield. From Trainee.

Season	Club	Apps	Goals
1987–88	Northampton T	2	—
1988–89		22	2
1989–90		29	1
1990–91		5	—
1990–91	Maidstone U	20	1
1991–92		37	7
1992–93	Port Vale	22	1
1993–94		9	—
1994–95		37	—
1995–96		1	—

SANDFORD, Lee

Born Basingstoke 22.4.68 Ht 6 0
Wt 13 03
Defender. From Apprentice. England Youth.

Season	Club	Apps	Goals
1985–86	Portsmouth	7	—
1986–87		—	—
1987–88		21	1
1988–89		31	—
1989–90		13	—
1989–90	Stoke C	23	2
1990–91		32	2
1991–92		38	—
1992–93		42	2
1993–94		42	1
1994–95		35	1
1995–96		46	—

SANSAM, Christian

Born Hull 26.12.75 Ht 6 0 Wt 11 00
Forward. From Trainee.

Season	Club	Apps	Goals
1993–94	Scunthorpe U	10	—
1994–95		6	—
1995–96		5	1
1995–96	Scarborough	6	—

SANSOME, Paul

Born N Addington 6.10.61 Ht 6 0
Wt 13 06
Goalkeeper. From Crystal Palace Apprentice.

Season	Club	Apps	Goals
1979–80	Millwall	—	—
1980–81		—	—
1981–82		8	—
1982–83		24	—
1983–84		31	—
1984–85		46	—
1985–86		36	—
1986–87		10	—
1987–88		1	—
1987–88	Southend U	6	—
1988–89		44	—
1989–90		46	—
1990–91		46	—
1991–92		45	—
1992–93		43	—
1993–94		42	—
1994–95		33	—
1995–96		—	—
1995–96	*Birmingham C*	1	—

SANTOS, Yazalde

Born Jersey 30.7.75
Forward.

Season	Club	Apps	Goals
1995–96	Bournemouth	3	—

SARGENT, Dave

Born Wembley 22.12.77 Ht 5 10
Wt 12 00
Defender. From Watford.

Season	Club	Apps	Goals
1995–96	Wycombe W	—	—

Season	Club	League Appearances/Goals	

SAUNDERS, Dean

Born Swansea 21.6.64 Ht 5 8 Wt 10 06
Forward. From Apprentice. Wales 52 full caps.

1982–83	Swansea C	—	—
1983–84		19	3
1984–85		30	9
1984–85	*Cardiff C*	4	—
1985–86	Brighton & HA	42	15
1986–87		30	6
1986–87	Oxford U	12	6
1987–88		37	12
1988–89		10	4
1988–89	Derby Co	30	14
1989–90		38	11
1990–91		38	17
1991–92	Liverpool	36	10
1992–93		6	1
1992–93	Aston Villa	35	12
1993–94		38	10
1994–95		39	15

To Galatasaray

SAUNDERS, Lee

Born Nuneaton 23.3.77 Ht 5 10 Wt 12 03
Defender. From Trainee.

1994–95	Doncaster R	—	—
1995–96		—	—

SAUNDERS, Mark

Born Reading 23.7.71 Ht 5 10 Wt 11 12
Midfield. From Tiverton.

1995–96	Plymouth Arg	10	1

SAVAGE, Dave

Born Dublin 30.7.73 Ht 6 2 Wt 12 07
Midfield. From Longford T. Eire Under-21, 5 full caps.

1994–95	Millwall	37	2
1995–96		27	—

SAVAGE, Rob

Born Wrexham 18.10.74 Ht 6 0 Wt 10 01
Forward. From Trainee. Wales Under-21, 3 full caps.

1993–94	Manchester U	—	—
1994–95	Crewe Alex	6	2
1995–96		30	7

SAVILLE, Andy

Born Hull 12.12.64 Ht 6 1 Wt 12 11
Forward. From Local.

1983–84	Hull C	1	—
1984–85		4	1
1985–86		9	1
1986–87		35	9
1987–88		31	6
1988–89		20	1
1988–89	Walsall	12	4
1989–90		26	1
1989–90	Barnsley	15	3
1990–91		45	12
1991–92		22	6
1991–92	Hartlepool U	1	—
1992–93		36	13
1992–93	Birmingham C	10	7
1993–94		39	10
1994–95		10	—
1994–95	*Burnley*	4	1
1995–96	Preston NE	44	29

SCAIFE, Nicky

Born Middlesbrough 14.5.75 Ht 6 1 Wt 13 13
Midfield. From Whitby.

1994–95	York C	1	—
1995–96		1	—

SCALES, John

Born Harrogate 4.7.66 Ht 6 2 Wt 13 05
Defender. England B, 3 full caps.

1984–85	Leeds U	—	—
1985–86	Bristol R	29	1
1986–87		43	1
1987–88	Wimbledon	25	1
1988–89		38	5
1989–90		28	2
1990–91		36	2
1991–92		41	—
1992–93		32	1
1993–94		37	—
1994–95		3	—
1994–95	Liverpool	35	2
1995–96		27	—

SCARGILL, Jon

Born Dewsbury 9.4.77 Ht 6 1 Wt 14 02
Goalkeeper. From Trainee.

1994–95	Sheffield W	—	—
1995–96		—	—

Season Club League Appearances/Goals

SCHMEICHEL, Peter

Born Gladsaxe 18.11.63 Ht 6 4 Wt 15 13
Goalkeeper. Denmark 87 full caps.

Season	Club	Apps	Goals
1984	Hvidovre	30	—
1985		28	6
1986		30	—
1987	Brondby	23	2
1988		26	—
1989		26	—
1990		26	—
1991		18	—
1991–92	Manchester U	40	—
1992–93		42	—
1993–94		40	—
1994–95		32	—
1995–96		36	—

SCHOFIELD, Jon

Born Barnsley 16.5.65 Ht 5 11 Wt 11 08
Midfield. From Gainsborough T.

Season	Club	Apps	Goals
1988–89	Lincoln C	29	2
1989–90		29	2
1990–91		42	3
1991–92		39	1
1992–93		40	—
1993–94		40	2
1994–95		12	1
1994–95	Doncaster R	27	1
1995–96		41	4

SCHOLES, Paul

Born Salford 16.11.74 Ht 5 7 Wt 11 00
Forward. From Trainee. England Youth.

Season	Club	Apps	Goals
1992–93	Manchester U	—	—
1993–94		—	—
1994–95		17	5
1995–96		26	10

SCIMECA, Riccardo

Born Leamington Spa 13.6.75 Ht 6 1
Wt 12 09
Defender. From Trainee. England Under-21.

Season	Club	Apps	Goals
1993–94	Aston Villa	—	—
1994–95		—	—
1995–96		17	—

SCOTT, Andy

Born Manchester 27.6.75 Ht 6 0 Wt 12 11
Defender. From Trainee.

Season	Club	Apps	Goals
1992–93	Blackburn R	—	—
1993–94		—	—
1994–95	Cardiff C	13	1
1995–96		1	—

SCOTT, Andy

Born Epsom 2.8.72 Ht 6 1 Wt 11 05
Forward. From Sutton U.

Season	Club	Apps	Goals
1992–93	Sheffield U	2	1
1993–94		15	—
1994–95		37	4
1995–96		7	—

SCOTT, Colin

Born Glasgow 19.5.70 Ht 6 1 Wt 12 04
Goalkeeper. From Dalry Thistle.

Season	Club	Apps	Goals
1987–88	Rangers	—	—
1988–89		—	—
1989–90		—	—
1990–91		—	—
1990–91	*Airdrieonians*	1	—
1991–92	Rangers	—	—
1992–93		—	—
1993–94		6	—
1994–95		4	—
1995–96		3	—

SCOTT, Gary

Born Liverpool 3.2.78
Defender. From Trainee.

Season	Club	Apps	Goals
1995–96	Tranmere R	—	—

SCOTT, Keith

Born London 9.6.67 Ht 6 3 Wt 14 00
Forward. From Leicester U.

Season	Club	Apps	Goals
1989–90	Lincoln C	10	2
1990–91		6	—
From Wycombe W			
1993–94	Wycombe W	15	10
1993–94	Swindon T	27	4
1994–95		24	8
1994–95	Stoke C	18	3
1995–96		7	—
1995–96	Norwich C	12	2
1995–96	*Bournemouth*	8	1

SCOTT, Kevin

Born Easington 17.12.66 Ht 6 2
Wt 14 03
Defender. From Middlesbrough.

Season	Club	Apps	Goals
1984–85	Newcastle U	—	—
1985–86		—	—

Season	Club	League Appearances	Goals
1986–87		3	1
1987–88		4	1
1988–89		29	—
1989–90		42	3
1990–91		42	—
1991–92		44	1
1992–93		45	2
1993–94		18	—
1993–94	Tottenham H	12	1
1994–95		4	—
1994–95	*Port Vale*	17	1
1995–96	Tottenham H	2	—

SCOTT, Martin

Born Sheffield 7.1.68 Ht 5 10 Wt 11 08
Midfield. From Apprentice.

Season	Club	League Appearances	Goals
1984–85	Rotherham U	3	—
1985–86		—	—
1986–87		12	—
1987–88		19	—
1987–88	*Nottingham F*	—	—
1988–89	Rotherham U	19	1
1989–90		28	1
1990–91		13	1
1990–91	Bristol C	27	1
1991–92		46	3
1992–93		35	3
1993–94		45	5
1994–95		18	2
1994–95	Sunderland	24	—
1995–96		43	6

SCOTT, Peter

Born London 1.10.63 Ht 5 9 Wt 12 03
Midfield. From Apprentice.

Season	Club	League Appearances	Goals
1981–82	Fulham	1	—
1982–83		—	—
1983–84		32	4
1984–85		19	1
1985–86		32	5
1986–87		30	6
1987–88		23	2
1988–89		37	3
1989–90		41	3
1990–91		23	2
1991–92		39	1
1992–93	Bournemouth	10	—
1993–94	Barnet	30	2
1994–95		28	—
1995–96		20	—

SCOTT, Richard

Born Dudley 29.9.74 Ht 5 9 Wt 12 08
Defender. From Trainee.

Season	Club	League Appearances	Goals
1992–93	Birmingham C	1	—
1993–94		6	—
1994–95		5	—
1994–95	Shrewsbury T	8	1
1995–96		36	6

SCOTT, Rob

Born Epsom 15.8.73 Ht 6 1 Wt 11 10
Forward. From Sutton U.

Season	Club	League Appearances	Goals
1993–94	Sheffield U	—	—
1994–95		1	—
1994–95	*Scarborough*	8	3
1995–96	Sheffield U	5	1
1995–96	*Northampton T*	5	—
1995–96	Fulham	21	5

SCOWCROFT, James

Born Bury St Edmunds 15.11.75 Ht 6 1
Wt 12 02
Forward. From Trainee.

Season	Club	League Appearances	Goals
1994–95	Ipswich T	—	—
1995–96		23	2

SCULLY, Pat

Born Dublin 23.6.70 Ht 6 1 Wt 13 07
Defender. From Trainee. Eire Schools, Youth, Under-21, Under-23, B, 1 full cap.

Season	Club	League Appearances	Goals
1987–88	Arsenal	—	—
1988–89		—	—
1989–90		—	—
1989–90	*Preston NE*	13	1
1990–91	Arsenal	—	—
1990–91	*Northampton T*	15	—
1990–91	Southend U	21	—
1991–92		44	3
1992–93		42	3
1993–94		8	—
1993–94	Huddersfield T	11	—
1994–95		38	1
1995–96		25	1

SCULLY, Tony

Born Dublin 12.6.76 Ht 5 7 Wt 11 12
Forward. From Trainee. Eire Under-21.

Season	Club	League Appearances	Goals
1993–94	Crystal Palace	—	—
1994–95		—	—
1994–95	*Bournemouth*	10	—

Season	Club	League Appearances	Goals
1995–96	Crystal Palace	2	—
1995–96	*Cardiff C*	14	—

SEABURY, Kevin

Born Shrewsbury 24.11.73 Ht 5 9
Wt 11 11
Defender. From Trainee.

Season	Club	League Appearances	Goals
1992–93	Shrewsbury T	1	—
1993–94		—	—
1994–95		30	—
1995–96		34	—

SEAGRAVES, Mark

Born Bootle 22.10.66 Ht 6 0 Wt 13 04
Defender. From Apprentice. England Schools, Youth.

Season	Club	League Appearances	Goals
1983–84	Liverpool	—	—
1984–85		—	—
1985–86		—	—
1986–87		—	—
1986–87	*Norwich C*	3	—
1987–88	Liverpool	—	—
1987–88	Manchester C	17	—
1988–89		23	—
1989–90		2	—
1990–91	Bolton W	32	—
1991–92		40	1
1992–93		37	5
1993–94		35	1
1994–95		13	—
1995–96	Swindon T	28	—

SEAL, David

Born Penrith NSW 26.1.72 Ht 5 11
Wt 12 01
Forward. From Aalst.

Season	Club	League Appearances	Goals
1994–95	Bristol C	9	—
1995–96		30	10

SEALEY, Les

Born Bethnal Green 29.9.57 Ht 6 1
Wt 13 06
Goalkeeper. From Apprentice.

Season	Club	League Appearances	Goals
1975–76	Coventry C	—	—
1976–77		11	—
1977–78		2	—
1978–79		36	—
1979–80		20	—
1980–81		35	—
1981–82		15	—
1982–83		39	—
1983–84	Luton T	42	—
1984–85		26	—
1984–85	*Plymouth Arg*	6	—
1985–86	Luton T	35	—
1986–87		41	—
1987–88		31	—
1988–89		32	—
1989–90		—	—
1989–90	*Manchester U*	2	—
1990–91	Manchester U	31	—
1991–92	Aston Villa	18	—
1991–92	*Coventry C*	2	—
1992–93	Aston Villa	—	—
1992–93	*Birmingham C*	12	—
1992–93	Manchester U	—	—
1993–94		—	—
1994–95	Blackpool	7	—
1994–95	West Ham U	—	—
1995–96		2	—

SEAMAN, David

Born Rotherham 19.9.63 Ht 6 4
Wt 14 10
Goalkeeper. From Apprentice. England Under-21, B, 29 full caps.

Season	Club	League Appearances	Goals
1981–82	Leeds U	—	—
1982–83	Peterborough U	38	—
1983–84		45	—
1984–85		8	—
1984–85	Birmingham C	33	—
1985–86		42	—
1986–87	QPR	41	—
1987–88		32	—
1988–89		35	—
1989–90		33	—
1990–91	Arsenal	38	—
1991–92		42	—
1992–93		39	—
1993–94		39	—
1994–95		31	—
1995–96		38	—

SEARLE, Damon

Born Cardiff 26.10.71 Ht 5 11 Wt 10 04
Defender. From Trainee. Wales Youth, Under-21.

Season	Club	League Appearances	Goals
1990–91	Cardiff C	35	—
1991–92		42	1
1992–93		42	1
1993–94		42	—
1994–95		32	—
1995–96		41	1

Season	Club	League Appearances/Goals	

SEATON, Andrew

Born Edinburgh 16.9.77
Midfield. From Stoneyburn Jun.

1995–96	Falkirk	1	—

SEBA, Jesus

Born Zaragoza 11.4.74 Ht 5 6 Wt 9 13
Midfield. From Zaragoza.

1995–96	Wigan Ath	20	3

SEDGEMORE, Ben

Born Wolverhampton 5.8.75 Ht 6 0
Wt 12 04
Midfield. From Trainee.

1993–94	Birmingham C	—	—
1994–95		—	—
1994–95	*Northampton T*	1	—
1995–96	Birmingham C	—	—
1995–96	*Mansfield T*	9	—
1995–96	Peterborough U	17	—

SEDGLEY, Steve

Born Enfield 26.5.68 Ht 6 1 Wt 13 13
Midfield. From Apprentice. England Under-21.

1986–87	Coventry C	26	—
1987–88		27	2
1988–89		31	1
1989–90	Tottenham H	32	—
1990–91		34	—
1991–92		34	—
1992–93		22	3
1993–94		42	5
1994–95	Ipswich T	26	4
1995–96		40	4

SEGERS, Hans

Born Eindhoven 30.10.61 Ht 5 11
Wt 12 07
Goalkeeper. From PSV Eindhoven.

1984–85	Nottingham F	28	—
1985–86		11	—
1986–87		14	—
1986–87	*Stoke C*	1	—
1987–88	Nottingham F	5	—
1987–88	*Sheffield U*	10	—
1987–88	*Dunfermline Ath*	4	—
1988–89	Nottingham F	—	—
1988–89	Wimbledon	33	—
1989–90		38	—
1990–91		37	—
1991–92		41	—
1992–93		41	—
1993–94		41	—
1994–95		32	—
1995–96		4	—

SELLARS, Neil

Born Kirkcaldy 9.5.77 Ht 5 8 Wt 9 11
Midfield. From Kirkcaldy YM.

1994–95	Raith R	—	—
1995–96		1	—

SELLARS, Scott

Born Sheffield 27.11.65 Ht 5 7 Wt 9 10
Midfield. From Apprentice. England Under-21.

1982–83	Leeds U	1	—
1983–84		19	3
1984–85		39	7
1985–86		17	2
1986–87	Blackburn R	32	4
1987–88		42	7
1988–89		46	2
1989–90		43	14
1990–91		9	1
1991–92		30	7
1992–93	Leeds U	7	—
1992–93	Newcastle U	13	2
1993–94		30	3
1994–95		12	—
1995–96		6	—
1995–96	Bolton W	22	3

SELLEY, Ian

Born Chertsey 14.6.74 Ht 5 9 Wt 10 01
Midfield. From Trainee. England Youth, Under-21.

1992–93	Arsenal	9	—
1993–94		18	—
1994–95		13	—
1995–96		—	—

SEMPLE, Ryan

Born Derry 2.7.77
Midfield. From Trainee.

1994–95	Peterborough U	2	—
1995–96		—	—

Season	Club	League Appearances/Goals	

SERRANT, Carl

Born Bradford 12.9.75
Defender. From Trainee.

1994–95	Oldham Ath	—	—
1995–96		20	1

SERTORI, Mark

Born Manchester 1.9.67 Ht 6 2 Wt 14 02
Midfield.

1986–87	Stockport Co	3	—
1987–88		1	—
1987–88	Lincoln C	—	—
1988–89		26	4
1989–90		24	5
1989–90	Wrexham	18	2
1990–91		29	—
1991–92		36	—
1992–93		12	—
1993–94		15	1
1994–95	Bury	2	—
1995–96		11	1

SETTER, Lee

Born Torquay 10.10.76 Ht 5 6 Wt 10 10
Midfield. From Trainee.

1995–96	Torquay U	—	—

SHAIL, Mark

Born Sweden 15.10.66 Ht 6 1 Wt 13 03
Defender. From Yeovil.

1992–93	Bristol C	4	—
1993–94		36	2
1994–95		38	2
1995–96		12	—

SHAKESPEARE, Craig

Born Birmingham 26.10.63 Ht 5 10
Wt 12 05
Midfield. From Apprentice.

1981–82	Walsall	—	—
1982–83		31	4
1983–84		46	6
1984–85		41	9
1985–86		32	4
1986–87		44	11
1987–88		45	8
1988–89		45	3
1989–90	Sheffield W	17	—
1989–90	WBA	18	1
1990–91		36	1
1991–92		44	8
1992–93		14	2
1993–94	Grimsby T	33	3
1994–95		19	3
1995–96		28	2

SHANNON, Rab

Born Bellshill 20.4.66 Ht 5 11 Wt 11 08
Defender. From St Columba's BC.
Scotland Youth, Under-21.

1982–83	Dundee	—	—
1983–84		6	—
1984–85		3	—
1985–86		33	—
1986–87		39	5
1987–88		41	—
1988–89		29	1
1989–90		36	1
1990–91		37	2
1991–92	*Middlesbrough*	1	—
1991–92	Dundee	3	—
1991–92	Dunfermline Ath	27	—
1992–93		42	—
1993–94	Motherwell	43	—
1994–95		25	3
1995–96	Dundee U	26	1

SHARP, Graeme

Born Glasgow 16.10.60 Ht 6 1 Wt 11 06
Forward. From Eastercraigs. Scotland
Under-21, 12 full caps.

1978–79	Dumbarton	6	1
1979–80		34	16
1979–80	Everton	2	—
1980–81		4	—
1981–82		29	15
1982–83		41	15
1983–84		28	7
1984–85		36	21
1985–86		37	19
1986–87		27	5
1987–88		32	13
1988–89		26	7
1989–90		33	6
1990–91		27	3
1991–92	Oldham Ath	42	12
1992–93		21	7
1993–94		34	9
1994–95		12	2
1995–96		—	—

Season	Club	League Appearances/Goals	

SHARP, Kevin

Born Ontario 19.9.74 Ht 5 9 Wt 10 07
Midfield. From Auxerre. England Youth.

1992–93	Leeds U	4	—
1993–94		10	—
1994–95		2	—
1995–96		1	—
1995–96	Wigan Ath	20	6

SHARP, Lee

Born Lincoln 18.12.76 Ht 6 2 Wt 14 00
Goalkeeper. From Lincoln U.

1995–96	QPR	—	—

SHARP, Ray

Born Stirling 16.11.69 Ht 5 11 Wt 12 04
Defender. From Gairdoch U. Scotland Under-21.

1986–87	Dunfermline Ath	—	—
1987–88		—	—
1988–89	*Stenhousemuir*	5	—
1988–89	Dunfermline Ath	9	—
1989–90		27	—
1990–91		31	—
1991–92		25	—
1992–93		27	—
1993–94		30	1
1994–95		2	—
1994–95	Preston NE	21	—
1995–96		1	—

SHARPE, John

Born Birmingham 9.8.75 Ht 5 11
Wt 11 06
Midfield. From Trainee.

1993–94	Manchester C	—	—
1994–95		—	—
1995–96		—	—
1995–96	*Exeter C*	14	1

SHARPE, Lee

Born Halesowen 27.5.71 Ht 6 0
Wt 12 06
Forward. From Trainee. England Under-21, B, 8 full caps.

1987–88	Torquay U	14	3
1988–89	Manchester U	22	—
1989–90		18	1
1990–91		23	2
1991–92		14	1
1992–93		27	1
1993–94		30	9
1994–95		28	3
1995–96		31	4

SHARPLES, John

Born Bury 26.1.73 Ht 6 01 Wt 11 03
Defender. From Manchester U Trainee.

1991–92	Hearts	—	—
1992–93		—	—
1993–94		—	—
1994–95	Ayr U	27	—
1995–96		26	4
1995–96	York C	10	—

SHAW, Graham

Born Newcastle under Lyme 7.6.67
Ht 5 9 Wt 11 04
Forward. From Apprentice.

1985–86	Stoke C	20	5
1986–87		18	2
1987–88		33	6
1988–89		28	5
1989–90	Preston NE	31	5
1990–91		44	10
1991–92		46	14
1992–93	Stoke C	29	5
1993–94		4	—
1994–95		3	—
1994–95	*Plymouth Arg*	6	—
1994–95	Rochdale	4	—
1995–96		18	—

SHAW, Greg

Born Dumfries 15.2.70 Ht 6 0 Wt 10 12
Forward. From Dalbeattie Star.

1988–89	Ayr U	2	—
1989–90		3	—
1990–91		9	—
1991–92		39	10
1992–93		5	—
1992–93	Falkirk	6	2
1993–94		28	10
1994–95		3	—
1995–96	Dunfermline Ath	28	12

SHAW, Paul

Born Burnham 4.9.73 Ht 5 11 Wt 12 02
Forward. From Trainee.

1991–92	Arsenal	—	—

Season Club League Appearances/Goals

Season	Club	Apps	Goals
1992–93		—	—
1993–94		—	—
1994–95		1	—
1994–95	*Burnley*	9	4
1995–96	Arsenal	3	—
1995–96	*Cardiff C*	6	—
1995–96	*Peterborough U*	12	5

SHAW, Richard

Born Brentford 11.9.68 Ht 5 9 Wt 12 08
Defender. From Apprentice.

Season	Club	Apps	Goals
1986–87	Crystal Palace	—	—
1987–88		3	—
1988–89		14	—
1989–90		21	—
1989–90	*Hull C*	4	—
1990–91	Crystal Palace	36	1
1991–92		10	—
1992–93		33	—
1993–94		34	2
1994–95		41	—
1995–96		15	—
1995–96	Coventry C	21	—

SHAW, Simon

Born Teeside 21.9.73 Ht 5 11 Wt 11 02
Midfield. From Trainee.

Season	Club	Apps	Goals
1991–92	Darlington	1	—
1992–93		23	4
1993–94		30	1
1994–95		12	1
1995–96		41	1

SHEARER, Alan

Born Newcastle 13.8.70 Ht 5 11
Wt 12 06
Forward. From Trainee. England Youth, Under-21, B, 28 full caps.

Season	Club	Apps	Goals
1987–88	Southampton	5	3
1988–89		10	—
1989–90		26	3
1990–91		36	4
1991–92		41	13
1992–93	Blackburn R	21	16
1993–94		40	31
1994–95		42	34
1995–96		35	31

SHEARER, Duncan

Born Fort William 28.8.62 Ht 5 10
Wt 10 09
Forward. From Inverness Clach. Scotland 7 full caps.

Season	Club	Apps	Goals
1983–84	Chelsea	—	—
1984–85		—	—
1985–86		2	1
1985–86	Huddersfield T	8	7
1986–87		42	21
1987–88		33	10
1988–89	Swindon T	36	14
1989–90		42	20
1990–91		44	22
1991–92		37	22
1991–92	Blackburn R	6	1
1992–93	Aberdeen	34	22
1993–94		43	17
1994–95		23	7
1995–96		30	3

SHEARER, Lee

Born Southend 23.10.77 Ht 6 4
Wt 12 01
Defender. From Trainee.

Season	Club	Apps	Goals
1994–95	Leyton Orient	2	—
1995–96		8	1

SHEARER, Peter

Born Birmingham 4.2.67 Ht 6 0 Wt 11 00
Forward. From Apprentice.

Season	Club	Apps	Goals
1984–85	Birmingham C	4	—
1985–86		—	—
1986–87	Rochdale	1	—
From Cheltenham T			
1988–89	Bournemouth	4	1
1989–90		34	4
1990–91		5	—
1991–92		8	1
1992–93		34	4
1993–94		—	—
1993–94	Birmingham C	2	—
1994–95		23	7
1995–96		—	—

SHEERIN, Paul

Born Edinburgh 28.8.74 Ht 5 10 Wt 12 00
Midfield. From Whitehill Welfare.
Scotland Under-21.

Season	Club	Apps	Goals
1992–93	Alloa	9	—

Season	Club	League Appearances/Goals	
1992–93	Southampton	—	—
1993–94		—	—
1994–95		—	—
1995–96		—	—

SHEFFIELD, Jon

Born Bedworth 1.2.69 Ht 6 0 Wt 12 08
Goalkeeper.

Season	Club	Apps	Goals
1986–87	Norwich C	—	—
1987–88		—	—
1988–89		1	—
1989–90		—	—
1989–90	*Aldershot*	11	—
1989–90	*Ipswich T*	—	—
1990–91	Norwich C	—	—
1990–91	*Aldershot*	15	—
1990–91	*Cambridge U*	2	—
1991–92	Cambridge U	13	—
1992–93		13	—
1993–94		—	—
1993–94	*Colchester U*	6	—
1993–94	*Swindon T*	2	—
1994–95	Cambridge U	28	—
1994–95	*Hereford U*	8	—
1995–96	Peterborough U	46	—

SHELTON, Gary

Born Nottingham 21.3.58 Ht 5 7
Wt 11 00
Midfield. From Apprentice. England Under-21.

Season	Club	Apps	Goals
1975–76	Walsall	2	—
1976–77		10	—
1977–78		12	—
1977–78	Aston Villa	—	—
1978–79		19	7
1979–80		4	—
1979–80	*Notts Co*	8	—
1980–81	Aston Villa	—	—
1981–82		1	—
1981–82	Sheffield W	9	1
1982–83		40	4
1983–84		40	5
1984–85		41	4
1985–86		31	1
1986–87		37	3
1987–88	Oxford U	32	—
1988–89		33	1
1989–90	Bristol C	43	9
1990–91		43	8
1991–92		19	3
1992–93		42	4
1993–94		3	—
1993–94	*Rochdale*	3	—
1994–95	Chester C	33	2
1995–96		11	1

SHEPHERD, Paul

Born Leeds 17.11.77
Forward. From Trainee. England Youth.

Season	Club	Apps	Goals
1995–96	Leeds U	—	—

SHEPHERD, Tony

Born Glasgow 16.11.66 Ht 5 9 Wt 10 00
Midfield. From Celtic BC. Scotland Schools, Youth.

Season	Club	Apps	Goals
1983–84	Celtic	—	—
1984–85		—	—
1985–86		1	—
1986–87		21	2
1987–88		6	1
1988–89		—	—
1989–90	*Bristol C*	3	—
1989–90	Carlisle U	31	2
1990–91		44	6
1991–92	Motherwell	5	—
1992–93		5	—
From Portadown			
1995–96	Ayr U	11	—
1995–96	Partick T	1	—
1995–96	Stranraer	2	—

SHEPPARD, James

Born Preston 18.9.75 Ht 5 8 Wt 10 10
Midfield. From Trainee.

Season	Club	Apps	Goals
1994–95	Blackpool	—	—
1995–96		—	—

SHEPPARD, Simon

Born Clevedon 7.8.73 Ht 6 4 Wt 14 03
Goalkeeper. From Trainee. England Youth.

Season	Club	Apps	Goals
1991–92	Watford	—	—
1992–93		5	—
1993–94		18	—
1993–94	*Scarborough*	9	—
1994–95	Watford	—	—
1994–95	Reading	—	—
1995–96		18	—

Season	Club	League Appearances/Goals	

SHERIDAN, Darren

Born Manchester 8.12.67 Ht 5 4 Wt 10 12
Midfield. From Winsford.

1993–94	Barnsley	3	—
1994–95		35	2
1995–96		41	—

SHERIDAN, John

Born Stretford 1.10.64 Ht 5 10 Wt 12 01
Midfield. From Local. Eire Youth, Under-21, Under-23, B, 34 full caps.

1981–82	Leeds U	—	—
1982–83		27	2
1983–84		11	1
1984–85		42	6
1985–86		32	4
1986–87		40	15
1987–88		38	12
1988–89		40	7
1989–90	Nottingham F	—	—
1989–90	Sheffield W	27	2
1990–91		46	10
1991–92		24	6
1992–93		25	3
1993–94		20	3
1994–95		36	1
1995–96		17	—
1995–96	*Birmingham C*	2	—

SHERINGHAM, Teddy

Born Highams Park 2.4.66 Ht 6 0 Wt 12 05
Forward. From Apprentice. England Youth, 20 full caps.

1983–84	Millwall	7	1
1984–85		—	—
1984–85	*Aldershot*	5	—
1985–86	Millwall	18	4
1986–87		42	13
1987–88		43	22
1988–89		33	11
1989–90		31	9
1990–91		46	33
1991–92	Nottingham F	39	13
1992–93		3	1
1992–93	Tottenham H	38	21
1993–94		19	14
1994–95		42	18
1995–96		38	16

SHERLOCK, Paul

Born Wigan 17.11.73 Ht 5 11 Wt 11 05
Defender. From Trainee.

1992–93	Notts Co	—	—
1993–94		7	—
1994–95		5	1
1994–95	Mansfield T	2	—
1995–96		18	2

SHERON, Mike

Born Liverpool 11.1.72 Ht 5 10 Wt 11 12
Forward. From Trainee. England Under-21.

1990–91	Manchester C	—	—
1990–91	*Bury*	5	1
1991–92	Manchester C	29	7
1992–93		38	11
1993–94		33	6
1994–95	Norwich C	21	1
1995–96		7	1
1995–96	Stoke C	28	15

SHERWOOD, Tim

Born St Albans 2.2.69 Ht 6 1 Wt 12 09
Midfield. From Trainee. England Under-21, B.

1986–87	Watford	—	—
1987–88		13	—
1988–89		19	2
1989–90	Norwich C	27	3
1990–91		37	7
1991–92		7	—
1991–92	Blackburn R	11	—
1992–93		39	3
1993–94		38	2
1994–95		38	6
1995–96		33	3

SHIELDS, Greg

Born Falkirk 21.8.76 Ht 5 9 Wt 10 10
Defender. From Rangers BC.

1994–95	Rangers	—	—
1995–96		1	—

SHILTON, Peter

Born Leicester 18.9.49 Ht 6 1 Wt 14 00
Goalkeeper. From Apprentice. England Schools, Youth, Under-23, 125 full caps. Football League.

1965–66	Leicester C	1	—

Season	Club	League Appearances	Goals
1966–67		4	—
1967–68		35	1
1968–69		42	—
1969–70		39	—
1970–71		40	—
1971–72		37	—
1972–73		41	—
1973–74		42	—
1974–75		5	—
1974–75	Stoke C	25	—
1975–76		42	—
1976–77		40	—
1977–78		3	—
1977–78	Nottingham F	37	—
1978–79		42	—
1979–80		42	—
1980–81		40	—
1981–82		41	—
1982–83	Southampton	39	—
1983–84		42	—
1984–85		41	—
1985–86		37	—
1986–87		29	—
1987–88	Derby Co	40	—
1988–89		38	—
1989–90		35	—
1990–91		31	—
1991–92		31	—
1991–92	Plymouth Arg	7	—
1992–93		23	—
1993–94		4	—
1994–95		—	—
1994–95	Wimbledon	—	—
1994–95	Bolton W	1	—
1995–96	Coventry C	—	—
1995–96	West Ham U	—	—

SHILTON, Sam

Born Nottingham 21.7.78 Ht 5 10 Wt 11 06
Midfield. From Schools.

Season	Club	League Appearances	Goals
1994–95	Plymouth Arg	2	—
1995–96		1	—
1995–96	Coventry C	—	—

SHIPP, Danny

Born Romford 25.9.76 Ht 5 11 Wt 11 13
Forward. From Trainee.

Season	Club	League Appearances	Goals
1995–96	West Ham U	—	—

SHIPPERLEY, Neil

Born Chatham 30.10.74 Ht 6 1 Wt 13 11
Forward. From Trainee. England Under-21.

Season	Club	League Appearances	Goals
1992–93	Chelsea	3	1
1993–94		24	4
1994–95		10	2
1994–95	*Watford*	6	1
1994–95	Southampton	19	4
1995–96		37	7

SHIRTLIFF, Peter

Born Barnsley 6.4.61 Ht 6 1 Wt 12 02
Defender. From Apprentice.

Season	Club	League Appearances	Goals
1978–79	Sheffield W	26	1
1979–80		3	—
1980–81		28	—
1981–82		31	2
1982–83		8	—
1983–84		36	1
1984–85		35	—
1985–86		21	—
1986–87	Charlton Ath	33	3
1987–88		36	2
1988–89		34	2
1989–90	Sheffield W	33	2
1990–91		39	2
1991–92		12	—
1992–93		20	—
1993–94	Wolverhampton W	39	—
1994–95		28	—
1995–96		2	—
1995–96	Barnsley	32	—

SHORE, Jamie

Born Bristol 1.9.77 Ht 5 9 Wt 10 09
Midfield. From Trainee. England Youth.

Season	Club	League Appearances	Goals
1994–95	Norwich C	—	—
1995–96		—	—

SHORT, Chris

Born Munster 9.5.70 Ht 5 10 Wt 12 04
Defender. From Pickering T.

Season	Club	League Appearances	Goals
1988–89	Scarborough	2	—
1989–90		41	1
1990–91		—	—
1990–91	*Manchester U*	—	—
1990–91	Notts Co	15	1
1991–92		27	—
1992–93		31	1

Season	Club	Apps	Goals
1993–94		6	—
1994–95		13	—
1994–95	*Huddersfield T*	6	—
1995–96	Notts Co	2	—
1995–96	Sheffield U	15	—

SHORT, Craig

Born Bridlington 25.6.68 Ht 6 3
Wt 13 08
Defender. From Pickering T. England Schools.

Season	Club	Apps	Goals
1987–88	Scarborough	21	2
1988–89		42	5
1989–90	Notts Co	44	2
1990–91		—	—
1990–91		43	—
1991–92		38	3
1992–93		3	1
1992–93	Derby Co	38	3
1993–94		43	3
1994–95		37	3
1995–96	Everton	23	2

SHOTTON, Malcolm

Born Newcastle 16.2.57 Ht 6 3 Wt 13 12
Defender. From Apprentice.

Season	Club	Apps	Goals
1974–75	Leicester C	—	—
1975–76		—	—
From Nuneaton			
1980–81	Oxford U	38	5
1981–82		40	4
1982–83		46	1
1983–84		43	1
1984–85		42	1
1985–86		42	—
1986–87		11	—
1987–88		1	—
1987–88	Portsmouth	10	—
1987–88	Huddersfield T	14	—
1988–89		2	1
1988–89	Barnsley	37	5
1989–90		29	1
1989–90	Hull C	16	2
1990–91		26	—
1991–92		17	—
1992–93	Ayr U	35	1
1993–94		38	2
1994–95	Barnsley	8	1
1995–96		2	—

SHOWLER, Paul

Born Doncaster 10.10.66 Ht 5 7
Wt 11 00
Midfield. From Sheffield W, Sunderland, Colne Dynamoes, Altrincham.

Season	Club	Apps	Goals
1991–92	Barnet	39	7
1992–93		32	5
1993–94	Bradford C	32	5
1994–95		23	2
1995–96		33	8

SHUTT, Carl

Born Sheffield 10.10.61 Ht 5 10
Wt 12 10
Forward. From Spalding U.

Season	Club	Apps	Goals
1984–85	Sheffield W	—	—
1985–86		19	9
1986–87		20	7
1987–88		1	—
1987–88	Bristol C	22	9
1988–89		24	1
1988–89	Leeds U	3	4
1989–90		20	2
1990–91		28	10
1991–92		14	1
1992–93		14	—
1993–94		—	—
1993–94	Birmingham C	26	4
1993–94	*Manchester C*	6	—
1994–95	Bradford C	32	4
1995–96		34	8

SHUTTLEWORTH, Barry

Born Accrington 9.7.77 Ht 5 8 Wt 11 00
Forward. From Trainee.

Season	Club	Apps	Goals
1995–96	Bury	—	—

SIGURDSSON, Larus

Born Akuveyni 4.6.73 Ht 6 0 Wt 12 06
Defender. From Thor.

Season	Club	Apps	Goals
1994–95	Stoke C	23	1
1995–96		46	—

SILENZI, Andrea

Born Rome 10.2.66 Ht 6 3 Wt 11 13
Forward. From Torino. Italy 1 full cap.

Season	Club	Apps	Goals
1995–96	Nottingham F	10	—

Season	Club	League Appearances/Goals	

SIMKIN, Darren

Born Walsall 24.3.70 Ht 6 0 Wt 13 08
Defender. From Blakenall.

1991–92	Wolverhampton W	—	—
1992–93		7	—
1993–94		8	—
1994–95		—	—
1994–95	Shrewsbury T	12	—
1995–96		—	—

SIMPSON, Colin

Born Oxford 30.4.76 Ht 6 1 Wt 11 05
Forward. From Trainee.

1994–95	Watford	—	—
1995–96		1	—

SIMPSON, Derek

Born Lanark 23.12.78 Ht 5 10 Wt 10 09
Midfield. From Trainee.

1995–96	Reading	—	—

SIMPSON, Fitzroy

Born Trowbridge 26.2.70 Ht 5 6 Wt 10 04
Midfield. From Trainee.

1988–89	Swindon T	7	—
1989–90		30	2
1990–91		38	3
1991–92		30	4
1991–92	Manchester C	11	1
1992–93		29	1
1993–94		15	—
1994–95		16	2
1994–95	*Bristol C*	4	—
1995–96	Manchester C	—	—
1995–96	Portsmouth	30	5

SIMPSON, Gary

Born Ashford 14.2.76 Ht 6 3 Wt 13 11
Defender. From Trainee.

1994–95	Luton T	—	—
1995–96		—	—
1995–96	*Fulham*	7	—

SIMPSON, Karl

Born Newmarket 12.10.76 Ht 5 11
Wt 11 06
Defender. From Trainee.

1994–95	Norwich C	—	—
1995–96		1	—

SIMPSON, Michael

Born Nottingham 28.2.74 Ht 5 9
Wt 10 08
Midfield. From Trainee.

1992–93	Notts Co	—	—
1993–94		6	1
1994–95		19	2
1995–96		23	—

SIMPSON, Paul

Born Carlisle 26.7.66 Ht 5 6 Wt 11 09
Forward. From Apprentice. England Youth, Under-21.

1982–83	Manchester C	3	—
1983–84		—	—
1984–85		10	6
1985–86		37	8
1986–87		32	3
1987–88		38	1
1988–89		1	—
1988–89	Oxford U	25	8
1989–90		42	9
1990–91		46	17
1991–92		31	9
1991–92	Derby Co	16	7
1992–93		35	12
1993–94		34	9
1994–95		42	8
1995–96		39	10

SIMPSON, Philip

Born London 18.10.69 Ht 5 9 Wt 11 12
Midfield. From Stevenage B.

1995–96	Barnet	24	1

SIMPSON, Robert

Born Luton 3.3.76 Ht 5 9 Wt 10 07
Forward. From Trainee. England Youth.

1993–94	Tottenham H	—	—
1994–95		—	—
1995–96		—	—

SINCLAIR, David

Born Dunfermline 6.10.69 Ht 5 11
Wt 12 10
Midfield. From Kelty U21.

1990–91	Raith R	23	1
1991–92		22	1
1992–93	*Portadown*	—	—
1992–93	Raith R	32	—

Season	Club	League Appearances	Goals
1993–94		36	2
1994–95		32	3
1995–96		32	3

SINCLAIR, Frank

Born Lambeth 3.12.71 Ht 5 9 Wt 12 09
Defender. From Trainee.

Season	Club	League Appearances	Goals
1989–90	Chelsea	—	—
1990–91		4	—
1991–92		8	1
1991–92	*WBA*	6	1
1992–93	Chelsea	32	—
1993–94		35	—
1994–95		35	3
1995–96		13	1

SINCLAIR, Ron

Born Stirling 19.11.64 Ht 5 11 Wt 12 03
Goalkeeper. From Apprentice. Scotland Schools, Youth.

Season	Club	League Appearances	Goals
1982–83	Nottingham F	—	—
1983–84		—	—
1983–84	*Wrexham*	11	—
1984–85	Nottingham F	—	—
1984–85	*Derby Co*	—	—
1985–86	Nottingham F	—	—
1985–86	*Sheffield U*	—	—
1985–86	*Leeds U*	—	—
1986–87	Leeds U	8	—
1986–87	*Halifax T*	4	—
1987–88	Leeds U	—	—
1988–89		—	—
1988–89	*Halifax T*	10	—
1989–90	Leeds U	—	—
1989–90	Bristol C	27	—
1990–91		17	—
1991–92		—	—
1991–92	*Walsall*	10	—
1991–92	Stoke C	26	—
1992–93		29	—
1993–94		—	—
1994–95		24	—
1994–95	*Bradford C*	—	—
1995–96	Stoke C	1	—

SINCLAIR, Trevor

Born Dulwich 2.3.73 Ht 5 10 Wt 12 05
Midfield. From Trainee. England Under-21.

Season	Club	League Appearances	Goals
1989–90	Blackpool	9	—
1990–91		31	1
1991–92		27	3
1992–93		45	11
1993–94	QPR	32	4
1994–95		33	4
1995–96		37	2

SINNOTT, Lee

Born Pelsall 12.7.65 Ht 6 1 Wt 13 07
Defender. From Apprentice. England Youth, Under-21.

Season	Club	League Appearances	Goals
1981–82	Walsall	4	—
1982–83		32	2
1983–84		4	—
1983–84	Watford	20	—
1984–85		30	—
1985–86		18	2
1986–87		10	—
1987–88	Bradford C	42	1
1988–89		42	2
1989–90		45	2
1990–91		44	1
1991–92	Crystal Palace	36	—
1992–93		19	—
1993–94		—	—
1993–94	Bradford C	18	—
1994–95		16	1
1994–95	Huddersfield T	25	1
1995–96		32	—

SINTON, Andy

Born Newcastle 19.3.66 Ht 5 8 Wt 11 05
Midfield. From Apprentice. England Schools, B, 12 full caps.

Season	Club	League Appearances	Goals
1982–83	Cambridge U	13	5
1983–84		34	6
1984–85		26	2
1985–86		20	—
1985–86	Brentford	26	3
1986–87		46	5
1987–88		46	11
1988–89		31	9
1988–89	QPR	10	3
1989–90		38	6
1990–91		38	3
1991–92		38	3
1992–93		36	7
1993–94	Sheffield W	25	3
1994–95		25	—
1995–96		10	—
1995–96	Tottenham H	9	—

Season	Club	League Appearances/Goals	

SKELTON, Aaron

Born Welwyn 22.11.74 Ht 6 0 Wt 12 06
Midfield. From Trainee.

Season	Club	Apps	Goals
1992–93	Luton T	—	—
1993–94		—	—
1994–95		5	—
1995–96		—	—

SKILLING, Mark

Born Irvine 6.10.72 Ht 5 9 Wt 10 13
Midfield. From Saltcoats Victoria. Scotland Under-21.

Season	Club	Apps	Goals
1992–93	Kilmarnock	40	4
1993–94		23	3
1994–95		17	3
1995–96		15	1

SKINGSLEY, Ross

Born Woolwich 10.1.77 Ht 5 11 Wt 12 00
Midfield. From Trainee.

Season	Club	Apps	Goals
1995–96	Middlesbrough	—	—

SKINNER, Craig

Born Bury 21.10.70 Ht 5 10 Wt 11 00
Forward. From Trainee.

Season	Club	Apps	Goals
1989–90	Blackburn R	—	—
1990–91		7	—
1991–92		9	—
1992–93	Plymouth Arg	13	1
1993–94		16	—
1994–95		24	3
1995–96	Wrexham	23	3

SKINNER, Justin

Born Hounslow 30.1.69 Ht 6 0 Wt 11 03
Midfield. From Apprentice.

Season	Club	Apps	Goals
1986–87	Fulham	3	—
1987–88		32	6
1988–89		38	8
1989–90		30	4
1990–91		32	5
1991–92	Bristol R	42	3
1992–93		12	—
1993–94		29	5
1994–95		38	2
1995–96		28	—

SKINNER, Justin

Born London 17.9.72 Ht 5 8 Wt 10 12
Defender. From Trainee.

Season	Club	Apps	Goals
1991–92	Wimbledon	—	—
1992–93		1	—
1993–94		—	—
1993–94	*Bournemouth*	16	—
1994–95	Wimbledon	—	—
1994–95	*Wycombe W*	5	—
1995–96	Wimbledon	1	—

SKIVERTON, Terry

Born Mile End 26.6.75 Ht 5 11 Wt 11 06
Defender. From Trainee.

Season	Club	Apps	Goals
1993–94	Chelsea	—	—
1994–95		—	—
1994–95	*Wycombe W*	10	—
1995–96	Chelsea	—	—
1995–96	Wycombe W	4	1

SLADE, Steve

Born Romford 6.10.75 Ht 5 10 Wt 10 10
Forward. From Trainee. England Under-21.

Season	Club	Apps	Goals
1994–95	Tottenham H	—	—
1995–96		5	—

SLATER, Darren

Born Bishop Auckland 4.1.79
Defender. From Trainee.

Season	Club	Apps	Goals
1995–96	Hartlepool U	1	—

SLATER, Robbie

Born Ormskirk 26.11.64 Ht 5 11 Wt 12 05
Midfield. From Lens. Australia full caps.

Season	Club	Apps	Goals
1994–95	Blackburn R	18	—
1995–96	West Ham U	22	2

SLATER, Stuart

Born Sudbury 27.3.69 Ht 5 9 Wt 11 06
Midfield. From Apprentice. England Under-21, B.

Season	Club	Apps	Goals
1986–87	West Ham U	—	—
1987–88		2	—
1988–89		18	1
1989–90		40	7
1990–91		40	3
1991–92		41	—

Season	Club	Apps	Goals
1992–93	Celtic	39	2
1993–94		4	1
1993–94	Ipswich T	28	1
1994–95		27	1
1995–96		17	2

SLAVIN, James

Born Lanark 18.1.75 Ht 6 2 Wt 14 00
Defender. From Giffnock North.

Season	Club	Apps	Goals
1992–93	Celtic	—	—
1993–94		—	—
1994–95		3	—
1995–96	Partick T	8	—

SLAWSON, Steve

Born Nottingham 13.11.72 Ht 6 0
Wt 12 11
Forward. From Trainee.

Season	Club	Apps	Goals
1991–92	Notts Co	13	1
1992–93		20	3
1992–93	*Burnley*	5	2
1993–94	Notts Co	4	—
1994–95		1	—
1994–95	*Shrewsbury T*	6	—
1995–96	Mansfield T	29	5

SLOAN, Scott

Born Wallsend 14.12.67 Ht 5 10
Wt 12 01
Forward. From Ponteland.

Season	Club	Apps	Goals
1988–89	Berwick R	26	4
1989–90		35	16
1990–91	Newcastle U	16	1
1991–92		—	—
1991–92	Falkirk	23	4
1992–93		29	6
1993–94		12	1
1993–94	*Cambridge U*	4	1
1994–95	Hartlepool U	29	2
1995–96		6	—

SMALL, Bryan

Born Birmingham 15.11.71 Ht 5 9
Wt 11 09
Defender. From Trainee. England Under-21.

Season	Club	Apps	Goals
1989–90	Aston Villa	—	—
1990–91		—	—
1991–92		8	—
1992–93		14	—
1993–94		9	—
1994–95		5	—
1994–95	*Birmingham C*	3	—
1995–96	Aston Villa	—	—
1995–96	Bolton W	1	—

SMART, Allan

Born Perth 8.7.74 Ht 6 2 Wt 12 10
Forward.

Season	Club	Apps	Goals
1994–95	Caledonian Th	4	—
1994–95	Preston NE	19	6
1995–96		2	—
1995–96	*Carlisle U*	4	—

SMILLIE, Neil

Born Barnsley 19.7.58 Ht 5 6 Wt 10 07
Forward. From Apprentice.

Season	Club	Apps	Goals
1975–76	Crystal Palace	—	—
1976–77		1	—
1976–77	*Brentford*	3	—
1977–78	Crystal Palace	1	—
1978–79		8	1
1979–80		8	1
1980–81		24	2
1981–82		41	3
1982–83	Brighton & HA	25	—
1983–84		26	2
1984–85		24	—
1985–86	Watford	16	3
1986–87		—	—
1986–87	Reading	16	—
1987–88		23	—
1988–89	Brentford	28	2
1989–90		43	5
1990–91		36	3
1991–92		44	7
1992–93		21	1
1993–94	Gillingham	38	2
1994–95		15	1
1995–96		—	—

SMITH, Alan

Born Birmingham 21.11.62 Ht 6 3
Wt 12 13
Forward. From Alvechurch. England B, 13 full caps. Football League.

Season	Club	Apps	Goals
1982–83	Leicester C	39	13
1983–84		40	15
1984–85		39	12
1985–86		40	19
1986–87		33	14

1986–87	*Leicester C*	9	3
1987–88	Arsenal	39	11
1988–89		36	23
1989–90		38	10
1990–91		37	22
1991–92		39	12
1992–93		31	3
1993–94		25	3
1994–95		19	2
1995–96		—	—

SMITH, Alex

Born Liverpool 15.2.76 Ht 5 8 Wt 9 09
Defender. From Trainee.

1994–95	Everton	—	—
1995–96		—	—
1995–96	Swindon T	8	—

SMITH, Andy

Born Aberdeen 22.11.68 Ht 6 1
Wt 12 07
Forward. From Peterhead.

1990–91	Airdrieonians	28	3
1991–92		29	4
1992–93		34	4
1993–94		38	7
1994–95		36	12
1995–96	Dunfermline Ath	19	9

SMITH, Chris

Born Birmingham 3.1.77 Ht 5 7
Wt 11 01
Forward. From Trainee.

1994–95	Walsall	—	—
1995–96		1	—

SMITH, Craig

Born Mansfield 2.8.76 Ht 6 0 Wt 13 07
Midfield. From Trainee.

1995–96	Derby Co	—	—

SMITH, David

Born Liverpool 26.12.70 Ht 5 10
Wt 12 02
Midfield. From Trainee.

1989–90	Norwich C	1	—
1990–91		3	—
1991–92		1	—
1992–93		6	—

Season Club League Appearances/Goals

1993–94		7	—
1994–95	Oxford U	42	—
1995–96		45	1

SMITH, David

Born Gloucester 29.3.68 Ht 5 8
Wt 10 08
Midfield. England Under-21.

1986–87	Coventry C	—	—
1987–88		16	4
1988–89		35	3
1989–90		37	6
1990–91		36	1
1991–92		24	4
1992–93		6	1
1992–93	*Bournemouth*	1	—
1992–93	Birmingham C	13	1
1993–94		25	2
1993–94	WBA	18	—
1994–95		22	—
1995–96		16	—

SMITH, David

Born Lambeth 13.9.76 Ht 5 11 Wt 11 07
Defender. From Trainee.

1995–96	Fulham	—	—

SMITH, Dean

Born West Bromwich 19.3.71 Ht 6 0
Wt 13 00
Defender. From Trainee.

1988–89	Walsall	15	—
1989–90		7	—
1990–91		33	—
1991–92		9	—
1992–93		42	1
1993–94		36	1
1994–95	Hereford U	35	3
1995–96		40	8

SMITH, Gary

Born Harlow 3.12.68 Ht 5 10 Wt 12 09
Midfield.

1985–86	Fulham	1	—
1986–87		—	—
1987–88	Colchester U	11	—

From Enfield, Wycombe W, Welling U

1993–94	Barnet	9	—
1994–95		4	—
1995–96		1	—

Season	Club	League Appearances/Goals	

SMITH, Gary

Born Glasgow 25.3.71 Ht 6 0 Wt 10 04
Defender. From Duntocher BC.

1988–89	Falkirk	3	—
1989–90		36	—
1990–91		31	—
1991–92	Aberdeen	16	1
1992–93		40	—
1993–94		21	—
1994–95		31	—
1995–96		33	—

SMITH, Gavin

Born Sheffield 24.9.77
Forward. From Trainee.

1994–95	Sheffield W	—	—
1995–96		—	—

SMITH, Henry

Born Lanark 10.3.56 Ht 6 2 Wt 12 00
Goalkeeper. From School. Scotland Under-21, 3 full caps.

1978–79	Leeds U	—	—
1979–80		—	—
1980–81		—	—
1981–82	Hearts	33	—
1982–83		39	—
1983–84		36	—
1984–85		36	—
1985–86		36	—
1986–87		43	—
1987–88		44	—
1988–89		36	—
1989–90		36	—
1990–91		23	—
1991–92		44	—
1992–93		25	—
1993–94		27	—
1994–95		15	—
1995–96		3	—

SMITH, Ian

Born Bury 28.11.76 Ht 6 0 Wt 12 00
Defender. From Trainee.

1993–94	Manchester C	—	—
1994–95		—	—
1995–96		—	—

Season	Club	League Appearances/Goals	

SMITH, James

Born Birmingham 17.9.74 Ht 5 6
Wt 10 08
Forward. From Trainee.

1993–94	Wolverhampton W	—	—
1994–95		25	—
1995–96		13	—

SMITH, Mark

Born Birmingham 2.1.73 Ht 6 1
Wt 13 09
Goalkeeper. From Trainee.

1991–92	Nottingham F	—	—
1992–93		—	—
1992–93	Crewe Alex	7	—
1993–94		32	—
1994–95		24	—
1995–96		—	—

SMITH, Martin

Born Sunderland 13.11.74 Ht 5 11
Wt 12 03
Forward. From Trainee. England Under-21.

1992–93	Sunderland	—	—
1993–94		29	8
1994–95		35	10
1995–96		20	2

SMITH, Mike

Born Liverpool 28.9.73 Ht 5 11 Wt 11 07
Midfield. From Runcorn.

1995–96	Doncaster R	13	—

SMITH, Neil

Born London 30.9.71 Ht 5 9 Wt 12 05
Midfield. From Trainee.

1990–91	Tottenham H	—	—
1991–92		—	—
1991–92	Gillingham	26	2
1992–93		39	3
1993–94		35	2
1994–95		33	1
1995–96		37	1

SMITH, Paul

Born Lewisham 2.11.71 Ht 6 1 Wt 11 12
Midfield. From Horsham.

1994–95	Barnet	—	—
1995–96		—	—

Season	Club	League Appearances/Goals	

SMITH, Paul

Born Lenham 18.9.71 Ht 5 11 Wt 14 00
Midfield. From Trainee.

Season	Club	Apps	Goals
1989–90	Southend U	10	1
1990–91		2	—
1991–92		—	—
1992–93		8	—
1993–94	Brentford	32	3
1994–95		35	3
1995–96		46	4

SMITH, Paul

Born Easington 22.1.76 Ht 6 0 Wt 13 03
Forward. From Trainee.

Season	Club	Apps	Goals
1993–94	Burnley	1	—
1994–95		—	—
1995–96		10	—

SMITH, Paul

Born Hastings 25.1.76 Ht 5 11 Wt 11 07
Midfield. From Hastings.

Season	Club	Apps	Goals
1994–95	Nottingham F	—	—
1995–96		—	—

SMITH, Paul

Born Edinburgh 2.11.62 Ht 5 11
Wt 12 00
Midfield. From Edinburgh BC.

Season	Club	Apps	Goals
1980–81	Dundee	—	—
1981–82		—	—
1982–83	Dundee U	—	—
1982–83	Raith R	16	2
1983–84		38	8
1984–85		38	19
1985–86		35	21
1986–87	Motherwell	44	9
1987–88		30	4
1988–89		4	—
1988–89	Dunfermline Ath	35	5
1989–90		33	4
1990–91		31	2
1991–92	Falkirk	32	2
1992–93		19	1
1992–93	Dunfermline Ath	16	1
1993–94		44	9
1994–95		34	6
1995–96		11	—
1995–96	Hearts	9	—

SMITH, Peter

Born Stone 12.7.69 Ht 6 0 Wt 12 01
Defender. From Alma Swanley.

Season	Club	Apps	Goals
1994–95	Brighton & HA	38	1
1995–96		31	1

SMITH, Richard

Born Leicester 3.10.70 Ht 5 11 Wt 13 03
Defender. From Trainee.

Season	Club	Apps	Goals
1988–89	Leicester C	—	—
1989–90		4	—
1989–90	*Cambridge U*	4	—
1990–91	Leicester C	4	—
1991–92		25	1
1992–93		44	—
1993–94		8	—
1994–95		12	—
1995–96		1	—
1995–96	Grimsby T	18	—

SMITH, Scott

Born Christchurch 6.3.75 Ht 5 8
Wt 11 00
Defender. From Trainee.

Season	Club	Apps	Goals
1993–94	Rotherham U	7	—
1994–95		4	—
1995–96		14	—

SMITH, Shaun

Born Leeds 9.4.71 Ht 5 10 Wt 11 00
Defender. From Trainee.

Season	Club	Apps	Goals
1988–89	Halifax T	1	—
1989–90		6	—
1990–91		—	—
1991–92	Crewe Alex	10	—
1992–93		36	4
1993–94		37	7
1994–95		45	8
1995–96		29	1

SMITH, Thomas

Born Glasgow 12.10.73 Ht 5 8 Wt 11 07
Midfield. From 'S' Form.

Season	Club	Apps	Goals
1990–91	Partick T	1	—
1991–92		—	—
1992–93		2	—
1993–94		8	1
1994–95		14	1
1995–96		25	2

SMITH, Tommy

Born Northampton 25.11.77 Ht 5 9
Wt 10 10
Midfield. From Trainee.

Season	Club	Apps	Goals
1994–95	Manchester U	—	—
1995–96		—	—

SMITH, Tony

Born Sunderland 21.9.71 Ht 5 11
Wt 11 09
Defender. From Trainee. England Youth.

Season	Club	Apps	Goals
1990–91	Sunderland	9	—
1991–92		2	—
1991–92	*Hartlepool U*	5	—
1992–93	Sunderland	7	—
1993–94		1	—
1994–95		1	—
1995–96	Northampton T	2	—

SMITHARD, Matthew

Born Leeds 13.6.76 Ht 5 9 Wt 10 09
Forward. From Trainee.

Season	Club	Apps	Goals
1992–93	Leeds U	—	—
1993–94		—	—
1994–95		—	—
1995–96		—	—

SNEEKES, Richard

Born Amsterdam 30.10.68 Ht 5 11
Wt 12 03
Midfield. Holland Under-21.

Season	Club	Apps	Goals
1985–86	Ajax	1	—
1986–87		1	—
1987–88		1	—
1988–89	Volendam	31	7
1989–90	Fortuna Sittard	32	2
1990–91		32	7
1991–92		33	5
1992–93		29	6
From Locarno, Fortuna Sittard.			
1994–95	Bolton W	38	6
1995–96		17	1
1995–96	WBA	13	10

SNELDERS, Theo

Born Westervoort 7.12.63 Ht 6 2
Wt 14 02
Goalkeeper. From Twente. Holland full caps.

Season	Club	Apps	Goals
1988–89	Aberdeen	36	—
1989–90		23	—
1990–91		21	—
1991–92		42	—
1992–93		41	—
1993–94		33	—
1994–95		24	—
1995–96		7	—
1995–96	Rangers	2	—

SNODIN, Glynn

Born Rotherham 14.2.60 Ht 5 6 Wt 11 00
Defender. From Apprentice.

Season	Club	Apps	Goals
1976–77	Doncaster R	4	—
1977–78		22	2
1978–79		34	3
1979–80		41	1
1980–81		44	3
1981–82		40	7
1982–83		38	14
1983–84		43	13
1984–85		43	18
1985–86	Sheffield W	28	1
1986–87		31	—
1987–88	Leeds U	35	7
1988–89		35	3
1989–90		4	—
1990–91		20	—
1991–92		—	—
1991–92	*Oldham Ath*	8	1
1991–92	Rotherham U	3	—
1991–92	Hearts	7	—
1992–93		27	—
1993–94	Barnsley	11	—
1994–95		14	—
1995–96		—	—
1995–96	Carlisle U	—	—

SNODIN, Ian

Born Rotherham 15.8.63 Ht 5 7 Wt 9 00
Midfield. From Apprentice. England Youth, Under-21.

Season	Club	Apps	Goals
1979–80	Doncaster R	9	1
1980–81		32	2
1981–82		33	2
1982–83		34	3
1983–84		39	9
1984–85		41	8
1985–86	Leeds U	37	5
1986–87		14	1
1986–87	Everton	16	—
1987–88		31	2
1988–89		23	—

Season	Club	League Appearances/Goals	
1989–90		25	—
1990–91		1	—
1991–92		—	—
1992–93		20	1
1993–94		29	—
1994–95		3	—
1994–95	*Sunderland*	6	—
1994–95	Oldham Ath	17	—
1995–96		26	—

SOLLITT, Adam

Born Sheffield 22.6.77 Ht 6 0 Wt 10 09
Goalkeeper. From Trainee.

1995–96	Barnsley	—	—

SOLOMAN, Jason

Born Welwyn 6.10.70 Ht 6 0 Wt 12 02
Midfield. From Trainee. England Youth.

1988–89	Watford	—	—
1989–90		—	—
1990–91		8	—
1991–92		29	—
1992–93		36	2
1993–94		25	3
1994–95		2	—
1994–95	*Peterborough U*	4	—
1994–95	Wycombe W	6	1
1995–96		7	—

SOMMER, Jurgen

Born New York 27.2.69 Ht 6 5 Wt 15 12
Goalkeeper. USA full caps.

1991–92	Luton T	—	—
1991–92	*Brighton & HA*	1	—
1992–93	Luton T	—	—
1992–93	*Torquay U*	10	—
1993–94	Luton T	43	—
1994–95		37	—
1995–96		2	—
1995–96	QPR	33	—

SOUTHALL, Neville

Born Llandudno 16.9.58 Ht 6 0
Wt 14 00
Goalkeeper. From Winsford. Wales Under-21, 86 full caps.

1980–81	Bury	39	—
1981–82	Everton	26	—
1982–83		17	—
1982–83	*Port Vale*	9	—
1983–84	Everton	35	—
1984–85		42	—
1985–86		32	—
1986–87		31	—
1987–88		32	—
1988–89		38	—
1989–90		38	—
1990–91		38	—
1991–92		42	—
1992–93		40	—
1993–94		42	—
1994–95		41	—
1995–96		38	—

SOUTHALL, Nicky

Born Teeside 28.1.72 Ht 5 10 Wt 12 12
Forward. From Trainee.

1990–91	Hartlepool U	—	—
1991–92		22	3
1992–93		39	6
1993–94		40	9
1994–95		37	6
1995–96	Grimsby T	33	2

SOUTHGATE, Gareth

Born Watford 3.9.70 Ht 6 0 Wt 12 08
Midfield. From Trainee. England 9 full caps.

1988–89	Crystal Palace	—	—
1989–90		—	—
1990–91		1	—
1991–92		30	—
1992–93		33	3
1993–94		46	9
1994–95		42	3
1995–96	Aston Villa	31	1

SPACKMAN, Nigel

Born Romsey 2.12.60 Ht 6 1 Wt 13 04
Midfield. From Andover.

1980–81	Bournemouth	44	3
1981–82		35	3
1982–83		40	4
1983–84	Chelsea	40	3
1984–85		42	1
1985–86		39	7
1986–87		20	1
1986–87	Liverpool	12	—
1987–88		27	—
1988–89		12	—
1988–89	QPR	16	1

Season	Club	League Appearances/Goals	
1989–90		13	—
1989–90	Rangers	21	1
1990–91		35	—
1991–92		42	—
1992–93		2	—
1992–93	Chelsea	6	—
1993–94		9	—
1994–95		36	—
1995–96		16	—

SPARROW, Paul

Born London 24.3.75 Ht 6 0 Wt 11 07
Defender. From Trainee.

1993–94	Crystal Palace	—	—
1994–95		—	—
1995–96		1	—
1995–96	Preston NE	13	—

SPEARE, James

Born Liverpool 5.11.76 Ht 6 1 Wt 13 00
Goalkeeper. From Trainee.

1995–96	Everton	—	—

SPEARING, Tony

Born Romford 7.10.64 Ht 5 7 Wt 12 00
Defender. From Apprentice. England Youth.

1982–83	Norwich C	—	—
1983–84		4	—
1984–85		—	—
1984–85	*Stoke C*	9	—
1984–85	*Oxford U*	5	—
1985–86	Norwich C	8	—
1986–87		39	—
1987–88		18	—
1988–89	Leicester C	36	—
1989–90		20	1
1990–91		17	—
1991–92	Plymouth Arg	30	—
1992–93		5	—
1992–93	Peterborough U	22	—
1993–94		34	1
1994–95		33	—
1995–96		9	1

SPEED, Gary

Born Hawarden 8.9.69 Ht 5 9 Wt 12 10
Midfield. From Trainee. Wales Under-21, 35 full caps.

Season	Club	League Appearances/Goals	
1988–89	Leeds U	1	—
1989–90		25	3
1990–91		38	7
1991–92		41	7
1992–93		39	7
1993–94		36	10
1994–95		39	3
1995–96		29	2

SPEIGHT, Martyn

Born Stockton 26.7.78
Defender. From Trainee.

1995–96	Doncaster R	1	—

SPENCER, John

Born Glasgow 11.9.70 Ht 5 6 Wt 11 07
Forward. From Rangers Am BC. Scotland Under-21, 12 full caps.

1986–87	Rangers	—	—
1987–88		—	—
1988–89		—	—
1988–89	*Morton*	4	1
From Lai Sun			
1990–91	Rangers	5	1
1991–92		8	1
1992–93	Chelsea	23	7
1993–94		19	5
1994–95		29	11
1995–96		28	13

SPENCER, Simon

Born Islington 10.9.76 Ht 5 10 Wt 11 04
Midfield. From Trainee. England Youth.

1995–96	Tottenham H	—	—

SPINK, Dean

Born Birmingham 22.1.67 Ht 6 1
Wt 14 08
Forward. From Halesowen.

1989–90	Aston Villa	—	—
1989–90	*Scarborough*	3	2
1989–90	*Bury*	6	1
1989–90	Shrewsbury T	13	5
1990–91		43	6
1991–92		40	1
1992–93		23	1
1993–94		40	18
1994–95		39	11
1995–96		34	6

SPINK, Nigel

Born Chelmsford 8.8.58 Ht 6 2 Wt 14 06
Goalkeeper. From Chelmsford C. England B, 1 full cap.

Season	Club	Apps	Goals
1976–77	Aston Villa	—	—
1977–78		—	—
1978–79		—	—
1979–80		1	—
1980–81		—	—
1981–82		—	—
1982–83		22	—
1983–84		28	—
1984–85		19	—
1985–86		31	—
1986–87		32	—
1987–88		44	—
1988–89		34	—
1989–90		38	—
1990–91		34	—
1991–92		23	—
1992–93		25	—
1993–94		15	—
1994–95		13	—
1995–96		2	—
1995–96	WBA	15	—

SPITERI, Denis

Born Cardiff 16.10.76
Defender. From Trainee.

Season	Club	Apps	Goals
1995–96	Swansea C	—	—

SPOONER, Nicky

Born Manchester 5.6.71 Ht 5 10 Wt 11 09
Defender. From Trainee.

Season	Club	Apps	Goals
1990–91	Bolton W	—	—
1991–92		15	1
1992–93		6	1
1993–94		1	—
1994–95		1	—
1995–96		—	—

SQUIRES, Jamie

Born Preston 15.11.75 Ht 6 1 Wt 13 11
Defender. From Trainee.

Season	Club	Apps	Goals
1993–94	Preston NE	4	—
1994–95		11	—
1995–96		7	—

SRNICEK, Pavel

Born Ostrava 10.3.68 Ht 6 2 Wt 14 07
Goalkeeper. From Banik Ostrava. Czech 3 full caps.

Season	Club	Apps	Goals
1990–91	Newcastle U	7	—
1991–92		13	—
1992–93		32	—
1993–94		21	—
1994–95		38	—
1995–96		15	—

STABB, Chris

Born Bradford 12.10.76 Ht 5 9 Wt 11 11
Defender. From Trainee.

Season	Club	Apps	Goals
1994–95	Bradford C	1	—
1995–96		—	—

STALLARD, Mark

Born Derby 24.10.74 Ht 6 0 Wt 12 09
Forward. From Trainee.

Season	Club	Apps	Goals
1991–92	Derby Co	3	—
1992–93		5	—
1993–94		—	—
1994–95		16	2
1994–95	*Fulham*	4	3
1995–96	Derby Co	3	—
1995–96	Bradford C	21	9

STAMP, Philip

Born Middlesbrough 12.12.75 Ht 5 10 Wt 12 05
Midfield. From Trainee. England Youth.

Season	Club	Apps	Goals
1992–93	Middlesbrough	—	—
1993–94		10	—
1994–95		3	—
1995–96		12	2

STAMPS, Scott

Born Edgbaston 20.3.75 Ht 5 10 Wt 11 02
Defender. From Trainee.

Season	Club	Apps	Goals
1992–93	Torquay U	2	—
1993–94		6	—
1994–95		25	1
1995–96		23	1

STANCLIFFE, Paul

Born Sheffield 5.5.58 Ht 6 2 Wt 13 04
Defender. From Apprentice.

Season	Club	Apps	Goals
1975–76	Rotherham U	42	2

Season	Club	League Appearances/Goals	
1976–77		46	—
1977–78		32	3
1978–79		33	—
1979–80		33	1
1980–81		44	—
1981–82		42	2
1982–83		13	—
1983–84	Sheffield U	43	1
1984–85		33	1
1985–86		40	1
1986–87		36	2
1987–88		41	3
1988–89		42	3
1989–90		40	1
1990–91		3	—
1990–91	*Rotherham U*	5	—
1990–91	Wolverhampton W	17	—
1991–92	York C	18	1
1992–93		41	1
1993–94		28	1
1994–95		4	—
1995–96		—	—

STANISLAUS, Roger

Born Hammersmith 2.11.68 Ht 5 11
Wt 13 02
Defender. From Trainee.

Season	Club	Apps	Goals
1986–87	Arsenal	—	—
1987–88	Brentford	37	2
1988–89		43	1
1989–90		31	1
1990–91	Bury	44	2
1991–92		40	3
1992–93		24	—
1993–94		35	—
1994–95		33	—
1995–96	Leyton Orient	21	—

STANNARD, Jim

Born London 6.10.62 Ht 6 2 Wt 15 08
Goalkeeper. From Local.

Season	Club	Apps	Goals
1980–81	Fulham	17	—
1981–82		2	—
1982–83		—	—
1983–84		15	—
1984–85		7	—
1984–85	*Charlton Ath*	1	—
1984–85	*Southend U*	17	—
1985–86	Southend U	46	—
1986–87		46	—
1987–88	Fulham	46	—
1988–89		45	—
1989–90		44	1
1990–91		42	—
1991–92		46	—
1992–93		43	—
1993–94		46	—
1994–95		36	—
1995–96	Gillingham	46	—

STANT, Phil

Born Bolton 13.10.62 Ht 5 11 Wt 13 04
Forward. From Camberley.

Season	Club	Apps	Goals
1982–83	Reading	4	2
From Army			
1986–87	Hereford U	9	1
1987–88		39	9
1988–89		41	28
1989–90	Notts Co	22	6
1990–91		—	—
1990–91	*Blackpool*	12	5
1990–91	*Lincoln C*	4	—
1990–91	*Huddersfield T*	5	1
1990–91	Fulham	19	5
1991–92	Mansfield T	40	26
1992–93		17	6
1992–93	Cardiff C	24	11
1993–94		36	10
1993–94	*Mansfield T*	4	1
1994–95	Cardiff C	19	13
1994–95	Bury	20	13
1995–96		34	9

STAPLETON, Simon

Born Oxford 10.12.68 Ht 6 0 Wt 13 01
Midfield. From Portsmouth Trainee.

Season	Club	Apps	Goals
1988–89	Bristol R	5	—
1989–90		—	—
From Wycombe W			
1993–94	Wycombe W	22	1
1994–95		26	2
1995–96		1	—

STARBUCK, Phil

Born Nottingham 24.11.68 Ht 5 10
Wt 13 03
Forward. From Apprentice.

Season	Club	Apps	Goals
1986–87	Nottingham F	5	2
1987–88		10	—
1987–88	*Birmingham C*	3	—
1988–89	Nottingham F	7	—
1989–90		2	—

Season	Club	League Appearances/Goals	
1989–90	*Hereford U*	6	—
1990–91	Nottingham F	12	—
1990–91	*Blackburn R*	6	1
1991–92	Huddersfield T	44	14
1992–93		38	9
1993–94		46	12
1994–95		9	1
1994–95	Sheffield U	23	1
1995–96		11	1
1995–96	*Bristol C*	5	1

STARK, Wayne

Born Derby 14.10.76
Midfield. From Trainee.

1993–94	Mansfield T	1	—
1994–95		—	—
1995–96		—	—

STATHAM, Brian

Born Zimbabwe 21.5.69 Ht 5 11 Wt 11 00
Defender. From Apprentice. England Youth, Under-21.

1987–88	Tottenham H	18	—
1988–89		6	—
1989–90		—	—
1990–91		—	—
1990–91	*Reading*	8	—
1991–92	Tottenham H	—	—
1991–92	*Bournemouth*	2	—
1991–92	*Brentford*	18	—
1992–93	Brentford	45	—
1993–94		31	1
1994–95		36	—
1995–96		17	—

STATHAM, Mark

Born Daveyhulme 7.3.76 Ht 6 2 Wt 13 03
Goalkeeper. From Trainee.

1992–93	Nottingham F	—	—
1993–94		—	—
1994–95	Wigan Ath	2	—
1995–96		—	—

STATON, Luke

Born Doncaster 10.3.79 Ht 5 7 Wt 9 10
Midfield. From Trainee.

1995–96	Blackburn R	—	—

STAUNTON, Steve

Born Drogheda 19.1.69 Ht 6 0 Wt 12 04
Defender. From Dundalk. Eire Under-21, 62 full caps.

1986–87	Liverpool	—	—
1987–88		—	—
1987–88	*Bradford C*	8	—
1988–89	Liverpool	21	—
1989–90		20	—
1990–91		24	—
1991–92	Aston Villa	37	4
1992–93		42	2
1993–94		24	2
1994–95		35	5
1995–96		13	—

STEELE, Tim

Born Coventry 1.12.67 Ht 5 10 Wt 11 04
Forward. From Apprentice.

1985–86	Shrewsbury T	2	—
1986–87		11	1
1987–88		33	3
1988–89		15	1
1988–89	Wolverhampton W	11	1
1989–90		15	1
1990–91		28	2
1991–92		17	3
1991–92	*Stoke C*	7	1
1992–93	Wolverhampton W	4	—
1993–94	Bradford C	11	—
1993–94	Hereford U	20	2
1994–95		5	—
1995–96		7	—

STEELE, Winnie

Born Basildon 28.2.77 Ht 5 8 Wt 11 02
Midfield. From Trainee.

1995–96	Bury	—	—

STEFANOVIC, Dejan

Born Yugoslavia 28.10.74 Ht 6 2 Wt 12 10
Defender. Yugoslavia 4 full caps.

1995–96	Sheffield W	6	—

STEIN, Mark

Born S. Africa 29.1.66 Ht 5 6 Wt 11 09
Forward. England Youth.

1983–84	Luton T	1	—
1984–85		1	—

Season	Club	League Appearances/Goals	
1985–86		6	—
1985–86	*Aldershot*	2	1
1986–87	Luton T	21	8
1987–88		25	11
1988–89	QPR	31	4
1989–90		2	—
1989–90	Oxford U	41	9
1990–91		34	8
1991–92		7	1
1991–92	Stoke C	36	16
1992–93		46	26
1993–94		12	8
1993–94	Chelsea	18	13
1994–95		24	8
1995–96		8	—

STENSGAARD, Michael

Born Denmark 1.9.74 Ht 6 2 Wt 13 04
Goalkeeper. From Hvidovre. Denmark Under-21.

Season	Club	League Appearances/Goals	
1994–95	Liverpool	—	—
1995–96		—	—

STEPHENSON, Ashlyn

Born South Africa 6.7.74
Goalkeeper.

Season	Club	League Appearances/Goals	
1995–96	Birmingham C	—	—
1995–96	Darlington	1	—

STEPHENSON, Paul

Born Wallsend 2.1.68 Ht 5 9 Wt 12 05
Midfield. From Apprentice. England Youth.

Season	Club	League Appearances/Goals	
1985–86	Newcastle U	22	1
1986–87		24	—
1987–88		7	—
1988–89		8	—
1989–90	Millwall	12	1
1989–90		23	2
1990–91		30	1
1991–92		28	2
1992–93		5	—
1992–93	*Gillingham*	12	2
1992–93	Brentford	11	—
1993–94		25	—
1994–95		34	2
1995–96	York C	27	2

STERLING, Worrell

Born Bethnal Green 8.6.65 Ht 5 7 Wt 11 02
Midfield. From Apprentice.

Season	Club	League Appearances/Goals	
1982–83	Watford	3	—
1983–84		10	1
1984–85		15	4
1985–86		24	3
1986–87		18	4
1987–88		21	2
1988–89		3	—
1988–89	Peterborough U	12	3
1989–90		46	5
1990–91		46	9
1991–92		45	4
1992–93		44	8
1993–94	Bristol R	43	5
1994–95		46	1
1995–96		30	—

STEVEN, Trevor

Born Berwick 21.9.63 Ht 5 8 Wt 10 09
Midfield. From Apprentice. England Under-21, 36 full caps.

Season	Club	League Appearances/Goals	
1980–81	Burnley	1	—
1981–82		36	3
1982–83		39	8
1983–84	Everton	27	1
1984–85		40	12
1985–86		41	9
1986–87		41	14
1987–88		36	6
1988–89		29	6
1988–89	Rangers	34	3
1989–90		19	2
1990–91		2	1
1991–92	Marseille	27	3
1992–93	Rangers	24	5
1993–94		32	4
1994–95		11	—
1995–96		6	—

STEVENS, Gary

Born Barrow 27.3.63 Ht 5 11 Wt 12 07
Defender. From Apprentice. England 46 full caps.

Season	Club	League Appearances/Goals	
1980–81	Everton	—	—
1981–82		19	1
1982–83		28	—
1983–84		27	1
1984–85		37	3

Season	Club	League Appearances/Goals	
1985–86		41	1
1986–87		25	2
1987–88		31	—
1988–89	Rangers	35	1
1989–90		35	1
1990–91		36	4
1991–92		43	2
1992–93		9	—
1993–94		29	—
1994–95	Tranmere R	37	1
1995–96		34	—

STEVENS, Ian

Born Malta 21.10.66 Ht 5 9 Wt 12 04
Forward. From Trainee.

Season	Club	Apps	Goals
1984–85	Preston NE	4	1
1985–86		7	1
1986–87	Stockport Co	2	—
From Lancaster C			
1986–87	Bolton W	8	2
1987–88		9	—
1988–89		21	5
1989–90		4	—
1990–91		5	—
1991–92	Bury	45	17
1992–93		32	14
1993–94		33	7
1994–95	Shrewsbury T	38	8
1995–96		32	12

STEVENS, Keith

Born Merton 21.6.64 Ht 6 0 Wt 12 12
Defender. From Apprentice.

Season	Club	Apps	Goals
1980–81	Millwall	1	—
1981–82		7	—
1982–83		26	—
1983–84		17	—
1984–85		41	—
1985–86		33	1
1986–87		35	1
1987–88		35	1
1988–89		23	—
1989–90		28	—
1990–91		42	1
1991–92		27	—
1992–93		31	2
1993–94		44	1
1994–95		20	—
1995–96		39	2

STEVENS, Shaun

Born Chertsey 8.3.76 Ht 5 10 Wt 11 07
Defender.

Season	Club	Apps	Goals
1994–95	Wycombe W	—	—
1995–96		—	—

STEWART, Billy

Born Liverpool 1.1.65 Ht 5 11 Wt 11 07
Goalkeeper. From Apprentice.

Season	Club	Apps	Goals
1982–83	Liverpool	—	—
1983–84		—	—
1984–85	Wigan Ath	6	—
1985–86		8	—
1986–87	Chester C	29	—
1987–88		27	—
1988–89		46	—
1989–90		46	—
1990–91		38	—
1991–92		37	—
1992–93		42	—
1993–94		7	—
1994–95	Northampton T	27	—
1994–95	*Chesterfield*	1	—
1995–96	Chester C	45	—

STEWART, Marcus

Born Bristol 7.11.72 Ht 5 10 Wt 10 06
Forward. From Trainee. Football League.

Season	Club	Apps	Goals
1991–92	Bristol R	33	5
1992–93		38	11
1993–94		29	5
1994–95		27	15
1995–96		44	21

STEWART, Paul

Born Manchester 7.10.64 Ht 5 11
Wt 11 10
Midfield. From Apprentice. England Youth, Under-21, B, 3 full caps.

Season	Club	Apps	Goals
1981–82	Blackpool	14	3
1982–83		38	7
1983–84		44	10
1984–85		31	7
1985–86		42	8
1986–87		32	21
1986–87	Manchester C	11	2
1987–88		40	24
1988–89	Tottenham H	30	12
1989–90		28	8
1990–91		35	3

Season	Club	League Appearances/Goals	
1991–92		38	5
1992–93	Liverpool	24	1
1993–94		8	—
1993–94	*Crystal Palace*	18	3
1994–95	Liverpool	—	—
1994–95	*Wolverhampton W*	8	2
1994–95	*Burnley*	6	—
1995–96	Liverpool	—	—
1995–96	Sunderland	12	1

STEWART, Simon

Born Leeds 1.11.73 Ht 6 2 Wt 13 08
Defender. From Trainee.

1992–93	Sheffield W	6	—
1993–94		—	—
1994–95		—	—
1995–96		—	—
1995–96	*Shrewsbury T*	4	—

STIMAC, Igor

Born Croatia 6.9.67 Ht 6 2 Wt 13 00
Defender. Croatia 18 full caps.

1995–96	Derby Co	27	1

STIMSON, Mark

Born Plaistow 27.12.67 Ht 5 10
Wt 12 06
Defender. From Trainee.

1984–85	Tottenham H	—	—
1985–86		—	—
1986–87		1	—
1987–88		—	—
1987–88	*Leyton Orient*	10	—
1988–89	Tottenham H	1	—
1988–89	*Gillingham*	18	—
1989–90	Newcastle U	37	1
1990–91		23	1
1991–92		24	—
1992–93		2	—
1992–93	*Portsmouth*	4	—
1993–94	Portsmouth	29	1
1994–95		15	—
1995–96		14	1
1995–96	*Barnet*	5	—
1995–96	Southend U	10	—

STIRLING, Jered

Born Stirling 13.10.76 Ht 6 0 Wt 11 06
Defender. From St Roch's.

1993–94	Partick T	—	—
1994–95		—	—
1995–96		2	—

STOCK, Russell

Born Great Yarmouth 25.6.77 Ht 6 1
Wt 13 01
Midfield. From Trainee.

1995–96	Cambridge U	17	1

STOCKWELL, Mick

Born Chelmsford 14.2.65 Ht 5 9
Wt 11 04
Midfield. From Apprentice.

1982–83	Ipswich T	—	—
1983–84		—	—
1984–85		—	—
1985–86		8	—
1986–87		21	1
1987–88		43	1
1988–89		23	2
1989–90		34	3
1990–91		44	6
1991–92		46	2
1992–93		39	4
1993–94		42	1
1994–95		15	—
1995–96		37	1

STOKER, Gareth

Born Bishop Auckland 22.2.73 Ht 5 10
Wt 10 12
Midfield. From Leeds U Trainee.

1991–92	Hull C	24	2
1992–93		6	—
1993–94		—	—
1994–95	Hereford U	10	—
1995–96		33	3

STOKES, Dean

Born Birmingham 23.5.70 Ht 5 9
Wt 10 05
Defender. From Halesowen.

1992–93	Port Vale	—	—
1993–94		21	—
1994–95		3	—
1995–96		18	—

Season	Club	League Appearances/Goals	

STOKOE, Graham

Born Newcastle 17.12.75 Ht 6 1
Wt 12 02
Midfield. From Birmingham C.

1994–95	Stoke C	—	—
1995–96		—	—
1995–96	*Hartlepool U*	8	—

STONE, Steve

Born Gateshead 20.8.71 Ht 5 8
Wt 12 05
Midfield. From Trainee. England 9 full caps.

1989–90	Nottingham F	—	—
1990–91		—	—
1991–92		1	—
1992–93		12	1
1993–94		45	5
1994–95		41	5
1995–96		34	7

STORER, Stuart

Born Harborough 16.1.67 Ht 5 11
Wt 12 13
Forward. From Local.

1983–84	Mansfield T	1	—
1984–85	Birmingham C	—	—
1985–86		2	—
1986–87		6	—
1986–87	Everton	—	—
1987–88		—	—
1987–88	*Wigan Ath*	12	—
1987–88	Bolton W	15	1
1988–89		23	2
1989–90		38	4
1990–91		35	5
1991–92		9	—
1992–93		3	—
1992–93	Exeter C	10	4
1993–94		44	2
1994–95		23	2
1994–95	Brighton & HA	2	1
1995–96		38	2

STOREY, Brett

Born Sheffield 7.7.77
Midfield. From Trainee.

1995–96	Sheffield U	—	—
1995–96	Lincoln C	2	1

STOWELL, Matthew

Born Reading 1.3.77 Ht 6 0 Wt 12 00
Defender. From Trainee.

1995–96	Reading	—	—

STOWELL, Mike

Born Preston 19.4.65 Ht 6 2 Wt 13 10
Goalkeeper. From Leyland Motors.

1984–85	Preston NE	—	—
1985–86		—	—
1985–86	Everton	—	—
1986–87		—	—
1987–88	*Chester C*	14	—
1987–88	*York C*	6	—
1987–88	*Manchester C*	14	—
1988–89	Everton	—	—
1988–89	*Port Vale*	7	—
1988–89	*Wolverhampton W*	7	—
1989–90	Everton	—	—
1989–90	*Preston NE*	2	—
1990–91	Wolverhampton W	39	—
1991–92		46	—
1992–93		26	—
1993–94		46	—
1994–95		37	—
1995–96		38	—

STRACHAN, Gordon

Born Edinburgh 9.2.57 Ht 5 6
Wt 10 06
Midfield.

1974–75	Dundee	1	—
1975–76		23	6
1976–77		36	7
1977–78	Aberdeen	12	2
1978–79		31	5
1979–80		33	10
1980–81		20	6
1981–82		30	7
1982–83		32	12
1983–84		25	13
1984–85	Manchester U	41	15
1985–86		28	5
1986–87		34	4
1987–88		36	8
1988–89		21	1
1988–89	Leeds U	11	3
1989–90		46	16
1990–91		34	7
1991–92		36	4
1992–93		31	4

Season	Club	Apps	Goals
1993–94		33	3
1994–95		6	—
1994–95	Coventry C	5	—
1995–96		12	—

STRATFORD, Lee

Born Barnsley 11.11.75 Ht 5 10
Wt 10 09
Midfield. From Trainee.

Season	Club	Apps	Goals
1992–93	Nottingham F	—	—
1993–94		—	—
1994–95		—	—
1995–96		—	—

STRODDER, Gary

Born Cleckheaton 1.4.65 Ht 6 1
Wt 13 03
Defender. From Apprentice.

Season	Club	Apps	Goals
1982–83	Lincoln C	8	—
1983–84		22	1
1984–85		26	2
1985–86		43	1
1986–87		33	2
1986–87	West Ham U	12	—
1987–88		30	1
1988–89		7	—
1989–90		16	1
1990–91	WBA	34	1
1991–92		37	3
1992–93		29	1
1993–94		21	2
1994–95		19	1
1995–96	Notts Co	43	3

STRONG, Greg

Born Bolton 5.9.75 Ht 6 2
Wt 11 12
Defender. From Trainee. England Youth.

Season	Club	Apps	Goals
1992–93	Wigan Ath	—	—
1993–94		18	1
1994–95		17	2
1995–96	Bolton W	1	—

STRONG, Steve

Born Watford 15.3.78
Forward. From Trainee.

Season	Club	Apps	Goals
1994–95	Bournemouth	1	—
1995–96		1	—

STUART, Graham

Born Tooting, London 24.10.70 Ht 5 9
Wt 11 09
Forward. From Trainee. FA Schools, England Under-21.

Season	Club	Apps	Goals
1989–90	Chelsea	2	1
1990–91		19	4
1991–92		27	—
1992–93		39	9
1993–94	Everton	30	3
1994–95		28	3
1995–96		29	9

STUART, Jamie

Born Southwark 15.10.76 Ht 5 10
Wt 11 00
Defender. From Trainee. England Youth, Under-21.

Season	Club	Apps	Goals
1994–95	Charlton Ath	12	—
1995–96		27	2

STUART, Mark

Born Hammersmith 15.12.66 Ht 5 10
Wt 11 03
Defender. From QPR Schoolboy.

Season	Club	Apps	Goals
1984–85	Charlton Ath	6	1
1985–86		30	12
1986–87		36	9
1987–88		31	6
1988–89		4	—
1988–89	Plymouth Arg	32	5
1989–90		25	6
1989–90	*Ipswich T*	5	2
1990–91	Bradford C	13	2
1991–92		16	3
1992–93		—	—
1992–93	Huddersfield T	15	3
1993–94	Rochdale	42	13
1994–95		31	2
1995–96		34	13

STUBBS, Alan

Born Kirkby 6.10.71 Ht 6 2 Wt 13 10
Defender. From Trainee.

Season	Club	Apps	Goals
1990–91	Bolton W	23	—
1991–92		32	1
1992–93		42	2
1993–94		41	1
1994–95		39	1
1995–96		25	4

STURGESS, Paul

Born Dartford 4.8.75 Ht 5 11 Wt 12 05
Defender. From Trainee.

Season	Club	Apps	Goals
1992–93	Charlton Ath	4	—
1993–94		8	—
1994–95		23	—
1995–96		13	—

STURRIDGE, Dean

Born Birmingham 27.7.73 Ht 5 7
Wt 11 13
Forward. From Trainee.

Season	Club	Apps	Goals
1991–92	Derby Co	1	—
1992–93		10	—
1993–94		—	—
1994–95		12	1
1994–95	*Torquay U*	10	5
1995–96	Derby Co	39	20

STURRIDGE, Simon

Born Birmingham 9.12.69 Ht 5 5
Wt 10 09
Forward. From Trainee.

Season	Club	Apps	Goals
1988–89	Birmingham C	21	3
1989–90		31	10
1990–91		38	6
1991–92		40	10
1992–93		20	1
1993–94		—	—
1993–94	Stoke C	13	—
1994–95		8	1
1995–96		41	13

SUCKLING, Perry

Born Leyton 12.10.65 Ht 6 2 Wt 13 02
Goalkeeper. From Apprentice. England Youth, Under-21.

Season	Club	Apps	Goals
1982–83	Coventry C	3	—
1983–84		24	—
1984–85		—	—
1985–86		—	—
1986–87	Manchester C	37	—
1987–88		2	—
1987–88	Crystal Palace	17	—
1988–89		27	—
1989–90		12	—
1989–90	*West Ham U*	6	—
1990–91	Crystal Palace	—	—
1991–92		3	—
1991–92	*Brentford*	8	—
1992–93	Watford	37	—
1993–94		2	—
1994–95	Doncaster R	9	—
1995–96		21	—

SULLEY, Chris

Born Camberwell 3.12.59 Ht 5 8
Wt 10 00
Defender. From Apprentice.

Season	Club	Apps	Goals
1978–79	Chelsea	—	—
1979–80		—	—
1980–81		—	—
1980–81	Bournemouth	8	—
1981–82		46	—
1982–83		46	1
1983–84		46	2
1984–85		23	—
1985–86		37	—
1986–87	Dundee U	7	—
1986–87	Blackburn R	13	—
1987–88		34	—
1988–89		19	—
1989–90		36	—
1990–91		25	3
1991–92		7	—
1992–93	Port Vale	40	1
1993–94	Preston NE	21	1
1994–95		—	—
1995–96		—	—

SULLIVAN, Neil

Born Sutton 24.2.70 Ht 6 0 Wt 12 01
Goalkeeper. From Trainee.

Season	Club	Apps	Goals
1988–89	Wimbledon	—	—
1989–90		—	—
1990–91		1	—
1991–92		1	—
1991–92	*Crystal Palace*	1	—
1992–93	Wimbledon	1	—
1993–94		2	—
1994–95		11	—
1995–96		16	—

SUMMERBEE, Nicky

Born Altrincham 26.8.71 Ht 5 11
Wt 12 08
Forward. From Trainee. England Under-21.

Season	Club	Apps	Goals
1989–90	Swindon T	1	—
1990–91		7	—
1991–92		27	—

Season	Club	League Appearances/Goals	
1992–93		39	3
1993–94		38	3
1994–95	Manchester C	41	1
1995–96		37	1

SUMMERBELL, Mark

Born Durham 30.10.76 Ht 5 10
Wt 11 09
Midfield. From Trainee.

Season	Club	Apps	Goals
1995–96	Middlesbrough	1	—

SUMMERFIELD, Kevin

Born Walsall 7.1.59 Ht 5 11 Wt 11 00
Midfield. From Apprentice.

Season	Club	Apps	Goals
1976–77	WBA	—	—
1977–78		—	—
1978–79		2	1
1979–80		3	1
1980–81		—	—
1981–82		4	2
1982–83	Birmingham C	5	1
1982–83	Walsall	21	9
1983–84		33	8
1984–85	Cardiff C	10	1
1984–85	Plymouth Arg	17	2
1985–86		26	7
1986–87		28	9
1987–88		37	5
1988–89		20	2
1989–90		10	1
1989–90	*Exeter C*	4	—
1990–91	Plymouth Arg	1	—
1990–91	Shrewsbury T	32	5
1991–92		44	7
1992–93		35	7
1993–94		33	3
1994–95		18	—
1995–96		1	—

SUND, Ulf

Born Finland 28.12.78
Midfield. From IFK Vasa.

Season	Club	Apps	Goals
1995–96	Crewe Alex	—	—

SUNDERLAND, Jon

Born Newcastle 2.11.75 Ht 6 0 Wt 11 13
Midfield. From Trainee.

Season	Club	Apps	Goals
1994–95	Blackpool	2	—
1995–96		—	—
1995–96	Scarborough	6	—

SUNDGOT, Ole

Born Norway 21.3.72
Midfield. From Molde.

Season	Club	Apps	Goals
1995–96	Oldham Ath	—	—

SUSSEX, Andy

Born Islington 23.11.64 Ht 6 3 Wt 13 08
Midfield. From Apprentice.

Season	Club	Apps	Goals
1981–82	Orient	8	1
1982–83		24	2
1983–84		29	6
1984–85		19	2
1985–86		36	4
1986–87		20	1
1987–88		8	1
1988–89	Crewe Alex	25	4
1989–90		33	9
1990–91		44	11
1991–92	Southend U	15	3
1992–93		23	4
1993–94		21	6
1994–95		15	1
1995–96		2	—
1995–96	*Brentford*	3	—

SUTCH, Daryl

Born Lowestoft 11.9.71 Ht 6 0 Wt 12 02
Midfield. From Trainee. England Youth, Under-21.

Season	Club	Apps	Goals
1989–90	Norwich C	—	—
1990–91		4	—
1991–92		9	—
1992–93		22	2
1993–94		3	—
1994–95		30	1
1995–96		13	—

SUTTON, Chris

Born Nottingham 10.3.73 Ht 6 3
Wt 13 07
Forward. From Trainee. England Under-21, B.

Season	Club	Apps	Goals
1990–91	Norwich C	2	—
1991–92		21	2
1992–93		38	8
1993–94		41	25
1994–95	Blackburn R	40	15
1995–96		13	—

Season	Club	League Appearances/Goals	

SUTTON, Steve

Born Hartington 16.4.61 Ht 6 1
Wt 14 08
Goalkeeper. From Apprentice.

1980–81	Nottingham F	1	—
1980–81	*Mansfield T*	8	—
1981–82	Nottingham F	1	—
1982–83		17	—
1983–84		6	—
1984–85		14	—
1984–85	*Derby Co*	14	—
1985–86	Nottingham F	31	—
1986–87		28	—
1987–88		35	—
1988–89		36	—
1989–90		30	—
1990–91		—	—
1990–91	*Coventry C*	1	—
1991–92	Nottingham F	—	—
1991–92	*Luton T*	14	—
1991–92	Derby Co	10	—
1992–93		25	—
1993–94		—	—
1994–95		20	—
1995–96		6	—
1995–96	*Reading*	2	—

SUTTON, Wayne

Born Derby 1.10.75 Ht 6 0 Wt 13 09
Defender. From Trainee.

1992–93	Derby Co	—	—
1993–94		—	—
1994–95		6	—
1995–96		1	—

SWAILES, Chris

Born Gateshead 19.10.70 Ht 6 2
Wt 12 07
Defender. From Ipswich T Trainee, Peterborough U, Boston U, Birmingham C, Bridlington T.

1993–94	Doncaster R	17	—
1994–95		32	—
1995–96	Ipswich T	5	—

SWAILES, Matthew

Born Bolton 28.10.76
Forward. From Trainee.

1995–96	Bury	—	—

Season Club League Appearances/Goals

SWALES, Steve

Born Whitby 26.12.73 Ht 5 8 Wt 10 03
Defender. From Trainee.

1991–92	Scarborough	4	—
1992–93		3	—
1993–94		26	—
1994–95		21	1
1995–96	Reading	9	—

SWALWELL, Andrew

Born Middlesbrough 29.3.79
Midfield. From Trainee.

1995–96	Middlesbrough	—	—

SWAN, Peter

Born Leeds 28.9.66 Ht 6 3 Wt 15 09
Defender. From Local.

1984–85	Leeds U	—	—
1985–86		16	3
1986–87		7	—
1987–88		25	8
1988–89		1	—
1988–89	Hull C	11	1
1989–90		31	11
1990–91		38	12
1991–92	Port Vale	33	3
1992–93		38	2
1993–94		40	—
1994–95	Plymouth Arg	27	2
1995–96		—	—
1995–96	Burnley	32	5

SYKES, Paul

Born Pontefract 13.1.77 Ht 6 2 Wt 12 00
Defender. From Trainee.

1994–95	Sheffield W	—	—
1995–96		—	—

SYMONS, Kit

Born Basingstoke 8.3.71 Ht 6 1
Wt 13 07
Defender. From Trainee. Wales Under-21, 22 full caps.

1988–89	Portsmouth	2	—
1989–90		1	—
1990–91		1	—
1991–92		46	1
1992–93		41	2
1993–94		29	3
1994–95		40	4

Season	Club	Apps	Goals
1995–96	....	1	—
1995–96	Manchester C............	38	2

SYMONS, Paul

Born North Shields 20.4.76 Ht 5 11
Wt 12 00
Forward. From Trainee.

Season	Club	Apps	Goals
1993–94	Blackpool	1	—
1994–95	....	—	—
1995–96	....	—	—

TAGGART, Gerry

Born Belfast 18.10.70 Ht 6 1
Wt 12 03
Defender. From Trainee. Northern Ireland Under-23, 35 full caps.

Season	Club	Apps	Goals
1988–89	Manchester C............	11	1
1989–90	....	1	—
1989–90	Barnsley......................	21	2
1990–91	....	30	2
1991–92	....	38	3
1992–93	....	44	4
1993–94	....	38	2
1994–95	....	41	3
1995–96	Bolton W......................	11	1

TAIT, Mick

Born Wallsend 30.9.56 Ht 5 11
Wt 12 10
Midfield. From Apprentice.

Season	Club	Apps	Goals
1974–75	Oxford U	4	—
1975–76	....	37	12
1976–77	....	23	11
1976–77	Carlisle U....................	13	3
1977–78	....	43	10
1978–79	....	46	7
1979–80	....	4	—
1979–80	Hull C..........................	33	3
1980–81	Portsmouth..................	38	8
1981–82	....	35	9
1982–83	....	44	6
1983–84	....	36	3
1984–85	....	33	1
1985–86	....	26	2
1986–87	....	28	1
1987–88	....	—	—
1987–88	Reading.......................	35	2
1988–89	....	36	4
1989–90	....	28	3
1990–91	Darlington...................	45	2
1991–92	....	34	—
1992–93	Hartlepool U...............	35	1
1993–94	....	26	—
From Gretna			
1994–95	....	20	—
1995–96	....	39	2

TAIT, Paul

Born Sutton Coldfield 31.1.71 Ht 6 1
Wt 10 00
Midfield. From Trainee.

Season	Club	Apps	Goals
1987–88	Birmingham C...........	1	—

Season	Club	League Appearances/Goals	
1988–89		10	—
1989–90		14	2
1990–91		17	3
1991–92		12	—
1992–93		28	2
1993–94		10	—
1993–94	*Millwall*	—	—
1994–95	Birmingham C	25	4
1995–96		27	3

TAIT, Paul

Born Newcastle 24.10.74 Ht 6 1
Wt 10 13
Forward. From Trainee.

Season	Club	Apps	Goals
1993–94	Everton	—	—
1994–95	Wigan Ath	5	—
1995–96		—	—

TALBOT, David

Born Stoke 12.10.76 Ht 6 3 Wt 11 05
Defender. From Trainee.

Season	Club	Apps	Goals
1995–96	Stoke C	—	—

TALBOT, Stuart

Born Birmingham 14.6.73 Ht 5 11
Wt 11 00
Forward. From Doncaster R, Moor Green.

Season	Club	Apps	Goals
1994–95	Port Vale	2	—
1995–96		20	—

TALBOYS, Steve

Born Bristol 18.9.66 Ht 5 10 Wt 11 06
Midfield. From Gloucester C.

Season	Club	Apps	Goals
1991–92	Wimbledon	—	—
1992–93		7	—
1993–94		7	—
1994–95		7	1
1995–96		5	—

TALIA, Frank

Born Melbourne 20.7.72 Ht 6 1
Wt 13 04
Goalkeeper. From Sunshine GC.

Season	Club	Apps	Goals
1992–93	Blackburn R	—	—
1992–93	*Hartlepool U*	14	—
1993–94	Blackburn R	—	—
1994–95		—	—
1995–96		—	—
1995–96	Swindon T	16	—

TALLON, Gary

Born Drogheda 5.9.73 Ht 5 10 Wt 11 12
Forward. Trainee.

Season	Club	Apps	Goals
1991–92	Blackburn R	—	—
1992–93		—	—
1993–94		—	—
1994–95		—	—
1995–96		—	—

TANKARD, Allen

Born Islington 21.5.69 Ht 5 10 Wt 11 07
Defender. From Trainee. England Youth.

Season	Club	Apps	Goals
1985–86	Southampton	3	—
1986–87		2	—
1987–88		—	—
1988–89	Wigan Ath	33	1
1989–90		45	1
1990–91		46	1
1991–92		44	—
1992–93		41	1
1993–94	Port Vale	26	—
1994–95		39	1
1995–96		29	—

TANNER, Adam

Born Maldon 25.10.73 Ht 6 0 Wt 12 01
Midfield. From Trainee.

Season	Club	Apps	Goals
1992–93	Ipswich T	—	—
1993–94		—	—
1994–95		10	2
1995–96		10	—

TARICCO, Mauricio

Born Buenos Aires 10.3.73 Ht 5 8
Wt 11 05
Defender. From Argentinos Juniors. Argentina Under-23.

Season	Club	Apps	Goals
1994–95	Ipswich T	—	—
1995–96		39	—

TARPEY, Ged

Born Manchester 28.4.77 Ht 6 0
Wt 13 00
Defender. From Trainee.

Season	Club	Apps	Goals
1995–96	Manchester C	—	—

TAYLOR, Alex

Born Baillieston 13.6.62 Ht 5 7
Wt 10 11
Midfield. From Blantyre St J.

Season	Club	Apps	Goals
1982–83	Dundee U	3	—

Season	Club	League Appearances/Goals	
1983–84		9	1
1984–85		21	5
1985–86		—	—
1986–87	Hamilton A	25	1
1987–88		41	4
1988–89	Walsall	13	3
1989–90		32	3
1990–91		—	—
1990–91	Falkirk	29	2
1991–92		22	1
1992–93		8	1
1992–93	Partick T	8	1
1993–94		32	4
1994–95		23	2
1995–96	Raith R	10	—

TAYLOR, Bob

Born Horden 3.2.67 Ht 5 9 Wt 11 13
Forward. From Horden CW.

Season	Club	League Appearances/Goals	
1985–86	Leeds U	2	—
1986–87		2	—
1987–88		32	9
1988–89		6	—
1988–89	Bristol C	12	8
1989–90		37	27
1990–91		39	11
1991–92		18	4
1991–92	WBA	19	8
1992–93		46	30
1993–94		42	18
1994–95		42	11
1995–96		42	17

TAYLOR, Gareth

Born Weston-Super-Mare 25.2.73 Ht 6 2
Wt 12 05
Forward. From Southampton Trainee.
Wales Under-21, 3 full caps.

Season	Club	League Appearances/Goals	
1991–92	Bristol R	1	—
1992–93		—	—
1993–94		—	—
1994–95		39	12
1995–96		7	4
1995–96	Crystal Palace	20	1
1995–96	Sheffield U	10	2

TAYLOR, Ian

Born Birmingham 4.6.68 Ht 6 1
Wt 12 00
Midfield. From Moor Green.

Season	Club	League Appearances/Goals	
1992–93	Port Vale	41	15
1993–94		42	13
1994–95	Sheffield W	14	1
1994–95	Aston Villa	22	1
1995–96		25	3

TAYLOR, Jamie

Born Bury 11.1.77 Ht 5 6 Wt 9 12
Forward. From Trainee.

Season	Club	League Appearances/Goals	
1993–94	Rochdale	10	1
1994–95		9	—
1995–96		16	3

TAYLOR, John

Born Norwich 24.10.64 Ht 6 3 Wt 13 09
Forward. From Local.

Season	Club	League Appearances/Goals	
1982–83	Colchester U	—	—
1983–84		—	—
1984–85		—	—
From Sudbury			
1988–89	Cambridge U	40	12
1989–90		45	15
1990–91		40	14
1991–92		35	5
1991–92	Bristol R	8	7
1992–93		42	14
1993–94		45	23
1994–95	Bradford C	36	11
1994–95	Luton T	9	3
1995–96		28	—

TAYLOR, Maik

Born Germany 4.9.71 Ht 6 5 Wt 13 08
Goalkeeper. From Farnborough T.

Season	Club	League Appearances/Goals	
1995–96	Barnet	45	—

TAYLOR, Mark

Born Saltburn 8.11.74 Ht 6 2 Wt 13 10
Defender. From Trainee.

Season	Club	League Appearances/Goals	
1992–93	Middlesbrough	—	—
1993–94		—	—
1994–95		—	—
1994–95	*Darlington*	8	—
1995–96	Fulham	7	—
1995–96	Northampton T	1	—

TAYLOR, Mark

Born Walsall 22.2.66 Ht 5 9 Wt 12 05
Midfield. From Local.

Season	Club	League Appearances/Goals	
1984–85	Walsall	4	—
1985–86		18	2

1986–87 17 —
1987–88 40 1
1988–89 34 1
1989–90 Sheffield W 9 —
1990–91 *Shrewsbury T* 19 2
1991–92 Shrewsbury T 29 2
1992–93 42 5
1993–94 41 2
1994–95 44 2
1995–96 38 1

TAYLOR, Martin

Born Tamworth 9.12.66 Ht 5 11
Wt 13 09
Goalkeeper. From Mile Oak R.

1986–87 Derby Co — —
1987–88 — —
1987–88 *Carlisle U* 10 —
1987–88 *Scunthorpe U* 8 —
1988–89 Derby Co — —
1989–90 3 —
1990–91 7 —
1991–92 5 —
1992–93 21 —
1993–94 46 —
1994–95 12 —
1995–96 — —

TAYLOR, Matthew

Born Maidstone 6.3.76 Ht 5 7 Wt 11 12
Defender. From Trainee.

1994–95 Burnley — —
1995–96 — —

TAYLOR, Paul

Born Manchester 5.8.77 Ht 5 10
Wt 12 02
Defender. From Trainee.

1995–96 Bury — —

TAYLOR, Robert

Born Norwich 30.4.71 Ht 6 1 Wt 13 08
Forward. From Trainee.

1989–90 Norwich C — —
1990–91 — —
1990–91 *Leyton Orient* 3 1
1991–92 Birmingham C — —
1991–92 Leyton Orient 11 1
1992–93 39 18
1993–94 23 1
1993–94 Brentford 5 2
1994–95 43 23
1995–96 42 11

TAYLOR, Ross

Born Southend 14.1.77 Ht 5 10
Wt 11 12
Defender. From Trainee. England Youth.

1995–96 Arsenal — —

TAYLOR, Scott

Born Chertsey 5.5.76 Ht 5 10 Wt 11 04
Forward. From Staines.

1994–95 Millwall 6 —
1995–96 22 —
1995–96 Bolton W 1 —

TAYLOR, Scott

Born Portsmouth 28.11.70 Ht 5 9
Wt 11 00
Midfield. From Trainee.

1988–89 Reading 3 —
1989–90 29 2
1990–91 32 1
1991–92 29 2
1992–93 32 5
1993–94 38 6
1994–95 44 8
1995–96 Leicester C 39 6

TAYLOR, Shaun

Born Plymouth 26.2.63 Ht 6 1 Wt 13 00
Defender. From Bideford.

1986–87 Exeter C 23 —
1987–88 41 1
1988–89 46 6
1989–90 45 5
1990–91 45 4
1991–92 Swindon T 42 4
1992–93 46 11
1993–94 42 4
1994–95 37 4
1995–96 43 7

TAYLOR, Steve

Born Stone 7.1.70 Ht 6 0 Wt 12 08
Forward. From Bromsgrove R.

1995–96 Northampton T 2 —

Season	Club	League Appearances/Goals	

TEALE, Shaun

Born Southport 10.3.64 Ht 6 0 Wt 14 00
Defender. From Southport, Northwich Vic, Weymouth.

1988–89	Bournemouth	20	—
1989–90		34	—
1990–91		46	4
1991–92	Aston Villa	42	—
1992–93		39	1
1993–94		38	1
1994–95		28	—
1995–96	Tranmere R	29	—

TEATHER, Paul

Born Rotherham 26.12.77 Ht 5 11
Wt 11 02
Midfield. From Trainee. England Youth.

1994–95	Manchester U	—	—
1995–96		—	—

TELFER, Paul

Born Edinburgh 21.10.71 Ht 5 9 Wt 11 06
Midfield. From Trainee. Scotland Under-21.

1988–89	Luton T	—	—
1989–90		—	—
1990–91		1	—
1991–92		20	1
1992–93		32	2
1993–94		45	7
1994–95		46	9
1995–96	Coventry C	31	1

TEN-HEUVEL, Laurens

Born Amsterdam 6.6.76 Ht 6 0 Wt 10 09
Forward. From Den Bosch.

1995–96	Barnsley	3	—

THACKERAY, Andy

Born Huddersfield 13.2.68 Ht 5 9
Wt 11 00
Midfield.

1985–86	Manchester C	—	—
1986–87	Huddersfield T	2	—
1986–87	Newport Co	11	3
1987–88		43	1
1988–89	Wrexham	35	2
1989–90		34	7
1990–91		41	2
1991–92		42	3
1992–93	Rochdale	41	6
1993–94		37	4
1994–95		41	3
1995–96		29	—

THATCHER, Ben

Born Swindon 30.11.75 Ht 5 11
Wt 12 07
Defender. From Trainee. England Youth, Under-21.

1992–93	Millwall	—	—
1993–94		8	—
1994–95		40	1
1995–96		42	—

THEW, Lee

Born Sunderland 23.10.74 Ht 5 10
Wt 12 08
Midfield. From Trainee.

1993–94	Doncaster R	11	1
1994–95		21	1
1995–96	Scarborough	14	—

THIRLBY, Anthony

Born Germany 4.3.76 Ht 5 8 Wt 10 05
Midfield. From Trainee.

1993–94	Exeter C	10	—
1994–95		27	2
1995–96		2	—

THOM, Andreas

Born Rudersdorf 7.9.65 Ht 5 8 Wt 11 10
Forward. From TSV Bayer 04 Leverkusen.

1995–96	Celtic	32	5

THOM, Stuart

Born Dewsbury 27.12.76 Ht 6 2
Wt 11 12
Defender. From Trainee.

1993–94	Nottingham F	—	—
1994–95		—	—
1995–96		—	—

THOMAS, David

Born Caerphilly 26.9.75 Ht 5 10
Wt 11 07
Forward. From Trainee.

1994–95	Swansea C	4	—
1995–96		16	1

Season Club League Appearances/Goals

THOMAS, Geoff

Born Manchester 5.8.64 Ht 6 1 Wt 12 03
Midfield. From Local. England B, 9 full caps.

Season	Club	Apps	Goals
1981–82	Rochdale	—	—
1982–83		1	—
1983–84		10	1
1983–84	Crewe Alex	8	1
1984–85		40	4
1985–86		37	6
1986–87		40	9
1987–88	Crystal Palace	41	6
1988–89		22	5
1989–90		35	1
1990–91		38	6
1991–92		30	6
1992–93		29	2
1993–94	Wolverhampton W	8	4
1994–95		14	1
1995–96		2	—

THOMAS, Glen

Born Hackney 6.10.67 Ht 6 1 Wt 13 03
Defender. From Apprentice.

Season	Club	Apps	Goals
1985–86	Fulham	—	—
1986–87		1	—
1987–88		27	—
1988–89		40	1
1989–90		17	1
1990–91		34	1
1991–92		45	3
1992–93		43	—
1993–94		37	—
1994–95		7	—
1994–95	Peterborough U	8	—
1994–95	Barnet	7	—
1995–96		16	—
1995–96	Gillingham	15	—

THOMAS, Jason

Born Swansea 22.2.77 Ht 5 8 Wt 10 12
Forward.

Season	Club	Apps	Goals
1995–96	Birmingham C	—	—

THOMAS, Kevin

Born Edinburgh 25.4.75 Ht 5 8
Wt 12 00
Forward. From Links U. Scotland Under-21.

Season	Club	Apps	Goals
1992–93	Hearts	4	2
1993–94		12	—
1994–95		18	5
1995–96		3	—

THOMAS, Mark

Born Tooting 22.11.74 Ht 5 9 Wt 10 10
Midfield. From Trainee.

Season	Club	Apps	Goals
1993–94	Wimbledon	—	—
1994–95		—	—
1995–96		—	—

THOMAS, Martin

Born Lyndhurst 12.9.73 Ht 5 8 Wt 11 04
Forward. From Trainee.

Season	Club	Apps	Goals
1992–93	Southampton	—	—
1993–94		—	—
1993–94	Leyton Orient	5	2
1994–95	Fulham	23	3
1995–96		37	5

THOMAS, Michael

Born Lambeth 24.8.67 Ht 5 9 Wt 12 06
Midfield. From Apprentice. England Schools, Youth, Under-21, B, 2 full caps.

Season	Club	Apps	Goals
1985–86	Arsenal	—	—
1986–87		12	—
1986–87	*Portsmouth*	3	—
1987–88	Arsenal	37	9
1988–89		37	7
1989–90		36	5
1990–91		31	2
1991–92		10	1
1991–92	Liverpool	17	3
1992–93		8	1
1993–94		7	—
1994–95		23	—
1995–96		27	1

THOMAS, Mitchell

Born Luton 2.10.64 Ht 6 2 Wt 13 00
Defender. From Apprentice. England Youth, Under-21, B.

Season	Club	Apps	Goals
1982–83	Luton T	4	—
1983–84		26	—
1984–85		36	—
1985–86		41	1
1986–87	Tottenham H	39	4
1987–88		36	—
1988–89		25	1
1989–90		26	1

Season Club League Appearances/Goals

Season	Club	Apps	Goals
1990–91	....	31	—
1991–92	West Ham U	35	3
1992–93	....	3	—
1993–94	....	—	—
1993–94	Luton T.....................	20	1
1994–95	....	36	—
1995–96	....	27	—

THOMAS, Rod

Born London 10.10.70 Ht 5 6 Wt 11 02
Forward. From Trainee. England Youth, Under-21.

Season	Club	Apps	Goals
1987–88	Watford.....................	4	—
1988–89	....	18	2
1989–90	....	32	6
1990–91	....	24	1
1991–92	....	5	—
1991–92	*Gillingham*...............	8	1
1992–93	Watford.....................	1	—
1993–94	Carlisle U..................	38	9
1994–95	....	36	6
1995–96	....	36	1

THOMAS, Scott

Born Bury 30.10.74 Ht 5 9 Wt 11 02
Midfield. From Trainee.

Season	Club	Apps	Goals
1991–92	Manchester C............	—	—
1992–93	....	—	—
1993–94	....	—	—
1994–95	....	2	—
1995–96	....	—	—

THOMAS, Tony

Born Liverpool 12.7.71 Ht 5 11
Wt 13 00
Defender. From Trainee.

Season	Club	Apps	Goals
1988–89	Tranmere R...............	9	2
1989–90	....	42	2
1990–91	....	33	3
1991–92	....	30	3
1992–93	....	16	—
1993–94	....	40	2
1994–95	....	26	—
1995–96	....	31	—

THOMAS, Wayne

Born Walsall 28.8.78 Ht 5 11 Wt 11 10
Forward. From Trainee.

Season	Club	Apps	Goals
1995–96	Torquay U	6	—

THOMPSON, Adrian

Born Sydney 13.3.77 Ht 5 9 Wt 11 12
Goalkeeper.

Season	Club	Apps	Goals
1994–95	Walsall	—	—
1995–96	....	—	—

THOMPSON, Alan

Born Newcastle 22.12.73 Ht 6 0
Wt 12 08
Midfield. From Trainee. England Youth, Under-21.

Season	Club	Apps	Goals
1990–91	Newcastle U	—	—
1991–92	....	14	—
1992–93	....	2	—
1993–94	Bolton W	27	6
1994–95	....	37	7
1995–96	....	26	1

THOMPSON, Andy

Born Cannock 9.11.67 Ht 5 4 Wt 10 06
Defender. From Apprentice.

Season	Club	Apps	Goals
1985–86	WBA...........................	15	1
1986–87	....	9	—
1986–87	Wolverhampton W....	29	8
1987–88	....	42	2
1988–89	....	46	6
1989–90	....	33	4
1990–91	....	44	3
1991–92	....	17	—
1992–93	....	20	—
1993–94	....	37	3
1994–95	....	31	9
1995–96	....	45	6

THOMPSON, David

Born Ashington 20.11.68 Ht 6 2
Wt 13 02
Defender. From Trainee.

Season	Club	Apps	Goals
1986–87	Millwall	—	—
1987–88	....	—	—
1988–89	....	15	1
1989–90	....	27	2
1990–91	....	17	3
1991–92	....	33	—
1992–93	Bristol C.....................	17	—
1993–94	....	—	—
1993–94	Brentford..................	10	1
1994–95	....	—	—
1994–95	Blackpool	17	—
1994–95	Cambridge U.............	7	—
1995–96	....	15	—

THOMPSON, David

Born Birkenhead 12.9.77 Ht 5 7
Wt 10 00
Midfield. From Trainee. England Youth.

Season	Club	Apps	Goals
1994–95	Liverpool	—	—
1995–96		—	—

THOMPSON, David

Born Manchester 27.5.62 Ht 5 8
Wt 11 12
Defender. From Local.

Season	Club	Apps	Goals
1981–82	Rochdale	2	—
1982–83		46	5
1983–84		40	4
1984–85		40	2
1985–86		27	2
1985–86	*Manchester U*	—	—
1986–87	Notts Co	46	7
1987–88		9	1
1987–88	Wigan Ath	27	2
1988–89		42	7
1989–90		39	5
1990–91	Preston NE	21	2
1991–92		25	2
1992–93	Chester C	39	3
1993–94		41	6
1994–95	Rochdale	40	6
1995–96		43	4

THOMPSON, Garry

Born Birmingham 7.10.59 Ht 6 1
Wt 14 04
Forward. From Apprentice. England Under-21.

Season	Club	Apps	Goals
1977–78	Coventry C	6	2
1978–79		20	8
1979–80		17	6
1980–81		35	8
1981–82		36	10
1982–83		20	4
1982–83	WBA	12	7
1983–84		37	13
1984–85		42	19
1985–86	Sheffield W	36	7
1986–87	Aston Villa	31	6
1987–88		24	11
1988–89		5	—
1988–89	Watford	21	7
1989–90		13	1
1989–90	Crystal Palace	9	2
1990–91		11	1
1991–92	QPR	15	1
1992–93		4	—
1993–94	Cardiff C	30	5
1994–95		13	—
1994–95	Northampton T	15	4
1995–96		34	2

THOMPSON, Neil

Born Beverley 2.10.63 Ht 5 11 Wt 13 08
Defender. From Nottingham F Apprentice.

Season	Club	Apps	Goals
1981–82	Hull C	23	—
1982–83		8	—
From Scarborough			
1987–88	Scarborough	41	6
1988–89		46	9
1989–90	Ipswich T	45	3
1990–91		38	6
1991–92		45	6
1992–93		31	3
1993–94		32	—
1994–95		10	—
1995–96		5	1

THOMPSON, Neil

Born Hackney 30.4.78
Defender. From Trainee.

Season	Club	Apps	Goals
1995–96	Barnet	2	—

THOMPSON, Steve

Born Oldham 2.11.64 Ht 5 11 Wt 13 05
Midfield. From Apprentice.

Season	Club	Apps	Goals
1982–83	Bolton W	3	—
1983–84		40	3
1984–85		34	4
1985–86		35	8
1986–87		44	7
1987–88		44	7
1988–89		43	9
1989–90		45	6
1990–91		45	5
1991–92		2	—
1991–92	Luton T	5	—
1991–92	Leicester C	34	3
1992–93		44	8
1993–94		30	7
1994–95		19	—
1994–95	Burnley	12	—
1995–96		18	—

Season Club League Appearances/Goals

THOMPSON, Steve

Born Plymouth 12.1.63 Ht 5 7 Wt 11 09
Midfield. From Slough T.

Season	Club	Apps	Goals
1981–82	Bristol C	1	1
1982–83		11	—
1982–83	Torquay U	1	—

From Slough T

Season	Club	Apps	Goals
1993–94	Wycombe W	27	1
1994–95		35	2
1995–96		—	—

THOMPSTONE, Ian

Born Manchester 17.1.71 Ht 6 0 Wt 13 00
Forward. From Trainee.

Season	Club	Apps	Goals
1987–88	Manchester C	1	1
1988–89		—	—
1989–90		—	—
1990–91	Oldham Ath	—	—
1991–92		—	—
1991–92	Exeter C	15	3
1992–93	Halifax T	31	9
1992–93	Scunthorpe U	11	2
1993–94		30	5
1994–95		19	1
1995–96	Rochdale	25	1

THOMSEN, Claus

Born Aarhus 31.5.70 Ht 6 3 Wt 13 06
Midfield. From Aarhus. Denmark Under-21, 6 full caps.

Season	Club	Apps	Goals
1994–95	Ipswich T	33	5
1995–96		37	2

THOMSON, Andrew

Born Swindon 28.3.74 Ht 6 3 Wt 14 12
Defender. From Trainee.

Season	Club	Apps	Goals
1992–93	Swindon T	—	—
1993–94		1	—
1994–95		21	—
1995–96		—	—
1995–96	Portsmouth	16	—

THOMSON, Andy

Born Motherwell 1.4.71 Ht 5 10
Wt 10 12
Forward. From Jerviston BC.

Season	Club	Apps	Goals
1989–90	Q of S	26	6
1990–91		37	11
1991–92		39	26
1992–93		38	21
1993–94		35	29
1994–95	Southend U	39	11
1995–96		33	6

THOMSON, Billy

Born Linwood 10.2.58 Ht 6 2 Wt 12 03
Goalkeeper. From Glasgow United.
Scotland Under-21, 7 full caps.

Season	Club	Apps	Goals
1975–76	Partick T	—	—
1976–77		—	—
1977–78		—	—
1978–79	St Mirren	34	—
1979–80		36	—
1980–81		36	—
1981–82		35	—
1982–83		35	—
1983–84		30	—
1984–85	Dundee U	11	—
1985–86		28	—
1986–87		42	—
1987–88		36	—
1988–89		36	—
1989–90		7	—
1990–91		5	—
1991–92	Motherwell	43	—
1992–93		9	—
1993–94		—	—
1994–95	Rangers	5	—
1995–96		1	—

THOMSON, Martin

Born Bradford 3.10.74 Ht 5 10 Wt 11 08
Defender. From Trainee.

Season	Club	Apps	Goals
1993–94	Sheffield U	—	—
1994–95		—	—
1995–96		—	—

THOMSON, Peter

Born Bury 30.6.77 Ht 6 3 Wt 13 04
Forward. From Stand Ath.

Season	Club	Apps	Goals
1995–96	Bury	—	—

THOMSON, Scott M

Born Aberdeen 29.1.72 Ht 5 10
Wt 11 10
Midfield. From Shrewsbury T Trainee.

Season	Club	Apps	Goals
1990–91	Brechin C	30	3
1991–92		11	3
1991–92	Aberdeen	—	—
1992–93		2	—
1993–94		3	—
1994–95		10	1

Season	Club	Apps	Goals
1995–96		4	—
1995–96	Raith R	9	1

THOMSON, Scott Y

Born Edinburgh 8.11.66 Ht 6 0
Wt 11 09
Goalkeeper. From Hutchison Vale BC.

Season	Club	Apps	Goals
1986–87	Dundee U	3	—
1987–88		—	—
1988–89		1	—
1989–90		2	—
1990–91		—	—
1991–92	Forfar Ath	44	—
1992–93		39	—
1993–94		5	—
1993–94	Raith R	34	—
1994–95		35	—
1995–96		26	—

THOMSON, Steven

Born Glasgow 23.1.78 Ht 5 8 Wt 10 09
Midfield. From Trainee.

Season	Club	Apps	Goals
1995–96	Crystal Palace	—	—

THORN, Andy

Born Carshalton 12.11.66 Ht 6 0
Wt 11 05
Defender. From Apprentice. England Under-21.

Season	Club	Apps	Goals
1984–85	Wimbledon	10	—
1985–86		28	—
1986–87		34	2
1987–88		35	—
1988–89	Newcastle U	26	1
1989–90		10	1
1989–90	Crystal Palace	17	1
1990–91		34	1
1991–92		33	—
1992–93		34	1
1993–94		10	—
1994–95		—	—
1994–95	Wimbledon	23	1
1995–96		14	—

THORNBER, Stephen

Born Dewsbury 11.10.65 Ht 5 9
Wt 11 07
Midfield. From Local.

Season	Club	Apps	Goals
1983–84	Halifax T	4	1
1984–85		31	3
1985–86		18	—
1986–87		16	—
1987–88		35	—
1988–89	Swansea C	31	—
1989–90		34	1
1990–91		19	1
1991–92		33	4
1992–93	Blackpool	24	—
1993–94	Scunthorpe U	24	2
1994–95		37	5
1995–96		16	—

THORNE, Gary

Born Reading 22.3.77 Ht 5 8 Wt 11 07
Defender. From Trainee.

Season	Club	Apps	Goals
1995–96	Swindon T	—	—

THORNE, Peter

Born Manchester 21.6.73 Ht 6 0
Wt 12 00
Forward. From Trainee.

Season	Club	Apps	Goals
1991–92	Blackburn R	—	—
1992–93		—	—
1993–94		—	—
1993–94	*Wigan Ath*	11	—
1994–95	Blackburn R	—	—
1994–95	Swindon T	20	9
1995–96		26	10

THORNLEY, Ben

Born Bury 21.4.75 Ht 5 9 Wt 11 12
Forward. From Trainee. England Under-21.

Season	Club	Apps	Goals
1992–93	Manchester U	—	—
1993–94		1	—
1994–95		—	—
1995–96		1	—
1995–96	Stockport Co	10	1
1995–96	*Huddersfield T*	12	2

THORNLEY, Timothy

Born Leicester 3.3.77
Goalkeeper. From Trainee.

Season	Club	Apps	Goals
1994–95	Torquay U	1	—
1995–96		—	—

THORNTON, Mark

Born Newcastle 17.11.76
Defender. From Trainee.

Season	Club	Apps	Goals
1995–96	Newcastle U	—	—

Season	Club	League Appearances/Goals	

THORP, Michael

Born Wallington 5.12.75 Ht 6 0
Wt 11 07
Defender. From Trainee.

1994–95	Reading	—	—
1995–96		2	—

THORPE, Andrew

Born Sheffield 9.3.77 Ht 5 11 Wt 12 02
Defender. From Trainee.

1995–96	Sheffield U	—	—

THORPE, Jeff

Born Whitehaven 17.11.72 Ht 5 11
Wt 12 08
Midfield. From Trainee.

1990–91	Carlisle U	13	—
1991–92		28	1
1992–93		28	—
1993–94		—	—
1994–95		28	4
1995–96		34	1

THORPE, Lee

Born Wolverhampton 14.12.75 Ht 6 0
Wt 11 06
Forward. From Trainee.

1993–94	Blackpool	1	—
1994–95		1	—
1995–96		1	—

THORPE, Tony

Born Leicester 10.4.74 Ht 5 9 Wt 12 04
Forward. From Leicester C.

1992–93	Luton T	—	—
1993–94		14	1
1994–95		4	—
1995–96		33	7

THORSTVEDT, Erik

Born Stavanger 28.10.62 Ht 6 4
Wt 14 03
Goalkeeper. From IFK Gothenburg.
Norway 97 full caps.

1988–89	Tottenham H	18	—
1989–90		34	—
1990–91		37	—
1991–92		24	—
1992–93		27	—
1993–94		32	—
1994–95		1	—
1995–96		—	—

TIERNEY, Francis

Born Liverpool 10.9.75 Ht 5 10
Wt 11 00
Midfield. From Trainee.

1992–93	Crewe Alex	1	—
1993–94		8	1
1994–95		20	4
1995–96		22	2

TIERNEY, Grant

Born Falkirk 11.10.61 Ht 6 0 Wt 11 06
Defender. From Bainsford F.

1978–79	Hearts	—	—
1979–80		—	—
1980–81	Cowdenbeath	32	1
1981–82		32	2
1982–83		32	2
1983–84		35	1
1984–85		25	3
1984–85	Meadowbank T	8	—
1985–86		35	4
1986–87		36	4
1987–88		36	2
1988–89		18	—
1988–89	Dunfermline Ath	18	1
1989–90		33	2
1990–91	Partick T	28	1
1991–92		13	1
1992–93		16	2
1993–94		22	1
1994–95		5	—
1995–96		1	—

TILER, Carl

Born Sheffield 11.2.70 Ht 6 4 Wt 12 10
Defender. From Trainee. England Under-21.

1987–88	Barnsley	1	—
1988–89		4	—
1989–90		21	1
1990–91		45	2
1991–92	Nottingham F	26	1
1992–93		37	—
1993–94		3	—
1994–95		3	—
1994–95	*Swindon T*	2	—
1995–96	Nottingham F	—	—
1995–96	Aston Villa	1	—

Season Club League Appearances/Goals

TILLEY, Anthony

Born Zambia 11.2.77
Forward.

Season	Club	Apps	Goals
1995–96	Portsmouth	—	—

TILLSON, Andy

Born Huntingdon 30.6.66 Ht 6 2
Wt 12 10
Defender. From Kettering T.

Season	Club	Apps	Goals
1988–89	Grimsby T	45	2
1989–90		42	3
1990–91		18	—
1990–91	QPR	19	2
1991–92		10	—
1992–93		—	—
1992–93	*Grimsby T*	4	—
1992–93	Bristol R	29	—
1993–94		13	—
1994–95		40	2
1995–96		38	1

TILSON, Steve

Born Wickford 27.7.66 Ht 5 11 Wt 12 10
Midfield. From Burnham.

Season	Club	Apps	Goals
1988–89	Southend U	16	2
1989–90		16	—
1990–91		38	8
1991–92		46	7
1992–93		31	3
1993–94		10	—
1993–94	*Brentford*	2	—
1994–95	Southend U	26	2
1995–96		28	3

TIMONS, Chris

Born Longworth 8.12.74 Ht 6 1 Wt 12 07
Defender. From Clipstone Welfare.

Season	Club	Apps	Goals
1993–94	Mansfield T	16	1
1994–95		6	—
1995–96		17	1

TINKLER, Mark

Born Bishop Auckland 24.10.74 Ht 5 10
Wt 13 03
Midfield. From Trainee. England Youth.

Season	Club	Apps	Goals
1991–92	Leeds U	—	—
1992–93		7	—
1993–94		3	—
1994–95		3	—
1995–96		9	—

TINNION, Brian

Born Stanley 23.2.68 Ht 6 1 Wt 13 00
Defender. From Apprentice.

Season	Club	Apps	Goals
1985–86	Newcastle U	—	—
1986–87		3	—
1987–88		16	1
1988–89		13	1
1988–89	Bradford C	14	1
1989–90		37	5
1990–91		41	5
1991–92		26	8
1992–93		27	3
1992–93	Bristol C	11	2
1993–94		41	5
1994–95		35	2
1995–96		30	3

TISDALE, Paul

Born Malta 14.1.73 Ht 5 9 Wt 11 13
Midfield. From School.

Season	Club	Apps	Goals
1991–92	Southampton	—	—
1992–93		—	—
1992–93	*Northampton T*	5	—
1993–94	Southampton	—	—
1994–95		7	—
1995–96		9	1

TITTERTON, David

Born Hatton 25.9.71 Ht 5 11 Wt 13 08
Defender. From Trainee. England Youth.

Season	Club	Apps	Goals
1989–90	Coventry C	1	—
1990–91		1	—
1991–92		—	—
1991–92	Hereford U	25	1
1992–93		26	—
1993–94	Wycombe W	18	1
1994–95		1	—
1995–96	Bury	—	—

TOD, Andrew

Born Dunfermline 4.11.71 Ht 6 3
Wt 12 00
Defender. From Kelty Hearts.

Season	Club	Apps	Goals
1993–94	Dunfermline Ath	22	11
1994–95		35	6
1995–96		36	5

TODD, Andrew

Born Nottingham 22.2.79
Midfield. From Trainee.

Season	Club	Apps	Goals
1995–96	Nottingham F	—	—

Season	Club	League Appearances/Goals	

TODD, Andy

Born Derby 21.9.74 Ht 5 10 Wt 10 11
Defender. From Trainee.

1991–92	Middlesbrough	—	—
1992–93		—	—
1993–94		3	—
1994–95		5	—
1994–95	*Swindon T*	13	—
1995–96	Bolton W	12	2

TODD, Lee

Born Hartlepool 7.3.72 Ht 5 5 Wt 10 03
Defender. From Hartlepool U Trainee.

1990–91	Stockport Co	14	—
1991–92		19	—
1992–93		39	—
1993–94		33	—
1994–95		37	2
1995–96		42	—

TODD, Mark

Born Belfast 4.12.67 Ht 5 9 Wt 10 04
Midfield. From Trainee. Northern Ireland Under-23.

1985–86	Manchester U	—	—
1986–87		—	—
1987–88	Sheffield U	12	—
1988–89		39	4
1989–90		16	1
1990–91		3	—
1990–91	*Wolverhampton W*	7	—
1991–92	Sheffield U	—	—
1991–92	Rotherham U	23	2
1992–93		16	4
1993–94		11	1
1994–95		14	—
1995–96	Scarborough	23	1
1995–96	Mansfield T	12	—

TOLSON, Neil

Born Wordley 25.10.73 Ht 6 2 Wt 11 12
Forward. From Trainee.

1991–92	Walsall	9	1
1991–92	Oldham Ath	—	—
1992–93		3	—
1993–94		—	—
1993–94	Bradford C	22	2
1994–95		10	2
1994–95	*Chester C*	4	—
1995–96	Bradford C	31	8

TOMAN, Andy

Born Northallerton 7.3.62 Ht 5 10 Wt 12 06
Midfield. From Bishop Auckland.

1985–86	Lincoln C	24	4
1986–87	Hartlepool U	21	5
1987–88		46	17
1988–89		45	6
1989–90	Darlington	—	—
1990–91		43	5
1991–92		43	4
1992–93		29	1
1992–93	*Scarborough*	6	—
1993–94	Scunthorpe U	15	5
1993–94	Scarborough	13	1
1994–95		6	—
1995–96		16	2

TOMLINSON, Graeme

Born Watford 10.12.75 Ht 5 9 Wt 11 05
Forward. From Trainee.

1993–94	Bradford C	17	6
1994–95	Manchester U	—	—
1995–96		—	—
1995–96	*Luton T*	7	—

TOMLINSON, Micky

Born Lambeth 15.9.72 Ht 5 8 Wt 11 00
Midfield. From Trainee.

1990–91	Leyton Orient	1	1
1991–92		1	—
1992–93		8	—
1993–94		4	—
1993–94	Barnet	11	—
1994–95		27	1
1995–96		25	2

TOMLINSON, Paul

Born Brierley Hill 22.2.64 Ht 6 2 Wt 14 04
Goalkeeper. From Middlewood R.

1983–84	Sheffield U	30	—
1984–85		2	—
1985–86		—	—
1986–87		5	—
1986–87	*Birmingham C*	11	—
1987–88	Bradford C	42	—
1988–89		38	—
1989–90		41	—
1990–91		43	—

Season	Club	League Appearances/Goals	
1991–92		45	—
1992–93		24	—
1993–94		23	—
1994–95		37	—
1995–96		—	—

TORPEY, Steve

Born Islington 8.12.70 Ht 6 3 Wt 14 03
Forward. From Trainee.

1988–89	Millwall	—	—
1989–90		7	—
1990–91		—	—
1990–91	Bradford C	29	7
1991–92		43	10
1992–93		24	5
1993–94	Swansea C	40	9
1994–95		41	11
1995–96		42	15

TORTOLANO, Joe

Born Stirling 6.4.66 Ht 5 8 Wt 11 02
Forward. From Apprentice. Scotland Under-21.

1983–84	WBA	—	—
1984–85		—	—
1985–86	Hibernian	20	3
1986–87		33	—
1987–88		21	4
1988–89		25	—
1989–90		7	—
1990–91		18	1
1991–92		25	1
1992–93		21	3
1993–94		18	1
1994–95		18	—
1995–96		16	—

TOTTEN, Alex

Born Southampton 1.10.76 Ht 5 8
Wt 10 07
Midfield. From Trainee.

1994–95	Portsmouth	4	—
1995–96		—	—

TOVEY, Paul

Born Wokingham 5.12.73 Ht 5 8
Wt 10 10
Midfield. From Trainee.

1992–93	Bristol R	—	—
1993–94		1	—

Season	Club	League Appearances/Goals	
1994–95		—	—
1995–96		8	—

TOWN, David

Born Bournemouth 9.12.76 Ht 5 7
Wt 11 13
Forward. From Trainee.

1993–94	Bournemouth	1	—
1994–95		5	—
1995–96		7	—

TOWNLEY, Leon

Born Loughton 16.2.76 Ht 6 0 Wt 12 09
Defender. From Trainee.

1994–95	Tottenham H	—	—
1995–96		—	—

TOWNSEND, Andy

Born Maidstone 27.7.63 Ht 5 11
Wt 12 07
Midfield. From Welling, Weymouth. Eire B, 60 full caps.

1984–85	Southampton	5	—
1985–86		27	1
1986–87		14	1
1987–88		37	3
1988–89	Norwich C	36	5
1989–90		35	3
1990–91	Chelsea	34	2
1991–92		35	6
1992–93		41	4
1993–94	Aston Villa	32	3
1994–95		32	1
1995–96		33	2

TOWNSEND, Quentin

Born Worcester 13.2.77 Ht 6 1 Wt 13 00
Defender. From Trainee.

1995–96	Wolverhampton W	—	—

TRACEY, Simon

Born Woolwich 9.12.67 Ht 6 0 Wt 13 08
Goalkeeper. From Apprentice.

1985–86	Wimbledon	—	—
1986–87		—	—
1987–88		—	—
1988–89		1	—
1988–89	Sheffield U	7	—
1989–90		46	—

Season	Club	League Appearances/Goals	
1990–91		31	—
1991–92		29	—
1992–93		10	—
1993–94		15	—
1994–95		5	—
1994–95	*Manchester C*	3	—
1994–95	*Norwich C*	1	—
1995–96	Sheffield U	11	—
1995–96	*Wimbledon*	1	—

TRAVIS, Simon

Born Preston 22.3.77
Forward. From Trainee.

1995–96	Torquay U	8	—

TREBBLE, Neil

Born Hitchin 16.2.69 Ht 6 3 Wt 13 10
Forward. From Stevenage Borough.

1993–94	Scunthorpe U	14	2
1994–95	Preston NE	19	4
1994–95	Scarborough	15	3
1995–96		32	5

TREES, Robert

Born Manchester 18.12.77 Ht 5 10
Wt 11 05
Midfield. From Trainee.

1995–96	Manchester U	—	—

TRETTON, Andrew

Born Derby 9.10.76 Ht 6 0 Wt 12 08
Defender. From Trainee.

1993–94	Derby Co	—	—
1994–95		—	—
1995–96		—	—

TREVITT, Simon

Born Dewsbury 20.12.67 Ht 5 11
Wt 12 06
Defender. From Apprentice.

1986–87	Huddersfield T	11	—
1987–88		37	1
1988–89		39	—
1989–90		7	—
1990–91		38	—
1991–92		41	1
1992–93		—	—
1993–94		31	1
1994–95		21	—
1995–96		4	—
1995–96	Hull C	25	—

TRINDER, Jason

Born Leicester 3.3.70 Ht 5 11
Wt 14 03
Goalkeeper. From Grimsby T.

1994–95	Mansfield T	7	—
1995–96		1	—

TROLLOPE, Paul

Born Swindon 3.6.72 Ht 5 8 Wt 11 09
Midfield. From Trainee.

1989–90	Swindon T	—	—
1990–91		—	—
1991–92		—	—
1991–92	*Torquay U*	10	—
1992–93	Torquay U	36	2
1993–94		42	10
1994–95		18	4
1994–95	Derby Co	24	4
1995–96		17	—

TUCK, Stuart

Born Brighton 1.10.74 Ht 5 11 Wt 11 02
Defender. From Trainee.

1993–94	Brighton & HA	11	—
1994–95		23	—
1995–96		8	—

TURKINGTON, Edmond

Born Merseyside 15.5.78
Midfield. From Trainee.

1995–96	Liverpool	—	—

TURLEY, Billy

Born Wolverhampton 15.7.73 Ht 6 3
Wt 14 12
Goalkeeper. From Evesham.

1995–96	Northampton T	2	—

TURNBULL, Lee

Born Stockton 27.9.67 Ht 6 0 Wt 12 07
Midfield. From Local.

1985–86	Middlesbrough	2	—
1986–87		14	4
1987–88		—	—
1987–88	Aston Villa	—	—
1987–88	Doncaster R	30	1

Season	Club	League Appearances	Goals
1988–89		32	4
1989–90		42	10
1990–91		19	6
1990–91	Chesterfield	19	9
1991–92		27	7
1992–93		33	8
1993–94		8	2
1993–94	Doncaster R	11	1
1993–94	Wycombe W	6	—
1994–95		5	1
1994–95	*Scunthorpe U*	10	3
1995–96	Scunthorpe U	23	3

TURNER, Andy

Born Woolwich 23.5.75 Ht 5 9 Wt 11 07
Midfield. From Trainee. Eire Under-21.

Season	Club	League Appearances	Goals
1991–92	Tottenham H	—	—
1992–93		18	3
1993–94		1	—
1994–95		1	—
1994–95	*Wycombe W*	4	—
1994–95	*Doncaster R*	4	1
1995–96	Tottenham H	—	—
1995–96	*Huddersfield T*	5	1
1995–96	*Southend U*	6	—

TURNER, Barry

Born Nottingham 1.12.78 Ht 5 9 Wt 10 03
Midfield. From Trainee.

Season	Club	League Appearances	Goals
1995–96	Nottingham F	—	—

TURNER, Darren

Born Derby 23.12.77 Ht 5 3 Wt 8 00
Midfield. From Trainee.

Season	Club	League Appearances	Goals
1994–95	Nottingham F	—	—
1995–96		—	—

TURNER, Mark

Born Bebbington 4.10.72 Ht 6 1 Wt 12 09
Midfield. From Trainee.

Season	Club	League Appearances	Goals
1991–92	Wolverhampton W	—	—
1992–93		1	—
1993–94		—	—
1994–95	Northampton T	4	—
1995–96		—	—

TURNER, Phil

Born Sheffield 12.2.62 Ht 5 8 Wt 11 00
Midfield. From Apprentice.

Season	Club	League Appearances	Goals
1979–80	Lincoln C	14	1
1980–81		38	4
1981–82		28	1
1982–83		40	3
1983–84		42	3
1984–85		36	3
1985–86		43	4
1986–87	Grimsby T	34	3
1987–88		28	5
1987–88	Leicester C	8	—
1988–89		16	2
1988–89	Notts Co	16	2
1989–90		44	6
1990–91		38	1
1991–92		29	1
1992–93		20	1
1993–94		40	3
1994–95		38	1
1995–96		12	1

TURNER, Robbie

Born Durham 18.9.66 Ht 6 2 Wt 13 12
Midfield. From Apprentice.

Season	Club	League Appearances	Goals
1984–85	Huddersfield T	1	—
1985–86	Cardiff C	34	7
1986–87		5	1
1986–87	*Hartlepool U*	7	1
1986–87	Bristol R	17	1
1987–88		9	1
1987–88	Wimbledon	4	—
1988–89		6	—
1988–89	Bristol C	19	6
1989–90		33	6
1990–91	Plymouth Arg	39	14
1991–92		25	3
1992–93		2	—
1992–93	Notts Co	8	1
1992–93	*Shrewsbury T*	9	—
1993–94	Notts Co	—	—
1993–94	Exeter C	22	3
1994–95		11	1
1995–96		12	3
1995–96	Cambridge U	10	3

TURNER, Tommy

Born Johnstone 11.10.63 Ht 5 9 Wt 10 07
Midfield. From Glentyan Thistle.

Season	Club	League Appearances	Goals
1983–84	Morton	—	—

Season	Club	Appearances	Goals
1984–85		13	1
1985–86		34	7
1986–87		38	4
1987–88		29	1
1988–89		31	10
1989–90		30	6
1990–91	St Johnstone	28	3
1991–92		33	3
1992–93		28	1
1993–94		39	—
1994–95		11	—
1994–95	Partick T	15	2
1995–96		22	3

TURPIN, Simon

Born Blackburn 11.8.75 Ht 6 3
Wt 11 08
Defender.

Season	Club	Appearances	Goals
1994–95	Crewe Alex	—	—
1995–96		—	—

TUTILL, Steve

Born Derwent 1.10.69 Ht 5 10
Wt 12 01
Defender. From Trainee. England Schools.

Season	Club	Appearances	Goals
1987–88	York C	21	—
1988–89		22	1
1989–90		42	—
1990–91		42	—
1991–92		39	1
1992–93		8	—
1993–94		46	4
1994–95		39	—
1995–96		25	—

TUTTLE, David

Born Reading 6.2.72 Ht 6 2
Wt 12 10
Defender. From Trainee. England Youth.

Season	Club	Appearances	Goals
1989–90	Tottenham H	—	—
1990–91		6	—
1991–92		2	—
1992–93		5	—
1992–93	*Peterborough U*	7	—
1993–94	Sheffield U	31	—
1994–95		6	—
1995–96		26	1
1995–96	Crystal Palace	10	1

TWEED, Steven

Born Edinburgh 8.8.72 Ht 6 3 Wt 13 02
Defender. From Hutchison Vale. Scotland Under-21.

Season	Club	Appearances	Goals
1991–92	Hibernian	1	—
1992–93		14	—
1993–94		29	3
1994–95		33	—
1995–96		31	—

TWIDDY, Chris

Born Pontyridd 19.1.76 Ht 5 10
Wt 11 06
Midfield. From Trainee. Wales Under-21.

Season	Club	Appearances	Goals
1994–95	Plymouth Arg	15	1
1995–96		2	—

TWISS, Michael

Born Salford 26.12.77 Ht 5 10 Wt 12 10
Forward. From Trainee.

Season	Club	Appearances	Goals
1995–96	Manchester U	—	—

TWYNHAM, Gary

Born Manchester 8.2.76 Ht 6 0 Wt 12 01
Midfield. From Trainee.

Season	Club	Appearances	Goals
1994–95	Manchester U	—	—
1995–96		—	—
1995–96	Darlington	2	—

TYLER, Mark

Born Norwich 2.4.77 Ht 5 11 Wt 12 00
Goalkeeper. From Trainee. England Youth.

Season	Club	Appearances	Goals
1994–95	Peterborough U	5	—
1995–96		—	—

Season Club League Appearances/Goals

UHLENBEEK, Gus

Born Paramaribo 20.8.70
Midfield. From TOPS SV.

Season	Club	Apps	Goals
1995–96	Ipswich T	40	4

ULLATHORNE, Robert

Born Wakefield 11.10.71 Ht 5 8
Wt 11 03
Midfield. From Trainee.

Season	Club	Apps	Goals
1989–90	Norwich C	—	—
1990–91		2	—
1991–92		20	3
1992–93		—	—
1993–94		16	2
1994–95		27	2
1995–96		29	—

UNSWORTH, David

Born Preston 16.10.73 Ht 6 0 Wt 14 00
Forward. From Trainee. England Youth, Under-21, 1 full cap.

Season	Club	Apps	Goals
1991–92	Everton	2	1
1992–93		3	—
1993–94		8	—
1994–95		38	3
1995–96		31	2

UNSWORTH, Lee

Born Eccles 25.2.73 Ht 6 0 Wt 11 00
Defender. From Ashton U.

Season	Club	Apps	Goals
1994–95	Crewe Alex	—	—
1995–96		29	—

UPSON, Matthew

Born Eye 18.4.79 Ht 6 1 Wt 11 05
Defender. From Trainee.

Season	Club	Apps	Goals
1995–96	Luton T	—	—

UTLEY, Darren

Born Barnsley 28.9.77 Ht 6 0 Wt 10 09
Midfield. From Trainee.

Season	Club	Apps	Goals
1995–96	Doncaster R	1	—

VALENTINE, Peter

Born Huddersfield 16.6.63 Ht 6 0
Wt 12 09
Defender. From Apprentice.

Season	Club	Apps	Goals
1980–81	Huddersfield T	—	—
1981–82		14	1
1982–83		5	—
1983–84	Bolton W	42	1
1984–85		26	—
1985–86	Bury	46	3
1986–87		46	2
1987–88		42	2
1988–89		30	1
1989–90		38	—
1990–91		42	2
1991–92		39	3
1992–93		36	3
1993–94	Carlisle U	20	2
1994–95		9	—
1994–95	Rochdale	27	2
1995–96		23	—

VAN BLERK, Jason

Born Sydney 16.3.68 Ht 6 1 Wt 13 00
Midfield. From Go Ahead. Australia full caps.

Season	Club	Apps	Goals
1994–95	Millwall	27	1
1995–96		42	1

VAN DER GAAG, Michel

Born Zutphen 27.10.71 Ht 6 2 Wt 12 04
Defender. From PSV Eindhoven.

Season	Club	Apps	Goals
1994–95	Motherwell	2	—
1995–96		12	1

VAN HEUSDEN, Arjan

Born Alphen 11.12.72 Ht 6 4 Wt 12 09
Goalkeeper. From Noordwijk.

Season	Club	Apps	Goals
1994–95	Port Vale	2	—
1995–96		7	—

VAN HOOIJDONK, Pierre

Born Steenbergen 29.11.69 Ht 6 4
Wt 13 05
Forward. From NAC Breda. Holland Under-21.

Season	Club	Apps	Goals
1994–95	Celtic	14	4
1995–96		34	26

Season Club League Appearances/Goals

VAN VOSSEN, Peter

Born Zieriksee 21.4.68
Forward. From Istanbulspor Kulubu.
Holland 18 full caps.

Season	Club	App	Gls
1995–96	Rangers	7	—

VAN DE KAMP, Guido

Born Den Bosch 8.2.64 Ht 6 2 Wt 13 01
Goalkeeper. From Den Bosch.

Season	Club	App	Gls
1991–92	Dundee U	27	—
1992–93		1	—
1993–94		25	—
1994–95	Dunfermline Ath	13	—
1995–96		26	—

VAN DER LAAN, Robin

Born Schiedam 5.9.68 Ht 5 11 Wt 13 08
Forward. From Wageningen.

Season	Club	App	Gls
1990–91	Port Vale	18	4
1991–92		43	5
1992–93		38	6
1993–94		33	4
1994–95		44	5
1995–96	Derby Co	39	6

VAN DER VELDEN, Carel

Born Arnheim 3.8.72 Ht 5 9 Wt 13 00
Midfield. From Den Bosch.

Season	Club	App	Gls
1995–96	Barnsley	7	—

VARADI, Imre

Born Paddington 8.7.59 Ht 5 9 Wt 12 03
Forward. From Letchworth GC.

Season	Club	App	Gls
1977–78	Sheffield U	—	—
1978–79		10	4
1978–79	Everton	—	—
1979–80		4	—
1980–81		22	6
1981–82	Newcastle U	42	18
1982–83		39	21
1983–84	Sheffield W	38	17
1984–85		38	16
1985–86	WBA	32	9
1986–87		—	—
1986–87	Manchester C	30	9
1987–88		32	17
1988–89		3	—
1988–89	Sheffield W	20	3
1989–90		2	—
1989–90	Leeds U	13	2
1990–91		6	2
1991–92		3	—
1991–92	*Luton T*	6	1
1992–93	Leeds U	4	1
1992–93	*Oxford U*	5	—
1992–93	Rotherham U	11	4
1993–94		39	19
1994–95		17	2
1995–96	Mansfield T	1	—
1995–96	Scunthorpe U	2	—

VARTY, Will

Born Workington 1.10.76 Ht 6 0
Wt 12 04
Defender. From Trainee.

Season	Club	App	Gls
1995–96	Carlisle U	—	—

VATA, Rudi

Born Shkoder 13.2.69 Ht 6 1 Wt 12 05
Midfield. From Dinamo Tirana. Albania full caps.

Season	Club	App	Gls
1992–93	Celtic	22	2
1993–94		10	1
1994–95		7	1
1995–96		6	—

VAUGHAN, John

Born Isleworth 26.6.64 Ht 5 10 Wt 13 01
Goalkeeper. From Apprentice.

Season	Club	App	Gls
1981–82	West Ham U	—	—
1982–83		—	—
1983–84		—	—
1984–85		—	—
1984–85	*Charlton Ath*	6	—
1985–86	West Ham U	—	—
1985–86	*Bristol R*	6	—
1985–86	*Wrexham*	4	—
1985–86	*Bristol C*	2	—
1986–87	Fulham	44	—
1987–88		—	—
1987–88	*Bristol C*	3	—
1988–89	Cambridge U	29	—
1989–90		46	—
1990–91		43	—
1991–92		33	—
1992–93		27	—
1993–94	Charlton Ath	6	—
1994–95	Preston NE	26	—
1995–96		40	—

Season	Club	League Appearances/Goals	

VAUGHAN, Tony

Born Manchester 11.10.75 Ht 6 1
Wt 11 02
Defender. From Trainee.

1994–95	Ipswich T	10	—
1995–96		25	1

VEART, Carl

Born Whyalla Adelaide 21.5.70 Ht 5 10
Wt 11 05
Forward. From Adelaide C. Australia full caps.

1994–95	Sheffield U	39	10
1995–96		27	5
1995–96	Crystal Palace	12	—

VENISON, Barry

Born Consett 16.8.64 Ht 5 10
Wt 12 03
Defender. From Apprentice. England Youth, Under-21, 2 full caps.

1981–82	Sunderland	20	1
1982–83		37	—
1983–84		41	—
1984–85		39	1
1985–86		36	—
1986–87	Liverpool	33	—
1987–88		18	—
1988–89		15	—
1989–90		25	—
1990–91		6	—
1991–92		13	1
1992–93	Newcastle U	44	—
1993–94		37	—
1994–95		28	1

From Galatasaray

1995–96	Southampton	22	—

VENUS, Mark

Born Hartlepool 6.4.67 Ht 6 0
Wt 11 08
Defender.

1984–85	Hartlepool U	4	—
1985–86	Leicester C	1	—
1986–87		39	—
1987–88		21	1
1987–88	Wolverhampton W	4	—
1988–89		35	—
1989–90		44	2
1990–91		6	—
1991–92		46	1
1992–93		12	—
1993–94		39	1
1994–95		39	3
1995–96		22	—

VICK, Leigh

Born Cardiff 8.1.78
Midfield. From Trainee.

1994–95	Cardiff C	2	—
1995–96		2	—

VICKERS, Steve

Born Bishop Auckland 13.10.67 Ht 6 1
Wt 12 12
Defender. From Spennymoor U.

1985–86	Tranmere R	3	—
1986–87		36	2
1987–88		46	1
1988–89		46	3
1989–90		42	3
1990–91		42	1
1991–92		43	1
1992–93		42	—
1993–94		11	—
1993–94	Middlesbrough	26	3
1994–95		44	3
1995–96		32	1

VICTORY, Jamie

Born London 14.11.75 Ht 5 11 Wt 12 02
Defender. From Trainee.

1994–95	West Ham U	—	—
1995–96	Bournemouth	16	1

VILJOEN, Nik

Born New Zealand 3.12.76 Ht 5 10
Wt 12 00
Forward. From Trainee.

1995–96	Rotherham U	8	2

VILSTRUP, Johnny

Born Copenhagen 27.2.69 Ht 6 0
Wt 13 02
Midfield. From Lyngby.

1995–96	Luton T	7	—

Season	Club	League Appearances/Goals	

VINCENT, Jamie

Born London 18.6.75 Ht 5 10 Wt 11 09
Defender. From Trainee.

1993–94	Crystal Palace	—	—
1994–95		—	—
1994–95	*Bournemouth*	8	—
1995–96	Crystal Palace	25	—

VINE, Darren

Born Sheffield 22.12.76 Ht 5 11
Wt 12 08
Forward. From Trainee.

1995–96	Sheffield U	—	—

VINNICOMBE, Chris

Born Exeter 20.10.70 Ht 5 8 Wt 10 12
Midfield. England Under-21.

1988–89	Exeter C	25	—
1989–90		14	1
1989–90	Rangers	7	—
1990–91		10	1
1991–92		2	—
1992–93		—	—
1993–94		4	—
1994–95	Burnley	29	1
1995–96		35	2

VIRGO, James

Born Brighton 21.12.76 Ht 5 10
Wt 12 10
Defender. From Trainee.

1995–96	Brighton & HA	—	—

VIVEASH, Adrian

Born Swindon 30.9.69 Ht 6 1 Wt 11 09
Defender. From Trainee.

1988–89	Swindon T	—	—
1989–90		—	—
1990–91		25	1
1991–92		10	—
1992–93		5	—
1992–93	*Reading*	5	—
1993–94	Swindon T	—	—
1994–95		14	1
1994–95	*Reading*	6	—
1995–96	Swindon T	—	—
1995–96	*Barnsley*	2	1
1995–96	Walsall	31	—

VONK, Michael

Born Alkmaar 28.10.68 Ht 6 3 Wt 13 05
Defender. From SW/Dordrecht.

1991–92	Manchester C	9	—
1992–93		26	2
1993–94		35	1
1994–95		21	—
1995–96		—	—
1995–96	*Oldham Ath*	5	1
1995–96	Sheffield U	17	—

VOWDEN, Colin

Born Newmarket 13.9.71 Ht 6 1
Wt 13 00
Defender. From Cambridge C.

1994–95	Cambridge U	—	—
1995–96		24	—

Season	Club	League Appearances/Goals	

WADDLE, Chris

Born Hedworth 14.12.60 Ht 6 1 Wt 13 03
Forward. From Tow Law T. England Under-21, 62 full caps. Football League.

1980–81	Newcastle U	13	1
1981–82		42	7
1982–83		37	7
1983–84		42	18
1984–85		36	13
1985–86	Tottenham H	39	11
1986–87		39	6
1987–88		22	2
1988–89		38	14
1989–90	Marseille	37	9
1990–91		35	6
1991–92		35	7
1992–93	Sheffield W	33	1
1993–94		19	3
1994–95		25	4
1995–96		32	2

WADDOCK, Gary

Born Alperton 17.3.62 Ht 5 10 Wt 12 05
Midfield. From Apprentice. Eire Youth, Under-21, Under-23, B, 20 full caps.

1979–80	QPR	16	1
1980–81		33	3
1981–82		35	—
1982–83		33	—
1983–84		36	3
1984–85		31	1
1985–86		15	—
1986–87		4	—
1987–88		—	—
From Charleroi			
1989–90	Millwall	18	—
1990–91		40	2
1991–92	QPR	—	—
1991–92	*Swindon T*	6	—
1992–93	QPR	—	—
1992–93	Bristol R	31	—
1993–94		39	1
1994–95		1	—
1994–95	Luton T	40	1
1995–96		36	—

WALES, Danny

Born London 17.11.77 Ht 5 10 Wt 10 12
Midfield. From Trainee.

1995–96	Crystal Palace	—	—

WALKER, Andy

Born Glasgow 6.4.65 Ht 5 8 Wt 10 07
Forward. From Baillieston Juniors. Scotland Under-21, 3 full caps.

1984–85	Motherwell	11	3
1985–86		22	4
1986–87		43	10
1987–88	Celtic	42	16
1988–89		22	8
1989–90		32	6
1990–91		11	—
1991–92		1	—
1991–92	*Newcastle U*	2	—
1991–92	Bolton W	24	15
1992–93		32	26
1993–94		11	3
1994–95	Celtic	26	6
1995–96		16	3
1995–96	Sheffield U	14	8

WALKER, Des

Born Hackney 26.11.65 Ht 5 11 Wt 11 11
Defender. From Apprentice. England Under-21, 59 full caps.

1983–84	Nottingham F	4	—
1984–85		3	—
1985–86		39	—
1986–87		41	—
1987–88		35	—
1988–89		34	—
1989–90		38	—
1990–91		37	—
1991–92		33	1
1992–93	Sampdoria	30	—
1993–94	Sheffield W	42	—
1994–95		38	—
1995–96		36	—

WALKER, Ian

Born Watford 31.10.71 Ht 6 1 Wt 12 09
Goalkeeper. From Trainee. England Youth, Under-21, 2 full caps.

1989–90	Tottenham H	—	—
1990–91		1	—
1990–91	*Oxford U*	2	—
1990–91	*Ipswich T*	—	—
1991–92	Tottenham H	18	—
1992–93		17	—
1993–94		11	—
1994–95		41	—
1995–96		38	—

Season	Club	League Appearances/Goals	

WALKER, James

Born Sutton-in-Ashfield 9.7.73 Ht 5 11
Wt 13 03
Goalkeeper. From Trainee.

1991–92	Notts Co	—	—
1992–93		—	—
1993–94	Walsall	31	—
1994–95		4	—
1995–96		26	—

WALKER, John

Born Glasgow 12.12.73 Ht 5 6 Wt 11 06
Midfield. From Clydebank BC.

1990–91	Rangers	—	—
1991–92		—	—
1992–93		—	—
1993–94	Clydebank	6	2
1994–95		21	—
1995–96		—	—
1995–96	Grimsby T	2	1

WALKER, Justin

Born Nottingham 6.9.75 Ht 5 10
Wt 12 12
Midfield. From Trainee. England Youth.

1992–93	Nottingham F	—	—
1993–94		—	—
1994–95		—	—
1995–96		—	—

WALKER, Keith

Born Edinburgh 17.4.66 Ht 6 0
Wt 12 08
Midfield. From ICI Juveniles.

1984–85	Stirling Albion	38	6
1985–86		32	5
1986–87		21	6
1987–88	St Mirren	19	3
1988–89		14	1
1989–90		10	2
1989–90	Swansea C	13	—
1990–91		24	—
1991–92		32	1
1992–93		42	2
1993–94		27	2
1994–95		28	—
1995–96		33	—

WALKER, Nicky

Born Aberdeen 29.9.62 Ht 6 2 Wt 11 12
Goalkeeper. From Elgin C. Scotland
Youth, 2 full caps.

1980–81	Leicester C	—	—
1981–82		6	—
1982–83	Motherwell	16	—
1983–84		15	—
1983–84	Rangers	8	—
1984–85		14	—
1985–86		34	—
1986–87		2	—
1987–88		5	—
1987–88	*Dunfermline Ath*	1	—
1988–89	Rangers	12	—
1989–90	Hearts	—	—
1990–91		13	—
1991–92		—	—
1991–92	*Burnley*	6	—
1992–93	Hearts	18	—
1993–94		17	—
1994–95		2	—
1994–95	Partick T	20	—
1995–96		33	—

WALKER, Paul

Born Kilwinning 20.8.77 Ht 5 5 Wt 9 07
Midfield. From Dundee U BC.

1994–95	Dundee U	—	—
1995–96		2	—

WALKER, Ray

Born North Shields 28.9.63 Ht 5 10
Wt 12 00
Midfield. From Apprentice. England
Youth.

1981–82	Aston Villa	—	—
1982–83		1	—
1983–84		8	—
1984–85		7	—
1984–85	*Port Vale*	15	1
1985–86	Aston Villa	7	—
1986–87	Port Vale	45	4
1987–88		42	6
1988–89		43	5
1989–90		40	—
1990–91		45	6
1991–92		26	2
1992–93		35	9
1993–94		—	—
1994–95		23	1

Season Club League Appearances/Goals

Season	Club	Apps	Goals
1994–95	*Cambridge U*	5	—
1995–96	Port Vale	35	—

WALKER, Richard

Born Cambridge 14.3.77
Midfield. From Trainee.

Season	Club	Apps	Goals
1994–95	Cambridge U	—	—
1995–96		—	—

WALKER, Richard

Born Derby 9.11.71 Ht 6 0 Wt 12 00
Defender. From Trainee.

Season	Club	Apps	Goals
1991–92	Notts Co	—	—
1992–93		12	3
1993–94		21	1
1994–95		7	—
1994–95	*Mansfield T*	4	—
1995–96	Notts Co	11	—

WALKER, Richard

Born Birmingham 8.11.77
Midfield. From Trainee.

Season	Club	Apps	Goals
1995–96	Aston Villa	—	—

WALLACE, Ray

Born Lewisham 2.10.69 Ht 5 7 Wt 11 04
Defender. From Trainee. England Under-21.

Season	Club	Apps	Goals
1987–88	Southampton	—	—
1988–89		26	—
1989–90		9	—
1990–91		—	—
1991–92	Leeds U	—	—
1991–92	*Swansea C*	2	—
1992–93	Leeds U	6	—
1993–94		1	—
1993–94	*Reading*	3	—
1994–95	Stoke C	20	1
1994–95	*Hull C*	7	—
1995–96	Stoke C	44	6

WALLACE, Rodney

Born Lewisham 2.10.69 Ht 5 7 Wt 11 03
Forward. From Trainee. England Under-21, B.

Season	Club	Apps	Goals
1987–88	Southampton	15	1
1988–89		38	12
1989–90		38	18
1990–91		37	14
1991–92	Leeds U	34	11
1992–93		32	7
1993–94		37	17
1994–95		32	4
1995–96		24	1

WALLEY, Mark

Born Barnsley 17.9.76 Ht 5 10 Wt 11 01
Forward. From Trainee. England Youth.

Season	Club	Apps	Goals
1993–94	Nottingham F	—	—
1994–95		—	—
1995–96		—	—

WALLING, Dean

Born Leeds 17.4.69 Ht 5 11 Wt 11 10
Defender.

Season	Club	Apps	Goals
1986–87	Leeds U	—	—
1987–88	Rochdale	12	2
1988–89		34	3
1989–90		19	3
From Guiseley			
1991–92	Carlisle U	37	5
1992–93		23	—
1993–94		40	5
1994–95		41	7
1995–96		43	2

WALLWORK, Ronnie

Born Manchester 10.9.77 Ht 5 9
Wt 12 09
Defender. From Trainee. England Youth.

Season	Club	Apps	Goals
1994–95	Manchester U	—	—
1995–96		—	—

WALSH, Colin

Born Hamilton 22.7.62 Ht 5 9 Wt 11 00
Midfield. From Apprentice. Scotland Youth, Under-21.

Season	Club	Apps	Goals
1979–80	Nottingham F	—	—
1980–81		16	4
1981–82		15	3
1982–83		37	5
1983–84		38	13
1984–85		13	1
1985–86		20	6
1986–87		—	—
1986–87	Charlton Ath	33	6
1987–88		11	3
1988–89		5	—
1988–89	*Peterborough U*	5	1

Season	Club	League Appearances/Goals	
1989–90	Charlton Ath	27	2
1990–91		13	—
1990–91	*Middlesbrough*	13	1
1991–92	Charlton Ath	42	4
1992–93		42	1
1993–94		35	4
1994–95		28	1
1995–96		6	—

WALSH, Gary

Born Wigan 21.3.68 Ht 6 3 Wt 14 13
Goalkeeper. From Apprentice. England Under-21.

Season	Club	League Appearances/Goals	
1984–85	Manchester U	—	—
1985–86		—	—
1986–87		14	—
1987–88		16	—
1988–89		—	—
1988–89	*Airdrie*	3	—
1989–90	Manchester U	—	—
1990–91		5	—
1991–92		2	—
1992–93		—	—
1993–94		3	—
1993–94	*Oldham Ath*	6	—
1994–95	Manchester U	10	—
1995–96	Middlesbrough	32	—

WALSH, Michael

Born Rotherham 5.8.77 Ht 6 0 Wt 12 07
Defender. From Trainee.

Season	Club	League Appearances/Goals	
1994–95	Scunthorpe U	3	—
1995–96		25	—

WALSH, Paul

Born Plumstead 1.10.62 Ht 5 8 Wt 10 04
Forward. From Apprentice. England Youth, Under-21, 3 full caps.

Season	Club	League Appearances/Goals	
1979–80	Charlton Ath	9	—
1980–81		40	11
1981–82		38	13
1982–83	Luton T	41	13
1983–84		39	11
1984–85	Liverpool	26	8
1985–86		20	11
1986–87		23	6
1987–88		8	—
1987–88	Tottenham H	11	1
1988–89		33	6
1989–90		26	2
1990–91		29	7
1991–92		29	3
1991–92	*QPR*	2	—
1992–93	Portsmouth	43	9
1993–94		30	5
1993–94	Manchester C	11	4
1994–95		39	12
1995–96		3	—
1995–96	Portsmouth	21	5

WALSH, Steve

Born Fulwood 3.11.64 Ht 6 3 Wt 14 06
Defender. From Local.

Season	Club	League Appearances/Goals	
1982–83	Wigan Ath	31	—
1983–84		42	1
1984–85		40	2
1985–86		13	1
1986–87	Leicester C	21	—
1987–88		32	7
1988–89		30	2
1989–90		34	3
1990–91		35	3
1991–92		43	7
1992–93		40	15
1993–94		10	4
1994–95		5	—
1995–96		37	4

WALTERS, Mark

Born Birmingham 2.6.64 Ht 5 9 Wt 11 08
Midfield. From Apprentice. England Youth, Under-21, B, 1 full cap.

Season	Club	League Appearances/Goals	
1981–82	Aston Villa	1	—
1982–83		22	1
1983–84		37	8
1984–85		36	10
1985–86		40	10
1986–87		21	3
1987–88		24	7
1987–88	Rangers	18	7
1988–89		31	8
1989–90		27	5
1990–91		30	12
1991–92	Liverpool	25	3
1992–93		34	11
1993–94		17	—
1993–94	*Stoke C*	9	2
1994–95	Liverpool	18	—
1994–95	*Wolverhampton W*	11	3
1995–96	Liverpool	—	—
1995–96	Southampton	5	—

Season	Club	League Appearances/Goals	

WALTON, David

Born Bedlingham 10.4.73 Ht 6 1
Wt 14 01
Defender. From Trainee.

1991–92	Sheffield U	—	—
1992–93		—	—
1993–94		—	—
1993–94	Shrewsbury T	27	5
1994–95		36	3
1995–96		35	—

WALTON, Paul

Born Sunderland 2.7.79
Forward. From Trainee.

1995–96	Hartlepool U	6	—

WANLESS, Paul

Born Banbury 14.12.73 Ht 6 1 Wt 13 04
Midfield. From Trainee.

1991–92	Oxford U	6	—
1992–93		7	—
1993–94		9	—
1994–95		10	—
1995–96	Lincoln C	8	—
1995–96	*Cambridge U*	14	1

WARBURTON, Ray

Born Rotherham 7.10.67 Ht 6 0
Wt 12 13
Defender. From Apprentice.

1984–85	Rotherham U	1	—
1985–86		—	—
1986–87		3	—
1987–88		—	—
1988–89		—	—
1989–90	York C	43	2
1990–91		22	4
1991–92		9	—
1992–93		10	3
1993–94		6	—
1993–94	*Northampton T*	17	1
1994–95	Northampton T	39	3
1995–96		44	3

WARD, Ashley

Born Manchester 24.11.70 Ht 6 1
Wt 12 01
Forward. From Trainee.

1989–90	Manchester C	1	—
1990–91		—	—
1990–91	*Wrexham*	4	2
1991–92	Leicester C	10	—
1992–93		—	—
1992–93	*Blackpool*	2	1
1992–93	Crewe Alex	20	4
1993–94		25	13
1994–95		16	8
1994–95	Norwich C	25	8
1995–96		28	10
1995–96	Derby Co	7	1

WARD, Darran

Born Kenton 13.9.78
Defender. From Trainee.

1995–96	Watford	1	—

WARD, Darren

Born Worksop 11.5.74 Ht 5 11 Wt 12 09
Goalkeeper. From Trainee. Wales Under-21.

1992–93	Mansfield T	13	—
1993–94		33	—
1994–95		35	—
1995–96	Notts Co	46	—

WARD, Gavin

Born Sutton Coldfield 30.6.70 Ht 6 3
Wt 14 05
Goalkeeper. From Aston Villa Trainee.

1988–89	Shrewsbury T	—	—
1989–90	WBA	—	—
1989–90	Cardiff C	2	—
1990–91		1	—
1991–92		24	—
1992–93		32	—
1993–94	Leicester C	32	—
1994–95		6	—
1995–96	Bradford C	36	—
1995–96	Bolton W	5	—

WARD, Mark

Born Prescot 10.10.62 Ht 5 6 Wt 10 00
Midfield. From Everton Apprentice, Northwich Vic.

1983–84	Oldham Ath	42	6
1984–85		42	6
1985–86	West Ham U	42	3
1986–87		37	1
1987–88		37	1
1988–89		30	2

Season	Club	Apps	Goals
1989–90		19	5
1989–90	Manchester C	19	3
1990–91		36	11
1991–92	Everton	37	4
1992–93		19	1
1993–94		27	1
1993–94	*Birmingham C*	9	1
1994–95	Birmingham C	41	3
1995–96		13	3
1995–96	Huddersfield T	8	—

WARD, Mitch

Born Sheffield 19.6.71 Ht 5 8 Wt 10 12
Midfield. From Trainee.

Season	Club	Apps	Goals
1989–90	Sheffield U	—	—
1990–91		4	—
1990–91	*Crewe Alex*	4	1
1991–92	Sheffield U	6	2
1992–93		26	—
1993–94		22	1
1994–95		14	2
1995–96		42	1

WARD, Peter

Born Durham 15.10.64 Ht 5 10
Wt 11 07
Forward. From Chester-le-Street.

Season	Club	Apps	Goals
1986–87	Huddersfield T	7	—
1987–88		26	2
1988–89		4	—
1989–90	Rochdale	40	5
1990–91		44	5
1991–92	Stockport Co	44	1
1992–93		35	3
1993–94		35	3
1994–95		28	3
1995–96	Wrexham	34	5

WARD, Richard

Born Middlesbrough 6.1.77 Ht 5 11
Wt 13 00
Midfield. From Trainee.

Season	Club	Apps	Goals
1993–94	Middlesbrough	—	—
1994–95		—	—
1995–96		—	—

WARD, Robert

Born Blackpool 16.3.77 Ht 5 8 Wt 11 04
Defender. From Trainee.

Season	Club	Apps	Goals
1995–96	Blackpool	—	—

Season Club League Appearances/Goals

WARE, Paul

Born Congleton 7.11.70 Ht 5 9 Wt 11 05
Midfield. From Trainee.

Season	Club	Apps	Goals
1987–88	Stoke C	1	—
1988–89		11	1
1989–90		16	—
1990–91		34	2
1991–92		24	3
1992–93		28	4
1993–94		1	—
1994–95		—	—
1994–95	Stockport Co	19	1
1995–96		27	3

WARHURST, Paul

Born Stockport 26.9.69 Ht 6 0 Wt 11 04
Defender. From Trainee. England Under-21.

Season	Club	Apps	Goals
1987–88	Manchester C	—	—
1988–89	Oldham Ath	4	—
1989–90		30	1
1990–91		33	1
1991–92	Sheffield W	33	—
1992–93		29	6
1993–94		4	—
1993–94	Blackburn R	9	—
1994–95		27	2
1995–96		10	—

WARK, John

Born Glasgow 4.8.57 Ht 5 11 Wt 12 12
Defender. From Apprentice. Scotland Under-21, 29 full caps.

Season	Club	Apps	Goals
1974–75	Ipswich T	3	—
1975–76		3	—
1976–77		33	10
1977–78		18	5
1978–79		42	6
1979–80		41	12
1980–81		40	18
1981–82		42	18
1982–83		42	20
1983–84		32	5
1983–84	Liverpool	9	2
1984–85		40	18
1985–86		9	3
1986–87		11	5
1987–88		1	—
1987–88	Ipswich T	7	—
1988–89		41	13
1989–90		41	10

Season	Club	League Appearances	Goals
1990–91	Middlesbrough	32	2
1991–92	Ipswich T	37	3
1992–93		37	6
1993–94		38	3
1994–95		26	4
1995–96		14	2

WARNER, Anthony

Born Liverpool 11.5.74 Ht 6 4 Wt 13 09
Goalkeeper. From School.

Season	Club	League Appearances	Goals
1993–94	Liverpool	—	—
1994–95		—	—
1995–96		—	—

WARNER, Michael

Born Harrogate 17.1.74 Ht 5 9 Wt 10 10
Midfield. From Tamworth.

Season	Club	League Appearances	Goals
1995–96	Northampton T	—	—

WARNER, Rob

Born Stratford 20.4.77 Ht 5 10 Wt 11 06
Defender. From Trainee.

Season	Club	League Appearances	Goals
1994–95	Hereford U	16	—
1995–96		—	—

WARNER, Vance

Born Leeds 3.9.74 Ht 6 0 Wt 13 02
Defender. From Trainee.

Season	Club	League Appearances	Goals
1991–92	Nottingham F	—	—
1992–93		—	—
1993–94		1	—
1994–95		1	—
1995–96		—	—
1995–96	*Grimsby T*	3	—

WARREN, Christer

Born Bournemouth 10.10.74 Ht 5 10
Wt 11 04
Midfield. From Cheltenham T.

Season	Club	League Appearances	Goals
1994–95	Southampton	—	—
1995–96		7	—

WARREN, Lee

Born Manchester 28.2.69 Ht 6 0
Wt 12 00
Midfield. From Trainee.

Season	Club	League Appearances	Goals
1987–88	Leeds U	—	—
1987–88	Rochdale	31	1
1988–89	Hull C	28	—
1989–90		10	—
1990–91		15	—
1990–91	*Lincoln C*	3	1
1991–92	Hull C	31	1
1992–93		36	—
1993–94		33	—
1994–95	Doncaster R	14	2
1995–96		42	—

WARREN, Mark

Born Clapton 12.11.74 Ht 6 05 Wt 11 07
Defender. From Trainee.

Season	Club	League Appearances	Goals
1991–92	Leyton Orient	1	—
1992–93		14	—
1993–94		6	—
1993–94	*West Ham U*	—	—
1994–95	Leyton Orient	31	3
1995–96		22	1

WARREN, Matt

Born Derby 14.2.76 Ht 5 10 Wt 13 06
Defender. From Trainee.

Season	Club	League Appearances	Goals
1994–95	Derby Co	—	—
1995–96		—	—

WARRINGTON, Andy

Born Sheffield 10.6.76 Ht 6 3 Wt 12 11
Goalkeeper. From Trainee.

Season	Club	League Appearances	Goals
1994–95	York C	—	—
1995–96		6	—

WASSALL, Darren

Born Edgbaston 27.6.68 Ht 6 0
Wt 12 07
Defender.

Season	Club	League Appearances	Goals
1987–88	Nottingham F	3	—
1987–88	*Hereford U*	5	—
1988–89	Nottingham F	—	—
1988–89	*Bury*	7	1
1989–90	Nottingham F	3	—
1990–91		7	—
1991–92		14	—
1992–93	Derby Co	24	—
1993–94		25	—
1994–95		32	—
1995–96		17	—

Season	Club	League Appearances/Goals	

WATERMAN, David

Born Guernsey 16.5.77 Ht 5 10
Wt 12 00
Defender. From Trainee.

1995–96	Portsmouth	—	—

WATKIN, Steve

Born Wrexham 16.6.71 Ht 5 10
Wt 11 10
Forward. From School.

1989–90	Wrexham	—	—
1990–91		9	1
1991–92		28	8
1992–93		33	18
1993–94		40	9
1994–95		32	4
1995–96		29	7

WATKISS, Stuart

Born Wolverhampton 8.5.66 Ht 6 1
Wt 13 09
Defender. From Apprentice.

1983–84	Wolverhampton W	2	—
From Rushall Olympic			
1993–94	Walsall	39	2
1994–95		8	—
1995–96		15	—
1995–96	Hereford U	19	—

WATSON, Alex

Born Liverpool 15.4.68 Ht 6 2 Wt 13 00
Defender. From Apprentice. England Youth.

1984–85	Liverpool	—	—
1985–86		—	—
1986–87		—	—
1987–88		2	—
1988–89		2	—
1989–90		—	—
1990–91		—	—
1990–91	*Derby Co*	5	—
1990–91	Bournemouth	23	3
1991–92		15	—
1992–93		46	1
1993–94		45	1
1994–95		22	—
1995–96		—	—
1995–96	*Gillingham*	10	1
1995–96	Torquay U	29	2

WATSON, Andy

Born Huddersfield 1.4.67 Ht 5 9
Wt 11 02
Defender. From Harrogate T.

1988–89	Halifax T	45	5
1989–90		38	10
1990–91	Swansea C	14	1
1991–92		—	—
1991–92	Carlisle U	35	14
1992–93		21	8
1992–93	Blackpool	15	2
1993–94		40	20
1994–95		33	15
1995–96		27	6

WATSON, Dave

Born Liverpool 20.11.61 Ht 6 0
Wt 13 07
Defender. From Amateur. England Under-21, 12 full caps.

1979–80	Liverpool	—	—
1980–81		—	—
1980–81	Norwich C	18	3
1981–82		38	3
1982–83		35	1
1983–84		40	1
1984–85		39	—
1985–86		42	3
1986–87	Everton	35	4
1987–88		37	4
1988–89		32	3
1989–90		29	1
1990–91		32	2
1991–92		35	3
1992–93		40	1
1993–94		28	1
1994–95		38	2
1995–96		34	1

WATSON, David

Born Barnsley 10.11.73 Ht 5 11
Wt 12 03
Goalkeeper. From Trainee. England Youth, Under-21.

1992–93	Barnsley	5	—
1993–94		9	—
1994–95		37	—
1995–96		45	—

Season	Club	League Appearances/Goals	

WATSON, Gordon

Born Sidcup 20.3.71 Ht 5 10 Wt 12 09
Forward. From Trainee. England Under-21.

1988–89	Charlton Ath	—	—
1989–90		9	—
1990–91		22	7
1990–91	Sheffield W	5	—
1991–92		4	—
1992–93		11	1
1993–94		23	12
1994–95		23	2
1994–95	Southampton	12	3
1995–96		25	3

WATSON, Gregg

Born Glasgow 21.9.70 Ht 5 9 Wt 10 09
Defender. From Aberdeen Lads. Scotland Youth.

1987–88	Aberdeen	—	—
1988–89		4	—
1989–90		4	—
1990–91		7	—
1991–92		8	—
1992–93		—	—
1993–94	Partick T	37	—
1994–95		29	—
1995–96		32	1

WATSON, Kevin

Born Hackney 3.1.74 Ht 5 9 Wt 12 06
Midfield. From Trainee.

1991–92	Tottenham H	—	—
1992–93		5	—
1993–94		—	—
1993–94	*Brentford*	3	—
1994–95	Tottenham H	—	—
1994–95	*Bristol C*	2	—
1994–95	*Barnet*	13	—
1995–96	Tottenham H	—	—

WATSON, Mark

Born Birmingham 28.12.73 Ht 5 9
Wt 11 00
Forward. From Sutton U.

1994–95	West Ham U	—	—
1995–96		1	—
1995–96	*Leyton Orient*	1	1
1995–96	*Cambridge U*	4	1
1995–96	*Shrewsbury T*	1	—
1995–96	Bournemouth	—	—

Season	Club	League Appearances/Goals	

WATSON, Paul

Born Hastings 4.1.75 Ht 5 8
Wt 10 08
Defender. From Trainee.

1992–93	Gillingham	1	—
1993–94		14	—
1994–95		39	2
1995–96		8	—

WATSON, Steve

Born North Shields 1.4.74 Ht 6 1
Wt 12 07
Defender. From Trainee. England Youth, Under-21.

1990–91	Newcastle U	24	—
1991–92		28	1
1992–93		2	—
1993–94		32	2
1994–95		27	4
1995–96		23	3

WATSON, Tommy

Born Liverpool 29.9.69 Ht 5 8
Wt 10 10
Midfield. From Trainee.

1987–88	Grimsby T	19	—
1988–89		21	4
1989–90		16	1
1990–91		41	9
1991–92		17	2
1992–93		24	4
1993–94		11	1
1994–95		21	3
1995–96		2	—
1995–96	*Hull C*	4	—

WATT, Michael

Born Aberdeen 27.11.70 Ht 6 1
Wt 11 10
Goalkeeper. From Cove R. Scotland Under-21.

1989–90	Aberdeen	7	—
1990–91		10	—
1991–92		2	—
1992–93		3	—
1993–94		4	—
1994–95		14	—
1995–96		30	—

Season	Club	League Appearances/Goals	

WATTS, Julian

Born Sheffield 17.3.71 Ht 6 3 Wt 13 07
Defender. From Trainee.

Season	Club	App	Goals
1990–91	Rotherham U	10	—
1991–92		10	1
1991–92	Sheffield W	—	—
1992–93		4	—
1992–93	*Shrewsbury T*	9	—
1993–94	Sheffield W	1	—
1994–95		—	—
1995–96		11	1
1995–96	Leicester C	9	—

WDOWCZYK, Dariusz

Born Warsaw 21.9.62 Ht 5 11 Wt 11 11
Defender. From Legia Warsaw. Poland full caps.

Season	Club	App	Goals
1989–90	Celtic	23	1
1990–91		24	—
1991–92		19	—
1992–93		25	3
1993–94		25	—
1994–95	Reading	38	—
1995–96		30	—

WEATHERS, Andrew

Born Liverpool 14.11.76
Midfield. From Trainee.

Season	Club	App	Goals
1995–96	Everton	—	—

WEAVER, Nicky

Born Sheffield 2.3.79 Ht 6 4 Wt 14 00
Goalkeeper. From Trainee.

Season	Club	App	Goals
1995–96	Mansfield T	1	—

WEBB, Matthew

Born Bristol 24.9.76 Ht 5 8 Wt 9 12
Midfield. From Trainee.

Season	Club	App	Goals
1994–95	Birmingham C	1	—
1995–96		—	—

WEBB, Neil

Born Reading 30.7.63 Ht 6 0 Wt 14 07
Midfield. From Apprentice. England Youth, Under-21, B, 26 full caps. Football League.

Season	Club	App	Goals
1979–80	Reading	5	—
1980–81		27	7
1981–82		40	15
1982–83	Portsmouth	42	8
1983–84		40	10
1984–85		41	16
1985–86	Nottingham F	38	14
1986–87		32	14
1987–88		40	13
1988–89		36	6
1989–90	Manchester U	11	2
1990–91		32	3
1991–92		31	3
1992–93		1	—
1992–93	Nottingham F	9	—
1993–94		21	3
1994–95		—	—
1994–95	*Swindon T*	6	—
1995–96	Nottingham F	—	—

WEBB, Simon

Born Castle Bar 19.1.78 Ht 5 11 Wt 12 02
Midfield. From Trainee.

Season	Club	App	Goals
1994–95	Tottenham H	—	—
1995–96		—	—

WEBBER, Damien

Born Rustington 8.10.68 Ht 6 4 Wt 14 00
Defender. From Bognor Regis T.

Season	Club	App	Goals
1994–95	Millwall	22	2
1995–96		16	—

WEBSTER, Simon

Born Earl Shilton 20.1.64 Ht 6 0 Wt 11 07
Defender. From Apprentice.

Season	Club	App	Goals
1981–82	Tottenham H	—	—
1982–83		2	—
1983–84		1	—
1983–84	*Exeter C*	26	—
1984–85	Tottenham H	—	—
1984–85	*Norwich C*	—	—
1984–85	Huddersfield T	16	1
1985–86		41	2
1986–87		39	1
1987–88		22	—
1987–88	Sheffield U	5	1
1988–89		12	2
1989–90		20	—
1990–91	Charlton Ath	40	—
1991–92		44	5
1992–93		43	2

Season	Club	League Appearances/Goals	
1993–94	West Ham U	—	—
1994–95		5	—
1994–95	*Oldham Ath*	7	—
1995–96	West Ham U	—	—
1995–96	*Derby Co*	3	—

WEGERLE, Roy

Born South Africa 19.3.64 Ht 5 11 Wt 11 00
Forward. From Tampa Bay R. USA full caps.

Season	Club	League Appearances/Goals	
1986–87	Chelsea	12	2
1987–88		11	1
1987–88	*Swindon T*	7	1
1988–89	Luton T	30	8
1989–90		15	2
1989–90	QPR	19	6
1990–91		35	18
1991–92		21	5
1991–92	Blackburn R	12	2
1992–93		22	4
1992–93	Coventry C	6	—
1993–94		21	6
1994–95		26	3
1995–96		—	—

WEIR, David

Born Falkirk 10.5.70 Ht 6 2 Wt 13 07
Defender. From Celtic BC.

Season	Club	League Appearances/Goals	
1992–93	Falkirk	30	1
1993–94		37	3
1994–95		32	1
1995–96		34	3

WEIR, Micky

Born Edinburgh 16.1.66 Ht 5 4 Wt 10 03
Midfield. From Portobello T.

Season	Club	League Appearances/Goals	
1982–83	Hibernian	—	—
1983–84		—	—
1984–85		12	—
1985–86		7	—
1986–87		24	4
1987–88		5	1
1987–88	Luton T	8	—
1987–88	Hibernian	13	2
1988–89		7	—
1989–90		18	3
1990–91		20	1
1991–92		31	11
1992–93		33	5

Season	Club	League Appearances/Goals	
1993–94		—	—
1994–95		19	1
1995–96		9	1
1995–96	Millwall	8	—

WELCH, Keith

Born Bolton 3.10.68 Ht 6 1 Wt 13 07
Goalkeeper. From Trainee.

Season	Club	League Appearances/Goals	
1986–87	Bolton W	—	—
1986–87	Rochdale	24	—
1987–88		46	—
1988–89		46	—
1989–90		46	—
1990–91		43	—
1991–92	Bristol C	26	—
1992–93		45	—
1993–94		45	—
1994–95		44	—
1995–96		35	—

WELLER, Paul

Born Brighton 6.3.75 Ht 5 8 Wt 11 02
Forward. From Trainee.

Season	Club	League Appearances/Goals	
1993–94	Burnley	—	—
1994–95		—	—
1995–96		25	1

WELLS, David

Born Portsmouth 29.12.77
Goalkeeper. From Trainee.

Season	Club	League Appearances/Goals	
1994–95	Bournemouth	1	—
1995–96		—	—

WELLS, Mark

Born Leicester 17.10.71 Ht 5 8 Wt 11 02
Midfield. From Trainee.

Season	Club	League Appearances/Goals	
1990–91	Notts Co	—	—
1991–92		1	—
1992–93		1	—
1993–94	Huddersfield T	23	4
1994–95	Scarborough	18	1
1995–96		14	1

WELSH, Brian

Born Edinburgh 23.2.69 Ht 6 2 Wt 12 01
Defender. From Tynecastle BC.

Season	Club	League Appearances/Goals	
1986–87	Dundee U	1	—

Season Club League Appearances/Goals

Season	Club	Apps	Goals
1987–88		1	1
1988–89		1	—
1989–90		5	—
1990–91		17	—
1991–92		11	1
1992–93		15	1
1993–94		37	1
1994–95		27	4
1995–96		23	1

WELSH, Steve

Born Glasgow 19.4.68 Ht 6 1
Wt 12 03
Defender. From Army.

Season	Club	Apps	Goals
1989–90	Cambridge U	—	—
1990–91		1	—
1991–92	Peterborough U	42	—
1992–93		45	1
1993–94		45	1
1994–95		14	—
1994–95	*Preston NE*	—	—
1994–95	Partick T	20	—
1995–96		35	—

WEST, Colin

Born Wallsend 13.11.62 Ht 6 0
Wt 13 12
Forward. From Apprentice.

Season	Club	Apps	Goals
1980–81	Sunderland	—	—
1981–82		18	6
1982–83		23	3
1983–84		38	9
1984–85		23	3
1984–85	Watford	12	7
1985–86		33	13
1986–87	Rangers	9	2
1987–88		1	—
1987–88	Sheffield W	25	7
1988–89		20	1
1988–89	WBA	17	8
1989–90		21	4
1990–91		28	8
1991–92		7	2
1991–92	*Port Vale*	5	1
1992–93	Swansea C	33	12
1993–94	Leyton Orient	43	14
1994–95		30	9
1995–96		39	16

WEST, Dean

Born Wakefield 5.12.72 Ht 5 8
Wt 12 02
Defender. From Leeds U Schoolboy.

Season	Club	Apps	Goals
1990–91	Lincoln C	1	1
1991–92		32	3
1992–93		19	3
1993–94		18	6
1994–95		41	6
1995–96		8	1
1995–96	Bury	37	1

WEST, Paul

Born Birmingham 22.6.70 Ht 5 11
Wt 12 07
Defender. From Alcester T.

Season	Club	Apps	Goals
1991–92	Port Vale	—	—
1992–93	Bradford C	—	—
1993–94	Wigan Ath	2	—
1994–95		1	—
1995–96		—	—

WESTLEY, Shane

Born Canterbury 16.6.65 Ht 6 2
Wt 13 08
Defender. From Apprentice.

Season	Club	Apps	Goals
1983–84	Charlton Ath	8	—
1984–85		—	—
1984–85	Southend U	12	—
1985–86		36	5
1986–87		32	—
1986–87	*Norwich C*	—	—
1987–88	Southend U	36	5
1988–89		28	—
1989–90	Wolverhampton W	37	—
1990–91		5	1
1991–92		—	—
1992–93		8	1
1992–93	Brentford	17	1
1993–94		31	—
1994–95		16	—
1994–95	*Southend U*	5	—
1995–96	Cambridge U	3	—
1995–96	Lincoln C	9	1

WESTON, Richard

Born Bristol 2.3.77 Ht 5 11 Wt 11 02
Goalkeeper. From Trainee.

Season	Club	Apps	Goals
1995–96	Birmingham C	—	—

WESTWATER, Ian

Born Loughborough 8.11.63 Ht 6 0
Wt 13 00
Goalkeeper. From Salvesen BC.

Season	Club	Apps	Goals
1980–81	Hearts	2	—
1981–82		—	—
1982–83		—	—
1983–84		—	—
1984–85	Dunfermline Ath	8	—
1985–86		38	—
1986–87		42	—
1987–88		28	—
1988–89		39	—
1989–90		36	—
1990–91		1	—
1991–92	Falkirk	40	—
1992–93		24	—
1993–94		3	—
1993–94	Dunfermline Ath	9	—
1994–95		17	—
1995–96		11	—

WESTWOOD, Ashley

Born Bridgnorth 31.8.76 Ht 5 10
Wt 10 08
Defender. From Trainee. England Youth.

Season	Club	Apps	Goals
1994–95	Manchester U	—	—
1995–96	Crewe Alex	33	4

WESTWOOD, Chris

Born Dudley 13.2.77 Ht 6 0
Wt 13 00
Defender. From Trainee.

Season	Club	Apps	Goals
1995–96	Wolverhampton W	—	—

WETHERALL, David

Born Sheffield 14.3.71 Ht 6 2 Wt 13 12
Defender. From School.

Season	Club	Apps	Goals
1989–90	Sheffield W	—	—
1990–91		—	—
1991–92	Leeds U	1	—
1992–93		13	1
1993–94		32	1
1994–95		38	3
1995–96		34	4

WHALLEY, Gareth

Born Manchester 19.12.73 Ht 5 10
Wt 11 06
Midfield. From Trainee.

Season	Club	Apps	Goals
1992–93	Crewe Alex	25	1
1993–94		15	1
1994–95		40	1
1995–96		44	2

WHARTON, Paul

Born Newcastle 26.6.77 Ht 5 4 Wt 9 09
Midfield. From Trainee.

Season	Club	Apps	Goals
1994–95	Leeds U	—	—
1995–96		—	—
1995–96	Hull C	9	—

WHEALING, Anthony

Born Manchester 3.9.76 Ht 5 9 Wt 10 02
Defender. From Trainee.

Season	Club	Apps	Goals
1995–96	Blackburn R	—	—

WHEELER, Adam

Born Sheffield 29.11.77
Midfield. From Newcastle U Trainee.

Season	Club	Apps	Goals
1995–96	Doncaster R	—	—

WHELAN, Noel

Born Leeds 30.12.74 Ht 6 2 Wt 12 03
Forward. From Trainee. England Under-21.

Season	Club	Apps	Goals
1992–93	Leeds U	1	—
1993–94		16	—
1994–95		23	7
1995–96		8	—
1995–96	Coventry C	21	8

WHELAN, Phil

Born Stockport 7.8.72 Ht 6 4 Wt 14 01
Defender. England Under-21.

Season	Club	Apps	Goals
1989–90	Ipswich T	—	—
1990–91		—	—
1991–92		8	2
1992–93		32	—
1993–94		29	—
1994–95		13	—
1994–95	Middlesbrough	—	—
1995–96		13	1

WHELAN, Ronnie

Born Dublin 25.9.61 Ht 5 9
Wt 12 03
Midfield. From Home Farm. Eire Schools, Youth, Under-21, B, 53 full caps.

Season	Club	Apps	Goals
1979–80	Liverpool	—	—
1980–81		1	1
1981–82		32	10
1982–83		28	2
1983–84		23	4
1984–85		37	7
1985–86		39	10
1986–87		39	3
1987–88		28	1
1988–89		37	4
1989–90		34	1
1990–91		14	1
1991–92		10	—
1992–93		17	1
1993–94		23	1
1994–95	Southend U	33	1
1995–96		1	—

WHELAN, Spencer

Born Liverpool 17.9.71 Ht 6 2
Wt 13 00
Defender. From Liverpool.

Season	Club	Apps	Goals
1990–91	Chester C	11	—
1991–92		32	—
1992–93		28	—
1993–94		22	—
1994–95		23	1
1995–96		39	2

WHISTON, Peter

Born Widnes 4.1.68 Ht 6 0
Wt 12 02
Defender.

Season	Club	Apps	Goals
1987–88	Plymouth Arg	—	—
1988–89		2	—
1989–90		8	—
1989–90	*Torquay U*	8	1
1990–91	Torquay U	28	—
1991–92		4	—
1991–92	Exeter C	36	3
1992–93		27	3
1993–94		22	1
1994–95	Southampton	1	—
1995–96		—	—
1995–96	Shrewsbury T	28	2

WHITBREAD, Adrian

Born Epping 22.10.71 Ht 6 2 Wt 11 13
Defender. From Trainee.

Season	Club	Apps	Goals
1989–90	Leyton Orient	8	—
1990–91		38	—
1991–92		43	1
1992–93		36	1
1993–94	Swindon T	35	1
1994–95		1	—
1994–95	West Ham U	8	—
1995–96		2	—
1995–96	*Portsmouth*	13	—

WHITE, Alan

Born Darlington 22.3.76
Defender.

Season	Club	Apps	Goals
1994–95	Middlesbrough	—	—
1995–96		—	—

WHITE, Darren

Born Easington 13.1.79
Midfield. From Trainee.

Season	Club	Apps	Goals
1995–96	Middlesbrough	—	—

WHITE, David

Born Manchester 30.10.67 Ht 6 1
Wt 12 09
Forward. England Youth, Under-21, B, 1 full cap.

Season	Club	Apps	Goals
1985–86	Manchester C	—	—
1986–87		24	1
1987–88		44	13
1988–89		45	6
1989–90		37	8
1990–91		38	16
1991–92		39	18
1992–93		42	16
1993–94		16	1
1993–94	Leeds U	15	5
1994–95		23	3
1995–96		4	1
1995–96	Sheffield U	28	7

WHITE, Devon

Born Nottingham 2.3.64 Ht 6 3
Wt 14 00
Forward. From Arnold T.

Season	Club	Apps	Goals
1984–85	Lincoln C	7	1
1985–86		22	3
1986–87		—	—

Season	Club	League Appearances/Goals	
From Boston U			
1987–88	Bristol R	39	15
1988–89		40	5
1989–90		43	12
1990–91		45	11
1991–92		35	10
1991–92	Cambridge U	2	—
1992–93		20	4
1992–93	QPR	7	2
1993–94		18	7
1994–95		1	—
1994–95	Notts Co	20	7
1995–96		20	8
1995–96	Watford	16	5

WHITE, Jason

Born Meriden 19.10.71 Ht 6 0 Wt 12 10
Forward. From Derby Co Trainee.

Season	Club	Apps	Goals
1991–92	Scunthorpe U	22	11
1992–93		37	5
1993–94		9	—
1993–94	*Darlington*	4	1
1993–94	Scarborough	24	9
1994–95		39	11
1995–96	Northampton T	45	16

WHITE, John

Born Honiton 9.9.74 Ht 5 8 Wt 11 03
Midfield. From Trainee.

Season	Club	Apps	Goals
1992–93	Watford	—	—
1993–94		—	—
1994–95		—	—
1995–96		—	—

WHITE, Steve

Born Chipping Sodbury 2.1.59 Ht 5 11
Wt 12 06
Forward. From Mangotsfield U.

Season	Club	Apps	Goals
1977–78	Bristol R	8	4
1978–79		27	10
1979–80		15	6
1979–80	Luton T	9	—
1980–81		21	7
1981–82		42	18
1982–83	Charlton Ath	29	12
1982–83	*Lincoln C*	3	—
1982–83	*Luton T*	4	—
1983–84	Bristol R	43	9
1984–85		18	3
1985–86		40	12
1986–87	Swindon T	35	15
1987–88		25	11
1988–89		43	13
1989–90		43	18
1990–91		35	9
1991–92		23	10
1992–93		34	7
1993–94		6	—
1994–95	Hereford U	36	15
1995–96		40	29

WHITE, Tom

Born Bristol 26.1.76 Ht 5 11 Wt 12 02
Defender. From Trainee.

Season	Club	Apps	Goals
1994–95	Bristol R	4	—
1995–96		2	—

WHITEHALL, Steve

Born Bromborough 8.12.66 Ht 5 9
Wt 11 05
Forward. From Southport.

Season	Club	Apps	Goals
1991–92	Rochdale	34	8
1992–93		42	14
1993–94		39	14
1994–95		42	10
1995–96		46	20

WHITEHEAD, Phil

Born Halifax 17.12.69 Ht 6 2 Wt 15 04
Goalkeeper. From Trainee.

Season	Club	Apps	Goals
1986–87	Halifax T	12	—
1987–88		—	—
1988–89		11	—
1989–90		19	—
1989–90	Barnsley	—	—
1990–91		—	—
1990–91	*Halifax T*	9	—
1991–92	Barnsley	3	—
1991–92	*Scunthorpe U*	8	—
1992–93	Barnsley	13	—
1992–93	*Scunthorpe U*	8	—
1992–93	*Bradford C*	6	—
1993–94	Barnsley	—	—
1993–94	Oxford U	39	—
1994–95		38	—
1995–96		34	—

WHITEHEAD, Russell

Born0.0.0 Ht 5 8 Wt 10 04
Defender.

Season	Club	Apps	Goals
1995–96	Liverpool	—	—

Season	Club	League Appearances/Goals	

WHITEHEAD, Stuart

Born Bromsgrove 17.7.76 Ht 5 11
Wt 12 04
Midfield. From Bromsgrove R.

1995–96	Bolton W	—	—

WHITEHOUSE, Dane

Born Sheffield 14.10.70 Ht 5 9 Wt 11 10
Midfield. From Trainee.

1988–89	Sheffield U	5	—
1989–90		12	1
1990–91		4	—
1991–92		34	7
1992–93		14	5
1993–94		38	5
1994–95		39	8
1995–96		38	4

WHITESIDE, Garry

Born Glasgow 6.9.73 Ht 5 7 Wt 10 08
Midfield. From St Roch's Jun.

1995–96	Falkirk	2	—

WHITINGTON, Craig

Born Brighton 3.9.70 Ht 5 11 Wt 13 03
Forward. From Crawley T.

1993–94	Scarborough	27	10
1994–95	Huddersfield T	1	—
1994–95	*Rochdale*	1	—
1995–96	Huddersfield T	—	—

WHITLEY, Jeffrey

Born Zambia 14.4.75
Midfield. From Trainee.

1995–96	Manchester C	—	—

WHITLEY, Jim

Born Zambia 14.4.75 Ht 5 9 Wt 11 00
Midfield. From Trainee.

1993–94	Manchester C	—	—
1994–95		—	—
1995–96		—	—

WHITLOW, Mike

Born Northwich 13.1.68 Ht 6 0 Wt 13 03
Defender. From Witton Alb.

1988–89	Leeds U	20	1
1989–90		29	1
1990–91		18	1
1991–92		10	1
1991–92	Leicester C	5	—
1992–93		24	1
1993–94		31	2
1994–95		28	2
1995–96		42	3

WHITNEY, Jonathan

Born Nantwich 23.12.70 Ht 5 10
Wt 12 03
Defender. From Winsford.

1993–94	Huddersfield T	14	—
1994–95		—	—
1994–95	*Wigan Ath*	12	—
1995–96	Huddersfield T	4	—
1995–96	Lincoln C	26	2

WHITNEY, Scott

Born Northampton 10.3.79
Defender. From Trainee.

1995–96	Nottingham F	—	—

WHITTAKER, Stuart

Born Liverpool 2.1.75 Ht 5 7 Wt 9 03
Midfield. From Liverpool Trainee.

1993–94	Bolton W	2	—
1994–95		1	—
1995–96		—	—

WHITTAM, Philip

Born Bolton 12.8.76 Ht 5 8 Wt 9 08
Defender. From Trainee.

1994–95	Manchester U	—	—
1995–96		—	—

WHITTINGHAM, Guy

Born Evesham 10.11.64 Ht 5 10
Wt 12 00
Forward. From Yeovil, Army.

1989–90	Portsmouth	42	23
1990–91		37	12
1991–92		35	11
1992–93		46	42
1993–94	Aston Villa	18	3
1993–94	*Wolverhampton W*	13	8
1994–95	Aston Villa	7	2
1994–95	Sheffield W	21	9
1995–96		29	6

Season	Club	League Appearances/Goals	

WHITTLE, Justin

Born Derby 18.3.71 Ht 6 1
Wt 12 08
Defender. From Celtic.

Season	Club	Apps	Goals
1994–95	Stoke C	—	—
1995–96		8	—

WHITTON, Steve

Born East Ham 4.12.60 Ht 6 0 Wt 13 07
Midfield. From Apprentice.

Season	Club	Apps	Goals
1978–79	Coventry C	—	—
1979–80		7	—
1980–81		1	—
1981–82		28	9
1982–83		38	12
1983–84	West Ham U	22	5
1984–85		17	1
1985–86		—	—
1985–86	*Birmingham C*	8	2
1986–87	Birmingham C	39	9
1987–88		33	14
1988–89		23	5
1988–89	Sheffield W	12	3
1989–90		19	1
1990–91		1	—
1990–91	Ipswich T	10	2
1991–92		43	9
1992–93		24	3
1993–94		11	1
1993–94	Colchester U	8	2
1994–95		36	10
1995–96		12	2

WHITWORTH, Neil

Born Ince 12.4.72 Ht 6 2
Wt 12 06
Defender. From Trainee. England Youth.

Season	Club	Apps	Goals
1989–90	Wigan Ath	2	—
1990–91	Manchester U	1	—
1991–92		—	—
1991–92	*Preston NE*	6	—
1991–92	*Barnsley*	11	—
1992–93	Manchester U	—	—
1993–94		—	—
1993–94	*Rotherham U*	8	1
1993–94	*Blackpool*	3	—
1994–95	Kilmarnock	30	3
1995–96		28	—

WHYTE, Chris

Born London 2.9.61 Ht 6 1 Wt 12 00
Defender. From Amateur. England Under-21.

Season	Club	Apps	Goals
1979–80	Arsenal	—	—
1980–81		—	—
1981–82		32	2
1982–83		36	3
1983–84		15	2
1984–85		—	—
1984–85	*Crystal Palace*	13	—
1985–86	Arsenal	7	1
From Los Angeles R			
1988–89	WBA	40	3
1989–90		44	4
1990–91	Leeds U	38	3
1991–92		41	1
1992–93		34	1
1993–94	Birmingham C	33	—
1994–95		31	1
1995–96		4	—
1995–96	*Coventry C*	1	—
1995–96	Charlton Ath	11	—

WHYTE, David

Born Greenwich 20.4.71 Ht 5 8
Wt 10 07
Forward. From Greenwich Borough.

Season	Club	Apps	Goals
1988–89	Crystal Palace	—	—
1989–90		—	—
1990–91		—	—
1991–92		11	1
1991–92	*Charlton Ath*	8	2
1992–93	Crystal Palace	—	—
1993–94		16	3
1994–95	Charlton Ath	38	19
1995–96		25	2

WHYTE, Derek

Born Glasgow 31.8.68 Ht 5 11 Wt 12 11
Defender. From Celtic BC. Scotland Schools, Youth, Under-21, B, 9 full caps.

Season	Club	Apps	Goals
1985–86	Celtic	11	—
1986–87		42	—
1987–88		41	3
1988–89		22	—
1989–90		35	1
1990–91		24	2
1991–92		40	1
1992–93		1	—
1992–93	Middlesbrough	35	—

Season Club League Appearances/Goals

Season	Club	Apps	Goals
1993–94		42	1
1994–95		36	1
1995–96		25	—

WICKS, Matthew

Born Reading 8.9.78 Ht 6 2 Wt 13 05
Defender. From Manchester U Trainee.

Season	Club	Apps	Goals
1995–96	Arsenal	—	—

WIDDRINGTON, Tommy

Born Newcastle 1.10.71 Ht 5 10
Wt 11 12
Defender. From Trainee.

Season	Club	Apps	Goals
1989–90	Southampton	—	—
1990–91		—	—
1991–92		3	—
1991–92	*Wigan Ath*	6	—
1992–93	Southampton	12	—
1993–94		11	1
1994–95		28	—
1995–96		21	2

WIEGHORST, Morten

Born Glostrup 25.2.71 Ht 6 3 Wt 14 00
Midfield. From Lyngby.

Season	Club	Apps	Goals
1992–93	Dundee	23	2
1993–94		24	2
1994–95		29	3
1995–96		14	4
1995–96	Celtic	11	1

WIETECHA, Dave

Born Colchester 1.11.74 Ht 6 3
Wt 15 00
Goalkeeper.

Season	Club	Apps	Goals
1993–94	Millwall	—	—
1993–94	*Crewe Alex*	—	—
1993–94	*Rotherham U*	—	—
1994–95	Millwall	—	—
1995–96		—	—

WIGG, Nathan

Born Newport 27.9.74 Ht 5 8 Wt 11 03
Midfield. From Trainee.

Season	Club	Apps	Goals
1993–94	Cardiff C	19	—
1994–95		19	1
1995–96		20	—

WILCOX, Jason

Born Bolton 15.7.71 Ht 6 0 Wt 11 00
Forward. From Trainee. England B, 1 full cap.

Season	Club	Apps	Goals
1989–90	Blackburn R	1	—
1990–91		18	—
1991–92		38	4
1992–93		33	4
1993–94		33	6
1994–95		27	5
1995–96		10	3

WILCOX, Russ

Born Hemsworth 25.3.64 Ht 6 0
Wt 12 10
Defender. From Apprentice.

Season	Club	Apps	Goals
1980–81	Doncaster R	1	—
From Cambridge U, Frickley Ath			
1986–87	Northampton T	35	1
1987–88		46	4
1988–89		11	1
1989–90		46	3
1990–91	Hull C	31	1
1991–92		40	4
1992–93		29	2
1993–94	Doncaster R	40	2
1994–95		37	4
1995–96		4	—
1995–96	Preston NE	27	1

WILDER, Chris

Born Stocksbridge 23.9.67 Ht 5 11
Wt 10 10
Defender. From Apprentice.

Season	Club	Apps	Goals
1985–86	Southampton	—	—
1986–87	Sheffield U	11	—
1987–88		25	—
1988–89		29	1
1989–90		8	—
1989–90	*Walsall*	4	—
1990–91	Sheffield U	16	—
1990–91	*Charlton Ath*	1	—
1991–92	Sheffield U	4	—
1991–92	*Charlton Ath*	2	—
1991–92	*Leyton Orient*	16	1
1992–93	Rotherham U	32	8
1993–94		37	2
1994–95		45	1
1995–96		18	—
1995–96	Notts Co	9	—

Season	Club	League Appearances/Goals	

WILKERSON, Paul

Born Hertford 11.12.74 Ht 6 3
Wt 13 11
Goalkeeper.

1993–94	Watford	—	—
1994–95		—	—
1995–96		—	—

WILKIE, Glen

Born Stepney 22.1.77
Defender. From Trainee.

1994–95	Leyton Orient	11	—
1995–96		—	—

WILKINS, Dean

Born Hillingdon 12.7.62 Ht 5 10
Wt 12 04
Midfield. From Apprentice.

1980–81	QPR	2	—
1981–82		1	—
1982–83		3	—
1983–84	Brighton & HA	2	—
1983–84	*Orient*	10	—
From PEC Zwolle			
1987–88	Brighton & HA	44	3
1988–89		43	1
1989–90		46	6
1990–91		46	7
1991–92		26	—
1992–93		35	3
1993–94		21	2
1994–95		14	—
1995–96		35	3

WILKINS, Ray

Born Hillingdon 14.9.56 Ht 5 8
Wt 11 00
Midfield. From Apprentice. England Under-21, Under-23, 84 full caps. Football League.

1973–74	Chelsea	6	—
1974–75		21	2
1975–76		42	11
1976–77		42	7
1977–78		33	7
1978–79		35	3
1979–80	Manchester U	37	2
1980–81		13	—
1981–82		42	1
1982–83		26	1
1983–84		42	3
1984–85	AC Milan	28	—
1985–86		29	2
1986–87		16	—
From Paris St Germain			
1987–88	Rangers	24	1
1988–89		31	1
1989–90		15	—
1989–90	QPR	23	1
1990–91		38	2
1991–92		27	1
1992–93		27	2
1993–94		39	1
1994–95	Crystal Palace	1	—
1994–95	QPR	2	—
1995–96		15	—

WILKINS, Richard

Born Streatham 28.5.65 Ht 6 0
Wt 12 01
Midfield. From Haverhill R.

1986–87	Colchester U	23	2
1987–88		46	9
1988–89		40	7
1989–90		43	4
1990–91	Cambridge U	41	3
1991–92		32	4
1992–93		1	—
1993–94		7	—
1994–95	Hereford U	35	2
1995–96		42	3

WILKINSON, Ian

Born Warrington 2.7.73 Ht 5 11
Wt 13 04
Goalkeeper. From Trainee.

1991–92	Manchester U	—	—
1992–93		—	—
1993–94	Stockport Co	—	—
1993–94	Crewe Alex	3	—
1994–95		—	—
1994–95	*Doncaster R*	—	—
1995–96	Crewe Alex	—	—

WILKINSON, Ian

Born Ferriby 19.9.77 Ht 6 2 Wt 13 00
Defender. From Trainee.

1995–96	Hull C	8	1

Season	Club	League Appearances/Goals	

WILKINSON, Paul

Born Louth 30.10.64 Ht 6 1 Wt 12 04
Forward. From Apprentice. England Under-21.

1982–83	Grimsby T	4	1
1983–84		37	12
1984–85		30	14
1984–85	Everton	5	2
1985–86		4	1
1986–87		22	4
1986–87	Nottingham F	8	—
1987–88		26	5
1988–89	Watford	45	19
1989–90		43	15
1990–91		46	18
1991–92	Middlesbrough	46	15
1992–93		41	13
1993–94		45	15
1994–95		31	6
1995–96		3	—
1995–96	*Oldham Ath*	4	1
1995–96	*Watford*	4	—
1995–96	*Luton T*	3	—

WILKINSON, Steve

Born Lincoln 1.9.68 Ht 5 10 Wt 11 07
Forward. From Apprentice.

1986–87	Leicester C	1	—
1987–88		5	1
1988–89		1	—
1988–89	*Rochdale*	—	—
1988–89	*Crewe Alex*	5	2
1989–90	Leicester C	2	—
1989–90	Mansfield T	37	15
1990–91		39	11
1991–92		30	14
1992–93		43	11
1993–94		42	10
1994–95		41	22
1995–96	Preston NE	42	10

WILLEMS, Ron

Born Epe 20.9.66 Ht 6 0 Wt 13 00
Forward.

1983–84	PEC Zwolle	14	1
1984–85		29	6
1985–86	Twente	22	—
1986–87		31	5
1987–88		32	11
1988–89	Ajax	1	—
1989–90		19	7
1990–91		22	6
1991–92		3	—
1992–93		2	2
1993–94	Grasshoppers	27	9
1994–95		29	9
1995–96	Derby Co	33	11

WILLGRASS, Alex

Born Scarborough 8.4.76 Ht 5 10
Wt 11 06
Midfield.

1994–95	Scarborough	—	—
1995–96		7	—

WILLIAMS, Adrian

Born Reading 16.8.71 Ht 6 2 Wt 12 06
Defender. From Trainee. Wales 7 full caps.

1988–89	Reading	8	—
1989–90		16	2
1990–91		7	—
1991–92		40	4
1992–93		31	4
1993–94		41	—
1994–95		22	1
1995–96		31	3

WILLIAMS, Andy

Born Birmingham 19.7.62 Ht 6 0
Wt 11 10
Midfield. From Dudley, Solihull B.

1985–86	Coventry C	8	—
1986–87		1	—
1986–87	Rotherham U	36	4
1987–88		36	6
1988–89		15	3
1988–89	Leeds U	18	1
1989–90		16	2
1990–91		12	—
1991–92		—	—
1991–92	*Port Vale*	5	—
1991–92	Notts Co	15	1
1992–93		22	1
1993–94		2	—
1993–94	*Huddersfield T*	6	—
1993–94	Rotherham U	34	2
1994–95		17	—
1995–96	Hull C	34	—

WILLIAMS, Carl

Born Cambridge 14.1.77 Ht 5 7
Wt 12 06
Midfield. From Trainee.

1995–96	Fulham	13	—

WILLIAMS, Darren

Born Middlebrough 28.4.77 Ht 5 8
Wt 11 00
Midfield. From Trainee.

1994–95	York C	1	—
1995–96		18	—

WILLIAMS, David

Born Liverpool 18.9.68 Ht 6 0 Wt 12 00
Goalkeeper. From Trainee.

1987–88	Oldham Ath	—	—
1987–88	Burnley	—	—
1988–89		7	—
1989–90		7	—
1990–91		3	—
1991–92		5	—
1991–92	*Rochdale*	6	—
1992–93	Burnley	2	—
1992–93	*Crewe Alex*	—	—
1993–94	Burnley	—	—
1994–95	Cardiff C	40	—
1995–96		42	—

WILLIAMS, Dean P

Born Lichfield 5.1.72 Ht 6 1 Wt 12 09
Goalkeeper. From Tamworth.

1993–94	Brentford	7	—
1994–95	Doncaster R	35	—
1995–96		17	—

WILLIAMS, Gareth

Born Isle of Wight 12.3.67 Ht 6 0
Wt 12 02
Forward. From Gosport Borough.

1987–88	Aston Villa	1	—
1988–89		1	—
1989–90		10	—
1990–91		—	—
1991–92	Barnsley	17	—
1992–93		8	5
1992–93	*Hull C*	4	—
1993–94	Barnsley	9	1
1993–94	*Hull C*	16	2
1994–95	Barnsley	—	—
1994–95	Bournemouth	1	—
1994–95	Northampton T	15	—
1995–96		35	1

WILLIAMS, Geraint

Born Cwmpare 5.1.62 Ht 5 7 Wt 12 06
Midfield. From Apprentice. Wales Youth, Under-21, 13 full caps.

1979–80	Bristol R	—	—
1980–81		28	1
1981–82		16	—
1982–83		35	3
1983–84		34	4
1984–85		28	—
1984–85	Derby Co	12	—
1985–86		40	4
1986–87		40	1
1987–88		40	1
1988–89		37	1
1989–90		38	—
1990–91		31	—
1991–92		39	2
1992–93	Ipswich T	37	—
1993–94		34	—
1994–95		38	1
1995–96		42	1

WILLIAMS, Jamie

Born Coventry 21.2.77 Ht 5 7 Wt 9 06
Midfield. From Trainee.

1995–96	Coventry C	—	—

WILLIAMS, John

Born Birmingham 11.5.68 Ht 6 0
Wt 13 01
Midfield. From Cradley T.

1991–92	Swansea C	39	11
1992–93	Coventry C	41	8
1993–94		32	3
1994–95		7	—
1994–95	*Notts Co*	5	2
1994–95	*Stoke C*	4	—
1994–95	*Swansea C*	7	2
1995–96	Coventry C	—	—
1995–96	Wycombe W	29	8

WILLIAMS, Lee

Born Birmingham 3.2.73 Ht 5 7
Wt 11 07
Midfield. From Trainee.

1991–92	Aston Villa	—	—

Season Club League Appearances/Goals

Season	Club	Apps	Goals
1992–93		—	—
1992–93	*Shrewsbury T*	3	—
1993–94	Aston Villa	—	—
1993–94	Peterborough U	18	—
1994–95		40	1
1995–96		33	—

WILLIAMS, Lee

Born Essex 13.3.77
Forward.

Season	Club	Apps	Goals
1995–96	Leyton Orient	3	—

WILLIAMS, Marc

Born Bangor 8.2.73 Ht 5 11 Wt 11 10
Forward. From Bangor C.

Season	Club	Apps	Goals
1994–95	Stockport Co	1	—
1995–96		17	1

WILLIAMS, Mark

Born Stalybridge 28.9.70 Ht 6 0
Wt 13 00
Defender. From Newtown.

Season	Club	Apps	Goals
1991–92	Shrewsbury T	3	—
1992–93		28	1
1993–94		36	1
1994–95		35	1
1995–96	Chesterfield	42	3

WILLIAMS, Mark

Born Johannesburg 11.8.66 Ht 5 10
Wt 11 03
Forward. From RWD Molenbeek. South Africa full caps.

Season	Club	Apps	Goals
1995–96	Wolverhampton W	12	—

WILLIAMS, Martin

Born Luton 12.7.73 Ht 5 9 Wt 11 12
Forward. From Leicester C Trainee.

Season	Club	Apps	Goals
1991–92	Luton T	1	—
1992–93		22	1
1993–94		15	1
1994–95		2	—
1994–95	*Colchester U*	3	—
1995–96	Reading	15	1

WILLIAMS, Michael

Born Bradford 21.11.69 Ht 5 11
Wt 11 04
Midfield. From Maltby.

Season	Club	Apps	Goals
1991–92	Sheffield W	—	—
1992–93		3	—
1992–93	*Halifax T*	9	1
1993–94	Sheffield W	4	—
1994–95		10	1
1995–96		5	—

WILLIAMS, Paul

Born Leicester 11.9.69 Ht 5 7 Wt 10 00
Forward. From Trainee.

Season	Club	Apps	Goals
1988–89	Leicester C	—	—
1989–90	Stockport Co	7	—
1990–91		24	2
1991–92		13	1
1992–93		26	1
1993–94	Coventry C	9	—
1993–94	*WBA*	5	—
1994–95	Coventry C	5	—
1994–95	*Huddersfield T*	9	—
1995–96	Plymouth Arg	46	2

WILLIAMS, Paul

Born London 16.8.65 Ht 5 7 Wt 10 09
Forward. From Woodford T. England Under-21, B.

Season	Club	Apps	Goals
1986–87	Charlton Ath	—	—
1987–88		12	—
1987–88	*Brentford*	7	3
1988–89	Charlton Ath	32	13
1989–90		38	10
1990–91	Sheffield W	46	15
1991–92		40	9
1992–93		7	1
1992–93	Crystal Palace	18	—
1993–94		24	7
1994–95		4	—
1994–95	*Sunderland*	3	—
1994–95	*Birmingham C*	11	—
1995–96	Charlton Ath	9	—
1995–96	*Torquay U*	9	—

WILLIAMS, Paul

Born Burton 26.3.71 Ht 6 0 Wt 12 10
Defender. From Trainee. England Under-21.

Season	Club	Apps	Goals
1989–90	Derby Co	10	1
1989–90	*Lincoln C*	3	—

Season Club League Appearances/Goals

Season	Club	Apps	Goals
1990–91	Derby Co	19	4
1991–92		41	13
1992–93		19	4
1993–94		34	1
1994–95		37	3
1995–96	Coventry C	32	2

WILLIAMS, Paul

Born Liverpool 25.9.70 Ht 5 11
Wt 12 02
Defender. From Trainee.

Season	Club	Apps	Goals
1988–89	Sunderland	1	—
1989–90		1	—
1990–91	*Swansea C*	12	1
1991–92	Sunderland	7	—
1992–93		—	—
1993–94	Doncaster R	1	—
1994–95		7	—
1995–96		—	—

WILLIAMS, Paul A

Born Sheffield 8.9.63 Ht 6 3 Wt 14 08
Forward. From Distillery, Leeds U, Grenaker R, Nuneaton. Northern Ireland 1 full cap.

Season	Club	Apps	Goals
1986–87	Preston NE	1	—
1987–88	Newport Co	26	3
1987–88	Sheffield U	6	—
1988–89		2	—
1989–90	Hartlepool U	8	—
1990–91	Stockport Co	24	14
1990–91	WBA	10	—
1991–92		34	5
1992–93		—	—
1992–93	*Coventry C*	2	—
1992–93	Stockport Co	16	3
1993–94		—	—
1993–94	Rochdale	11	2
1994–95		14	5
1995–96		12	—
1995–96	*Doncaster R*	3	1

WILLIAMS, Philip

Born Salford 1.10.78
Goalkeeper.

Season	Club	Apps	Goals
1995–96	Doncaster R	—	—

WILLIAMS, Ryan

Born Sutton 31.8.78 Ht 5 3 Wt 9 10
Forward. From Trainee.

Season	Club	Apps	Goals
1995–96	Mansfield T	10	3

WILLIAMS, Scott

Born Bangor 7.8.74 Ht 6 0 Wt 12 00
Defender. From Trainee. Wales Under-21.

Season	Club	Apps	Goals
1992–93	Wrexham	1	—
1993–94		14	—
1994–95		10	—
1995–96		—	—

WILLIAMS, Steven

Born Aberystwyth 16.10.74 Ht 6 3
Wt 12 12
Goalkeeper. From Coventry C.

Season	Club	Apps	Goals
1993–94	Cardiff C	18	—
1994–95		6	—
1995–96		4	—

WILLIAMS, Steven

Born Sheffield 3.11.75 Ht 6 1 Wt 11 07
Forward. From Trainee.

Season	Club	Apps	Goals
1993–94	Lincoln C	8	1
1994–95		6	1
1995–96		3	—
1995–96	Peterborough U	3	—

WILLIAMSON, Danny

Born London 5.12.73 Ht 5 10 Wt 11 06
Midfield. From Trainee.

Season	Club	Apps	Goals
1992–93	West Ham U	—	—
1993–94		3	1
1993–94	*Doncaster R*	13	1
1994–95	West Ham U	4	—
1995–96		29	4

WILLIS, Adam

Born Nuneaton 21.9.76 Ht 6 1 Wt 12 02
Midfield. From Trainee.

Season	Club	Apps	Goals
1995–96	Coventry C	—	—

WILLIS, Jimmy

Born Liverpool 12.7.68 Ht 6 2 Wt 12 04
Defender. From Blackburn R.

Season	Club	Apps	Goals
1986–87	Halifax T	—	—
1987–88	Stockport Co	10	—
1987–88	Darlington	9	—
1988–89		41	2
1989–90		—	—
1990–91		28	2
1991–92		12	2
1991–92	Leicester C	10	—

Season	Club	League Appearances/Goals	
1991–92	*Bradford C*	9	1
1992–93	Leicester C	—	—
1993–94		9	1
1994–95		29	2
1995–96		12	—

WILLIS, Roger

Born Sheffield 17.6.67 Ht 6 1 Wt 12 00
Defender.

Season	Club	Apps	Goals
1989–90	Grimsby T	9	—
From Barnet			
1991–92	Barnet	38	12
1992–93		6	1
1992–93	Watford	32	2
1993–94		4	—
1993–94	Birmingham C	16	5
1994–95		3	—
1994–95	Southend U	21	4
1995–96		10	3

WILLMOTT, Chris

Born Bedford 30.9.77
Defender. From Trainee.

Season	Club	Apps	Goals
1995–96	Luton T	—	—

WILMOT, Rhys

Born Newport 21.2.62 Ht 6 1 Wt 12 00
Goalkeeper. From Apprentice. Wales Youth, Under-21.

Season	Club	Apps	Goals
1979–80	Arsenal	—	—
1980–81		—	—
1981–82		—	—
1982–83		—	—
1982–83	*Hereford U*	9	—
1983–84	Arsenal	—	—
1984–85	*Orient*	46	—
1985–86	Arsenal	2	—
1986–87		6	—
1987–88		—	—
1988–89		—	—
1988–89	*Swansea C*	16	—
1988–89	*Plymouth Arg*	17	—
1989–90	Plymouth Arg	46	—
1990–91		36	—
1991–92		34	—
1992–93	Grimsby T	33	—
1993–94		—	—
1994–95	Crystal Palace	6	—
1995–96		—	—

WILSON, Barry

Born Kirkcaldy 16.2.71 Ht 5 11 Wt 12 04
Forward. From Ross Co.

Season	Club	Apps	Goals
1994–95	Raith R	26	5
1995–96		13	—

WILSON, Clive

Born Manchester 13.11.61 Ht 5 7
Wt 10 00
Midfield. From Local.

Season	Club	Apps	Goals
1979–80	Manchester C	—	—
1980–81		—	—
1981–82		4	—
1982–83		—	—
1982–83	*Chester*	21	2
1983–84	Manchester C	11	—
1984–85		27	4
1985–86		25	5
1986–87		31	—
1986–87	Chelsea	—	—
1986–87	*Manchester C*	11	—
1987–88	Chelsea	31	2
1988–89		32	3
1989–90		18	—
1990–91	QPR	13	1
1991–92		40	3
1992–93		41	3
1993–94		42	3
1994–95		36	2
1995–96	Tottenham H	28	—

WILSON, Danny

Born Wigan 1.1.60 Ht 5 6 Wt 11 00
Midfield. From Wigan Ath. Northern Ireland 24 full caps.

Season	Club	Apps	Goals
1977–78	Bury	12	1
1978–79		46	7
1979–80		32	—
1980–81	Chesterfield	33	3
1981–82		43	3
1982–83		24	7
1982–83	Nottingham F	10	1
1983–84	*Scunthorpe U*	6	3
1983–84	Brighton & HA	26	10
1984–85		38	5
1985–86		33	11
1986–87		38	7
1987–88	Luton T	38	8
1988–89		37	9
1989–90		35	7
1990–91	Sheffield W	36	6

Season	Club	League Appearances/Goals	
1991–92	....	36	3
1992–93	....	26	2
1993–94	Barnsley........................	43	—
1994–95	....	34	2
1995–96	....	—	—

WILSON, Kevin

Born Banbury 18.4.61 Ht 5 8 Wt 11 03
Forward. From Banbury U. Northern Ireland 42 full caps.

Season	Club	Apps	Goals
1979–80	Derby Co....................	4	—
1980–81	....	27	7
1981–82	....	24	9
1982–83	....	22	4
1983–84	....	32	2
1984–85	....	13	8
1984–85	Ipswich T....................	17	7
1985–86	....	39	7
1986–87	....	42	20
1987–88	Chelsea........................	25	5
1988–89	....	46	13
1989–90	....	37	14
1990–91	....	22	7
1991–92	....	22	3
1991–92	Notts Co......................	8	1
1992–93	....	32	1
1993–94	....	29	1
1993–94	*Bradford C*..................	5	—
1994–95	Walsall........................	42	16
1995–96	....	46	15

WILSON, Mark

Born Scunthorpe 9.2.79 Ht 5 11 Wt 12 01
Forward. From Trainee.

Season	Club	Apps	Goals
1995–96	Manchester U	—	—

WILSON, Paul

Born London 29.6.64 Ht 5 9 Wt 12 00
Defender. From West Ham U, Billericay, Barking.

Season	Club	Apps	Goals
1991–92	Barnet........................	25	1
1992–93	....	9	—
1993–94	....	34	3
1994–95	....	36	3
1995–96	....	33	4

WILSON, Paul

Born Maidstone 22.2.77
Forward. From Trainee.

Season	Club	Apps	Goals
1994–95	Gillingham..................	2	—
1995–96	....	—	—

WILSON, Paul

Born Bradford 2.8.68 Ht 5 11 Wt 12 00
Defender. From Trainee.

Season	Club	Apps	Goals
1985–86	Huddersfield T...........	7	—
1986–87	....	8	—
1987–88	Norwich C..................	—	—
1987–88	Northampton T..........	15	1
1988–89	....	39	1
1989–90	....	27	—
1990–91	....	44	3
1991–92	....	16	1
1991–92	Halifax T....................	23	5
1992–93	....	22	2
1992–93	Burnley......................	20	—
1993–94	....	11	—
1994–95	....	—	—
1994–95	York C........................	22	—
1995–96	Scunthorpe U............	40	1

WILSON, Steve

Born Hull 24.4.74 Ht 5 10 Wt 10 10
Goalkeeper. From Trainee.

Season	Club	Apps	Goals
1990–91	Hull C........................	2	—
1991–92	....	3	—
1992–93	....	26	—
1993–94	....	9	—
1994–95	....	20	—
1995–96	....	19	—

WINDASS, Dean

Born Hull 1.4.69 Ht 5 9 Wt 12 03
Forward. From N Ferriby.

Season	Club	Apps	Goals
1991–92	Hull C........................	32	6
1992–93	....	41	7
1993–94	....	43	23
1994–95	....	44	17
1995–96	....	16	4
1995–96	Aberdeen....................	20	6

WINNIE, David

Born Glasgow 26.10.66 Ht 6 1 Wt 12 07
Defender. From 'S' Form.

Season	Club	Apps	Goals
1983–84	St Mirren....................	8	—
1984–85	....	30	3
1985–86	....	20	1
1986–87	....	14	—
1987–88	....	26	2
1988–89	....	30	—
1989–90	....	17	—
1990–91	....	1	—

Season	Club	Apps	Goals
1990–91	Aberdeen	—	—
1991–92		28	1
1992–93		21	—
1993–94		16	—
1993–94	*Middlesbrough*	1	—
1994–95	Aberdeen	8	—
1995–96	Hearts	6	—

WINSTANLEY, Mark

Born St Helens 22.1.68 Ht 6 1 Wt 12 08
Defender. From Trainee.

Season	Club	Apps	Goals
1984–85	Bolton W	—	—
1985–86		3	—
1986–87		13	—
1987–88		8	1
1988–89		44	—
1989–90		43	1
1990–91		32	—
1991–92		27	—
1992–93		29	1
1993–94		21	—
1994–95	Burnley	44	2
1995–96		45	3

WINTER, Paul

Born Salford 15.8.76 Ht 5 10 Wt 12 03
Midfield.

Season	Club	Apps	Goals
1995–96	Bury	—	—

WINTER, Steve

Born Bristol 26.10.73 Ht 5 8 Wt 10 10
Defender. From Taunton T.

Season	Club	Apps	Goals
1995–96	Torquay U	36	—

WINTERBURN, Nigel

Born Coventry 11.12.63 Ht 5 8 Wt 11 04
Defender. From Local. England Youth, Under-21, B, 2 full caps.

Season	Club	Apps	Goals
1981–82	Birmingham C	—	—
1982–83		—	—
1983–84	Oxford U	—	—
1983–84	Wimbledon	43	1
1984–85		41	4
1985–86		39	1
1986–87		42	2
1987–88	Arsenal	17	—
1988–89		38	3
1989–90		36	—
1990–91		38	—
1991–92		41	1
1992–93		29	1
1993–94		34	—
1994–95		39	—
1995–96		36	2

WINTERS, Robert

Born East Kilbride 4.11.74 Ht 5 10
Wt 11 06
Forward. From Muirend Amateurs.

Season	Club	Apps	Goals
1993–94	Dundee U	—	—
1994–95		13	2
1995–96		35	7

WISE, Dennis

Born Kensington 16.12.66 Ht 5 6
Wt 10 00
Forward. From Southampton Apprentice. England Under-21, B, 12 full caps.

Season	Club	Apps	Goals
1984–85	Wimbledon	1	—
1985–86		4	—
1986–87		28	4
1987–88		30	10
1988–89		37	5
1989–90		35	8
1990–91	Chelsea	33	10
1991–92		38	10
1992–93		27	3
1993–94		35	4
1994–95		19	6
1995–96		35	7

WISHART, Fraser

Born Johnstone 1.3.65 Ht 5 8 Wt 10 00
Defender. From Pollok.

Season	Club	Apps	Goals
1983–84	Motherwell	6	—
1984–85		—	—
1985–86		26	—
1986–87		44	3
1987–88		43	1
1988–89		35	1
1989–90	St Mirren	20	—
1990–91		22	—
1991–92		9	—
1992–93	Falkirk	24	2
1993–94	Rangers	5	—
1994–95		4	—
1994–95	Hearts	8	—
1995–96		1	—

Season	Club	League Appearances/Goals	

WITHE, Chris

Born Liverpool 25.9.62 Ht 5 10
Wt 11 12
Defender. From Apprentice.

Season	Club	App	Goals
1980–81	Newcastle U	2	—
1981–82		—	—
1982–83		—	—
1983–84	Bradford C	45	1
1984–85		45	—
1985–86		33	—
1986–87		18	1
1987–88		2	—
1987–88	Notts Co	35	2
1988–89		45	1
1989–90	Bury	31	1
1990–91		—	—
1990–91	*Chester C*	2	—
1990–91	*Mansfield T*	11	—
1990–91	Mansfield T	10	—
1991–92		10	1
1992–93		45	4
1993–94	Shrewsbury T	26	—
1994–95		31	2
1995–96		32	—

WITTER, Tony

Born London 12.8.65 Ht 6 2 Wt 13 02
Defender. From Grays Ath.

Season	Club	App	Goals
1990–91	Crystal Palace	—	—
1991–92	QPR	—	—
1991–92	*Millwall*	—	—
1991–92	*Plymouth Arg*	3	1
1992–93	QPR	—	—
1993–94		1	—
1993–94	*Reading*	4	—
1994–95	QPR	—	—
1994–95	Millwall	27	1
1995–96		31	1

WOAN, Ian

Born Wirrall 14.12.67 Ht 5 10 Wt 12 02
Midfield. From Runcorn.

Season	Club	App	Goals
1989–90	Nottingham F	—	—
1990–91		12	3
1991–92		21	5
1992–93		28	3
1993–94		24	5
1994–95		37	5
1995–96		33	8

WOOD, Paul

Born Middlesbrough 1.11.64 Ht 5 9
Wt 11 06
Forward. From Apprentice.

Season	Club	App	Goals
1982–83	Portsmouth	—	—
1983–84		8	1
1984–85		6	1
1985–86		25	4
1986–87		8	—
1987–88		—	—
1987–88	Brighton & HA	31	4
1988–89		35	1
1989–90		26	3
1989–90	Sheffield U	17	3
1990–91		7	—
1990–91	*Bournemouth*	21	—
1991–92	Sheffield U	4	—
1991–92	Bournemouth	35	9
1992–93		27	4
1993–94		16	5
1993–94	Portsmouth	12	1
1994–95		5	1
1995–96		15	1

WOOD, Paul

Born Sheffield 14.10.77
Midfield. From Trainee.

Season	Club	App	Goals
1995–96	Sheffield U	—	—

WOOD, Simon

Born Hull 24.9.76 Ht 5 9 Wt 11 08
Midfield. From Trainee.

Season	Club	App	Goals
1993–94	Coventry C	—	—
1994–95		—	—
1995–96		—	—
1995–96	Mansfield T	10	1

WOOD, Steve

Born Bracknell 2.2.63 Ht 6 1 Wt 13 00
Defender. From Apprentice.

Season	Club	App	Goals
1979–80	Reading	2	—
1980–81		6	—
1981–82		32	—
1982–83		18	—
1983–84		37	3
1984–85		46	1
1985–86		46	4
1986–87		32	1
1987–88	Millwall	22	—
1988–89		35	—

Season	Club	League Appearances	Goals
1989–90		21	—
1990–91		25	—
1991–92		7	—
1991–92	Southampton	15	—
1992–93		4	—
1993–94		27	—
1994–95	Oxford U	2	—
1995–96		11	—

WOOD, Trevor

Born Jersey 3.11.68 Ht 6 0 Wt 13 04
Goalkeeper. From Apprentice. Northern Ireland 1 full cap.

Season	Club	League Appearances	Goals
1986–87	Brighton & HA	—	—
1987–88		—	—
1988–89	Port Vale	2	—
1989–90		3	—
1990–91		32	—
1991–92		—	—
1992–93		5	—
1993–94		—	—
1994–95	Walsall	39	—
1995–96		20	—

WOODMAN, Andy

Born Denmark Hill 11.8.71 Ht 6 3
Wt 13 07
Goalkeeper. From Apprentice.

Season	Club	League Appearances	Goals
1989–90	Crystal Palace	—	—
1990–91		—	—
1991–92		—	—
1992–93		—	—
1993–94		—	—
1994–95	Exeter C	6	—
1994–95	Northampton T	10	—
1995–96		44	—

WOODMAN, Clayton

Born Bristol 6.2.77
Defender. From Trainee.

Season	Club	League Appearances	Goals
1995–96	Norwich C	—	—

WOODS, Billy

Born Cork 24.10.73 Ht 6 0 Wt 12 00
Forward. From Cork C.

Season	Club	League Appearances	Goals
1995–96	Tranmere R	—	—

WOODS, Chris

Born Boston 14.11.59 Ht 6 2 Wt 14 12
Goalkeeper. From Apprentice. England Under-21, B, 43 full caps.

Season	Club	League Appearances	Goals
1976–77	Nottingham F	—	—
1977–78		—	—
1978–79		—	—
1979–80	QPR	41	—
1980–81		22	—
1980–81	*Norwich C*	10	—
1981–82	Norwich C	42	—
1982–83		42	—
1983–84		42	—
1984–85		38	—
1985–86		42	—
1986–87	Rangers	42	—
1987–88		39	—
1988–89		24	—
1989–90		32	—
1990–91		36	—
1991–92	Sheffield W	41	—
1992–93		39	—
1993–94		10	—
1994–95		9	—
1995–96		8	—
1995–96	*Reading*	5	—

WOODS, Matthew

Born Gosport 9.9.76
Defender. From Trainee.

Season	Club	League Appearances	Goals
1995–96	Everton	—	—

WOODS, Neil

Born York 30.7.66 Ht 6 0 Wt 12 11
Forward. From Apprentice.

Season	Club	League Appearances	Goals
1982–83	Doncaster R	4	—
1983–84		7	1
1984–85		6	2
1985–86		30	7
1986–87		18	6
1986–87	Rangers	3	—
1987–88	Ipswich T	19	4
1988–89		1	—
1989–90		7	1
1989–90	Bradford C	14	2
1990–91		—	—
1990–91	Grimsby T	44	12
1991–92		37	8
1992–93		30	4
1993–94		11	—
1994–95		37	14
1995–96		33	3

Season Club League Appearances/Goals

WOODS, Ray

Born Birkenhead 7.6.65 Ht 5 10
Wt 11 09
Forward. From Apprentice.

Season	Club	Apps	Goals
1982–83	Tranmere R	1	—
1983–84		6	2
From Colne D			
1988–89	Wigan Ath	8	—
1989–90		—	—
1990–91		20	3
1990–91	Coventry C	12	1
1991–92		9	—
1992–93		—	—
1992–93	*Wigan Ath*	13	—
1993–94	Coventry C	—	—
1993–94	*Shrewsbury T*	9	1
1994–95	Shrewsbury T	19	—
1995–96		23	—

WOODS, Stephen

Born Davenham 15.12.76 Ht 5 11
Wt 11 12
Defender. From Trainee.

Season	Club	Apps	Goals
1995–96	Stoke C	—	—

WOODSFORD, Jamie

Born Ipswich 9.11.76 Ht 5 10 Wt 12 00
Forward. From Trainee. England Youth.

Season	Club	Apps	Goals
1994–95	Luton T	7	—
1995–96		3	—

WOODTHORPE, Colin

Born Ellesmere Pt 13.1.69 Ht 5 11
Wt 11 08
Defender. From Apprentice.

Season	Club	Apps	Goals
1986–87	Chester C	30	2
1987–88		35	—
1988–89		44	3
1989–90		46	1
1990–91	Norwich C	1	—
1991–92		15	1
1992–93		7	—
1993–94		20	—
1994–95	Aberdeen	14	—
1995–96		15	1

WOODWARD, Andy

Born Stockport 23.9.73 Ht 6 0 Wt 13 06
Defender. From Trainee.

Season	Club	Apps	Goals
1992–93	Crewe Alex	6	—
1993–94		12	—
1994–95		2	—
1994–95	Bury	8	—
1995–96		1	—

Season Club League Appearances/Goals

WOOLGAR, Matthew

Born Bedford 5.1.76 Ht 5 10 Wt 11 10
Midfield. From Trainee.

Season	Club	Apps	Goals
1994–95	Luton T	—	—
1995–96		—	—

WOOLSEY, Jeff

Born Upminster 8.11.77 Ht 5 11
Wt 12 03
Defender. From Trainee.

Season	Club	Apps	Goals
1995–96	Arsenal	—	—

WORBOYS, Gavin

Born Doncaster 14.7.74 Ht 6 2 Wt 12 00
Forward. From Trainee.

Season	Club	Apps	Goals
1991–92	Doncaster R	7	2
1992–93	Notts Co	—	—
1993–94		—	—
1993–94	*Exeter C*	4	1
1994–95	Notts Co	—	—
1994–95	Darlington	27	6
1995–96		14	2
1995–96	Northampton T	13	1

WORMULL, Simon

Born Crawley 1.12.76 Ht 5 10 Wt 12 03
Midfield. From Trainee.

Season	Club	Apps	Goals
1995–96	Tottenham H	—	—

WORRALL, Ben

Born Swindon 7.12.75 Ht 5 7 Wt 11 06
Midfield. From Trainee. England Youth.

Season	Club	Apps	Goals
1994–95	Swindon T	3	—
1995–96		—	—

WORRELL, David

Born Dublin 12.1.78 Ht 5 10 Wt 11 08
Defender. From Trainee.

Season	Club	Apps	Goals
1994–95	Blackburn R	—	—
1995–96		—	—

WORTHINGTON, Nigel

Born Ballymena 4.11.61 Ht 5 11
Wt 12 08
Defender. From Ballymena U. Northern Ireland Youth, 64 full caps.

Season	Club	Apps	Goals
1981–82	Notts Co	2	—
1982–83		41	3
1983–84		24	1
1983–84	Sheffield W	14	1
1984–85		38	1
1985–86		15	—
1986–87		35	—
1987–88		38	—
1988–89		28	—
1989–90		32	2
1990–91		33	1
1991–92		34	5
1992–93		40	1
1993–94		31	1
1994–95	Leeds U	27	1
1995–96		16	—

WOSAHLO, Bradley

Born Ipswich 14.2.75 Ht 5 10 Wt 10 06
Midfield. From Trainee.

Season	Club	Apps	Goals
1993–94	Brighton & HA	1	—
1994–95		—	—
1995–96	Cambridge U	4	—

WOTTON, Paul

Born Plymouth 17.8.77 Ht 5 10
Wt 12 00
Defender. From Trainee.

Season	Club	Apps	Goals
1994–95	Plymouth Arg	7	—
1995–96		1	—

WRACK, Darren

Born Cleethorpes 5.5.76 Ht 5 9
Wt 12 00
Forward. From Trainee.

Season	Club	Apps	Goals
1994–95	Derby Co	16	1
1995–96		10	—

WRAY, Shaun

Born Birmingham 14.3.78 Ht 6 0
Wt 12 11
Forward. From Trainee.

Season	Club	Apps	Goals
1995–96	Shrewsbury T	3	—

WRIGHT, Alan

Born Ashton-U-Lyme 28.9.71 Ht 5 4
Wt 9 05
Defender. From Trainee. England Schools, Youth, Under-21.

Season	Club	Apps	Goals
1987–88	Blackpool	1	—
1988–89		16	—
1989–90		24	—
1990–91		45	—
1991–92		12	—
1991–92	Blackburn R	33	1
1992–93		24	—
1993–94		12	—
1994–95		5	—
1994–95	Aston Villa	8	—
1995–96		38	2

WRIGHT, Andrew

Born Leeds 21.10.78
Midfield. From Trainee.

Season	Club	Apps	Goals
1995–96	Leeds U	—	—

WRIGHT, Dale

Born Middlesbrough 21.12.74 Ht 6 0
Wt 12 01
Defender. From Trainee.

Season	Club	Apps	Goals
1991–92	Nottingham F	—	—
1992–93		—	—
1993–94		—	—
1994–95		—	—
1995–96		—	—

WRIGHT, George

Born South Africa 22.12.69 Ht 5 7
Wt 10 02
Defender. From Hutchison Vale BC.

Season	Club	Apps	Goals
1987–88	Hearts	—	—
1988–89		—	—
1989–90		1	—
1990–91		17	2
1991–92		24	1
1992–93		12	—
1993–94		12	—
1994–95		1	—
1995–96		2	—
1995–96	Falkirk	2	—
1995–96	Livingston	10	—

Season Club League Appearances/Goals

Season Club League Appearances/Goals

WRIGHT, Ian

Born Woolwich 3.11.63 Ht 5 9
Wt 11 08
Forward. From Greenwich Borough. England B, 20 full caps.

Season	Club	Apps	Goals
1985–86	Crystal Palace	32	9
1986–87		38	8
1987–88		41	20
1988–89		42	24
1989–90		26	8
1990–91		38	15
1991–92		8	5
1991–92	Arsenal	30	24
1992–93		31	15
1993–94		39	23
1994–95		31	18
1995–96		31	15

WRIGHT, Ian

Born Lichfield 10.3.72 Ht 6 0
Wt 12 07
Defender. From Trainee.

Season	Club	Apps	Goals
1989–90	Stoke C	1	—
1990–91		1	—
1991–92		3	—
1992–93		1	—
1993–94		—	—
1993–94	Bristol R	29	—
1994–95		7	1
1995–96		18	—

WRIGHT, Jermaine

Born Greenwich 21.10.75 Ht 5 9
Wt 10 03
Forward. From Trainee. England Youth.

Season	Club	Apps	Goals
1992–93	Millwall	—	—
1993–94		—	—
1994–95		—	—
1994–95	Wolverhampton W	6	—
1995–96		7	—
1995–96	*Doncaster R*	13	—

WRIGHT, Johnny

Born Belfast 24.11.75 Ht 5 9
Wt 11 05
Defender. From Trainee.

Season	Club	Apps	Goals
1994–95	Norwich C	2	—
1995–96		1	—

WRIGHT, Keith

Born Edinburgh 17.5.65 Ht 5 11
Wt 11 00
Forward. From Melbourne Th. Scotland 1 full cap.

Season	Club	Apps	Goals
1983–84	Raith R	37	5
1984–85		38	22
1985–86		39	21
1986–87		17	13
1986–87	Dundee	20	10
1987–88		42	15
1988–89		35	8
1989–90		34	11
1990–91		36	18
1991–92	Hibernian	40	9
1992–93		42	11
1993–94		42	16
1994–95		19	10
1995–96		28	9

WRIGHT, Mark

Born Dorchester 1.8.63 Ht 6 2
Wt 13 03
Defender. From Amateur. England Under-21, 45 full caps.

Season	Club	Apps	Goals
1980–81	Oxford U	—	—
1981–82		10	—
1981–82	Southampton	3	—
1982–83		39	2
1983–84		29	1
1984–85		36	—
1985–86		33	3
1986–87		30	1
1987–88		—	—
1987–88	Derby Co	38	3
1988–89		33	1
1989–90		36	6
1990–91		37	—
1991–92	Liverpool	21	—
1992–93		33	2
1993–94		31	1
1994–95		6	—
1995–96		28	2

WRIGHT, Nick

Born Derby 15.10.75 Ht 5 9
Wt 11 07
Forward. From Trainee.

Season	Club	Apps	Goals
1994–95	Derby Co	—	—
1995–96		—	—

WRIGHT, Paul

Born East Kilbride 17.8.67 Ht 5 8
Wt 10 08
Forward. From 'S' Form. Scotland Youth, Under-21.

Season	Club	Apps	Goals
1983–84	Aberdeen	1	—
1984–85		—	—
1985–86		10	2
1986–87		25	4
1987–88		9	4
1988–89		23	6
1989–90	QPR	15	5
1989–90	Hibernian	3	1
1990–91		33	6
1991–92	St Johnstone	41	18
1992–93		42	14
1993–94		17	7
1994–95		12	1
1994–95	Kilmarnock	7	1
1995–96		36	13

WRIGHT, Richard

Born Ipswich 5.11.77 Ht 6 2
Wt 13 00
Goalkeeper. From Trainee. England Youth.

Season	Club	Apps	Goals
1994–95	Ipswich T	3	—
1995–96		23	—

WRIGHT, Robert

Born London 17.9.77
Goalkeeper. From QPR Trainee.

Season	Club	Apps	Goals
1995–96	Charlton Ath	—	—

WRIGHT, Stephen

Born Bellshill 27.8.71 Ht 5 10
Wt 10 10
Defender. From Aberdeen Lads. Scotland Under-21, 2 full caps.

Season	Club	Apps	Goals
1987–88	Aberdeen	—	—
1988–89		—	—
1989–90		1	—
1990–91		17	1
1991–92		23	—
1992–93		36	—
1993–94		36	—
1994–95		34	1
1995–96	Rangers	6	—

WRIGHT, Tommy

Born Dunfermline 10.1.66 Ht 5 7
Wt 11 04
Forward. From Apprentice. Scotland Under-21.

Season	Club	Apps	Goals
1982–83	Leeds U	4	1
1983–84		25	8
1984–85		42	14
1985–86		10	1
1986–87		—	—
1986–87	Oldham Ath	28	7
1987–88		41	9
1988–89		43	7
1989–90	Leicester C	41	3
1990–91		44	7
1991–92		44	12
1992–93	Middlesbrough	36	5
1993–94		16	—
1994–95		1	—
1995–96	Bradford C	34	4

WRIGHT, Tommy

Born Belfast 29.8.63 Ht 6 1 Wt 14 05
Goalkeeper. From Linfield. Northern Ireland 22 full caps. Football League.

Season	Club	Apps	Goals
1987–88	Newcastle U	—	—
1988–89		9	—
1989–90		14	—
1990–91		—	—
1990–91	*Hull C*	6	—
1991–92	Newcastle U	33	—
1992–93		14	—
1993–94		3	—
1993–94	Nottingham F	10	—
1994–95		—	—
1995–96		—	—

WYATT, Mike

Born Bristol 12.9.74 Ht 5 10 Wt 11 03
Forward. From Trainee.

Season	Club	Apps	Goals
1993–94	Bristol C	10	—
1994–95		3	—
1995–96	Bristol R	4	—

Season Club League Appearances/Goals

YALLOP, Frank

Born Watford 4.4.64 Ht 5 11 Wt 12 00
Defender. From Apprentice. England Youth, Canada full caps.

Season	Club	Apps	Goals
1981–82	Ipswich T	—	—
1982–83		—	—
1983–84		6	—
1984–85		10	—
1985–86		34	—
1986–87		31	—
1987–88		41	2
1988–89		40	2
1989–90		31	—
1990–91		45	—
1991–92		17	—
1992–93		6	2
1993–94		7	—
1994–95		41	1
1995–96		7	—
1995–96	*Blackpool*	3	—

YATES, Dean

Born Leicester 26.10.67 Ht 6 2 Wt 12 06
Defender. From Apprentice. England Under-21.

Season	Club	Apps	Goals
1984–85	Notts Co	8	—
1985–86		44	4
1986–87		42	9
1987–88		46	2
1988–89		41	6
1989–90		45	6
1990–91		41	4
1991–92		25	2
1992–93		—	—
1993–94		1	—
1994–95		21	—
1994–95	Derby Co	11	1
1995–96		38	2

YATES, Steve

Born Bristol 29.1.70 Ht 5 10 Wt 12 02
Defender. From Trainee.

Season	Club	Apps	Goals
1986–87	Bristol R	2	—
1987–88		—	—
1988–89		35	—
1989–90		42	—
1990–91		34	—
1991–92		39	—
1992–93		44	—
1993–94		1	—
1993–94	QPR	29	—
1994–95		23	1
1995–96		30	—

YEBOAH, Tony

Born Kumasi 6.6.66 Ht 5 11 Wt 13 13
Forward. From Corner Stores, Okwawu U. Ghana full caps.

Season	Club	Apps	Goals
1988–89	Saarbrucken	28	9
1989–90		37	17
1990–91	Eintracht Frankfurt	26	8
1991–92		34	15
1992–93		27	20
1993–94		22	18
1994–95		14	7
1994–95	Leeds U	18	12
1995–96		22	12

YORKE, Dwight

Born Tobago 3.11.71 Ht 5 11 Wt 11 13
Forward. From St Clair's, Tobago.

Season	Club	Apps	Goals
1989–90	Aston Villa	2	—
1990–91		18	2
1991–92		32	11
1992–93		27	6
1993–94		12	2
1994–95		37	6
1995–96		35	17

YOUDS, Eddie

Born Liverpool 3.5.70 Ht 6 3 Wt 14 00
Defender. From Trainee.

Season	Club	Apps	Goals
1988–89	Everton	—	—
1989–90		—	—
1989–90	*Cardiff C*	1	—
1989–90	*Wrexham*	20	2
1990–91	Everton	8	—
1991–92		—	—
1991–92	Ipswich T	1	—
1992–93		16	—
1993–94		23	1
1994–95		10	—
1994–95	Bradford C	17	3
1995–96		30	4

YOUNG, Eric

Born Singapore 25.3.60 Ht 6 3 Wt 13 04
Defender. From Slough T. Wales 21 full caps.

Season	Club	Apps	Goals
1982–83	Brighton & HA	—	—
1983–84		30	4

Season	Club	League Appearances/Goals	
1984–85		35	3
1985–86		32	2
1986–87		29	1
1987–88	Wimbledon	29	3
1988–89		35	1
1989–90		35	5
1990–91	Crystal Palace	34	3
1991–92		30	1
1992–93		38	6
1993–94		46	5
1994–95		13	—
1995–96		—	—
1995–96	Wolverhampton W	30	2

YOUNG, Neil

Born Harlow 31.8.73 Ht 5 9 Wt 12 00
Defender. From Trainee.

Season	Club	League Appearances/Goals	
1991–92	Tottenham H	—	—
1992–93		—	—
1993–94		—	—
1994–95	Bournemouth	32	—
1995–96		41	—

YOUNG, Scott

Born Tonypandy 14.1.76 Ht 6 2
Wt 12 04
Forward. From Trainee. Wales Under-21.

Season	Club	League Appearances/Goals	
1993–94	Cardiff C	6	—
1994–95		22	—
1995–96		41	—

YOUNG, Stuart

Born Hull 16.12.72 Ht 5 10 Wt 12 10
Forward. From Arsenal Trainee.

Season	Club	League Appearances/Goals	
1991–92	Hull C	15	2
1992–93		4	—
1992–93	Northampton T	8	2
1993–94	Scarborough	28	9
1994–95		13	1
1994–95	Scunthorpe U	14	2
1995–96		14	1

YURAN, Sergei

Born Kiev 11.6.69
Forward. From Porto. Russia full caps.

Season	Club	League Appearances/Goals	
1995–96	Millwall	13	1

ZELIC, Ned

Born Australia 4.7.71 Ht 6 2 Wt 13 00
Midfield. From Australian Institute of Sport.

Season	Club	League Appearances/Goals	
1992–93	Borussia Dortmund	19	—
1993–94		18	1
1994–95		4	—
1995–96	QPR	4	—

ZUMRUTEL, Soner

Born Islington 6.10.74 Ht 5 6 Wt 11 00
Forward. From Trainee.

Season	Club	League Appearances/Goals	
1993–94	Arsenal	—	—
1994–95		—	—
1995–96		—	—
1995–96	Cambridge U	—	—